CIMA

STUDY TEXT

STRATEGIC
PAPER F3

FINANCIAL STRATEGY

Our text is designed to help you study **effectively** and **efficiently**.

In this edition we:

- **Highlight** the **most important elements** in the syllabus and the **key skills** you will need
- **Signpost** how each chapter links to the syllabus and the learning outcomes
- **Provide** lots of **exam alerts** explaining how what you're learning may be tested
- **Include examples** and **questions** to help you apply what you've learnt
- **Emphasise key points** in **section summaries**
- **Test your knowledge** of what you've studied in **quick quizzes**
- **Examine your understanding** in our **exam question bank**
- **Reference all the important topics** in the **full index**

FOR EXAMS UNTIL SEPTEMBER 2013

BPP LEARNING MEDIA

First edition 2009
Fourth edition June 2012

ISBN 9781 4453 9607 1
(Previous ISBN 9780 7517 9480 9)

e-ISBN 9781 4453 9264 6

British Library Cataloguing-in-Publication Data
A catalogue record for this book
is available from the British Library

Published by

BPP Learning Media Ltd
BPP House, Aldine Place
London W12 8AA

www.bpp.com/learningmedia

Printed in the United Kingdom

Your learning materials, published by BPP Learning Media Ltd, are printed on paper sourced from sustainable, managed forests.

All our rights reserved. No part of this publication may be reproduced, stored in a retrieval system or transmitted, in any form or by any means, electronic, mechanical, photocopying, recording or otherwise, without the prior written permission of BPP Learning Media Ltd.

We are grateful to the Chartered Institute of Management Accountants for permission to reproduce past examination questions. The suggested solutions in the exam answer bank have been prepared by BPP Learning Media Ltd.

©
BPP Learning Media Ltd
2012

A note about copyright

Dear Customer

What does the little © mean and why does it matter?

Your market-leading BPP books, course materials and e-learning materials do not write and update themselves. People write them: on their own behalf or as employees of an organisation that invests in this activity. Copyright law protects their livelihoods. It does so by creating rights over the use of the content.

Breach of copyright is a form of theft – as well being a criminal offence in some jurisdictions, it is potentially a serious breach of professional ethics.

With current technology, things might seem a bit hazy but, basically, without the express permission of BPP Learning Media:

- Photocopying our materials is a breach of copyright

- Scanning, ripcasting or conversion of our digital materials into different file formats, uploading them to facebook or emailing them to your friends is a breach of copyright

You can, of course, sell your books, in the form in which you have bought them – once you have finished with them. (Is this fair to your fellow students? We update for a reason.) But the e-products are sold on a single user licence basis: we do not supply 'unlock' codes to people who have bought them second-hand.

And what about outside the UK? BPP Learning Media strives to make our materials available at prices students can afford by local printing arrangements, pricing policies and partnerships which are clearly listed on our website. A tiny minority ignore this and indulge in criminal activity by illegally photocopying our material or supporting organisations that do. If they act illegally and unethically in one area, can you really trust them?

Contents

	Page
Introduction	
How our Study Text can help you pass	iv
Our other products	iv
CIMA Distance Learning	iv
Features in our Study Text	v
Streamlined studying	vi
Syllabus and learning outcomes	vii
Studying F3	xiv
The exam paper	xviii
Part A Formulation of financial strategy	1
1 Objectives of organisations	3
2 Constraints on financial strategy	19
3 Forecasting and analysis	33
4 Financial strategies	59
Part B Financing decisions	75
5 Equity finance	77
6 Debt finance	101
7 Leasing	119
8 The cost of capital	135
9 The capital structure decision	161
10 Treasury function	181
Part C Investment decisions and project control	197
11 Investment appraisal techniques	199
12 International investment appraisal	229
13 Specific investment appraisal scenarios	249
14 Control of investment projects	271
15 Business valuations	287
16 Amalgamations and restructuring	321
Appendix 1: Discounted cash flow	357
Appendix 2: Mathematical tables and exam formulae	365
Exam question bank	373
Exam answer bank	401
Sample Pre-seen Question	459
Index	475
Review form	

How our Study Text can help you pass

| Streamlined studying | • We show you the best ways to study efficiently
• Our Text has been designed to ensure you can easily and quickly navigate through it
• The different features in our Text emphasise important knowledge and techniques |
|---|---|
| Exam expertise | • **Studying F3** on page xiv introduces the key themes of the syllabus and summarises how to pass
• We highlight throughout our Text how topics may be tested and what you'll have to do in the exam
• We help you see the complete picture of the syllabus, so that you can answer questions that range across the whole syllabus
• Our Text covers the syllabus content – no more, no less |
| Regular review | • We frequently summarise the key knowledge you need
• We test what you've learnt by providing questions and quizzes throughout our Text |

Our other products

BPP Learning Media also offers these products for the F3 exam:

Practice and Revision Kit	Providing lots more question practice and helpful guidance on how to pass the exam
Passcards	Summarising what you should know in visual, easy to remember, form
Success CDs	Covering the vital elements of the F3 syllabus in less than 90 minutes and also containing exam hints to help you fine tune your strategy
i-Pass	Providing computer-based testing in a variety of formats, ideal for self-assessment
Interactive Passcards	Allowing you to learn actively with a clear visual format summarising what you must know

You can purchase these products by visiting www.bpp.com/cimamaterials

CIMA Distance Learning

BPP's distance learning packages provide flexibility and convenience, allowing you to study effectively, at a pace that suits you, where and when you choose. There are four great distance learning packages available.

Online classroom	Through live interactive online sessions it provides you with the traditional structure and support of classroom learning, but with the convenience of attending classes wherever you are
Online classroom live	Through pre-recorded online lectures it provides you with the classroom experience via the web with the tutor guidance & support you'd expect from a face to face classroom
Basics Plus	A guided self study package containing a wealth of rich e-learning & physical content
Basics Online	A guided self study package containing a wealth of rich e-learning content

You can find out more about these packages by visiting www.bpp.com/cimadistancelearning

BPP LEARNING MEDIA

Features in our Study Text

Section Introductions explain how the section fits into the chapter

KEY TERM — Key Terms are the core vocabulary you need to learn

KEY POINT — Key Points are points that you have to know, ideas or calculations that will be the foundations of your answers

Exam Alerts show you how subjects are likely to be tested

Exam Skills are the key skills you will need to demonstrate in the exam, linked to question requirements

LEARN — Formulae To Learn are formulae you must remember in the exam

EXAM — Exam Formulae are formulae you will be given in the exam

Examples show how theory is put into practice

Questions give you the practice you need to test your understanding of what you've learnt

CASE STUDY — Case Studies link what you've learnt with the real-world business environment

Links show how the syllabus overlaps with other parts of the qualification, including Knowledge Brought Forward that you need to remember from previous exams

Website References link to material that will enhance your understanding of what you're studying

Further Reading will give you a wider perspective on the subjects you're covering

Section Summaries allow you to review each section

BPP LEARNING MEDIA

Streamlined studying

What you should do	In order to
Read the Chapter and Section Introductions	See why topics need to be studied and map your way through the chapter
Go quickly through the explanations	Gain the depth of knowledge and understanding that you'll need
Highlight the Key Points, Key Terms and Formulae To Learn	Make sure you know the basics that you can't do without in the exam
Focus on the Exam Skills and Exam Alerts	Know how you'll be tested and what you'll have to do
Work through the Examples and Case Studies	See how what you've learnt applies in practice
Prepare Answers to the Questions	See if you can apply what you've learnt in practice
Revisit the Section Summaries in the Chapter Roundup	Remind you of, and reinforce, what you've learnt
Answer the Quick Quiz	Find out if there are any gaps in your knowledge
Answer the Question(s) in the Exam Question Bank	Practise what you've learnt in depth

Should I take notes?

Brief notes may help you remember what you're learning. You should use the notes format that's most helpful to you (lists, diagrams, mindmaps).

Further help

BPP Learning Media's *Learning to Learn Accountancy* provides lots more helpful guidance on studying. It is designed to be used both at the outset of your CIMA studies and throughout the process of learning accountancy. It can help you **focus your studies on the subject and exam**, enabling you to **acquire knowledge, practise and revise efficiently and effectively**.

Syllabus and learning outcomes

Paper F3 Financial Strategy

The syllabus comprises:

Topic and Study Weighting

A	Formulation of financial strategy	25%
B	Financing decisions	30%
C	Investment decisions and project control	45%

Learning Outcomes

Lead	Component	Syllabus content
A	**Formulation of financial strategy**	
1 Discuss potential strategic financial objectives, and the relationships among and constraints on the elements of financial strategy	(a) Discuss the potential strategic financial objectives of an organisation (b) Discuss the interrelationships between decisions concerning investment, financing and dividends (c) Discuss the impact of internal and external constraints on financial strategy, including the impact of regulation on business combinations	(i) The financial and non-financial objectives of different organisations (eg value for money, maximising shareholder wealth, providing a surplus) (ii) The three key decisions of financial management (investment, financing and dividend) and their links (iii) Benefits of matching characteristics of investment and financing in the longer term, (eg in cross-border investment) and in short-term hedging strategies (iv) Considerations in the formulation of dividend policy and dividend decisions, including meeting the cash needs of the business (v) External constraints on financial strategy (eg funding, regulatory bodies, investor relations, strategy, and economic factors) (vi) Developing financial strategy in the context of regulatory requirements (eg price and service controls exercised by industry regulators) and international operations (vii) The implications of regulation for business combinations. (Detailed knowledge of the City Code and EU competition rules will not be tested)

2	Evaluate the strategic financial strategies and objectives of an organisation and the extent of their attainment	(a)	Identify an organisation's objectives in financial terms	(i)	The financial objectives of an organisation and the economic forces affecting its financial plans (eg interest, inflation and exchange rates)
		(b)	Evaluate the attainment of an organisation's financial objectives	(ii)	Assessing attainment of financial objectives
		(c)	Evaluate current and forecast performance taking account of potential variations in economic and business factors	(iii)	Use of financial analysis in the external assessment of the a company (eg in assessing creditworthiness and compliance with financing covenants)
		(d)	Evaluate alternative financial strategies for an organisation taking account of external assessment of the organisation by financiers and other stakeholders, including likely changes to such assessment in the light of developments in reporting	(iv)	Modelling and forecasting cash flows and financial statements based on expected values for economic variables (eg interest rates) and business variables (eg volume and margins) over a number of years
				(v)	Analysis of sensitivity to changes in expected values in the above models and forecasts
				(vi)	Assessing the implications for shareholder value of alternative financial strategies, including dividend policy (Modigliani and Miller's theory of dividend irrelevancy will be tested in broad terms. The mathematical proof of the model will not be required, but some understanding of the graphical method is expected)
				(vii)	The lender's assessment of creditworthiness
				(viii)	Current and emerging issues in financial reporting (eg proposals to amend or introduce new accounting standards) and in other forms of external reporting (eg environmental accounting)

B	Financing decisions				
1	Evaluate the financing requirements of an organisation and strategies for meeting those requirements	(a)	Analyse the short- and long-term financing requirements of an organisation	(i)	Identifying financing requirements (both in respect of domestic and international operations) and the impacts of different types of finance on models and forecasts of performance and position
		(b)	Evaluate alternative methods of meeting financing requirements, taking account of the implications for the organisation's financial statements, its tax position and financial stakeholders	(ii)	Working capital management strategies. (No detailed testing of cash and stock management models will be set since these are covered at a lower level within the syllabus)
		(c)	Evaluate the weighted average cost of capital of an organisation	(iii)	Types and features of domestic and international long-term finance: share capital (ordinary and preference shares, warrants), long-term debt (bank borrowing and forms of securitised debt, eg convertibles) and finance leases, and methods of issuing securities
		(d)	Recommend methods of funding specific investments, taking account of basic tax considerations and risk exposures (to interest and currency exchange rate fluctuations)	(iv)	The operation of stock exchanges (eg how share prices are determined, what causes share prices to rise or fall, and the efficient market hypothesis) (No detailed knowledge of any specific country's stock exchange will be tested)
		(e)	Recommend optimal strategies for the management of working capital and satisfaction of longer term financing requirements	(v)	The impact of changing capital structure on the market value of a company. (An understanding of Modigliani and Miller's theory of gearing, with and without taxes, will be expected, but proof of their theory will not be examined)
				(vi)	The capital asset pricing model (CAPM): calculation of the cost of equity using the dividend growth model (knowledge of methods of calculating and estimating dividend growth will be expected), the ability to gear and un-gear betas and comparison to the arbitrage pricing model

			(vii)	The ideas of diversifiable risk (unsystematic risk) and systematic risk (use of the two-asset portfolio formula will not be tested)
			(viii)	The cost of redeemable and irredeemable debt, including the tax shield on debt
			(ix)	The weighted average cost of capital (WACC): calculation, interpretation and uses
			(x)	The lease or buy decision (with both operating and finance leases)
			(xi)	Criteria for selecting sources of finance, including finance for international investments
			(xii)	The effect of financing decisions on balance sheet structure and on ratios of interest to investors and other financiers (gearing, earnings per share, price/earnings ratio, dividend yield, dividend cover gearing, interest cover)
2	Discuss the treasury function	(a) Discuss the role and management of the treasury function	(i)	The role of the treasury function in terms of setting corporate objectives, liquidity management, funding management, and currency management
			(ii)	The advantages and disadvantages of establishing treasury departments as profit centres or cost centres, and their control

C	Investment decisions and project control				
1	Evaluate investment choices	(a)	Analyse relevant costs, benefits and risks of an investment project	(i)	Identification of a project's relevant costs (eg infrastructure, marketing and human resource development needs), benefits (including incremental effects on other activities as well as direct cash flows) and risks (ie financial and non-financial, including reputation risk arising from ethical considerations and risks of legal change or uncertainty)
		(b)	Evaluate investment projects (domestic and international), including their financial and strategic implications, taking account of potential variations in business and economic factors		
		(c)	Evaluate potential investments in organisations of different types and intangible assets	(ii)	Linking investments with customer requirements and product/service design
		(d)	Recommend investment choice in the presence of capital rationing and/or real options	(iii)	Linking investment in IS/IT with strategic, operational and control needs (particularly where risks and benefits are difficult to quantify)
				(iv)	Calculation of a project's net present value and internal rate of return, including techniques for dealing with cash flows denominated in a foreign currency and use of the weighted average cost of capital
				(v)	The modified internal rate of return based on a project's 'terminal value' (reflecting an assumed reinvestment rate)
				(vi)	The effects of taxation (including foreign direct and withholding taxes), potential changes in economic factors (inflation, interest and exchange rates) and potential restrictions on remittances on these calculations
				(vii)	Recognising risk using the certainty equivalent method (when given a risk free rate and certainty equivalent values)
				(viii)	Adjusted present value. (The two step method may be tested for debt introduced permanently and debt in place for the duration of the project)

(ix) Valuation bases for assets (eg historic cost, replacement cost and realisable value), earnings (eg price/earnings multiples and earnings yield) and cash flows (eg discounted cash flow, dividend yield and the dividend growth model)

(x) The strengths and weaknesses of each valuation method and when each is most suitable, eg by reference to type of investee organisation (service, capital intensive etc)

(xi) Forms of intangible asset (including intellectual property rights, brands etc) and methods of valuation

(xii) Application of the efficient market hypothesis to business valuations

(xiii) Selection of an appropriate cost of capital for use in valuation

(xiv) Capital investment real options (ie to make follow-on investment, abandon or wait)

(xv) Single period capital rationing for divisible and non-divisible projects (Multiperiod rationing will not be tested)

2	Evaluate opportunities for merger, acquisition and divestment	(a)	Evaluate the financial and strategic implications of proposals for mergers and acquisitions, including their terms, post-transaction values and processes, and exit strategies	(i)	Recognition of the interests of different stakeholder groups in mergers, acquisitions and company valuations
				(ii)	The reasons for merger or acquisitions (eg synergistic benefits)
		(b)	Evaluate the financial and strategic implications of demergers and divestments	(iii)	Forms of consideration and terms for acquisitions (eg cash, shares, convertibles and earn-out arrangements), and their financial effects
				(iv)	The post-merger or post-acquisition integration process (eg management transfer and merger of systems)
				(v)	The function/role of management buy-outs and venture capitalists
				(vi)	Types of exit strategy and their implications
				(vii)	The reasons for (eg strategic change, opportunity cost of investment) and mechanisms of demerger or divestment
3	Evaluate procedures for investment projects	(a)	Evaluate procedures for the implementation and control of investment projects	(i)	Project implementation and control in the conceptual stage, the development stage, the construction stage and initial manufacturing/operating stage
				(ii)	Post completion audit of investment projects

Studying F3

1 What's F3 about?

1.1 Formulation of financial strategy

In Chapters 1 to 4, we are concerned with how **financial objectives** of different types of organisation are identified and achieved. We look at the links between investment, financing and dividend decisions and the **constraints** on formulating financial strategy. In Chapter 3 we look at the techniques of **ratio analysis** and **forecasting**. The emphasis in this exam is always on **discussion** of techniques you employ and using your calculations to support your **analysis.**

Probably the most important learning outcome in this paper is that you should be able to **recommend alternative financial strategies** and Chapter 4 takes you through the key features of this process.

1.2 Financing decisions

In Part B of this book we consider various aspects of financing decisions, starting with a look at the determination of **long-term capital structure** in the form of debt finance, equity finance and leasing. We look at how **securities markets** work and towards the end of this part of the book, the role of the treasury function.

There are some essential techniques that you need to use such as calculating the **cost of capital** and using the **capital asset pricing model**.

1.3 Investment decisions and project control

Part C of this book looks firstly at issues connected with **investment appraisal**. The basic techniques involved should be revision but we do then go on to introduce more complex calculations and techniques which need to be practised.

The rest of the book is then concerned with **methods of valuing different types** of organisations. The most important use of these techniques is in a merger or acquisition situation and this area is frequently examined.

2 What's required

You need to show understanding and ability to use techniques, and set your answers in context, above all in linking investment, financing and dividend decisions. Key higher level skills being tested are **analysis**, **evaluation** and **advice**.

The examiners are looking for:

- **Clear presentation** and **conclusions**
- **Understanding** of the key issues and tools
- Ability to **analyse** data and information (going beyond a description of the issues)
- Answers focused on the scenarios

2.1 What the examiner means

The table below has been prepared by CIMA to help you interpret the syllabus and learning outcomes and the meaning of exam questions.

You will see that there are five levels of Learning Objective, ranging from Knowledge to Evaluation, reflecting the level of skill you will be expected to demonstrate. At Paper F3 level, the entire hierarchy will be used.

At the start of each chapter in your Study Text is a Topic List relating the coverage in the chapter to the level of skill you may be called on to demonstrate during the exam.

Learning objectives	Verbs used	Definition
1 Knowledge What are you expected to know	• List • State • Define	• Make a list of • Express, fully or clearly, the details of/facts of • Give the exact meaning of
2 Comprehension What you are expected to understand	• Describe • Distinguish • Explain • Identify • Illustrate	• Communicate the key features of • Highlight the differences between • Make clear or intelligible/state the meaning of • Recognise, establish or select after consideration • Use an example to describe or explain something
3 Application How you are expected to apply your knowledge	• Apply • Calculate/ compute • Demonstrate • Prepare • Reconcile • Solve • Tabulate	• Put to practical use • Ascertain or reckon mathematically • Prove with certainty or to exhibit by practical means • Make or get ready for use • Make or prove consistent/compatible • Find an answer to • Arrange in a table
4 Analysis How you are expected to analyse the detail of what you have learned	• Analyse • Categorise • Compare and contrast • Construct • Discuss • Interpret • Prioritise • Produce	• Examine in detail the structure of • Place into a defined class or division • Show the similarities and/or differences between • Build up or compile • Examine in detail by argument • Translate into intelligible or familiar terms • Place in order of priority or sequence for action • Create or bring into existence

Learning objectives	Verbs used	Definition
5 Evaluation		
How you are expected to use your learning to evaluate, make decisions or recommendations	• Advise • Evaluate • Recommend	• Counsel, inform or notify • Appraise or assess the value of • Propose a course of action

3 How to pass

3.1 Study the whole syllabus

You need to be comfortable with **all areas of the syllabus** as questions, particularly in compulsory Section A, will often span a number of syllabus areas.

3.1.1 Lots of question practice

You can **develop application skills** by attempting questions in the Exam Question Bank and later on questions in the BPP Learning Media Practice and Revision Kit.

3.1.1.1 Analysing questions

For F3 it's particularly important to focus on **how long** to spend on each part of the question and avoid spending too much time doing the calculations at the expense of the written parts. Make sure you pick up **scenario details** eg size of company, listed or unlisted, attitude to risk, dividend policy.

3.1.1.2 Answering questions

You need to show understanding and ability to use relevant techniques, but most importantly make sure that you **set your answers in context** and don't make recommendations which are unsuitable for the organisation in question.

3.1.1.3 Exam technique

The following points of exam technique are particularly relevant to this paper.

- Analyse questions during the 20 minutes' reading time – for example by putting notes in the question margin
- Make sure workings are presented clearly
- If short on time on an investment appraisal, remember that you will score significantly more method marks for calculating all the flows for 2 years, rather than a couple of the flows for 10 years
- Remember that doing calculations is not enough – you have to be able to comment on them as well. The error that a lot of students make is to overemphasise the theories and numbers in this paper.

4 Brought forward knowledge

The examiner may test knowledge or techniques you've learnt at Certificate, Operational or Management level. As F3 is part of the Financial pillar, the content of papers F1 and F2 will be significant. However material from other papers is relevant as well, particularly information systems from E1, and investment appraisal from P1.

Remember however that brought forward knowledge will only be useful if it is linked to the particular organisation in the question.

5 Links with other Strategic level papers

Remember that the **financial strategies** chosen must fulfil the same criteria as business strategy – for example they should be acceptable, suitable and feasible – and financial strategy will be determined by the **financial risks**.

The exam paper

Format of the paper

		Number of marks
Section A:	A maximum of 4 compulsory questions, totalling 50 marks, all relating to a pre-seen study and further new un-seen case material	50
Section B:	2 out of 3 questions, 25 marks each	50
		100

Time allowed: 3 hours, plus 20 minutes' reading time

CIMA guidance

The examiners have stated that in all questions marks will be available for structure and presentation, and marks will be allocated for correct structure and approach. The marking scheme will apply 0.5 to 3 marks per valid point.

Numerical content

The paper may have up to 50% numerical content, and may require calculations that are not specified in questions.

Knowledge from other syllabuses

Candidates should also bring in their knowledge from other Strategic level papers. One aim of this paper is to prepare candidates for the TOPCIMA exam.

May 2012

Section A

1 Financial performance, dividend policy, international investment appraisal, risks of overseas investment

Section B

2 M&M theory, business valuation, capital structure
3 Working capital management, creditworthiness
4 Investment appraisal, consideration of other project factors

March 2012 (resit exam)

Section A

1 Cost of equity, business valuations, impact of takeover, defensive tactics

Section B

2 Efficient markets hypothesis, dividend policy, scrip dividends, financial strategies
3 Conversion value, cost of debt, WACC, convertible debt versus equity, treasury department
4 Validity of investment appraisal, real options, use of discount rate

November 2011

Section A

1   Investment decisions (uses of funds), business valuations, competition authorities

Section B

2   Financial objectives, treasury function
3   Rights issues
4   International investment decisions (NPV), post completion audit

September 2011 (resit exam)

Section A

1   Cash flow forecast, exchange rate movements, dividend policy, sources of finance, liquidity issues

Section B

2   Business valuations, amalgamations and restructuring
3   Cost of capital, NPV, APV
4   MBOs, business valuations, venture capital

May 2011

Section A

1   NPV, payback, investment decisions, real options

Section B

2   Dividend policy, IPO, implications of becoming a listed company, financing and dividend strategies
3   Different types of financing for investment – debt, finance lease, operating lease
4   Cost of equity, WACC, valuation of a business division

March 2011 (resit exam)

Section A

1   Investment appraisal (NPV), lease or buy decision, real options

Section B

2   Currency movements and their impact on results, calculation of operating cycle, working capital financing
3   WACC, appropriateness of WACC as discount rate, NPV
4   IPO and private placing, efficient market hypothesis

November 2010

Section A

1   Cash flow forecast, business valuations, strategic implications of sale of business

Section B

2   Cost of equity, yield to maturity, evaluation of different sources of finance
3   Capital rationing (NPV, PI), discount rate for foreign investment and currency, key financial ratios in foreign investment decisions
4   M&M cost of capital theories v traditional theory, calculation of cost of equity and WACC using M&M with tax model

September 2010 (resit exam)

Section A

1   Business valuations, evaluation of initial offer price, integration issues, choice of finance

Section B

2   Role of Treasury Department, sources of finance
3   Investment appraisal (NPV, IRR, MIRR)
4   Dividend policy, M&M dividend irrelevance theory

May 2010

Section A

1   International investment appraisal (NPV), choice of currency

Section B

2   Financing requirements, WACC, alternative approaches to financing
3   Management buyouts
4   Risk, CAPM, asset and equity betas

Specimen paper

Section A

1   NPV with exchange rates and tax rates; divestments

Section B

2   Lease or buy decision; post completion audit
3   Role of treasury department; company objectives
4   Forecast income statement; cash flow forecast

FORMULATION OF FINANCIAL STRATEGY

Part A

OBJECTIVES OF ORGANISATIONS

In Part A of this Study Text, we are concerned with how **financial objectives** of different types of organisation are identified and attained; the links between the investment, financing and dividend decisions; the **constraints** on formulating financial strategy; **non-financial objectives** and non-financial information; the analysis of the **performance of organisations**.

Remember the most important learning objective of this paper is that you should **recommend alternative financial strategies** for an organisation. What the first few chapters provide you with are factors you should consider and tools you can use when formulating your recommendations.

In this chapter the key question is **what are we trying to achieve?** You need to understand what the most important objectives are and how you recognise that they have been achieved. However don't assume that you will always be asked about the financial objectives of businesses. Questions may ask you to consider the objectives of non-commercial bodies or public sector bodies such as hospitals.

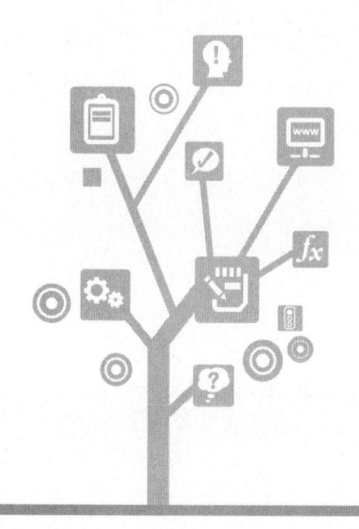

topic list	learning outcomes	syllabus references	ability required
1 Objectives of companies	A(1)(a)	A(1)(i)	analysis
2 Stakeholders and objectives	A(1)(a)	A(1)(i)	analysis
3 Objectives of publicly owned and non-commercial bodies	A(1)(a)	A(1)(i)	analysis
4 Financial management decisions	A(1)(b)	A(1)(ii)(iii)	analysis

1 Objectives of companies 11/11

Introduction

In this section we identify the main objectives of company. **Profit maximisation** is often assumed to be the main objective of a business but shareholders may still be disappointed even when profits are rising. Are other objectives therefore also important?

1.1 Strategic financial management

KEY TERMS

STRATEGIC FINANCIAL MANAGEMENT is 'the identification of the possible strategies capable of maximising an organisation's net present value, the allocation of scarce capital resources among the competing opportunities and the implementation and monitoring of the chosen strategy so as to achieve stated objectives'. *(CIMA Official Terminology)*

Strategy depends on stated **objectives** or **targets**. Therefore, an obvious starting point is the identification and formulation of these objectives.

STRATEGY is a course of action, including the specification of resources required, to achieve a specific objective. *(CIMA Official Terminology)*

CASE STUDY

The following statements of strategy were taken from recent Annual Reports and Accounts.

Tate & Lyle (Manufacturer of renewable food and industrial ingredients)

Tate & Lyle's strategy is to grow our business and create long-term value for our shareholders. To deliver this growth, we focus on five key business objectives.

- Serve our customers
- Operate efficiently and safely
- Invest in acquisitions and partnerships
- Invest in technology and people
- Grow the contribution from value added products

Kingfisher (Home improvement retail group)

Four strategic priorities:

- Strengthening
- Expanding
- Establishing
- Capitalising

Lloyds TSB (Financial services)

- Phase 1 – focus on core markets
- Phase 2 – build customer franchises
- Phase 3 – expand from strength

1.2 Financial objectives of a company

KEY POINT

It is assumed that the main objective of a company should be to **maximise the wealth** of its **ordinary shareholders**.

A company is financed by ordinary shareholders, preferred shareholders, bond holders and other long-term and short-term payables. All surplus funds, however, belong to the legal owners of the company, its ordinary shareholders. Any retained profits are undistributed wealth of these equity shareholders.

1.3 Measuring wealth and value

If the financial objective of a company is to **maximise the value** of the company, and in particular the value of its ordinary shares, we need to be able to put values on a company and its shares. How do we do it?

Methods of company valuation	
Going concern basis	Based on the company's balance sheet. Rising retained profits are an indication of potential dividends
Break-up basis	Only of interest if company is threatened with insolvency, or if individual assets are being sold to raise cash
Market values	Trading prices of stocks and shares, most relevant to financial objectives. Shareholder's return on investment comes from dividends received and increases in market value of shares (determined by expectations of future dividends)

When shares are in a **non-quoted company**, it can be hard to measure their value as there is **no market price** available. However the priorities of non-quoted shareholders will be the same, and therefore a company should be looking to maximise their wealth.

1.4 Increasing value

If a company's shares are **traded on a stock market**, the wealth of shareholders is increased when the **share price goes up**. The price of a company's shares should go up when the company is expected to make **additional profits**, which it will pay out as dividends or re-invest in the business to achieve future profit growth and dividend growth.

However, to increase the share price the company should achieve its profits without taking excessive **business risks** and **financial risks** that worry shareholders.

1.5 Financial targets

If there is an increase in earnings and dividends, management can hope for an increase in the share price too, so that shareholders benefit from both higher revenue (dividends) and also capital gains (higher share prices).

Management should set **financial targets** for factors which they can influence directly, such as cash flows, profits and dividend growth.

Examples of financial targets	
Increasing earnings per share	EPS should increase by 6% per annum
Borrowing levels	Ratio of debt: equity shouldn't exceed 1:1 or finance costs shouldn't be higher than 25% of profit from operations
Profit retention	Dividend cover (profit for the year: dividends) should exceed 2.5
Profit from operations	Target profit from operations: revenue ratio or minimum return on capital employed
Cash generation	Operating cash flow should increase by 2% more than inflation

These financial targets are not primary targets, but they can act as **subsidiary targets** or constraints that should help a company to achieve its main financial objective without incurring excessive risks.

1.6 Short-term and long-term targets

In the **long-term** companies should be looking to **maximise shareholder wealth**.

Short-term targets can encourage a company to pursue short-term objectives at the **expense** of long-term ones. For example, by deferring new capital investments, or spending only small amounts on research and development and on training.

1.7 Multiple financial targets

A major problem with setting a number of different financial targets, either primary targets or supporting secondary targets, is that they might not all be **consistent** with each other, and so might not all be achievable at the same time. When this happens, some **compromises** will have to be accepted.

Example: Evaluation of the attainment of financial objectives

Lion Grange Co has recently introduced a formal scheme of long range planning. At a meeting called to discuss the first draft plans, the following estimates emerged.

(a) Revenue in the current year reached £10,000,000, and forecasts for the next five years are £10,600,000, £11,400,000, £12,400,000, £13,600,000 and £15,000,000.

(b) The ratio of profit for the year to revenues is 10%, and this is expected to continue throughout the planning period.

(c) Total assets less current liabilities will remain at around 125% of sales. The current year equity is £8.75m.

It was also suggested that:

(d) If profits rise, dividends should rise by at least the same percentage

(e) An earnings retention rate of 50% should be maintained

(f) The ratio of long-term borrowing to long-term funds (debt plus equity) is limited (by the market) to 30%, which happens also to be the current gearing level of the company

Prepare a financial analysis of the draft long range plan and suggested policies for dividends, retained earnings and gearing.

Solution

The draft financial plan, for profits, dividends, assets required and funding, can be drawn up in a table, as follows.

	Current year £m	Year 1 £m	Year 2 £m	Year 3 £m	Year 4 £m	Year 5 £m
Revenues	10.00	10.60	11.40	12.40	13.60	15.00
Profit for the year	1.00	1.06	1.14	1.24	1.36	1.50
Dividends (50% of profit after tax)	0.50	0.53	0.57	0.62	0.68	0.75
Retained earnings						
Total assets less current liabilities (125% of sales)	12.50	13.25	14.25	15.50	17.00	18.75

	Current year £m	Year 1 £m	Year 2 £m	Year 3 £m	Year 4 £m	Year 5 £m
Equity (increased by retained earnings)	8.75	9.28	9.85	10.47	11.15	11.90
Maximum debt (30% of long term funds)	3.75	3.98	4.22	4.49	4.78	5.10
	12.50	13.26	14.07	14.96	15.93	17.00
Funds available/(Shortfall in funds)*	0.00	0.01	(0.18)	(0.54)	(1.07)	(1.75)

* Given maximum gearing of 30% and no new issue of shares = funds available minus total assets less current liabilities.

These figures show that the financial objectives of the company are not compatible with each other, and adjustments will have to be made.

(a) Given the assumptions about sales, profits, dividends and assets required, there will be an increasing shortfall of funds from year 2 onwards, unless new shares are issued or the gearing level rises above 30%.

(b) In years 2 and 3, the shortfall can be eliminated by retaining a greater percentage of profits, but this may have a serious adverse effect on the share price. In year 4 and year 5, the shortfall in funds cannot be removed even if dividend payments are reduced to nothing.

(c) The net asset turnover appears to be low. The situation would be eased if investments were able to generate higher revenues, so that fewer non-current assets and less working capital would be required to support the projected level of revenues.

(d) If net asset turnover cannot be improved, it may be possible to increase the profit to revenues ratio by reducing costs or increasing selling prices.

(e) If a new issue of shares is proposed to make up the shortfall in funds, the amount of funds required must be considered very carefully. Total dividends would have to be increased in order to pay dividends on the new shares. The company seems unable to offer prospects of suitable dividend payments, and so raising new equity might be difficult.

(f) It is conceivable that extra funds could be raised by issuing new debt, so that the level of gearing would be over 30%. It is uncertain whether investors would be prepared to lend money so as to increase gearing. If more funds were borrowed, profits would fall so that the share price might also be reduced.

1.8 Non-financial objectives

KEY POINT

Non-financial objectives such as quality measures, innovation measures and customer-based measures can also be important for a profit-making entity.

This is the balanced scorecard approach which is covered in the *E3 Enterprise Strategy* paper.

A company's non-financial objectives may include the following.

Non-financial objectives	
Customer satisfaction	A key target, because of the adverse financial consequences if businesses switch suppliers
Welfare of employees	Competitive wages and salaries, comfortable and safe working conditions, good training and career development
Welfare of management	High salaries, company cars, perks
Welfare of society	Concern for environment
Provision of service to minimum standard	For example regulations affecting utility companies (water, electricity providers)
Responsibilities to suppliers	Not exploiting power as buyer unscrupulously
Leadership in research and development	Failure to innovate may have adverse long-term financial consequences
Maintaining competitive position and market share	Preventing rivals from becoming too large and enjoying benefits of size such as economies of scale

Section summary

- In financial management of businesses, the key objective is the **maximisation of shareholders' wealth**.
- **Non-financial objectives** such as welfare, service provision and fulfilment of responsibilities are also important for businesses.

2 Stakeholders and objectives

Introduction

As you will have gathered from Section 1, many objectives and targets are set in terms of satisfying the requirements of interested parties or stakeholders. In this section we consider in more depth the importance of stakeholders and their role.

2.1 Stakeholder groups

KEY TERM

STAKEHOLDERS are those persons and organisations that have an interest in the strategy of an organisation. Stakeholders normally include shareholders, customers, staff and the local community.

(*CIMA Official Terminology*)

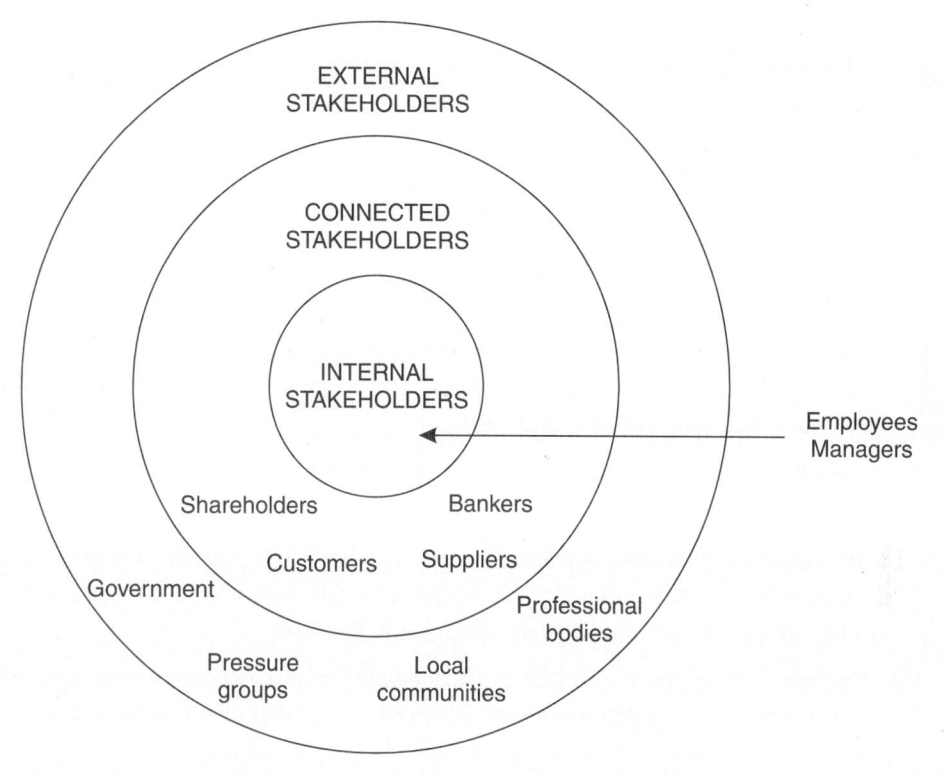

Concentric circles diagram:
- **Internal Stakeholders** (innermost): Employees, Managers
- **Connected Stakeholders** (middle): Shareholders, Bankers, Customers, Suppliers
- **External Stakeholders** (outermost): Government, Pressure groups, Local communities, Professional bodies

Exam skills

You may be told in a question that a company aims to respect the interests of stakeholders, and determines its policies in the light of that aim. Even if you aren't, you will see at various times in this text circumstances when stakeholder interests become particularly important, for example in a merger and acquisition situation, or when a business is linking investments with customer desires.

2.2 Objectives of stakeholder groups

The various groups of stakeholders in a firm will have different goals which will depend in part on the situation of the organisation.

Stakeholder goals	
Shareholders	Providers of risk capital, aim to maximise wealth
Suppliers	Often other businesses, aim to be paid full amount by date agreed, but want to continue long-term trading relationship, and so may accept later payment
Long-term lenders	Wish to receive payments of interest and capital on loan by due date for repayment
Employees	Maximise rewards paid to them in salaries and benefits, also prefer continuity in employment
Government	Political objectives such as sustained economic growth and high employment. The effect of government policies on organisations will be discussed in Chapter 2
Management	Maximising their own rewards

2.3 Stakeholder groups and strategy

The greater the power of stakeholders, the greater their influence will be. Each stakeholder group will have different expectations about what it wants, and the expectations of the various groups may conflict. Each group, however, will influence strategic decision-making.

> **Question 1.1** — Stakeholders
>
> Learning outcomes: A(1)(a)
>
> Describe and discuss the significance of the main stakeholders of a commercial bank.

2.4 The agency problem

KEY TERM

AGENCY THEORY is the hypothesis that attempts to explain elements of organisational behaviour through an understanding of the relationships between **principals** (such as shareholders) and **agents** (such as **company managers and accountants**).

A **conflict** may exist between the actions undertaken by agents in furtherance of their own self-interest, and those required to promote the interests of the principals. *(CIMA Official Terminology)*

The relationship between management and shareholders is sometimes referred to as an **agency relationship**, in which managers act as agents for the shareholders, using delegated powers to run the affairs of the company in the shareholders' best interests.

The agency relationship arising from the separation of ownership from management is sometimes characterised as the **agency problem**. For example, if managers hold none or very little of the equity shares of the company they work for, what is to stop them from:

- Working inefficiently?
- Not bothering to look for profitable new investment opportunities?
- Giving themselves high salaries and perks?

One power that shareholders possess is the **right to remove the directors from office**. However, shareholders have to take the initiative to do this, and in many companies, the shareholders lack the energy and organisation to take such a step.

2.5 Goal congruence

KEY TERM

In a control system, GOAL CONGRUENCE is the state which leads individuals or groups to take actions which are in their self-interest and also in the best interest of the entity. *(CIMA Official Terminology)*

Goal congruence may be better achieved, and the 'agency problem' better dealt with, by providing managers with incentives that are related to profits or share price, such as:

(a) **Performance related pay** either related to profit or a strategic performance measure

(b) Rewarding managers with **share options** (where selected employees are given a number of share options, each of which gives the holder the right after a certain date to subscribe for shares in the company at a fixed price)

In the UK, **corporate governance** regulations have been designed to monitor the actions of management (see Chapter 2).

2.6 Shareholder value analysis

Shareholder value analysis (SVA) was developed during the 1980s from the work of *Rappaport* and focuses on value creation using the net present value (NPV) approach. Thus, SVA assumes that **the value of a business is the net present value of its future cash flows, discounted at the appropriate cost of capital**. Many leading companies (including, for example, Pepsi, Quaker and Disney) have used SVA as a way of linking management strategy and decisions to the creation of value for shareholders.

> **KEY TERM**
>
> SHAREHOLDER VALUE ANALYSIS is an approach to financial management which focuses on total return to shareholders in terms of both dividends and price growth, calculated as the present value of future free cash flows of the business discounted at the weighted average cost of capital of the business less the market value of its debt.

SVA takes the following approach.

(a) Key decisions with implications for cash flow and risk are specified. These may be **strategic, operational, related to investment** or **financial**.

(b) **Value drivers** are identified as the factors having the greatest impact on shareholder value, and management attention is focused on the decisions which influence the value drivers. Value drivers include:

    (i) Sales growth and margin
    (ii) Working capital and fixed capital investment
    (iii) The cost of capital

SVA may help managers to concentrate on **activities which create value** rather than on short-term profitability. A problem with the approach is that of specifying a terminal value at the end of the planning horizon, which will extend for perhaps five or ten years.

Section summary

- One of the most important influences on strategy is the **goals of different interest groups**, or **stakeholder groups**.
    - **Internal** – managers, employees
    - **Connected** – shareholders, banks, customers, suppliers
    - **External** – government, pressure groups, local communities

- The **agency problem** arises when agents (managers) do not act in the best interests of their principals (shareholders).

- The system of corporate governance – which is the directors' responsibility – should seek to ensure **goal congruence** between the objectives of the organisation and those of its teams or departments or individual team members.

---

3 Objectives of publicly owned and non-commercial bodies

Introduction

Many organisations are **not-for-profit** and a more appropriate objective is to make sure the organisation is getting good **value for money**.

3.1 Not-for-profit organisations

Some organisations are set up with a prime objective which is not related to making profits. Charities and government organisations are examples. These organisations exist to pursue **non-financial aims**, such as providing a service to the community. However, there will be **financial constraints** which limit what any such organisation can do.

(a) A not-for-profit organisation needs finance to pay for its operations, and the major financial constraint is the **amount of funds that it can obtain** from its donors (its 'customers').

(b) Having obtained funds, a not-for-profit organisation will use the funds to help its 'clients', for example by alleviating suffering. It should seek to use the funds:

  (i) **Economically**: not spending $2 when the same thing can be bought for $1
  (ii) **Efficiently**: getting the best use out of what money is spent on
  (iii) **Effectively**: spending funds so as to achieve the organisation's objectives

Value for money and the three E's are covered in Paper P3 *Performance Strategy*.

3.2 Government departments

Financial management in **government departments** is different from financial management in an industrial or commercial company for a number of reasons.

(a) Government departments **do not operate to make a profit**, and the objectives of a department or of a programme of spending cannot be expressed in terms of maximising the return on capital employed.

(b) Government services are provided **without the commercial pressure of competition**. There are no competitive reasons for controlling costs, being efficient or, when services are charged for (such as medical prescriptions), keeping prices down.

(c) Government departments have full-time professional civil servants as their **managers**, but decisions are also taken by **politicians**.

(d) The government gets its money for spending from **taxes, other sources of income and borrowing** (such as issuing gilts) and the nature of its fund-raising differs substantially from fund-raising by companies.

Since managing government is different from managing a company, a different framework is needed for planning and control. This is achieved by:

(a) **Setting objectives** for each department
(b) **Careful planning** of public expenditure proposals
(c) Emphasis on getting **value for money**

In the UK, **internal markets** have been created in the health sector whereby purchasers are separated from providers of health care and the providers of hospital and other healthcare facilities compete for purchasers' funds. The idea is that those providing the best value for money will gain an increasing share of funds available.

3.3 Setting objectives

There are a number of issues to consider when objectives are set for not-for-profit organisations.

(a) **Who are the main stakeholders?**

There may be a complex mix of stakeholders, especially in the public sector. For example, a local government entity will be directed by a group of local politicians, controlled by the political party that won the last election. The local population will be the main stakeholders together with employees and central government.

(b) **Which are the most important objectives?**

Not-for-profit organisations tend to have **multiple objectives** so that even if they can all be clearly identified, it is impossible to say which is the overriding objective.

(c) **How will achievement of objectives be measured?**

Outputs can seldom be measured in a way that is generally agreed to be **meaningful.** (Are good exam results alone an adequate measure of the quality of teaching? How does one quantify the easing of pain following a successful operation?)

Bodies like local government and health services can **compare** their performance **against each other** and against the historical results of their predecessors.

Question 1.2   Voluntary sector

Learning outcome: A(1)(a)

Summarise the main strengths and weaknesses of a voluntary sector organisation.

Exam alert

You must always discuss the specific needs of the organisation in a scenario and make sure the issues you discuss are relevant.

Section summary

- The prime objective of publicly owned and non-commercial bodies will not be to make a profit but they will have to meet **financial targets**
- **Value for money** will be a more appropriate objective

4 Financial management decisions

Introduction

In this very important section we look at a framework for maximising shareholder wealth. An organisation must take sensible investment, financing and investment decisions. These decisions are **inter-related**.

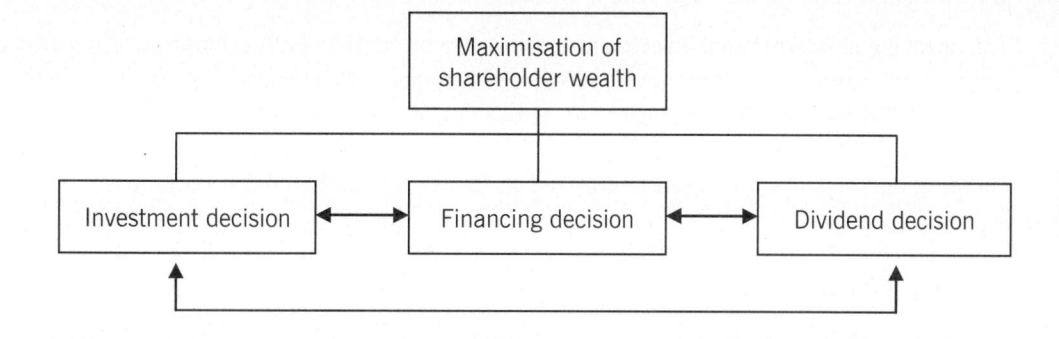

```
                    Maximisation of
                    shareholder wealth
                           |
       ┌───────────────────┼───────────────────┐
       │                   │                   │
Investment decision ◄──► Financing decision ◄──► Dividend decision
```

4.1 Investment decisions

The financial manager will need to **identify** investment opportunities, **evaluate** them and decide on the **optimum allocation of scarce funds** available between investments.

Investment decisions may be on the undertaking of **new projects** within the existing business, the **takeover** of, or the **merger** with, another company or the **selling off** of a part of the business.

Managers have to take decisions in the light of strategic considerations such as whether the business wants to **expand internally** (through investment in existing operations) or **externally** (through expansion).

4.2 Interaction of investment with financing and dividend decisions

Managers will need to consider whether **extra finance** will be required, and what will be the consequences of obtaining it. They will have to consider the demands of **providers of finance**, particularly of equity shareholders who require **dividends**. Will equity shareholders be content with projects that maximise their long-term returns, or will they require a minimum return or dividend each year?

4.3 Financing decisions

Financing decisions include those for both the long term (**capital structure**) and the short term (**working capital management**).

The financial manager will need to determine the **source, cost** and effect on **risk** of the possible sources of long-term finance. A balance between **profitability** and **liquidity** (ready availability of funds if required) must be taken into account when deciding on the optimal level of short-term finance.

4.4 Interaction of financing with investment and dividend decisions

When taking financial decisions, managers will have to fulfil the **requirements of the providers of finance**, otherwise finance may not be made available. This may be particularly difficult in the case of equity shareholders, since dividends are paid at the company's discretion. If equity shareholders do not receive the dividends they want, they will look to sell their shares, the share price will fall and the company will have more difficulty raising funds from share issues in future.

Although there may be risks in obtaining extra finance, the long-term risks to the business of **failing to invest** may be even greater and managers will have to balance these up. Investment may have direct consequences for decisions involving the **management of finance**. Extra working capital may be required if investments are made and sales expand as a consequence. Managers must be sensitive to this and ensure that a balance is maintained between receivables and inventory, and cash.

A further issue managers will need to consider is the **matching** of the **characteristics** of investment and finance. **Time** is a critical aspect; an investment which earns returns in the long-term should be matched with finance which requires repayment in the long-term.

The **financing of international investments** should also be considered. A company which expects to receive a substantial amount of income in a **foreign currency** will be concerned that this currency may weaken. **Short-term hedging strategies** can be used to deal with this risk.

Hedging and risk management is covered in Paper P3 *Performance Strategy*.

4.5 Dividend decisions

Dividend decisions may affect the view that shareholders have of the long-term prospects of the company, and thus the **market value of the shares**.

4.6 Interaction of dividend with investment and financing decisions

The amount of surplus cash paid out as **dividends** will have a direct impact on **finance** available for **investment**. Managers thus have a difficult decision to make. How much do they pay out to shareholders each year to keep them happy, and what level of funds do they retain in the business to invest in projects that will yield long-term income?

Funds available from **retained profits** may be needed if debt finance is likely to be unavailable, or if taking on more debt would expose the company to undesirable risks.

We will consider all of these decisions in more detail throughout this Study Text.

Exam alert

This area has been regularly examined in the past. Any exam answer must always focus on the specific entities involved rather than a regurgitation of text book knowledge.

Section summary

In seeking to maximise shareholder wealth, a financial manager has to make the following inter-related decisions:

- Investment
- Financing
- Dividends

Chapter Roundup

- ✓ In financial management of businesses, the key objective is the **maximisation of shareholders' wealth**.
- ✓ **Non-financial objectives** such as welfare, service provision and fulfilment of responsibilities are also important for businesses.
- ✓ One of the most important influences on strategy is the **goals of different interest groups**, or **stakeholder groups**.
    - **Internal** – managers, employees
    - **Connected** – shareholders, banks, customers, suppliers
    - **External** – government, pressure groups, local communities
- ✓ The **agency problem** arises when agents (managers) do not act in the best interests of their principals (shareholders).
- ✓ The system of corporate governance – which is the directors' responsibility – should seek to ensure **goal congruence** between the objectives of the organisation and those of its teams or departments or individual team members.
- ✓ The prime objective of publicly owned and non-commercial bodies will not be to make a profit but they will have to meet **financial targets**.
- ✓ **Value for money** will be a more appropriate objective.
- ✓ In seeking to maximise shareholder wealth, a financial manager has to make the following inter-related decisions:
    - Investment
    - Financing
    - Dividends

Quick Quiz

1. On what management objective is the theory of company finance primarily based?

2. Identify **three** non-financial and three financial objectives that might be pursued by a major international airline.

3. List six types of stakeholder group.

4. **Fill in the blanks**

   ………………………… theory sees employees as individuals, each with their own objectives, the relationship between managers and shareholders being an ………………………… relationship. If achieving individual and departmental objectives leads to achievement of the organisation's objectives, there is …………………………

5. Where external financing limits apply government-owned industries are not usually set financial targets.

   True ☐

   False ☐

6. To obtain value for money, a not-for-profit organisation should aim for the '**Three Es**', which are (**fill in the blanks**):

   E ……

   E ……

   E ……

7. In the context of managing performance in 'not for profit' organisations, which of the following definitions is incorrect?

   A   Value for money means providing a service in a way which is economical, efficient and effective.

   B   Economy means doing things cheaply: not spending $2 when the same thing can be bought for $1.

   C   Efficiency means doing things quickly: minimising the amount of time that is spent on a given activity.

   D   Effectiveness means doing the right things: spending funds so as to achieve the organisation's objectives.

8. **Fill in the blanks**

   Decisions of the financial manager
   - ………… decisions
   - ………… decisions
   - ………… decisions

9. ………………………… is a course of action, including the specification of resources required, to achieve a specific objective.

Answers to Quick Quiz

1   The objective of management is to maximise the market value of the enterprise and the shareholders' wealth.

2   Possible **non-financial objectives** that might be pursued by a major international airline include (choose any three):

   - Strengthening business image with clients or customers
   - Having a better reputation than rival airlines
   - Reducing carbon emissions (Singapore Airlines have introduced initiatives to reduce emissions by approximately 550,000 tonnes)
   - Better 'product offering' than rivals (eg Singapore Airlines' 'Better than First Class' service)
   - Expand destinations offered
   - Better customer service than rivals
   - Improving punctuality

   Possible financial objectives include (choose any three):

   - Revenue growth year-on-year
   - Stable earnings for the future
   - Increase dividends per share (or start paying dividends)
   - Containing costs

3   Any six from the following:

   Employees, managers, shareholders, bankers, customers, suppliers, government, local communities, pressure groups, professional bodies.

4   Agency; agency; goal congruence

5   False

6   Economy; efficiency; effectiveness

7   C   Efficiency means doing things well: getting the best use out of what money is spent on

8   Investment; financing; dividend

9   Strategy

Answers to Questions

1.1 Stakeholders

(a) **Customers**

Customers are very significant to the bank because this group directly provides **income** for the business. Some customers, for example large corporate customers, are more significant than others.

(b) **Employees**

This group looks to the bank to be a good employer, offering fair and continuing employment. This group is very significant to the company, as banks are people-intensive businesses and good performance by employees can impact directly on customer satisfaction and hence company profitability.

(c) **Suppliers**

These may provide the company with **key technologies** that enable the bank to have a competitive advantage.

(d) **Government agencies**

There is a widespread feeling that banks abuse their position and exploit customers, for example through **cartel-type** agreements on cash machine charges. Government agencies may have powers to control activities of the bank. The competition authorities may recommend that a proposed takeover planned by the bank be blocked.

(e) **Intermediaries**

The bank sells some of its services (for example insurance policies) through intermediaries whose continued support is of significance.

1.2 Voluntary sector

Strengths

- There are **no shareholders** who would expect a short-term return on their investment.
- There is less chance of **conflict** between social goals and profit goals.
- Voluntary organisations may be **trusted** more by users than a comparable private sector organisation, for whom users may be suspicious of the company's profit motives.
- There may be greater **dedication** from staff who share the voluntary organisation's vision.
- 'Staff' may be prepared to give their services for **free**.

Weaknesses

- The **absence** of a **profit motive** may lead to **unfocused** management whose results are difficult to monitor.
- There may be a reluctance to act in a **business-like way**, thereby resulting in poor services to users.
- Users may **not** expect to **pay** for services provided, but overhead costs must still be covered.
- Voluntary workers may be **less committed** to their job as they will not lose pay for poor performance.

Now try this question from the Exam Question Bank

Number	Level	Marks	Time
Q1	Examination	25	45 mins

CONSTRAINTS ON FINANCIAL STRATEGY

We now examine the range of **factors** which may constrain financial strategy.

It is important to see how changes or differences in these factors may influence strategy. For example, a **change in government legislation** may limit (or maybe open up) opportunities. When seeking **investment opportunities in other countries**, the particular external factors which are important there will need to be considered.

Interest rates are a key influence on **investment** decisions, and you need to appreciate the main factors affecting interest rates, and why rates differ across the economy.

As well as influencing business decisions, many of the constraints will require direct action by businesses, possibly **costs of complying** with them, or (possibly costly) action to limit their effects.

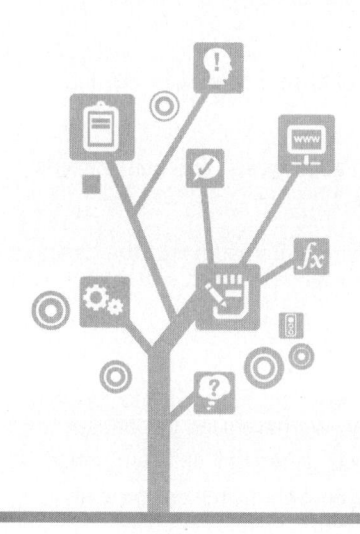

topic list	learning outcomes	syllabus references	ability required
1 Constraints on financial strategy	A(1)(c)	A(v)	analysis
2 Regulatory bodies	A(1)(c)	A(v),(vi)	analysis
3 Economic constraints	A(1)(c)	A(v)	analysis
4 International constraints	A(1)(c)	A(v)	analysis

19

1 Constraints on financial strategy

> **Introduction**
>
> In this section we look at factors inside and outside an organisation which may hold it back from implementing its financial strategies. These factors include funding, investor relations, regulatory bodies and economic factors. We will look at the last two in more detail in Sections 2 and 3.

1.1 Funding constraints

Businesses may be reluctant to **obtain extra funds themselves** for a variety of reasons. In smaller non-listed companies, equity funding from the small group of owners will be a significant source of finance. However owners may not have the **financial resources** to provide significant equity injections, and may also require the company to pay them a regular source of income.

Larger companies listed on a stock exchange may be constrained when they are contemplating a share issue by fears that the issue **will not be fully taken up** or that they will have to issue shares at a **low price** in order to ensure full take-up.

Directors of companies of any size may be reluctant to obtain further **debt finance** because:

(a) They fear that the company may be unable to **service the debt**, to make the required capital and interest payments on time

(b) The tax position is such that they will be unable to use the **tax shield**, to obtain any tax benefit from interest payments

(c) The company lacks the **asset base** to be able to **generate additional cash** if needed or provide **sufficient security**

(d) The company wishes to **maintain access** to the capital markets on **good terms**, and hence needs a good credit rating

Smaller companies may be deterred from **obtaining debt finance** by lender requirements that the directors offer personal security.

1.2 Investor relations

Financial constraints are bound up with the need to **keep investors happy**. We have seen in Chapter 1 that investors need to be convinced that companies are investing in projects generating sufficient long-term returns, and that en route the company will also be able to generate enough dividends to satisfy investor requirements.

1.3 Agency theory

The ability of an entity to maximise shareholder wealth may be constrained by the actions of managers who sometimes have different objectives. This is the **agency problem** that we covered in Chapter 1.

1.4 Business strategy

Obviously a business's financial strategy is not independent of its overall business strategy. There may be occasions when an organisation departs from what appears to be the optimum financial strategy. It may for instance depart from its optimal capital structure to **raise funds** to seize a potentially **valuable investment opportunity**.

An entity may also suffer from a **shortage of key skills** or **limited production capacity**, both of which may limit its ability to operate to its maximum wealth generating capacity.

Exam skills

An exam scenario could give details of potential investments and you may need to discuss the internal and external constraints affecting the investment decision. A fundamental problem with such questions has been the amount of material in the answers that appeared to have been lifted straight from study texts without applying that knowledge to the scenario provided.

Section summary

Constraints on financial strategy include funding, investor relations, business strategy and economic factors.

2 Regulatory bodies

Introduction

A powerful **external constraint** on the ability of a company to create wealth for its shareholders are local or overseas governments, or government regulators.

2.1 The impact of legislation

As you have seen in your earlier studies, legislation which impacts on entities includes:

- Companies Acts
- Health and safety regulations
- Consumer protection laws
- Contract and agency laws
- Employment law
- Protection of the environment laws

2.2 Compliance with legislation

Organisations need to consider carefully the financial aspects of compliance with the law. Compliance with legislation may involve **extra costs**, including the extra procedures and investment necessary to conform to safety standards, staff training costs and legal costs.

Higher costs of compliance, as well as costs of labour may mean that companies **relocate** to countries where costs and regulatory burdens are lower. However these costs may also act as a **significant barrier to entry**, benefiting companies that are already in the industry.

Businesses that fail to comply with the law run the risk of financial **penalties** and the financial consequences of accompanying **bad publicity**.

2.3 Corporate governance

The **corporate governance debate** impacts upon the way companies make decisions, their financial organisation and their relations with investors and auditors.

KEY TERM

CORPORATE GOVERNANCE is the system by which companies and other entities are directed and controlled. **Boards of directors** are responsible for the governance of their companies. The **shareholders'** role in governance is to appoint the directors and the **auditors** and to satisfy themselves that an appropriate governance structure is in place.

The responsibilities of the board include:

- Setting the company's **strategic aims**
- Providing the **leadership** to put them into effect
- Supervising the **management** of the business
- **Reporting** to shareholders on their stewardship

The board's actions are subject to laws, regulations and the shareholders in general meeting.

(CIMA Official Terminology)

Corporate governance has emerged as a major issue in the last ten to fifteen years in the light of several high profile collapses. Guidance has been given because of the lack of confidence perceived in financial reporting and in the ability of auditors to provide the assurances required by the users of financial accounts.

Paper P3 *Performance Strategy* covers this area and you can use relevant information from the other areas you have studied in the *Financial Strategy* exam.

2.3.1 Impact of corporate governance requirements on businesses

The consequences of **failure to obey corporate governance regulations** should be considered along with failure to obey any other sort of legislation. In regimes where corporate governance rules are **guidelines** rather than regulations, businesses will consider what the consequences might be of non-compliance, in particular the **impact** on **share prices**.

Obedience to requirements or guidelines can also have consequences for businesses. For example increased disclosure regulations have highlighted **director remuneration packages** that investors have thought to be excessively generous.

2.4 Competition regulation

The government can influence a market through **regulations**, eg using an **industry regulator** or a **competition authority**.

2.4.1 Industry regulators

Where a market is not competitive, industry regulatory authorities have the role of ensuring that **consumers' interests** are not subordinated to those of other stakeholders, such as employees, shareholders and tax authorities.

The two main methods used to regulate monopoly industries are as follows.

(a) **Price control**

   The regulator **agreeing the output prices** with the industry. Typically, the price is **progressively reduced** in **real terms** each year by setting price increases at a rate below that of inflation. This has been used with success by regulators in the UK but can be confrontational.

(b) **Profit control**

   The regulator **agreeing the maximum profit** which the industry can make. A typical method is to fix maximum profit at x% of capital employed, but this does not provide any incentive to making more efficient use of assets: the higher the capital employed, the higher the profit.

In addition the regulator will be concerned with:

(a) Actively **promoting competition** by encouraging new firms in the industry and preventing unreasonable barriers to entry

(b) Addressing **quality** and **safety** issues and considering the **social implications** of service provision and pricing

2.4.2 Regulation of takeovers

Competition authorities such as the UK Competition Commission aim to protect competition within a market. It will make in-depth enquiries into mergers and markets to ensure that one company cannot dominate a market. Where a potential merger is **sufficiently large** to warrant an investigation, the competition authority will look at whether the merger will be **against the public interest** in terms of:

(a) **Effective competition** within the industry

(b) The interests of consumers, purchasers and users of the goods and services of that industry in respect of **quality**, **price** and **variety**

(c) The **reduction of costs** and the introduction of new products and techniques

We will look at the regulation of takeovers again in Chapter 16.

Section summary

- A powerful **external constraint** on the ability of a company to create wealth for its shareholders is local or overseas governments, or government regulators.

- The **corporate governance** debate impacts upon the way companies make decisions, their financial organisation and their relations with investors and auditors.

- The government can influence a market through **regulations**, eg using an industry regulator or a competition authority.

---

3 Economic constraints

Introduction

Economic constraints on strategy will be imposed by **inflation, interest rates** and **exchange rates**. You will be expected to have a good understanding of how economic factors can impact on an entity and be able to discuss the effect on financial strategies.

3.1 Effects of inflation

Inflation can affect all the financial areas of a business and impact upon its **profit performance** in a variety of ways.

(a) The rate of inflation will **affect the prices** that a business must pay for all the factors of production and the prices that it is able to charge to its customers. It will therefore affect the level of reported profits.

(b) When inflation is high, **regular price reviews** will be necessary so as to ensure that there is no erosion of real returns. In times of low inflation it may be difficult to achieve any price increases due to a reduced level of inflationary expectations.

(c) Where there is a high level of inflation, there is also a **high level of uncertainty** about the future. This tends to make businesses wary of committing themselves to new long-term investments.

(d) Inflation places **pressure on cash flow**, particularly where the prices of raw materials are rising ahead of prices charged to customers. Even where sales prices do keep up, additional cash will still be required to cover the increased payments to suppliers that will have to be made in advance of monies being received in respect of credit sales.

(e) Companies may **increase their level of investment in inventory** as a hedge against anticipated price rises. This will also increase the amount of working capital required and restrict the funds available for new investment.

(f) Different approaches may need to be taken to **financial reporting** and evaluation methods, such as current cost accounting techniques, which make it easier to understand the changing performance of a company over time.

(g) The relationship between **inflation rates** and **interest rates** means that interest rates tend to rise during a period of inflation. This has implications both for the capital structure decisions and investment appraisal criteria used by companies.

3.2 Interest rates

Interest rates are an important element in the economic environment, and are of particular relevance for financial managers.

(a) Interest rates **measure the cost of borrowing**. If a company wants to raise money, it must pay interest on its borrowing, and the rate of interest payable will be one which is 'current' at the time the borrowing takes place. When interest rates go up, companies will pay more interest on some of their borrowing (for example on bank overdrafts).

(b) Interest rates in a country **influence the foreign exchange value** of the country's currency.

(c) Interest rates act as a **guide to the sort of return** that a company's shareholders might want, and changes in market interest rates will affect share prices.

3.2.1 Nominal rates and real rates of interest

Nominal rates of interest are the actual rates of interest paid. **Real rates of interest** are rates of interest adjusted for the rate of inflation. The real rate is therefore a measure of the increase in the real wealth, expressed in terms of **buying power**, of the investor or lender.

The relationship between nominal rates and real rates of interest was originally explored by *Fisher* and can be expressed as follows:

> (1 + nominal rate of interest) = (1 + real rate of interest) x (1 + inflation rate)
>
> This formula is often referred to as the *Fisher equation*.

The real rate of interest can be calculated as:

$$\text{Real rate of interest} = \frac{1 + \text{nominal rate of interest}}{1 + \text{rate of inflation}} - 1$$

If the nominal rate of interest is 12% and the rate of inflation is 8%, the real rate of interest would be 1.12/1.08 − 1 = 0.037 = 3.7%.

3.2.2 The general level of interest rates

Interest rates on any one type of financial asset will vary over time. In other words, the general level of interest rates might go up or down. The general level of interest rates is affected by several factors.

(a) **Need for a real return**

Investors normally want to **earn a 'real' rate of return** on their investment. The appropriate 'real' rate of return will depend on factors such as investment risk.

(b) **Inflation**

Nominal rates of interest should be sufficient to **cover expected rates of inflation** over the term of the investment and to provide a real return.

(c) **Uncertainty about future rates of inflation**

When investors are uncertain about inflation and therefore about what future nominal and real interest rates will be, they are likely to require **higher interest yields** to persuade them to take the risk of investing, especially in the longer term.

(d) **Liquidity preference of investors and the demand for borrowing**

Higher interest rates have to be offered to persuade savers to invest their surplus money. When the demand to borrow increases, interest rates will rise.

(e) **Balance of payments**

When a country has a continuing deficit on the current account of its balance of payments, and the authorities are unwilling to allow the exchange rate to depreciate by more than a certain amount, interest rates may have to be raised to **attract capital** into the country. The country can then finance the deficit by borrowing from abroad.

(f) **Monetary policy**

From mid-1997, decisions over UK interest rate policy have been made by the Monetary Policy Committee of the Bank of England. The Bank of England influences very short-term money market rates by means of **open market operations**. Usually longer term money market rates, and then banks' base rates, will respond to the authorities' wish for interest rate changes.

(g) **Interest rates abroad**

The rate of interest in one country will be influenced by **external factors**, such as interest rates in other countries and expectations about the exchange rate. When interest rates in overseas countries are high, interest rates on domestic currency investments must also be comparably high, to avoid capital transfers abroad and a fall in the exchange rate of the domestic currency.

3.2.3 Interest rates in different markets and market segments

(a) **Risk**

Higher risk borrowers must pay higher rates on their borrowing, to compensate lenders for the greater risk involved.

(b) **The need to make a profit on re-lending**

Financial intermediaries make their profits from re-lending at a higher rate of interest than the cost of their borrowing.

(c) **The duration of the lending**

Normally, long-term loans will earn a higher yield than short-term loans. You should be familiar with the reasons for this term structure of interest rates as illustrated by the **yield curve**, from your previous studies; the main points are summarised below.

(d) **The size of the loan**

Deposits above a certain amount with a bank or building society might attract higher rates of interest than smaller deposits.

(e) **Different types of financial asset**

Different types of financial asset attract different rates of interest. This reflects the competition for deposits between different types of financial institution.

3.2.4 The term structure of interest rates: the yield curve

Interest rates depend on the **term to maturity** of the asset. For example, government bonds might be short-dated, medium-dated, or long-dated depending on when the bonds are to be redeemed and the investor repaid.

The **term structure of interest rates** refers to the way in which the yield on a security varies according to the term of the borrowing, as shown by the **yield curve**.

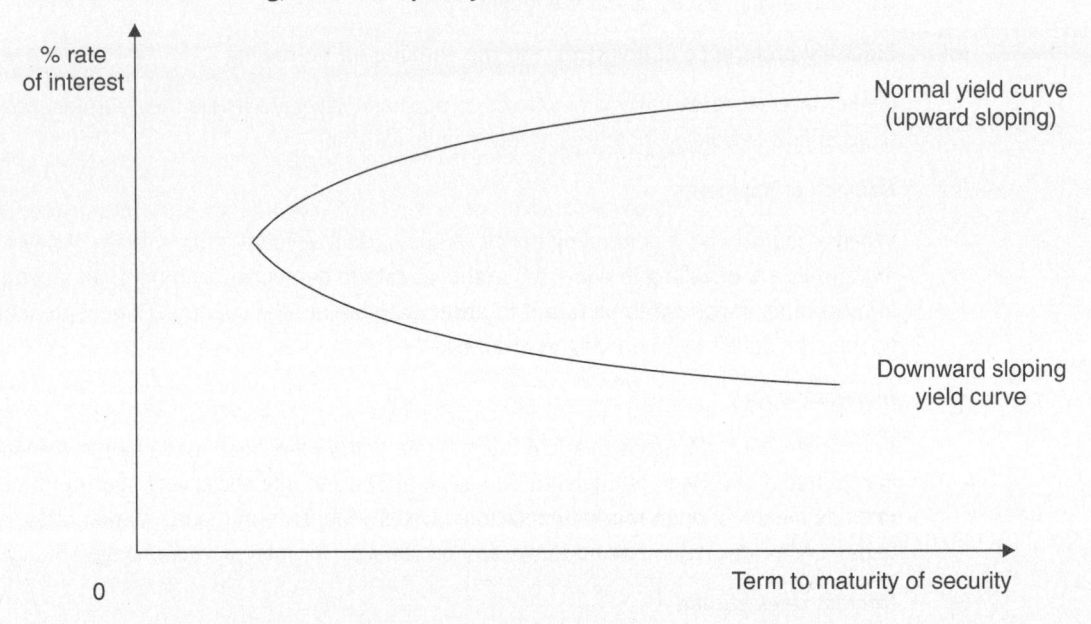

The reasons why, in theory, the yield curve will normally be upward sloping, so that long-term financial assets offer a higher yield than short-term assets, are as follows.

(a) **The investor must be compensated for tying up his money in the asset for a longer period of time**. The only way to overcome this **liquidity preference** of investors is to compensate them for the loss of liquidity; in other words, to offer a higher rate of interest on longer dated bonds.

(b) **There is a greater risk in lending long-term than in lending short-term**. To compensate investors for this risk, they might require a higher yield on longer dated investments.

A yield curve might **slope downwards**, with short-term rates higher than longer term rates for a number of reasons.

(a) **Expectations**. When interest rates are expected to fall, short-term rates might be higher than long-term rates, and the yield curve would be downward sloping.

(b) **Government policy**. A policy of keeping interest rates relatively high might have the effect of forcing short-term interest rates higher than long-term rates.

(c) The **market segmentation theory**. The slope of the yield curve will reflect conditions in different segments of the market. This theory holds that the major investors are confined to a particular segment of the market and will not switch segment even if the forecast of likely future interest rates changes.

3.2.5 Interest rates and share prices

When interest rates change, the **return expected** by investors from shares will also change. For example, if interest rates fell from 14% to 12% on government bonds, and from 15% to 13% on company bonds, the return expected from shares (dividends and capital growth) would also fall. This is because shares and debt are alternative ways of investing money. **If interest rates fall, shares become more attractive to buy**. As demand for shares increases, their prices rise too, and so the dividend return gained from them falls in percentage terms.

3.2.6 Changes in interest rates and financing decisions

Interest rates are important for financial decisions by companies.

(a) **When interest rates are low**, it might be financially prudent:

   (i) To **borrow more**, preferably at a fixed rate of interest, and so increase the company's gearing

   (ii) To **borrow for long periods** rather than for short periods

   (iii) To **pay back loans which incur a high interest rate**, if it is within the company's power to do so, and take out new loans at a lower interest rate

(b) **When interest rates are higher:**

   (i) A company might decide to **reduce the amount of its debt finance**, and to substitute equity finance, such as retained earnings

   (ii) A company which has a large surplus of cash and liquid funds to invest might switch some of its **short-term investments** out of equities and into interest-bearing securities

   (iii) A company might opt to raise new finance by borrowing short-term funds and debt at a **variable interest rate** (for example on overdraft) rather than long-term funds at fixed rates of interest, in the hope that interest rates will soon come down again

3.2.7 Interest rates and new capital investments

When interest rates go up, and so the cost of finance to a company goes up, **the minimum return** that a company will require on its own new capital investments will go up too. Some new capital projects might be in the pipeline, with purchase contracts already signed with suppliers, and so there will often be a time lag before higher interest rates result in **fewer new investments**.

A company's management should give close consideration, when interest rates are high, to keeping **investments in assets**, particularly unwanted or inefficient non-current assets, inventories and receivables, down **to a minimum**, in order to reduce the company's need to borrow.

3.2.8 Other impacts of higher interest rates

Businesses are likely to face lower demand for the following reasons:

(a) Consumer spending falling because the higher interest rates **raise the cost of capital**

(b) The **value of investors' financial assets falling**, and their maintaining their total wealth by saving more and spending less

(c) The **exchange rate rising** as a result of an influx of foreign capital, attracted by higher interest rates. This rise will result in exports becoming more expensive.

However the influx of foreign funds may also eventually mean that **more capital** is available for domestic companies.

3.3 Exchange rates

EXCHANGE RATE is the rate at which a national currency exchanges for other national currencies, being set by the interaction of demand and supply of the various currencies in the foreign exchange markets (**floating** exchange rate) or by government intervention in order to maintain a constant rate of exchange (**fixed** exchange rate).
(CIMA Official Terminology)

Exchange rates between different currencies on the world's foreign exchange markets are continually changing, and often by large amounts.

Foreign exchange rates are important for a business and its financial management because they affect:

- The cost of imports
- The value of exports
- The costs and benefits of international borrowing and lending

3.3.1 Impact of changes in exchange rates

Changes in the value of a currency will affect the cost of goods from abroad. For example, if a consignment of goods is shipped from the USA to Germany and the invoice price is US$420,000:

- If the euro-dollar exchange rate is €1 = $1.50, the cost of the imports would be €280,000
- If the euro fell in value to €1 = $1.25, the cost of the imports would be higher, at €336,000

Changes in the value of a currency affect buying costs, companies and households alike, because a large proportion of the raw materials, components and finished goods that we consume is imported.

Exchange rates affect **exporting companies**, for similar reasons, because changes in exchange rates affect the price of exported goods to foreign buyers.

(a) **When the local currency, say the yen, goes up in value**, goods sold abroad by Japanese exporters, and invoiced in yen, will cost more to the foreign buyers (who must purchase yens with their own currency in order to pay).

(b) **When the yen falls in value,** goods sold abroad by Japanese exporters and invoiced in yen will become cheaper to foreign buyers.

To the extent that demand is influenced by price, the demand for exports will therefore vary with changes in the exchange rate.

Similarly if you are going on holiday or on a shopping trip abroad you will be interested in movements in the exchange rate. When you are buying currency, you want your own currency to appreciate as this means you will get more of the foreign currency for every unit of your own currency. For example, if £1 is worth $1.5066 and you purchased £500 worth of dollars, you would receive $753.30. However if sterling appreciated to £1 = $1.5300, you would receive $765.

However when you are exchanging foreign currency into your home currency, you want your home currency to depreciate. For example, if you came back from holiday with $50 and £1 = $1.5300, you would receive £32.68 ($50/$1.5300). If sterling depreciated to £1 = $1.5066, you would receive £33.19.

Exchange rate risk is covered in Paper P3 *Performance Strategy* and you should use your knowledge from this paper if it is appropriate.

Section summary

Economic constraints on strategy will be imposed by **inflation**, **interest rates** and **exchange rates**.

4 International constraints

Introduction

An exam scenario may concern an entity which trades internationally. You need to be able to discuss the particular factors that will impact on such an entity's financial strategy, such as the risks of interference in its business.

4.1 Trading abroad

Compared with companies that trade entirely within one country, companies that trade overseas will have to deal with a variety of international constraints.

4.1.1 Foreign exchange constraints

As we have already seen, any company that exports or imports faces the risk of **higher costs** or **lower revenues** because of adverse movements in foreign exchange rates. A company that owns assets in different countries (subsidiaries abroad) faces the risk of accounting losses due to adverse movements in exchange rates causing a fall in the value of those assets, as expressed in domestic currency.

4.1.2 Political issues

A company which trades abroad can face risks of **economic or political measures** being taken by governments, affecting the operations of its subsidiaries abroad. An example was the import restrictions imposed by the USA on the British cashmere industry during 1999, in retaliation for EU restrictions on banana imports.

Political risk is covered in Paper P3 *Performance Strategy*.

4.1.3 Geographical separation

The **geographical separation** of the **parent company** from its subsidiaries adds to the problems of management control of the group of companies as a whole. Separation may enhance problems caused by **language** and **cultural differences**.

4.1.4 Litigation

The risk of litigation varies in different countries and to minimise this risk, attention should be paid to **legislation** and **regulations** covering the products sold in different countries. Care should be taken to comply with contract terms.

4.2 Multinationals

A MULTINATIONAL COMPANY or enterprise is one which owns or controls production facilities or subsidiaries or service facilities outside the country in which it is based. Thus, a company does not become 'multinational' simply by virtue of exporting or importing products – **ownership and control of facilities abroad** is involved.

Examples of multinational companies include:

Food and drink	Hospitality and leisure	Car manufacturers	Technology	Pharmaceuticals
Coca Cola	Hilton	Ford	Microsoft	GlaxoSmithKline
McDonald's	Marriott	Toyota	Dell	Pfizer

CASE STUDY

An excerpt from the Coca Cola annual report 2008 highlights the multinational nature of the company:

'We have the benefit of being one of the world's most global companies. With operations spanning more than 200 countries, we are able to transfer what has been successful in any given market to other countries and operating groups.'

McDonald's reports on its Canadian web site that it operates in more than 119 countries.

(Source: *www.mcdonalds.ca*)

Exam skills

It is essential to ensure that any discussion concerning a multinational entity recognises its size and complexity. For example, potential losses from unfavourable tax rates or exchange rate movements are immaterial for a large multi-national group. Also, the impact of exchange rate movements relating to a project could be largely immaterial to group gearing levels due to the small size of the project in relation to the size of the group.

Section summary

Entities which trade **internationally** must be aware of additional external constraints such as foreign exchange risk, political risk, geographical separation and litigation.

Chapter Roundup

- ✓ Constraints on financial strategy include funding, investor relations, business strategy and economic factors
- ✓ A powerful **external constraint** on the ability of a company to create wealth for its shareholders are local or overseas governments, or government regulators.
- ✓ The **corporate governance** debate impacts upon the way companies make decisions, their financial organisation and their relations with investors and auditors.
- ✓ The government can influence a market through **regulations**, eg using an industry regulator or a competition authority.
- ✓ **Economic constraints** on strategy will be imposed by **inflation, interest rates** and **exchange rates**.
- ✓ Entities which trade **internationally** must be aware of additional external constraints such as foreign exchange risk, political risk, geographical separation and litigation.

Quick Quiz

1. List two principal methods of regulating a monopoly industry.
2. Draw a 'normal' yield curve, labelling axes.
3. Fill in the following at (A), (B) and (C) in the equation below
   - Nominal rate of interest
   - Real rate of interest
   - Rate of inflation

PART A FORMULATION OF FINANCIAL STRATEGY   2: Constraints on financial strategy   **31**

$$\frac{1+(A)}{1+(B)} - 1 = (C)$$

4   What effect does a high interest rate have on the exchange rate?

5   **Fill in the blank**

   Corporate governance is ....

6   What is the best way to achieve a division of responsibilities at the head of a company?

7   What is the definition of a multinational entity?

Answers to Quick Quiz

1   Price control; profit control.

2

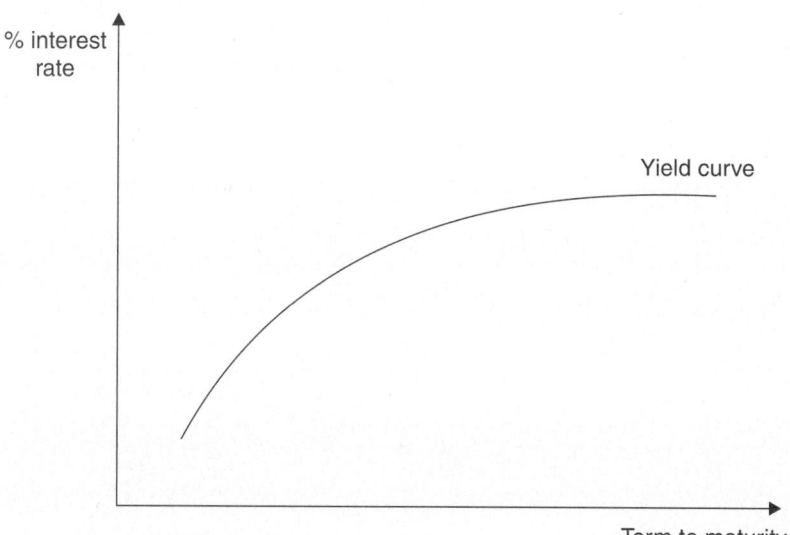

Yield curve (% interest rate vs Term to maturity)

3   (A) Nominal rate of interest
    (B) Rate of inflation
    (C) Real rate of interest

4   It attracts foreign investment, thus increasing the demand for the currency. The exchange rate rises as a result.

5   The system by which companies are directed and controlled

6   Separation of the posts of Chairman and Chief Executive

7   A multinational entity is one which owns or controls production facilities or subsidiaries or service facilities outside the country in which it is based.

Now try this question from the Exam Question Bank

Number	Level	Marks	Time
Q2	Examination	25	45 mins

FORECASTING AND ANALYSIS

We start this chapter by **revising ratio analysis** and other methods of **performance measurement**. You are unlikely to get a question that solely involves calculating and analysing ratios in this paper. You may be asked for example, to use ratio analysis to ascertain whether an organisation has **met its objectives.**

Cash forecasting is vital to ensure that **sufficient funds** will be **available** when they are needed to sustain the activities of an enterprise, at an acceptable cost.

Although you will have encountered forecasts before, again don't neglect this chapter as the examiners have highlighted this topic as important. You may well get a compulsory question on forecasting.

In Section 3 we look at how you should prepare forecast financial statements.

Section 5 deals with the links between the cash requirements forecast and decisions on financing.

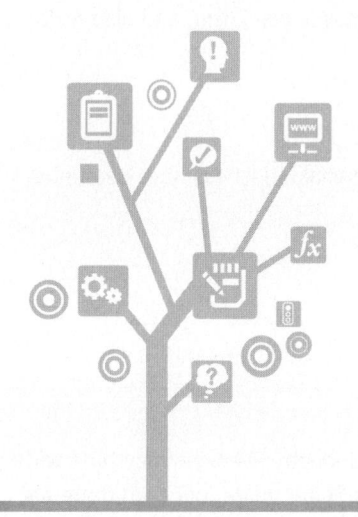

topic list	learning outcomes	syllabus references	ability required
1 Performance analysis	A(2)(a)(b)(c)	A(2)(i)(ii)(iii)	evaluation
2 Cash forecasts	A(2)(c)(d)	A(2)(iv)	evaluation
3 Forecast financial statements: example	A(2)(c)(d)	A(2)(iv)	evaluation
4 Sensitivity analysis and changes in variables	A2(c)(d)	A(v)	evaluation
5 Financing requirements	B(1)(a)	B(1)(i)	evaluation

1 Performance analysis

Introduction

In Chapter 1 we looked at financial objectives. The aim of this chapter is to determine whether an entity will **meet** its objectives. Ratios provide a means of systematically analysing financial statements. You will have covered much of this section in your earlier studies so the material here is designed to refresh your memory.

1.1 Uses of ratio analysis

The key to obtaining meaningful information from ratio analysis is **comparison**: comparing ratios over time within the same business to establish whether the business is **improving** or **declining**, and comparing ratios between similar businesses to see whether the company you are analysing is better or worse than average within its own business sector.

A vital element in effective ratio analysis is understanding the needs of the person for whom the ratio analysis is being undertaken.

(a) **Investors** will be interested in the **risk and return** relating to their investment, so will be concerned with dividends, market prices, level of debt vs equity etc.

(b) **Suppliers** and **loan creditors** are interested in receiving the payments due to them, so will want to know how liquid the business is.

(c) **Managers** are interested in ratios that indicate how well the business is being run, and also how the business is doing in relation to its **competitors**.

Exam alert

Exam questions often ask you to use ratio analysis to assess whether financial objectives have been met.

1.2 Limitations of ratio analysis

Although ratio analysis can be a very useful technique, it is important to realise its limitations.

(a) **Availability of comparable information**

When making comparisons with other companies in the industry, industry averages may hide **wide variations** in figures. Figures for 'similar' companies may provide a better guide, but then there are problems identifying which companies are similar, and obtaining enough detailed information about them.

(b) **Use of historical/out-of-date information**

Comparisons with the previous history of a business may be of limited use, if the business has recently undergone, or is about to undergo, **substantial changes**.

(c) **Ratios are not definitive**

'Ideal levels' vary industry by industry, and even they are not definitive. Companies may be able to exist without any difficulty with ratios that are rather worse than the industry average.

(d) **Need for careful interpretation**

For example, if comparing two businesses' liquidity ratios, one business may have higher levels. This might appear to be 'good', but further investigation might reveal that the higher ratios are a result of higher inventory and receivable levels which are a result of poor working capital management by the business with the 'better' ratios.

(e) **Manipulation**

Any ratio including profit may be distorted by **choice of accounting policies**. For smaller companies, working capital ratios may be distorted depending on whether a big customer pays, or a large supplier is paid, before or after the year-end.

(f) **Other information**

Ratio analysis on its own is not sufficient for interpreting company accounts, and there are other items of information that should be looked at. We shall consider this further below.

Exam skills

Bear these limitations in mind when calculating and interpreting ratios, as examiners' reports give many examples of misapplication of ratio analysis, and over-simplistic and misleading interpretations.

1.2.1 Use of financial statements for financial analysis

When assessing the performance of a company, the most readily available information to many stakeholders is the annual report.

Analysis using financial statements is not a precise science. The nature of accounting information means that distortions and differences will always exist between sets of accounts not only from entity to entity but also over time.

Information in published accounts is generally summarised information and detailed information may be needed to make informed decisions. Many items in the accounts will be included at their historic cost. Historic cost information may not be the most appropriate for the decision for which the analysis is being undertaken. Always remember that 'profit' and 'net assets' are fairly arbitrary figures and can be affected by manipulation.

Different firms **use different accounting policies** and have different methods of estimating balances. This means statements from two organisations may not be comparable. In addition, comparability may be impaired where estimates and judgments are used.

A further complication is using accounting loopholes to allow an organisation to obtain finance without it needing to be reported in the statement of financial position.

1.3 Categorisation of ratios

You may remember that ratios can be grouped into the following four categories:

- Profitability and return
- Debt and gearing
- Liquidity: control of cash and other working capital items
- Shareholders' investment ratios (or 'stock market ratios')

1.4 Profitability and return

> Knowledge brought forward from earlier studies

Return on capital employed

$$\text{ROCE} = \frac{\text{PBIT}}{\text{Capital employed}}\% = \frac{\text{Profit from operations}}{\text{Total assets less current liabilities}}\%$$

Where capital employed = shareholders' funds + long-term debt finance

When **interpreting** ROCE look for the following.

- How risky is the business?
- How capital intensive is it?
- What ROCE do similar businesses have?
- How does it compare with current market borrowing rates, is it earning enough to be able to cover the costs of extra borrowing?

Problems: which items to consider to achieve comparability:

- Revaluation of assets
- Accounting policies, eg goodwill, research and development
- Whether bank overdraft is classified as a short/long-term liability

Return on equity (return on net assets)

$$\text{ROE} = \frac{\text{Profit after interest and tax}}{\text{Book value of shareholders' funds}}\%$$

This gives a more **restricted view** of capital than ROCE, but the same principles apply.

ROCE = Asset turnover × Profit margin

Asset turnover

$$\text{Asset turnover} = \frac{\text{Sales}}{\text{Capital employed}} \text{ or } \frac{\text{Sales}}{\text{Total assets less current liabilities}}$$

This measures how efficiently the assets have been used. Amend to just non-current assets for capital intensive businesses.

Profit margin

$$\text{Profit margin} = \frac{\text{PBIT}}{\text{Sales}}\% \qquad \text{Gross profit margin} = \frac{\text{Gross profit}}{\text{Sales}}\%$$

It is useful to compare profit margin to gross profit % to investigate movements which do not match.

Gross profit margin

- Sales prices, sales volume and sales mix
- Purchase prices and related costs (discount, carriage etc)
- Production costs, both direct (materials, labour) and indirect (overheads both fixed and variable)
- Inventory levels and valuation, including errors, cut-off and costs of running out of goods

Net profit margin

- Sales expenses in relation to sales levels
- Administrative expenses, including salary levels
- Distribution expenses in relation to sales levels

PART A FORMULATION OF FINANCIAL STRATEGY   3: Forecasting and analysis

1.5 Debt and gearing

Knowledge brought forward from earlier studies

Debt ratio

$$\text{Debt ratio} = \frac{\text{Current and non-current liabilities}}{\text{Current and non-current assets}} \% \;(>50\%=\text{high})$$

Debt/equity

$$\text{Debt/equity ratio} = \frac{\text{Interest bearing net debts}}{\text{Shareholders' funds}} \% \;(>100\% = \text{high})$$

Or simply $\dfrac{\text{Value of debt}}{\text{Value of equity}}$

Operating gearing (leverage)

$$\text{Gearing} = \frac{\text{Contribution (sales minus variable cost of sales)}}{\text{PBIT}}$$

Demonstrates relationship between cost operating structure and profitability. Indication of business risks from rises or falls in volume.

Interest cover

$$\text{Interest cover} = \frac{\text{PBIT (incl int receivable)}}{\text{Interest payable}} \;\text{or}\; \frac{\text{Profit from operations}}{\text{Finance costs}}$$

Is this a better way to measure gearing? Company must generate enough profit to cover interest. Certainly it's important to bankers and lenders.

We shall consider gearing and investor ratios further in Chapter 9.

1.6 Liquidity

Knowledge brought forward from earlier studies

Current ratio

$$\text{Current ratio} = \frac{\text{Current assets}}{\text{Current liabilities}}$$

Assume assets realised at book level ∴ theoretical. 2:1 acceptable? 1.5:1? It depends on the industry. Remember that excessively large levels can indicate excessive receivables and inventories, and poor control of working capital.

Quick ratio

$$\text{Quick ratio (acid test)} = \frac{\text{Current assets - inventory}}{\text{Current liabilities}}$$

Eliminates illiquid and subjectively valued inventory. Care is needed: it could be high if **overtrading** with receivables, but no cash. Is 1:1 OK? Many supermarkets operate on 0.3, as inventories of goods are very liquid and inventory turnover is very fast.

Receivables collection period (receivables days)

$$\text{Average collection period} = \frac{\text{Trade receivables}}{\text{Credit sales}} \times 365$$

Is it **consistent** with quick/current ratio? If not, investigate.

Inventory days

$$\text{Inventory days} = \frac{\text{Inventory}}{\text{Cost of sales}} \times 365$$

Note that cost of sales excludes depreciation of any production equipment

The quicker the turnover the better? But remember:

- Lead times
- Seasonal fluctuations in orders
- Alternative uses of warehouse space
- Bulk buying discounts
- Likelihood of inventory perishing or becoming obsolete

Payables payment period (payables days)

$$\text{Payables payment period} = \frac{\text{Trade payables}}{\text{Purchases}} \times 365$$

Use **cost of sales (excluding depreciation)** if purchases are not disclosed.

Cash operating cycle

= Average time raw materials are in inventory

− Period of credit taken from suppliers

+ Time taken to produce goods

+ Time taken by customers to pay for goods

Reasons for changes in liquidity

- Credit control efficiency altered
- Altering payment period of suppliers as a source of funding
- Reducing inventory holdings to maintain liquidity

We shall look at the management of working capital in Chapter 4.

1.7 Shareholder investor ratios

Knowledge brought forward from earlier studies

Dividend yield

$$\text{Dividend yield} = \frac{\text{Dividend per share}}{\text{Market price per share}} \%$$

- **Low yield**: the company retains a large proportion of profits to reinvest
- **High yield**: this is a risky company or slow-growing

Dividend yield is generally less than interest yield. Shareholders will expect price rises, and wish for return (dividends + capital gains) to exceed return investors get from fixed interest securities.

Earnings per share (EPS)

$$\text{EPS} = \frac{\text{Profits distributable to ordinary shareholders}}{\text{Number of ordinary shares issued}}$$

Investors look for growth; earnings levels need to be sustained to pay dividends and invest in the business. In order for comparisons over time to be valid, must be consistent basis of calculation. EPS can be manipulated.

Need to consider possibility of dilution through exercise of warrants or options, or conversion of bonds.

Dividend cover

$$\text{Dividend cover} = \frac{\text{EPS}}{\text{Dividend per share}}$$

This shows **how safe the dividend is**, or the extent of profit retention. Variations are due to maintaining dividend when profits are declining.

The converse of dividend cover is the **dividend payout ratio**.

$$\text{Dividend payout ratio} = \frac{\text{Dividend per share}}{\text{EPS}}$$

P/E ratio

$$\text{P/E ratio} = \frac{\text{Market price per share}}{\text{EPS}}$$

The **higher the better** here: it reflects the confidence of the market in high earnings growth and/or low risk. A rise in EPS will cause an increase in P/E ratio, but maybe not to same extent.

P/E ratio will be affected by interest rate changes; a rise in rates will mean a fall in the P/E ratio as shares become less attractive. P/E ratio also depends on market expectations and confidence.

Earnings yield

$$\text{Earnings yield} = \frac{\text{EPS}}{\text{Market price per share}} \%$$

This shows the dividend yield if there is no retention of profit. It allows you to compare companies with **different dividend policies**, showing growth rather than earnings.

Net assets per share

$$\text{Net assets per share} = \frac{\text{Net assets}}{\text{No of shares}}$$

This is a crude measure of value of a company, liable to distortion.

Return on shareholders' funds

$$\text{Return on shareholders' funds (equity)} = \frac{\text{Earnings}}{\text{Shareholders' funds}} \times 100$$

Earnings are after interest, tax and any preference dividends. A high return on shareholders' funds suggests that the company is profitable and has more funds available for equity shareholders.

Total shareholder return

Total shareholder return = dividend yield + capital gain.

As the name suggests, this is a measure of the total return to shareholders over a one year period.

> **Other factors**
>
> Investors are also interested in current market price, past and future returns and security of investment.

We shall look at the major investor ratios again in Chapter 9.

Question 3.1 — Ratios

Learning outcomes: A(2)(c)

Calculate liquidity and working capital ratios from the accounts of a manufacturer of products for the construction industry, and comment on the ratios.

	20X8 $m	20X7 $m
Revenue	2,065.0	1,788.7
Less cost of sales	1,478.6	1,304.0
Gross profit	586.4	484.7
Current assets		
Inventory	119.0	109.0
Receivables (note 1)	400.9	347.4
Short-term investments	4.2	18.8
Cash at bank and in hand	48.2	48.0
	572.3	523.2
Creditors: amounts falling due within one year		
Loans and overdrafts	49.1	35.3
Taxes	62.0	46.7
Dividend	19.2	14.3
Payables (note 2)	370.7	324.0
	501.0	420.3
Net current assets	71.3	102.9

Notes

		20X8 $m	20X7 $m
1	Trade receivables	329.8	285.4
2	Trade payables	236.2	210.8

1.8 Other information

As well as ratios, other **financial** and **non-financial information** can give valuable indicators of a company's performance and position.

(a) **The revaluation of non-current assets**

Non-current assets may be stated in the statement of financial position at cost less accumulated depreciation. They may also be revalued from time to time to a current market value, which will lead to an increased depreciation charge.

(b) **Share capital and reserves**

The nature of any increase in share capital and accumulated profits will be of interest including **share issues** and **substantial profit retentions**. If a company has **issued shares in the form of a dividend**, are there obvious reasons why this should be so? For example, does the company need to retain capital within the business because of poor trading in the previous year, making the directors reluctant to pay out more cash dividend than necessary?

(c) **Loans and other liabilities**

Two aspects to look out for are whether or not loans are **secured** and the **redemption dates** of loans.

(d) **Contingencies**

Contingencies are conditions which exist at the balance sheet date where the outcome will be confirmed only on the occurrence or non-occurrence of one or more uncertain future events. For example, a pending lawsuit.

(e) **Events after the statement of financial position date**

Significant events occurring after statement of financial position date include mergers and acquisitions or the purchase and sales of major non-current assets and investments. Knowledge of such events allows the analyst to 'update' the latest published figures by taking account of their potential impact.

Section summary

Ratios provide a means of systematically analysing financial statements. They can be grouped under the headings **profitability**, **liquidity**, **gearing** and **shareholders' investment**.

---

2 Cash forecasts 9/11

Introduction

Forecasting is used to set shareholder expectations, for performance evaluation and to analyse financing requirements. In the exam you could be expected to produce a forecast statement of comprehensive income, a forecast statement of financial position and/or a cash flow forecast.

2.1 Cash budgets

A CASH BUDGET (or FORECAST) is a detailed budget of estimated cash inflows and outflows incorporating both revenue and capital items. *(CIMA Official Terminology)*

Cash forecasts (or budgets) provide an early warning of liquidity problems, by estimating:

- How much cash is required
- When it is required
- How long it is required for
- Whether it will be available from anticipated sources

A company must know **when** it might need to borrow and **for how long**, not just **what amount** of funding could be required.

2.2 Estimating a future statement of financial position

Statement of financial position based forecasts can be used to assess the scale of funding requirements or cash surpluses expected over time, and to act as a check on the realism of cash flow based forecasts.

This forecast calls for some prediction of the amount/value of each item in the company's statement of financial position, **excluding cash and short-term investments**, as these are what we are trying to predict. A forecast is prepared by taking each item in the statement of financial position, and estimating what its value might be at the future date. The assumptions used are critical, and the following guidelines are suggested.

(a) **Intangible non-current assets and long term investments**

If there are any, they should be taken at their current value unless there is good reason for another treatment.

(b) **Property, plant and equipment**

Some estimate of **asset purchases** (and disposals) will be required. Revaluations can be ignored as they are not cash flows.

(c) **Current assets**

Estimates of **inventory** and **receivables** are sometimes based on fairly simple assumptions, such as the following:

(i) **Same** as current amounts. This is unlikely if business has boomed

(ii) **Increase by a certain percentage**, to allow for growth in business volume. For example, the volume of receivables might be expected to increase by a similar amount

(iii) **Decrease by a certain percentage**, to allow for tighter management control over working capital

(iv) Assume to be a **certain percentage** of the company's estimated **annual sales revenue** for the year

(v) The firm can assume that the **operating cycle** will more or less **remain the same**

In other words, if a firm's customers take two months to pay, this relationship can be expected to continue. Therefore, if total annual sales are $12m and customers take two months to pay, receivables at the year end will be $2/12 \times \$12m = \$2m$.

If revenue increases to $18m, and the collection period stays at two months, receivables will amount to $2/12 \times \$18m = \$3m$. Similar relationships might be plotted for inventory and hence purchases and suppliers.

(d) **Current liabilities**

Some itemising of current liabilities will be necessary, because no single set of assumptions can accurately estimate them collectively.

(i) **Trade payables and accruals** can be estimated in a similar way to current assets, as indicated above.

(ii) Current liabilities include **bank loans** due for repayment within 12 months. These can be identified individually.

(iii) **Bank overdraft facilities**. Often there will be no overdraft in the forecast balance sheet. Any available overdraft facility can be considered when the company's overall cash needs are identified.

(iv) **Taxation**. Any tax on profits payable should be estimated from anticipated profits and based on an estimated percentage of those profits.

(v) **Dividends payable**. Any ordinary dividend payable should be estimated from anticipated profits, and any preference dividend payable can be predicted from the coupon rate of dividend for the company's preference shares.

(vi) **Other creditors** can be included if required and are of significant value.

(e) **Non-current creditors**

Non-current creditors are likely to consist of non-current loans, bonds and any other non-current finance debt. Unless the company has already arranged further non-current borrowing, this item should include just existing long-term debts, minus debts that will be repaid before the statement of financial position date (or debts transferred from long-term to short-term creditors).

(f) **Share capital and reserves**

With the exception of accumulated profits (retained earnings), the estimated figures for share capital and other reserves should be the same as their current amount, unless it is expected or known that a new issue of shares will take place, in which case the total amount raised (net of issue expenses) should be added to the share capital/other reserves total.

(g) **Accumulated profits**

An estimate is required of the change in the company's **accumulated profits** in the period up to the statement of financial position date. This reserve should be calculated as:

(i) The existing value of the retained earnings

(ii) **Plus** further retained profits anticipated in the period to the statement of financial position date (ie post tax profits minus estimated dividends)

2.3 Compiling a statement of financial position

The various estimates should now be brought together into a statement of financial position. The figures on each side will not be equal, and there will be one of the following.

(a) A surplus of share capital and reserves over net assets (total assets minus total liabilities). If this occurs, the company will be forecasting a **cash surplus**.

(b) A surplus of net assets over share capital and reserves. If this occurs, the company will be forecasting a **funding deficit**.

Alpha has an existing statement of financial position and an estimated forecast in one year's time **before the necessary extra funding is taken into account**, as follows.

	Existing €'000	Existing €'000	Forecast after one year €'000	Forecast after one year €'000
ASSETS				
Non-current assets		100		180
Current assets		90		100
Total assets		190		280
EQUITY AND LIABILITIES				
Share capital and reserves				
€1 ordinary shares	50		50	
Other reserves	20		20	
Accumulated profits	30		50	
		100		120
Non-current liabilities				
5% bonds	20		20	
Deferred tax	10		10	
		30		30
Current liabilities		60		90
Total equity and liabilities		190		240

The company is expecting to increase its total assets in the next year by €90,000 (€280,000 – €190,000) but expects accumulated profits for the year to be €20,000 (€50,000 – €30,000) and current liabilities to increase by €30,000. There is an excess of net assets over share capital and reserves amounting to €40,000 (€280,000 – €240,000), which is a **funding deficit**. The company must consider ways of obtaining extra cash (eg by borrowing) to cover the deficit. If it cannot, it will need to keep its assets below the forecast amount, or to have higher short-term payables.

A revised projected statement of financial position can then be prepared by introducing these new sources of funds. This should be checked for realism (eg by **ratio analysis**) to ensure that the proportion of the statement made up by non-current assets and working capital, etc is sensible.

2.4 Deriving cash flow from statement of comprehensive income and statement of financial position information

The previous paragraphs concentrated on preparing a forecast statement of financial position, with estimated figures for receivables, payables and inventory. Cash requirements might therefore be presented as the 'balancing figure'. However, it is possible to derive a forecast figure for cash flows using both the statement of comprehensive income and statement of financial position. The profit from operations is adjusted first of all for items not involving cash, such as depreciation. This is further adjusted for changes in the levels of working capital (eg receivables and payables) to arrive at operational cash flows.

This is illustrated in the example below. For the time being, assume that there is no depreciation. The task is to get from profit to operational cash flow, by taking into account movements in working capital.

			Profit $	Operational cash flow $
Sales			200,000	200,000
Opening receivables (∴ received in year)				15,000
Closing receivables (outstanding at year end)				(24,000)
Cash in				191,000
Cost of sales			170,000	170,000
Closing inventory (purchased, but not used, in year)				21,000
Opening inventory (used, but not purchased, in year)				(12,000)
Purchases in year				179,000
Opening payables (∴ paid in year)				11,000
Closing payables (outstanding at year end)				(14,000)
Cash out				176,000
Profit/operational cash flow			30,000	15,000

This may be summarised as:

			$	$
Profit				30,000
(Increase)/Decrease in inventory	Opening		12,000	
	Closing		(21,000)	
				(9,000)
(Increase)/Decrease in receivables	Opening		15,000	
	Closing		(24,000)	
				(9,000)
Increase/(Decrease) in payables	Closing		14,000	
	Opening		(11,000)	
				3,000
Operational cash flow				15,000

Section summary

- **Cash forecasting** should ensure that sufficient funds will be available when needed, to sustain the activities of an enterprise at an acceptable cost.

- **Statement of financial position based forecasts** can be used to assess the scale of funding requirements or cash surpluses expected over time, and to act as a check on the realism of cash flow based forecasts.

3 Forecast financial statements: example

Introduction

In this paper, you could be presented with a requirement to construct forecast financial statements, which need not be presented in published accounts format, based upon first or base year data. Below, we work through such a question in detail.

Exam alert

Do not worry about the **format** of the statements. You will probably be given abbreviated statements of financial position and comprehensive income which you can copy. Any **clear format** for the cash flow statement will be acceptable.

Example: Financial statement forecasting

You are a consultant working for a company called CC Drains, which started trading four years ago in 20X3 and which manufactures plastic rainwater drainage goods. You have the following information.

(a) Revenue and cost of sales are expected to increase by 10% in each of the financial years ending 31 December 20X7, 20X8 and 20X9. Operating expenses are expected to increase by 5% each year.

(b) The company expects to continue to be liable for tax at the marginal rate of 30%. You can assume that tax is paid or refunded 12 months after the year end.

(c) The ratios of receivables to sales and trade payables to cost of sales will remain the same for the next three years.

(d) Non-current assets comprise land and buildings, for which no depreciation is provided. Other assets used by the company, such as machinery and vehicles, are hired on operating leases.

(e) The company plans for dividends to grow at 25% in each of the financial years 20X7, 20X8 and 20X9.

(f) The company plans to purchase new machinery to the value of $500,000 during 20X7, to be depreciated straight line over ten years. The company charges a full year's depreciation in the first year of purchase of its assets. Tax allowable depreciation at 25% reducing balance is available on this expenditure.

(g) Inventory was purchased for $35,000 at the beginning of 20X7. The value of inventory after this purchase is expected to remain at $361,000 for the foreseeable future.

(h) No decision has been made on the type of finance to be used for the expansion programme. The company's directors believe that they can raise new medium-term secured bonds if necessary.

(i) The average P/E ratio of listed companies in the same industry as CC Drains is 15.

The company's objectives include the following.

(a) To earn a pre-tax return on the closing book value of shareholders' funds of 35% pa
(b) To increase dividends per share by 25% per year
(c) To obtain a quotation on a recognised stock exchange within the next three years

A summary of the financial statements for the year to 31 December 20X6 is set out below.

CC DRAINS

SUMMARISED STATEMENT OF COMPREHENSIVE INCOME
FOR THE YEAR TO 31 DECEMBER 20X6

	$'000
Revenue	1,560
Less cost of sales	950
Gross profit	610
Less operating expenses	325
Less interest	30
Less tax liability	77
Net profit	178
Dividends declared	68

SUMMARISED STATEMENT OF FINANCIAL POSITION AT 31 DECEMBER 20X6

	$'000
Non-current assets (net book value)	750
Current assets	
Inventories	326
Receivables	192
Cash and bank	50
Total assets	1,318
Financing	
Ordinary share capital (ordinary shares of $1)	500
Retained profits to 31 December 20X5	128
Retentions for the year to 31 December 20X6	110
10% loan note redeemable 20Z0	300
	1,038
Current liabilities	
Trade payables	135
Other payables (including tax and dividends)	145
Total equity and liabilities	1,318

Required

Using the information given:

(a) Prepare forecast statements of comprehensive income for the years 20X7, 20X8 and 20X9, and calculate whether the company is likely to meet its stated financial objective (return on shareholders' funds) for these three years.

(b) Prepare cash flow forecasts for the years 20X7, 20X8 and 20X9, and estimate the amount of funds which will need to be raised by the company to finance its expansion.

Notes

(1) You should ignore interest or returns on surplus funds invested during the three-year period of review.

(2) You may ignore the timing of cash flows within each year and you should not discount the cash flows.

PART A FORMULATION OF FINANCIAL STRATEGY 3: Forecasting and analysis **47**

Solution

(a) CC DRAINS STATEMENTS OF COMPREHENSIVE INCOME

	Actual 20X6 $'000	20X7 $'000	Forecast 20X8 $'000	20X9 $'000
Revenue (increase 10% pa)	1,560	1,716	1,888	2,076
Less cost of sales (increase 10% pa)	950	1,045	1,150	1,264
Gross profit	610	671	738	812
Less: operating expenses (increase 5% pa)	325	341	358	376
depreciation (10% pa × $500,000)		50	50	50
Profit from operations	285	280	330	386
Less interest (assumed constant)	30	30	30	30
Profit before tax	255	250	300	356
Less taxation (see working below)	77	53	77	101
Net profit	178	197	223	255
Less dividend (25% growth pa)	68	85	106	133
Retained profit	110	112	117	122
Reserves b/f	128	238	350	467
Reserves c/f	238	350	467	589
Share capital	500	500	500	500
Year end reserves	238	350	467	589
Year end shareholders' funds	738	850	967	1,089
Pre-tax return on shareholders' funds	34.6%	29.4%	31.0%	32.7%

On the basis of these figures, the financial objective of a pre-tax return of 35% of year-end shareholders' funds is not achieved in any of the years.

Working

It is assumed that the company does not account for deferred taxation.

	Actual 20X6 $'000	20X7 $'000	Forecast 20X8 $'000	20X9 $'000
Profit before tax	255	250	300	356
Add back depreciation		50	50	50
Less tax allowance (25% reducing balance)		(125)	(94)	(70)
Taxable profit	255	175	256	336
Tax at 30%	77	53	77	101

(b) **Cash flow forecasts**

Exam skills

There are many ways of computing the cash flow forecasts. However, some ways are quicker than others. Our answer shows one of the quickest methods first. Remember that you will need to complete calculations in the exam as quickly as possible.

The 20X6 statement of financial position figure for 'other payables (including tax and dividends)' is simply the sum of tax and dividends in the statement of comprehensive income. It is assumed that this will continue to be the case in the following three years. The annual change in net current assets can be computed as follows.

3: Forecasting and analysis

Changes in net current assets

	Actual 20X6 $'000	Forecast 20X7 $'000	Forecast 20X8 $'000	Forecast 20X9 $'000
Inventories (scenario note (7))	326	361	361	361
Receivables (12.31% of sales) *	192	211	232	256
Trade payables (14.21% of cost of sales) *	(135)	(148)	(163)	(180)
Tax and dividends payable (sum of the figures)	(145)	(138)	(183)	(234)
Net current assets	238	286	247	203
Increase/(decrease) net current assets		48	(39)	(44)

* Alternatively receivables and payables can be computed as a 10% increase each year.

The cash flow forecasts can then be constructed.

Cash flow forecasts

	20X7 $'000	20X8 $'000	20X9 $'000
Retained profit for the year	112	117	122
Add back depreciation	50	50	50
(Investment in net current assets)/release of net current assets (see working)	(48)	39	44
Expenditure on non-current assets	(500)		
Surplus/(deficit) for the year	(386)	206	216
Cash/(deficit) b/f	50	(336)	(130)
Cash/(deficit) c/f	(336)	(130)	86

The company will need to find finance of $338,000 in 20X7 but this can be completely repaid in the following two years. However, interest costs have been ignored in this computation.

Exam skills

Alternative presentations include:

- A detailed statement of cash receipts and payments, or
- A cash flow statement in IAS 7 format.

Answers by both of these methods are shown here, for comparison, but you should practise producing forecasts as quickly as possible.

Appendices

1 **Cash receipts and payments**

	20X7 $'000	20X8 $'000	20X9 $'000
Receipts			
Cash from sales (revenue + opening receivables – closing receivables)	1,697	1,867	2,053
Payments			
For purchases (cost of sales + opening payables – closing payables)	1,032	1,135	1,248
Operating expenses	341	358	376
Additional inventory purchase	35		
Machinery	500		
Interest (current year)	30	30	30
Tax (previous year)	77	53	77
Dividends (previous year)	68	85	106
Total payments	2,083	1,661	1,837

PART A FORMULATION OF FINANCIAL STRATEGY 3: Forecasting and analysis

	20X7 $'000	20X8 $'000	20X9 $'000
Net cash flow	(386)	206	216
Cash/(deficit) b/f	50	(336)	(130)
Cash/(deficit) c/f	(336)	(130)	86

2   **IAS 7 format**

	20X7 $'000	20X8 $'000	20X9 $'000
Net cash inflow from operations (see working)	290	373	429
Less: interest paid	30	30	30
dividends paid	68	85	106
tax paid	77	53	77
Net cash inflow	115	205	216
Investing activities			
Non-current assets	500		
Net cash flow before financing	(385)	205	216

Working: net cash inflow from operations

	20X6 $'000	20X7 $'000	20X8 $'000	20X9 $'000
Inventory	326	361	361	361
Receivables	192	211	232	256
Less payables	(135)	(149)	(163)	(180)
	383	423	430	437
Incremental working capital		(40)	(7)	(7)
Gross profit before depreciation		671	738	812
Less operating expenses		341	358	376
Net cash inflow from operations		290	373	429

Question 3.2   Forecast financial statements

Learning outcomes: A(2)(c)(d)

Triassic produces smoke alarms for residential and office premises. The most recent statement of financial position of the company is set out below.

Statement of financial position as at 30 November 20X2

	€m	€m	€m
Non-current assets			
Freehold buildings at cost		24.4	
Less: accumulated depreciation		4.4	20.0
Plant and machinery at cost		37.9	
Less: accumulated depreciation		12.9	25.0
			45.0
Current assets			
Inventory	39.0		
Trade receivables	20.0		
Bank	8.3	67.3	
Less: payables: amounts falling due within one year			
Trade payables	12.0		
Taxation	4.5		
Dividends	7.8	24.3	
			43.0
			88.0

Capital and reserves

	€m
Ordinary €1 shares	20.0
Accumulated profits	68.0
	88.0

During the year to 30 November 20X2, the sales revenue for the business was €240m.

As a result of recent changes in government legislation, it has been predicted that the market for smoke alarms will increase significantly in the short-term. The directors of Triassic are planning to expand the business significantly during the forthcoming year in order to exploit these new market conditions. The following forecasts and assumptions for the forthcoming year have been prepared by the directors.

(i) Sales for the forthcoming year will be 25% higher than the previous year. Sales are expected to be spread evenly over the year.

(ii) The gross profit margin will be 30% of sales.

(iii) To prepare for the expansion in output, new machinery costing €57m will be purchased at the beginning of the year and a long-term loan will be taken out immediately to help finance this purchase. At the end of the year, the long-term debt to equity ratio is planned to be 1:3.

(iv) The average receivables collection period will be three times that of previous years and the average payment period for creditors will be one and a half months.

(v) The value of inventory at the end of the year will be €18m lower than at the beginning of the year.

(vi) Depreciation charges for freehold buildings and plant and machinery are calculated using the reducing balance method and will be 5% and 20% respectively. Other expenses for the period will be €54.6m. There will be no prepayments or accruals at the end of the year.

(vii) Dividends will be announced at the end of the year and the dividend payout ratio will be 50% which is in line with previous years. The tax rate will be 30% of net profits before taxation. The dividend and tax will be paid after the year end.

All workings should be in €millions and should be made to one decimal place. Workings must be clearly shown.

Required

(a) Prepare in as much detail as the information allows:

　　(i) A forecast statement of comprehensive income for the year ended 30 November 20X3, and
　　(ii) A forecast balance statement of financial position sheet as at 30 November 20X3.

(b) Comment briefly on the financial performance and position of the business using the financial statements prepared in (a) above.

Exam alert

The discussion/explanation part of a forecasting question will be worth a significant proportion of the marks on offer, so make sure you practise answering these parts, in addition to the calculations.

PART A FORMULATION OF FINANCIAL STRATEGY   3: Forecasting and analysis

4 Sensitivity analysis and changes in variables

> **Introduction**
>
> As part of a business's risk analysis, different forecasts should be prepared with **changing financial** or **business variables**. The links between these variables and the figures in the forecasts may not be straightforward.

4.1 Sensitivity analysis

In a well-designed forecast a great number of **'what-if'** questions can be asked and answered quickly by carrying out **sensitivity analysis** and changing the relevant data or variables. In a cash flow forecast model, managers may wish to know the cash flow impact if sales growth per month is nil, ½%, 1%, 1½%, 2½% or minus 1% and so on.

However businesses will also want to estimate the magnitude of changes in sales and ultimately profits if economic or business variables change. This will be more problematic.

4.2 Changes in economic variables

Businesses need to be aware of likely changes in inflation, interest rates and so on. Governments and central banks issue regular updates and forecasts, and the financial press is also helpful.

However businesses will also need to forecast:

- How the **predicted changes** will **affect demand**. The links may not be easy to forecast. Businesses should consider separately the effect of major increases on each type of product.

- How the **business** will **respond to changes in variables**. For example will the business automatically adjust prices upwards by the rate of inflation, or will it try to hold prices? What will its competitors do? If raw material prices increase, will the business try to change suppliers? What effect will this have on payment patterns?

4.3 Changes in business variables

Economic variables will clearly impact upon business variables such as **sales volumes** or **profit margins**. Businesses need to be aware of the other factors, such as changes in the competitive environment that could affect these variables and how this effect might work.

The original forecast should itself have been based on **demand forecasts**, determined by **market surveys** and **statistical models** based on past changes in demand. However if factors such as taste change, businesses need to recognise this might not just require marginal changes in forecasts, but a re-visiting of the base data, since the changes will ultimately render the previous surveys or models redundant.

CASE STUDY

Singapore Airlines provide sensitivity analysis in their annual reports. For example, an extract from their 2010/11 annual report shows the sensitivity of passenger revenue to changes in key variables.

Sensitivity of passenger revenue to a one percentage point change in passenger load factor and a one percentage point change in passenger yield is as follows:

	SG$m
One percentage point change in passenger load factor, if yield and seat capacity remain constant	110.6
One percentage point change in passenger yield, if passenger traffic remains constant	86.8

A change in the price of fuel of US$1 per barrel affects Singapore Airlines' annual fuel cost by about SG$36 million.

> **Section summary**
> - Current and forecast information can be evaluated taking account of variation in **economic** (eg interest rates) and **business** (eg volume and margins) factors.
> - The **sensitivity** of changes in expected values in the forecasts can be analysed.

5 Financing requirements 9/11

> **Introduction**
>
> Cash deficits will be funded in different ways, depending on whether they are short or long-term. Sources of finance will be covered in detail in later chapters of the Study Text. Businesses should also have procedures for investing surpluses with appropriate levels of risk and return.

5.1 Deficiencies

Any forecast **deficiency** of cash will have to be funded.

(a) **Borrowing**. If borrowing arrangements are not already secured, a source of funds will have to be found. If a company cannot fund its cash deficits it could be wound up.

(b) The firm can make arrangements to **sell any short-term marketable financial investments** to raise cash.

(c) The firm can delay payments to suppliers, or pull in payments from customers. This is sometimes known as **leading and lagging**.

Because cash forecasts cannot be entirely accurate, companies should have **contingency funding**, available from a surplus cash balance and liquid investments, or from a bank facility. The approximate size of contingency margin will vary from company to company, according to the cyclical nature of the business and the approach of its cash planners.

Forecasting gives management **time** to arrange its funding. If planned in advance, instead of a panic measure to avert a cash crisis, a company can more easily choose when to borrow, and will probably obtain a lower interest rate.

5.2 Cash surpluses

If a **cash surplus** is forecast, having an idea of both its size and how long it will exist could help decide how best to invest it.

In some cases, the amount of **interest** earned from surplus cash could be significant for the company's earnings. The company might then need a forecast of its interest earnings in order to indicate its prospective **earnings per share** to stock market analysts and institutional investors.

The entity must have procedures for investing surpluses which consider both **risk** and **return**.

> **Section summary**
>
> Once a cash forecast has been prepared, decisions on **financing** can then be made.

PART A FORMULATION OF FINANCIAL STRATEGY 3: Forecasting and analysis

Chapter Roundup

- **Ratios** provide a means of systematically analysing financial statements. They can be grouped under the headings **profitability, liquidity, gearing** and **shareholders' investment**.
- **Cash forecasting** should ensure that sufficient funds will be available when needed, to sustain the activities of an enterprise at an acceptable cost.
- **Statement of financial position based forecasts** can be used to assess the scale of funding requirements or cash surpluses expected over time, and to act as a check on the realism of cash flow based forecasts.
- Current and forecast information can be evaluated taking account of variation in **economic** (eg interest rates) and **business** (eg volume and margins) factors.
- The **sensitivity** of changes in expected values in the forecasts can be analysed.
- Once a cash forecast has been prepared, decisions on **financing** can then be made.

Quick Quiz

1. What are the main limitations of ratio analysis?
2. Return on equity = ?
3. What are the components of the cash operating cycle?
4. Give three methods of funding a deficiency of cash.
5. What variables should typically be included in a cash budgeting model?
6. If a business is in financial difficulties, what type of assets should be sold off first?
7. From what sources might a business be able to obtain contingency funds?

Answers to Quick Quiz

1. - Lack of comparable industry information
   - Historical information used for comparison may be out-of-date
   - Ratio levels may not indicate situation fairly
   - Ratios need careful interpretation
   - Ratios can be manipulated
   - Some ratios can be calculated in different ways
   - Ratios shouldn't be used in isolation

2. Return on equity = $\dfrac{\text{Profit after interest and tax}}{\text{Book value of shareholders' funds}} \times 100\%$

3. **Cash operating cycle**

   = Average time raw materials are in inventory
   − Period of credit taken from suppliers
   + Time taken to produce goods
   + Time taken by customers to pay for goods

4. Borrowing; selling short-term financial investments; leading and lagging payables and receivables.

5
- Total sales
- Cash sales, perhaps as a percentage of total sales
- Credit sales, perhaps as a percentage of total sales
- Rate of growth in sales, or seasonal variations in sales
- Time taken by receivables to pay what they owe
- Purchases on credit
- Wages and salaries
- Other cash expenses
- Dividends
- Taxation payments
- Capital expenditure

6   Short-term marketable financial investments

7
- Surplus cash balances
- Liquid investments
- Bank facility

Answers to Questions

3.1 Ratios

	20X8	20X7
Current ratio	$\dfrac{572.3}{501.0} = 1.14$	$\dfrac{523.2}{420.3} = 1.24$
Quick ratio	$\dfrac{453.3}{501.0} = 0.90$	$\dfrac{414.2}{420.3} = 0.99$
Receivables collection period	$\dfrac{329.8}{2,065.0} \times 365 = 58$ days	$\dfrac{285.4}{1,788.7} \times 365 = 58$ days
Inventory turnover period	$\dfrac{119.0}{1,478.6} \times 365 = 29$ days	$\dfrac{109.0}{1,304.0} \times 365 = 31$ days
Payables payment period	$\dfrac{236.2}{1,478.6} \times 365 = 58$ days	$\dfrac{210.8}{1,304.0} \times 365 = 59$ days

As a manufacturing group serving the construction industry, the company would be expected to have a comparatively **lengthy receivables collection period**, because of the relatively poor cash flow in the construction industry. It is clear that the company compensates for this by ensuring that it does not pay for raw materials and other costs before they have sold their inventories of finished goods (hence the similarity of receivables' and payables' turnover periods).

The company's current ratio is a little lower than average but its quick ratio is better than average and very little less than the current ratio. This suggests that **inventory levels are strictly controlled**, which is reinforced by the low inventory turnover period. It would seem that working capital is **tightly managed**, to avoid the poor liquidity which could be caused by a high receivables' turnover period and comparatively high payables.

3.2 Forecast financial statements

(a) (i) There is no information about the cost of loan interest, and it is assumed that this cost is included within other expenses.

TRIASSIC

FORECAST STATEMENT OF COMPREHENSIVE INCOME FOR THE YEAR TO 30 NOVEMBER 20X3

	€m	€m
Revenue (€240m × 1.25)		300.0
Cost of sales (70%)		210.0
Gross profit (30%)		90.0
Expenses	54.6	
Depreciation of buildings (5% of €20m)	1.0	
Depreciation of plant and machinery (20% of €(25m + 57m))	16.4	
		72.0
Profit before taxation		18.0
Taxation (30%)		5.4
Profit after taxation		12.6
Dividend (50%)		6.3
Retained profit		6.3

(ii) TRIASSIC

FORECAST STATEMENT OF FINANCIAL POSITION AS AT 30 NOVEMBER 20X3

	€m	€m	€m
Non-current assets			
Freehold buildings at cost		24.4	
Less accumulated depreciation		5.4	
			19.0
Plant and machinery at cost		94.9	
Less accumulated depreciation (12.9 + 16.4)		29.3	
			65.6
			84.6
Current assets			
Inventory (39 – 18)		21.0	
Trade receivables (W1)		75.0	
		96.0	
Payables: amounts falling due within one year			
Bank overdraft (W4)	19.2		
Trade payables (W2)	24.0		
Taxation payable	5.4		
Dividend payable	6.3		
		54.9	
			41.1
			125.7
Payables: amounts falling due after more than one year			
Loan (W3)			31.4
Total net assets			94.3
Share capital and reserves			
Ordinary shares of €1			20.0
Accumulated profits (68 + 6.3)			74.3
Total equity and reserves			94.3

Workings

(1) *Trade receivables*

Average debt collection period in year to 30.11.20X2 = (20/240) × 12 months = 1 month.

Average debt collection period in year to 30.11.20X3 = 3 times one month = 3 months.

Trade receivables as at 30 November 20X3 = (3/12) × €300 million = €75 million.

(2) *Trade payables*

Purchases in the year = closing inventory + cost of sales − opening inventory.

Purchases are therefore (given an €18m reduction in inventory levels)

21m + 210m − 39m = €192 million.

Trade payables at 30.11.20X3 = (1.5/12) × €192 million = €24 million.

(3) *Loan*

	€m
Share capital	20.0
Reserves as at 30 November 20X2	68.0
Accumulated profit, 20X3	6.3
Share capital and reserves at 30.11.20X3	94.3
Loan at 30.11.20X3 (1/3 of €94.3m)	31.4
Original loan	57.0
Loan repaid in the year	25.6

(4) *Cash*

> **Tutorial note**. The cash balance can be calculated as the 'missing figure' to make the net assets equal the share capital and reserves. A proof of the cash position, however, is shown here.

	€m	€m
Operating profit		18.0
Add back depreciation (1.0 + 16.4)		17.4
		35.4
Reduction in inventory	18.0	
Increase in receivables (75 − 20)	(55.0)	
Increase in trade payables (24 − 12)	12.0	
		(25.0)
Cash flow from operations		10.4
Tax paid		
Dividends paid		
Machinery purchase		
Loan raised		57.0
Loan repaid		(25.6)
Cash flow in the year		(27.5)
Cash at start of year		8.3
Cash at end of year		(19.2)

PART A FORMULATION OF FINANCIAL STRATEGY

(b) **The profit after tax next year** will be €12.6 million, giving a return on equity of (12.6/94.3) 13.4% and a profit margin on sales of (12.6/300) 4.2%. In the previous year, the profit after tax was €15.6 million (double the dividend), with a ROE of (15.6/88) 17.7% and a profit/sales ratio of (15.6/240) 6.5%.

The forecast profit is therefore lower, with a lower ROE and a lower profit/sales ratio, despite a 25% increase in sales.

Liquidity is also expected to deteriorate. The company is forecasting a bank overdraft of €19.2 million at the end of November 20X3, compared to a positive cash balance the previous year. The company will have to ensure that bank overdraft facilities are available if it goes ahead with its plan to increase sales.

The company will also have some long-term debt capital, having been ungeared in the year to 30 November 20X2.

On the basis of the forecasts, it is questionable whether there is any financial benefit to be obtained from expanding sales, and the company management should review its plans urgently, before implementing them.

Now try these questions from the Exam Question Bank

Number	Level	Marks	Time
Q3	Examination	25	45 mins
Q4	Introductory	n/a	35 mins

FINANCIAL STRATEGIES

Probably the most important learning outcome in this paper is that you should be able to '**recommend alternative financial strategies** for an organisation.' The syllabus requires you to assess the implications for shareholder value of alternative financial strategies. We start by looking at short-term financial strategy in the form of **working capital management**.

As we've already seen, **dividend policy** is a key element in overall financial strategy, and in Section 2 we consider dividend policy in depth, in particular whether the amounts of profits that a company distributes has much or little impact on shareholders.

Section 3 deals with **recent developments in financial reporting**. You won't be asked questions requiring a detailed knowledge of financial reporting standards; however you will be expected to know how recent changes and current issues might affect the financial strategies that organisations choose.

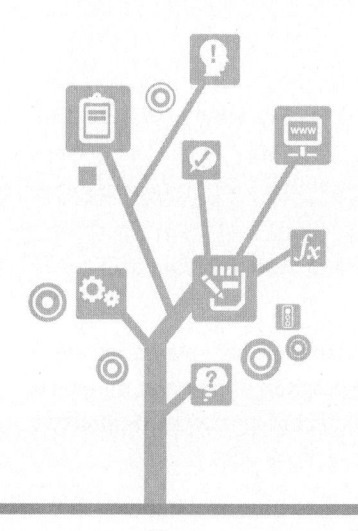

topic list	learning outcomes	syllabus references	ability required
1 Short-term financial strategy	B(1)(a)	B(1)(ii)	evaluation
2 Dividend policy	A(1)(c),(2)d	A(1)(iv),(2)(vi)	analysis
3 Issues in financial reporting	A(2)(d)	A(2)(viii)	evaluation

1 Short-term financial strategy

> **Introduction**
>
> All entities need **liquid resources** to fund working capital needs. Short-term financial strategy involves planning to ensure enough day-to-day cash flow and is determined by **working capital management**. It involves achieving a balance between the requirement to minimise the **risk** of insolvency and the requirement to **maximise profit**.

1.1 Working capital management

Exam alert

Questions on working capital management in this paper will focus more on the overall approach to management rather than the operational issues that are examined at lower levels. However be aware that the March 2011 (resit) exam had a 9 mark section of a 25 mark question on calculating an operating cycle. Working capital management is an important area in this paper.

The working capital that an organisation holds has to be financed, and investment in working capital can be a significant drain on the resources that a business has. Working capital policy involves **investment** decisions and **financing** decisions.

1.2 Working capital investment

Organisations have to decide what are the most important **risks** relating to working capital, and therefore whether to adopt a **conservative** or **aggressive** approach.

1.2.1 Conservative working capital management

A **conservative** working capital management policy aims to **reduce the risk of system breakdown** by holding high levels of working capital.

Customers are allowed **generous payment terms** to stimulate demand, **finished goods inventories** are high to **ensure availability** for customers, and **raw materials and work in progress** are **high** to **minimise the risk** of running out of **inventory** and consequent downtime in the manufacturing process. **Suppliers** are **paid promptly** to ensure their goodwill, again to minimise the chance of stock-outs.

However, the cumulative effect on these policies can be that the firm carries a high burden of **unproductive assets**, resulting in a **financing cost** that can destroy profitability. A period of rapid expansion may also cause **severe cash flow problems** as working capital requirements outstrip available finance. Further problems may arise from inventory obsolescence and lack of flexibility to customer demands.

1.2.2 Aggressive working capital management

An **aggressive** working capital investment policy aims to reduce this financing cost and increase profitability by **cutting inventories**, **speeding up collections from customers**, and **delaying payments to suppliers**.

The potential disadvantage of this policy is an increase in the chances of **system breakdown** through running out of inventory or **loss of goodwill** with customers and suppliers. However, modern manufacturing techniques encourage inventory and work in progress reductions through just-in-time policies, flexible production facilities and improved quality management. Improved customer satisfaction through quality and effective response to customer demand can also mean that credit periods are shortened.

1.3 Working capital financing

There are different ways in which the funding of the current and non-current assets of a business can be achieved by **employing long and short-term sources of funding**.

Short-term finance is usually **cheaper** than long-term finance (under a normal yield curve).

The diagram below illustrates three alternative types of policy A, B and C. The dotted lines A, B and C are the cut-off levels between short-term and long-term financing for each of the policies A, B and C respectively: assets above the relevant dotted line are financed by short-term funding while assets below the dotted line are financed by long-term funding.

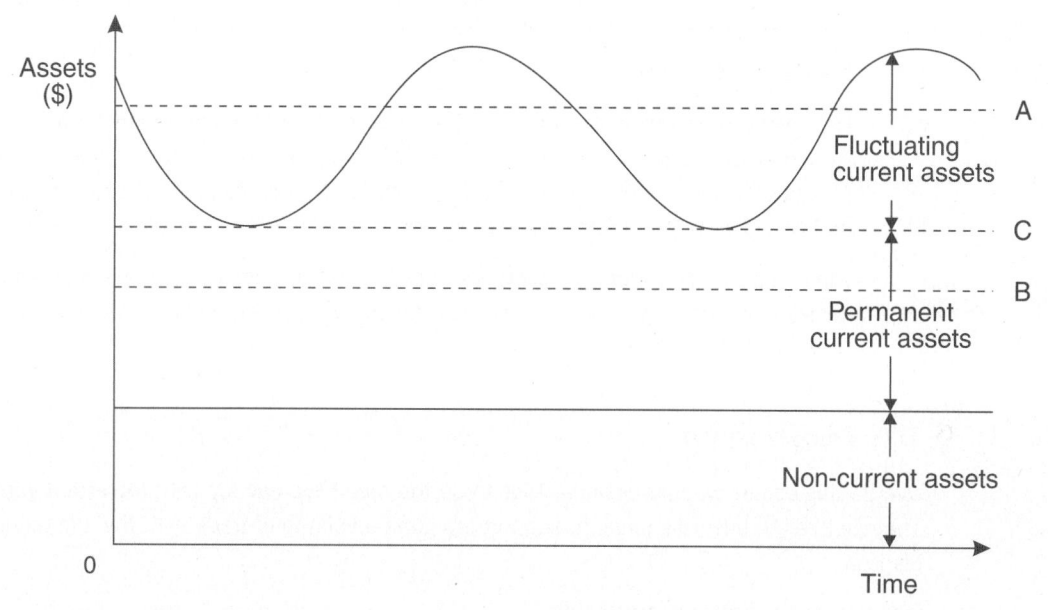

Fluctuating current assets together with **permanent current assets** (the core level of investment in inventory and receivables) form part of the working capital of the business, which may be financed by either long-term funding (including equity capital) or by current liabilities (short-term funding). This can be seen in terms of policies A, B and C. Once again a conservative or an aggressive approach can be followed.

(a) Policy A can be characterised as a **conservative approach** to financing working capital. All non-current assets and permanent current assets, as well as part of the fluctuating current assets, are financed by long-term funding. There is only a need to call upon short-term financing at times when fluctuations in current assets push total assets above the level of dotted line A. At times when fluctuating current assets are low and total assets fall below line A, there will be **surplus cash** which the company will be able to invest in marketable securities.

(b) Policy B is a more **aggressive approach** to financing working capital. Not only are fluctuating current assets all financed out of short-term sources, but so are some of the permanent current assets. This policy represents an **increased risk of liquidity and cash flow problems**, although potential returns will be increased if short-term financing can be obtained more cheaply than long-term finance. It enables **greater flexibility** in financing.

(c) A **balance** between risk and return might be best achieved by the **moderate approach** of policy C, a policy of maturity matching in which long-term funds finance permanent assets while short-term funds finance non-permanent assets.

1.4 Other factors

The trend of overall working capital management will be complicated by the following factors:

(a) **Industry norms**

These are of particular importance for the **management of receivables**. It will be difficult to offer a much shorter payment period than competitors.

(b) **Products**

The **production process**, and hence the amount of work in progress is obviously much greater for some products and in some industries.

(c) **Management issues**

How **working capital** is **managed** may have a significant impact upon the actual length of the working capital cycle whatever the overall strategy might be. Factors to consider include the degree of centralisation (which may allow a more aggressive approach to be adopted, depending though on how efficient the centralised departments actually are).

Differences in the **nature of assets** also need to be considered. Businesses adopting a more conservative strategy may well hold permanent safety inventory and cash balances, whereas there is no safety level of receivables balances.

1.5 Overtrading

Overtrading occurs when a business tries to **do too much too quickly** with **too little long-term capital**. The result is the business trying to support too large a volume of trade with the capital resources at its disposal.

Symptoms of overtrading are as follows.

(a) There is a **rapid increase in turnover**.

(b) There is a **rapid increase in the volume of current assets** and possibly also non-current assets. Inventory turnover and accounts receivable turnover might slow down, in which case the rate of increase in inventories and accounts receivable would be even greater than the rate of increase in sales.

(c) There is **only a small increase in proprietors' capital** (perhaps through retained profits). Most of the increase in assets is financed by credit, especially:

   (i) **Trade accounts payable** - the payment period to accounts payable is likely to lengthen

   (ii) A **bank overdraft**, which often reaches or even exceeds the limit of the facilities agreed by the bank

(d) Some **debt ratios** and **liquidity ratios** alter dramatically.

   (i) The **proportion** of **total assets** financed by proprietors' capital falls, and the proportion financed by credit rises.

   (ii) The **current ratio** and the **quick ratio** fall.

   (iii) The business might have a **liquid deficit**, that is, an excess of current liabilities over current assets.

Even if an overtrading business operates at a profit, it could fail as a result of such liquidity problems. Suitable **solutions** to the problem would be measures to reduce the degree of overtrading.

(a) **New capital** from the shareholders could be injected.

(b) **Better control** could be applied to inventories and accounts receivable.

(c) The company could **abandon ambitious plans** for increased sales and more non-current asset purchases until the business has had time to consolidate its position, and build up its capital base with retained profits.

1.6 Multinational working capital management

Multinational entities will find effective management of working capital more difficult due to a number of factors.

(a) **Longer distances involved**

(b) The **number of parties** involved

(c) The **political risk** from governments placing restrictions on the transfer of funds out of some countries, or the imposition of quotas or tariffs

(d) **Exchange rate fluctuations** between the time of sale and the time the debt is collected will increase the risks from granting credit

(e) **Managing inventory is more complex** as customer demand is harder to analyse, taxes may be payable on inventory holdings and there may be an increased risk of expropriation

Exam alert

A past exam question has required advice on whether management of working capital should be carried out in a foreign country or maintained as a centralised function in the UK. Use your practical common sense in such situations as well as technical knowledge.

Section summary

Short-term financial strategy is determined by **working capital management**. It involves achieving a balance between the requirement to minimise the risk of insolvency and the requirement to maximise profit.

2 Dividend policy   9/10, 5/11, 9/11, 3/12, 5/12

Introduction

In Chapter 1, we identified the three main types of decisions facing financial managers: investment decisions, financing decisions and dividend decisions. In this section we are going to look in more detail at the dividend decision.

KEY TERM

A DIVIDEND is a distribution of profits to the holders of equity investments in proportion to their holdings of a particular class of capital.   *(IAS 18)*

Exam alert

Dividend policy has been regularly examined as a minor issue to comment on.

2.1 Dividend payments

Shareholders normally have the power to vote to **reduce** the size of the dividend at the AGM, but not the power to **increase** the dividend. The directors of the company are therefore in a strong position, with regard to shareholders, when it comes to determining dividend policy. For practical purposes, shareholders will usually be obliged to accept the dividend policy that has been decided on by the directors, or otherwise to sell their shares.

2.2 Factors influencing dividend policy

The amount of surplus cash paid out as dividends will have a **direct impact** on **finance available for investment**.

When deciding upon the dividends to pay out to shareholders, one of the main considerations of the directors will be the amount of earnings they wish to retain to meet **financing needs**.

Question 4.1 — Retained earnings

Learning outcomes: A(2)(d)

What are the major reasons for using the cash from retained earnings to finance new investments, rather than to pay higher dividends and then raise new equity funds for the new investments?

As well as future financing requirements, the decision on how much of a company's profits should be retained, and how much paid out to shareholders, will be influenced by:

(a) The **need to remain profitable**. (Dividends are paid out of profits, and an unprofitable company cannot for ever go on paying dividends out of retained profits made in the past).

(b) The **law on distributable profits**.

(c) Any **dividend restraints** that might be imposed by loan agreements.

(d) The **effect of inflation**, and the need to retain some profit within the business just to maintain its operating capability unchanged.

(e) The company's **gearing level**. (If the company wants extra finance, the sources of funds used should strike a balance between equity and debt finance).

(f) The company's **liquidity position**. (Dividends are a cash payment, and a company must have enough cash to pay the dividends it declares).

(g) The need to **repay debt** in the near future.

(h) The ease with which the company could raise **extra finance** from sources other than retained earnings – see below re life cycle issues.

(i) The **signalling effect** of dividends to shareholders and the financial markets in general – see below.

2.3 Life cycle issues

Young companies usually have a **residual** dividend policy which means they choose to rely on internally generated equity to finance any new projects. As a result, dividend payments can come out of the residual or leftover equity only after all project capital requirements are met so dividends are **rarely paid**.

Mature companies usually have a **stable growth** dividend policy. They have less need to invest in new projects and investments can and should be financed by **debt.** (We will look at life cycle issues and financing in Chapter 9).

2.4 Dividends as a signal to investors

The ultimate objective in any financial management decisions is to **maximise shareholders' wealth**. This wealth is basically represented by the **current market value** of the company, which should largely be determined by the **cash flows arising from the investment decisions** taken by management.

Although the market would **like** to value shares on the basis of underlying cash flows on the company's projects, such information is **not readily available to investors**. But the directors do have this information.

The dividend declared can be interpreted as a **signal** from directors to shareholders about the strength of underlying project cash flows.

Investors usually expect a **consistent dividend policy** from the company, with stable dividends each year or, even better, **steady dividend growth**. A large rise or fall in dividends in any year can have a marked effect on the company's share price. Stable dividends or steady dividend growth are usually needed for share price stability. A cut in dividends may be treated by investors as signalling that the future prospects of the company are weak. Thus, the dividend which is paid acts, possibly without justification, as a **signal** of the future prospects of the company.

The signalling effect of a company's dividend policy may also be used by management of a company which faces a possible **takeover**. The dividend level might be increased as a defence against the takeover: investors may take the increased dividend as a signal of improved future prospects, thus driving the share price higher and making the company more expensive for a potential bidder to take over.

CASE STUDY

Almost 20 years after its inception, Microsoft announced that it would pay a dividend for the first time in an attempt to address calls for the company to release some of its $43.4 billion cash surplus to its shareholders. Despite this news, Microsoft's share price fell by 3% ($1.71). This suggests that the markets may have took the announcement as a signal of a reduction in profitable future investment opportunities for the company.

Exam skills

You should show, whenever relevant in exam answers, that you appreciate the signalling effect of dividends. However, don't mention it if you're dealing with a private company as it won't be relevant.

2.5 Theories of dividend policy

2.5.1 Residual theory

A **'residual' theory** of **dividend policy** can be summarised as follows.

- If a company can identify projects with positive net present values, it should invest in them.
- Only when these investment opportunities are exhausted should dividends be paid.

2.5.2 Traditional view

The **'traditional' view** of dividend policy, implicit in our earlier discussion, is to focus on the effects on **share price**. The price of a share depends upon the mix of dividends, given shareholders' required rate of return, and growth.

2.5.3 Irrelevancy theory

In contrast to the traditional view, **Modigliani and Miller** (MM) proposed that in a tax-free world, shareholders are **indifferent** between dividends and capital gains, and the value of a company is determined solely by the 'earning power' of its assets and investments.

MM argued that if a company with investment opportunities decides to pay a dividend, so that **retained earnings** are **insufficient** to finance all its investments, the shortfall in funds will be made up by **obtaining additional funds** from outside sources. As a result of obtaining outside finance instead of using retained earnings:

Loss of value in existing shares = Amount of dividend paid

In answer to criticisms that certain shareholders will show a preference either for high dividends or for capital gains, MM argued that if a company pursues a **consistent dividend policy**, 'each corporation would tend to attract to itself a clientele consisting of those preferring its particular payout ratio, but one clientele would be entirely as good as another in terms of the valuation it would imply for the firm'.

2.5.4 The case in favour of the relevance of dividend policy (and against MM's views)

There are strong arguments **against** MM's view that dividend policy is irrelevant as a means of affecting shareholder's wealth.

(a) **Differing rates** of **taxation** on **dividends** and **capital gains** can create a **preference** for a **high dividend** or one for **high earnings retention**.

(b) **Dividend retention** should be **preferred** by companies in a period of **capital rationing**.

(c) Due to imperfect markets and the possible difficulties of selling shares easily at a fair price, shareholders might need **high dividends** in order to have funds to **invest** in **opportunities** outside the company.

(d) **Markets** are **not perfect**. Because of **transaction costs** on the sale of shares, investors who want some cash from their investments will prefer to receive dividends rather than to sell some of their shares to get the cash they want.

(e) Information available to shareholders is imperfect, and they are not aware of the **future investment plans** and **expected profits** of their company. Even if management were to provide them with profit forecasts, these forecasts would not necessarily be accurate or believable.

(f) Perhaps the strongest argument against the MM view is that shareholders will tend to **prefer a current dividend** to future capital gains (or deferred dividends) because the future is more uncertain.

Exam skills

Even if you accept that dividend policy may have some influence on share values, there may be other, more important, influences. Don't be tempted to regurgitate chunks of theory in the exam, you must focus on the entities involved.

Question 4.2 — Dividend policy

Learning outcomes: A(2)(d)

Ochre is a company that is still managed by the two individuals who set it up 12 years ago. In the current year the company was launched on the stock market. Previously, all of the shares had been owned by its two founders and certain employees. Now, 40% of the shares are in the hands of the investing public. The company's profit growth and dividend policy are set out below. Will a continuation of the same dividend policy as in the past be suitable now that the company is quoted on the stock market?

Year	Profits £'000	Dividend £'000	Shares in issue
4 years ago	176	88	800,000
3 years ago	200	104	800,000
2 years ago	240	120	1,000,000
1 year ago	290	150	1,000,000
Current year	444	222 (proposed)	1,500,000

2.6 Scrip dividends

SCRIP DIVIDEND is a dividend paid by the issue of additional company shares, rather than by cash.
(CIMA Official Terminology)

A scrip dividend effectively converts retained earnings into **issued share capital**. When the directors of a company would prefer to retain funds within the business but consider that they must pay at least a certain amount of dividend, they might offer equity shareholders the choice of a **cash dividend** or a **scrip dividend**. Each shareholder would decide separately which to take.

2.6.1 Advantages of scrip dividends

(a) They can **preserve** a company's **cash position** if a substantial number of shareholders take up the share option.

(b) Investors may be able to obtain **tax advantages** if dividends are in the form of shares.

(c) Investors looking to **expand their holding** can do so **without incurring** the **transaction costs** of buying more shares.

(d) A small scrip issue will **not dilute the share price significantly.** If however cash is not offered as an alternative, empirical evidence suggests that the share price will tend to fall.

(e) A share issue will **decrease** the company's **gearing**, and may therefore **enhance** its **borrowing capacity.**

2.7 Share repurchase (share buyback)

In many countries companies have the right to **buy back shares from shareholders** who are willing to sell them, subject to certain conditions.

For a **smaller company** with few shareholders, the reason for buying back the company's own shares may be that there is no immediate willing purchaser at a time when a shareholder wishes to sell shares.

For a **public company**, share repurchase could provide a way of withdrawing from the share market and 'going private'.

2.7.1 Benefits of a share repurchase scheme

(a) Finding a **use for surplus cash**, which may be a 'dead asset'.

In 2012, Apple's Board of Directors authorised a $10 billion share repurchase program, over three years, to commence from September 2012. Tim Cook, the CEO, stated this was a use of surplus cash and that there was plenty of cash remaining to run the business.

(b) **Increase in earnings per share** through a reduction in the number of shares in issue. This should lead to a higher share price than would otherwise be the case, and the company should be able to increase dividend payments on the remaining shares in issue.

(c) **Increase in gearing.** Repurchase of a company's own shares allows debt to be substituted for equity, so raising gearing. This will be of interest to a company wanting to increase its gearing without increasing its total long-term funding.

(d) **Readjustment of the company's equity base** to more appropriate levels, for a company whose business is in decline.

(e) Possibly **preventing a takeover** or enabling a quoted company to withdraw from the stock market.

2.7.2 Drawbacks of a share repurchase scheme

(a) It can be **hard to arrive at a price** that will be fair both to the vendors and to any shareholders who are not selling shares to the company.

(b) A repurchase of shares could be seen as an **admission** that the company **cannot make better use of the funds** than the shareholders.

(c) Some shareholders may suffer from being **taxed on a capital gain** following the purchase of their shares rather than receiving dividend income.

Exam alert

Previous exam questions have asked for a discussion of the comparative advantages of a share repurchase versus a one-off dividend payment. Beware of making generalised comments in such a discussion and textbook style answers out of context.

Section summary

- **Retained earnings** are the most important single source of finance for companies, and financial managers should take account of the proportion of earnings that are retained as opposed to being paid as dividends.
- Companies generally **smooth out dividend payments** by adjusting only gradually to changes in earnings: large fluctuations might **undermine investors' confidence**.
- The dividends a company pays may be treated as a **signal** to investors. A company needs to take account of different **clienteles** of shareholders in deciding what dividends to pay.
- Purchase by a company of its own shares can take place for various reasons and must be in accordance with any **requirements of legislation**.

3 Issues in financial reporting

Introduction

In this section we look at some current issues in financial reporting which may impact on the financial strategy of an entity. Relevant issues may affect **individual items** (share-based payments) or the **whole basis** of accounts (value-based accounting), or may develop **new types of accounting** (environmental or human resource accounting).

3.1 Problems with performance reporting

The International Accounting Standards Board (IASB) was established in 2001 and is responsible for setting international accounting standards (IFRSs).

One of its key high-priority projects involved **performance reporting** but this is a highly problematic area.

(a) There are problems **defining** gains, revenue, income and losses.

(b) Economic and accounting **definitions of income** differ.

(c) It is difficult to deal with the consequences of **decision usefulness** and **fair-value accounting** in the statement of comprehensive income.

(d) Income statements which cover operational and financial gains and losses, as well as recognised but not realised gains and losses on operational and financial assets and liabilities, are very **complex**.

(e) It is difficult to establish a **bottom line**.

3.2 Financial Review

Annual reports do not purely contain the financial statements. IAS 1 encourages (but does not require) the inclusion of a financial review, which is a commentary by management on financial performance for the period.

Including a financial review in the financial statements has the following advantages.

(a) Companies appear willing to communicate and also have increased **transparency.**

(b) The **reputation** of a company may be improved through the production of voluntary information.

(c) It can be used to **explain** the background to the published statements. It may be especially useful to explain any unexpected balances or why performance is not as bad as the figures would otherwise suggest.

However there are also disadvantages from the inclusion of a financial review.

(a) Production of the review consumes a significant **amount** of senior management time.

(b) The review may be biased and the information given may be carefully selected. This can reduce the **reliability** of the review.

(c) Due to a lack of required content, reviews will not be **comparable** across similar entities.

Note: This review may also be known as an operating and financial review (OFR) or a business review.

3.3 Inclusion of published forecasts

Many believe that companies should publish forecast information in the annual report. However, published forecasts have certain disadvantages.

(a) The **information** contained in them **may be manipulated** by unscrupulous managers wishing to show a favourable impression.

(b) They are **only as good as the assumptions on which they are based**. Clearly there is an element of subjectivity and uncertainty involved in preparing them. However, users of forecasts should be aware of their limitations.

(c) Forecasts are **very difficult to audit**, because they are **based on subjective prediction**. However, auditors can assess the accounting principles adopted and the consistency with which they are applied.

(d) It is possible that **competitors could make use of the information** disclosed in a forecast, although if they were compulsory for all companies no single company would benefit from this advantage.

(e) If **markets** are **fully efficient**, arguably the impact of publishing forecasts will be limited. However if markets are not efficient, an over-optimistic forecast may result in the **directors coming under fire** if the company does not achieve its targets; over-pessimistic estimates may however result in **immediate falls in the company's share price.**

(f) Providing such additional information would be **costly** in terms of obtaining the information and also action taken by investors, customers and suppliers.

3.4 Environmental accounting

In their capacity as information providers, accountants may be required to report on a firm's environmental impact and possible consequences. Most listed companies now produce environmental reports but **disclosures are voluntary**.

3.4.1 Environmental issues

Examples of environmental issues affecting the work of an accountant include the following.

(a) **Environmental taxes** have to be dealt with (for example a charge for air or water pollution).

(b) **Investment appraisal** needs to incorporate environmental factors.

(c) **Pollution controls** need to be **costed** before being implemented.

(d) **Forecasts** need to incorporate the impact of changes in demand from 'green' consumers.

(e) **Contingent liabilities** may arise from environmental disasters or litigation due to noise or waste pollution.

3.4.2 Environmental reporting

More companies are now producing an external report for external stakeholders, covering:

- What the **business does** and how it impacts on the environment.
- **Environmental objectives** (eg use of 100% recyclable materials within x years).
- The **company's approach** to achieving and monitoring these objectives.
- An **assessment of its success** towards achieving the objectives.
- An **independent verification** of **claims made**.

There is **no obligation** to carry out an **environmental audit** and, if they are carried out, they are confidential and do not have to be published.

3.4.3 Widening the scope of environmental accounting

Companies are acknowledging the advantages of having an environmental policy, including **reduction/management of risk to the business, motivating staff** and corporate reputation enhanced by being a **good citizen**. Many believe that development of a policy will mean a **long term improvement in profitability**. According to Shell plc 'we believe long-term competitive success depends on being trusted to meet society's expectations.' Chemical, oil, steel and other high-polluting industries tend to be seen as more responsible for reporting on environmental issues.

Pressure is increasing on companies to widen their scope of corporate public accountability. This pressure stems from **increasing expectations of stakeholders** and knowledge about the consequences of ignoring such pressures. There is an increasing expectation on companies to follow social policies of their business in addition to economic and environmental policies.

Environmental regulations and demands from the public are increasing and companies therefore have to be increasingly aware of the costs of their actions.

3.5 Reporting of social issues

Social accounting is a way of measuring and reporting on an organisation's social and ethical performance. Many companies now prepare **social accounting reports** and appendices to their annual report as a matter of routine.

The activities of an organisation may result in positive effects on the environment – for example, it may provide employment that will result in social benefits to a particular area.

As well as social benefits, organisations' activities may lead to social costs, such as:

- Pollution (for example, excessive noise)
- Unemployment (for example, if a site is closed)
- Reduction in 'green' sites (for example, building houses on parkland)

CASE STUDY

In July 2001, the FTSE Group launched the FTSE4Good Index Series in response to the increasing focus placed by investors on corporate social responsibility (CSR). To qualify for inclusion in the index series, companies must disclose how they identify, manage and report their material social and environmental risks to their stakeholders.

Companies must satisfy a range of CSR criteria based on the following three broad principles:

- Developing positive relationships with stakeholders
- Up-holding and supporting universal human rights
- Working towards environmental sustainability

The index series excludes tobacco, nuclear power and arms manufacturing companies.

The **Corporate Report** published in 1975 suggested that a number of supplementary reports should be published.

(a) Statement of corporate objectives including **all stakeholders'** objectives

(b) The **employment report** with details of employees, wage rates, training etc

(c) **Statement of future prospects**, which was acknowledged as being difficult to produce but would provide extremely useful information to potential investors

(d) **Value-added reports** showing how various stakeholders have benefitted from the company's activities

Such information would be **costly** to provide and would need to be **independently audited**. As yet, the provision of this information is **voluntary** and very **variable**.

3.6 Human capital

The success of most companies at least partially relies on such staff-related factors as good management skills, technical ability (think Microsoft and Bill Gates for example) and general business 'know-how'. The success of such businesses as football clubs almost entirely relies on the playing and coaching staff. If this is the case, shouldn't such businesses be accounting for the value of their employees?

The easy answer is of course 'yes', but a more difficult question then follows – 'how do we value human capital?'

We cannot use the wages and salaries paid to employees as these are written off annually as an expense in the Income Statement. As employees are 'assets' of the company, we would expect them to appear in the Statement of Financial Position (Balance Sheet) of the company and be valued in line with other assets – whether by historic cost or replacement value to name but two.

3.6.1 Historic cost

If historic cost was used, all costs associated with recruiting, training and developing an employee would be capitalised. These costs would then be depreciated over the life of the 'asset'.

One of the problems with this method is that cost and depreciation do not necessarily correspond with the benefits generated by the employee. However it is a method used by many football clubs when valuing their players and coaching staff.

3.6.2 Replacement cost

Replacement cost of employees represents the cost of bringing new staff to the level of ability of existing staff. However this is very subjective as some staff have knowledge and ability that can only be gained through experience rather than training.

> **Section summary**
>
> Companies must **carefully assess** the impact of **changes** in **accounting standards**. Changes may affect individual items (share-based payments) or the whole basis of accounts (value-based accounting), or may develop new types of accounting (environmental or human resource accounting).

Chapter Roundup

- ✓ Short-term financial strategy is determined by **working capital management**. It involves achieving a balance between the requirement to minimise the risk of insolvency and the requirement to maximise profit.

- ✓ **Retained earnings** are the most important single source of finance for companies, and financial managers should take account of the proportion of earnings that are retained as opposed to being paid as dividends.

- ✓ Companies generally **smooth out dividend payments** by adjusting only gradually to changes in earnings: large fluctuations might **undermine investors' confidence**.

- ✓ The dividends a company pays may be treated as a **signal** to investors. A company needs to take account of different **clienteles** of shareholders in deciding what dividends to pay.

- ✓ Purchase by a company of its own shares can take place for various reasons and must be in accordance with any **requirements of legislation**.

- ✓ Companies must **carefully assess** the impact of **changes** in **accounting standards**. Changes may affect individual items (share-based payments) or the whole basis of accounts (value-based accounting), or may develop new types of accounting (environmental or human resource accounting).

Quick Quiz

1. What is the aim of a conservative working capital management policy?
2. What are permanent current assets?
3. **Fill in the blank**

   Particular companies may attract particular types of shareholders. This is called the .... effect.

4. Give a definition of 'signalling' in the context of dividends policy.
5. **Fill in the blank**

   A .... is a dividend payment which takes the form of new shares instead of cash.

6. Why might shareholders prefer a current dividend to a future capital gain?
7. Why would a company buy back shares from shareholders?
8. What disclosures might be included in an environmental accounting report?

Answers to Quick Quiz

1. To reduce the risk of system breakdown by holding high levels of working capital.

2. The core level of investment in inventory and receivables. This is the minimum level of current assets that an entity needs to continue operation.

3. Clientele

4. The use of dividend policy to indicate the future prospects of an enterprise

5. Scrip dividend

6. Tax advantages or because the future capital gain will be uncertain

7.
    - To find a use for surplus cash
    - To increase EPS
    - To increase gearing
    - To readjust the equity base to more appropriate levels
    - To prevent a takeover
    - To withdraw from the stock market

8.
    - How what the company does impacts upon the environment
    - The environmental objectives
    - The approach to monitoring and achieving those objectives
    - Assessment of success in achieving its objectives
    - Verification of claims made

Answers to Questions

4.1 Retained earnings

(a) The dividend policy of a company is in practice often determined by the directors. From their standpoint, funds from retained earnings are an attractive source of finance because investment projects can be undertaken without involving either the shareholders or any outsiders.

(b) The use of retained earnings as opposed to new shares or debentures avoids issue costs.

(c) The use of funds from retained earnings avoids the possibility of a change in control resulting from an issue of new shares.

4.2 Dividend policy

Year	Dividend per share pence	Dividend as % of profit
4 years ago	11.0	50%
3 years ago	13.0	52%
2 years ago	12.0	50%
1 year ago	15.0	52%
Current year	14.8	50%

The company appears to have pursued a dividend policy of paying out half of after-tax profits in dividend. This policy is only suitable when a company achieves a stable EPS or steady EPS growth. Investors do not like a fall in dividend from one year to the next, and the fall in dividend per share in the current year is likely to be unpopular, and to result in a fall in the share price.

The company would probably serve its shareholders better by paying a dividend of at least 15p per share, possibly more, in the current year, even though the dividend as a percentage of profit would then be higher.

Now try these questions from the Exam Question Bank

Number	Level	Marks	Time
Q5	Examination	25	45 mins
Q6	Examination	20	36 mins

FINANCING DECISIONS

Part B

EQUITY FINANCE

In Part B of this study text we consider various aspects of financing decisions. In the first few chapters of this part, we shall look at how businesses determine their long-term capital structure, before moving on to examine the consequences of choosing a particular capital structure.

When sources of **long-term finance** are used, large sums are usually involved, and so the financial manager needs to consider all the options available with care, looking at the possible effects on the company in the long term.

In this chapter, we describe the different forms of **share capital**, and go on to consider other long-term sources of finance in Chapters 6 and 7. The learning outcomes require you to identify and evaluate optimal strategies for the satisfaction of long-term financing requirements. You should therefore concentrate on the **reasons** why different methods are used and their **advantages** and **disadvantages**.

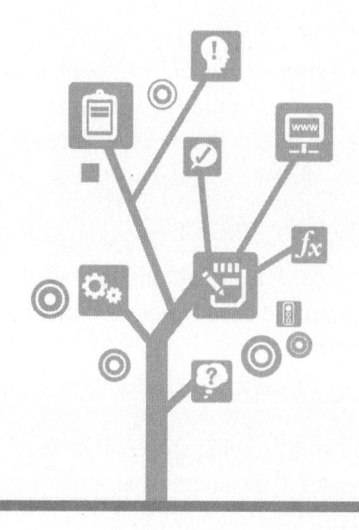

topic list	learning outcomes	syllabus references	ability required
1 Capital markets	B(1)(a),(b)	B(1)(iii)	evaluation
2 Rights issues	B(1)(b)	B(1)(iii)	evaluation
3 Scrip dividends, bonus issues and share splits	B(1)(b)	B(1)(iii)	evaluation
4 Share prices and investment returns	B(1)(b)	B(1)(iv)	evaluation
5 The efficient market hypothesis	B(1)(b)	B(1)(iv)	evaluation

1 Capital markets

> **Introduction**
>
> The aim of this section is to give you an insight into the **role of capital markets** in helping businesses and introducing you to some important terminology.

1.1 Stock markets

Capital markets are markets for trading in **long-term finance**, in the form of long-term financial instruments. In the UK, the principal capital markets are the **Stock Exchange 'main market'** (for companies with a full Stock Exchange listing) and the more loosely regulated 'second tier' **Alternative Investment Market (AIM)** which is also regulated by the Stock Exchange. Apart from regulating these two markets, the Stock Exchange is also the market for dealings in **government securities** (gilts).

The stock markets serve the following main purposes.

(a) **Primary markets**

As **primary markets** they enable organisations to **raise new finance**, by issuing new shares or new debentures. Capital markets make it easier for companies to raise new long-term finance than if they had to raise funds privately by contacting investors individually. In the UK, a company must have public company status (be a plc) to be allowed to raise finance from the public on a capital market.

(b) **Secondary markets**

As **secondary markets** they enable existing investors to sell their investments, should they wish to do so. The **marketability** of securities is a very important feature of the capital markets, because investors are more willing to buy investments if they know that they could sell them easily, should they wish to.

(c) **Realisation of value**

When a company comes to the stock market for the first time, and 'floats' its shares on the market, the **owners** of the company can **realise** some of the **value** of their shares in cash, because they will offer a proportion of their personally-held shares for sale to new investors.

(d) **Takeovers by share exchange**

When one company wants to take over another, it is common to do so by issuing shares to finance the takeover. Takeovers by means of a share exchange are only feasible if the shares that are offered can be readily traded on a stock market, and so have an identifiable market value.

1.2 Institutional investors

KEY TERM

INSTITUTIONAL INVESTORS are institutions which have large amounts of funds which they want to invest, and they will invest in bonds and shares or any other assets which offer satisfactory returns and security.

The institutional investors are now the biggest investors on many stock markets. The major institutional investors in the UK are pension funds, insurance companies, investment trusts, unit trusts, private equity and venture capital organisations.

1.3 Capital market participants

The various participants in the capital markets are summarised in the diagram below.

Capital markets

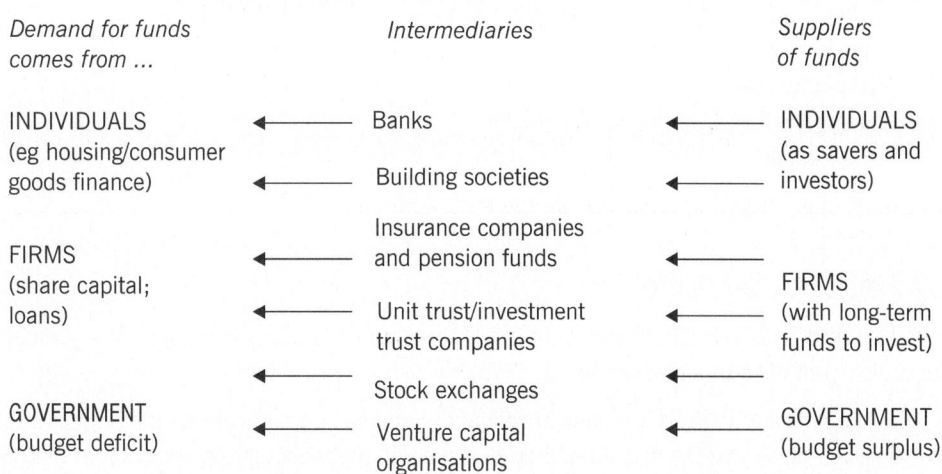

Demand for funds comes from ...	Intermediaries	Suppliers of funds
INDIVIDUALS (eg housing/consumer goods finance)	← Banks ← Building societies	← INDIVIDUALS (as savers and investors)
FIRMS (share capital; loans)	← Insurance companies and pension funds ← Unit trust/investment trust companies ← Stock exchanges	← FIRMS (with long-term funds to invest)
GOVERNMENT (budget deficit)	← Venture capital organisations	← GOVERNMENT (budget surplus)

1.4 Advantages of a stock market listing

WHY SEEK A STOCK MARKET LISTING?

- Access to a wider pool of finance
- Improved marketability of shares
- Easier to seek growth by acquisition
- Enhanced public image
- Original owners selling holding to obtain funds for other projects
- Original owners realising holding

1.5 Disadvantages of a stock market listing

The owners of a company seeking a stock market listing must take the following disadvantages into account:

(a) There will be significantly greater **public regulation, accountability** and **scrutiny.** The legal requirements the company faces will be greater, and the company will also be subject to the rules of the stock exchange on which its shares are listed.

(b) A **wider circle of investors** with more exacting requirements will hold shares.

(c) There will be additional costs involved in making share issues, including **brokerage commissions** and **underwriting fees.**

1.6 Methods of obtaining a listing

The process of making shares available to investors by obtaining a quotation on a stock exchange is called **flotation**.

An unquoted company can obtain a listing on the stock market by means of:

- **Offer for sale**
- **Prospectus issue**
- **Placing**
- **Introduction**

Of these an offer for sale or a placing are the most common.

1.7 Initial public offer

An **INITIAL PUBLIC OFFER (IPO)** is an invitation to the public to apply for shares in a company based on information contained in a prospectus.

An Initial Public Offer (IPO) is a means of selling the shares of a company to the public at large. When companies 'go public' for the first time, a **large** issue will probably take the form of an IPO. Subsequent issues are likely to be **placings** or **rights issues**, described later.

An IPO entails the **acquisition by an issuing house** of a large block of shares of a company, with a view to offering them for sale to the public.

An **issuing house** is usually an investment bank (or sometimes a firm of stockbrokers). It may acquire the shares either as a direct allotment from the company or by purchase from existing members. In either case, the issuing house publishes an invitation to the public to apply for shares, either at a fixed price or on a tender basis. The issuing house **accepts responsibility** to the public, and gives the support of its own reputation and standing to the issue.

In May 2012 Facebook launched one of the largest IPO's ever on the Nasdaq stock exchange, at $38 per share, valuing the company at $104 billion. Many questioned whether this was overly ambitious, given that the company's previous year net income figure was $1 billion. As a result the share price fell in early trading and after one week the share price was around $33.

1.7.1 Offers for sale by tender

It is often very difficult to decide upon the price at which the shares should be offered to the general public. One way of trying to ensure that the issue price reflects the value of the shares as perceived by the market is to make an **offer for sale by tender**. A **minimum price** will be fixed and subscribers will be invited to tender for shares at prices equal to or above the minimum. The shares will be **allotted at the highest price** at which they will **all be taken up**. This is known as the **striking price**.

Example: Offer for sale by tender

Byte Henderson is a new company that is making its first public issue of shares. It has decided to make the issue by means of an offer for sale by tender. The intention is to issue up to 4,000,000 shares (the full amount of authorised share capital) at a minimum price of 300 pence. The money raised, net of issue costs of £1,000,000, would be invested in projects which would earn benefits with a present value equal to 130% of the net amount invested.

The following tenders have been received. (Each applicant has made only one offer.)

Price tendered per share £	Number of shares applied for at this price
6.00	50,000
5.50	100,000
5.00	300,000
4.50	450,000
4.00	1,100,000
3.50	1,500,000
3.00	2,500,000

(a) How many shares would be issued, and how much in total would be raised, if Byte Henderson chooses:

   (i) To maximise the total amount raised?
   (ii) To issue exactly 4,000,000 shares?

(b) Harvey Goldfinger, a private investor, has applied for 12,000 shares at a price of £5.50 and has sent a cheque for £66,000 to the issuing house that is handling the issue. In both cases (a)(i) and (ii), how many shares would be issued to Mr Goldfinger, assuming that any partial acceptance of offers would mean allotting shares to each accepted applicant in proportion to the number of shares applied for? How much will Mr Goldfinger receive back out of the £66,000 he has paid?

Solution

(a) We begin by looking at the cumulative tenders.

Price £	Cumulative number of shares applied for	Amount raised if price is selected, before deducting issue costs £
6.00	50,000	300,000
5.50	150,000	825,000
5.00	450,000	2,250,000
4.50	900,000	4,050,000
4.00	2,000,000	8,000,000
3.50	3,500,000	12,250,000
3.00	6,000,000 (4,000,000 max)	12,000,000

   (i) To maximise the total amount raised, the issue price should be £3.50. The total raised before deducting issue costs would be £12,250,000.

   (ii) To issue exactly 4,000,000 shares, the issue price must be £3.00. The total raised would be £12,000,000, before deducting issue costs.

(b) (i) Harvey Goldfinger would be allotted 12,000 shares at £3.50 per share. He would receive a refund of 12,000 × £2 = £24,000 out of the £66,000 he has paid.

   (ii) If 4,000,000 shares are issued, applicants would receive two thirds of the shares they tendered for. Harvey Goldfinger would be allotted 8,000 shares at £3 per share and would receive a refund of £42,000 out of the £66,000 he has paid.

1.8 Prospectus issue

Issues where the issuing firm sells shares directly to the general public tend to be quite rare on many stock exchanges, and the issues that are made tend to be quite large. These issues are sometimes known as **offers by prospectus**. This type of issue is very risky, because of the lack of guarantees that all shares will be taken up.

1.9 A placing

A **placing** is an arrangement whereby the shares are not all offered to the public, but instead, the sponsoring market maker arranges for most of the issue to be bought by a **small number of investors**, usually institutional investors such as pension funds and insurance companies.

1.9.1 The choice between an offer for sale and a placing

Is a company likely to prefer an offer for sale of its shares, or a placing?

(a) **Placings** are much **cheaper**. Approaching institutional investors privately is a much cheaper way of obtaining finance, and thus placings are often used for smaller issues.

(b) Placings are likely to be **quicker**.

(c) Placings are likely to involve **less disclosure** of **information.**

(d) However, most of the shares will be placed with a **relatively small number of (institutional) shareholders**, which means that most of the shares are **unlikely to be available for trading** after the flotation, and that **institutional shareholders** will have control of the **company**.

(e) When a company first comes to the market in the UK, the **maximum proportion of shares** that can be **placed** is **75%**, to ensure some shares are available to a wider public.

1.10 An introduction

By this method of obtaining a quotation, no shares are made available to the market, neither existing nor newly created shares; nevertheless, the stock market grants a quotation. This will only happen where shares in a large company are already widely held, so that a market can be seen to exist. A company might want an **introduction** to obtain **greater marketability** for the shares, a known share valuation for inheritance tax purposes and easier access in the future to additional capital.

1.11 Underwriting

A company about to issue new securities in order to raise finance might decide to have the issue underwritten. **Underwriters** are financial institutions which agree (in exchange for a fixed fee, perhaps 2.25% of the finance to be raised) to buy at the issue price any securities which are **not subscribed** for by the investing public.

Underwriters **remove** the **risk** of a share issue's being under-subscribed, but at a cost to the company issuing the shares. It is not compulsory to have an issue underwritten. Ordinary offers for sale are most likely to be underwritten although rights issues may be as well.

1.12 Costs of share issues on stock market

Companies may incur the following costs when issuing shares.

- Underwriting costs
- Stock market listing fee (the initial charge) for the new securities
- Fees of the issuing house, solicitors, auditors and public relations consultant
- Charges for printing and distributing the prospectus
- Advertising in national newspapers

1.13 Pricing shares for a stock market launch

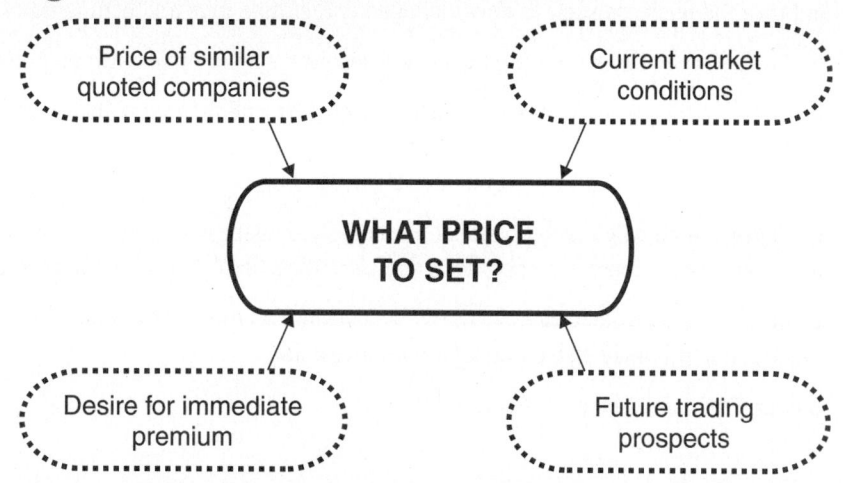

Factors influencing **WHAT PRICE TO SET?**:
- Price of similar quoted companies
- Current market conditions
- Desire for immediate premium
- Future trading prospects

Companies will be keen to avoid **over-pricing an issue**, which could result in the **issue** being **under subscribed**, leaving underwriters with the unwelcome task of having to buy up the unsold shares. On the other hand, if the **issue price** is **too low** then the issue will be **oversubscribed** and the company would have been able to raise the required capital by issuing fewer shares.

The share price of an issue is usually advertised as being based on a certain P/E ratio, the ratio of the price to the company's most recent earnings per share figure in its audited accounts. The issuer's P/E ratio can then be compared by investors with the P/E ratios of similar quoted companies.

1.14 Venture capital

KEY TERM

VENTURE CAPITAL is risk capital, normally provided in return for an equity stake.

Venture capital companies (such as 3i group) make funding available to **young, unquoted companies** to help them to expand.

The requirements are **very high growth potential** and **very high returns** (in excess of 30% per annum). This return arises when the company that has been financed is **floated** on the stock market or **sold**.

Venture capitalists have been accused of **short-termism** by requiring early reported profits and an early exit. Failure to hit targets set by the venture capitalist can lead to an **equity ratchet** where extra shares are transferred to their ownership at no additional cost to the venture capitalist.

When a company's directors look for help from a venture capital institution, they must recognise that:

(a) The institution will want an **equity stake** in the company.

(b) It will need convincing that the company can be successful (management buyouts of companies which already have a record of **successful trading** have been increasingly favoured by venture capitalists in recent years).

(c) It may want to have a **representative** appointed to the company's board, to look after its interests, or an **independent director** (the 3i group runs an Independent Director Scheme).

1.15 Private equity

Private equity describes a group of companies that raises funds from investors, typically pension funds, and uses the money to buy companies which they **run privately**.

Private equity deals are much bigger than venture capitalists' and typically use a **high proportion of debt** when making acquisitions. This debt is placed on the balance sheet of the acquired company. Once a private equity firm has owned a company for six months or a year, it will **refinance** all the debt and pay some cash back to its investors. The private equity firm makes a series of often drastic changes to improve the business such as new management, cutting jobs and getting rid of loss-making divisions.

In the same way as venture capitalists, exit involves sale or flotation three to five years later.

Investors in private equity are increasingly turning to emerging markets to generate their returns since private equity returns in developed countries have been dented by the lack of debt financing available as well as near-zero growth rates in both the US and Europe.

In contrast, emerging market buyouts seldom rely on debt, with returns typically achieved by introducing new technology, improving operations and benefiting from steady increases in consumer spending.

Latin America (excluding Brazil) is seen by investors as the most attractive new destination, with Indonesia and Turkey also on popular with investors.

Source Financial Times 12 April 2012

1.16 Preference shares

PREFERENCE SHARES are shares carrying a fixed rate of dividends, the holders of which, subject to the conditions of issue, have a prior claim to any company profits available for distribution. They are an example of prior charge capital.

Preferred shareholders may also have a prior claim to the repayment of capital in the event of winding up.

PRIOR CHARGE CAPITAL is capital which has a right to the receipt of interest or of preferred dividends in precedence to any claim on distributable earnings on the part of the ordinary shareholders. On winding up, the claims of holders of prior charge capital also rank before those of ordinary shareholders.

Preference shares' dividends will **not be paid** if there are **no profits** whereas interest payments must be met whether or not the entity has made a profit. Preference dividends are not **tax-deductible** whereas debt interest is. A company therefore will tend to prefer to pay a fixed charge on bonds, for which the interest charge is net of tax, than on preference shares.

Section summary

- Capital markets are markets for trading in **long-term** finance
- A company can obtain a stock market listing through an **offer for sale**, a **prospectus issue**, a **placing** or an **introduction**
- **Venture capital** and **private equity** are also sources of long term equity finance

2 Rights issues   9/10, 11/10, 11/11

Introduction

A **rights issue** is a way for a company to raise funds. You will need to understand how it works and be able to do the necessary price calculations.

KEY TERMS

A RIGHTS ISSUE is the raising of new capital by giving existing shareholders the right to subscribe to new shares in proportion to their current holdings. These shares are usually issued at a discount to market price. A shareholder not wishing to take up a rights issue may sell the rights.

A DILUTION is the reduction in the earnings and voting power per share caused by an increase or potential increase in the number of shares in issue. *(CIMA Official Terminology)*

2.1 Advantages of rights issues

(a) Rights issues are **cheaper** than offers for sale to the general public. This is partly because no **prospectus** is generally required (provided that the issue is for less than 10% of the class of shares concerned), partly because the **administration** is **simpler** and partly because the cost of underwriting will be less.

(b) Rights issues are **more beneficial** to **existing shareholders** than issues to the general public. New shares are issued at a **discount** to the current market price, to make them attractive to investors. A rights issue secures the discount on the market price for existing shareholders, who may either keep the shares or sell them if they wish.

(c) **Relative voting rights** are **unaffected** if shareholders all take up their rights.

(d) The finance raised may be used to **reduce gearing** in book value terms by increasing share capital and/or to pay off long-term debt which will reduce gearing in market value terms.

2.2 Disadvantages of rights issues

(a) The **amount of finance** that can be **raised** by rights issues of unquoted companies is limited by the funds available to existing shareholders.

(b) **Choosing the best issue price** may **be problematic**. If the price is considered too high, the issue may not be fully subscribed; if too low, the company will not have raised all the funds it conceivably could have done.

(c) During the time between the **announcement of the rights issue** and the **date of subscription** the **market price of shares** may **fall**, and the issue price of rights will be above the market price, with the result that the rights issue will fail.

(d) Rights issues **can't be used** to **widen the base** of shareholders.

2.3 Pricing a rights issue

A company making a rights issue must set a price which is low enough to **secure the acceptance** of shareholders, who are being asked to provide extra funds, but not so low that earnings per share are excessively diluted. Other possible problems include getting the issue **underwritten** and an excessive **fall** in the **share price.**

Exam alert

A question might ask for discussion on the effect of a rights issue, as well as calculations, eg of the effect on EPS.

Example: Rights issue (1)

Seagull can achieve a profit after tax of 20% on the capital employed. At present its capital structure is as follows.

	£
200,000 ordinary shares of £1 each	200,000
Retained earnings	100,000
	300,000

The directors propose to raise an additional £126,000 from a rights issue. The current market price is £1.80.

Required

(a) Calculate the number of shares that must be issued if the rights price is:
£1.60; £1.50; £1.40; £1.20.

(b) Calculate the dilution in earnings per share in each case.

Solution

The earnings at present are 20% of £300,000 = £60,000. This gives earnings per share of 30p. The earnings after the rights issue will be 20% of £426,000 = £85,200.

Rights price £	No of new shares (£126,000 ÷ rights price)	EPS (£85,200 ÷ total no of shares) Pence	Dilution Pence
1.60	78,750	30.6	+ 0.6
1.50	84,000	30.0	–
1.40	90,000	29.4	– 0.6
1.20	105,000	27.9	– 2.1

Note that at a high rights price the earnings per share are increased, not diluted. The breakeven point (zero dilution) occurs when the rights price is equal to the capital employed per share:

£300,000 ÷ 200,000 = £1.50.

2.4 The market price of shares after a rights issue: the theoretical ex-rights price

After the announcement of a rights issue, **share prices generally fall**. This temporary fall is due to **uncertainty in the market about** the consequences of the issue, with respect to future profits, earnings and dividends. After the issue has actually been made, the market price per share will normally fall, because there are more shares in issue and the new shares were issued at a discount price.

When a rights issue is announced, all existing shareholders have the **right to subscribe for new shares**, and so there are **rights attached to the existing shares**. The shares are therefore described as being traded as 'cum rights'. On the first day of dealings in the newly issued shares, the rights no longer exist and the old shares are now 'ex rights' (without rights attached).

In theory, the new market price will be the consequence of an adjustment to allow for the discount price of the new issue, and a **theoretical ex rights price** can be calculated (the shares are ex rights because the new shares have been issued and the rights no longer exist).

Example: Rights issue (2)

Fundraiser has 1,000,000 ordinary shares of £1 in issue, which have a market price on 1 September of £2.10 per share. The company decides to make a rights issue, and offers its shareholders the right to subscribe for one new share at £1.50 each for every four shares already held. After the announcement of the issue, the share price fell to £1.95, but by the time just prior to the issue being made, it had recovered to £2 per share. This market value just before the issue is known as the cum rights price. What is the theoretical ex-rights price?

Solution

Value of the portfolio for a shareholder with 4 shares before the rights issue:

	£
4 shares @ £2.00	8.00
1 share @ £1.50	1.50
	9.50

so the value per share after the rights issue (or TERP) is: $\frac{£9.50}{5} = £1.90$

An alternative method would be to use the formula given to you in the exam.

Theoretical ex-rights price = $\frac{1}{N+1}\left((N \times \text{cum rights price}) + \text{issue price}\right)$

where N = number of shares required to buy one new share.

Theoretical ex-rights price = $\frac{1}{4+1}((4 \times £2) + £1.50) = \frac{£9.50}{5} = £1.90$

2.5 Yield adjusted ex-rights price

We have assumed so far that the additional funds raised by the rights issue will generate the **same rate of return as existing funds**. If the new funds are likely to earn a **different return** from what is currently being earned, the **yield-adjusted** theoretical ex-rights price should be calculated. The yield-adjusted price demonstrates how the market will view the rights issue, and what will happen to the market value.

Yield-adjusted theoretical ex-rights price = $\left[\frac{\text{Cum rights price} \times N}{(N+1)}\right] + \left[\frac{\text{Issue price}}{(N+1)} \times \frac{\text{Yield on new funds}}{\text{Yield on existing funds}}\right]$

Example: Rights issue (3)

Using the same data for Fundraiser as above, with the additional information that rate of return on new funds = 12%, and on existing funds = 8%, calculate the yield-adjusted theoretical ex-rights price.

Solution

Yield-adjusted theoretical ex-rights price = $\left[\frac{2 \times 4}{5}\right] + \left[\frac{1.50}{5} \times \frac{0.12}{0.08}\right] = £2.05$

Exam skills

An exam question may give you the net present value of the project which the rights issue has been raised for. The yield adjusted ex rights price will then simply be:

$$\frac{\text{Original market capitalisation of the company} + \text{NPV of the project} + \text{proceeds of rights issue}}{\text{New number of shares in issue}}$$

2.6 The value of rights

$$\text{Value of a right} = \frac{\text{Theoretical ex-rights price} - \text{Issue price}}{N}$$

Where N = the number of rights required to buy one share

Using the above example:

$$\text{Value of a right} = \frac{2.00 - 1.50}{5} = \frac{1.90 - 1.50}{4} = 10p$$

This means that the value of a right attaching to each **existing** share is 10p. If a holder of four existing shares exercises his rights to buy one new share, and then sells it, his gain will be 1.90 – 1.50 = 40p, in other words (4 × 10p) or the difference between the theoretical ex-rights price and the rights issue price.

The value of rights is the **theoretical gain** a shareholder would make by exercising his rights.

Question 5.1 — Effects of rights issue

Learning outcomes: B(1)(b)

Devonian has the following long-term capital structure as at 30 November 20X3.

	$m
Ordinary shares 25c fully paid	50.0
General reserve	22.5
Retained profit	25.5
	98.0

The company has no long-term loans.

In the year to 30 November 20X3, the profit from operations (net profit before interest and taxation) was $40m and it is expected that this will increase by 25 per cent during the forthcoming year. The company is listed on a major stock exchange and the current share price is $2.10.

The company wishes to raise $72m in order to re-equip one of its factories and is considering making a one-for-five rights issue at a discounted price of $1.80 per share. It is expected that the price earnings (P/E) ratio will remain the same for the forthcoming year.

Assume a tax rate of 30 per cent.

Required

(a) Assuming the rights issue of shares is made, calculate

    (i) The theoretical ex-rights price of an ordinary share in Devonian, and

    (ii) The value of the rights for each original ordinary share.

(b) Calculate the price of an ordinary share in Devonian in one year's time assuming a rights issue is made.

2.7 Shareholder options

Possible courses of action open to shareholders:

(a) **'Take up' or 'exercise' the rights**

This means buying the new shares at the rights price. Shareholders who do this will maintain their percentage holdings in the company by subscribing for the new shares.

(b) **'Renounce' the rights and sell them on the market**

Shareholders who do this will have lower percentage holdings of the company's equity after the issue than before the issue, and the total value of their shares will be less (on the assumption that the actual market price after the issue is close to the theoretical ex rights price).

(c) **Renounce part of the rights and take up the remainder**

For example, a shareholder may sell enough of his rights to enable him to buy the remaining rights shares he is entitled to with the sale proceeds, and so keep the total market value of his shareholding in the company unchanged.

(d) **Do nothing**

Shareholders may be protected from the consequences of their inaction because rights not taken up are sold on a shareholder's behalf by the company. The Stock Exchange rules state that if new securities are not taken up, they should be sold by the company to new subscribers for the benefit of the shareholders who were entitled to the rights.

The decision by individual shareholders as to whether they take up the offer will therefore depend on:

(a) The **expected rate of return** on the investment (and the risk associated with it)
(b) The **return obtainable** from other investments (allowing for the associated risk)

Question 5.2 — Rights issue

Learning outcomes: B(1)(b)

Gopher has issued 3,000,000 ordinary shares of £1 each, which are at present selling for £4 per share. The company plans to issue rights to purchase one new equity share at a price of £3.20 per share for every three shares held. A shareholder who owns 900 shares thinks that he will suffer a loss in his personal wealth because the new shares are being offered at a price lower than market value. On the assumption that the actual market value of shares will be equal to the theoretical ex rights price, what would be the effect on the shareholder's wealth if:

(a) He sells all the rights
(b) He exercises half of the rights and sells the other half
(c) He does nothing at all

Exam skills

Make sure you practise the calculations in this chapter so that you can do them competently and quickly if required.

Section summary

A **rights issue** is an offer to existing shareholders for them to buy more shares, usually at lower than the current share price.

3 Scrip dividends, bonus issues and share splits

Introduction
This section explains some more terminology that you need to be familiar with.

3.1 Scrip dividends
We discussed scrip dividends, the dividends paid by the issue of additional company shares, in section 2.6 of the previous chapter.

3.2 Bonus issues

KEY TERM

A BONUS/SCRIP/CAPITALISATION ISSUE is the capitalisation of the reserves of an entity by the issue of additional shares to existing shareholders, in proportion to their holdings. Such shares are normally fully paid-up with no cash called for from the shareholders. *(CIMA Official Terminology)*

For example, if a company with issued share capital of 100,000 ordinary shares of £1 each made a one for five bonus issue, 20,000 new shares would be issued to existing shareholders, one new share for every five old shares held. Issued share capital would be increased by £20,000, and reserves (probably share premium account, if there is one) reduced by this amount.

By creating more shares in this way, a bonus issue does not raise new funds, but does have the advantage of making shares **cheaper** and therefore (perhaps) **more easily marketable** on the Stock Exchange. For example, if a company's shares are priced at £6 on the Stock Exchange, and the company makes a one for two bonus issue, we should expect the share price after the issue to fall to £4 each. Shares at £4 each might be more easily marketable than shares at £6 each.

3.3 Share splits

Another way to create cheaper shares with a greater marketability is to **split** the ordinary shares into a **larger number** with a **lower nominal value**. For example, each ordinary share of £1 is split into two shares of 50p each.

The difference between a bonus issue and a share split is that a **bonus issue converts equity reserves into share capital**, whereas a **share split leaves reserves unaffected**.

Section summary
Scrip dividends, bonus issues and share splits are not methods of raising new equity funds, but they are methods of altering the share capital of a company, or in the case of scrip dividends and scrip issues, increasing the issued share capital of a company.

4 Share prices and investment returns   11/11

Introduction
In this section we look at how share prices are determined. As we shall see, there are various theories which seek to explain share price movements.

4.1 Ordinary (equity) shares

KEY TERMS

EQUITY is share capital, retained earnings and other reserves of a single entity, plus minority interests in a group, representing the investment made in the entity by the owners.

EQUITY SHARE CAPITAL is a company's issued share capital less capital which carries preferential rights. Equity share capital normally comprises ordinary shares.

Ordinary (equity) shares are those of the owners of a company.

The ordinary shares of UK companies have a **nominal** or 'face' value, typically £1 or 50p. Outside the UK it is not uncommon for a company's shares to have no nominal value.

The market value of a quoted company's shares bears **no relationship** to their **nominal value**, except that when ordinary shares are issued for cash, the issue price must be equal to or (more usually) more than the nominal value of the shares.

4.2 Book value versus market value

The **book value** of equity is the ordinary share capital in the balance sheet plus the value of shareholders' reserves. The book value is a **historical figure** which reflects accounting adjustments and procedures.

The book value may be very different to the **market value** of the shares. This is the share price multiplied by the number of shares in issue which reflects **investors' expectations of future earnings**.

4.3 Theories of share price behaviour

There are the following differing views about share price movements.

- The fundamental analysis theory
- Technical analysis (chartist theory)
- Random walk theory

These different theories about how share prices are reached in the market, especially fundamental analysis, have important consequences for financial management.

4.4 The fundamental analysis theory of share values

The fundamental theory of share values is based on the theory that the 'realistic' market price of a share can be derived from a **valuation of estimated future dividends** (the dividend valuation model). The value of a share will be the discounted present value of all future expected dividends on the share, discounted at the shareholders' cost of capital (see Chapter 9).

KEY TERM

FUNDAMENTAL ANALYSIS is the analysis of external and internal influences that directly affect the operations of a company with a view to assisting in investment decisions. Information accessed might include fiscal/monetary policy, financial statements, industry trends, competitor analysis, etc.

(CIMA Official Terminology)

In general terms, fundamental analysis seems to be valid. This means that if an investment analyst can foresee before anyone else that:

(a) A **company's future profits** and **dividends** are going to be different from what is currently expected
(b) **Shareholders' cost of capital** will **rise or fall** (for example in response to interest rate changes)

then the analyst will be able to predict a future share price movement, and so recommend clients to buy or sell the share before the price change occurs.

In practice however, share price movements are affected by **day to day fluctuations**, reflecting

- Supply and demand in a particular period
- Investor confidence
- Market interest rate movements

Investment analysts want to be able to predict these fluctuations in prices, but fundamental analysis might be inadequate as a technique.

4.5 Charting or technical analysis

Chartists or **'technical analysts'** attempt to predict share price movements by assuming that past price patterns will be repeated. There is no real theoretical justification for this approach, but it can at times be spectacularly successful. Studies have suggested that the degree of success is greater than could be expected merely from chance.

TECHNICAL ANALYSIS is the analysis of past movements in the prices of financial instruments, currencies, commodities etc, with a view to, by applying analytical techniques, predicting future price movements.

(CIMA Official Terminology)

Chartists do not attempt to predict every price change. They are primarily interested in trend reversals, for example when the price of a share has been rising for several months but suddenly starts to fall.

One of the main problems with chartism is that it is often difficult to see a **new trend** until **after it has happened**. By the time the chartist has detected a signal, other chartists will have as well, and the resulting mass movement to buy or sell will push the price so as to eliminate any advantage.

With the use of sophisticated computer programs to simulate the work of a chartist, academic studies have found that the results obtained were **no better or worse** than those obtained from a simple 'buy and hold' strategy of a **well diversified portfolio** of shares.

4.6 Random walk theory

Random walk theory is consistent with the fundamental theory of share values. It accepts that a share should have an intrinsic price dependent on the fortunes of the company and the expectations of investors. One of its underlying assumptions is that **all relevant information about a company is available to all potential investors** who will act upon the information in a **rational** manner.

The key feature of random walk theory is that although share prices will have an **intrinsic or fundamental value**, this value will be altered as new information becomes available, and that the behaviour of investors is such that the actual share price will fluctuate from day to day around the intrinsic value.

Section summary

- **Fundamental analysis** is based on the theory that share prices can be derived from an analysis of **future dividends**.
- **Technical analysts** or **chartists** work on the basis that past price patterns will be repeated.
- **Random walk theory** is based on the idea that share prices will alter when **new information** becomes **available**.

5 The efficient market hypothesis 3/11, 3/12

Introduction

The efficient market hypothesis also attempts to explain share price movements. The ability of stock markets to price shares accurately has been tested to see if they correspond to one of three levels of efficiency.

5.1 The definition of efficiency

KEY TERM

EFFICIENT MARKET HYPOTHESIS is the hypothesis that the stock market responds immediately to all available information, with the effect that an individual investor cannot, in the long run, expect to obtain greater than average returns from a diversified portfolio of shares. *(CIMA Official Terminology)*

Different types of efficiency can be distinguished in the context of the operation of financial markets.

(a) **Allocative efficiency**

If financial markets allow funds to be directed towards firms which make the most productive use of them, then there is **allocative efficiency** in these markets.

(b) **Operational efficiency**

Transaction costs are incurred by **participants** in financial markets, for example commissions on share transactions, margins between interest rates for lending and for borrowing, and loan arrangement fees. Financial markets have **operational efficiency** if transaction costs are kept as low as possible. Transaction costs are kept low where there is open competition between brokers and other market participants.

(c) **Informational processing efficiency**

The **information processing efficiency** of a stock market means the ability of a stock market to price stocks and shares fairly and quickly. An efficient market in this sense is one in which the market prices of all securities reflect all the available information.

5.2 Features of efficient markets

It has been argued that the UK and US stock markets are **efficient** capital markets, that is, markets in which:

(a) The prices of securities bought and sold **reflect all the relevant information** which is available to the buyers and sellers: in other words, share prices change quickly to reflect all new information about future prospects.

(b) No **individual dominates** the market.

(c) **Transaction costs** of buying and selling are not so high as to discourage trading significantly.

(d) Investors are **rational.**

(e) There are low, or no, costs of **acquiring information.**

5.3 Impact of efficiency on share prices

If the stock market is efficient, share prices should vary in a **rational** way.

(a) If a company makes an investment with a **positive net present value**, shareholders will get to know about it and the market price of its shares will rise in anticipation of future dividend increases.

(b) If a company makes a **bad investment** shareholders will find out and so the **price** of its **shares will fall**.

(c) If interest rates rise, **shareholders will want a higher return** from their investments, so market prices will fall.

5.4 Varying degrees of efficiency

There are three degrees or 'forms' of **efficiency**: **weak form**, **semi-strong form** and **strong form**.

5.4.1 Weak form efficiency

Under the weak form hypothesis of market efficiency, share prices reflect all available information about **past** changes in the share price.

Since new information arrives unexpectedly, changes in share prices should occur in a **random fashion.** If it is correct, then using technical analysis to study past share price movements will not give anyone an advantage, because the information they use to predict share prices is already reflected in the share price.

5.4.2 Semi-strong form efficiency

If a stock market displays semi-strong efficiency, current share prices reflect both:

- All relevant information about past price movements and their implications, and
- All knowledge which is available publicly

This means that individuals cannot 'beat the market' by reading the newspapers or annual reports, since the information contained in these will be reflected in the share price.

Tests to prove semi-strong efficiency have concentrated on the speed and accuracy of stock market response to information and on the ability of the market to **anticipate share price changes** before new information is formally announced. For example, if two companies plan a merger, share prices of the two companies will inevitably change once the merger plans are formally announced. The market would show semi-strong efficiency, however, if it were able to anticipate such an announcement, so that share prices of the companies concerned would change in advance of the merger plans being confirmed.

Research in both the UK and the USA has suggested that market prices anticipate mergers several months before they are formally announced, and the conclusion drawn is that the stock markets in these countries **do** exhibit semi-strong efficiency.

5.4.3 Strong form efficiency

If a stock market displays a strong form of efficiency, share prices reflect **all** information whether publicly available or not.

- From past price changes
- From public knowledge or anticipation
- From specialists' or experts' insider knowledge (eg investment managers)

5.5 Implications of efficient market hypothesis for the financial manager

If the markets are quite strongly efficient, the main consequence for financial managers will be that they simply need to **concentrate** on **maximising the net present value** of the **company's investments** in order to maximise the wealth of shareholders. Managers need not worry, for example, about the effect on share prices of financial results in the published accounts because investors will make **allowances** for **low profits** or **dividends** in the current year if higher profits or dividends are expected in the future.

If the market is strongly efficient, there is little point in financial managers attempting strategies that will attempt to mislead the markets.

(a) There is no point for example in trying to identify a correct date when **shares** should be **issued**, since share prices will always reflect the true worth of the company.

(b) The market will identify any attempts to **window dress the accounts** and put an optimistic spin on the figures.

(c) The market will decide what **level of return** it requires for the risk involved in making an investment in the company. It is pointless for the company to try to change the market's view by issuing different types of capital instruments.

Similarly if the company is looking to expand, the directors will be wasting their time if they seek as **takeover targets** companies whose shares are undervalued, since the market will fairly value all companies' shares.

Only if the market is semi-strongly efficient, and the financial managers possess **inside information** that would significantly alter the price of the company's shares if released to the market, could they perhaps gain an advantage. However attempts to take account of this inside information may breach insider dealing laws.

The different characteristics of a semi-strong form and a strong form efficient market thus affect the **timing** of share price movements, in cases where the relevant information becomes available to the market eventually. The difference between the two forms of market efficiency concerns **when** the share prices change, not by how much prices eventually change.

Exam skills

Bear the efficient market hypothesis in mind when discussing how a company's value might be affected by the financing or investment decisions it takes. Knowledge of **what** and **when** information will be incorporated into a quoted share price is likely to influence how and when information regarding financial management decisions is made public.

In particular, since current share prices can be crucial to the success or otherwise of takeover **bids and new share issues**, it will be important to be aware of how the market is likely to react to varying levels of information released. The market may not react predictably, nor in a way a business wants it to, if it does not have full information.

Section summary

The theory behind share price movements can be explained by the three forms of the **efficient market hypothesis**.

- **Weak form efficiency** implies that prices reflect all relevant information about past price movements and their implications.
- **Semi-strong form efficiency** implies that prices reflect past price movements and publicly available knowledge.
- **Strong form efficiency** implies that prices reflect past price movements, publicly available knowledge and inside knowledge.

Chapter Roundup

- Capital markets are markets for trading in **long-term** finance
- A company can obtain a stock market listing through an **offer for sale**, a **prospectus issue**, a **placing** or an **introduction**
- **Venture capital** and **private equity** are also sources of long term equity finance
- A **rights issue** is an offer to existing shareholders for them to buy more shares, usually at lower than the current share price.
- **Scrip dividends**, **bonus issues** and **share splits** are not methods of raising new equity funds, but they are methods of altering the share capital of a company, or in the case of scrip dividends and scrip issues, increasing the issued share capital of a company.
- **Fundamental analysis** is based on the theory that share prices can be derived from an analysis of **future dividends**.
- **Technical analysts** or **chartists** work on the basis that past price patterns will be repeated.
- **Random walk theory** is based on the idea that share prices will alter when **new information** becomes available.
- The theory behind share price movements can be explained by the three forms of the **efficient market hypothesis.**
    - **Weak form efficiency** implies that prices reflect all relevant information about past price movements and their implications.
    - **Semi-strong form efficiency** implies that prices reflect past price movements and publicly available knowledge.
    - **Strong form efficiency** implies that prices reflect past price movements, publicly available knowledge and inside knowledge.

Quick Quiz

1 Which of the following sources of finance to companies is the most widely used in practice?

    A   Bank borrowings
    B   Rights issues
    C   New share issues
    D   Retained earnings

2 Identify four reasons why a company may seek a stock market listing.

3 A company's shares have a nominal value of £1 and a market value of £3. In a rights issue, one new share would be issued for every three shares at a price of £2.60. What is the theoretical ex-rights price?

4 A company offers to pay a dividend in the form of new shares which are worth more than the cash alternative which is also offered. What is this dividend in the form of shares called?

5 Match A/B to (i)/(ii), to express the difference between a share split and a bonus issue.

    A   A bonus issue ....   (i)   .... converts equity reserves into share capital
    B   A share split ....   (ii)   .... leaves reserves unaffected

PART B FINANCING DECISIONS   5: Equity finance

6   Which of the following is least likely to be a reason for seeking a stock market flotation?

    A   Improving the existing owners' control over the business
    B   Access to a wider pool of finance
    C   Enhancement of the company's image
    D   Transfer of capital to other uses

7   Which of the following is not true of a rights issue by a listed company?

    A   Rights issues do not require a prospectus
    B   The rights issues price can be at a discount to market price
    C   If shareholders do not take up the rights, the rights lapse
    D   Relative voting rights are unaffected if shareholders exercise their rights

8   Which theory of share price behaviour does the following statement describe?

    'The analysis of external and internal influences upon the operations of a company with a view to assisting in investment decisions.'

    A   Technical analysis
    B   Random walk theory
    C   Fundamental analysis theory
    D   Chartism

9   What is meant by 'efficiency', in the context of the efficient market hypothesis?

10 The different 'forms' of the efficient market hypothesis state that share prices reflect *which* types of information? Tick all that apply.

	Form of EMH		
	Weak	Semi-strong	Strong
No information	☐	☐	☐
All information in past share price record	☐	☐	☐
All other publicly available information	☐	☐	☐
Specialists' and experts' 'insider' knowledge	☐	☐	☐

Answers to Quick Quiz

1   D   Retained earnings

2   Four of the following five: access to a wider pool of finance; improved marketability of shares; transfer of capital to other uses (eg founder members liquidating holdings); enhancement of company image; making growth by acquisition possible

3   ((£3 × 3) + £2.60) ÷ 4 = £2.90

4   An enhanced scrip dividend

5   A(i); B(ii)

6   A   Flotation is likely to involve a significant loss of control to a wider circle of investors.

7   C   Shareholders have the option of renouncing the rights and selling them on the market.

8   C   Fundamental analysis theory

9   Efficiency in processing information in the pricing of stocks and shares

10

	Form of EMH		
	Weak	Semi-strong	Strong
No information	☐	☐	☐
All information in past share price record	✓	✓	✓
All other publicly available information	☐	✓	✓
Specialists' and experts' 'insider' knowledge	☐	☐	✓

Answers to Questions

5.1 Effects of rights issue

(a)

	$
Current market value of 5 existing shares (× $2.10)	10.50
Rights issue price of one new share	1.80
Theoretical value of 6 shares	12.30

(i) Theoretical ex-rights price = $12.30/6 shares = $2.05 per share.

(ii) The value of the rights for each new share is $2.05 − $1.80 = $0.25. The value of the rights for each existing share is therefore $0.25/5 shares = $0.05 per share.

(b) (i) Rights issue

	Million
Number of shares in issue ($50 million/$0.25 per share)	200
New shares in rights issue (1 for 5)	40
Total number of shares after the issue	240

Current earnings = $40 million less 30% tax = $28 million.
Current EPS = $28 million/200 million shares = $0.14
Current P/E ratio = 2.1/0.14 = 15 times.

	$m
Profit before taxation (+ 25%)	50
Taxation at 30%	(15)
Profit after tax (earnings)	35

Earnings per share = $35 million/240 million shares = $0.146
Assumed P/E ratio (no change) = 15
Assumed share price in one year's time: $0.146 × 15 = $2.19

5.2 Rights issue

Value of the portfolio for a shareholder with 3 shares before the rights issue

	£
3 shares @ £4.00	12.00
1 share @ £3.20	3.20
4	15.20

So the value per share after the rights issue (or TERP) is 15.20/4 = £3.80.

Alternative solution

The theoretical ex rights price = $\frac{1}{3+1}((3 \times £4) + £3.20)) = £3.80$ per share

	£
Theoretical ex rights price	3.80
Price per new share	3.20
Value of rights per new share	0.60

The value of the rights attached to each existing share is $\frac{£0.60}{3} = £0.20$.

We will assume that a shareholder is able to sell his rights for £0.20 per existing share held.

(a) If the shareholder **sells all his rights**:

	£
Sale value of rights (900 × £0.20)	180
Market value of his 900 shares, ex rights (× £3.80)	3,420
Total wealth	3,600
Total value of 900 shares cum rights (× £4)	£3,600

The shareholder would neither gain nor lose wealth. He would not be required to provide any additional funds to the company, but his shareholding as a proportion of the total equity of the company will be lower.

(b) If the shareholder **exercises half of the rights** (buys 450/3 = 150 shares at £3.20) and sells the other half:

	£
Sale value of rights (450 × £0.20)	90
Market value of his 1,050 shares, ex rights (× £3.80)	3,990
	4,080
Total value of 900 shares cum rights (× £4)	3,600
Additional investment (150 × £3.20)	480
	4,080

The shareholder would neither gain nor lose wealth, although he will have increased his investment in the company by £480.

(c) If the shareholder **does nothing**, but all other shareholders either exercise their rights or sell them, he would lose wealth as follows.

	£
Market value of 900 shares cum rights (× £4)	3,600
Market value of 900 shares ex rights (× £3.80)	3,420
Loss in wealth	180

It follows that the shareholder, to protect his existing investment, should either **exercise his rights** or **sell them** to another investor. If he does not exercise his rights, the new securities he was entitled to subscribe for might be sold for his benefit by the company, and this would protect him from losing wealth.

Now try this question from the Exam Question Bank

Number	Level	Marks	Time
Q7	Examination	20	36 mins

DEBT FINANCE

As well as being financed by its owners, the **shareholders**, a company is likely to be financed by lenders who provide it with **debt finance**. We look in this chapter at the most important forms of long-term debt finance. We examine the **practical factors** that determine whether lenders provide finance, how much they provide and on what terms. Remember that you may need to use the detail in this chapter to explain **why** organisations choose particular sources of finance.

Go slowly through the calculations, to confirm your understanding, as calculations remain an important element in this paper. Discounted cash flow techniques are revised in the appendix on page 343.

You must always make recommendations that are suitable for the **specific type of entity** so the last two sections look at the specific financing for multi-nationals and small entities.

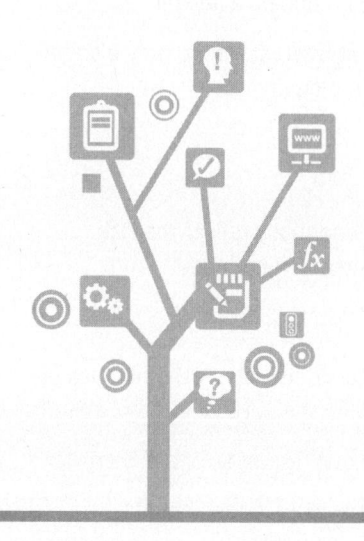

topic list	learning outcomes	syllabus references	ability required
1 Medium-term finance	A(2)(d), B(1)(b)	A(2)(vii), B(1)(iii)	evaluation
2 Long-term debt	B(1)(b)	B(1)(iii)	evaluation
3 Convertible securities	B(1)(b)	B(1)(iii)	evaluation
4 Warrants	B(1)(b)	B(1)(iii)	evaluation
5 International debt finance	B(1)(d)	B(1)(iii)	evaluation
6 Small and medium-sized entities	B(i)(d)	B(1)(iii)	evaluation

1 Medium-term finance

> **Introduction**
>
> This section explains loan finance and how a lender will decide what interest rate to charge a customer.

1.1 Term loans

Banks often provide term loans as medium or long-term financing for customers. The customer borrows a fixed amount and pays it back with interest over a period or at the end of it. You will hopefully remember that this contrasts with an overdraft facility, when a customer, through its current account, can borrow money on a short-term basis up to a certain amount. Overdrafts are repayable on demand.

The **advantages** of a term loan are as follows.

(a) They are **easy and quick** to negotiate and arrange.
(b) **Flexible repayment schedules** may be offered by banks.
(c) They are particularly useful for **small entities** who can have problems raising capital.

1.2 Mezzanine finance

This is unsecured loans that rank after secured debt but ahead of equity in a liquidation. It is commonly used for **management buy-outs** (see Chapter 16), where there is a need to **bridge the gap** between the amount of loans that banks are prepared to make and the amount of equity funding available.

It is **higher risk** lending than bank loans so tends to attract a **higher rate of interest**. There may also be warrants attached (see Section 4) entitling the holder to subscribe for future equity.

1.3 Creditworthiness   5/12

From the lender's viewpoint, the interest rate charged on loan finance will normally reflect the **risk** associated with the loan and an assessment of a company's creditworthiness will be made.

Risk issue	Factors that will cause the interest rate to be higher
Purpose	If the lender assesses that the project is risky or is concerned about the abilities of the management team
Amount	If the amount of the loan is high relative to the financial resources of the borrower
Repayment	If repayment of capital is at the end of the loan, rather than in instalments
Time period	If the loan is for a long time period
Security	If there are no assets available against which the loan can be secured

> **Section summary**
>
> Bank loans tend to be a **source** of **medium-term finance**, linked with the purchase of specific assets. Interest and repayments will be set in advance.

2 Long-term debt

> **Introduction**
>
> In this section we look at the terminology used to describe long-term debt and the different types of debt finance that are available.

2.1 Bonds

The term **bonds** describes various forms of long-term debt a company may issue. Bonds come in various forms, including redeemable, irredeemable, floating rate, zero coupon and convertible.

Bonds have a **nominal value**, which is the debt owed by the company, and interest is paid at a stated **'coupon'** on this amount. For example, if a company issues 10% bonds, the coupon will be 10% of the nominal value of the bonds, so that £100 of bonds will receive £10 interest each year. The rate quoted is the gross rate, before tax.

Unlike shares, debt is often issued **at par**, ie with £100 payable per £100 nominal value. Where the coupon rate is fixed at the time of issue, it will be set according to prevailing market conditions given the credit rating of the company issuing the debt. Subsequent changes in market (and company) conditions will cause the **market value of the bond to fluctuate**, although the coupon will stay at the **fixed percentage** of the nominal value.

Some European companies and banks are taking advantage of low interest rates, healthy cash reserves and receptive investors to repay some old debt ahead of schedule and, in many cases, replace it with longer-term bonds to smooth repayment schedules.

Banks have been using loans from the European Central Bank to buy back some of their bonds at a discount, which eases their debt load and generates extra capital on their balance sheet.

While banks are mainly taking advantage of the depressed value of their debt, particularly "subordinated debt" that is at risk in any restructuring, most corporate bonds trade at a premium in the market.

However, companies enjoy exceptionally low borrowing costs, thanks to burgeoning investor interest and rock-bottom interest rates for safer government bonds, which serve as a benchmark against which debts are priced. This allows many to exchange old bonds with a higher pre-financial crisis coupon with less expensive instruments.

Source Financial Times 22 April 2012

2.2 Debentures

A DEBENTURE is a written acknowledgement of a debt by a company, usually given under its seal and normally containing provisions as to payment of interest and the terms of repayment of principal. A bond may be secured on some or all of the assets of the company or its subsidiaries.

Debentures are defined as the written acknowledgement of a debt incurred by a company, normally containing provisions about the payment of interest and the eventual repayment of capital. The terms of the bond are set out in a **trust deed**.

One example of a debenture is the existence of 'debenture tickets' for the All England Lawn Tennis Club (Wimbledon). An investor who has lent money to the club to fund capital improvements (such as the retractable roof on Centre Court) is not paid interest but is instead given seats in prime locations on either Centre Court or No 1 Court. These debenture tickets are the only tickets that can be legally transferred or sold by the holder to another party.

2.3 Security

Bonds will often be secured. **Security** may take the form of either a **fixed charge** or a **floating charge**.

(a) **Fixed charge**

Security would be related to a **specific asset** or group of assets, typically land and buildings. The company would be unable to dispose of the asset without providing a substitute asset for security, or without the lender's consent.

(b) **Floating charge**

With a floating charge on **certain assets** of the company (for example inventory or receivables), the lender's security in the event of a default of payment is whatever assets of the appropriate class the company then owns (provided that another lender does not have a prior charge on the assets). The company would be able, however, to dispose of its assets as it chose until a default took place. In the event of default, the lender would probably appoint a receiver to run the company rather than lay claim to a particular asset.

Not all bonds are secured. Investors are likely to expect a **higher yield** with **unsecured bonds** to compensate them for the extra risk. The rate of interest on unsecured bonds may be around 1% or more higher than for secured debt.

2.4 Deep discount bonds

DEEP DISCOUNT BOND is a bond offered at a large discount on the face value of the debt so that a significant proportion of the return to the investor comes by way of a capital gain on redemption, rather than through interest payment. *(CIMA Official Terminology)*

Deep discount bonds will be redeemable at par (or above par) when they eventually mature. For example a company might issue £1,000,000 of bonds in 2002, at a price of £50 per £100, and redeemable at par in the year 2017. For a company with specific cash flow requirements, the **low servicing costs** during the currency of the bond may be an attraction, coupled with a high cost of redemption at maturity.

Investors might be attracted by the **large capital gain** offered by the bonds, which is the difference between the issue price and the redemption value. However, deep discount bonds will carry a much **lower rate of interest** than other types of bonds. The only tax advantage is that the gain gets taxed (as **income**) in one lump on maturity or sale, not as amounts of interest each year.

2.5 Zero coupon bonds

ZERO COUPON BOND is a bond offering no interest payments, all investor return being gained through capital appreciation. *(CIMA Official Terminology)*

Zero coupon bonds are bonds that are issued at a discount to their redemption value, but no interest is paid on them. The investor gains from the difference between the issue price and the redemption value, and there is an implied interest rate in the amount of discount at which the bonds are issued (or subsequently re-sold on the market).

(a) The advantage for borrowers is that zero coupon bonds can be used to **raise cash immediately**, and there is no cash repayment until redemption date. The cost of redemption is known at the time of issue, and so the borrower can plan to have funds available to redeem the bonds at maturity.

(b) The advantage for lenders is restricted, unless the rate of discount on the bonds **offers a high yield**. The only way of obtaining cash from the bonds before maturity is to sell them, and their market value will depend on the remaining term to maturity and current market interest rates.

The tax advantage of zero coupon bonds is the same as that for deep discount bonds.

2.6 The redemption of bonds

Bonds are usually **redeemable**. They are issued for a term of ten years or more, and perhaps 25 to 30 years. At the end of this period, they will 'mature' and become redeemable (at par or possibly at a value above par).

KEY TERM

REDEMPTION is repayment of the principal amount (for example a bond) at the date of maturity.
(CIMA Official Terminology)

Some redeemable bonds have an earliest and a latest redemption date. For example, 12% Loan Notes 2013/15 are redeemable at any time between the earliest specified date (in 2013) and the latest date (in 2015). The issuing company can choose the date. The decision by a company when to redeem a debt will depend on **how much cash** is available to the company to repay the debt, and on the **nominal rate of interest** on the debt.

Some bonds do not have a redemption date, and are '**irredeemable**' or '**undated**'. Undated bonds might be redeemed by a company that wishes to pay off the debt, but there is no obligation on the company to do so.

2.6.1 Valuation of redeemable bonds

Valuation depends upon **future expected receipts**.

LEARN

Value of debt = (Interest earnings × Annuity factor) + (Redemption value × Discounted cash flow factor)

The principles of discounting future cash flows have been covered in Paper P1 *Performance Operations* and we will also be using these techniques in Chapters 7 and 11. If you need to refresh your knowledge of these techniques, please work through the Appendix: Discounted cash flow.

Example: Valuation of debt

Furry has in issue 12% bonds with par value $100,000 and redemption value $110,000, with interest payable quarterly. The redemption yield on the bonds is 8% annually and 2% quarterly. The bonds are redeemable on 30 June 20X4 and it is now 31 December 20X0.

Required

Calculate the market value of the bonds.

Solution

You need to use the redemption yield cost of debt as the discount rate, and remember to use an annuity factor for the interest. We are discounting over 14 periods using the quarterly discount rate (8%/4).

Period		Cash flow $	Discount factor 2%	Present value $
1–14	Interest	3,000	12.106	36,318
14	Redemption	110,000	0.758	83,380
				119,698

Market value is $119,698.

2.6.2 Yield to maturity

The yield to maturity (or **redemption yield**) is the effective yield on a redeemable bond which allows for the time value of money and is effectively the **internal rate of return** of the cash flows.

For example, a five year unsecured bond with a coupon of 5% per annum, redeemable at par and issued at a 6% discount to par will have a yield to maturity of 6.47%. This is calculated by assuming a nominal value of $100 and calculating NPVs at 5% and 7% discount rates.

Year	Cash flow $m	Discount factor @ 5%	Present value $m	Discount factor @ 7%	Present value $m
0	(94)	1.000	(94.00)	1.000	(94.00)
1–5	5	4.329	21.64	4.100	20.50
5	100	0.784	78.40	0.713	71.30
NPV			6.04		(2.20)

$$\text{Yield to maturity} = 5\% + \left(\frac{6.04}{(6.04+2.20)}\right) \times 2\% = 6.47\%$$

For **irredeemable** debt the yield to maturity (YTM) can be calculated as

YTM = Annual interest / Current market value × 100%

For example an irredeemable bond with a coupon of 4% and a current market price of $93 has a YTM of

4 / 93 × 100% = 4.30%

2.6.3 Yield to maturity on foreign currency bonds

The yield to maturity becomes more complicated if a company issues foreign currency bonds. First, let's consider a company that is based in Europe, but issues irredeemable bonds denominated in US $100. Assume the coupon rate is 6%. If the exchange rate is expected to remain constant then the calculation is as before. However, if the US $ is expected to strengthen by 2% per year against the euro, the cost of the interest to the company will be 2% higher each year.

Therefore the YTM would be

[(1.06 × 1.02) − 1] = 0.0812 = 8.12%

The calculation for redeemable foreign currency bonds is more complicated as the cash flows need to be converted into the home currency first before the IRR calculation is made. This will be demonstrated by the use of an example.

Example: Yield to maturity for a redeemable foreign currency bond

Fluffy has in issue 6% bonds with par value $100 and redemption value $108, with interest payable annually. Fluffy's home currency is GBP. The bonds are redeemable on 30 September 20X8 and it is now 30 September 20X4. The current market value is equal to the par value of the bonds. The current spot rate is GBP/USD 1.6000. The dollar is expected to strengthen against sterling by 2% per year.

Required

Calculate the yield to maturity (in GBP) of the bonds.

Solution

First you need to calculate the GBP cash flows for each year.

Period		USD Cash flow $	Exchange rate	GBP Cash flow £
0	Market value	(100)	1.6000	(62.50)
1	Interest	6	1.6000/1.02 = 1.5686	3.83
2	Interest	6	1.5686/1.02 = 1.5378	3.90
3	Interest	6	1.5378/1.02 = 1.5076	3.98
4	Interest and redemption	114	1.5076/1.02 = 1.4780	77.13

Then these cash flows can be used in the IRR calculation

Period	GBP Cash flow	DF 8%	PV	DF 10%	
0	(62.50)	1.000	(62.50)	1.000	
1					
2					
3	3.98	0.794	3.16	0.751	
4	77.13	0.735	56.69	0.683	
			4.24		

YTM = 8% + [4.24/(4.24 + 0.13)] × 2% = 9.94%

2.6.4 How will a company finance the redemption of long-term debt?

There is no guarantee that a company will be able to raise a new loan to pay off a maturing debt, and one item to look for in a company's balance sheet is the **redemption date** of **current loans**, to establish how much new finance is likely to be needed by the company, and when.

(a) If the redemption is to take place using **current funds** (assuming there are enough available), the business needs to consider the **alternative uses** to which these funds could be put.

(b) The company may decide to issue **new debt** to replace the old debt. The company will incur **issue costs** using new debt, and will also need to consider the **future pattern of interest rates**.

(c) Alternatively the company could use an issue of **equity** to provide the funds for redemption. **Issue costs** will again be a factor, and the directors will need to consider whether to issue shares to **new shareholders**, or use a **rights issue** to existing shareholders.

(d) If the redeemable debt has been **issued** on the stock market, it can be bought and hence redeemed by the company at any time. The directors will choose to redeem it if other possible sources of finance have a lower cost.

2.7 Irredeemable debt

In some cases, debts are irredeemable, whereby the company will continue to pay interest every year indefinitely (in perpetuity).

Ignoring tax, the value of irredeemable debt is:

$$P_0 = \frac{i}{k_d}$$

Where P_0 is the ex-interest market value of debt
i is the annual interest charge
k_d is the cost of debt (required return by debt holders)

> **With tax, the value of irredeemable debt is:**
>
> $$P_0 = \frac{i(1-t)}{K_{dnet}}$$
>
> Where t is the tax rate
> K_{dnet} is the cost of debt after tax

Section summary

- The term **bonds** describes various forms of long-term debt a company may issue. Bonds come in various forms, including redeemable, irredeemable, floating rate, zero coupon and convertible
- The yield to maturity (or **redemption yield**) is the effective yield on a redeemable bond which allows for the time value of money and is effectively the **internal rate of return** of the cash flows

3 Convertible securities   11/10, 3/12

Introduction

Convertible securities are a **hybrid** of debt and equity. They can be converted to ordinary shares at some future date.

3.1 Convertible bonds

CONVERTIBLE DEBT is a liability that gives the holder the right to convert into another instrument, normally ordinary shares, at a pre-determined price/rate and time. *(CIMA Official Terminology)*

Conversion terms often vary over time. For example, the conversion terms of convertible bonds might be that on 1 April 20X0, £2 of bonds can be converted into one ordinary share, whereas on 1 April 20X1, the conversion price will be £2.20 of bonds for one ordinary share. Once converted, convertible securities cannot be converted back into the original fixed return security.

3.2 The conversion value and the conversion premium

The current market value of ordinary shares into which a unit of bonds may be converted is known as the conversion value. The **conversion value** will be below the value of the bonds at the date of issue, but will be expected to increase as the date for conversion approaches on the assumption that a company's shares ought to increase in market value over time.

Conversion value = Conversion ratio × market price per ordinary share

Conversion premium = Current market value − current conversion value

Question 6.1
Convertible debt

Learning outcome: B(1)(b)

The 10% convertible bonds of Starchwhite are quoted at £142 per £100 nominal. The earliest date for conversion is in four years time, at the rate of 30 ordinary shares per £100 nominal. The share price is currently £4.15. Annual interest on the bonds has just been paid.

Required

(a) Calculate the current conversion value.
(b) Calculate the conversion premium and comment on its meaning.

3.3 The issue price and the market price of convertible bonds

A company will aim to issue bonds with the **greatest possible conversion premium** as this will mean that, for the amount of capital raised, it will, on conversion, have to issue the lowest number of new ordinary shares. The premium that will be accepted by potential investors will depend on the company's growth potential and so on prospects for a sizeable increase in the share price.

Convertible bonds issued at par normally have a **lower coupon rate of interest** than straight debt. This lower yield is the price the investor has to pay for the conversion rights. It is, of course, also one of the reasons why the issue of convertible bonds is attractive to a company, particularly one with tight cash flows around the time of issue, but an easier situation when the notes are due to be converted.

When convertible bonds are traded on a stock market, their **minimum market price** or **floor value** will be the price of straight bonds with the same coupon rate of interest. If the market value falls to this minimum, it follows that the market attaches no value to the conversion rights.

The actual market price of convertible bonds will depend on

- The **price of straight debt**
- The **current conversion value**
- The **length of time** before conversion may take place
- The **market's expectation** as to future equity returns and the risk associated with these returns

Most companies issuing convertible bonds expect them to be **converted**. They view the notes as **delayed equity**. They are often used either because the company's ordinary share price is considered to be particularly depressed at the time of issue or because the issue of equity shares would result in an immediate and significant drop in earnings per share. There is no certainty, however, that the security holders will exercise their option to convert; therefore the bonds may run their full term and need to be redeemed.

Example: Convertible bonds

CD has issued 50,000 units of convertible bonds, each with a nominal value of $100 and a coupon rate of interest of 10% payable yearly. Each $100 of convertible bonds may be converted into 40 ordinary shares of CD in three years time. Any bonds not converted will be redeemed at 110 (that is, at $110 per $100 nominal value of bond).

Estimate the likely current market price for $100 of the bonds, if investors in the bonds now require a pre-tax return of only 8%, and the expected value of CD ordinary shares on the conversion day is:

(a) $2.50 per share
(b) $3.00 per share

Solution

(a) Shares are valued at $2.50 each

If shares are only expected to be worth $2.50 each on conversion day, the value of 40 shares will be $100, and investors in the debt will presumably therefore redeem their debt at 110 instead of converting them into shares.

The market value of $100 of the convertible debt will be the discounted present value of the expected future income stream.

Year		Cash flow $	Discount factor 8%	Present value $
1	Interest	10	0.926	9.26
2	Interest	10	0.857	8.57
3	Interest	10	0.794	7.94
3	Redemption value	110	0.794	87.34
				113.11

The estimated market value is $113.11 per $100 of debt. This is also the floor value.

(b) Shares are valued at $3 each

If shares are expected to be worth $3 each, the debt holders will convert their debt into shares (value per $100 of stock = 40 shares × $3 = $120) rather than redeem their debt at 110.

Year		Cash flow/value $	Discount factor 8%	Present value $
1	Interest	10	0.926	9.26
2	Interest	10	0.857	8.57
3	Interest	10	0.794	7.94
3	Value of 40 shares	120	0.794	95.28
				121.05

The estimated market value is $121.05 per $100 of debt.

3.4 Advantages of convertibles

(a) Convertibles serve as a **sweetener** for debt by allowing the investor to participate in increases in price of share capital.

(b) The issuer can pay **lower interest** than on straight debt. This may be significant if funds are tight during the early years of issue of the bonds. They are usually issued by **high growth companies** who do not want the burden of high interest payments.

(c) The **attractions of the conversion rights**, the possibility of a significant capital gain and the hedge against risk (the right to have the debt repaid if conversion is not worthwhile), should mean the lender is willing to accept fewer other conditions.

(d) Convertibles may provide a means of issuing equity ultimately at a **higher price** than **current** market price.

(e) There may be provisions in the issue terms allowing the issuer to **force conversion** if the market price of the bonds is greater than the conversion price.

(f) If the company issued straight bonds initially and then equity to redeem the bonds, two lots of issue costs would be paid, whereas with convertible debt, issue costs would only be **paid once**.

(g) The **debt ratio** is **reduced** if conversion takes place.

3.5 Disadvantages of convertibles

(a) If the company had waited for funds, and the **market price increases significantly** above the conversion price, it would be better off issuing shares at a higher price, rather than having to issue shares at the lower conversion terms.

(b) The company has to **repay the debt** if the share price does not increase.

(c) Some borrowers may be reluctant to invest because of the **lower yield** on convertible shares compared with securities not having conversion rights.

(d) As compared with warrants, the exercise of convertibles does **not provide extra funds** to the firm, whereas the exercise of warrants does.

Section summary

- **Convertible debt** can, at the holder's option, be converted to ordinary shares at some future date instead of being held to maturity
- Convertibles are **debt sweeteners** as they allow a lower rate of interest to be paid on the debt

---

4 Warrants

Introduction

Share warrants are another form of debt sweetener which give their holder the right to apply for new shares at a specified exercise price in the future.

4.1 Purpose of warrants

A **warrant** is a right given by a company to an investor, **allowing him** to **subscribe** for new shares at a future date at a fixed, pre-determined price (the **exercise price**).

Warrants are usually issued as part of a package with unsecured bonds: an investor who buys bonds will also acquire a certain number of warrants. The purpose of warrants is to make the bonds more attractive.

Once issued, warrants are detachable from the bonds and can be sold and bought separately before or during the 'exercise period' (the period during which the right to use the warrants to subscribe for shares is allowed). The market value of warrants will depend on expectations of actual share prices in the future.

4.2 Advantages of warrants

(a) Warrants themselves **do not involve** the **payment** of any **interest or dividends**. Furthermore, when they are initially attached to bonds, the interest rate on the bonds will be lower than for a comparable straight debt.

(b) Warrants make a bond issue more attractive and may make an issue of unsecured bonds possible where **adequate security is lacking**.

(c) Warrants provide a means of **generating additional equity** funds in the future without any immediate dilution in earnings per share. The cost will be the right that warrants holders to buy at the **possibly reduced exercise price**.

4.3 Disadvantages of warrants

The disadvantages of warrants are:

(a) When exercised, they will result in the **dilution** of **share capital.**

(b) Warrants may be exercised when a business **does not need additional capital**.

(c) The company has **less control** over the exercise of warrants than it does over the exercise of share capital.

> **Section summary**
>
> **Share warrants** give their holder the right to apply for new shares at a specified exercise price in the future. They can be issued as an 'add-on' to a new issue of bonds.

5 International debt finance

> **Introduction**
>
> Large companies with excellent credit ratings use the Euromarkets to borrow in any foreign currency using unregulated markets organised by merchant banks. This market is much bigger than the market for domestic bonds.

5.1 International borrowing

Borrowing markets are becoming increasingly internationalised, particularly for larger companies. Companies are able to borrow long-term funds on the **eurocurrency (money) markets** and on the markets for **eurobonds**. These markets are collectively called '**euromarkets**'. Large companies can also borrow on the **syndicated loan market** where a syndicate of banks provides medium to long-term currency loans.

If a company is receiving income in a foreign currency or has a long-term investment overseas, it can try to **limit the risk** of adverse exchange rate movements by **matching**. It can take out a long-term loan and use the foreign currency receipts to repay the loan.

5.2 Eurocurrency markets

KEY TERMS

EUROCURRENCY is currency which is held by individuals and institutions outside the country of issue of that currency.

EURODOLLARS are US dollars deposited with, or borrowed from, a bank outside the USA.

(CIMA Official Terminology)

A UK company might borrow money from a bank or from the investing public, in sterling. However it might also borrow in a foreign currency, especially if it trades abroad, or if it already has assets or liabilities abroad denominated in a foreign currency. When a company borrows in a foreign currency, the loan is known as a **eurocurrency loan**. (As with euro-equity, it is not only the euro that is involved, and so the 'euro-' prefix is a misnomer.) Banks involved in the euro currency market are **not subject to central bank reserve requirements** or regulations in respect of their involvement.

The eurocurrency markets involve the **depositing of funds** with a **bank outside the country** of the currency in which the funds are denominated and **re-lending these funds for a fairly short term**, typically three months, normally at a floating rate of interest.

Eurocredits are medium to long-term international bank loans which may be arranged by individual banks or by **syndicates of banks**. Syndication of loans increases the amounts available to hundreds of millions, while reducing the exposure of individual banks.

5.3 Eurobonds

A EUROBOND is a bond sold outside the jurisdiction of the country in whose currency the bond is denominated. *(CIMA Official Terminology)*

In recent years, a strong market has built up which allows very large companies to borrow in this way, long-term or short-term. Again, the market is not subject to national regulations.

Eurobonds are **long-term loans raised by international companies** or other institutions and **sold to investors in several countries** at the same time. Eurobonds are normally repaid after 5–15 years, and are for major amounts of capital ie $10 million or more.

Exam alert

Don't make the common mistake of thinking that eurobonds are issued in Europe or only denominated in euros.

5.3.1 How are Eurobonds issued?

STEP 1 A lead manager is appointed from a major merchant bank; the lead manager liaises with the credit rating agencies and organises a **credit rating** of the Eurobond.

STEP 2 The lead manager organises an **underwriting syndicate** (of other merchant banks) who agree the terms of the bond (eg interest rate, maturity date) and buy the bond.

STEP 3 The underwriting syndicate then organise the sale of the bond; this normally involves **placing** the bond with **institutional investors**.

5.3.2 Advantages of Eurobonds

(a) Eurobonds are '**bearer instruments**', which means that the owner does not have to declare his identity.

(b) Interest is paid gross and this has meant that Eurobonds have been used by investors to avoid tax.

(c) Eurobonds create a liability in a foreign currency to **match** against a foreign currency asset.

(d) They are often **cheaper** than a foreign currency bank loan because they can be sold on by the investor, who will therefore accept a lower yield in return for this greater liquidity.

(e) They are also extremely **flexible**. Most eurobonds are fixed rate but they can be floating rate or linked to the financial success of the company.

(f) They are typically issued by companies with excellent credit ratings and are normally **unsecured**, which makes it easier for companies to raise debt finance in the future.

(g) Eurobond issues are not normally advertised because they are **placed** with institutional investors and this reduces issue costs.

5.3.3 Disadvantages of Eurobonds

Like any form of debt finance there will be **issue costs** to consider (approximately 2% of funds raised in the case of Eurobonds) and there may also be problems if gearing levels are too high.

A borrower contemplating a eurobond issue must consider the **foreign exchange risk** of a long-term foreign currency loan. If the money is to be used to purchase assets which will earn revenue in a currency different to that of the bond issue, the borrower will run the risk of exchange losses if the currency of the loan strengthens against the currency of the revenues out of which the bond (and interest) must be repaid.

Exam skills

Since Eurobonds are a major source of finance, they may feature in exam questions. For example, you may be required to compare euro bank loans and a euro-denominated Eurobond or to discuss the advantages and disadvantages of different methods of funding, including a euro-denominated Eurobond.

Section summary

Large companies will have access to international debt such as **Eurobonds**.

6 Small and medium-sized entities

Introduction

In this exam you must always suggest suitable finance for the specific needs of the entity in the scenario. Small and medium-sized entities have specific problems obtaining finance which are very different to large, multinational entities.

The options open to small and medium-sized enterprises (SMEs) may be particularly limited. They face **competition** for funds, as investors have opportunities to invest in all sizes of organisation, also overseas and in government debt. In this competition they are handicapped by the problem of **uncertainty**.

(a) Whatever the details provided to potential investors, SMEs have **neither** the **business** history **nor larger track record** that larger organisations possess.

(b) Larger enterprises are subject by law to **more public scrutiny**; their accounts have to contain more detail and be audited, they receive more press coverage and so on.

(c) Because of the uncertainties involved, banks often use **credit scoring** systems to **control exposure.**

(d) **The costs of monitoring** small businesses may be **excessive for banks**, particularly if they are facing **difficult conditions themselves**.

(e) Banks face **regulatory pressures** with regulators classifying **lending to the small business sector** as being a **higher risk investment**.

A common problem is often that banks will be **unwilling** to increase **loan funding** without an increase in **security given** (which the owners may be unwilling or unable to give), or an increase in **equity funding** (which may be difficult to obtain).

Certain trends in various countries may be more helpful for small businesses.

(a) The **development of the non-bank sector**, with some organisations specialising in lending to small businesses.

(b) **Government aid** includes loan guarantee schemes, grants and enterprise capital funds.

Exam alert

Make sure that your financing recommendations are suitable for the type of entity in the scenario and not just a 'brain-dump' of types of finance.

PART B FINANCING DECISIONS   6: Debt finance   **115**

You are not expected to have knowledge of any specific government scheme but you may gain credit in the exam for relevant discussion of available schemes in your own country.

Section summary

Small and medium-sized entities often find it difficult to obtain finance due to the **risks** involved for lenders.

Chapter Roundup

- Bank loans tend to be a **source** of **medium-term finance**, linked with the purchase of specific assets. Interest and repayments will be set in advance

- The term **bonds** describes various forms of long-term debt a company may issue. Bonds come in various forms, including redeemable, irredeemable, floating rate, zero coupon and convertible

- The yield to maturity (or **redemption yield**) is the effective yield on a redeemable bond which allows for the time value of money and is effectively the **internal rate of return** of the cash flows

- **Convertible debt** can, at the holder's option, be converted to ordinary shares at some future date instead of being held to maturity

- Convertibles are **debt sweeteners** as they allow a lower rate of interest to be paid on the debt

- **Share warrants** give their holder the right to apply for new shares at a specified exercise price in the future. They can be issued as an 'add-on' to a new issue of bonds

- **Large companies** will have access to international debt such as **Eurobonds**

- Small and medium-sized entities often find it difficult to obtain finance due to the **risks** involved for lenders

Quick Quiz

1. Which of the following comparisons between bonds and preference shares is not a true statement?

    A   Bonds are cheaper to service since interest is tax-deductible.
    B   Bonds are more attractive to investors because they are secured against assets.
    C   Bonds holders rank above preference shareholders in the event of a liquidation.
    D   Bonds are more similar to equity than preference shares.

2. Holders of bonds are long-term receivables of the company.

    True ☐

    False ☐

3. A company has 12% bonds in issue, which have a market value of £135 per £100 nominal value. What is:

    (a) The coupon rate?
    (b) The amount of interest payable per annum per £100 nominal?

4. An investor has the option of redeeming a company's 11% loan notes 2008/2010 at any date between 1 January 2008 and 31 December 2010 inclusive.

    True ☐

    ☐

False

5 Convertible securities are fixed return securities that may be converted into zero coupon bonds/ordinary shares/warrants. (Delete as appropriate.)

6 Which of the following statements about convertible securities is false?

   A   They are fixed return securities.
   B   They must be converted into shares before the redemption date.
   C   The price at which they will be converted into shares is predetermined.
   D   Issue costs are lower than for equity.

7 Do borrowers benefit from floating rate bonds when interest rates are rising or falling?

8 What is the value of £100 12% debt redeemable in 3 years time at a premium of 20p per £ if the debtholder's required return is 10%?

9 What are the main factors lenders will consider when deciding whether to offer loan finance?

Answers to Quick Quiz

1 D

2 False. They are long-term payables of the company.

3 (a) 12%
   (b) £12

4 False. The company will be able to choose the date of redemption.

5 Ordinary shares

6 B The holder has the option to convert, but he will only convert if it is advantageous for him to do so. If the share price falls, the bonds may run their full term and need to be redeemed in the same way as other forms of debt.

7 Falling

8

Years		£	Discount factor @ 10%	Present value £
1–3	Interest	12	2.487	29.84
3	Redemption premium	120	0.751	90.12
				119.96

   Value of debt = £119.96

9 **P**urpose
   Amount
   Repayment
   Term
   Security

PART B FINANCING DECISIONS   6: Debt finance

Answers to Questions

6.1 Convertible debt

(a) Conversion ratio is £100 bond = 30 ordinary shares

   Conversion value = 30 × £4.15 = £124.50

(b) Conversion premium = £(142 − 124.50) = £17.50

   or $\dfrac{17.50}{124.50} \times 100\% = 14\%$

   The share price would have to rise by 14% before the conversion rights became attractive.

Now try these questions from the Exam Question Bank

Number	Level	Marks	Time
Q8	Examination	19	34 mins
Q9	Introductory	n/a	35 mins

LEASING

In this chapter, we consider the option of **leasing** an asset.

As well as looking at the **advantages** and **disadvantages** of different types of lease compared with **other forms of credit finance**, we shall be discussing the tax and cash flow implications of leasing. You need to know how to determine whether an organisation should **lease** or **buy** an asset.

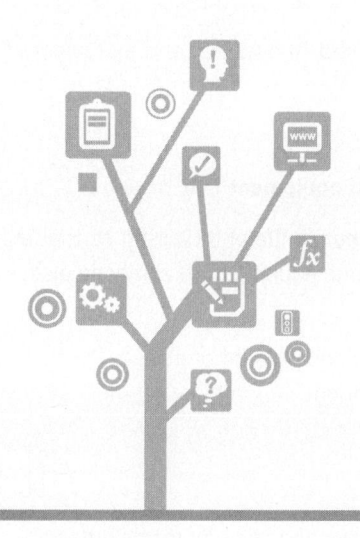

topic list	learning outcomes	syllabus references	ability required
1 Leasing as a source of finance	B(1)(b)	B(1)(iii)	evaluation
2 Lease or buy decisions	B(1)(d)	B(1)(x)	evaluation

119

1 Leasing as a source of finance

> **Introduction**
>
> **Leasing** is a commonly used source of finance, especially for small or medium-sized entities. It is a form of debt finance that can be very useful where capital is rationed.

1.1 The nature of leasing

Rather than buying an asset outright, using either available cash resources or borrowed funds, a business may lease an asset.

KEY TERM

LEASING is a contract between lessor and lessee for hire of a specific asset selected from a manufacturer or vendor of such assets by the lessee.

(a) The **lessor** retains ownership of the asset.

(b) The **lessee** has possession and use of the asset on payment of specified rentals over a period.

(c) Many lessors are **financial intermediaries** such as banks and insurance companies.

(d) The **range of assets leased** is wide, including office equipment and computers, cars and commercial vehicles, aircraft, ships and buildings.

1.2 Operating leases

Operating leases are rental agreements between the user of the leased asset (the lessee) and a provider of finance (the lessor) whereby:

(a) The **lessor supplies the equipment** to the lessee.

(b) The **lessor is responsible** for **servicing and maintaining the leased equipment.**

(c) The **period of the lease** is fairly **short, less** than the **expected economic life** of the asset, so that at the end of one lease agreement, the lessor can either lease the same equipment to someone else, and obtain a good rent for it, or sell the equipment second-hand.

With an operating lease, the lessor, often a finance house, purchases the equipment from the manufacturer and then leases it to the user (the lessee) for the agreed period.

1.3 Finance leases

KEY TERM

FINANCE LEASE is a lease agreement that transfers substantially all the risks and rewards incidental to ownership of an asset from the lessor to the lessee. *(CIMA Official Terminology)*

Finance leases are lease agreements between a **lessor** and **lessee**, for most or all of the asset's expected useful life.

Suppose that a company decides to obtain a company car and to finance the acquisition by means of a finance lease. A **car dealer** will **supply the car**. A finance house will agree to act as lessor in a finance leasing arrangement, and so will purchase the car from the dealer and lease it to the company. The company will take possession of the car from the car dealer, and make regular payments (monthly, quarterly, six monthly or annually) to the finance house under the terms of the lease.

There are other important characteristics of a finance lease.

(a) The **lessee** is normally **responsible** for the **upkeep**, servicing and maintenance of the asset. For a car this would mean repairs and servicing, road tax insurance and garaging. The lessor is not involved in this at all.

(b) The **lease** has a **primary period**, which covers all or most of the useful economic life of the asset. At the end of this primary period, the lessor would not be able to lease the asset to someone else, because the asset would be worn out. The lessor must therefore ensure that the lease payments during the primary period pay for the full cost of the asset as well as providing the lessor with a suitable return on his investment.

(c) The lessee may be able to continue to lease the asset for an **indefinite secondary period**, in return for a very low nominal rent, sometimes called a 'peppercorn rent'. Alternatively, the lessee might be allowed to sell the asset on a lessor's behalf (since the lessor is the owner) and to keep most of the sale proceeds, paying only a small percentage (perhaps 10%) to the lessor.

Example: Finance lease

On 1 January 20X0, Gordon Co leased an asset with a fair value of $38 million. The lease term was five years and the interest rate implicit in the lease was 10%. The company is required to make five annual instalments of $10 million on 31 December, with the first payment on 31 December 20X0.

Solution

Interest is calculated as 10% of the outstanding *capital* balance at the beginning of each year. The outstanding capital balance reduces each year by the capital element comprised in each instalment. The outstanding capital balance at 1 January 20X0 is the $38 million fair value at which both the asset and liability are initially recorded.

	$m
Balance 1 January 20X0	38.0
Interest 10%	3.8
Instalment 31 December 20X0	(10.0)
Balance outstanding 31 December 20X0	31.8
Interest 10% (rounded)	3.2
Instalment 31 December 20X1	(10.0)
Balance outstanding 31 December 20X1	25.0
Interest 10%	2.5
Instalment 31 December 20X2	(10.0)
Balance outstanding 31 December 20X2	17.5
Interest 10% (rounded)	1.7
Instalment 31 December 20X3	(10.0)
Balance outstanding 31 December 20X3	9.2
Interest 10% (rounded)	0.8
Instalment 31 December 20X4	(10.0)
	–

1.4 Allocating the finance charge – the actuarial method

The actuarial method of allocating the finance charge uses a periodic interest rate to calculate interest on the outstanding amount of the lease.

At the beginning of the lease, the capital invested is equal to the fair value of the asset (less any initial deposit paid by the lessee).

This amount reduces as each instalment is paid. Interest is charged on the reducing balance of the capital. It follows that the interest accruing is greatest in the early part of the lease term and gradually reduces as capital is repaid. The example below illustrates this point.

Example: Actuarial method

On 1 January 20X5 Jennifer Co acquired a machine from Alice Co under a finance lease. The cash price of the machine was $7,710 while the minimum payments in the lease agreement totalled $10,000. The agreement required the immediate payment of a $2,000 deposit with the balance being settled in four equal annual instalments commencing on 31 December 20X5. The finance charge of $2,290 represents interest of 15% per annum, calculated on the remaining balance of the liability during each accounting period. Depreciation on the plant is to be provided for at the rate of 20% per annum on a straight line basis assuming a residual value of nil.

Required

Show the breakdown of each instalment between interest and capital, using the actuarial method.

Solution

Interest is calculated as 15% of the outstanding *capital* balance at the beginning of each year. The outstanding capital balance reduces each year by the capital element comprised in each instalment. The outstanding capital balance at 1 January 20X5 is $5,710 ($7,710 fair value less $2,000 deposit).

	Total $	Capital $	Interest $
Capital balance at 1 Jan 20X5		5,710	
1st instalment (interest = $5,710 × 15%)	2,000	1,144	856
Capital balance at 1 Jan 20X6		4,566	
2nd instalment (interest = $4,566 × 15%)	2,000	1,315	685
Capital balance at 1 Jan 20X7		3,251	
3rd instalment (interest = $3,251 × 15%)	2,000	1,512	488
Capital balance at 1 Jan 20X8		1,739	
4th instalment (interest = $1,739 × 15%)	2,000	1,739	261
	8,000	–	2,290
Capital balance at 1 Jan 20X9			

1.5 Allocating the finance charge – the sum of digits method

The **sum of digits** method splits the total interest (without reference to a rate of interest) in such a way that the greater proportion falls in the earlier years. This method is quicker and easier to calculate than the actuarial method. The procedure is as follows.

STEP 1 Assign a digit to each instalment. The digit 1 should be assigned to the final instalment, 2 to the penultimate instalment and so on.

STEP 2 Add the digits. A quick method of adding the digits is to use the formula $n(n+1)/2$ where n is the number of periods of borrowing.

STEP 3 Calculate the interest charge included in each instalment. Do this by multiplying the total interest accruing over the lease term by the fraction:

$$\frac{\text{Digit applicable to the payment}}{\text{Sum of the digits}}$$

Example: Sum of digits method

Using the same information as the previous example of Jennifer Co

Required

Show the interest payments in each year, using the sum of digits method.

Solution

Assign digits to the borrowing periods:

20X5	4
20X6	3
20X7	2
20X8	1

Add the digits:

$1 + 2 + 3 + 4 = 10$

Or $(4 \times 5)/2 = 10$

Calculate the interest charge:

The total interest paid is $10,000 − $7,710 = $2,290. The amount charged to each year is

20X5	4/10 × $2,290 = $916
20X6	3/10 × $2,290 = $687
20X7	2/10 × $2,290 = $458
20X8	1/10 × $2,290 = $229

1.6 Attractions of leasing

The attractions of leases to the supplier of the equipment, the lessee and the lessor are as follows.

(a) The **supplier** of the **equipment** is **paid in full** at the **beginning**. The equipment is sold to the lessor, and apart from obligations under guarantees or warranties, the supplier has no further financial concern about the asset.

(b) The **lessor invests finance** by **purchasing assets** from suppliers and makes a return out of the lease payments from the lessee. Provided that a lessor can find lessees willing to pay the amounts he wants to make his return, the lessor can make good profits. He will also get capital allowances on his purchase of the equipment.

(c) **Leasing** might be **attractive** to the **lessee**:

   (i) If the lessee does not have enough cash to pay for the asset, and would have difficulty obtaining a bank loan to buy it, and so has to rent it in one way or another if he is to have the use of it at all

   (ii) As finance leases are **cheaper** than **bank loans**. Surveys suggest that this is a major reason why leases are used. The logic is that the lessor is prepared to **lend** at a **lower cost** because he possesses greater security ie the ownership of the asset

   (iii) As leases, once negotiated, are **legally binding** and **cannot be withdrawn** with immediate effect in the way an overdraft facility might be

   (iv) The lessee may find the **tax relief** available advantageous

Operating leases have these further advantages.

(a) The leased equipment does **not** have to be **shown** in the **lessee's published balance sheet**, and so the lessee's balance sheet shows no increase in its gearing ratio.

(b) The **equipment** is **leased** for a **shorter period** than its expected useful life. In the case of high-technology equipment, if the equipment becomes out of date before the end of its expected life, the lessee does not have to keep on using it, and it is the lessor who must bear the risk of having to sell obsolete equipment secondhand.

(c) The lessor deals with **servicing**, **maintenance** and **administration**.

Not surprisingly perhaps, a major growth area in operating leasing has been in computers and office equipment (such as photocopiers and fax machines) where technology is continually improving.

CASE STUDY

The aircraft leasing industry has come to the fore after several aviation downturns in recent years. Lessors' ownership of the world's civil aircraft fleet has increased from 12 per cent in 1990 to 36 per cent in 2010, according to Boeing, the plane maker.

Some aircraft lessors are predicting their share of the global fleet will rise to as much as 50 per cent by 2015, partly because some airlines may find it harder to secure financing for their jets due to economic circumstances. Lessors make most of their money through the charges paid by airlines that use their jets.

Source Financial Times 17 January 2012

1.7 Sale and leaseback arrangements

A company which owns its own premises can obtain finance by selling the property to an insurance company or pension fund for immediate cash and renting it back, usually for at least 50 years with rent reviews every few years.

A company would raise more cash from a **sale and leaseback agreement** than from a mortgage, but it should only make such an agreement if it cannot raise sufficient funds any other way.

Disadvantages of sale and leaseback are as follows.

(a) The company **loses ownership** of a valuable asset which is almost certain to appreciate over time.

(b) The **future borrowing capacity** of the firm will be reduced, since the property if owned could be used to provide security for a loan.

(c) The company is **contractually committed** to occupying the property for many years ahead, and this can be restricting.

(d) The **real cost** is likely to be high, particularly as there will be frequent rent reviews.

1.8 Hire purchase

Hire purchase is a **vendor credit arrangement** similar to leasing, with the exception that ownership of the goods passes to the hire purchase customer on payment of the final credit instalment, whereas a lessee never becomes the owner of the goods.

Question 7.1 — Lease v loan

Learning outcomes: B(1)(b)

Explain the cash flow characteristics of a finance lease, and compare it with the use of a bank loan. Your answer should include some comment on the significance of a company's anticipated tax position on lease versus buy decisions.

PART B FINANCING DECISIONS   7: Leasing   **125**

> **Section summary**
>
> **Leasing** is a commonly used source of finance. Major types of leases are **operating leases** (**lessor** responsible for maintaining asset), **finance leases** (**lessee** responsible for maintenance), and **sale and leaseback** arrangements.

2 Lease or buy decisions   9/10, 3/11, 5/11

> **Introduction**
>
> Leasing as a source of debt finance needs to carefully analysed against other forms of debt finance using discounted cash flow techniques.

The principles of discounting future cash flows have been covered in Paper P1 *Performance Operations* and we will also be using these techniques in Chapter 11.

These techniques are revised in the appendix: Discounted cash flow.

2.1 Lease or buy calculations

The decision whether to buy or lease an asset is made once the **decision to invest** in the asset has been made.

Discounted cash flow techniques are used to evaluate the lease or buy decision so that the **least-cost financing option** can be chosen.

The cost of capital that should be applied to the cash flows for the financing decision is the **cost of borrowing**. We assume that if the organisation decided to purchase the equipment, it would finance the purchase by borrowing funds (rather than out of retained funds). We therefore compare the **cost of borrowing** with the **cost of leasing** by applying this cost of borrowing to the financing cash flows.

The cost of borrowing **does not include the interest repayments on the loan** as this is dealt with via the cost of capital.

2.2 A simple example

Brown Co has decided to invest in a new machine which has a ten year life and no residual value. The machine can either be purchased now for $50,000, or it can be leased for ten years with lease rental payments of $8,000 per annum payable at the end of each year.

The cost of capital to be applied is 9% and taxation should be ignored.

Solution

Present value of leasing costs

PV =   Annuity factor at 9% for 10 years × $8,000
    =   6.418 × $8,000
    = $51,344

If the machine was purchased now, it would cost $50,000. The purchase is therefore the least-cost financing option.

2.3 An example with taxation

Mallen and Mullins Inc has decided to install a new milling machine. The machine costs $20,000 and it would have a useful life of five years with a trade-in value of $4,000 at the end of the fifth year. A decision has now to be taken on the method of financing the project.

(a) The company could purchase the machine for cash, using bank loan facilities on which the current rate of interest is 13% before tax.

(b) The company could lease the machine under an agreement which would entail payment of $4,800 at the end of each year for the next five years.

The rate of tax is 30%. If the machine is purchased, the company will be able to claim a tax depreciation allowance of 100% in Year 1. Tax is payable with a year's delay.

Solution

Cash flows are discounted at the after-tax cost of borrowing, which is at 13% × 70% = 9.1%, say 9%.

The present value (PV) of purchase costs

Year	Item	Cash flow $	Discount factor @ 9%	PV $
0	Equipment cost	(20,000)	1.000	(20,000)
5	Trade-in value	4,000	0.650	2,600
2	Tax savings, from allowances 30% × $20,000	6,000	0.842	5,052
			NPV of purchase	(12,348)

The PV of leasing costs

It is assumed that the lease payments are fully tax-allowable.

Year	Lease payment $	Savings in tax (30%) $	Discount factor @ 9%	PV $
1–5	(4,800) pa		3.890	(18,672)
2–6		1,440 pa	3.569 (W)	5,139
			NPV of leasing	(13,533)

Working

	$
6 year cumulative present value factor 9%	4.486
1 year present value factor 9%	(0.917)
	3.569

The cheapest option would be to purchase the machine.

An alternative method of making lease or buy decisions is to carry out a single financing calculation with the payments for one method being negative and the receipts being positive, and vice versa for the other method.

Year	0 $m	1 $m	2 $m	3 $m	4 $m	5 $m	6 $m
Saved equipment cost	20,000						
Lost trade-in value						(4,000)	
Lost tax savings from allowances			(6,000)				
Lease payments		(4,800)	(4,800)	(4,800)	(4,800)	(4,800)	
Tax allowances			1,440	1,440	1,440	1,440	1,440
Net cash flow	20,000	(4,800)	(9,360)	(3,360)	(3,360)	(7,360)	1,440
Discount factor 9%	1.000	0.917	0.842	0.772	0.708	0.650	0.596
PV	20,000	(4,402)	(7,881)	(2,594)	(2,379)	(4,784)	858
NPV	(1,182)						

The **negative NPV** indicates that the **lease is unattractive** and the **purchasing decision is better**, as the net savings from not leasing outweigh the net costs of purchasing.

Exam skills

In this exam, speed is of the essence and you may find it much quicker to do a single calculation, especially if you then have to do a sensitivity analysis.

2.4 A more complicated example with taxation

Using the information from Example 2.3 (apart from the tax payment date) now assume that the company can claim tax depreciation allowances of 25% on a reducing balance basis over the machine's five year life if it is purchased.

Depreciation is tax deductible and Mallen and Mullins Inc uses straight line depreciation in its accounts. The interest element of the lease payments is also tax deductible.

The rate of tax is 30%, payable in the year of the relevant profits.

Exam skills

Tax treatment of leases varies in different countries and you need to read the information in an exam question very carefully. The examiners have commented that the tax aspects of these calculations have caused difficulties.

Solution

Tax depreciation allowances

Year	Value at start of year $	25% depreciation $	30% tax allowance $
1	20,000	5,000	1,500
2	15,000	3,750	1,125
3	11,250	2,813	844
4	8,437	2,109	633
5	8,437 − 2,109 − 4,000	Balance 2,328	698

Present value of purchase costs

Year	0	1	2	3	4	5
	$	$	$	$	$	$
Purchase cost	(20,000)					
Tax allowances		1,500	1,125	844	633	698
Trade-in value						4,000
Net cash flow	(20,000)	1,500	1,125	844	633	4,698
Discount factor 9%	1.000	0.917	0.842	0.772	0.708	0.650
PV	(20,000)	1,376	947	652	448	3,054
Total	(13,523)					

Leasing cost

Depreciation costs = $\dfrac{20,000 - 4,000}{5}$ = $3,200

Tax relief @ 30% = 960

In order to calculate the **interest implicit** in the lease, we need to calculate the implicit interest rate by using an IRR calculation:

Year		Cash flow	Discount factor @ 6%	PV	Discount factor @ 7%	PV
		$		$		$
0	Purchase cost	(20,000)	1.000	(20,000)	1.000	(20,000)
1–5	Lease payments	4,800	4.212	20,218	4.100	19,680
				218		(320)

IRR = 6% + $\dfrac{218}{(218 - 320)}$ × 1 = 6.4%

Opening balance	Implicit interest at 6.4%	End of year debt	Repayment	Closing balance
$	$	$	$	$
20,000	1,280	21,280	4,800	16,480
16,480	1,055	17,535	4,800	12,735
12,735	815	13,550	4,800	8,750
8,750	560	9,310	4,800	4,510
4,510	289	4,799	4,800	(1)

Rounding means that the final closing balance does not exactly equal zero.

NPV of leasing costs

	Year 1	Year 2	Year 3	Year 4	Year 5
	$	$	$	$	$
Lease payments	(4,800)	(4,800)	(4,800)	(4,800)	(4,800)
Tax relief on depreciation	960	960	960	960	960
Tax relief on implicit interest	384	317	245	168	87
Net cash flows	(3,456)	(3,523)	(3,595)	(3,672)	(3,753)
Discount factor @ 9%	0.917	0.842	0.772	0.708	0.650
PV	(3,169)	(2,966)	(2,775)	(2,600)	(2,439)
Total	(13,949)				

2.5 Evaluating a lease or buy decision

Lease or buy decisions are not purely a matter of calculations. We discussed above why leasing might be attractive to a business; the following issues are also relevant to a lease or buy decision.

(a) **Effect on cash flow**

The organisation's liquidity at the time the **decision** is made may be **important**. If the business is suffering cash-flow difficulties, lease payments may offer a smoother cash flow than one big lump sum.

(b) **Cost of capital**

The decision on whether to **obtain use** of the asset may be **dependent upon the appraisal method or cost of capital used**. A decision not to invest taken using the company's overall cost of capital may be reversed if a significantly lower cost of leasing is used in the cash flow.

(c) **Running expenses**

Lease or buy calculations normally assume that the **running costs** are the **same** under each alternative. This may not be so. **Expenses like maintenance and insurance** may differ between the alternatives.

(d) **Trade in value**

The organisation will gain the (uncertain) benefits of a **trade-in value** if it chooses the purchase option.

(e) **Effect on reported profits**

Annual profits are reported on an **accruals basis**, after the deduction of depreciation. The effect of the alternatives on reported profits should be considered since this could, if significant, affect **dividend policy** and the **valuation of shares**.

(f) **Alternative uses of funds**

Lease or buy decisions will not be taken in **isolation**. If the business has limited funds available, there may be **better uses** for those funds than obtaining the asset, even if the asset does yield net positive cash flows.

2.6 The position of the lessor

So far, we have looked at examples of leasing decisions from the viewpoint of the lessee. You might be asked to evaluate a leasing arrangement from the position of the **lessor**. This is rather like a **mirror image** of the lessee's position.

Assuming that it is purchasing the asset, the lessor will receive capital allowances on the expenditure, and the lease payments will be taxable income.

2.7 Example: lessor's position

Continuing the same case of Mallen and Mullins from Example 2.3, suppose that the lessor's required rate of return is 12% after tax. The lessor's cash flows will be as follows.

	Cash flow £	Discount factor @ 12%	PV £
Purchase costs (see above)			
Year 0	(20,000)	1.000	(20,000)
Year 5 trade-in	4,000	0.567	2,268
Tax savings			
Year 2	6,000	0.797	4,782
Lease payments: years 1–5	4,800	3.605	17,304
Tax on lease payments: years 2–6			
(discount factor = 4.111 – 0.893)	(1,440)	3.218	(4,634)
NPV			(280)

Conclusion. The leasing payments proposed are not justifiable for the lessor if it seeks a required rate of return of 12%, since the resulting NPV is negative.

Question 7.2 — Lease or buy

Learning outcomes: B(1)(d)

The management of a company has decided to acquire Machine X which costs £63,000 and has an operational life of four years. The expected scrap value would be zero. Tax is payable at 30% on operating cash flows one year in arrears. Capital allowances are available at 100% in Year 1.

Suppose that the company has the opportunity either to purchase the machine or to lease it under a finance lease arrangement, at an annual rent of £20,000 for four years, payable at the end of each year. The company can borrow to finance the acquisition at 10%. Should the company lease or buy the machine?

Section summary

- The decision whether to **lease or buy** an asset is a **financing decision** which interacts with the investment decision to buy the asset.
- Identify the **least-cost financing option** by comparing the cash flows of purchasing and leasing. The cash flows are discounted at an **after-tax cost of borrowing**.

Chapter Roundup

- ✓ **Leasing** is a commonly used source of finance. Major types of leases are **operating leases** (lessor responsible for maintaining asset), **finance leases** (lessee responsible for maintenance), and **sale and leaseback** arrangements.
- ✓ The decision whether to **lease or buy** an asset involves a **financing decision** which interacts with the investment decision to buy the asset.
- ✓ Identify the **least-cost financing option** by comparing the cash flows of purchasing and leasing. The cash flows are discounted at an **after-tax cost of borrowing**.

PART B FINANCING DECISIONS

Quick Quiz

1   Operating leases and finance leases are distinguished for accounting purposes. Which of the following statements is not true of an operating lease?

    A   The lessor supplies the equipment to the lessee.
    B   The period of the lease is less than the expected economic life of the asset.
    C   The lessee is normally responsible for servicing and maintaining the leased equipment.
    D   The lessor retains most of the risks and rewards of ownership.

2   Who is responsible for the servicing of a leased asset in the case of:

    (a) An operating lease?
    (b) A finance lease?

    | The lessee | or | The lessor |

3   Why should operating leases be popular for users of high technology equipment?

4   Cemstone has decided to acquire a new grinding machine. It cannot afford to purchase the machine outright, and has therefore arranged to pay for it in regular instalments using a finance house. What type of arrangement is this?

    A   Finance lease
    B   Operating lease
    C   Lender credit
    D   Vendor credit

5   A hire purchase contract is a contract for the hire of an asset that contains a provision giving the hirer an option to acquire legal title to the asset upon the fulfilment of certain conditions stated in the contract.

    True   ☐
    False ☐

Answers to Quick Quiz

1   C   The lessor is normally responsible for maintaining the equipment.

2   (a) The lessor
    (b) The lessee

3   Because such equipment may soon become obsolete.

4   D   This is also known as hire purchase.

5   True

Answers to Questions

7.1 Lease v loan

A finance lease is an agreement between the user of the leased asset and a provider of finance that covers the majority of the asset's useful life. Key features of a finance lease are as follows.

(a) The provider of finance is usually a **third party finance house** and not the original provider of the equipment.

(b) The **lessee is responsible for the upkeep**, servicing and maintenance of the asset.

(c) The lease has a **primary period**, which covers all or most of the useful economic life of the asset. At the end of the primary period the lessor would not be able to lease the equipment to someone else because it would be worn out.

(d) It is common at the end of the primary period to allow the lessee to continue to lease the asset for an indefinite **secondary period**, in return for a very low nominal rent, sometimes known as a 'peppercorn' rent.

The cash flow implications of this form of lease are therefore as follows.

(a) **Regular payments** to the **lessor**, which comprise interest and principal. This can be very useful to the lessee from a cash flow management point of view.

(b) **Costs of maintenance** and so on, which may be less predictable in terms of both timing and amount.

(c) **Tax-allowable depreciation** cannot be claimed on the purchase cost of the equipment, but the lease payments are fully allowable for tax purposes. This may be of benefit to a company that is unable to make full use of its tax-allowable depreciation.

If the equipment is acquired using a **medium term bank loan**, the cash flow patterns would be similar to those that would arise using a finance lease. However, if the loan were subject to a **variable rate of interest**, this would introduce a further source of variability into the cash flows. The main difference between the two approaches would be that the company could claim **tax-allowable depreciation** on the purchase cost of the equipment. The **interest element** of the repayments would also be allowable against tax, but the repayments of principal would not.

7.2 Lease or buy

The financing decision will be appraised by discounting the relevant cash flows at the after-tax cost of borrowing, which is $10\% \times 70\% = 7\%$.

(a) **Purchase option**

Year	Item	Cash flow £	Discount factor 7%	Present value £
0	Cost of machine	(63,000)	1.000	(63,000)
2	Tax saved from tax-allowable depreciation 30% × £63,000	18,900	0.873	16,500
				(46,500)

(b) **Leasing option**

It is assumed that the lease payments are tax-allowable in full.

Year	Item	Cash flow £	Discount factor 7%	Present value £
1–4	Lease costs	(20,000)	3.387	(67,740)
2–5	Tax savings on lease costs (× 30%)	6,000	3.165	18,990
				(48,750)

The purchase option is cheaper, using a cost of capital based on the after-tax cost of borrowing. On the assumption that investors would regard borrowing and leasing as equally risky finance options, the purchase option is recommended.

Now try this question from the Exam Question Bank

Number	Level	Marks	Time
Q10	Introductory	n/a	30 mins

THE COST OF CAPITAL

In this chapter we examine the concept of the **cost of capital**, which can be used as a **discount rate** in evaluating the investments of an organisation.

We firstly base cost of equity calculations on the **dividend valuation model**. We then look at a way of establishing the cost of equity that takes risk into account: the **capital asset pricing model**.

Don't neglect the **cost of debt** though as this often causes students problems, in particular the distinction between the cost of irredeemable and cost of redeemable debt.

In the exam you may be asked to calculate the **weighted average cost of capital** and its component costs, either as a separate sub-question, or as part of a larger question, most likely an investment appraisal. Remember that questions won't just involve calculations; you may be asked to discuss the problems with the methods of calculation you've used or the relevance of the costs of capital to investment decisions.

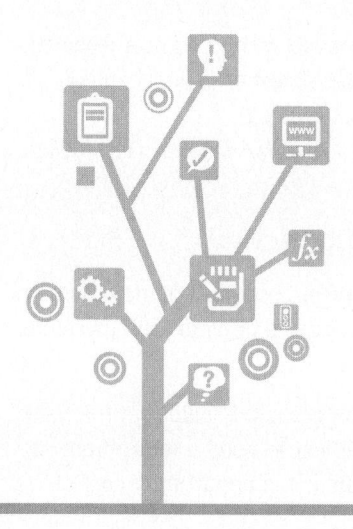

topic list	learning outcomes	syllabus references	ability required
1 Investment decisions, financing and the cost of capital	B(1)(c)	B(1)(vi)	evaluation
2 The dividend valuation model	B(1)(c)	B(1)(vi)	evaluation
3 The capital asset pricing model (CAPM)	B(1)(c)	B(1)(vi)(vii)	evaluation
4 The cost of debt	B(1)(c)	B(1)(viii)	evaluation
5 The weighted average cost of capital	B(1)(c)	B(1)(ix)	evaluation

1 Investment decisions, financing and the cost of capital

> **Introduction**
> The cost of capital is the **rate of return** that the entity must pay to satisfy the providers of funds, and it reflects the **riskiness** of the finance used.

1.1 The cost of capital

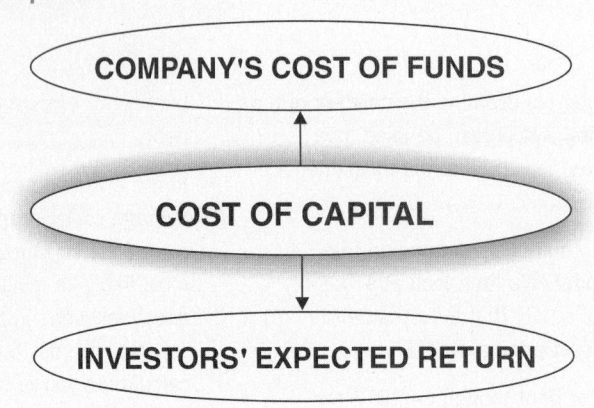

```
COMPANY'S COST OF FUNDS
        ↕
   COST OF CAPITAL
        ↕
INVESTORS' EXPECTED RETURN
```

It is thus the **minimum return** that a company should make on its own investments, to earn the cash flows out of which investors can be paid their return.

KEY TERM

COST OF CAPITAL is the minimum acceptable return on an investment, generally computed as a discount rate for use in investment appraisal exercises. The computation of the optimal cost of capital can be complex, and many ways of determining this opportunity cost have been suggested.

(CIMA Official Terminology)

1.2 The cost of capital as an opportunity cost of finance

The cost of capital, however it is measured, is an **opportunity cost of finance,** because it is the minimum return that investors require. If they do not get this return, they will transfer some or all of their investment somewhere else. Here are two examples.

(a) If a bank offers to lend money to a company, the interest rate it charges is the **yield** that the bank wants to receive from **investing** in the company, because it can get just as good a return from lending the money to someone else. In other words, the interest rate is the **opportunity cost** of lending for the bank.

(b) When shareholders invest in a company, the returns that they can expect must be sufficient to persuade them not to sell some or all of their shares and invest the money somewhere else. The yield on the shares is therefore the **opportunity cost** to the shareholders of not investing somewhere else.

1.3 The cost of capital and risk

The cost of capital has three elements.

Risk-free rate of return +
Premium for business risk +
Premium for financial risk

COST OF CAPITAL

(a) **Risk-free rate of return**

This is the return which would be required from an investment if it were completely free from risk. Typically, a risk-free yield would be the **yield on government securities**.

(b) **Premium for business risk**

This is an increase in the required rate of return due to the existence of **uncertainty about** the future and about a **firm's business prospects**. The actual returns from an investment may not be as high as they are expected to be. Business risk will be higher for some firms than for others, and some types of project undertaken by a firm may be more risky than other types of project that it undertakes.

(c) **Premium for financial risk**

This relates to the danger of high debt levels (high gearing). For ordinary shareholders, financial risk is evident in the variability of earnings after deducting payments to holders of debt capital. The higher the gearing of a company's capital structure, the greater will be the financial risk to ordinary shareholders, and this should be reflected in a higher risk premium and therefore a higher cost of capital.

Because different companies are in different types of business (varying **business risk**) and have different capital structures (varying **financial risk**) the cost of capital applied to one company may differ radically from the cost of capital of another.

Section summary

The cost of capital is the **cost of funds** that a company raises and uses, and is the **minimum return** it should make on its investments.

2 The dividend valuation model 11/10

Introduction

We will now go on to look at the **calculation** of the cost of capital. We start by calculating the **cost of equity** using the dividend valuation model.

2.1 The cost of ordinary share capital

New funds from equity shareholders are obtained either from **new issues of shares** or from **retained earnings**. Both of these sources of funds have a cost.

(a) Shareholders will **not** be prepared to **provide funds** for a **new issue** of **shares** unless the return on their investment is sufficiently attractive.

(b) Retained earnings also have a cost. This is an **opportunity cost**, the dividend forgone by shareholders.

Equity is a **high-risk investment** as ordinary shareholders are the last to be paid in a liquidation. Equity is therefore the **most expensive** form of finance.

2.2 The dividend valuation model

Cum dividend or **CUM DIV** means the purchaser of shares is entitled to receive the next dividend payment.

Ex dividend or **EX DIV** means that the purchaser of shares is not entitled to receive the next dividend payment.

If we begin by ignoring share issue costs, the cost of equity, both for new issues and retained earnings, could be estimated by means of a **dividend valuation model**, on the assumption that the market value of shares is directly related to expected future dividends on the shares.

If the future dividend per share is expected to be **constant** in amount, then the **ex dividend** share price will be calculated by the formula:

$$P_0 = \frac{d}{(1+k_e)} + \frac{d}{(1+k_e)^2} + \frac{d}{(1+k_e)^3} + \ldots = \frac{d}{k_e}, \text{ so } k_e = \frac{d}{P_0}$$

Where k_e is the shareholders' cost of capital

d is the annual dividend per share, starting at year 1 and then continuing annually in perpetuity.

P_0 is the ex-dividend share price (the price of a share where the share's new owner is **not** entitled to the dividend that is soon to be paid).

Cost of ordinary (equity) share capital, paying an annual dividend d in perpetuity, and having a current ex div price P_0:

$$k_e = \frac{d}{P_0}$$

We shall look at the dividend valuation model again in Chapter 15, in the context of valuation of shares.

Example: Dividend valuation model

Cygnus has a dividend cover ratio of 4.0 times and expects zero growth in dividends. The company has one million £1 ordinary shares in issue and the market capitalisation (value) of the company is £50 million. After-tax profits for next year are expected to be £20 million.

What is the expected rate of return from the ordinary shares?

Solution

Total dividends = $\frac{£20 \text{ million}}{4}$ = £5 million

$k_e = \frac{£5 \text{ million}}{£50 \text{ million}} = 10\%$

2.3 The dividend growth model

Shareholders will normally expect dividends to increase year by year and not to remain constant in perpetuity. The **fundamental theory of share values** states that the market price of a share is the present value of the discounted future cash flows of revenues from the share, so the market value given an expected constant annual growth in dividends would be:

$$P_0 = \frac{d_0(1+g)}{(1+k_e)} + \frac{d_0(1+g)^2}{(1+k_e)^2} + \ldots$$

Where P_0 is the current market price (ex div)
  d_0 is the current net dividend
  k_e is the shareholders' cost of capital
  g is the expected annual growth in dividend payments

and both k_e and g are expressed as proportions.

It is often convenient to assume a constant expected dividend growth rate in perpetuity. The formula above then simplifies to:

$$P_0 = \frac{d_0(1+g)}{(k_e - g)}$$

Re-arranging this, we get a formula for the ordinary shareholders' cost of capital.

EXAM

Cost of ordinary (equity) share capital, having a current ex div price, P_0, having just paid a dividend, d_0, with the dividend growing in perpetuity by a constant g% per annum:

$$k_e = \frac{d_0(1+g)}{P_0} + g \text{ or } k_e = \frac{d_1}{P_0} + g$$

Where d_1 is the dividend in year 1, so that:

$d_1 = d_0(1+g)$

Question 8.1   Cost of equity

Learning outcomes: B(1)(c)

A share has a current market value of 96p, and the last dividend was 12p. If the expected annual growth rate of dividends is 4%, calculate the cost of equity capital.

2.4 Estimating the growth rate

There are two methods for estimating the growth rate that you need to be familiar with.

2.4.1 Historic growth

Firstly, the future growth rate can be predicted from an **analysis of the growth in dividends** over the past few years.

Year	Dividends €	Earnings €
20X1	150,000	400,000
20X2	192,000	510,000
20X3	206,000	550,000
20X4	245,000	650,000
20X5	262,350	700,000

Dividends have risen from €150,000 in 20X1 to €262,350 in 20X5. The increase represents four years' growth. (Check that you can see that there are four years' growth, and not five years' growth, in the table.) The average growth rate, g, may be calculated as follows. Assume the current market price is €3.35.

$$\text{Dividend in 20X1} \times (1+g)^4 = \text{Dividend in 20X5}$$

$$(1+g)^4 = \frac{\text{Dividend in 20X5}}{\text{Dividend in 20X1}}$$

$$= \frac{€262{,}350}{€150{,}000}$$

$$= 1.749$$

$$1+g = \sqrt[4]{1.749} = 1.15$$

$$g = 0.15, \text{ ie } 15\%$$

The growth rate over the last four years is assumed to be expected by shareholders into the indefinite future, so the cost of equity, k_e, is:

$$\frac{d_0(1+g)}{P_0} + g = \frac{0.26235(1.15)}{3.35} + 0.15 = 0.24, \text{ ie } 24\%$$

Alternatively, the historic growth formula can be written as:

> **LEARN**
>
> $$g = \sqrt[n]{\frac{\text{dividend in year x}}{\text{dividend in year x-n}}} - 1$$
>
> Where n is the number of years' growth
>   year x is the final year's dividend

Question 8.2 — Growth rate

Learning outcomes: B(1)(c)

The following figures have been extracted from the accounts of Mezzo:

Year	Dividends €	Earnings €
20X1	100,000	350,000
20X2	125,000	400,000
20X3	125,000	370,000
20X4	160,000	450,000
20X5	200,000	550,000

You have been asked to calculate the cost of equity for the company. What growth rate would you use in the calculations?

2.4.2 Current re-investment level

Alternatively, the growth rate can be estimated using the **current re-investment level** (Gordon's growth approximation).

Retained profits will earn a certain rate of return and so growth will come from the yield on the retained funds. The rate of growth in dividends is expressed as:

> **LEARN**
>
> $g = bR$
>
> where b is proportion of profits retained for reinvestment
>   g is the annual growth rate in dividends
>   R is yield on new investments (this is often taken to be the accounting rate of return)

So, if a company retains 65% of its earnings for capital investment projects it has identified, and these projects are expected to have an average return of 8%:

g = bR = 65% × 8% = 5.2%

2.5 Cost of preference shares

For preference shares the future cash flows are the dividend payments in perpetuity so that:

$$k_{pref} = \frac{d}{P_0}$$

Where P_0 is the current market price of preference share capital after payment of the current dividend
       d   is the dividend received
       k_{pref} is the cost of preference share capital

Exam skills

Don't forget that tax relief is **not given** for preference share dividends.

When calculating the weighted average cost of capital (see Section 5), the cost of preferred shares is a separate component and should not be combined with the cost of debt or the cost of equity.

Section summary

- The **dividend valuation model** can be used to estimate a cost of equity, on the assumption that the market value of shares is directly related to the expected future dividends on the shares.
- The **dividend growth rate** can be calculated using historic growth or current re-investment levels.

3 The capital asset pricing model (CAPM) 5/10, 3/12

Introduction

We now look at the other method of calculating the cost of equity which uses the capital asset pricing model (CAPM). This model incorporates **risk**.

3.1 Systematic risk and unsystematic risk 5/10, 3/12

Whenever an investor invests in some shares, or a company invests in a new project, there will be some **risk** involved. The actual return on the investment might be better or worse than that hoped for. To some extent, risk is unavoidable (unless the investor settles for risk-free securities such as gilts).

Provided that the investor **diversifies** his investments in a suitably wide **portfolio**, the investments which perform well and those which perform badly should tend to cancel each other out, and much risk can be diversified away. In the same way, a company which invests in a number of projects will find that some do well and some do badly, but taking the whole portfolio of investments, average returns should turn out much as expected.

Risks that can be diversified away are referred to as **unsystematic risk**. But there is another sort of risk too. Some investments are by their very nature more risky than others. This has nothing to do with chance variations up or down in actual returns compared with what an investor should expect. This **inherent risk** – the **systematic risk** or **market risk** – **cannot be diversified away**.

KEY TERMS

MARKET or SYSTEMATIC RISK is risk that cannot be diversified away. NON-SYSTEMATIC or UNSYSTEMATIC RISK applies to a single investment or class of investments, and can be reduced or eliminated by diversification.
(CIMA Official Terminology)

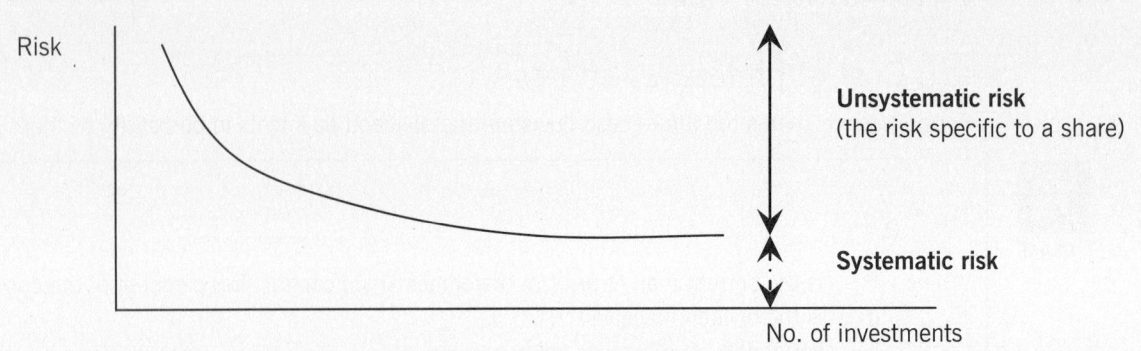

Risk

Unsystematic risk
(the risk specific to a share)

Systematic risk

No. of investments

In return for accepting systematic risk, a risk-averse investor will expect to earn a return which is **higher** than the return on a risk-free investment.

The amount of systematic risk in an investment varies between different types of investment.

3.2 Systematic risk and unsystematic risk: implications for investments

The implications of systematic risk and unsystematic risk are as follows.

(a) If an investor wants to **avoid risk** altogether, he must **invest entirely** in **risk-free securities**

(b) If an investor **holds shares in just a few companies**, there will be **some unsystematic risk** as well as systematic risk in his portfolio, because he will not have spread his risk enough to diversify away the unsystematic risk. To eliminate unsystematic risk, he must build up a well diversified portfolio of investments.

(c) If an investor holds a **balanced portfolio** of all the stocks and shares on the stock market, he will incur systematic risk which is exactly equal to the average systematic risk in the stock market as a whole.

(d) **Shares in individual companies** will have **different systematic risk characteristics** to this market average. Some shares will be less risky and some will be more risky than the stock market average. Similarly, some investments will be more risky and some will be less risky than a company's 'average' investments.

3.3 The beta factor

The capital asset pricing model is mainly concerned with how systematic risk is measured, and how systematic risk affects required returns and share prices. **Systematic risk** is measured using **beta factors**.

KEY TERM

BETA FACTOR is the measure of the systematic risk of a security relative to the market portfolio. If a share price were to rise or fall at double the market rate, it would have a beta factor of 2.0. Conversely, if the share price moved at half the market rate, the beta factor would be 0.5. *(CIMA Official Terminology)*

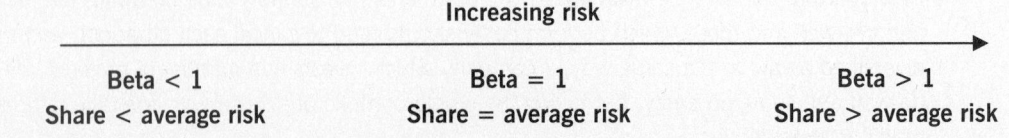

Increasing risk →

| Beta < 1 | Beta = 1 | Beta > 1 |
| Share < average risk | Share = average risk | Share > average risk |

CASE STUDY

The following are examples of beta factors of well-known companies. Note the differences in betas between companies within the same sector and the differences in betas across sectors.

Company	Sector	Beta factor
Qantas	Airlines	1.4100
Cathay Pacific	Airlines	0.9282
Singapore Airlines	Airlines	0.7589
GlaxoSmithKline	Pharmaceuticals	0.4280
Pfizer	Pharmaceuticals	0.7154
Audi	Auto and truck manufacturers	0.6246
Honda	Auto and truck manufacturers	1.1200
Toyota	Auto and truck manufacturers	1.0500
Lloyds Banking Group	Banks	1.9500
Royal Bank of Scotland Group	Banks	2.3600
Santander	Banks	1.4500

Source: *ft.com* (20 April 2012)

3.4 Risk and returns

CAPM theory includes the following propositions.

(a) Investors in shares require a **return** in **excess of the risk-free rate**, to compensate them for systematic risk.

(b) Investors should **not require** a **premium** for **unsystematic risk**, because this can be diversified away by holding a wide portfolio of investments.

(c) Because systematic risk varies between companies, investors will require a **higher return** from shares in those companies where the systematic risk is bigger.

The same propositions can be applied to capital investments by companies.

(a) Companies will want a **return on a project** to **exceed** the **risk-free rate**, to compensate them for systematic risk.

(b) **Unsystematic risk** can be **diversified away**, and so a premium for unsystematic risk should not be required.

(c) Companies should want a **bigger return** on projects where **systematic risk is greater**.

A major **assumption in CAPM** is that there is a linear relationship between the return obtained from an individual security and the average return from all securities in the market.

3.5 Example: CAPM (1)

The following information is available about the performance of an individual company's shares and the stock market as a whole.

	Individual company	Stock market as a whole
Price at start of period	105.0	480.0
Price at end of period	110.0	490.0
Dividend during period	7.6	39.2

The expected return on the company's shares R_i and the expected return on the 'market portfolio' of shares R_m may be calculated as:

$$\frac{\text{Capital gain (or loss)} + \text{dividend}}{\text{Price at start of period}}$$

$$R_i = \frac{(110-105)+7.6}{105} = 0.12 \qquad R_m = \frac{(490-480)+39.2}{480} = 0.1025$$

A statistical analysis of 'historic' returns from a security and from the 'average' market may suggest that a **linear relationship** can be assumed to exist between them. A series of comparative figures could be prepared (month by month) of the return from a company's shares and the average return of the market as a whole. The results could be drawn on a scattergraph and a 'line of best fit' drawn (using linear regression techniques) as shown in the diagram below.

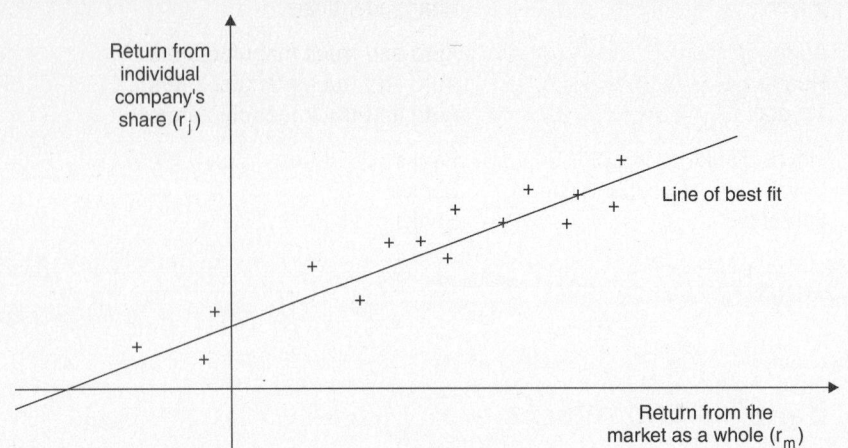

This analysis would show three things.

(a) The return from the security and the return from the market as a whole will tend to **rise or fall together**.

(b) The return from the security may be higher or lower than the market return. This is because the **systematic risk** of the individual security differs from that of the market as a whole.

(c) The scattergraph may not give a good line of best fit, unless a large number of data items are plotted, because actual returns are affected by **unsystematic risk** as well as by systematic risk.

Note that returns can be negative. A share price fall represents a capital loss, which is a negative return.

The conclusion from this analysis is that individual securities will be either **more or less risky** than the market average in a fairly **predictable** way. The measure of this relationship between market returns and an individual security's returns, reflecting differences in systematic risk characteristics, can be developed into a beta factor for the individual security.

3.6 The market risk premium

MARKET RISK PREMIUM is the difference between the expected rate of return on a market portfolio and the risk-free rate of return over the same period. *(CIMA Official Terminology)*

The market risk premium ($R_m - R_f$) represents the excess of market returns over those associated with investing in risk-free assets.

The CAPM makes use of the principle that **returns on shares** in the **market as a whole** are expected to be higher than the returns on risk-free investments. The difference between market returns and risk-free returns is called an **excess return**. For example, if the return on British Government bonds is 9% and market returns are 13%, the excess return on the market's shares as a whole is 4%.

The difference between the risk-free return and the expected return on an individual security can be measured as the **excess return for the market as a whole multiplied by the security's beta factor**.

3.7 The CAPM formula

The capital asset pricing model is a statement of the principles explained above. It can be stated as follows.

PART B FINANCING DECISIONS 8: The cost of capital 145

EXAM

$k_e = R_f + (R_m - R_f) \beta$

Where k_e is the cost of equity capital
  R_f is the risk-free rate of return
  R_m is the return from the market as a whole
  β is the beta factor of the individual security

Example: CAPM (1)

Shares in Louie and Dewie have a beta of 0.9. The expected returns to the market are 10% and the risk-free rate of return is 4%. What is the cost of equity capital for Louie and Dewie?

Solution

$$\begin{aligned} k_e &= R_f + (R_m - R_f) \beta \\ &= 4 + ((10 - 4) \times 0.9) \\ &= 9.4\% \end{aligned}$$

Example: CAPM (2)

Investors have an expected rate of return of 8% from ordinary shares in Algol, which have a beta of 1.2. The expected returns to the market are 7%.

What will be the expected rate of return from ordinary shares in Rigel, which have a beta of 1.8?

Solution

Algol: $k_e = R_f + (R_m - R_f) \beta$
  $8 = R_f + (7 - R_f) \times 1.2$
  $8 = R_f + 8.4 - 1.2 R_f$
  $0.2 R_f = 0.4$
  $R_f = 2$

Rigel: $k_e = 2 + (7 - 2) 1.8$
  $= 11\%$

Question 8.3 Returns

Learning outcomes: B(1)(c)

The risk-free rate of return is 7%. The average market return is 11%.

(a) What will be the return expected from a share whose β factor is 0.9?

(b) What would be the share's expected value if it is expected to earn an annual dividend of 5.3c, with no capital growth?

3.7.1 Alpha values

The **alpha value** can be seen as a measure of how wrong the CAPM is.

Alpha values:

(a) Reflect only temporary, abnormal returns, if CAPM is a realistic model

(b) Can be positive or negative

(c) Over time, will tend towards zero for any individual share, and for a well-diversified portfolio taken as a whole will be 0

(d) May exist due to the inaccuracies and limitations of the CAPM

If the **alpha value** is **positive**, investors who don't hold shares will be tempted to buy them (to take advantage of the abnormal return), and investors who do hold shares will want to hold on to them so share prices will rise. If the **alpha value** is **negative**, investors won't want to buy them, and current holders will want to sell them, so share prices will fall.

3.7.2 Example: Alpha values

ABC plc's shares have a beta value of 1.2 and an alpha value of +2%. The market return is 10% and the risk-free rate of return is 6%.

Required return 6% + (10% − 6%) × 1.2 = 10.8%

Current return = expected return ± alpha value = 10.8% + 2% = 12.8%

3.8 Problems with applying the CAPM in practice

(a) The need to **determine** the **excess return** ($R_m - R_f$). Expected, rather than historical, returns should be used, although historical returns are often used in practice.

(b) The need to **determine** the **risk-free rate**. A risk-free investment might be a government security. However, interest rates vary with the term of the lending.

(c) **Errors** in the **statistical analysis used** to calculate β values. Betas may also **change over** time.

(d) The CAPM is also **unable to forecast accurately returns** for companies with **low price/earnings** ratios and to take account of seasonal 'month-of-the-year' effects and 'day-of-the-week' effects that appear to influence returns on shares.

Question 8.4 — Beta factor

Learning outcomes: B(1)(c)

(a) What does beta measure, and what do betas of 0.5, 1 and 1.5 mean?
(b) What factors determine the level of beta which a company may have?

Section summary

- The **capital asset pricing model** can be used to calculate a cost of equity and incorporates **risk**
- The CAPM is based on a comparison of the **systematic risk** of **individual investments** with the risks of **all shares** in the **market**
- The **beta factor** measures a share's volatility in terms of market risk
- Problems of CAPM include **unrealistic assumptions** and the **required estimates being difficult to make**

4 The cost of debt

Introduction

In this section we look at another component of the cost of capital. The **cost of debt** is lower than the cost of equity as debt finance offers a higher degree of **security** to its holders. We need to use different techniques to calculate **redeemable** and **irredeemable** debt costs.

4.1 The cost of debt capital

Debt finance offers a **higher degree of security** as interest has to be paid, there may be a security for the debt and it will be repaid ahead of equity in a liquidation. Interest also attracts **tax relief** so the cost of debt will be **lower** than the cost of equity.

Exam alert

Remember that different types of debt have different costs. The cost of a bond will not be the same as the cost of a bank loan.

4.2 Irredeemable debt capital

Using the same logic as for preferred shares:

Cost of irredeemable debt capital (k_d), paying interest i in perpetuity, and having a current ex-div price P_0:

$$k_d = \frac{i}{P_0} \quad \text{(given in the exam as } P_0 = \frac{i}{k_d}\text{)}$$

Example: Cost of debt (no tax)

Lepus has issued bonds of $100 nominal value with annual interest of 9% per year, based on the nominal value. The current market price of the bonds is $90. What is the cost of the bonds?

Solution

$k_d = 9/90 = 10\%$

4.3 Redeemable debt capital

If the debt is **redeemable** then in the year of redemption the interest payment will be received by the holder as well as the amount payable on redemption, so:

$$P_0 = \frac{i}{(1+k_{d\,net})} + \frac{i}{(1+k_{d\,net})^2} + \ldots + \frac{i + p_n}{(1+k_{d\,net})^n}$$

Where p_n = the amount payable on redemption in year n.

The above equation cannot be simplified, so 'r' will have to be calculated by trial and error, as an **internal rate of return (IRR)**.

You will find it helpful to lay out the cash flows so they look like a project:

Time	Cash flow
0	(Market value)
1–n	Interest
N	Redemption value

To calculate the IRR:

STEP 1 Calculate the net present value using a 10% discount rate.

STEP 2 Calculate the NPV using a second discount rate.
(a) If the NPV is **positive**, use a second rate that is **greater** than the first rate
(b) If the NPV is **negative**, use a second rate that is **less** than the first rate

STEP 3 Use the two NPV values to **estimate the IRR**. The formula to apply is as follows.

$$IRR \approx a + \left(\left(\frac{NPV_a}{NPV_a - NPV_b}\right)(b-a)\right)\%$$

Where   a = the lower of the two rates of return used
b = the higher of the two rates of return used
NPV_a = the NPV obtained using rate a
NPV_b = the NPV obtained using rate b

Example: Cost of redeemable debt (no tax)

Owen Allot has in issue 10% bonds of a nominal value of $100. The market price is $90 ex interest. Calculate the cost of this capital if the bond is:

(a) Irredeemable
(b) Redeemable at par after 10 years

Ignore taxation.

Solution

(a) **The cost of irredeemable debt capital** is $\frac{i}{P_0} = \frac{\$10}{\$90} \times 100\% = 11.1\%$

(b) The cost of redeemable debt capital

Year		Cash flow $	Discount factor @ 10%	PV $	Discount factor @ 12%	PV $
0	Market value	(90)	1.000	(90.00)	1.000	(90.00)
1–10	Interest	10	6.145	61.45	5.650	56.50
10	Capital repayment	100	0.386	38.60	0.322	32.20
				10.05		(1.30)

The approximate cost of redeemable debt capital is, therefore:

$$10 + \left[\frac{10.05}{(10.05 - -1.30)}\right] \times 2 = 11.77\%$$

4.4 Debt capital and taxation

The interest on debt capital is likely to be an allowable deduction for purposes of taxation and this **tax relief on interest** must be recognised in computations. The after-tax cost of irredeemable debt capital is:

$$k_{d\,net} = \frac{i(1-t)}{P_0}$$

Where $k_{d\,net}$ is the cost of debt capital

i is the annual interest payment

P_0 is the current market price of the debt capital ex interest (that is, after payment of the current interest)

t is the rate of corporation tax

Therefore if a company pays $10,000 a year interest on irredeemable debt with a nominal value of $100,000 and a market price of $80,000, and the rate of tax is 30%, the cost of the debt would be:

$$\frac{10,000}{80,000}(1 - 0.30) = 0.0875 = 8.75\%$$

The higher the rate of tax is, the greater the tax benefits in having debt finance will be compared with equity finance. In the example above, if the rate of tax had been 50%, the cost of debt would have been, after tax:

$$\frac{10,000}{80,000}(1 - 0.50) = 0.0625 = 6.25\%$$

In the case of **redeemable debt**, the capital repayment is not allowable for tax. To calculate the cost of the debt capital to include in the weighted average cost of capital, it is necessary to calculate an internal rate of return which takes account of tax relief on the interest.

Example: Cost of redeemable debt (with tax)

Goodies Co has €100,000 6% redeemable bonds in issue. Interest is paid annually on 31 December. The ex-interest market value of the bonds on 1 January 20X5 is €93 and the bonds are redeemable at a 10% premium on 31 December 20X9. the effective rate of tax is 30%.

What is the cost of debt?

Solution

Year		Cash flow €	Discount factor @ 10%	PV €	Discount factor @ 5%	PV €
0	Market value	(93)	1.000	(93.00)	1.000	(93.00)
1–5	Interest after tax	6 × (1 – 0.3)	3.791	15.92	4.329	18.18
5	Capital repayment	110	0.621	68.31	0.784	86.24
				(8.77)		11.42

The approximate cost of redeemable debt capital is, therefore:

$$5 + \left[\frac{11.42}{(11.42 - 8.77)} \times 5\right] = 7.82\%$$

Exam alert

Make sure that you know the difference in methods for calculating the cost of irredeemable **and** redeemable debt, as this is often a weakness in exams.

4.5 The cost of floating rate debt

If a firm has variable or **'floating rate' debt**, then the cost of an equivalent fixed interest debt should be substituted. 'Equivalent' usually means fixed interest debt with a similar term to maturity in a firm of similar standing, although if the cost of capital is to be used for project appraisal purposes, there is an argument for using debt of the same duration as the project under consideration.

4.6 The cost of short-term funds

The cost of short-term funds such as bank loans and overdrafts is the **current interest** being charged on such funds.

Section summary

The **cost of debt** is the return an enterprise must pay to its lenders.

- For **irredeemable debt**, this is the (post-tax) interest as a percentage of the ex interest market value of the bonds.
- For **redeemable debt**, the cost is given by the internal rate of return of the cash flows involved.

5 The weighted average cost of capital   5/10, 11/10, 3/11, 5/11, 3/12

We have looked at the costs of individual sources of capital for a company. But how does this help us to work out the cost of capital as a whole, or the discount rate to apply in DCF investment appraisals? We now need to calculate a weighted average cost of capital (WACC) which **combines** together the costs of two or more types of capital.

5.1 Calculating the WACC

A company's funds may be viewed as a **pool of resources**. Money is withdrawn from this pool of funds to invest in new projects and added to the pool as new finance is raised or profits are retained.

KEY TERM

WEIGHTED AVERAGE COST OF CAPITAL is the average cost of the company's finance (equity, debentures, bank loans) weighted according to the proportion each element bears to the total pool of capital. Weighting is usually based on market valuations, current yields and costs after tax.

(CIMA Official Terminology)

A general formula for the weighted average cost of capital (or k_0) is as follows.

$$\text{WACC} = k_e \left[\frac{V_E}{V_E + V_D} \right] + k_d (1-t) \left[\frac{V_D}{V_E + V_D} \right]$$

Where k_e is the cost of equity
 k_d is the cost of debt
 V_E is the market value of issued shares (market capitalisation)
 V_D is the market value of debt

Preference shares can be added in if necessary as in the example below.

Example: Weighted average cost of capital

An entity has the following information in its statement of financial position.

	$'000
Ordinary shares of 50¢	2,500
8% preference shares of $1 each	1,500
12% unsecured bonds	1,000

The ordinary shares are currently quoted at 130¢ each, the bonds are trading at $72 per $100 nominal and the preference shares at 52¢ each. The ordinary dividend of 15¢ has just been paid with an expected growth rate of 10%. Corporation tax is currently 30%.

Calculate the weighted average cost of capital for this entity.

Solution

Market values

		$'000
Equity (V_E):	$\frac{2,500}{0.5} \times 1.30$	6,500
Preference shares (V_P):	$1,500 \times 0.52$	780
Bonds (V_D):	$1,000 \times 0.72$	720
		8,000

Cost of equity

$$k_e = \frac{d_0(1+g)}{P_0} + g = \frac{0.15(1+0.1)}{1.3} + 0.1 = 0.2269 = 22.69\%$$

Cost of preference shares

$$k_p = \frac{d}{P_0} = \frac{0.08}{0.52} = 0.1538 = 15.38\%$$

Cost of bonds

$$k_d = \frac{i(1-t)}{P_o} = \frac{0.12(1-0.3)}{0.72} = 0.1167 = 11.67\%$$

Weighted average cost of capital

$$k_o = k_e\left(\frac{V_E}{V_E + V_P + V_D}\right) + k_p\left(\frac{V_P}{V_E + V_P + V_D}\right) + k_d\left(\frac{V_D}{V_E + V_P + V_D}\right)$$

$$V_E + V_P + V_D = 8{,}000$$

$$k_o = \left(22.69\% \times \frac{6{,}500}{8{,}000}\right) + \left(15.38\% \times \frac{780}{8{,}000}\right) + \left(11.67\% \times \frac{720}{8{,}000}\right)$$

$$= 18.43\% + 1.5\% + 1.05\% = 20.98\%$$

5.2 Weighting

Two methods of weighting could be used.

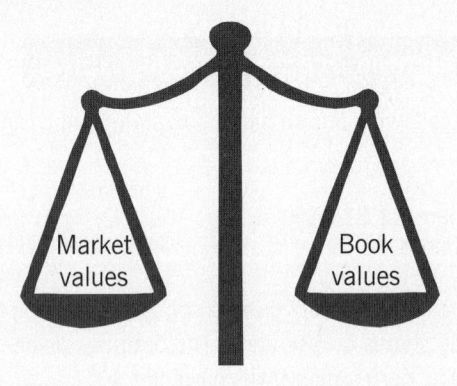

Market values | Book values

Although book values are often easier to obtain they are of doubtful economic significance. It is, therefore, more **meaningful to use market values** when data are available. For unquoted companies estimates of market values are likely to be extremely subjective and consequently book values may be used. When using market values it is not possible to split the equity value between share capital and reserves and only one cost of equity can be used. This removes the need to estimate a separate cost of retained earnings.

Exam skills

Always use market values in an exam question unless you are told otherwise.

You may need to calculate the market value of equity using the capitalisation of earnings at the cost of capital.

5.3 Using the WACC in investment appraisal

The weighted average cost of capital can be used in investment appraisal if we make the following assumptions.

(a) New investments must be **financed** by **new sources of funds**: retained earnings, new share issues, new loans and so on.

(b) The cost of capital to be applied to project evaluation must **reflect** the **marginal cost** of new capital.

(c) The weighted average cost of capital **reflects** the **company's long-term future capital structure**, and capital costs. If this were not so, the current weighted average cost would become irrelevant because eventually it would not relate to any actual cost of capital.

5.4 Arguments against using the WACC

The arguments against using the WACC as the cost of capital for investment appraisal (as follows) are based on criticisms of the assumptions that are used to justify use of the WACC.

(a) New investments undertaken by a company might have different **business risk** characteristics from the company's existing operations. As a consequence, the return required by investors might go up (or down) if the investments are undertaken, because their business risk is perceived to be higher (or lower).

(b) The finance that is raised to fund a new investment might substantially change the capital structure and the perceived **financial risk** of investing in the company. Depending on whether the project is financed by equity or by debt capital, the perceived financial risk of the entire company might change. This must be taken into account when appraising investments.

(c) Many companies raise **floating rate** debt capital as well as fixed interest debt capital. With floating rate debt capital, the interest rate is variable, and is altered every three or six months or so in line with changes in current market interest rates. The cost of debt capital will therefore fluctuate as market conditions vary.

Floating rate debt is difficult to incorporate into a WACC computation, and the best that can be done is to substitute an 'equivalent' fixed interest debt capital cost in place of the floating rate debt cost.

5.5 Marginal cost of capital approach

The **marginal cost of capital** approach involves calculating a marginal cut-off rate for acceptable investment projects by:

(a) **Establishing rates of return** for each component of capital structure, except retained earnings, based on its value if it were to be raised under current market conditions

(b) **Relating dividends or interest** to these values to obtain a marginal cost for each component

(c) **Applying the marginal cost** to each component depending on its proportionate weight within the capital structure and adding the resultant costs to give a weighted average

It can be argued that the current weighted average cost of capital should be used to evaluate projects, where a company's capital structure changes **only very slowly** over time; then the marginal cost of new capital should be roughly equal to the weighted average cost of current capital.

Where gearing levels fluctuate significantly, or the finance for new project carries a significantly **different level of risks** to that of the existing company, there is good reason to seek an alternative marginal cost of capital.

Example: Marginal cost of capital

Georgebear has the following capital structure:

Source	After tax cost %	Market value $m	After tax cost × Market value
Equity	12	10	1.2
Preference	10	2	0.2
Existing bonds	7.5	8	0.6
New bonds		20	2.0

$$\text{Weighted average cost of capital} = \frac{2 \times 100\%}{20}$$
$$= 10\%$$

Georgebear's directors have decided to embark on major capital expenditure, which will be financed by a major issue of funds. The estimated project cost is $3,000,000, $1/3$ of which will be financed by equity, 2/3 of which will be financed by bonds. As a result of undertaking the project, the cost of equity (existing and new shares) will rise from 12% to 14%. The cost of preference shares and the cost of existing bonds will remain the same, while the after tax cost of the new bonds will be 9%.

Required

Calculate the company's new weighted average cost of capital, and its marginal cost of capital.

Solution

New weighted average cost of capital

Source	After tax cost %	Market value $m	After tax cost × Market value
Equity	14.0	11	1.54
Preference	10.0	2	0.20
Existing bonds	7.5	8	0.60
New bonds	9.0	2	0.18
		23	2.50

$$\text{WACC} = \frac{2.52 \times 100\%}{23}$$
$$= 11.0\%$$

$$\text{Marginal cost of capital} = \frac{(2.52 - 2.0) \times 100\%}{23 - 20}$$
$$= 17.3\%$$

Question 8.5 — WACC

Learning outcomes: B(1)(c)

(a) What is meant by the 'weighted average cost of capital' of a company? Why do many companies use it as a discount rate in investment appraisal?

(b) Explain how this cost of capital is calculated and discuss the components required. (Detailed mathematical calculations are not required.)

Section summary

- The **weighted average cost of capital** can be used to evaluate a business's investment projects if:
    - The project is small relative to the business
    - The existing capital structure will be maintained (same financial risk)
    - The project has the same business risk as the business

- The weighted average cost of capital is influenced by the **risk-free rate of return**, and the need to provide for extra return to compensate for the business and financial risks the organisation faces

PART B FINANCING DECISIONS8: The cost of capital

Chapter Roundup

- ✓ The cost of capital is the **cost of funds** that a company raises and uses, and is the **minimum return** it should make on its investments

- ✓ The **dividend valuation model** can be used to estimate a cost of equity, on the assumption that the market value of shares is directly related to the expected future dividends on the shares.

- ✓ The **dividend growth rate** can be calculated using historic growth or current re-investment levels

- ✓ The **capital asset pricing model** can be used to calculate a cost of equity and incorporates **risk**

- ✓ The CAPM is based on a comparison of the **systematic risk** of **individual investments** with the risks of **all shares** in the **market**

- ✓ The **beta factor** measures a share's volatility in terms of market risk

- ✓ Problems of CAPM include **unrealistic assumptions** and the **required estimates being difficult to make**

- ✓ The **cost of debt** is the return an enterprise must pay to its lenders.

    - For **irredeemable debt**, this is the (post-tax) interest as a percentage of the ex interest market value of the bonds.

    - For **redeemable debt**, the cost is given by the internal rate of return of the cash flows involved.

- ✓ The **weighted average cost of capital** can be used to evaluate a business's investment projects if:

    - The project is small relative to the business
    - The existing capital structure will be maintained (same financial risk)
    - The project has the same business risk as the business

- ✓ The weighted average cost of capital is influenced by the **risk-free rate of return**, and the need to provide for extra return to compensate for the business and financial risks the organisation faces

Quick Quiz

1. The cost of capital has three elements. Which of the following is not one of these elements?

    A   The market rate of return
    B   The premium for business risk
    C   The premium for financial risk
    D   The risk-free rate of return

2. 'The minimum acceptable return on an investment, generally computed as a hurdle rate for use in investment appraisal exercises' *(CIMA Official Terminology)*. What does this define?

3. A share has a current market value of 120c and the last dividend was 10c. If the expected annual growth rate of dividends is 5%, calculate the cost of equity capital.

4. The risk free rate of return is 8%, average market return is 14% and a share's beta factor is 0.5. What is the cost of equity?

5. Identify the variables k_e, d_1, P_0 and g in the following dividend valuation model formula.

$$k_e = \frac{d_1}{P_0} + g$$

6   Identify the variables k_e, k_d, V_E and V_D in the following weighted average cost of capital formula.

$$\text{WACC} = k_e \left[\frac{V_E}{V_E + V_D} \right] + k_d (1-t) \left[\frac{V_D}{V_E + V_D} \right]$$

7   When calculating the weighted average cost of capital, which of the following is the preferred method of weighting?

   A   Book values of debt and equity
   B   Average levels of the market values of debt and equity (ignoring reserves) over five years
   C   Current market values of debt and equity (ignoring reserves)
   D   Current market values of debt and equity (plus reserves)

8   What is the cost of $1 irredeemable debt capital paying an annual rate of interest of 7%, and having a current market price of $1.50?

Answers to Quick Quiz

1   A   The market rate of return

2   The cost of capital

3   $\dfrac{10(1+0.05)}{120} + 0.05 = 13.75\%$

4   $k_e = 8 + ((14 - 8) \times 0.5) = 11\%$

5   k_e is the shareholders' cost of capital

   d_1 is the dividend in year 1

   P_0 is the current market price (ex div)

   g is the expected annual growth in dividend payments

6   k_e is the cost of equity

   k_d is the cost of debt

   V_E is the market value of equity in the firm

   V_D is the market value of debt in the firm

7   C   Current market values of debt and equity (ignoring reserves)

8   Cost of debt = $\dfrac{0.07}{1.50}$ = 4.67%

Answers to Questions

8.1 Cost of equity

$$\text{Cost of equity capital} = \frac{12(1 + 0.04)}{96} + 0.04$$

$$= 0.13 + 0.04$$
$$= 0.17$$
$$= 17\%$$

8.2 Growth rate

Let 'g' = rate of growth in dividends.

Dividend in 20X1 × $(1 + g)^4$	= Dividend in 20X5
$(1 + g)^4$	= Dividend in 20X5 ÷ Dividend in 20X1
$(1 + g)^4$	= 200,000 ÷ 100,000
$(1 + g)^4$	= 2.0
$1 + g$	= $\sqrt[4]{2}$
$1 + g$	= 1.19
g	= 19%

8.3 Returns

(a) $7\% + ((11\% - 7\%) \times 0.9) = 10.6\%$

(b) $\dfrac{5.3c}{10.6\%} = 50c$

8.4 Beta factor

(a) **Beta measures** the systematic risk of a risky investment such as a share in a company. The total risk of the share can be sub-divided into two parts, known as **systematic (or market) risk** and **unsystematic (or unique) risk**. The systematic risk depends on the sensitivity of the return of the share to general economic and market factors such as periods of boom and recession. The capital asset pricing model shows how the return which investors expect from shares should depend only on systematic risk, not on unsystematic risk, which can be eliminated by holding a well-diversified portfolio.

Beta is calibrated such that the average risk of stock market investments has a **beta of 1**. Thus shares with betas of 0.5 or 1.5 would have half or 1½ times the average sensitivity to market variations respectively.

This is reflected by higher volatility of share prices for shares with a beta of 1.5 than for those with a beta of 0.5. For example, a 10% increase in general stock market prices would be expected to be reflected as a 5% increase for a share with a beta of 0.5 and a 15% increase for a share with a beta of 1.5, with a similar effect for price reductions.

(b) The beta of a company will be the **weighted average** of the beta of its shares and the beta of its debt. The beta of debt is very low, but not zero, because corporate debt bears default risk, which in turn is dependent on the volatility of the company's cash flows.

Factors determining the beta of a company's equity shares include:

(i) **Sensitivity** of the company's **cash flows** to economic factors, as stated above. For example sales of new cars are more sensitive than sales of basic foods and necessities.

(ii) The company's **operating gearing**. A high level of fixed costs in the company's cost structure will cause high variations in operating profit compared with variations in sales.

(iii) The company's **financial gearing**. High borrowing and interest costs will cause high variations in equity earnings compared with variations in operating profit, increasing the equity beta as equity returns become more variable in relation to the market as a whole. This effect will be countered by the low beta of debt when computing the weighted average beta of the whole company.

8.5 WACC

(a) The **weighted average cost of capital** (WACC) is the **average cost** of the different elements within the capital structure of a company, using weightings based on the market values of each of the different elements.

In many cases it will be difficult to associate a particular project with a particular form of finance. A company's funds may be viewed as a pool of resources. Money is withdrawn from this pool of funds to invest in new projects and added to the pool as new finance is raised or profits are retained. Under these circumstances it might seem appropriate to use an average cost of capital as a discount rate.

The correct cost of capital to use in investment appraisal is the **marginal cost** of the funds raised (or earnings retained) to finance the investment. The WACC might be considered the most reliable guide to the marginal cost of capital, but only on the assumption that the company continues to invest in the future, in projects of a standard level of business risk, by raising funds in the same proportions as its existing capital structure.

(b) The WACC can be expressed using the formula:

$$WACC = k_e \left[\frac{V_E}{V_E + V_D} \right] + k_d (1-t) \left[\frac{V_D}{V_E + V_D} \right]$$

Where k_e = cost of equity
k_d = cost of debt
V_E = market value of issued shares
V_D = market value of debt
t = tax rate

The cost of capital is the **cost of funds** that a company raises and uses, and the return that investors expect to be paid for putting funds into the company. It is therefore the minimum return that a company should make on its own investments to earn the cash flows out of which investors can be paid their return.

New equity funds are obtained from new issues of shares and from retained earnings. The costs of these funds are effectively the rate of return required by shareholders. In the case of retained earnings, the cost is the opportunity cost of the dividend forgone by the shareholders.

The cost of equity, both for new issues and retained earnings, is often estimated using the **dividend valuation model**, on the assumption that the market value of shares is directly related to expected future dividends on the shares.

Estimating the cost of **fixed interest** or fixed dividend capital is much easier than estimating the cost of ordinary share capital because the interest received by the holder of the security is fixed by contract and will not fluctuate.

The cost of debt capital already issued is the **rate of interest** (the internal rate of return) which equates the current market price with the discounted future cash receipts from the security.

Since the interest on debt capital is an **allowable deduction** for tax purposes, this should be taken into account in computing the cost of debt capital so as to make it properly comparable with the cost of equity.

If a firm has **floating rate debt**, the cost of an equivalent fixed interest debt should be substituted. This means debt with a similar term to maturity in a firm of similar standing. The cost of short-term funds such as bank loans and overdrafts is the current rate of interest being charged on such funds.

Weightings should be based on **market values** where possible because they have greater economic significance than book values.

Now try these questions from the Exam Question Bank

Number	Level	Marks	Time
Q11	Introductory	15	27 mins
Q12	Introductory	15	27 mins

THE CAPITAL STRUCTURE DECISION

This chapter looks at the impact of capital structure on **key ratios** of interest to investors and on the market value of a company. Choosing the best possible capital structure is a key strategic decision.

We also look at the effects of changing capital structure on the **cost of capital**. The technique of **gearing and ungearing betas** is important for this exam and will be looked at again later in the context of **business valuations**.

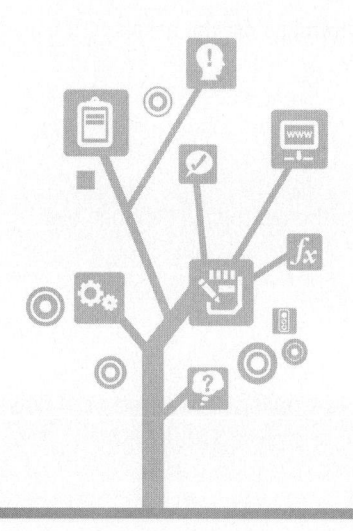

topic list	learning outcomes	syllabus references	ability required
1 The capital structure decision	B(1)(e)	B(1)(xii)	evaluation
2 Effect of capital structure on ratios	B(1)(e)	B(1)(xii)	evaluation
3 Theories of capital structure	B(1)(e)	B(1)(v)	evaluation
4 Project specific cost of capital	B(1)(e)	B(1)(vi)	evaluation

1 The capital structure decision

> **Introduction**
>
> We have previously looked at the sources and costs of debt and equity finance. We now need to look at what **proportion of debt and equity** an entity should use. Debt finance can create valuable **tax savings** which can reduce the cost of capital and increase shareholder value. However, too much debt increases **financial risk**.

1.1 Capital structure

KEY TERM

CAPITAL STRUCTURE refers to the way in which an organisation is financed, by a combination of long-term capital (ordinary shares and reserves, preferred shares, bonds, bank loans, convertible bonds and so on) and short-term liabilities, such as a bank overdraft and trade payables. The mix of finance can be measured by **gearing** ratios.

The assets of a business must be financed somehow. When a business is growing, the additional assets must be financed by additional capital.

1.2 The advantages of using debt finance

(a) Debt is a **cheaper form of finance** than shares because, unlike preferred shares, debt interest is tax-deductible in most tax regimes.

(b) Debt should be **more attractive** to investors because it will be **secured** against the assets of the company.

(c) **Debt holders** rank above **shareholders** in the event of a liquidation.

(d) **Issue costs** should be **lower** for debt than for shares.

(e) There is **no immediate change** in the existing structure of control, although this will change over time as conversion rights are exercised.

(f) There is **no immediate dilution** in earnings and dividends per share.

(g) Lenders do not participate in high profits compared with shares.

(h) Debt acts as a **discipline on management** as careful management of working capital and cash flow is needed.

1.3 Disadvantages of debt

(a) **Interest** has to be paid on debt no matter what the company's profits in a year are. In particular the company may find itself locked into long-term debt at unfavourable rates of interest. The company is not legally obliged to pay dividends.

(b) If the business struggles to pay the interest on debt, **direct financial distress costs** may be incurred in the form of higher debt payments and costs of managing the liquidation process.

(c) **Indirect financial distress costs** can include a loss of sales, higher costs from suppliers or sale of inventory at below market value.

(d) **Agency costs** occur when managers may be reluctant to invest if gearing levels are already high.

(e) Money has to be made available for **redemption** or **repayment** of debt.

(f) Heavy borrowing **increases the financial risks** for ordinary shareholders who may demand a **higher rate of return** because an increased interest burden increases the risks that dividends will not be paid.

(g) There might be restrictions on a company's power to borrow. The **company's constitution** may limit borrowing. These borrowing limits cannot be altered except with the approval of the shareholders at a general meeting of the company. **Trust deeds of existing loan notes** may **limit borrowing**. These limits can only be overcome by redeeming the loan notes.

1.4 Company circumstances

One determinant of how suitable the gearing mix is the stability of the company. It may seem obvious, but it is worth stressing that debt financing will be more appropriate when:

- The company is in a **healthy competitive position**
- **Cash flows** and **earnings** are stable
- **Profit margins** are **reasonable**
- The **bulk of the company's assets** are **tangible**
- The **liquidity** and **cash flow position** is **strong**
- The **debt-equity ratio** is low
- **Share prices** are **low**

Life cycle issues are therefore important. Young, growing companies tend to have **unpredictable and unstable cash flows** so debt finance is less appropriate than for mature companies.

CASE STUDY

Historically, gearing levels - as measured by net debt as a proportion of shareholders funds - have run at an average of about 30% over the past 20 years. Peak levels were reached in the past few years as companies took advantage of cheap credit. Current predictions see it coming down to about 20% - and staying there for a good while to come.

One of the most immediate concerns to heavily indebted companies is whether, in a recessionary environment, they will be able to generate the profit and cash flows to service their debts.

Analysts say that for a typical industrial company banks are likely in future to make debt covenants stricter, so that net debt cannot exceed two-and-a-half to three times EBITDA, compared with a current average of three to four times.

Gearing levels vary from sector to sector as well. Oil companies prefer low levels given their exposure to the volatility of oil prices. BP's net debt-shareholders' funds ratio of 21% is at the low end of a 20-30% range it considers prudent.

Miners' gearing is on a clear downward trend already. Xstrata, the mining group, stressed last month that its £4.1 billion rights issue would cut gearing from 40% to less than 30%. A week later, BHP said its $13 billion (£8.8bn) of first-half cash flows had cut gearing to less than 10%. Rio, which had gearing of 130% at the last count in August 2008, is desperately trying to cut it by raising fresh equity.

Utilities tend to be highly geared because they can afford to borrow more against their typically reliable cash flows. But even here the trend is downwards. Severn Trent, the UK water group, says its appropriate long-term gearing level is 60%. But 'given ongoing uncertainties . . . it is prudent in the near term to retain as much liquidity and flexibility as possible'. It does not expect to pursue that target until credit markets improve.

Reducing gearing is not easy, especially for the most indebted companies that need to the most: shareholders will be more reluctant to finance replacement equity in companies with highly leveraged balance sheets.

Financial Times 11 February 2009

Section summary

Debt finance can create valuable tax savings which can **reduce the cost of capital** and **increase shareholder value.** However, too much debt increases **financial risk** and incurs **financial distress costs.**

2 Effect of capital structure on ratios

Introduction

This section links to forecasting and analysis that we covered in Chapter 3. If an entity changes its capital structure, it will impact on a number of key ratios such as gearing, interest cover and EPS.

2.1 Gearing

In Chapter 3, we revised gearing briefly. You should remember that the financial risk of a company's capital structure can be measured by a **gearing ratio**, a **debt ratio** or **debt/equity ratio** and by the **interest cover**. A gearing ratio should not be given without stating how it has been defined.

Exam skills

You need to be able to explain and calculate the level of financial gearing using alternative measures. The question may specify how gearing should be calculated eg debt to total value of entity using market values.

Financial gearing measures the relationship between shareholders' capital plus reserves, and either prior charge capital or borrowings or both.

Commonly used measures of financial gearing are based on the statement of financial position values of the fixed interest and equity capital. They include:

$$\frac{\text{Prior charge capital}}{\text{Equity capital (including reserves)}} \quad \text{and} \quad \frac{\text{Prior charge capital}}{\text{Total capital employed *}}$$

* Either including or excluding minority interests, deferred tax and deferred income.

With the first definition above, a company is low geared if the gearing ratio is less than 100%, highly geared if the ratio is over 100% and neutrally geared if it is exactly 100%. With the second definition, a company is neutrally geared if the ratio is 50%, low geared below that, and highly geared above that.

Question 9.1 — Gearing

Learning outcome: B(1)(e)

From the following statement of financial position, compute the company's financial gearing ratio.

	$'000	$'000	$'000
Non-current assets			12,400
Current assets		1,000	
Payables: amounts falling due within one year			
Loans	120		
Bank overdraft	260		
Trade payables	430		
Bills of exchange	70		
		880	
Net current assets			120
Total assets less current liabilities			12,520
Payables: amounts falling due after more than one year			
Bonds		4,700	
Bank loans		500	
			(5,200)
Provisions for liabilities and charges: deferred taxation			(300)
Deferred income			(250)
Total net assets			6,770

| | $'000 | $'000 | $'000 |

Capital and reserves

	$'000
Called up share capital	
Ordinary shares	1,500
Preferred shares	500
	2,000
Share premium account	760
Revaluation reserve	1,200
Accumulated profits	2,810
Total share capital and reserves	6,770

2.1.1 Gearing ratios based on market values

An alternative method of calculating a gearing ratio is one based on **market values**:

$$\frac{\text{Market value of debt (including preference shares)}}{\text{Market value of equity + Market value of debt}}$$

The advantage of this method is that potential investors in a company are able to judge the further debt capacity of the company more clearly by **reference** to **market values** than they could by looking at statement of financial position values.

The disadvantage of a gearing ratio based on market values is that it **disregards** the **value** of the company's **assets**, which might be used to secure further loans. A gearing ratio based on statement of financial position values arguably gives a better indication of the **security for lenders** of fixed interest capital.

2.1.2 Changing financial gearing

Financial gearing is an attempt to quantify the **degree of risk** involved in holding equity shares in a company, both in terms of the company's ability to remain in business and in terms of expected ordinary dividends from the company.

The more geared the company is, the **greater the risk** that little (if anything) will be available to distribute by way of dividend to the ordinary shareholders. The more geared the company, the greater the percentage change in profit available for ordinary shareholders for any given percentage change in profit before interest and tax.

This means that there will be greater **volatility** of amounts available for ordinary shareholders, and presumably therefore greater volatility in dividends paid to those shareholders, where a company is highly geared. That is the risk. You may do extremely well or extremely badly without a particularly large movement in the profit from operations of the company.

Gearing ultimately measures the company's ability to **remain in business**. A highly geared company has a large amount of interest to pay annually. If those borrowings are 'secured' in any way then the holders of the debt are perfectly entitled to force the company to realise assets to pay their interest if funds are not available from other sources. Clearly, the more highly geared a company, the more likely this is to occur when and if profits fall.

2.1.3 Operating gearing

Financial risk, as we have seen, can be measured by financial gearing. **Business risk** refers to the risk of making only low profits, or even losses, due to the nature of the business that the company is involved in. One way of measuring business risk is by calculating a company's **operating gearing** or 'operational gearing'.

$$\text{Operating gearing or leverage} = \frac{\text{Contribution}}{\text{Profit before interest and tax (PBIT)}}$$

Contribution is sales minus variable cost of sales.

The significance of operating gearing is as follows.

(a) **If contribution is high but PBIT is low**, fixed costs will be high, and only just covered by contribution. Business risk, as measured by operating gearing, will be high.

(b) **If contribution is not much bigger than PBIT**, fixed costs will be low, and fairly easily covered. Business risk, as measured by operating gearing, will be low.

2.2 Interest cover

Like gearing, **interest cover** is a measure of financial risk which is designed to show the risks in terms of profit rather than in terms of capital values.

$$\text{Interest cover} = \frac{\text{Profit before interest and tax}}{\text{Interest payable}}$$

As a general guide, an interest cover of **less than three times** is considered low, indicating that profitability is too low given the gearing of the company.

Example: Effect of a change in capital structure on ratios

You need to be able to demonstrate the **impact of changing capital structures on investor ratios.** The following example illustrates how such a question could be set out.

A summarised statement of financial position of Rufus is as follows.

	£m
Assets less current liabilities	150
Debt capital	(70)
	80
Share capital (20 million shares of £1)	20
Reserves	60
	80

The company's profits in the year just ended are as follows.

	£m
Profit from operations	21.0
Interest	6.0
Profit before tax	15.0
Taxation at 30%	4.5
Profit after tax (earnings)	10.5
Dividends	6.5
Retained profits	4.0

The company is now considering an investment of £25 million. This will add £5 million each year to profits before interest and tax.

(a) There are two ways of financing this investment. One would be to borrow £25 million at a cost of 8% per annum in interest. The other would be to raise the money by means of a 1 for 4 rights issue.

(b) Whichever financing method is used, the company will increase dividends per share next year from 32.5p to 35p.

(c) The company does not intend to allow its gearing level, measured as debt finance as a proportion of equity capital plus debt finance, to exceed 55% as at the end of any financial year. In addition, the company will not accept any dilution in earnings per share.

Assume that the rate of taxation will remain at 30% and that debt interest costs will be £6 million plus the interest cost of any new debt capital.

Required

(a) Produce a profit forecast for next year, assuming that the new project is undertaken and is financed (i) by debt capital or (ii) by a rights issue.

(b) Calculate the earnings per share next year, with each financing method.

(c) Calculate the effect on gearing as at the end of next year, with each financing method.

(d) Explain whether either or both methods of funding would be acceptable.

Solution

Current earnings per share are £10.5 million/20 million shares = 52.5 pence.

If the project is financed by £25 million of debt at 8%, interest charges will rise by £2 million. If the project is financed by a 1 for 4 rights issue, there will be 25 million shares in issue.

	Finance with debt £m	Finance with rights issue £m
Profit before interest and tax (+ 5.0)	26.00	26.00
Interest	8.00	6.00
	18.00	20.00
Taxation (30%)	5.40	6.00
Profit after tax	12.60	14.00
Dividends (35p per share)	7.00	8.75
Retained profits	5.60	5.25
Earnings (profits after tax)	£12.6 m	£14.0 m
Number of shares	20 million	25 million
Earnings per share	63 p	56 p

The projected statement of financial position as at the end of the year will be:

	Finance with debt £m	Finance with rights issue £m
Assets less current liabilities	180.6	180.25
(150 + new capital 25 + retained profits)		
Debt capital	(95.0)	(70.00)
	85.6	110.25
Share capital	20.0	25.00
Reserves	65.6	* 85.25
	85.6	110.25

* The rights issue raises £25 million, of which £5 million is represented in the statement of financial position by share capital and the remaining £20 million by share premium. The reserves are therefore the current amount (£60 million) plus the share premium of £20 million plus accumulated profits of £5.25 million.

	Finance with debt	Finance with rights issue
Debt capital	95.0	70.0
Debt capital plus equity finance	(95.0 + 85.6)	(70.0 + 110.25)
Gearing	53%	39%

Either financing method would be acceptable, since the company's requirements for no dilution in EPS would be met with a rights issue as well as by borrowing, and the company's requirement for the gearing level to remain below 55% is (just) met even if the company were to borrow the money.

> **Section summary**
>
> - **Financial gearing** measures the relationship between **shareholders' funds** and **prior charge capital**.
> - **Operating gearing** measures the relationship between **contribution** and **profit before interest and tax**.
> - If a company can generate returns on capital in excess of the interest payable on debt, financial gearing will **raise the EPS**. Gearing will, however, also increase **the variability of returns** for shareholders and increase the chance of **corporate failure**.

3 Theories of capital structure

> **Introduction**
>
> There are two main theories which attempt to explain the effect of changes in capital structure on cost of capital and therefore the market value of a company. These are the **traditional theory** and the **net operating income approach** (Modigliani and Miller).

3.1 The traditional view of WACC

The **traditional view** is as follows:

(a) As the **level of gearing increases**, the **cost of debt** remains **unchanged** up to a certain level of gearing. Beyond this level, the cost of debt will increase as interest cover falls, the amount of assets available for security falls and the risk of bankruptcy increases.

(b) The **cost of equity** rises as the level of **gearing increases** and **financial risk increases**.

(c) The **weighted average cost of capital** does **not remain constant**, but rather falls initially as the proportion of debt capital increases, and then begins to increase as the rising cost of equity (and possibly of debt) becomes more significant.

(d) The **optimum level of gearing** is where the **company's weighted average cost of capital is minimised**.

The traditional view about the cost of capital is illustrated in the following figure. It shows that the weighted average cost of capital will be minimised at a particular level of gearing P.

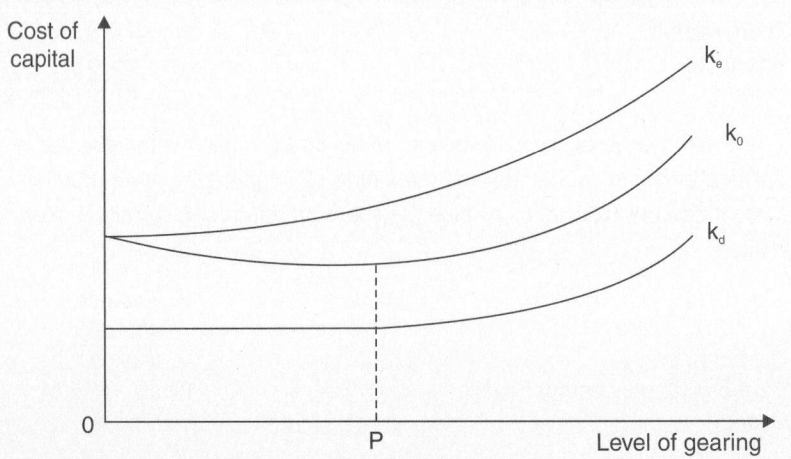

Where k_e is the cost of equity in the geared company
        k_d is the cost of debt
        k_0 is the weighted average cost of capital.

The traditional view is that the weighted average cost of capital, when plotted against the level of gearing, is saucer shaped. The optimum capital structure is where the weighted average cost of capital is lowest, at point P.

3.2 The net operating income (Modigliani-Miller (MM)) view of WACC

The net operating income approach takes a different view of the effect of gearing on WACC. In their 1958 theory, Modigliani and Miller (MM) proposed that the total market value of a company, in the absence of tax, will be determined only by two factors:

- The **total earnings** of the company
- The **level of operating (business) risk** attached to those earnings

The total market value would be computed by discounting the total earnings at a rate that is appropriate to the level of operating risk. This rate would represent the WACC of the company.

Thus Modigliani and Miller concluded that **the capital structure of a company would have no effect on its overall value or WACC**.

3.2.1 Assumptions of net operating income approach

Modigliani and Miller made various assumptions in arriving at this conclusion, including:

(a) A **perfect capital market** exists, in which investors have the same information, upon which they act rationally, to arrive at the same expectations about future earnings and risks.

(b) There are no **tax or transaction costs**.

(c) **Debt is risk-free** and freely available at the same cost to investors and companies alike.

Modigliani and Miller justified their approach by the use of **arbitrage**.

KEY TERM

ARBITRAGE is the simultaneous purchase and sale of a security in different markets, with the aim of making a risk-free profit through the exploitation of any price difference between the markets.
(CIMA Official Terminology)

Arbitrage can be used to show that once all opportunities for profit have been exploited, the market values of two companies with the same earnings in equivalent business risk classes will have moved to an equal value.

If Modigliani and Miller's theory holds, it implies:

(a) The **cost of debt remains unchanged** as the level of gearing increases.
(b) The **cost of equity rises** in such a way as to keep the **weighted average cost of capital constant**.

This would be represented on a graph as shown below.

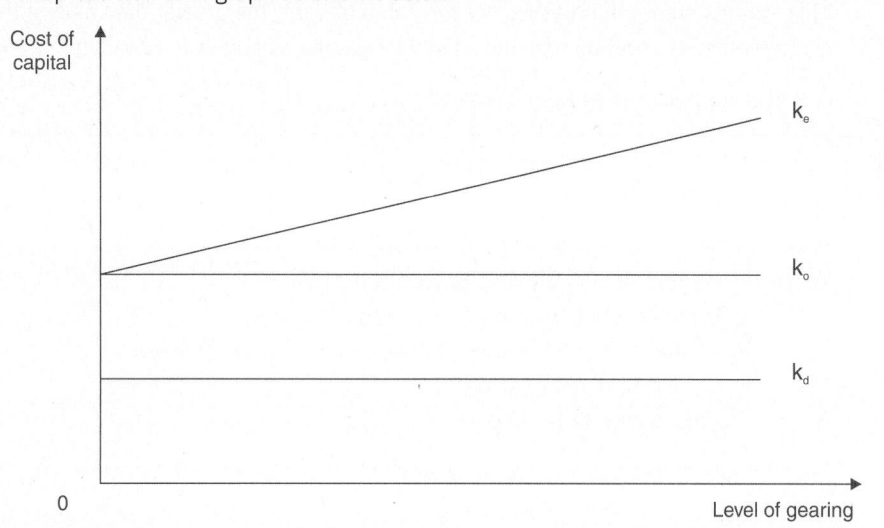

3.3 Modigliani-Miller theory adjusted for taxation

Having argued that debt has no benefit in the absence of taxation, MM then went on to demonstrate that debt can be beneficial where tax relief applies.

Allowing for **taxation reduces the cost of debt capital** by multiplying it by a factor (1 – t) where t is the rate of tax (assuming the debt to be irredeemable).

MM modified their theory to admit that tax relief on interest payments does makes debt capital cheaper to a company, and therefore **reduces the weighted average cost of capital** where a company has debt in its capital structure. They claimed that the weighted average cost of capital will continue to fall, up to gearing of 100%.

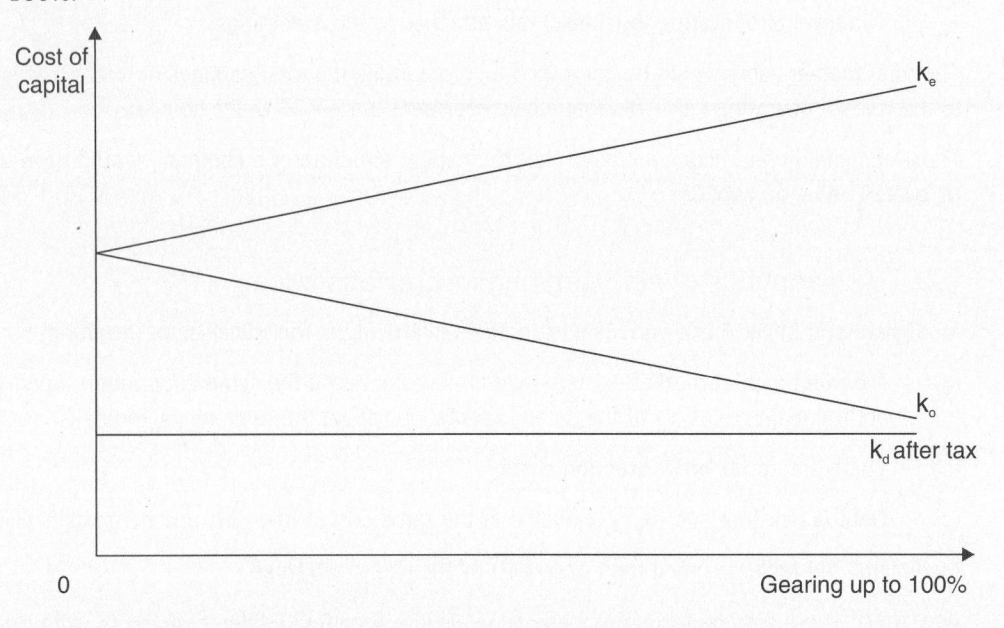

3.4 Formulae and MM theory

M&M developed the following formula as part of their with-taxation theory

$$V_g = V_u + TB$$

Where V_g = value of debt plus equity in geared company
V_u = value of equity in an equivalent ungeared company
TB = tax shield on debt (T is the corporate tax rate and B is the market value of the geared company's debt)

This formula shows that the greater the value of debt, the greater the value of the company and so supports the idea that a company should be geared as highly as possible to maximise its value.

A further formula arising from MM theory is

$$k_{eg} = k_{eu} + (k_{eu} - k_d)\frac{V_d}{V_e}(1-T)$$

Where k_{eg} is the cost of equity in a geared company
k_{eu} is the cost of equity in an ungeared company
V_d, V_e are the market values of debt and equity respectively
k_d is the cost of debt pre-tax
T is the corporate tax rate

This formula shows that the cost of equity will increase when the relative value of debt to equity increases.

MM also came up with an adjusted cost of capital formula as follows

$$k_{adj} = k_{eu}(1 - tL)$$

Where k_{adj} is the weighted average cost of capital in a geared company
k_{eu} is is the cost of equity in an ungeared company
t is the corporate tax rate
L is the gearing ratio measured by debt/(debt + equity)

This formula shows that WACC is reduced when gearing increases ie when more debt is taken on.

3.5 Weaknesses in MM theory

MM theory has been criticised as follows.

(a) MM theory assumes that **capital markets are perfect**. For example, a company will always be able to raise finance to fund worthwhile projects. This ignores the danger that higher gearing can lead to **financial distress costs** and **agency problems** (see Section 1.3).

(b) **Transaction costs** will restrict the arbitrage process.

(c) Investors are **assumed to act rationally** which may not be the case in practice.

3.6 Capital structure in the real world

In the real world some of the theoretical assumptions in MM theory **do not hold**. The most unrealistic are that perfect capital markets exist and that debt is risk free. Almost every borrower would agree that there is **greater risk** at very high levels of gearing and lenders will feel the same. This risk is that the borrower will not be able to service its interest payments and the company may become **insolvent**.

In reality there are a number of factors that can influence the capital structure.

3.6.1 Debt capacity

Debt capacity refers to the maximum amount of debt that a company can support or obtain. A company will have a greater capacity to borrow if it has a number of assets that can be offered as security on the debt.

A company can only increase its borrowing if there are lenders willing to **provide finance**. This may not necessarily always be easy depending on the **financial position** of the company and the state of the **economy**.

3.6.2 Debt covenants

Existing debt may have covenants attached, which require certain **targets** to be met by the borrower and therefore **reduce the flexibility** of management. Existing covenants may **prevent** or limit opportunities for further borrowing. Examples of financial covenants include target interest cover ratios or cash flow / earnings target levels. Breaching covenants may trigger an early repayment of the debt or other penalties.

3.6.3 Increasing debt costs

MM theory assumes that the cost of debt is unchanged at all levels of gearing. In reality as a borrower takes on greater levels of debt, and is perceived to be **riskier**, the lender's required rate of return is likely to **increase**.

3.6.4 Tax exhaustion

The benefit of tax relief on debt is only available whilst the borrower is making a taxable profit. If gearing is high enough, there will be a point where the interest payments will reduce taxable profit to zero and any further debt will not benefit from tax relief. This is known as **tax exhaustion**.

However as the borrower would be making a loss, this would also be likely to cause debt covenants to be breached, which may create more important problems for the company.

3.7 Capital structure conclusions

The practical implications of these capital structure theories can be generalised as follows.

Level of gearing

Low ←——————————————————————→ High

Young company	Mature company
Volatile cash flows	Stable cash flows
Tax benefits < financial distress costs	Tax benefits > financial distress costs

Exam skills

You may need to be able to discuss whether the choice of capital structure for an entity is likely to affect its overall value.

Section summary

- The **traditional theory of cost of capital** suggests that WACC is influenced by gearing; **Modigliani and Miller** disagree.
- Under the **traditional theory of cost of capital**, the cost declines initially and then rises as gearing increases. The **optimal capital structure** will be the point at which WACC is lowest.
- Modigliani and Miller stated that, in the absence of tax, a company's **capital structure** would have **no impact** upon its WACC.
- Modigliani and Miller went on to demonstrate that debt can be beneficial where **tax relief** applies and a company should use as much debt finance as possible.

---

4 Project specific cost of capital   5/10

Introduction

MM theory can be used to calculate the cost of capital in situations where an investment has **differing business and finance risks** from the existing business. Remember from the last chapter that if an entity is investing in projects with different business risk, it is not appropriate to use the WACC.

4.1 Beta values and the effect of gearing

If a company is geared and its **financial risk is therefore higher** than the risk of an all-equity company, then the β value of the geared company's equity will be higher than the β value of a similar ungeared company's equity.

4.2 Geared betas and ungeared betas

The connection between MM theory and the CAPM means that it is possible to establish a mathematical relationship between the β value of an ungeared company and the β value of a similar, but geared, company. The β value of a geared company will be higher than the β value of a company identical in every respect except that it is ungeared and therefore all-equity financed. This is because of the extra financial risk caused by using debt finance. The mathematical relationship between the 'ungeared' (or asset) and 'geared' betas is as follows.

$$\beta_u = \beta_g \frac{V_E}{V_E + V_D(1-t)} + \beta_d \frac{V_D(1-t)}{V_E + V_D(1-t)}$$

Where β_u is the beta factor of an ungeared company: the ungeared beta
β_g is the beta factor of equity in a similar, but geared company: the geared beta
β_d is the beta factor of debt in the geared company
V_D is the market value of the debt capital in the geared company
V_E is the market value of the equity capital in the geared company
t is the rate of corporate tax

Debt is often assumed to be risk-free and its beta (β_d) is then taken as zero, in which case the formula above reduces to the following form.

$$\beta_u = \beta_g \times \frac{V_E}{V_E + V_D(1-t)} \quad \text{or, without tax,} \quad \beta_u = \beta_g \times \frac{V_E}{V_E + V_D}$$

4.3 Using the geared and ungeared beta formula to calculate WACC

If a company plans to invest in a project which involves diversification into a new business, the investment will involve a different level of **systematic risk** from that applying to the company's existing business. A discount rate should be calculated which is **specific to the project**, and which takes account of both the project's systematic risk and the company's gearing level.

There are **two methods** which can be used to calculate a project specific cost of capital both of which start by calculating an ungeared beta.

4.3.1 Approach 1

STEP 1 Find a company's equity beta in the area the business is moving into and strip out the effect of gearing to create an ungeared beta

$$\beta_u = \beta_g \frac{V_E}{V_E + V_D(1-t)}$$

STEP 2 Use the ungeared beta to calculate the ungeared k_e

STEP 3 Use this ungeared k_e to calculate the WACC using the MM formula

$$k_{adj} = k_{eu}(1 - tL)$$

Where k_{adj} is the weighted average cost of capital of a geared company
k_{eu} is the cost of equity and the WACC of a similar ungeared company

> t is the tax saving due to interest payments expressed as a decimal, usually equal to the tax rate
>
> L is equivalent to $\dfrac{V_D}{V_D + V_E}$

Example: Approach 1

A company's debt: equity ratio, by market values, is 2:5. The corporate debt, which is assumed to be risk-free, yields 11% before tax. The beta value of the company's equity is currently 1.1. The average returns on stock market equity are 16%.

The company is now proposing to invest in a project which would involve diversification into a new industry, and the following information is available about this industry.

(a) Average beta coefficient of equity capital = 1.59
(b) Average debt: equity ratio in the industry = 1:2 (by market value)

The rate of corporation tax is 30%. What would be a suitable cost of capital to apply to the project?

Solution

STEP 1 Find a company's equity beta in the area the business is moving into and strip out the effect of gearing to create an ungeared beta

The beta value for the industry is 1.59.

$$\beta_u = 1.59 \left(\dfrac{2}{2 + (1(1-0.30))} \right) = 1.18$$

STEP 2 Use the ungeared beta to calculate the ungeared k_{eu}

$k_{eu} = 11\% + ((16 - 11) \times 1.18) = 16.9\%$

STEP 3 Use this ungeared k_{eu} to calculate the WACC using the MM formula

$k_{adj} = k_{eu}(1 - tL)$

The project will presumably be financed in a gearing ratio of 2:5 debt to equity, and so

$$L = \dfrac{2}{2+5}$$

$k_{adj} = 16.9\% \times (1 - (0.3 \times 2/7)) = 15.45\%$

4.3.2 Approach 2

STEP 1 Find a company's equity beta in the area the business is moving into and strip out the effect of gearing to create an ungeared beta

$$\beta_u = \beta_g \dfrac{V_E}{V_E + V_D(1-t)}$$

STEP 2 Regear the beta using the company's gearing using the formula

$$\beta_g = \beta_u + (\beta_u - \beta_d) \dfrac{V_D(1-t)}{V_E}$$

and calculate the k_e geared

PART B FINANCING DECISIONS　　　　　　　　　　　　　　　　　　　9: The capital structure decision　　**175**

STEP 3 Use this k_e geared to calculate the WACC using the formula below

EXAM

$$\text{WACC} = k_e \left[\frac{V_E}{V_E + V_D} \right] + k_d (1-t) \left[\frac{V_D}{V_E + V_D} \right]$$

Example: Approach 2

Using the information from the example above, the second approach can be used as follows.

STEP 1
$$\beta_u = 1.59 \left(\frac{2}{2 + (1(1 - 0.30))} \right) = 1.18$$

STEP 2 Regear the beta to reflect the company's own gearing level of 2:5.

$\beta_g = 1.18 + 1.18 \times [(2 \times 0.70)/5] = 1.51$

This is a project-specific beta for the firm's equity capital, and so using the CAPM, we can estimate the project-specific cost of equity as:

$k_{eg} = 11\% + (16\% - 11\%)\,1.51 = 18.55\%$

STEP 3 The project will presumably be financed in a gearing ratio of 2:5 debt to equity, and so the project-specific cost of capital ought to be:

$[^5/_7 \times 18.55\%] + [^2/_7 \times 70\% \times 11\%] = 15.45\%$

Exam alert

You will need to be able to ungear and regear a beta in order to calculate a value for a business.

Question 9.2　　　　　　　　　　　　　　　　　　　　　　　　　　　Geared and ungeared betas (1)

Learning outcome: B(1)(e)

Two companies are identical in every respect except for their capital structure. XY has a debt: equity ratio of 1:3, and its equity has a β value of 1.20. PQ has a debt:equity ratio of 2:3. Corporation tax is at 30%. Estimate a β value for PQ's equity.

Question 9.3　　　　　　　　　　　　　　　　　　　　　　　　　　　Geared and ungeared betas (2)

Learning outcome: B(1)(e)

Backwoods is a major international company with its head office in the UK, wanting to raise ☐150 million to establish a new production plant in the eastern region of Germany. Backwoods evaluates its investments using NPV, but is not sure what cost of capital to use in the discounting process for this project evaluation.

The company is also proposing to increase its equity finance in the near future for UK expansion, resulting overall in little change in the company's market-weighted capital gearing.

BPP LEARNING MEDIA

The summarised financial data for the company before the expansion are shown below.

Statement of consolidated income for the year ended 31 December 20X1

	£m
Revenue	1,984
Gross profit	432
Profit after tax	81
Dividends	37
Retained earnings	44

Statement of financial position as at 31 December 20X1

	£m
Non-current assets	846
Working capital	350
	1,196
Medium term and long term loans (see note below)	210
	986

Shareholders' funds

	£m
Issued ordinary shares of £0.50 each nominal value	225
Reserves	761
	986

Note on medium term and long term loans

These include £75m 14% fixed rate bonds due to mature in five years' time and redeemable at par. The current market price of these bonds is £120.00 and they have a cost of debt of 9%. Other medium and long-term loans are floating rate UK bank loans at LIBOR plus 1%, with a cost of debt of 7%.

Company rate of tax may be assumed to be at the rate of 30%. The company's ordinary shares are currently trading at 376 pence.

The equity beta of Backwoods is estimated to be 1.18. The systematic risk of debt may be assumed to be zero. The risk free rate is 7.75% and market return 14.5%.

The estimated equity beta of the main German competitor in the same industry as the new proposed plant in the eastern region of Germany is 1.5, and the competitor's capital gearing is 35% equity and 65% debt by book values, and 60% equity and 40% debt by market values.

Required

Estimate the cost of capital that the company should use as the discount rate for its proposed investment in eastern Germany. State clearly any assumptions that you make.

Section summary

Geared betas can be used to obtain an appropriate required return. They are calculated by **ungearing** an industry beta and then converting the ungeared beta back into a geared beta that reflects the company's own gearing ratio.

Chapter Roundup

- Debt finance can create valuable tax savings which can **reduce the cost of capital** and **increase shareholder value**. However, too much debt increases **financial risk** and incurs **financial distress costs**.
- **Financial gearing** measures the relationship between **shareholders' funds** and **prior charge capital**.
- **Operating gearing** measures the relationship between **contribution** and **profit before interest and tax**.
- If a company can generate returns on capital in excess of the interest payable on debt, financial gearing will **raise the EPS**. Gearing will, however, also increase **the variability of returns** for shareholders and increase the chance of **corporate failure**.
- The **traditional theory of cost of capital** suggests that WACC is influenced by gearing; **Modigliani and Miller** disagree.
- Under the **traditional theory of cost of capital**, the cost declines initially and then rises as gearing increases. The **optimal capital structure** will be the point at which WACC is lowest.
- Modigliani and Miller stated that, in the absence of tax, a company's **capital structure** would have **no impact** upon its WACC.
- Modigliani and Miller went on to demonstrate that debt can be beneficial where **tax relief** applies and a company should use as much debt finance as possible.
- **Geared betas** can be used to obtain an appropriate required return. They are calculated by **ungearing** an industry beta and then converting the ungeared beta back into a geared beta that reflects the company's own gearing ratio.

Quick Quiz

1. Fill in the blanks.

    .... gearing = $\dfrac{\text{Prior charge capital}}{\text{Total capital employed}}$

    .... gearing = $\dfrac{\text{Contribution}}{\text{Profit before interest and tax}}$

2. Fill in the blank.

    Interest cover = ...

3. Are preference shares prior charge or equity capital?

4. According to the traditional view of WACC, what happens to WACC as gearing increases?

5. What three steps are involved in calculating a project specific cost of capital?

Answers to Quick Quiz

1. Financial gearing = $\dfrac{\text{Prior charge capital}}{\text{Total capital employed}}$

   Operating gearing = $\dfrac{\text{Contribution}}{\text{Profit before interest and tax}}$

2. Interest cover = $\dfrac{\text{Profit before interest and tax}}{\text{Interest paid}}$

3. Prior charge capital

4. As gearing increases, WACC declines initially until there is an optimal capital structure. WACC then rises.

5. Either:

   STEP 1 Find a company's equity beta in the area the business is moving into and strip out the effect of gearing to create an ungeared beta.

   $$\beta_u = \beta_g \dfrac{V_E}{V_E + V_D(1 - t)}$$

   STEP 2 Use the ungeared beta to calculate the ungeared k_e

   STEP 3 Use this ungeared ke to calculate the WACC using the MM formula

   $$k_{adj} = k_{eu}(1 - tL)$$

   Or:

   STEP 1 Find a company's equity beta in the area the business is moving into and strip out the effect of gearing to create an ungeared beta.

   STEP 2 Regear the beta using the company's gearing using the formula using the formula

   $$\beta_g = \beta_u + (\beta_u - \beta_d)\dfrac{V_D(1 - t)}{V_E}$$

   and calculate the k_e geared

   STEP 3 Use this k_e geared to calculate the WACC

PART B FINANCING DECISIONS   9: The capital structure decision   **179**

Answers to Questions

9.1 Gearing

	$'000
Prior charge capital	
Preferred shares	500
Bonds	4,700
Long-term bank loans	500
Prior charge capital, ignoring short-term debt	5,700
Short-term loans	120
Overdraft	260
Prior charge capital, including short-term interest bearing debt	6,080

Either figure, $6,080,000 or $5,700,000, could be used. If gearing is calculated with capital employed in the denominator, and capital employed is non-current assets plus net current assets, it would be better to exclude short-term interest bearing debt from prior charge capital. This is because short-term debt is set off against current assets in arriving at the figure for net current assets.

Equity = 1,500 + 760 + 1,200 + 2,810 = $6,270,000

The gearing ratio can be calculated in any of the following ways.

(a) $\dfrac{\text{Prior charge capital}}{\text{Equity}} \times 100\% = \dfrac{6,080}{6,270} \times 100\% = 97\%$

(b) $\dfrac{\text{Prior charge capital}}{\text{Equity plus prior charge capital}} \times 100\% = \dfrac{6,080}{(6,080+6,270)} \times 100\% = 49.2\%$

(c) $\dfrac{\text{Prior charge capital}}{\text{Total capital employed}} \times 100\% = \dfrac{5,700}{12,520} \times 100\% = 45.5\%$

9.2 Geared and ungeared betas (1)

Estimate an ungeared beta from XY data.

$\beta_a = 1.20 \left(\dfrac{3}{3+(1(1-0.30))} \right) = 0.973$

Estimate a geared beta for PQ using this ungeared beta.

$\beta_e = 0.973 \left(\dfrac{3+(2(1-0.30))}{3} \right) = 1.427$

9.3 Geared and ungeared betas (2)

The discount rate that should be used is the weighted average cost of capital (WACC), with weightings based on market values. The cost of capital should take into account the systematic risk of the new investment, and therefore it will not be appropriate to use the company's existing equity beta. Instead, the estimated equity beta of the main German competitor in the same industry as the new proposed plant will be ungeared, and then the capital structure of Backwoods applied to find the WACC to be used for the discount rate.

Since the systematic risk of debt can be assumed to be zero, the German equity beta can be 'ungeared' using the following expression.

$$\beta_u = \beta_g \frac{V_E}{V_E + V_D(1-t)}$$

Where: β_u = asset beta
β_g = equity beta
V_E = proportion of equity in capital structure
V_D = proportion of debt in capital structure
t = tax rate

For the German company:

$$\beta_u = 1.5 \left(\frac{60}{60 + 40(1-0.30)} \right) = 1.023$$

The next step is to calculate the debt and equity of Backwoods based on market values.

		£m
Equity	450m shares at 376p	1,692.0
Debt: bank loans	(210 – 75)	135.0
Debt: bonds	(75 million × 1.20)	90.0
Total debt		225.0
Total market value		1,917.0

The beta can now be re-geared

β_g = 1.023 + 1.023 × [(225 × 0.7)/1,692] = 1.118

This can now be substituted into the capital asset pricing model (CAPM) to find the cost of equity.

$k_e = R_f + [R_m - R_f]\beta$

Where: k_e = cost of equity
R_f = risk free rate of return
R_m = market rate of return
k_e = 7.75% + (14.5% – 7.75%) × 1.118 = 15.30%

The WACC can now be calculated:

$$\left(15.3 \times \frac{1,692}{1,917} \right) + \left(7 \times \frac{135}{1,917} \right) + \left(9 \times \frac{90}{1,917} \right) = 14.4\%$$

Note. You have been given both costs of debt. In the exam you may well be asked to calculate the cost of debt.

Now try this question from the Exam Question Bank

Number	Level	Marks	Time
Q13	Introductory	25	45 mins

TREASURY FUNCTION

In the last part of Part B we consider the role of the treasury function. In larger organisations it is responsible for higher level strategic development plus operational issues involving special skills such as dealing with derivatives.

The key decisions relating to the treasury department – centralised or decentralised, cost centre or profit centre – are good territory for a discussion question in the exam.

The last section in this chapter looks at the relationship between **risk and reward**.

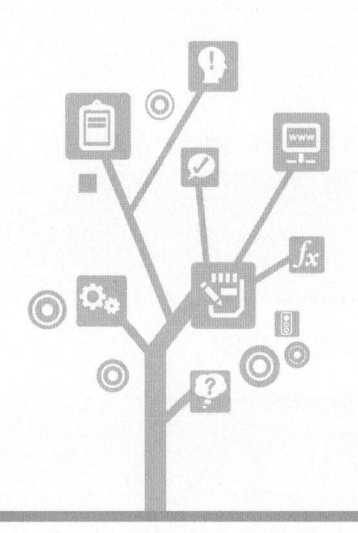

10

topic list	learning outcomes	syllabus references	ability required
1 The treasury function	B(2)(a)	B(2)(i),(ii)	Analysis
2 Risk and reward	B(1)(d)	B(1)vii	Evaluation

1 The treasury function   9/10, 11/11, 3/12

Introduction

Treasury management in a modern large entity covers a number of areas including liquidity management, funding management, currency management and corporate finance. This section looks at the these roles and then goes on to examine the advantages and disadvantages of establishing treasury departments as profit centres or cost centres.

1.1 Treasury management

Large companies rely heavily for both long-term and short-term funds on the financial and currency markets. To manage cash (funds) and currency efficiently, many large companies have set up a separate **treasury department**.

The Association of Corporate Treasurers' **definition of treasury management** is 'the corporate handling of all financial matters, the generation of external and internal funds for business, the management of currencies and cash flows, and the complex strategies, policies and procedures of corporate finance'.

A treasury department, even in a large company, is likely to be quite small, with perhaps a staff of three to six qualified accountants, bankers or corporate treasurers working under a Treasurer, who is responsible to the Finance Director. In some cases, where the company or organisation handles very large amounts of cash or foreign currency dealings, and often has large cash surpluses, the treasury department might be larger.

1.2 The role of the treasurer

The diagrams below are based on the Association of Corporate Treasurers' list of experience it requires from its student members before they are eligible for full membership of the Association. Required experience gives a good indication of the roles of treasury departments.

(a) **Corporate financial objectives**

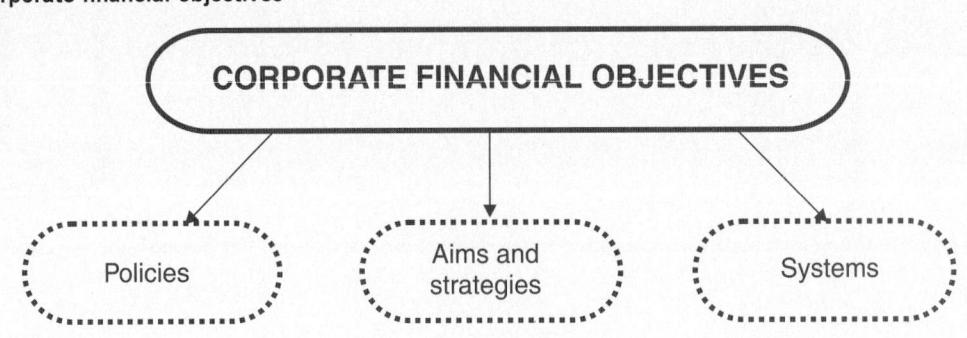

```
          CORPORATE FINANCIAL OBJECTIVES
           /              |              \
      Policies      Aims and         Systems
                    strategies
```

PART B FINANCING DECISIONS   10: Treasury function **183**

(b) **Liquidity management**: making sure the company has the liquid funds it needs, and invests any surplus funds, even for very short terms.

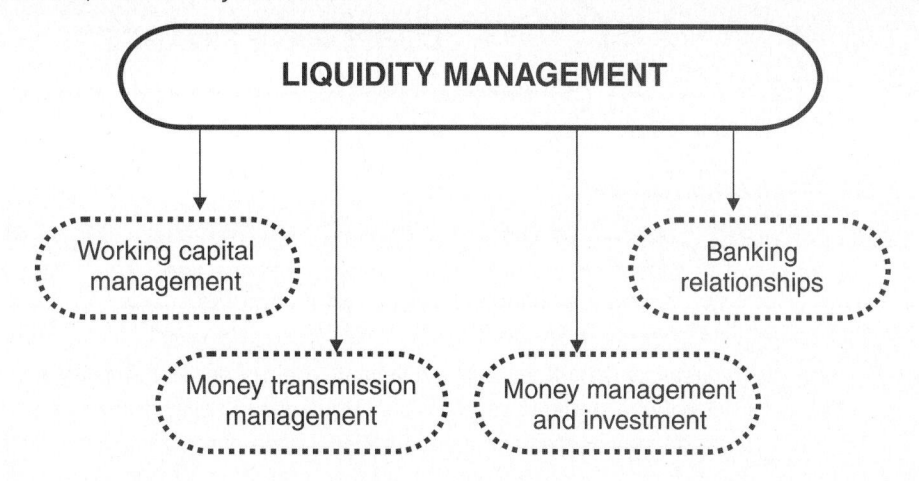

```
                    LIQUIDITY MANAGEMENT
           ┌─────────────┬─────────────┬─────────────┐
   Working capital   Money transmission   Money management   Banking
   management        management           and investment     relationships
```

(c) **Funding management**

```
   Where funds     Length of time/    Interest rate        Security
   obtainable      funds available

                          FUNDING MANAGEMENT

   Funding policies   Funding procedures   Sources        Types
```

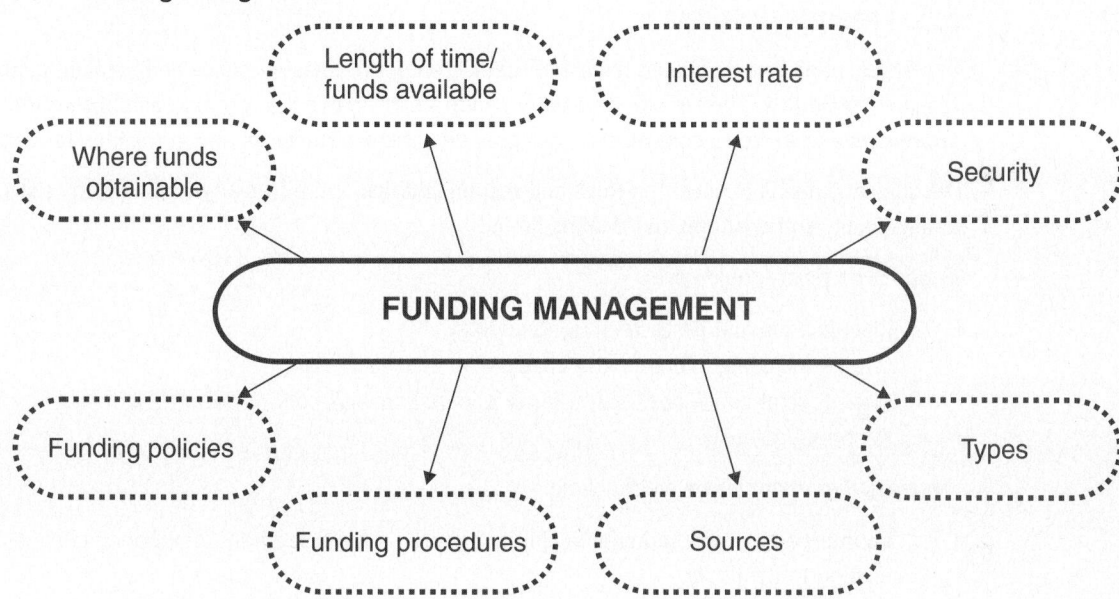

Funding management is concerned with all forms of borrowing, and alternative sources of funds, such as leasing and factoring.

(d) **Currency management**

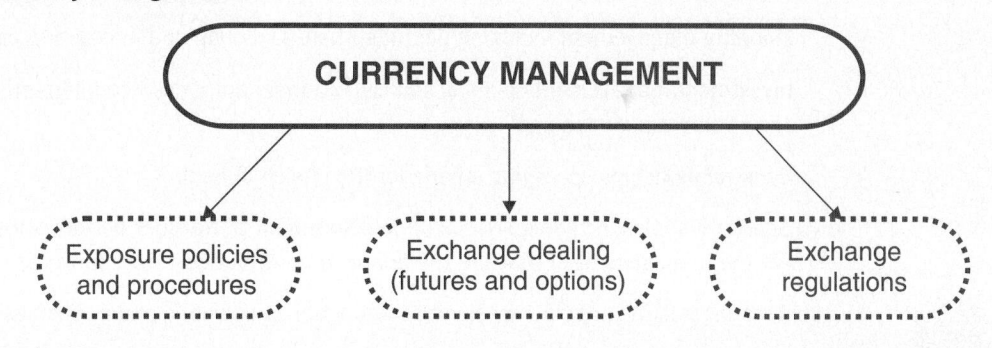

```
                    CURRENCY MANAGEMENT
          ┌──────────────────┬──────────────────┐
   Exposure policies    Exchange dealing      Exchange
   and procedures       (futures and options) regulations
```

Currency dealings can save or cost a company considerable amounts of money, and the success or shortcomings of the corporate treasurer can have a significant impact on the income statement of a company which is heavily involved in foreign trade.

(e) **Corporate finance**

```
                    ┌─────────────────────┐
                    │  CORPORATE FINANCE  │
                    └─────────────────────┘
         ↙                   ↓   ↓                  ↘
  Raising share                                        Dividend policies
    capital
         ↓                   ↓                     ↓
  Obtaining a stock    Project finance and    Mergers, acquisitions
  exchange listing       joint ventures       and business sales
```

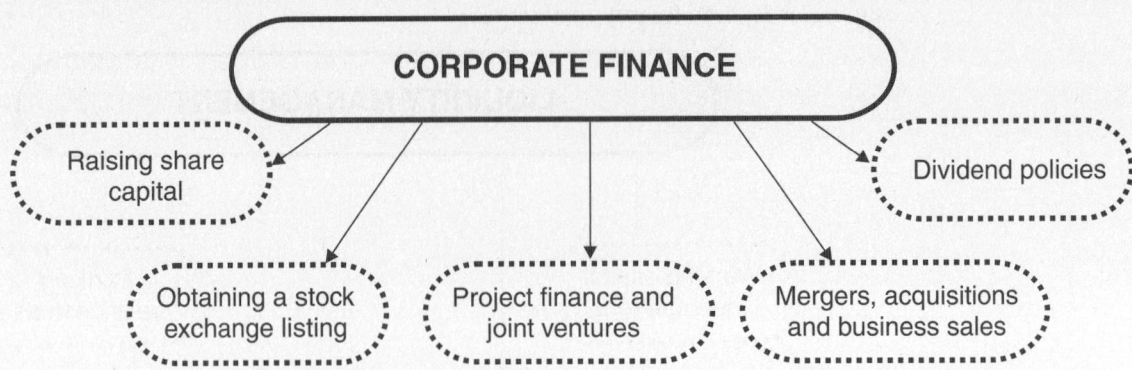

The treasury department has a role in all levels of decision-making within the company. It is involved with **strategic** decisions such as dividend policy or the raising of capital, **tactical** decisions such as risk management, and **operational** decisions such as the investment of surplus funds.

1.3 Treasury policy

All treasury departments should have a formal statement of treasury policy and detailed guidance on treasury procedures. The aims of a treasury policy are to enable managers to **establish direction**, **specify parameters** and **exercise control**, and also **provide a clear framework and guidelines for decisions**.

The guidance needs to cover the **roles** and **responsibilities** of the **treasury function**, the **risks** requiring management, **authorisation** and **dealing** limits.

Guidance on **risks** should cover:

- Identification and assessment methodology
- Criteria including tolerable and unacceptable levels of risk
- Management guidelines, covering risk elimination, risk control, risk retention and risk transfer
- Reporting guidelines

The areas that might be covered include:

- **Counterparty exposure** including limits for each counterparty and monitoring of exposures in relation to the limits

- **Currency and interest rate risk** such as hedging methods, authorised instruments and exposure limits

- **Funding risk** including limits and targets for different sources of funding

- **Liquidity management** including permitted banks, netting and inter-group procedures

- **Investment management** covering sources of funds, authorised counterparties and instruments, and inter-company funding

- **Bank relationships** specifying criteria for the choice of bank

The guidance must also include guidance on **measurement** of **treasury performance**. Measurement must cover both the **management of risk** and the **financial contribution** the department makes.

CASE STUDY

Treasury management can be a very significant function with public bodies such as local authorities.

Good financial practice requires Councils in the UK to produce an annual Treasury Management Strategy. This is approved prior to the commencement of the financial year.

Chichester District Council Treasury Management Strategy for 2010/11 to 2013/14 included the following:

Investment Counterparty Selection Criteria - The primary principle governing the Council's investment criteria is the security of its investments, although the yield or return on the investment is also a key consideration.

After this main principle the Council will ensure:

- It maintains a policy covering both the categories of investment types it will invest in, criteria for choosing investment counterparties with adequate security, and monitoring their security.

- It has sufficient liquidity in its investments. For this purpose it will set out procedures for determining the maximum periods for which funds may prudently be committed. These procedures also apply to the Council's prudential indicators covering the maximum principal sums invested.

1.4 Advantages of a separate treasury department

Advantages of having a treasury function which is **separate from the financial control function** are as follows.

(a) Centralised liquidity management avoids mixing cash surpluses and overdrafts in different localised bank accounts.

(b) Bulk cash flows allow **lower bank charges** to be negotiated.

(c) Larger volumes of cash can be invested, giving **better short-term investment opportunities**.

(d) Borrowing can be agreed in bulk, probably at **lower interest rates** than for smaller borrowings.

(e) Currency risk management should be improved, through **matching of cash flows in different subsidiaries**. There should be less need to use expensive hedging instruments such as option contracts.

(f) A specialist department can employ staff with a **greater level of expertise** than would be possible in a local, more broadly based, finance department.

(g) The company will be able to benefit from the use of **specialised cash management software**.

(h) Access to treasury expertise should **improve the quality of strategic planning and decision making**.

1.5 Centralised or decentralised cash management?

A large company may have a number of subsidiaries and divisions. In the case of a multinational, these will be located in different countries. It will be necessary to decide whether the treasury function should be centralised.

With **centralised cash management**, the central Treasury department effectively acts as the bank to the group. The central Treasury has the job of ensuring that individual operating units have all the funds they need at the right time.

1.5.1 Advantages of a specialist centralised treasury department

(a) **Centralised liquidity management** avoids having a mix of cash surpluses and overdrafts in different local bank accounts and facilitates bulk cash flows, so that lower bank charges can be negotiated.

(b) Larger volumes of cash are available to invest, giving better **short-term investment opportunities** (for example, money market deposits, high interest accounts and Certificates of Deposit).

(c) Any borrowing can be arranged **in bulk**, at lower interest rates than for smaller borrowings, and perhaps on the eurocurrency or eurobond markets.

(d) **Foreign currency risk management** is likely to be improved in a group of companies. A central treasury department can match foreign currency income earned by one subsidiary with expenditure in the same currency by another subsidiary. In this way, the risk of losses on adverse exchange rate changes can be avoided without the expense of forward exchange contracts or other 'hedging' (risk-reducing) methods.

(e) A specialist treasury department will employ **experts** with knowledge of dealing in futures, eurocurrency markets, taxation, transfer prices and so on. Localised departments would not have such expertise.

(f) The centralised pool of **funds required for precautionary purposes** will be smaller than the sum of separate precautionary balances which would need to be held under decentralised treasury arrangements.

(g) Through having a separate **profit centre**, attention will be focused on the contribution to group profit performance that can be achieved by good cash, funding, investment and foreign currency management.

(h) Centralisation provides a means of exercising **better control** through use of **standardised procedures** and **risk monitoring**. Standardised practices and performance measures can also create productivity benefits.

1.5.2 Possible advantages of decentralised cash management

(a) Sources of finance can be **diversified** and can be **matched with local assets**.

(b) Greater **autonomy** can be given to subsidiaries and divisions because of the closer relationships they will have with the decentralised cash management function.

(c) The decentralised Treasury function may be able to be **more responsive** to the needs of individual operating units.

However, since cash balances will not be aggregated at group level, there will be **more limited opportunities to invest** such balances on a short-term basis.

1.5.3 Centralised cash management in the multinational firm

If cash management within a **multinational firm** is centralised, each subsidiary holds only the minimum cash balance required for transaction purposes. All excess funds will be remitted to the central Treasury department.

Funds held in the central pool of funds can be returned quickly to the local subsidiary by telegraphic transfer or by means of worldwide bank credit facilities. The firm's bank can instruct its branch office in the country in which the subsidiary is located to advance funds to the subsidiary.

Exam skills

Always read the question very carefully and make sure you answer the specific question. Don't be tempted to answer the discussion question that you wanted rather than what is required!

Question 10.1 — Treasury centralisation

Learning outcome: B(2)(a)

Touten is a US registered multinational company with subsidiaries in 14 countries in Europe, Asia and Africa. The subsidiaries have traditionally been allowed a large amount of autonomy, but Touten is now proposing to centralise most of the group treasury management operations.

PART B FINANCING DECISIONS

Required

Acting as a consultant to Touten prepare a memo suitable for distribution from the group finance director to the senior management of each of the subsidiaries explaining:

(a) The potential benefits of treasury centralisation; and

(b) How the company proposes to minimise any potential problems for the subsidiaries that might arise as a result of treasury centralisation

1.6 The treasury department as cost centre or profit centre

A treasury department might be managed either as a **cost centre** or as a **profit centre**. For a group of companies, this decision may need to be made for treasury departments in separate subsidiaries as well as for the central corporate treasury department.

In a cost centre, managers have an incentive only to **keep the costs** of the department within **budgeted spending targets**. The cost centre approach implies that the treasury is there to perform a service of a certain standard to other departments in the enterprise. The treasury is treated much like any other service department.

However, some companies (including BP, for example) are able to make significant profits from their treasury activities. Treating the treasury department as a profit centre recognises the fact that treasury activities such as speculation may earn **revenues** for the company, and may as a result make treasury staff more motivated. It also means that treasury departments have to operate with a greater degree of commercial awareness, in for example the management of working capital.

Question 10.2 — Treasury profit centre

Learning outcome: B(2)(a)

Suppose that your company is considering plans to establish its treasury function as a profit centre. In what ways are the following issues of potential importance to these plans?

(a) How can we ensure that high quality treasury staff can be recruited?

(b) How might costly errors and overexposure to risk be prevented?

(c) Why will the treasury team need extensive market information to be successful?

(d) Could there be a danger that attitudes to risk in the treasury team will differ from those of the Board? If so, how?

(e) What is the relevance of internal charges?

(f) What problems could there be in evaluating performance of the treasury team?

CASE STUDY

The treasury function policy of Tesco plc as stated in its 2011 Annual Report is as follows:

'Financial risks relating to underlying business needs are mandated to our Treasury function which has clear policies and operating parameters and its activities are routinely reviewed and audited'

> **Section summary**
>
> - **Treasury management** in a modern enterprise covers a number of areas including **liquidity management**, **funding management**, **currency management** and **corporate finance**.
> - **Centralising** the treasury management function allows businesses to **employ experts**, **deal in bulk cash flows** and hence take **advantage of lower bank charges** and **avoid a mix of surpluses and deficits**. **Decentralised** cash management can be **more responsive to local needs** however.
> - The treasury department is usually run as a **cost centre** if its main focus is to keep costs within budgeted spending targets. It may be run as a **profit centre** if there is a high level of foreign exchange transactions, or the business wishes to make speculative profits.

2 Risk and reward

> **Introduction**
>
> There is **trade-off** between **risk** and **reward**. Investors in riskier assets expect to be compensated for the risk. We have already looked how risk can be incorporated into the cost of capital using the capital asset pricing model. We will now look at two other theories concerning risk and return.

2.1 Portfolios and portfolio theory

A **portfolio** is the collection of different investments that make up an investor's total holding. A portfolio might be:

- The investments in stocks and shares of an investor
- The investments in capital projects of a company

Portfolio theory, which originates from the work of *Markowitz*, is concerned with establishing guidelines for building up a portfolio of stocks and shares, or a portfolio of projects. The same theory applies to both stock market investors and to companies with capital projects to invest in.

2.1.1 Factors in the choice of investments

There are five major factors to be considered when any investor chooses investments.

Choosing investments	
Security	Investments at least maintaining their capital value
Liquidity	If investments are with short-term funds, should be convertible back into cash at short notice
Return	Make highest return compatible with safety
Spreading risks	Spreading investments over several types of security, so losses on some offset by gains on others
Growth prospects	Most profitable investments are in businesses with good growth prospects

2.1.2 Portfolios: Expected return and risk

When investors have portfolios of securities, they will expect the portfolios to provide a certain return on their investments.

The **expected return of a portfolio** will be a weighted average of the expected returns of the investments in the portfolio, weighted by the proportion of total funds invested in each.

The **risk** in an investment, or in a portfolio of investments, is the risk that the actual return will not be the same as the expected return. The actual return may be higher, but it may be lower. A prudent investor will want to avoid too much risk, and will hope that the actual returns from his portfolio are much the same as what he expected them to be.

2.1.3 Correlation between investments

Portfolio theory states that individual investments cannot be viewed simply in terms of their risk and return. The relationship between the return from one investment and the return from other investments is just as important.

The relationship between investments can be one of three types.

(a) **Positive correlation**

When there is positive correlation between investments, if one investment does well (or badly) it is likely that the other will perform likewise. Thus if you buy shares in one company making umbrellas and in another which sells raincoats you would expect both companies to do badly in dry weather.

(b) **Negative correlation**

If one investment does well the other will do badly, and vice versa. Thus if you hold shares in one company making umbrellas and in another which sells ice cream, the weather will affect the companies differently.

(c) **No correlation**

The performance of one investment will be independent of how the other performs. If you hold shares in a mining company and in a leisure company, it is likely that there would be no relationship between the profits and returns from each.

This relationship between the returns from different investments is measured by the correlation coefficient. A figure close to +1 indicates high positive correlation, and a figure close to −1 indicates high negative correlation. A figure of 0 indicates no correlation.

If investments show high negative correlation, then by combining them in a portfolio overall risk would be reduced. Risk will also be reduced by combining in a portfolio investments which have no significant correlation.

2.1.4 Should companies try to diversify?

Our discussion of portfolio theory has concentrated mainly on portfolios of stocks and shares. Investors can reduce their investment risk by diversifying, but what about individual companies choosing a range of businesses or projects to invest in?

You can probably think of examples of large companies today which concentrate mainly on a single industry or product range (for example, British Airways) and those which are **widely diversified** (for example, Virgin, which lends its name to such diverse products and services as mobile phones, holidays and wines).

Disadvantages of diversification include the following.

(a) A company may employ people with particular skills, and it will get the best out of its employees by allowing them to stick to doing **what they are good at**. A manager with expert knowledge of the electronics business, for example, might not be any good at managing a retailing business.

(b) When companies try to grow, they will often find the **best opportunities** to make extra profits in **industries or markets** with which they are **familiar.**

(c) Conglomerates are vulnerable to takeover bids where the buyer plans to **'unbundle'** the **companies** in the group and **sell them off individually** at a profit. Conglomerates' returns will often be mediocre rather than high, and so the stock market will value the shares on a fairly low P/E ratio, making them vulnerable to acquirers. Separate companies within the group would be valued according to their individual performance and prospects, often at P/E ratios that are much higher than for the conglomerate as a whole.

(d) A company can reduce its investment risk by diversifying and **lower investment risk** would **protect the company's shareholders**; however, a shareholder does not need the company to reduce investment risk on his behalf. Investors can probably **reduce investment risk more efficiently** than companies. They have a wider range of investment opportunities. Investments with uncorrelated or negatively correlated returns will be easier to identify. Estimates of beta factors will be more reliable for quoted companies' shares than for companies' capital expenditure projects.

2.1.5 Limitations of portfolio analysis for the financial manager

Portfolio analysis offers a way in which the financial manager can deal with risk by diversifying through the investment decisions which are made by the firm. However, portfolio theory applied to the selection of investment proposals has a number of limitations.

(a) In practice, it may require guesswork to **estimate probabilities** of different outcomes, for example when a new product is to be developed. In other cases, such as machine replacement, sufficient information may however be available to make relatively good probability estimates.

(b) It will be difficult in practical cases to know what are **shareholders' preferences** between risk and return and therefore to reflect these preferences in decision-making.

(c) The '**agency problem**' in management's relationship to the company is relevant. Managers have the security of their jobs to consider, while the shareholder can easily buy and sell securities. It is arguable that managers are as a result more risk-averse than shareholders, and this may distort managers' investment decisions.

(d) Projects may be of such a size that they are not **easy to divide** in accordance with recommended diversification principles.

(e) The theory assumes that there are **constant returns** to scale, in other words that the percentage returns provided by a project are the same however much is invested in it. In practice, there may be economies of scale to be gained from making a larger investment in a single project.

(f) **Other aspects** of risk **not covered** by the theory may need to be considered, eg bankruptcy costs.

2.2 The arbitrage pricing model

The capital asset pricing model (CAPM) is seen as a useful analytical tool by financial managers as well as by financial analysts. However, critics suggest that the relationship between risk and return is more complex than is assumed in the CAPM. One model which could replace the CAPM in the future is the **arbitrage pricing model (APM)**.

Exam skills

What is important here is to be aware that there are other models apart from the CAPM, and to know the benefits and limitations of the arbitrage pricing model (APM) relative to the CAPM.

Unlike the CAPM, which analyses the returns on a share as a function of a single factor – the return on the market portfolio – the APM assumes that the return on each security is based on a number of independent factors. The required return on an asset is shown as:

PART B FINANCING DECISIONS 10: Treasury function

LEARN

$$E(k_e) = r_f + \lambda_1\beta_1 + \lambda_2\beta_2 + \ldots \lambda_n\beta_n$$

Where $E(k_e)$ is the required return on an asset

r_f is the risk-free rate of return

λ is the 'market price' for each risk factor ie the difference between the actual and expected value of each factor

β is the sensitivity of the asset's returns to changes in the value of each factor

KEY POINT

Arbitrage pricing theory is a model which assumes that the return on a security is based on a number of independent factors, to each of which a particular risk premium is attached.

Factor analysis is used to ascertain the factors to which security returns are sensitive. Key factors identified by researchers include:

- Unanticipated inflation
- Changes in the expected level of industrial production
- Changes in the default premium on bonds (debentures)
- Unanticipated changes in the term structure of interest rates
- Long-run growth in the economy
- Changes in the price of oil

It has been demonstrated that when no further arbitrage opportunities exist, the expected return $E(r_j)$ can be shown as:

$$E(r_j) = r_f + \beta_1(r_1 - r_f) + \beta_2(r_2 - r_f) \ldots$$

where r_f is the risk-free rate of return

r_1 is the expected return on a portfolio with unit sensitivity to factor 1 and no sensitivity to any other factor

r_2 is the expected return on a portfolio with unit sensitivity to factor 2 and no sensitivity to any other factor

2.2.1 APM in practice

With the APM, the CAPM's problem of identifying the market portfolio is avoided, but this is replaced with the problem of identifying the macroeconomic factors (since they are not specified by the model) and their risk sensitivities. As with the CAPM, the available empirical evidence is inconclusive and neither proves nor disproves the theory of the APM. Both the CAPM and the APM do however provide a means of analysing how risk and return may be determined in conditions of competition and uncertainty. The simplicity of CAPM is likely to mean it is preferred to APM until empirical testing supports the superiority of APM.

Section summary

- There is a **trade-off** between **risk and return**. Investors in riskier assets expect to be compensated for the risk.

- **Portfolio theory** takes account of the fact that many investors have a range of investments that are unlikely all to change values in step. The investor should be concerned with his or her overall position, not with the performance of individual investments.

- In the future the **arbitrage pricing model** could replace the CAPM as a tool for analysing the determination of risk and returns.

Chapter Roundup

- ✓ **Treasury management** in a modern enterprise covers a number of areas including **liquidity management, funding management, currency management** and **corporate finance**.

- ✓ **Centralising** the treasury management function allows businesses to **employ experts**, **deal in bulk cash flows** and hence take **advantage of lower bank charges** and **avoid a mix of surpluses and deficits**. **Decentralised** cash management can be **more responsive to local needs** however.

- ✓ The treasury department is usually run as a **cost centre** if its main focus is to keep costs within budgeted spending targets. It may be run as a **profit centre** if there is a high level of foreign exchange transactions, or the business wishes to make speculative profits.

- ✓ There is a **trade-off** between **risk and return**. Investors in riskier assets expect to be compensated for the risk.

- ✓ **Portfolio theory** takes account of the fact that many investors have a range of investments that are unlikely all to change values in step. The investor should be concerned with his or her overall position, not with the performance of individual investments.

- ✓ In the future the **arbitrage pricing model** could replace the CAPM as a tool for analysing the determination of risk and returns.

Quick Quiz

1 **Fill in the blanks** in the statement below, using the words in the box. (Words may be used more than once.)

- Treasury management may be defined as 'the corporate handling of all (1) .... matters, the generation of external and internal (2) .... for business, the management of (3) .... and cash flow, and the complex strategies, policies and procedures of (4) ....

- A treasury department may be managed either as a (5) .... centre or a (6) .... centre.

- A (7) .... treasury department has the role of ensuring that individual operating units have all the funds they need at the right time.

- Futures and options might be employed in (8) .... risk management.

- Acquisitions and sales of businesses fall within the area of (9) ....

- Money transmission management is an aspect of (10) .... management.

• Corporate finance	• Centralised	• Profit	• Financial
• Liquidity	• Cost	• Currency/ies	• Funds

2 Why might a treasurer choose *not* to 'hedge' against the risk of a foreign exchange movement?

3 Give three possible advantages of decentralisation of the treasury function.

4 Give an example of a risk-free security.

PART B FINANCING DECISIONS　　　　　　　　　　　　　　　　　　　　　　　10: Treasury function

5　　Which of the following is an argument in favour of diversification by a company?

　　　A　　Employees of the company are likely to possess specialised skills
　　　B　　Investors can probably reduce investment risk more efficiently than companies
　　　C　　Conglomerates are vulnerable to takeover bids with the purpose of 'unbundling'
　　　D　　The risk of variable profits may be reduced

6　　Negative correlation is where the performance of the investment is independent of how the other performs

　　　True　　☐

　　　False　　☐

7　　Which model assumes that the return on a security is based on a number of independent factors, to each of which a risk premium is attached?

Answers to Quick Quiz

1　　(1) Financial (2) Funds (3) Currencies (4) Corporate finance (5) Cost (6) Profit (7) Centralised (8) Currency (9) Corporate finance (10) Liquidity

2　　Because they think it likely that a profit will be made in refraining from hedging the risk.

3　　• Diversification of sources of finance and matching with local assets
　　　• Greater autonomy for subsidiaries and divisions
　　　• Greater responsiveness to the needs of individual operating units

4　　Government bonds are generally considered to be virtually risk-free

5　　D　　The risk of variable profits may be reduced

6　　False: no correlation is the situation where performance is independent

7　　Arbitrage pricing theory

Answers to Questions

10.1 Treasury centralisation

MEMORANDUM

To:　Directors of all foreign subsidiaries
From:　Group Finance Director
Date:　1 July 20X0

Centralisation of treasury management operations

At its last meeting, the board of directors of Touten made the decision to centralise group treasury management operations. A further memo giving detailed plans will be circulated shortly, but my objective in this memo is to outline the potential benefits of treasury centralisation and how any potential problems arising at subsidiaries can be minimised. Most of you will be familiar with the basic arguments, which we have been discussing informally for some time.

What it means

Centralisation of treasury management means that most decisions on borrowing, investment of cash surpluses, currency management and financial risk management will be taken by an enhanced central treasury team, based at head office, instead of by subsidiaries directly. In addition we propose to set most transfer prices for inter-company goods and services centrally.

The potential benefits

The main benefits are:

(a) **Cost savings** resulting from reduction of unnecessary banking charges
(b) **Reduction of the group's total taxation charge**
(c) **Enhanced control over financial risk**

Reduction in banking charges will result from:

(a) **Netting off inter-company debts before settlement**. At the moment we are spending too much on foreign exchange commission by settling inter-company debts in a wide range of currencies through the banking system.

(b) **Knowledge of total group currency exposure from transactions**. Amounts receivable in one subsidiary can hedge payables in another, eliminating unnecessary hedging by subsidiaries.

(c) **Knowledge of the group's total cash resources and borrowing requirement**. This will reduce the incidence of one company lending cash while a fellow subsidiary borrows at a higher interest rate and will also eliminate unnecessary interest rate hedging. It will also facilitate higher deposit rates and lower borrowing rates.

Reduction in the group's tax charge will be made possible by a comprehensive centrally-set **transfer pricing policy**.

Enhanced control over financial risks will be possible because we will be able to develop a central team of specialists who will have a clear-cut strategy on hedging and risk management. Many of you have requested help in this area.

This team will be able to ensure that decisions are taken in line with **group strategy** and will also be able to provide you with enhanced financial information to assist you with your own decision making.

Potential problems for subsidiaries and their solution

Our group culture is one of **decentralisation** and **enablement of management at individual subsidiary level**. There is no intention to change this culture. Rather, it is hoped that releasing you from specialist treasury decisions will enable you to devote more time to developing your own business units.

The system can only work properly, however, if **information exchange** between head office and subsidiaries is swift and efficient. Enhanced computer systems are to be provided at all centres to assist you with daily reports. It is also important that you keep head office informed of all local conditions that could be beneficial to the treasury function, such as the availability of local subsidised loans, as well as potential local risks such as the threat of exchange control restrictions.

You will find that movements in your cash balances will be affected by **group policy**, as well as reported profitability. Any adjustments made by head office will be eliminated when preparing the performance reports for your own business units and we will ensure that joint venture partners are not penalised by group policy.

Please contact me with any further comments that you may have on our new treasury policy.

10.2 Treasury profit centre

If a profit centre approach is being considered, the following issues should be addressed.

(a) **Competence of staff**

Local managers may not have sufficient expertise in the area of treasury management to carry out speculative treasury operations competently. Mistakes in this specialised field may be costly. It may only be appropriate to operate a larger **centralised** treasury as a profit centre, and additional specialist staff demanding high salaries may need to be recruited.

(b) **Controls**

Adequate controls must be in place to prevent costly errors and overexposure to risks such as foreign exchange risks. It is possible to enter into a very large foreign exchange deal over the telephone.

(c) **Information**

A treasury team which trades in futures and options or in currencies is competing with other traders employed by major financial institutions who may have better knowledge of the market because of the large number of customers they deal with. In order to compete effectively, the team needs to have detailed and up-to-date market information.

(d) **Attitudes to risk**

The more aggressive approach to risk-taking which is characteristic of treasury professionals may be difficult to reconcile with the more measured approach to risk which may prevail within the board of directors. The recognition of treasury operations as profit making activities may not fit well with the main business operations of the company.

(e) **Internal charges**

If the department is to be a true profit centre, then market prices should be charged for its services to other departments. It may be difficult to put realistic prices on some services, such as arrangement of finance or general financial advice.

(f) **Performance evaluation**

Even with a profit centre approach, it may be difficult to measure the success of a treasury team for the reason that successful treasury activities sometimes involve **avoiding** the incurring of costs, for example when a currency devalues. For example, a treasury team which hedges a future foreign currency receipt over a period when the domestic currency undergoes devaluation may avoid a substantial loss for the company.

Now try these questions from the Exam Question Bank

Number	Level	Marks	Time
Q14	Introductory	n/a	20 mins
Q15	Introductory	n/a	25 mins

INVESTMENT DECISIONS AND PROJECT CONTROL

Part C

INVESTMENT APPRAISAL TECHNIQUES

In this chapter we go through the principles of **appraising investments** numerically. Although you may feel that these topics are familiar, it is worth working through the examples again to confirm that you do understand them. Examiners' reports often highlight basic errors of principle in answers to investment appraisal questions. It is likely that **NPV calculations** will be set somewhere on virtually every paper, often in the compulsory question.

We then show some of the different methods of assessing and taking account of the **risk and uncertainty** associated with a project.

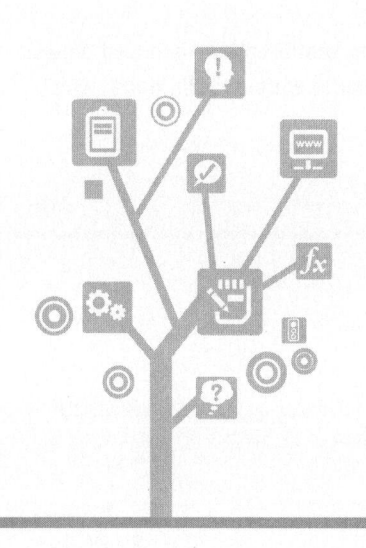

topic list	learning outcomes	syllabus references	ability required
1 Capital investment appraisal	C(1)(a),(b)	C(1)(i),(iv),(v),(vi)	Evaluation
2 Risk and uncertainty	C(1)(a),(b)	C(1)(i),(vii)	Evaluation

199

1 Capital investment appraisal 5/10, 9/10, 3/11, 5/11, 5/12

Introduction
This section revises material that you have covered before and it is essential that you are completely happy with all of the techniques. There is a brief revision of each technique and questions for you to brush up your knowledge.

You will have covered these techniques in Paper P1 *Performance Operations*.

The techniques are also covered in the Appendix: Discounted cash flow.

1.1 Accounting rate of return

This is also referred to as **return on capital employed (ROCE)** or **return on investment (ROI)**.

It is a **traditional** approach to evaluating investments which uses **financial accounting based figures** in arriving at a rate of return on a project. This is compared with a target rate of return to decide on its acceptability.

There are various **definitions** of the ARR, the most common of which is:

$$\text{ARR} = \frac{\text{Estimated average annual profit, after depreciation, before interest and tax}}{\text{Average book value of capital employed}} \times 100\%$$

The main disadvantages of the ARR are that it uses **subjective accounting profits** rather than cash flows; it does not take account of the **timing** of flows, and it can be computed under **various definitions**, which makes comparisons difficult.

Question 11.1   ARR

Learning outcome: C(1)(b)

A company has a target accounting rate of return of 20% (using the definition given above), and is now considering the following project.

Capital cost of asset	$80,000
Estimated life	4 years

Estimated profit before depreciation $
Year 1   20,000
Year 2   25,000
Year 3   35,000
Year 4   25,000

The capital asset would be depreciated by 25% of its cost each year, and will have no residual value. Should the project be undertaken?

PART C INVESTMENT DECISIONS AND PROJECT CONTROL   11: Investment appraisal techniques

1.2 Payback method   5/11

The **payback period** is the time required for the cash inflows from a capital investment project to equal the cash outflows. Either payback periods of different projects are compared, or the period is measured against an 'acceptable' period.

The payback should not be used as the sole appraisal method, as it ignores the cash flows after the payback period, but may be used as a **first screening method**, particularly when applied to risky projects.

The payback period may be estimated by computing the **accumulated cash inflows** year by year until the initial capital investment is covered.

The **discounted payback period** is a modification of payback; the future cash flows are discounted when the period is calculated.

1.3 Net present value   9/10, 3/11, 5/11, 9/11, 3/12

Net present value (NPV) is an appraisal technique which uses **cash flows**, takes account of both the **time value** of money and also the **total profitability** over a project's life, and is thus a method superior to both the ARR and payback methods.

1.3.1 Relevant costs

The cash flows used are those that are **relevant** ie those that arise as a **consequence** of the investment decision:

(a) **Cash flows** only are relevant so depreciation is ignored.

(b) Any costs incurred in the **past** or any **committed costs** which will be incurred regardless of whether the investment is undertaken are **not** relevant.

(c) Ignore costs that are **centrally allocated** eg overheads as they will be incurred regardless of whether the investment is undertaken.

(d) Remember to include **opportunity costs**. These are costs incurred or revenues lost from diverting existing resources from their existing use eg lost contribution.

1.3.2 Discounting

The **timing of cash flows** is taken into account by **discounting** them. This converts a future value into a **present value.**

The **discount rate** used is the **cost of capital.** The net present value is the value obtained by discounting all cash outflows and inflows of a capital investment project by the cost of capital. A **positive** NPV implies the project is acceptable.

> **EXAM**
>
> Future value S, of a sum X, invested for n periods, compounded at r% interest $S = X(1+r)^n$
>
> Present value of $1 payable or receivable in n years, discounted at r% per annum:
>
> $$PV = \frac{1}{(1+r)^n}$$
>
> Present value of an annuity of $1 per annum, receivable or payable in n years, discounted at r% per annum:
>
> $$PV = \frac{1}{r}\left[1 - \frac{1}{(1+r)^n}\right]$$

Question 11.2
Learning outcome: C(1)(b)

NPVs

What are the net present values of the following?

(a) $5,000 payable in 2 years' time, cost of capital 17%
(b) $5,000 payable in 3 years' time, cost of capital 8.5%
(c) $5,000 payable each year for five years beginning in a year's time, cost of capital 16%
(d) $5,000 payable each year for five years beginning in two year's time, cost of capital 16%
(e) $5,000 payable each year for five years beginning today, cost of capital 16%
(f) $5,000 payable each year for five years beginning in a year's time, cost of capital 16.5%

Question 11.3
Learning outcome: C(1)(b)

Purchase of material

LCH Inc manufactures product X which it sells for $5 a unit. Variable costs of production are currently $3 a unit, and fixed costs 50c a unit. A new machine is available which would cost $90,000 but which could be used to make product X for a variable cost of only $2.50 a unit. Fixed costs, however, would increase by $7,500 a year as a direct result of purchasing the machine. The machine would have an expected life of four years and a resale value after that time of $10,000. Sales of product X are estimated to be 75,000 units a year. If LCH expects to earn at least 12% a year from its investments, should the machine be purchased? (Ignore taxation.)

1.3.3 The timing of cash flows: conventions used in DCF

The following guidelines may be applied unless a question indicates that they should not be.

(a) A cash outlay to be incurred at the beginning of an investment project, that is now, occurs in year 0. The present value of $1 in year 0 is $1.

(b) A cash outlay, saving or inflow which occurs during the course of a time period (say, one year) is assumed to occur all at once at the end of the time period. Therefore receipts of $10,000 during the first year are taken to occur at the end of that year. That point in time is called 'year 1'.

(c) A cash outlay, saving or inflow which occurs at the beginning of a time period (say at the beginning of the second year) is taken to occur at the end of the previous year. Therefore a cash outlay of $5,000 at the beginning of the second year is taken to occur at year 1.

1.3.4 Other formulae

You may also find the following formulae useful.

(a) For **non-annual cash flows**, the period interest rate r is related to the annual interest rate R by the following formula.

$$r = \sqrt[n]{1+R} - 1$$

where n is the number of periods per annum.

For example, if the annual interest rate is 18%, the monthly interest rate $r = \sqrt[12]{1.18} - 1 = 0.0139$, ie 1.39%.

PART C INVESTMENT DECISIONS AND PROJECT CONTROL   11: Investment appraisal techniques

(b) **Changes in interest rate** can be reflected as in the following example.

In years 1, 2 and 3, the interest rate is 10%, 12% and 14% respectively.

Then, Year 3 discount factor $= \dfrac{1}{(1+r_1)(1+r_2)(1+r_3)}$

$= \dfrac{1}{1.10 \times 1.12 \times 1.14} = 0.712$

Question 11.4   Non-annual cash flows

Learning outcome: C(1)(b)

Calculate the net present value of the following short-duration investment.

Cost ($2,000,000)

Revenues

2 months $700,000
4 months $300,000
6 months $1,000,000
One year $250,000

The company's annual cost of capital is 16%

1.3.5 NPV layout

Exam alert

The examiners have often complained that students fail to layout NPV calculations in a clear format. The following proforma will help you to use a logical approach and gain as many marks as possible.

	Year 0	Year 1	Year 2	Year 3	Year 4
Sales receipts		X	X	X	
Costs	—	(X)	(X)	(X)	—
Sales less costs		X	X	X	
Taxation		(X)	(X)	(X)	(X)
Capital expenditure	(X)				
Scrap value				X	
Working capital	(X)			X	
Tax benefit of tax dep'n		X	X	X	X
	(X)	X	X	X	(X)
Discount factors @ post-tax cost of capital	X	X	X	X	X
Present value	(X)	X	X	X	(X)

We will now look at the working capital and taxation workings in more detail.

1.3.6 Working capital

Increases in working capital **reduce** the net cash flow of the period to which they relate. The relevant cash flows are the **incremental cash flows** from one year's requirement to the next. So for example, if a project lasts for five years with a €20,000 working capital requirement at the end of year 1, rising to €30,000 at the end of year 2, the DCF calculation will show €20,000 as a year 1 cash outflow and €10,000 (30,000 – 20,000) as a year 2 cash outflow.

Working capital is assumed to be **recovered** at the end of the project. In the example above, this will be shown by a €30,000 cash inflow at year 5.

Question 11.5 — NPV with working capital

Learning outcome: C(1)(b)

Elsie is considering the manufacture of a new product which would involve the use of both a new machine (costing £150,000) and an existing machine, which cost £80,000 two years ago and has a current net book value of £60,000. There is sufficient capacity on this machine, which has so far been under-used.

Annual sales of the product would be 5,000 units, selling at £32 a unit. Unit costs would be as follows.

	£
Direct labour (4 hours at £2)	8
Direct materials	7
Fixed costs including depreciation	9
	24

The project would have a five year life, after which the new machine would have a net residual value of £10,000. Because direct labour is continually in short supply, labour resources would have to be diverted from other work which currently earns a contribution of £1.50 per direct labour hour. The fixed overhead absorption rate would be £2.25 an hour (£9 a unit) but actual expenditure on fixed overhead would not alter.

Working capital requirements would be £10,000 in the first year, rising to £15,000 in the second year and remaining at this level until the end of the project, when it will all be recovered. The company's cost of capital is 20%. Ignore taxation.

Is the project worthwhile?

1.3.7 Taxation

Tax allowable depreciation is used to reduce taxable profits, and the consequent reduction in a tax payment should be treated as a **cash saving** arising from the acceptance of a project.

For example, suppose tax-allowable depreciation is allowed on the cost of plant and machinery at the rate of 25% on a reducing balance basis. Thus if a company purchases plant costing $80,000, the subsequent writing down allowances would be as follows.

Year		Tax-allowable depreciation $	Reducing balance $
1	(25% of cost)	20,000	60,000
2	(25% of RB)	15,000	45,000
3	(25% of RB)	11,250	33,750
4	(25% of RB)	8,438	25,312

When the plant is eventually sold, the difference between the sale price and the reducing balance amount at the time of sale will be treated as:

(a) A taxable profit if the sale price exceeds the reducing balance, and
(b) A tax-allowable loss if the reducing balance exceeds the sale price

The cash saving on the tax-allowable depreciation (or the cash payment for the charge) is calculated by multiplying the depreciation (or charge) by the tax rate.

PART C INVESTMENT DECISIONS AND PROJECT CONTROL   11: Investment appraisal techniques

Assumptions about tax-allowable depreciation could be simplified in an exam question. For example, you might be told that tax-allowable depreciation can be claimed at the rate of 25% of cost on a straight line basis (that is, over four years).

Exam alert

In investment appraisal, tax is often assumed to be payable **one year in arrears,** but you should read the question details carefully.

Tax allowable depreciation details should be checked in any question you attempt.

Example: Taxation

A company is considering whether or not to purchase an item of machinery costing £40,000 in 20X5. It would have a life of four years, after which it would be sold for £5,000. The machinery would create annual cost savings of £14,000.

The machinery would attract tax-allowable depreciation of 25% on the reducing balance basis which could be claimed against taxable profits of the current year, which is soon to end. A balancing allowance or charge would arise on disposal. The tax rate is 30%. Tax is payable half in the current year, half one year in arrears. The after-tax cost of capital is 8%.

Should the machinery be purchased?

Solution

Tax-allowable depreciation is first claimed against year 0 profits.

Cost: £40,000

Year	Tax-allowable depreciation £	Reducing balance (RB) £	
(0) 20X5 (25% of cost)	10,000	30,000	(40,000 – 10,000)
(1) 20X6 (25% of RB)	7,500	22,500	(30,000 – 7,500)
(2) 20X7 (25% of RB)	5,625	16,875	(22,500 – 5,625)
(3) 20X8 (25% of RB)	4,219	12,656	(16,875 – 4,219)
(4) 20X9 (25% of RB)	3,164	9,492	(12,656 – 3,164)

	£
Sale proceeds, end of fourth year	5,000
Less reducing balance, end of fourth year	9,492
Balancing allowance	4,492

Having calculated the depreciation each year, the tax savings can be computed. The year of the cash flow is one year after the year for which the allowance is claimed.

Year of claim	Tax-allowable depreciation £	Tax saved £	Year of tax payment/ saving (50% in each)
0	10,000	3,000	0/1
1	7,500	2,250	1/2
2	5,625	1,688	2/3
3	4,219	1,266	3/4
4	7,656	2,297	4/5
	35,000 *		

* Net cost £(40,000 – 5,000) = £35,000

These tax savings relate to tax-allowable depreciation. We must also calculate the extra tax payments on annual savings of £14,000.

The net cash flows and the NPV are now calculated as follows.

	Year 0 £	Year 1 £	Year 2 £	Year 3 £	Year 4 £	Year 5 £
Purchase of equipment	(40,000)					
Cost savings		14,000	14,000	14,000	14,000	
Tax on savings		(2,100)	(4,200)	(4,200)	(4,200)	(2,100)
Tax saved on tax-allowable dep'n	1,500	2,625	1,969	1,477	1,782	1,148
Net cash flow	(38,500)	14,525	11,769	11,277	16,582	(952)
Discount factor @ 8%	1.000	0.926	0.857	0.794	0.735	0.681
Present value	(38,500)	13,450	10,086	8,954	12,188	(648)

NPV = £5,530   The NPV is positive and so the purchase appears to be worthwhile.

1.3.8 An alternative and quicker method of calculating tax payments or savings

In the above example, the tax computations could have been combined, as follows.

	Year 0 £	Year 1 £	Year 2 £	Year 3 £	Year 4 £
Cost savings	0	14,000	14,000	14,000	14,000
Tax-allowable depreciation	10,000	7,500	5,625	4,219	7,656
Taxable profits	(10,000)	6,500	8,375	9,781	6,344
Tax at 30%	3,000	(1,950)	(2,512)	(2,934)	(1,903)

The net cash flows would then be as follows.

Year	Equipment £	Savings £	Tax £	Net cash flow £
0	(40,000)		1,500	(38,500)
1		14,000	525	14,525
2		14,000	(2,231)	11,769
3		14,000	(2,723)	11,277
4	5,000	14,000	(2,418)	16,582
5			(952)	(952)

The net cash flows are exactly the same as calculated previously.

Question 11.6   NPV with taxation

Learning outcome: C(1)(b)

A project requires an initial investment in machinery of $300,000. Additional cash inflows of $120,000 at current price levels are expected for three years, at the end of which time the machinery will be scrapped. The machinery will attract tax-allowable depreciation of 25% on the reducing balance basis, which can be claimed against taxable profits of the current year, which is soon to end. A balancing charge or allowance will arise on disposal.

The tax rate is 50% and tax is payable 50% in the current year, 50% one year in arrears. The pre-tax cost of capital is 22% and the rate of inflation is 10%. Assume that the project is 100% debt financed.

Required

Assess whether the project should be undertaken.

1.3.9 Inflation

In an inflationary environment, cash flows in a project may be given in **money terms** (the actual cash that will arise) or **real terms** (in today's currency).

Similarly, the required rate of return on an investment may be given as a **money** rate of return (including an allowance for a general rate of inflation) or as a **real** rate of return (the return required over and above inflation).

If cash flows are given in **money terms**, the **money rate** should be used to discount them (remember: 'money at money'); if the flows are in **real terms**, the **real rate** of return may be used to discount them ('real at real'), although this may not always result in the same answer.

If some of the cost or revenues relating to the project **inflate at rates different from the general rate of inflation**, it is **not** appropriate to discount real flows at the real rate. Instead, **money flows must be computed**, by applying the relevant rates of inflation to the real flows, which must then be discounted at the money required return.

> The two rates of return and the inflation rate are linked by the equation:
>
> (1 + nominal (money) rate of return) = (1 + real interest rate)(1 + inflation rate)
>
> This is often referred to as the *Fisher* Equation.

Question 11.7 — NPV with inflation

Learning outcome: C(1)(b)

Rice is considering a project which would cost £5,000 now. The annual benefits, for four years, would be a fixed income of £2,500 a year, plus other savings of £500 a year in year 1, rising by 5% each year because of inflation. Running costs will be £1,000 in the first year, but would increase at 10% each year because of inflating labour costs. The general rate of inflation is expected to be 7½% and the company's required money rate of return is 16%. Is the project worthwhile? (Ignore taxation.)

1.3.10 Expectations of inflation and the effects of inflation

When managers evaluate a particular project, or when shareholders evaluate their investments, they can only guess at what the rate of inflation is going to be. Their expectations will probably be wrong, at least to some extent, because it is extremely difficult to forecast the rate of inflation accurately. The only way in which uncertainty about inflation can be allowed for in project evaluation is by **risk and uncertainty analysis**.

We stated earlier that costs and benefits may rise at levels different from the general rate of inflation: inflation may be **general,** affecting prices of all kinds, or **specific** to particular prices. Generalised inflation has the following effects.

(a) Since non-current assets, inventories and other working capital will increase in money value, the same quantities of assets or working capital must be financed by increasing amounts of capital.

(b) Inflation means higher costs and higher selling prices. The effect of higher prices on demand is not necessarily easy to predict. A company that raises its prices by 10% because the general rate of inflation is running at 10% might suffer a serious fall in demand.

(c) Inflation, because it affects financing needs, is also likely to affect gearing, and so the cost of capital.

1.4 IRR

We covered the IRR technique in Chapter 8 when we looked at the cost of redeemable debt.

The IRR approach is to calculate the **discount rate at which the NPV of the project would be zero**, indicating the maximum cost of capital at which the project would be viable. Provided the investing business's cost of capital is less than this, the project may be accepted.

The IRR is found approximately by using interpolation, using the results from NPV computations at two different discount rates:

$$IRR = a + \frac{NPV_a}{NPV_a - NPV_b} (b - a)$$

where a = lower discount rate used with NPV_a

b = higher discount rate used with NPV_b

Question 11.8 — IRR

Learning outcome: C(1)(b)

A company is trying to decide whether to buy a machine for $80,000 which will save $20,000 a year for five years and which will have a resale value of $10,000 at the end of year 5. What is the IRR of the investment project?

1.5 NPV or IRR?

Given that there are two methods of using DCF, the NPV method and the IRR method, the relative merits of each method have to be considered. Which is better?

The **main advantage** of the **IRR** method is that the information it provides is more easily understood by managers, especially non-financial managers. For example, it is fairly easy to understand the meaning of the following statement.

'The project has an initial capital outlay of $100,000, and will earn a yield of 25%. This is in excess of the target yield of 15% for investments.'

It is not so easy to understand the meaning of this statement.

'The project will cost $100,000 and have an NPV of $30,000 when discounted at the minimum required rate of 15%.'

In other respects, the IRR method has serious disadvantages.

(a) It might be tempting to **confuse the IRR** and the **accounting ROCE**. The accounting ROCE and the IRR are two completely different measures. If managers were given information about both ROCE (or ROI) and IRR, it might be easy to get their meanings and significance mixed up.

(b) It ignores the relative size of investments. Both the following projects have an IRR of 18%.

	Project A £	Project B £
Cost, year 0	350,000	35,000
Annual savings, years 1–6	100,000	10,000

Clearly, project A is bigger (ten times as big) and so more profitable but if the only information on which the projects were judged were to be their IRR of 18%, project B would seem just as beneficial as project A.

(c) If the cash flows from a project are **not conventional** (with an outflow at the beginning resulting in inflows over the life of a project) there may be more than one IRR. This could be very difficult for managers to interpret. For example, the following project has cash flows which are not conventional, and as a result has two IRRs of approximately 7% and 35%.

Year	Project X £'000
0	(1,900)
1	4,590
2	(2,735)

This deficiency can be overcome by using the modified internal rate of return. This method assumes that all cash flows after the initial investment can be reinvested at the cost of capital, and converts all the flows to a single cash inflow at the end of the project's life.

(d) The IRR method should not be used to select between mutually exclusive projects. This follows on from point (b) and it is the most significant and damaging criticism of the IRR method.

Example: Mutually exclusive options

A company is considering two mutually exclusive options, option A and option B. The cash flows for each would be as follows.

Year		Option A £	Option B £
0	Capital outlay	(10,200)	(35,250)
1	Net cash inflow	6,000	18,000
2	Net cash inflow	5,000	15,000
3	Net cash inflow	3,000	15,000

The company's cost of capital is 16%. Which option should be chosen?

Solution

The NPV of each project is calculated below.

Year	Discount factor @ 16%	Option A Cashflow £	Option A Present value £	Option B Cashflow £	Option B Present value £
0	1.000	(10,200)	(10,200)	(35,250)	(35,250)
1	0.862	6,000	5,172	18,000	15,516
2	0.743	5,000	3,715	15,000	11,145
3	0.641	3,000	1,923	15,000	9,615
NPV			+610		+1,026

However, the IRR of option A is 20% and the IRR of option B is only 18% (workings not shown). On a comparison of NPVs, option B would be preferred but, on a comparison of IRRs, option A would be preferred.

Option B should be chosen. This is because the differences in the cash flows between the two options, when discounted at the cost of capital of 16%, show that the present value of the incremental benefits from option B compared with option A exceed the PV of the incremental costs. This can be re-stated in the following ways.

(a) The NPV of the differential cash flows (option B cash flows minus option A cash flows) is positive, and so it is worth spending the extra capital to get the extra benefits.

(b) The IRR of the differential cash flows exceeds the cost of capital of 16%, and so it is worth spending the extra capital to get the extra benefits.

1.5.1 Reinvestment assumption

An assumption underlying the NPV method is that any net cash inflows generated during the life of the project will be reinvested elsewhere at the cost of capital (that is, the discount rate). The IRR method, on the other hand, assumes these **cash flows** can be **reinvested elsewhere** to earn a return equal to the IRR of the original project.

If the IRR is **considerably higher** than the **cost of capital** this is an unlikely assumption. If the assumption is not valid the IRR method overestimates the project's return.

1.6 Modified internal rate of return (MIRR) 9/10

The MIRR overcomes the problem of the **reinvestment assumption** and the fact that **changes in the cost of capital over the life of the project** cannot be incorporated in the IRR method.

Consider a project requiring an initial investment of $24,500, with cash inflows of $15,000 in years 1 and 2 and cash inflows of $3,000 in years 3 and 4. The cost of capital is 10%.

If we calculate the IRR:

Year	Cash flow $	Discount factor @ 10%	Present value $	Discount factor @ 25%	Present value $
0	(24,500)	1.000	(24,500)	1.000	(24,500)
1	15,000	0.909	13,635	0.800	12,000
2	15,000	0.826	12,390	0.640	9,600
3	3,000	0.751	2,253	0.512	1,536
4	3,000	0.683	2,049	0.410	1,230
			5,827		(134)

$$\text{IRR} = 10\% + \left[\frac{5,827}{5,827+134} \times (25\% - 10\%)\right] = 24.7\%$$

The MIRR is calculated on the basis of **investing the inflows** at the **cost of capital**.

The table below shows the **values of the inflows if they were immediately reinvested at 10%.** For example the $15,000 received at the end of year 1 could be reinvested for three years at 10% pa (multiply by $1.1 \times 1.1 \times 1.1 = 1.331$).

Year	Cash inflows $	Interest rate multiplier	Amount when reinvested $
1	15,000	1.331	19,965
2	15,000	1.21	18,150
3	3,000	1.1	3,300
4	3,000	1.0	3,000
			44,415

The total cash outflow in year 0 ($24,500) is compared with the possible inflow at year 4, and the resulting figure of 24,500/44,415 = 0.552 is the discount factor in year 4. By looking along the year 4 row in present value tables you will see that this gives a return of 16%. This means that the $44,415 received in year 4 is equivalent to $24,500 in year 0 if the discount rate is 16%.

Alternatively, instead of using discount tables, we can calculate the MIRR as follows.

$$\text{Total return} = \frac{44,415}{24,500} = 1.813$$

$$\text{MIRR} = \sqrt[4]{1.813} - 1 = 1.16 - 1 = 16\%$$

In theory the MIRR of 16% will be a **better measure** than the IRR of 24.7%.

1.6.1 Advantages of MIRR

MIRR has the advantage over IRR that it assumes the **reinvestment rate** is the **company's cost of capital**. IRR assumes that the reinvestment rate is the IRR itself, which is usually untrue.

In many cases where there is conflict between the NPV and IRR methods, the MIRR will give the same indication as NPV, which is the **correct theoretical method**. This helps when explaining the appraisal of a project to managers, who often find the concept of rate of return easier to understand than that of net present value.

1.6.2 Disadvantages of MIRR

However, MIRR, like all rate of return methods, suffers from the problem that it may lead an investor to reject a project which has a **lower rate of return** but, because of its size, generates a **larger increase in wealth**.

In the same way, a **high-return** project with a **short life** may be preferred over a **lower-return** project with a longer life.

1.7 The use of appraisal methods in practice

A survey carried out by CIMA in 2009 showed the following usage of different investment appraisal techniques:

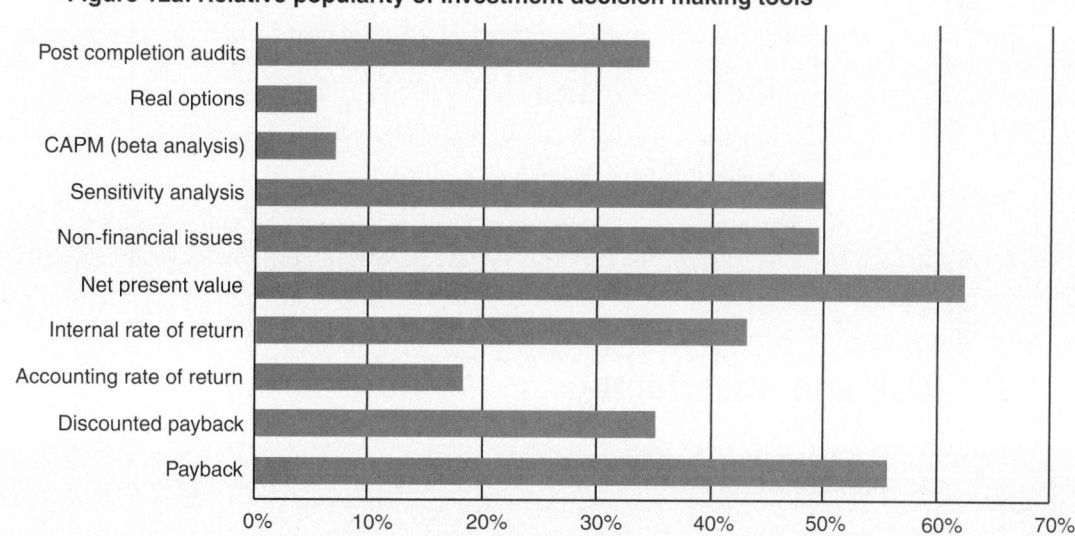

Figure 12a: Relative popularity of investment decision making tools

Source: *Management Accounting Tools for Today and Tomorrow*, CIMA, 2009

It was noted that respondents used on average between three and four of the investment decision-making tools included in the survey. NPV is unsurprisingly the most frequently used, but look at the popularity of payback despite its considerable limitations. It would appear that companies are willing to overlook these limitations in favour of simplicity and ease of understanding.

> **Section summary**
>
> - The **payback method** of project appraisal and the **ARR/ROCE/ROI method** of project appraisal are popular appraisal techniques despite their limitations.
> - There are two methods of using **discounted cash flow** to appraise investment projects, the NPV method and the IRR method.
> - The **NPV method** of project appraisal is to accept projects with a positive NPV.
> - In investment appraisal, tax is often assumed to be payable **one year in arrears,** but you should read the question details carefully.
> - (1+ money rate of return) = (1 + real rate of return) × (1 + rate of inflation)
> - **Real cash flows** should be discounted at a **real discount rate** ('real at real').
> - **Money cash flows** should be discounted at a **money discount rate** ('money at money').
> - The **IRR method** of project appraisal is to accept projects whose IRR (the rate at which the NPV is zero) exceeds a target rate of return. The IRR is estimated either from a graph or using interpolation. The formula to apply is:
>
> $$\text{IRR} = a + \frac{\text{NPV}_a}{\text{NPV}_a - \text{NPV}_b}(b - a).$$
>
> - When compared with the NPV method, the **IRR method** has a number of **disadvantages**.
>   - It **ignores** the **relative size** of investments.
>   - It is difficult to use if a project has **non-conventional cashflows** or when deciding between **mutually exclusive projects**.
>   - **Discount rates** that **differ** over the life of a project cannot be included in IRR calculations, although the **modified internal rate of return** (MIRR) method can incorporate them.

2 Risk and uncertainty

> **Section summary**
>
> Only if management know for certain what is going to happen in the future can they appraise a project in the knowledge that there is no risk. However the future is uncertain by nature. There are, nevertheless, techniques which can be used to enable managers to make a judgement on risk and uncertainty.

Again, you will have covered some of this material and techniques in Paper P1 *Performance Operations*

You will also cover risk in detail in Paper P3 *Performance Strategy* and should use relevant knowledge from that paper in discussions about the desirability of particular investments.

2.1 Risk v uncertainty

A distinction should be made between the terms risk and uncertainty.

Risk	• Several possible outcomes • On basis of past relevant experience, assign probabilities to outcomes • Increases as the variability of returns increases
Uncertainty	• Several possible outcomes • Little past experience, thus difficult to assign probabilities to outcomes • Increases as project life increases

A risky situation is one where we can say that there is a 70% probability that returns from a project will be in excess of $100,000 but a 30% probability that returns will be less than $100,000. If, however, no information can be provided on the returns from the project, we are faced with an uncertain situation.

In general, risky projects are those whose future cash flows, and hence the project returns, are likely to be variable. The greater the **variability** is, the greater the risk. The problem of risk is more acute with capital investment decisions than other decisions for the following reasons.

(a) Estimates of **capital expenditure** might be for **several years ahead**, such as for major construction projects. Actual costs may escalate well above budget as the work progresses.

(b) Estimates of **benefits** will be for **several years ahead**, sometimes 10, 15 or 20 years ahead or even longer, and such long-term estimates can at best be approximations.

2.2 Sensitivity analysis

The NPV could depend on a number of uncertain independent variables.

- Selling price
- Sales volume
- Cost of capital
- Initial cost
- Operating costs
- Benefits

The basic approach of sensitivity analysis is to **calculate the project's NPV** under **alternative assumptions** to determine how sensitive it is to changing conditions. An indication is thus provided of those variables to which the NPV is most sensitive (**critical variables**) and the **extent** to which those variables **may change** before the investment results in a negative NPV.

Sensitivity analysis therefore provides an indication of why a project might fail. Management should review critical variables to assess whether or not there is a strong possibility of events occurring which will lead to a negative NPV. Management should also pay particular attention to controlling those variables to which the NPV is particularly sensitive, once the decision has been taken to accept the investment.

A simple approach to deciding which variables the NPV is particularly sensitive to is to calculate the sensitivity of each variable:

$$\text{Sensitivity} = \frac{\text{NPV}}{\text{Present value of project variable}} \%$$

The lower the percentage, the more sensitive is NPV to that project variable as the variable would need to change by a smaller amount to make the project non-viable.

Example: Sensitivity analysis

Kenney Co is considering a project with the following cash flows.

Year	Initial investment $'000	Variable costs $'000	Cash inflows $'000	Net cash flows $'000
0	7,000			
1		(2,000)	6,500	4,500
2		(2,000)	6,500	4,500

Cash flows arise from selling 650,000 units at $10 per unit. Kenney Co has a cost of capital of 8%.

Required

Measure the sensitivity of the project to changes in variables.

Solution

The PVs of the cash flow are as follows.

Year	Discount factor 8%	PV of initial investment $'000	PV of variable costs $'000	PV of cash inflows $'000	PV of net cash flow $'000
0	1.000	(7,000)			(7,000)
1	0.926		(1,852)	6,019	4,167
2	0.857		(1,714)	5,571	3,857
		(7,000)	(3,566)	11,590	1,024

The project has a positive NPV and would appear to be worthwhile. The sensitivity of each project variable is as follows.

(a) **Initial investment**

$$\text{Sensitivity} = \frac{1,024}{7,000} \times 100 = 14.6\%$$

(b) **Sales volume**

$$\text{Sensitivity} = \frac{1,024}{11,590 - 3,566} \times 100 = 12.8\%$$

(c) **Selling price**

$$\text{Sensitivity} = \frac{1,024}{11,590} \times 100 = 8.8\%$$

(d) **Variable costs**

$$\text{Sensitivity} = \frac{1,024}{3,566} \times 100 = 28.7\%$$

(e) **Cost of capital.** We need to calculate the IRR of the project. Let us try discount rates of 15% and 20%.

Year	Net cash flow $'000	Discount factor 15%	PV $'000	Discount factor 20%	PV $'000
0	(7,000)	1	(7,000)	1	(7,000)
1	4,500	0.870	3,915	0.833	3,749
2	4,500	0.756	3,402	0.694	3,123
			NPV = 317		NPV = (128)

$$IRR = 0.15 + \left[\frac{317}{317+128} \times (0.20 - 0.15)\right] = 18.56\%$$

The cost of capital can therefore increase by 132% before the NPV becomes negative.

The elements to which the NPV appears to be most sensitive are the selling price followed by the sales volume. Management should thus pay particular attention to these factors so that they can be carefully monitored.

2.2.1 Weaknesses of this approach to sensitivity analysis

These are as follows.

(a) The method requires that **changes** in each key variable are **isolated**. However management is more interested in the combination of the effects of changes in two or more key variables.

(b) Looking at factors in isolation is unrealistic since they are often **interdependent**.

(c) Sensitivity analysis does not examine the **probability** that any particular variation in costs or revenues might occur.

(d) **Critical factors** may be those over which managers have no control.

(e) In itself it does not provide a decision rule. Parameters defining **acceptability** must be laid down by managers.

Question 11.9 — Sensitivity analysis

Learning outcome: C(1)(a)(b)

Nevers Ure Co has a cost of capital of 8% and is considering a project with the following 'most-likely' cash flows.

Year	Purchase of plant $	Running costs $	Savings $
0	(7,000)		
1		2,000	6,000
2		2,500	7,000

Required

Measure the sensitivity (in percentages) of the project to changes in the levels of expected costs and savings.

2.3 Certainty equivalents

KEY TERM

CERTAINTY EQUIVALENT METHOD is an approach to dealing with risk in a capital budgeting context. It involves expressing risky future cash flows in terms of the certain cash flow which would be considered, by the decision-maker, as their equivalent, ie the decision-maker would be indifferent between the risky amount and the (lower) riskless amount considered to be its equivalent. *(CIMA Official Terminology)*

Another method of allowing for risk in investment appraisal is the **certainty equivalent approach**. By this method, the expected cash flows of the project are **converted to equivalent riskless amounts**. The greater the risk of an expected cash flow, the smaller the certainty equivalent value (for receipts) or the larger the certainty equivalent value (for payments).

The **disadvantage** of the certainty equivalent approach is that the amount of the adjustment to each cash flow is decided **subjectively** by management.

As the cash flows are reduced to supposedly certain amounts they should then be discounted at a **risk free rate**.

Example: Certainty equivalents

Dark Ages, whose cost of capital is 10%, is considering a project with the following expected cash flows.

	Year 0 £	Year 1 £	Year 2 £	Year 3 £
Cash flow	(10,000)	7,000	5,000	5,000
Discount factor @ 10%	1.000	0.909	0.826	0.751
Present value	(10,000)	6,363	4,130	3,755

NPV = £4,248

The project would seem to be worthwhile. However, because of the uncertainty about the future cash flows, the management decides to reduce them to certainty equivalents by taking only 70%, 60% and 50% of the years 1, 2 and 3 cash flows respectively. The risk free rate is 5%.

Solution

The risk-adjusted NPV of the project would be as follows.

	Year 0 £	Year 1 £	Year 2 £	Year 3 £
Cash flow	(10,000)	7,000	5,000	5,000
Certainty equivalent	1.00	0.70	0.60	0.50
Risk adjusted cash flow	(10,000)	4,900	3,000	2,500
Discount factor @ 5% risk free rate	1.000	0.952	0.907	0.864
Present value	(10,000)	4,665	2,721	2,160

NPV = (454)

The project is too risky and should be rejected.

2.4 Probability analysis

A **probability distribution** of '**expected cash flows**' can often be estimated, recognising there are several possible outcomes, not just one. This may be used to do the following.

STEP 1 Calculate an expected value of the NPV

STEP 2 Measure risk, for example in the following ways.

(a) By calculating the worst possible outcome and its probability
(b) By calculating the probability that the project will fail to achieve a positive NPV

Example: Probability estimates of cash flows

A company is considering a project involving the outlay of $300,000 which it estimates will generate cash flows over its two year life at the probabilities shown in the following table.

Cash flows for project

	Cash flow $	Probability
Year 1	100,000	0.25
	200,000	0.50
	300,000	0.25
		1.00

	If cash flow in Year 1 is: $	there is a probability of:	that the cash flow in Year 2 will be: $
Year 2	100,000	0.25	NIL
		0.50	100,000
		0.25	200,000
		1.00	
	200,000	0.25	100,000
		0.50	200,000
		0.25	300,000
		1.00	
	300,000	0.25	200,000
		0.50	300,000
		0.25	350,000
		1.00	

The cost of capital is 10% for this type of project.

You are required to calculate the expected value (EV) of the project's NPV and the probability that the NPV will be negative.

Solution

STEP 1 Calculate expected value of the NPV.

First we need to draw up a probability distribution of the expected cash flows. We begin by calculating the present values of the cash flows.

Year	Cash flow $'000	Discount factor 10%	Present value $'000
1	100	0.909	90.9
1	200	0.909	181.8
1	300	0.909	272.7
2	100	0.826	82.6
2	200	0.826	165.2
2	300	0.826	247.8
2	350	0.826	289.1

Year 1 PV of cash flow $'000	Probability	Year 2 PV of cash flow $'000	Probability	Joint probability	Total PV of cash inflows $'000	EV of PV of cash inflows $'000
(a)	(b)	(c)	(d)	(b) × (d)	(a) + (c)	
90.9	0.25	0.0	0.25	0.0625	90.9	5.681
90.9	0.25	82.6	0.50	0.1250	173.5	21.688
90.9	0.25	165.2	0.25	0.0625	256.1	16.006
181.8	0.50	82.6	0.25	0.1250	264.4	33.050
181.8	0.50	165.2	0.50	0.2500	347.0	86.750
181.8	0.50	247.8	0.25	0.1250	429.6	53.700
272.7	0.25	165.2	0.25	0.0625	437.9	27.369
272.7	0.25	247.8	0.50	0.1250	520.5	65.063
272.7	0.25	289.1	0.25	0.0625	561.8	35.113
						344.420

	$
EV of PV of cash inflows	344,420
Less project cost	300,000
EV of NPV	44,420

STEP 2 Measure risk.

Since the EV of the NPV is positive, the project should go ahead unless the risk is unacceptably high. The probability that the project will have a negative NPV is the probability that the total PV of cash inflows is less than $300,000. From the column headed 'Total PV of cash inflows', we can establish that this probability is 0.0625 + 0.125 + 0.0625 + 0.125 = 0.375 or 37.5%. This might be considered an unacceptably high risk.

2.4.1 Problems with expected values

There are the following problems with using expected values in making investment decisions

- An investment may be **one-off**, and 'expected' NPV may never actually occur
- **Assigning probabilities** to events is highly **subjective**
- Expected values **do not evaluate the range** of possible NPV outcomes

PART C INVESTMENT DECISIONS AND PROJECT CONTROL   11: Investment appraisal techniques

2.4.2 Decision trees

You will remember from other studies that decision trees are used to model a finite number of possible outcomes where more than one variable that affects the ultimate outcome is uncertain. In addition the value of some variables may be dependent on the value of other variables.

2.5 Simulation models

Simulation will overcome problems of having a very large number of possible outcomes, also the correlation of cash flows (a project which is successful in its early years is more likely to be successful in its later years).

Example: Simulation model

The following probability estimates have been prepared for a proposed project.

	Year	Probability	$
Cost of equipment	0	1.00	(40,000)
Revenue each year	1–5	0.15	40,000
		0.40	50,000
		0.30	55,000
		0.15	60,000
Running costs each year	1–5	0.10	25,000
		0.25	30,000
		0.35	35,000
		0.30	40,000

The cost of capital is 12%. Assess how a simulation model might be used to assess the project's NPV.

Solution

A simulation model could be constructed by assigning a range of random number digits to each possible value for each of the uncertain variables. The random numbers must exactly match their respective probabilities. This is achieved by working upwards cumulatively from the lowest to the highest cash flow values and assigning numbers that will correspond to probability groupings as follows.

Revenue				Running costs		
$	Prob	Random numbers		$	Prob	Random numbers
40,000	0.15	00 – 14	*	25,000	0.10	00 – 09
50,000	0.40	15 – 54	**	30,000	0.25	10 – 34
55,000	0.30	55 – 84	***	40,000	0.35	35 – 69
60,000	0.15	85 – 99		40,000	0.30	70 – 99

*   Probability is 0.15 (15%). Random numbers are 15% of range 00 – 99.
**   Probability is 0.40 (40%). Random numbers are 40% of range 00 – 99 but starting at 15.
***   Probability is 0.30 (30%). Random numbers are 30% of range 00 – 99 but starting at 55.

For revenue, the selection of a random number in the range 00 and 14 has a probability of 0.15. This probability represents revenue of $40,000. Numbers have been assigned to cash flows so that when numbers are selected at random, the cash flows have exactly the same probability of being selected as is indicated in their respective probability distribution above.

Random numbers would be generated, for example by a computer program, and these would be used to assign values to each of the uncertain variables.

For example, if random numbers 378420015689 were generated, the values assigned to the variables would be as follows.

Calculation	Revenue Random number	Value $	Costs Random number	Value $
1	37	50,000	84	40,000
2	20	50,000	01	25,000
3	56	55,000	89	40,000

A computer would calculate the NPV may times over using the values established in this way with more random numbers, and the results would be analysed to provide the following.

(a) An **expected NPV** for the project
(b) A **statistical distribution** pattern for the possible variation in the NPV above or below this average

The decision whether to go ahead with the project would then be made on the basis of **expected return** and **risk**.

2.6 Adjusted payback

The payback method of investment appraisal recognises uncertainty in investment decisions by focusing on the near future. Short-term projects are preferred to long-term projects and liquidity is emphasised.

One way of dealing with risk is to **shorten** the payback period required. A **maximum payback period** can be set to reflect the fact that risk increases the longer the time period under consideration. However, the disadvantages of payback as an investment appraisal method mean that adjusted payback cannot be recommended as a method of adjusting for risk.

2.7 Risk-adjusted discount rates

Investors want higher returns for higher risk investments. The greater the risk attached to future returns, the greater the risk premium required. Investors also prefer cash now to later and require a higher return for longer time periods.

In investment appraisal, a **risk-adjusted discount rate** can be used for particular types or **risk classes** of investment projects to reflect their relative risks. For example, a **high discount rate** can be used so that a cash flow which occurs quite some time in the future will have less effect on the decision. Alternatively, with the launch of a new product, a higher **initial** risk premium may be used with a decrease in the discount rate as the product becomes established.

Section summary

- **Risk** can be applied to a situation where there are several possible outcomes and, on the basis of past relevant experience, probabilities can be assigned to the various outcomes that could prevail.
- **Uncertainty** can be applied to a situation where there are several possible outcomes but there is little past relevant experience to enable the probability of the possible outcomes to be predicted.
- There are a wide range of techniques for incorporating risk into project appraisal.
- **Sensitivity analysis** assesses how responsive the project's NPV is to changes in the variables used to calculate that NPV.
- Project cash flows can be converted to equivalent riskless amounts under the **certainty equivalent approach**.
- A **probability analysis** of expected cash flows can often be estimated and used both to calculate an expected NPV and to measure risk.
- Other risk adjustment techniques include the use of **simulation** models, **adjusted payback** and **risk-adjusted discount rates**.

Chapter Roundup

- ✓ The **payback method** of project appraisal and the **ARR/ROCE/ROI method** of project appraisal are popular appraisal techniques despite their limitations.

- ✓ There are two methods of using **discounted cash flow** to appraise investment projects, the NPV method and the IRR method.

- ✓ The **NPV method** of project appraisal is to accept projects with a positive NPV.

- ✓ In investment appraisal, tax is often assumed to be payable **one year in arrears,** but you should read the question details carefully.

- ✓ (1+ money rate of return) = (1 + real rate of return) × (1 + rate of inflation)

- ✓ **Real cash flows** should be discounted at a **real discount rate** ('real at real').

- ✓ **Money cash flows** should be discounted at a **money discount rate** ('money at money').

- ✓ The **IRR method** of project appraisal is to accept projects whose IRR (the rate at which the NPV is zero) exceeds a target rate of return. The IRR is estimated either from a graph or using interpolation. The formula to apply is:

    $$IRR = a + \frac{NPV_a}{NPV_a - NPV_b} (b - a).$$

- ✓ When compared with the NPV method, the **IRR method** has a number of **disadvantages**.
    - It **ignores** the **relative size** of investments.
    - It is difficult to use if a project has **non-conventional cashflows** or when deciding between **mutually exclusive projects**.
    - **Discount rates** that **differ** over the life of a project cannot be included in IRR calculations, although the **modified internal rate of return** (MIRR) method can incorporate them.

- ✓ **Risk** can be applied to a situation where there are several possible outcomes and, on the basis of past relevant experience, probabilities can be assigned to the various outcomes that could prevail.

- ✓ **Uncertainty** can be applied to a situation where there are several possible outcomes but there is little past relevant experience to enable the probability of the possible outcomes to be predicted.

- ✓ There are a wide range of techniques for incorporating risk into project appraisal.

- ✓ **Sensitivity analysis** assesses how responsive the project's NPV is to changes in the variables used to calculate that NPV.

- ✓ Project cash flows can be converted to equivalent riskless amounts under the **certainty equivalent approach**.

- ✓ A **probability analysis** of expected cash flows can often be estimated and used both to calculate an expected NPV and to measure risk.

- ✓ Other risk adjustment techniques include the use of **simulation** models, **adjusted payback** and **risk-adjusted discount rates**.

Quick Quiz

1. Fill in the blank.

   .... is 'the time required for the cash inflows from a capital investment project to equal the cash outflows.'

2. Group the following items that occur in investment appraisal questions under the following headings.

   ☐ Include in investment appraisal   ☐ Exclude from investment appraisal

   - Depreciation
   - Sunk costs
   - Opportunity costs
   - Allocated costs and revenues
   - After tax incremental cash flows
   - Effect of tax allowances
   - Dividend/interest
   - Working capital requirements

3. Which equation links the money rate of return and the real rate of return?

4. Are cash flows that are given in terms of today's $s being given in money or real terms?

5. On what assumption is the Modified Internal Rate of Return based?

6. Give three examples of uncertain independent variables upon which the NPV of a project may depend.

7. How are simulation models constructed?

8. Describe in a sentence each three ways in which managers can reduce risk.

9. Sensitivity analysis allows for uncertainty in project appraisal by assessing the probability of changes in the decision variables.

   True ☐
   False ☐

10. Fill in the blank.

    The .... is where expected cashflows are converted to riskless equivalent amounts.

11. Give two examples of ways that risk can be measured in probability analysis.

12. Expected values can help an accountant evaluate the range of possible Net Present Value outcomes.

    True ☐
    False ☐

Answers to Quick Quiz

1. The payback period

2. | **Include** in **investment appraisal** | **Exclude** from **investment appraisal** |
   |---|---|
   | • Opportunity costs | • Depreciation |
   | • After tax incremental cash flows | • Sunk costs |
   | • Effect of tax allowances | • Allocated costs and revenues |
   | • Working capital requirements | • Dividends/interest |

3. (1 + money (nominal) rate of return) = (1 + real rate) (1 + inflation rate)

4. Real terms

5. Cash inflows are invested at the cost of capital

6. (a) Selling price
   (b) Sales volume
   (c) Cost of capital
   (d) Initial cost
   (e) Operating costs
   (f) Benefits

7. By assigning a range of random number digits to each possible value of each of the uncertain variables.

8. (a) Set maximum payback period.
   (b) Use high discounting rate.
   (c) Use sensitivity analysis to determine the critical factors within the decision-making process.
   (d) Use pessimistic estimates.

9. False. Sensitivity analysis does not assess probability.

10. Certainty-equivalent approach.

11. Calculating the worst possible outcome and its probability.

    Calculating the probability that the project will fail to achieve a positive NPV.

12. False

Answers to Questions

11.1 ARR

	$
Total profit before depreciation over four years	105,000
Total profit after depreciation over four years	25,000
Average annual profit after depreciation	6,250
Original cost of investment	80,000
Average net book value over the four year period $\dfrac{(80,000 + 0)}{2}$	40,000

The average ARR is 6,250 ÷ 40,000 = 15.625%.

The project would not be undertaken because it would fail to yield the target return of 20%.

11.2 NPVs

(a) $5,000 × 17% year 2 discount factor = $5,000 × 0.731 = $3,655

(b) $5,000 × 8.5% year 3 discount factor = $5,000 × $\dfrac{1}{(1.085)^3}$ = $3,915

(c) $5,000 × 16% year 5 cumulative discount factor (cdf) = 5,000 × 3.274 = $16,370

(d) $5,000 × (16% year 6 cdf − year 1 cdf) = 5,000 × (3.685 − 0.862) = $14,115

(e) $5,000 × (1 + 16% year 4 cdf) = 5,000 × (1 + 2.798) = $18,990

(f) $5,000 × 16.5% cdf = 5,000 × $\dfrac{(1 - (1 + 0.165)^{-5})}{0.165}$ = $16,182

11.3 Purchase of material

Savings are 75,000 × $(3.00 − 2.50) = $37,500 a year.

Additional costs are $7,500 a year.

Net cash savings are therefore $30,000 a year.

It is assumed that the machine will be sold for $10,000 at the end of year 4.

Year	Year 0 $	Year 1 $	Year 2 $	Year 3 $	Year 4 $
Cash flow	(90,000)	30,000	30,000	30,000	40,000
Discount factor @ 12%	1.000	0.893	0.797	0.712	0.636
Present value	(90,000)	26,790	23,910	21,360	25,440
NPV	7,500				

The NPV is positive and so the project is expected to earn more than 12% a year and is therefore acceptable.

11.4 Non-annual cash flows

Two months

Interest rate = $\sqrt[6]{1+0.16} - 1 = 2.50\%$

Discount factor = $\dfrac{1}{1.025} = 0.976$

Four months

Interest rate = $\sqrt[3]{1+0.16} - 1 = 5.07\%$

Discount factor = $\dfrac{1}{1.0507} = 0.952$

Six months

Interest rate = $\sqrt[2]{1+0.16} - 1 = 7.70\%$

Discount factor = $\dfrac{1}{1.0770} = 0.928$

Time (months)	Cash flow $	Discount factor @ 16%	Present value $
0	(2,000,000)	1.000	(2,000,000)
2	700,000	0.976	683,200
4	300,000	0.952	285,600
6	1,000,0000	0.928	928,000
1	250,000	0.862	215,500
			112,300

11.5 NPV with working capital

Working

Years 1–5   Contribution from new product £
5,000 × £(32 – 15)   85,000
Less contribution forgone
5,000 (4 × £1.50)   30,000
                                                55,000

	Year 0 £	Year 1 £	Years 1–5 £	Year 5 £
Contribution			55,000	
Equipment	(150,000)			10,000
Working capital	(10,000)	(5,000)		15,000
Net cash flows	(160,000)	(5,000)	55,000	25,000
Discount factor @ 20%	1.000	0.833	2.991*	0.402
Present value	(160,000)	(4,165)	164,505	10,050
NPV	**10,390**			

The NPV is positive and the project is worthwhile.

* The discount factor 2.991 applied to the annual contribution is an example of an **annuity factor**, which can be used for a series of equal annual cash flows starting at time 0. Annuity factors may be found from the table or from the formula, both given in the Appendix at the end of this text.

11.6 NPV with taxation

	Year 0 $	Year 1 $	Year 2 $	Year 3 $	Year 4 $
Purchase	(300,000)				
Inflation factor	1.000	1.100	1.210	1.331	
Cash flow after inflation	(300,000)	132,000	145,200	159,720	
Tax on cash inflow		(33,000)	(69,300)	(76,230)	(39,930)
Tax saved on tax-allowable depn (W)	18,750	32,813	24,609	42,187	31,640
Net cash flow	(281,250)	131,813	100,509	125,677	(8,290)
Discount factor at 11%	1.000	0.901	0.812	0.731	0.659
Present value	(281,250)	118,764	81,613	91,870	(5,463)

NPV = $5,534

The project should be undertaken at least from the financial viewpoint.

Workings

Tax-allowable depreciation (Initial cost $300,000)

Year		Tax-allowable depreciation $	Reducing balance (RB) $
0	(25% at cost)	75,000	225,000
1	(25% of RB)	56,250	168,750
2	(25% of RB)	42,188	126,562
3	(25% of RB)	31,641	94,921

Balancing allowance

	$
Sale proceeds, end of third year	–
RB, end of third year	94,921
Balancing allowance	94,921

Tax saved on tax-allowable depreciation

Year of claim	Tax-allowable depreciation claimed $	Tax saved $	Year of tax saving
0	75,000	37,500	0/1
1	56,250	28,125	1/2
2	42,188	21,094	2/3
3	126,562	63,281	3/4
	300,000		

11.7 NPV with inflation

The cash flows at inflated values are as follows.

Year	Fixed income £	Other savings £	Running costs £	Net cash flow £
1	2,500	500	1,000	2,000
2	2,500	525	1,100	1,925
3	2,500	551	1,210	1,841
4	2,500	579	1,331	1,748

The NPV of the project is as follows.

	Year 0 £	Year 1 £	Year 2 £	Year 3 £	Year 4 £
Net cash flow	(5,000)	2,000	1,925	1,841	1,748
Discount factor @ 16%	1.000	0.862	0.743	0.641	0.552
Present value	(5,000)	1,724	1,430	1,180	965
NPV	**299**				

The NPV is positive and the project would appear to be worthwhile.

11.8 IRR

Year	Cash flow $	Discount factor @ 10%	PV of cash flow $
0	(80,000)	1.000	(80,000)
1–5	20,000	3.791	75,820
5	10,000	0.621	6,210
NPV			2,030

This is fairly close to zero. It is also positive, which means that the IRR is more than 10%. We will try 12% next.

Year	Cash flow $	Discount factor @ 12%	PV of cash flow $
0	(80,000)	1.000	(80,000)
1–5	20,000	3.605	72,100
5	10,000	0.567	5,670
NPV			(2,230)

This is fairly close to zero and negative. The IRR is therefore greater than 10% but less than 12%. We shall now use the two NPV values to estimate the IRR, using the formula.

Internal rate of return = $10 + \left[\frac{2,030}{2,030 - 2,230} \times (12 - 10) \right]$ = 10.95%, say 11%

11.9 Sensitivity analysis

The PVs of the cash flows are as follows.

Year	Discount factor @ 8%	PV of plant cost $	PV of running costs $	PV of savings $	PV of net cash flow $
0	1.000	(7,000)			(7,000)
1	0.926		(1,852)	5,556	3,704
2	0.857		(2,143)	5,999	3,856
		(7,000)	(3,995)	11,555	560

The project has a positive NPV and would appear to be worthwhile. Sensitivity of the project to changes in the levels of expected costs and savings is as follows.

(a) **Plant costs sensitivity** = $\dfrac{560}{7,000} \times 100 = 8\%$

(b) **Running costs sensitivity** = $\dfrac{560}{3,995} \times 100 = 14\%$

(c) **Savings sensitivity** = $\dfrac{560}{11,555} \times 100 = 4.8\%$

Now try these questions from the Exam Question Bank

Number	Level	Marks	Time
Q16	Introductory	20 marks	35 mins
Q17	Introductory	n/a	35 mins
Q18	Examination	25 marks	45 mins

INTERNATIONAL INVESTMENT APPRAISAL

This chapter looks at the important issues that an entity has to consider when investing abroad. It exposes the entity to a wider range of risks.

International investment appraisal is highly examinable and adds more complications to the NPV calculations. A step-by-step logical approach is required and this chapter takes you through the techniques.

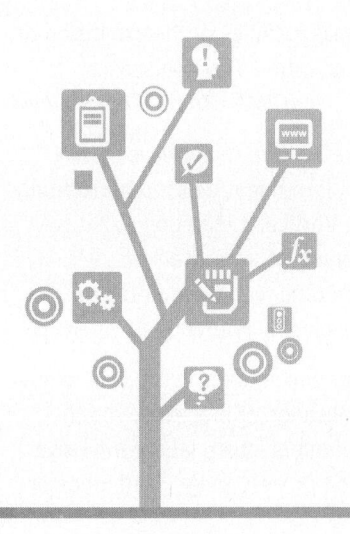

12

topic list	learning outcomes	syllabus references	ability required
1 International investment	C(1)(a)(b)	C(1)(i),(iv),(vi)	evaluation
2 International investment appraisal	C(1)(a)(b)	C(1)(i),(iv),(vi)	evaluation

1 International investment

> **Introduction**
> In this section we look at the reasons why an entity would choose to invest overseas and the risks and complications involved.

1.1 Why invest overseas?

We can summarise the reasons for overseas investment using 5 Cs:

The 5 Cs	Explanation
Company	An expansion strategy may create economies of scale as the company gets bigger.
Country	The company could locate near to high quality local supplies or access cheaper labour and government grants.
Customer	The company could locate closer to its end customer to enable shorter lead times.
Competition	Overseas markets may have weaker competition.
Currency	International investments can create costs which can be matched against revenues from that country and help to manage exchange rate risk.

We can summarise the reasons for overseas investment using 5 Cs:

KEY TERM

FOREIGN DIRECT INVESTMENT key (FDI) is the establishment of new overseas facilities or the expansion of existing overseas facilities, by an investor. FDI may be inward (domestic investment by overseas companies) or outward (overseas investment by domestic companies)   *(CIMA Official Terminology)*

FDI provides an alternative to growth restricted to a firm's domestic market. A firm might develop FDI provides an alternative to growth restricted to a firm's domestic market. A firm might develop **horizontally** in different countries, replicating its existing operations on a global basis. **Vertical** integration might have an international dimension through FDI to acquire raw material or component sources overseas (**backwards integration**) or to establish final production and distribution in other countries (**forward integration**). **Diversification** might alternatively provide the impetus to developing international interests.

FDI is likely to take place in the context of a **worldwide corporate strategy** which takes account of relative costs and revenues, tax considerations and **process specialisation** (specialisation of processes within particular production facilities). For example, some motor vehicle manufacturers locate labour-intensive processes in lower wage countries, leaving the final stage of the production process to be located nearer the intended market.

Strategy development is covered in Paper E3 *Enterprise Strategy* and your knowledge from this paper will be very useful in discussion questions on international investment.

1.2 Forms of overseas operations

Different forms of expansion overseas are available to meet various strategic objectives.

(a) Firms may expand by means of new **'start-up' investments**, for example the setting up of an **overseas subsidiary** to operate a manufacturing plant. This does allow flexibility, although it may be slow to achieve, expensive to maintain and slow to yield satisfactory results.

(b) A firm might **take over or merge with established firms abroad**. This provides a means of **purchasing market information**, **market share** and **distribution channels**. However, the better acquisitions will only be available at a premium.

(c) A **joint venture** with a local overseas partner might be entered into.

1.3 Joint ventures

KEY TERM

JOINT VENTURE is a contractual arrangement whereby two or more parties undertake an economic activity which is subject to joint control.
(IAS 31)

The two distinct types of joint venture are **industrial co-operation (contractual)**, and **joint-equity**. A contractual joint venture is for a fixed period and the duties and responsibility of the parties are contractually defined. A joint-equity venture involves investment, is of no fixed duration and continually evolves. It may be the best route in countries where full foreign ownership is discouraged.

There is a growing trend towards a contractual form of joint venture as a consequence of the **high research and development costs** and the **'critical mass'** necessary to take advantage of economies of scale in industries such as automobile engineering.

CASE STUDY

In March 2010, construction and engineering company McDermott International Inc announced its power generation subsidiary Babcock and Wilcox Co had formed a joint venture with Thermax Ltd in India. The purpose of the joint venture is to supply equipment for the Indian electricity generation market.

As well as enabling engineering, manufacture and management of large power projects in the Indian power section, Babcock and Wilcox will also license its technology to the venture. A new facility in India will also be built as part of the agreement.

1.4 Foreign subsidiaries

The basic structure of many multinationals consists of a parent company (a holding company) with subsidiaries in several countries. The subsidiaries may be wholly owned or just partly owned, and some may be owned through other subsidiaries.

1.4.1 The purpose of setting up subsidiaries abroad

The following are some reasons why a parent company might want to set up subsidiary companies in other countries.

- The location of markets
- The need for a sales organisation
- The opportunity to produce goods more cheaply
- The need to avoid import controls
- The need to obtain access to raw materials
- The availability of grants and tax concessions

1.4.2 Extracting profits

Whatever the reason for setting up subsidiaries abroad, the aim is to **increase the profits** of the **multinational's parent company**. However there are different approaches to increasing profits that the multinational might take.

(a) At one extreme, the **parent company** might **choose** to get **as much money** as it can **from the subsidiary**, and as quickly as it can. This would involve the transfer of all or most of the subsidiary's profits to the parent company.

(b) At the other extreme, the parent company might **encourage** a **foreign subsidiary** to **develop its business gradually**, to achieve long-term growth in sales and profits. To encourage growth, the subsidiary would be allowed to retain a large proportion of its profits, instead of remitting the profits to the parent company. A further consequence is that the economy of the country in which the subsidiary operates should be improved, with higher output adding to the country's gross domestic product and increasing employment.

1.4.3 Obtaining cash returns from an overseas subsidiary

If a subsidiary earns a profit, but then retains and reinvests the profits, the parent company will not get any cash at all. Various ways of obtaining a cash return are as follows.

(a) The subsidiary could make a profit and pay a **dividend** out of profits.

(b) The parent company could sell goods or services to the subsidiary and obtain payment. The amount of this payment will depend on the volume of sales and also on the **transfer price** for the sales.

(c) A parent company which grants a subsidiary the right to make goods protected by patents can charge a **royalty** on any goods that the subsidiary sells. The size of any royalty can be adjusted to suit the wishes of the parent company's management.

(d) If the parent company makes a **loan** to a subsidiary, it can set the interest rate high or low, thereby affecting the profits of both companies. A high rate of interest on a loan, for example, would improve the parent company's profits to the detriment of the subsidiary's profits.

(e) **Management charges** may be levied by the parent company for costs incurred in the management of international operations.

When the subsidiary is in a country where there are exchange control regulations, the parent company may have difficulty getting cash from the subsidiary.

1.4.4 Transfer pricing

When a foreign subsidiary makes a profit from goods/services supplied by its parent company, the profit will be included in the total profits of the multinational group. The management of the parent company must decide, however how the total profit of the group should be **divided** between the parent company and each of its subsidiaries, which is likely to depend on the **transfer prices** adopted.

Transfer pricing was covered in Paper P2 *Performance Management*.

1.5 Alternatives to FDI

(a) **Exporting** may be direct selling by the firm's own export division into the overseas markets, or it may be indirect through agents, distributors, trading companies and various other such channels. Exporting may be unattractive because of tariffs, quotas or other import restrictions in overseas markets, and local production may be the only feasible option in the case of bulky products such as cement and flat glass.

(b) **Licensing** involves conferring rights to make use of the licensor company's production process on producers located in the overseas market in return for royalty payments. Licensing can allow fairly rapid penetration of overseas markets and has the advantage that substantial financial resources will not be required. Many multinationals use a combination of various methods of servicing international markets, depending on the particular circumstances.

One famous example of licensing is Coca Cola which produces concentrate and sells it to licensed Coca Cola bottlers worldwide. These bottlers, which have exclusive territorial rights with the company, produce the finished products in bottles and cans using the 'secret formula' concentrate, filtered water and sweeteners. They are also responsible for selling and distributing the products to retailers and vending machines in their territory.

1.6 Countertrade

Countertrade is a general term used to describe a variety of commercial arrangements for reciprocal international trade or barter between companies or other organisations (eg state controlled organisations) in two or more countries.

COUNTERTRADE is a form of trading activity based on other than an arm's-length goods for cash exchange. Types of countertrade include:

- BARTER: the direct exchange of goods and services between two parties without the use of money

- COUNTERPURCHASE: a trading agreement in which the primary contract vendor agrees to make purchases of an agreed percentage of the primary contract value, from the primary contract purchaser, through a linked counterpurchase contract

- OFFSETS: a trading agreement in which the purchaser becomes involved in the production process, often acquiring technology supplied by the vendor

(CIMA Official Terminology)

Countertrade is **costly for the exporter**; it creates lengthy and cumbersome **administrative problems**, just to set up a countertrade arrangement. It is fraught with **uncertainty**, and deals can easily collapse or go wrong. Small and medium-sized firms might be unable and unwilling to accept the costs and administrative burdens of exporting by means of countertrade arrangements. However, in some situations, countertrade might be the **only way of securing export orders**.

1.7 Financing overseas investments   5/10, 9/10

The financing decision for overseas investments is crucial to the company as the correct decision can help to minimise the risks of such investments (discussed in the next section).

1.7.1 Financing overseas subsidiaries

There are several ways in which such subsidiaries may be financed.

(a) **Using free cash flows**

This is only suitable when the subsidiary has been established. The subsidiary will use its own internally generated funds to finance further investment programmes although this may not be enough for the required level of growth.

(b) **Using the parent company's home currency**

The parent company can raise the necessary finance in its own home capital markets and transfer this to the subsidiary via either equity or loans. The main advantage of this method is the likelihood of being able to raise funds more quickly as the capital markets will be familiar and the company is likely to be well known in these markets.

However there are several problems with this method of financing. There is no matching of foreign currency investment with foreign currency finance, thus exposing the company to significant risk. In addition, there may be exchange controls in place that limit the amount of foreign currency that is brought into the country.

(c) **Using the subsidiary's home currency**

Rather than raising finance in the parent company's home currency, the overseas investment could be raised in the currency of the subsidiary's location. This has the advantage of matching the finance currency with the investment currency, thus reducing (but not totally eliminating) foreign currency risk. The ease with which finance can be raised will depend on how well-developed the host country's capital markets are.

The use of the host country's finance may make the investment more acceptable to that country as not all of the subsidiary's profits will be sent back to the home country. Perhaps due to specific country exchange restrictions, there may be limitations on the amount of money that can be repatriated.

(d) **Using other countries' capital markets**

There is no reason why finance cannot be raised in a completely separate country. The mobility of funds means that finance for an investment in Hong Kong, for example, by a UK company may be raised in the USA, perhaps via a US subsidiary. This may happen if interest rates are more favourable in the 'independent' country, although this benefit will be counteracted by the strength of its currency relative to that of the home country.

1.8 The risks of overseas investments   11/10, 11/11, 5/12

The risks include the following.

(a) **Foreign exchange risks**

Any company that exports or imports faces the risk of **higher costs** or **lower revenues** because of adverse movements in foreign exchange rates.

A company that owns assets in different countries (subsidiaries abroad) faces the risk of accounting losses due to adverse movements in exchange rates causing a fall in the value of those assets, as expressed in domestic currency. Such companies may undertake foreign currency hedging activities to protect them from these losses (this is covered in detail in Paper P3 *Performance Strategy* and in outline below).

(b) **Political risks and country risks**

Economic or **political measures** could be taken by governments affecting the operations of its subsidiaries abroad. An example was the import restrictions imposed by the USA on the British cashmere industry during 1999, in retaliation for EU restrictions on banana imports.

(c) **Geographical separation**

The **geographical separation** of the **parent company** from its subsidiaries adds to the problems of management control of the group of companies as a whole.

(d) **Litigation risk**

The risk of litigation varies in different countries and to minimise this risk, attention should be paid to **legislation** and **regulations** covering the products sold in different countries. Care should be taken to comply with contract terms.

(e) **Risk of loss of goods in transit**

It may be possible to **insure** against this risk.

1.9 Hedging foreign exchange risk

As noted above, foreign exchange risk is a major factor in overseas investments. Exposure to exchange rate movements can result in significant transaction risk – the risk between the date of a transaction and its settlement date.

Example: Transaction risk

Minnie plc sells materials to a US customer and invoices in US dollars, exchanging these dollars for sterling when the transaction is settled. The customer receives an invoice for $105,000. The current exchange rate (spot rate) is £/$1.50 (that is, £1 = $1.50) and the customer will settle the invoice in one month's time.

One month later, the exchange rate has moved to £1/$1.52 (that is, £1 = $1.52). When the transaction was entered into, the sterling value of the materials was $105,000/$1.50 = £70,000. However when the transaction came to be settled, Minnie plc only received £69,078. Minnie plc thus lost £922 through exchange rate movements.

To protect themselves against foreign exchange risk, companies may use either internal or external **hedging** techniques.

1.9.1 Internal hedging techniques

(a) **Invoicing in the home currency**

This transfers the risk from your own company to your customers. In the example above, Minnie plc would have invoiced the customer for £70,000 (the sterling value of the materials) and the customer would have to exchange dollars for sterling in order to pay the invoice. However this method may make the company uncompetitive if there are other suppliers willing to invoice in dollars.

(b) **Matching**

This is the same as financing overseas investments in the host country's currency. The payments in a foreign currency are matched with receipts in the same currency. It is most commonly used by multinational companies where considerable inter-company trading takes place between subsidiaries. This type of internal hedging may benefit from a foreign currency bank account held either with the parent's company's own bank or with a bank in the host country. However, exact matching may be difficult, especially where there are few foreign currency transactions.

(c) **Leading and lagging**

This form of internal hedging involves taking advantage of exchange rate movements by altering the timing of payments or receipts.

Leading may involve a company reducing the time allowed to a customer for payment, if the company's home currency (in which the transaction will be settled) is weakening against the customer's currency. Lagging may involve a company extending longer payment terms to a customer if the company's home currency is weakening against the customer's currency and payment will be received in the latter.

In order for this technique to work effectively, it must be possible to make exchange rate predictions with some degree of confidence.

(d) **Netting**

This is similar to matching and is used principally by multinational companies.

Bilateral netting occurs where two companies within the same group net off their payments and receipts to each other.

Multilateral netting occurs when several companies within the same group interact with head office and the central treasury department to net off their transactions.

The process involves establishing a '**base**' currency to record all intra-group transactions and all subsidiaries inform the central treasury department of their transactions with each other. Central treasury will then inform each subsidiary of the outstanding amount payable or receivable to settle the intra-group transactions.

Whilst this procedure has the advantages of reducing the number of transactions (and thus transactions costs) and also reducing foreign currency risk, it requires strict control procedures from central treasury. In addition there are countries with severe restrictions on, or even prohibition of, netting, as well as legal and tax issues to consider.

1.9.2 External hedging techniques

Companies may use the external financial markets to hedge their foreign currency risk. The most popular techniques are summarised below.

(a) **Forward contracts**

A forward contract allows a company to arrange for a bank to buy or sell a quantity of foreign currency at a future date (for example in three months' time) at an exchange rate determined when the contract is entered into. This rate is known as the 'forward rate'. The company will therefore know in advance how much local currency it will receive (if selling foreign currency) or how much home currency must be paid (if buying foreign currency). Regardless of what the spot rate is at the time of maturity (known as the **settlement date**), the contract must be exercised.

Example: Forward contract

Ally plc has purchased materials for €250,000 from a German supplier with payment due in three months' time. Payment is required in euros. Ally plc is considering entering into a forward contract to hedge against movements in the £/€ exchange rate. The three month forward rate is 1.0900 – 1.0950.

How much will the materials cost in sterling if Ally plc enters into a three month forward contract?

Solution

The exchange rate in three months' time is £/€1.0900 (that is, £1 = €1.0900), therefore €250,000 will cost:

€250,000/1.0900 = £229,358

Note that even if the spot rate when the transaction was settled was, for example, £/€1.10 (which would have meant that the materials would only have cost £227,272) Ally plc must buy the euros at the **contracted** rate.

(b) **Money market hedge**

There is a close relationship between forward exchange rates and interest rates in the currencies involved in a transaction. It is therefore possible to 'manufacture' a forward rate by using the spot exchange rate and money market lending or borrowing. This is known as a 'money market hedge'.

There are four steps involved in setting up a money market hedge for foreign currency payments.

STEP 1 Determine how much foreign currency must be deposited now to have sufficient funds to pay supplier at the payment date

STEP 2 Determine how much this will cost in your home currency using the prevailing spot rate

STEP 3 When the time comes to pay
(a) Pay the supplier out of the foreign currency bank account
(b) Repay the home currency loan

Example: Money market hedge

Westwood plc buys goods from a Danish supplier with payment of Kr500,000 due in three months' time. The spot exchange rate is £/Kr 7.5509 – 7.5548. Westwood plc can borrow in sterling at the rate of 5% per annum and can deposit kroner at the rate of 7% per annum. What is the cost in sterling with a money market hedge and what effective forward rate would this represent?

Solution

The 3 month rates for sterling and kroner are 1.25% and 1.75% respectively.

(i) How many kroner must be deposited now to obtain Kr500,000 in 3 months' time?

Kr500,000/1.0175 = Kr491,400

(ii) How much will this cost in sterling at a spot rate of 7.5509?

Kr491,400/7.5509 = £65,078

(iii) Borrow £65,078 now at a rate of 1.25% for 3 months

Cost = £65,078 × 1.0125 = £65,891

(iv) Pay the Danish supplier using the money deposited in the kroner bank account and repay the sterling loan.

At the date of payment, Kr500,000 is paid to the Danish supplier which has cost Westwood plc £65,891. The effective forward rate is therefore Kr500,000/£65,891 = £/Kr7.588.

FUTURES CONTRACTS are contracts to buy or sell an amount of foreign currency at a future date.

(c) **Futures**

Futures contracts are conceptually similar to forward contracts but have certain important differences.

(i) Futures contracts are traded in organised, centralised exchanges such as the Chicago Mercantile Exchange, whereas forward contracts are traded '**over the counter**' in a geographically dispersed market.

(ii) Futures contracts are standardised in terms of the currencies that can be traded, the amounts and the maturity dates. Forward contracts can be **customised** to meet particular customer needs.

(iii) Futures contracts are '**marked to market**' and adjusted daily. There are initial and maintenance margins and daily cash settlements. Forward contracts do not require any cash payment until maturity.

(iv) As the futures exchange quotes daily prices for futures contracts, these contracts may be sold before their delivery date. However the contracts must be for specific amounts of currency and there are limited delivery dates. Forward contracts are customised for particular customers and are therefore not saleable.

A **CURRENCY OPTION** s an agreement that gives the holder the right, but not the obligation, to buy (call option) or sell (put option) a certain amount of currency at a stated rate of exchange (the strike price) at some point in the future.

AN AMERICAN OPTION can be exercised at any point up to and including the exercise date. A **European option** can only be exercised on the agreed exercise date.

(d) **Options**

Buying a currency option involves paying a premium, the level of which will depend on a number of factors.

(i) **The strike price**

The strike price might be in one of three states:

In the money – where the agreed price is more favourable to the holder than the currently available spot rate. The premium is likely to be higher in this case.

At the money – where the agreed price is the same as the currently available spot rate.

Out of the money – where the agreed price is less favourable to the holder than the currently available spot rate. The premium is likely to be low (maybe zero) in this case.

(ii) **Volatility of the spot rate**

The greater the volatility, the higher the premium is likely to be.

(iii) **Maturity**

The greater the time to maturity, the higher the premium is likely to be, as the holder is being protected from increasing uncertainty and risk.

(iv) **Other factors**

These include liquidity in the market, judgmental factors and sentiment.

Example: Options and forward contracts

Crabtree Inc is expecting to receive 20 million South African rands (R) in one month's time. The current spot rate is £/R 19.3383 – 19.3582. Compare the results of the following actions.

(a) The receipt is hedged using a forward contract at the rate 19.3048.

(b) The receipt is hedged by buying an over-the-counter (OTC) option from the bank, exercise price £/R 19.300, premium cost 12 pence per 100 schillings.

(c) The receipt is not hedged.

In each case compute the results if, in one month, the exchange rate moves to:

(i) 21.0000
(ii) 17.6000

Solution

The target receipt at today's spot rate is 20,000,000/19.3582 = £1,033,154.

(a) The receipt using a forward contract is fixed with certainty at 20,000,000/19.3048 = £1,036,012. This applies to both exchange rate scenarios.

(b) The cost of the option is 20,000,000/100 × 12/100 = £24,000. This must be paid at the start of the contract.

The results under the two scenarios are as follows.

Scenario	(i)	(ii)
Exchange rate	21.0000	17.6000
Strike price	19.3000	19.3000
Exercise option?	YES	NO
Exchange rate used	19.3000	17.6000
	£	£
Sterling received	1,036,269	1,136,364
Less option premium	24,000	24,000
Net receipt	1,012,269	1,112,364

(c) The results of not hedging under the two scenarios are as follows.

Scenario	(i)	(ii)
Exchange rate	21.0000	17.6000
Sterling received	$952,381	$1,136,364

Summary. The option gives a result between that of the forward contract and no hedge.

- If the South African rand weakens to 21.0000, the best result would have been obtained using the forward market (£1,036,012).

- If it strengthens to 17.6000, the best course of action would have been to take no hedge (£1,136,364).

- In both cases the option gives the second best result, being £24,000 below the best because of its premium cost.

1.10 Implications of international investment

You should be aware of the **strategic** implications of international expansion from your other CIMA strategic studies such as specific country factors and economies of scale.

There are a couple of financial implications of international investment that should also be considered:

(a) International investments will usually be more risky than domestic investments. Therefore the **cost of capital** is likely to increase as a result.

(b) If the assets of the investment are denominated in a foreign currency then they will have to be converted to the reporting currency for consolidation. This is an example of **translation risk**.

1.11 Tax implications of international investment

Taxation issues can influence the manner in which the foreign investment is set up and returns received by the parent company (eg by **transfer pricing).**

If a company makes investments abroad it will be liable to income tax in the home country on the profits made, the taxable amount being before the deduction of any foreign taxes. The profits may be any of the following.

- **Profits of an overseas branch** or agency
- **Income from foreign securities**, for example debentures in overseas companies
- **Dividends from overseas subsidiaries**
- **Gains** made on disposals of foreign assets

In many instances, a company will be potentially subject to overseas taxes as well as to local income tax on the same profits. There are however various ways that this may be avoided partly or wholly.

Exam alert

Assume any intercompany cash flows are allowable for tax purposes in an exam question, unless the question specifically states otherwise. State this assumption in your answer.

1.12 Double taxation relief (DTR)

A DOUBLE TAXATION AGREEMENT is an agreement between two countries intended to avoid the double taxation of income which would otherwise be subject to taxation in both. *(CIMA Official Terminology)*

Typical provisions of double taxation agreements based on the OECD Model Agreement are as follows.

(a) DTR is given to taxpayers in their **country of residence** by way of a credit for tax suffered in the country where income arises. This may be in the form of relief for withholding tax only or, given a holding of specified size in a foreign company, for the underlying tax on the profits out of which dividends are paid.

(b) **Total exemption from tax** is given in the country where income arises in the hands of, for example:
   (i) Visiting diplomats
   (ii) Teachers on exchange programmes

(c) **Preferential rates of withholding tax** are applied to, for example, payments of rent, interest and dividends. The usual rate is frequently replaced by 15% or less.

(d) There are **exchange of information** clauses so that tax evaders can be chased internationally.

(e) There are **rules to determine** a person's residence and to prevent dual residence (tie-breaker clauses).

(f) There are **clauses** which render certain profits taxable in only one rather than both of the contracting states.

(g) There is a **non-discrimination clause** so that a country does not tax foreigners more heavily than its own nationals.

Example: Double taxation relief

Suppose the tax rate on profits in the Federal West Asian Republic is 20%, the UK company tax is 30%, and there is a double taxation agreement between the two countries.

A subsidiary of a UK firm operating in the Federal West Asian Republic earns the equivalent of £1 million in profit, and therefore pays £200,000 in tax on profits. When the profits are remitted to the UK, the UK parent can claim a credit of £200,000 against the full UK tax charge of £300,000, and hence will only pay £100,000.

Exam skills

There are a number of different approaches you can take with taxation in an International NPV exam question. If you are stuck in the exam, the best approach is to make it clear you recognise the principle of double taxation relief, make a simplifying assumption and move on.

> **Section summary**
>
> - Reasons for overseas investment can be explained by the 5 Cs: Company, Country, Customer, Competition, Currency.
> - **Foreign direct investment (FDI)** will generally be undertaken if exporting is more costly than overseas production.
> - Overseas investments may be financed by:
>   - Free cash flow from the subsidiary
>   - Funds raised in the parent company's home capital markets and its own currency
>   - Funds raised in the host country's capital markets and in that country's currency
>   - Funds raised in other countries' capital markets
> - The **risks** of overseas investment include exchange rate risk, political risk, geographical separation, litigation risk and risk of loss of good in transit.
> - Internal hedging techniques include:
>   - Invoicing in the home currency
>   - Matching
>   - Leading and lagging
>   - Netting
> - External hedging techniques include:
>   - Forward contracts
>   - Money market hedge
>   - Futures
>   - Options
> - **Double taxation relief** is where governments give a tax credit for foreign tax paid on overseas profits.

2 International investment appraisal   5/10, 11/11, 5/12

Introduction

In this section we look at the complications in investment appraisal calculations where there is an international element. These include exchange rates, differing inflation rates and taxation.

Exam alert

In the exam, if you are given an exchange rate of US$/£0.89 this means that US$1 = £0.89.

2.1 Forecasting exchange rates

Inflation rates are often used in exams to forecast exchange rate movements.

Purchasing power parity

$$\text{Future spot rate A\$/B\$} = \text{Spot rate A\$/B\$} \times \frac{1 + \text{country B inflation rate}}{1 + \text{country A inflation rate}}$$

Example: Forecasting exchange rates

The $/£ exchange rate in January 2010 was 0.645 (that is, $1 = £0.645); inflation in the US was 2.6% and 3.4% in the UK.

Required

Calculate the forecast spot rate in each of the next three years for the $/£.

Solution

Year 1: 0.645 × 1.034/1.026 = 0.650

Year 2: 0.650 × 1.034/1.026 = 0.655

Year 3: 0.655 × 1.034/1.026 = 0.660

Question 12.1 — Forecasting exchange rates

Learning outcome: C(1)(b)

The £/€ exchange rate in April 2010 was £/€1.138 (that is, £1 = €1.138); inflation in Europe was 1.5% and 3.7% in the UK

Required

Calculate the forecast spot rate in each of the next three years for the £/€.

2.1.1 An alternative approach

You may be given an exchange rate and told that one of the currencies is appreciating/depreciating against the other. The way you calculate the new rates depends on which currency is appreciating/depreciating. It is important to identify the **base currency**.

Example: Appreciating/depreciating currencies

The currency exchange rate £/$ is £1 = $1.55. Consider the following separate situations.

(a) Suppose you are told that the $ will appreciate against the £ by 3% for the next two years.

The $ is not the base currency (that is, it is not quoted as $1 = £X), therefore you will **divide** the current spot rate by 1.03 (to indicate that it now takes 3% fewer $ to purchase £1).

Year	Exchange rate
0	£1 = $1.55
1	£1 = $1.55/1.03 = $1.505
2	£1 = $1.505/1.03 = $1.461

(b) You are now told that the $ will depreciate against the £ by 5% for the next two years.

You will therefore **divide** the current spot rate by 0.95 (to indicate that it now takes 5% more $ to purchase £1).

Year	Exchange rate
0	£1 = $1.55
1	£1 = $1.55/0.95 = $1.632
2	£1 = $1.632/0.95 = $1.718

(c) The £ is expected to appreciate by 4% against the $.

As the £ is the base currency, we will **multiply** the current spot rate by 1.04 (to indicate that £1 can buy 4% more $ than the previous year).

Year	Exchange rate
0	£1 = $1.55
1	£1 = $1.55 x 1.04 = $1.612
2	£1 = $1.612 x 1.04 = $1.676

(d) The £ is expected to depreciate by 3% against the $.

We will multiply the spot rate by 0.97 (to indicate that £1 can buy 3% fewer $ than the previous year).

Year	Exchange rate
0	£1 = $1.55
1	£1 = $1.55 x 0.97 = $1.504
2	£1 = $1.504 x 0.97 = $1.459

Exam skills

Examiners have commented that the calculation of forward rates and conversion of currencies has been surprisingly poor. Make sure you are confident with these calculations as they are likely to be required in your exam.

If **interest rates** are given instead of inflation rates, you can use the following formula:

Interest rate parity (Expectations theory)

$$\text{Future spot rate A\$/B\$} = \text{Spot rate A\$/B\$} \times \frac{1 + \text{nominal country B interest rate}}{1 + \text{nominal country A interest rate}}$$

2.2 The techniques for foreign project appraisal

Depending upon the information which is available, two alternative NPV methods are available. Both methods produce the NPV in domestic currency terms. For a UK company investing overseas, we can:

(a) **Convert the project cash flows** into **sterling** and then discount at a sterling discount rate to calculate the NPV in sterling terms, or

(b) **Discount the cash flows** in the **host country's currency** from the project at an **adjusted discount rate** for that currency and then convert the resulting NPV at the spot exchange rate.

12: International investment appraisal

Adjusted discount rate to use in international budgeting (International Fisher effect)

$$\frac{1 + \text{annual discount rate B\$}}{1 + \text{annual discount rate A\$}} = \frac{\text{Future spot rate A\$/B\$ in 12 months' time}}{\text{Spot rate A\$/B\$}}$$

The approach to be chosen will depend on the available information and the extent to which **forecasts are reliable**. Both approaches should give the same answer, provided that the approach used to predict future exchange rates (interest rate parity or purchasing power parity) holds true.

Example: Overseas investment appraisal

Bromwich, a UK company, is considering undertaking a new project in Horavia. This will require initial capital expenditure of H$1,250m, with no scrap value envisaged at the end of the five year lifespan of the project. There will also be an initial working capital requirement of H$500m, which will be recovered at the end of the project. Pre-tax net cash inflows of H$800m are expected to be generated each year from the project.

Company tax will be charged in Horavia at a rate of 40%, with depreciation on a straight-line basis being an allowable deduction for tax purposes. Horavian tax is paid at the end of the year following that in which the taxable profits arise.

There is a double taxation agreement between the UK and Horavia, which means that no UK tax will be payable on the project profits.

The spot rate is £/H$336 (that is, £1 = H$336), and the Horavian dollar is expected to appreciate against the £ by 5% per year.

A project of similar risk recently undertaken by Bromwich in the UK had a required post-tax rate of return of 16%.

Should the Horavian project be undertaken?

Solution

Method 1 – conversion of flows into sterling and discounting at sterling discount rate

	Time 0	Time 1	Time 2	Time 3	Time 4	Time 5	Time 6
H$m flows							
Capital	(1,750)					500	
Net cash inflows		800	800	800	800	800	
Taxation (W1)			(220)	(220)	(220)	(220)	(220)
	(1,750)	800	580	580	580	1,080	(220)
Exchange rate (W2)	336	319	303	288	274	260	247
£m flows	(5.21)	2.51	1.91	2.01	2.12	4.15	(0.89)
16% df	1.000	0.862	0.743	0.641	0.552	0.476	0.410
PV	(5.21)	2.16	1.42	1.29	1.17	1.98	(0.36)

NPV = £2.45m

Workings

(1) Taxation

	H$m
Net cash inflow	800
Less: depreciation (1,250/5)	(250)
	550 @ 40% = H$220m

(2) *Exchange rate*

Current spot = £/H$336 (that is, £1 = H$336). If the H$ is *appreciating* against the £, this means that the H$ is getting more valuable in terms of £, ie there will be more £ per H$ or *less* H$ per £.

Thus in one year's time the £/H$ rate will fall by 5%, to 95% × 336 = 319, etc.

Method 2 – discounting foreign cash flows at an adjusted discount rate

If we are to keep the cash flows in H$, and they need to be discounted at a rate that takes account of both the domestic discount rate (16%) and the rate at which the exchange rate is expected to decrease (5%).

$$\frac{1 + \text{Horavian disount rate}}{1 + \text{UK discount rate}} = \frac{\text{Future spot rate £ / H\$}}{\text{Spot rate £ / H\$}}$$

$$\frac{1 + I_H}{1.16} = \frac{319}{336}$$

$$1 + I_H = 1.10$$

Thus the adjusted discount rate is 10%.

Discounting the H$ flows at this rate:

	Time 0	Time 1	Time 2	Time 3	Time 4	Time 5	Time 6
H$m flows							
Capital	(1,750)	800	580	580	580	1,080	(220)
10% df	1	0.909	0.826	0.751	0.683	0.621	0.564
PV	(1,750)	727.1	479.1	435.6	396.1	670.7	(124.1)

NPV = H$834.6m

Translating this present value at the spot rate gives H$834.6/336 = £2.48m

This method is useful if the currency flows are annuities and the adjusted discount rate is a round number, as the computation can be reduced by the use of annuity tables.

Question 12.2 — Overseas investment appraisal

Learning outcome: C(1)(b)

Donegal is considering whether to establish a subsidiary in Ruritania, at a cost of Ruritanian $2,400,000. This would be represented by non-current assets of $2,000,000 and working capital of $400,000. The subsidiary would produce a product which would achieve annual sales of $1,600,000 and incur cash expenditures of $1,000,000 a year.

The company has a planning horizon of four years, at the end of which it expects the realisable value of the subsidiary's non-current assets to be $800,000. It expects also to be able to sell the rights to make the product for $500,000 at the end of four years.

It is the company's policy to remit the maximum funds possible to the parent company at the end of each year.

Tax is payable at the rate of 35% in Ruritania and is payable one year in arrears.

Tax allowable depreciation is at a rate of 25% on a straight line basis on all non-current assets.

Administration costs of £100,000 per annum will be incurred each year in the UK over the expected life of the project.

The UK taxation rate on taxable profits made in Ruritania and remitted to the UK, and on UK income and expenditure is 30%, payable one year in arrears.

The exchange rate is £/Ruritanian$5 (that is, £1 = Ruritanian $5)..

The company's cost of capital for the project is 10%.

Calculate the NPV of the project.

Section summary

To appraise overseas projects do ONE of the following:

- **Convert the project cash flows** into **the domestic currency** and then discount at a domestic discount rate to calculate the NPV in domestic currency terms

- **Discount the cash flows** in the **host country's currency** from the project at an **adjusted discount rate** for that currency and then convert the resulting NPV at the spot exchange rate.

Chapter Roundup

- Reasons for overseas investment can be explained by the 5 Cs: Company, Country, Customer, Competition, Currency.

- **Foreign direct investment (FDI)** will generally be undertaken if exporting is more costly than overseas production.

- Overseas investments may be financed by:
  - Free cash flow from the subsidiary
  - Funds raised in the parent company's home capital markets and its own currency
  - Funds raised in the host country's capital markets and in that country's currency
  - Funds raised in other countries' capital markets

- The risks of overseas investment include exchange rate risk, political risk, geographical separation, litigation risk and risk of loss of good in transit.

- Internal hedging techniques include:
  - Invoicing in the home currency
  - Matching
  - Leading and lagging
  - Netting

- External hedging techniques include:
  - Forward contracts
  - Money market hedge
  - Futures
  - Options

- **Double taxation relief** is where governments give a tax credit for foreign tax paid on overseas profits.

- To appraise overseas projects do ONE of the following:
  - **Convert the project cash flows** into **the domestic currency** and then discount at a domestic discount rate to calculate the NPV in domestic currency terms
  - **Discount the cash flows** in the **host country's currency** from the project at an **adjusted discount rate** for that currency and then convert the resulting NPV at the spot exchange rate.

Quick Quiz

1. What are the 5 C reasons for overseas investment?
2. Give three examples of political risk.
3. Give three examples of countertrade.
4. What is a double taxation agreement?
5. How should the domestic discount rate be adjusted if the foreign project flows are to be discounted?

Answers to Quick Quiz

1. Company, Country, Customer, Competition, Currency
2. Political risk is the risk of a foreign government increasing interest rates or corporation tax or seizing assets.
3. Countertrade can be barter, counterpurchase or offsets
4. An agreement between countries to avoid or minimise double taxation on profits earned abroad which are also taxable in the investor's home country
5. (1 + adjusted discount rate) = (1 + domestic discount rate) (1 + expected rate at which foreign exchange rate is expected to change)

Answers to Questions

12.1 Forecasting exchange rates

1.138 × 1.015/1.037 = 1.114

1.114 × 1.015/1.037 = 1.090

1.090 × 1.015/1.037 = 1.067

Note: The exchange rate is quoted as £ to € so the € inflation rate is divided by the £ inflation rate.

12.2 Overseas investment appraisal

	Time					
	0	1	2	3	4	5
$'000 cash flows						
Sales receipts		1,600	1,600	1,600	1,600	
Costs		(1,000)	(1,000)	(1,000)	(1,000)	
Tax allowable depreciation (brought in to calculate taxable profit)		(500)	(500)	(500)	(500)	
$ taxable profit		100	100	100	100	
Taxation			(35)	(35)	(35)	(35)
Add back tax allowable depreciation (as not a cash flow)		500	500	500	500	
Capital expenditure	(2,000)					
Scrap value					800	
Tax on scrap value (W1)						(280)
Terminal value					500	
Tax on terminal value						(175)
Working capital	(400)				400	
	(2,400)	600	565	565	2,265	(490)
Exchange rates	5:1	5:1	5:1	5:1	5:1	5:1
£'000 cash flows						
From/(to) Ruritania	(480)	120	113	113	453	(98)
Additional UK tax (W2)			(6)	(6)	(6)	(84)
Additional UK expenses/income		(100)	(100)	(100)	(100)	
UK tax effect of UK expenses/income			30	30	30	30
Net sterling cash flows	(480)	20	37	37	377	(152)
UK discount factors	1	0.909	0.826	0.751	0.683	0.621
Present values	(480)	18	31	28	257	(94)

NPV = (£240,000), therefore the company should not proceed.

Workings

(1) Tax is payable on $800,000 as tax written down value = $2,000,000 − (4 × $500,000) = 0

(2) Years 1–3

$ taxable profit = $100,000

At £/Ruritanian$5 exchange rate = £20,000

Tax at 30% = £6,000

Year 4

$ taxable profit = $100,000 + $800,000 + $500,000 = $1,400,000

At £/Ruritanian$5 exchange rate = £280,000

Tax at 30% = £84,000

Assume tax is fully payable in both countries.

Now try these questions from the Exam Question Bank

Number	Level	Marks	Time
Q19	Examination	20 marks	35 mins
Q20	Introductory	n/a	30 mins

SPECIFIC INVESTMENT APPRAISAL SCENARIOS

In this chapter, we examine some further **applications of discounted cash flow (DCF)** techniques. An enterprise may be faced with more investment opportunities than it can finance with the capital available, and we look first at how **capital rationing** may affect the investment decision.

We then examine various techniques that can be used to deal with complications in investment decisions. The **equivalent annual cost** method can be used when maintenance costs are an important element in an investment decision. **Real option theory** can be used to assist when organisations have to or can make further decisions after the initial investment decision. The **adjusted present value method** provides a better means of taking into account the effects of using loan finance than simple NPV analysis does.

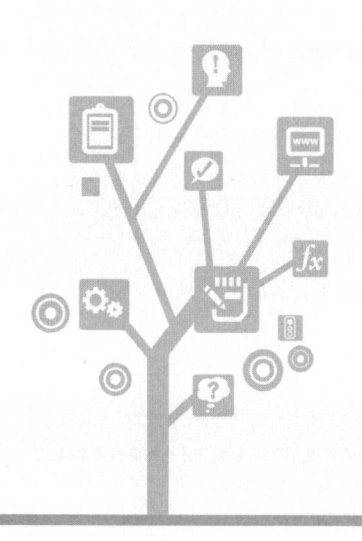

topic list	learning outcomes	syllabus references	ability required
1 Capital rationing	C(1)(d)	C(1)(xv)	evaluation
2 Equivalent annual cost	C(1)(a)(c)	C(1)(i),(iv)	evaluation
3 Real options	C(1)(d)	C(1)(xiv)	evaluation
4 Adjusted present value	C(1)(b)(c)	C(1)(viii)	evaluation

1 Capital rationing

Introduction

We have seen in the last two chapters that the decision rule with DCF techniques is to accept all projects which result in positive NPVs when discounted at the company's cost of capital. If an entity suffers capital rationing, it will not be able to enter into all projects with positive NPVs because there is not enough capital for all the investments. In this section we look at techniques to deal with this problem.

KEY TERM

CAPITAL RATIONING is a restriction on an organisation's ability to invest capital funds, caused by an internal budget ceiling being imposed on such expenditure by management (**soft capital rationing**), or by external limitations being applied to the company, as when additional borrowed funds cannot be obtained (**hard capital rationing**). *(CIMA Official Terminology)*

If an organisation is in a capital rationing situation it will not be able to invest in all available projects which have positive NPVs because there is not enough capital for all of the investments. Capital is a **limiting factor**.

1.1 Soft and hard capital rationing

Capital rationing may be necessary in a business due to **internal factors** (soft capital rationing) or **external factors** (hard capital rationing).

Soft capital rationing may arise for one of the following reasons.

(a) Management may be **reluctant to issue additional share capital** because of concern that this may lead to outsiders gaining control of the business.

(b) Management may be **unwilling to issue additional share capital** if it will lead to a dilution of earnings per share.

(c) Management may **not want to raise additional debt capital** because they do not wish to be committed to large fixed interest payments.

(d) There may be a desire within the organisation to **limit investment** to a level that can be financed solely from retained earnings.

(e) **Capital expenditure budgets** may restrict spending.

Note that whenever an organisation adopts a policy that restricts funds available for investment, such a policy may be less than optimal as the organisation may reject projects with a positive net present value and forgo opportunities that would have enhanced the market value of the organisation.

Hard capital rationing may arise for one of the following reasons.

(a) Raising money through the stock market may not be possible if **share prices are depressed**.

(b) There may be **restrictions on bank lending** due to government control.

(c) Lending institutions may consider an organisation to be too **risky** to be granted further loan facilities.

(d) The **costs** associated with making small issues of capital may be too great.

1.2 Divisible and non-divisible projects

(a) **Divisible projects** are those which can be undertaken completely or in fractions. Suppose that project A is divisible and requires the investment of $15,000 to achieve an NPV of $4,000. $7,500 invested in project A will earn an NPV of ½ × $4,000 = $2,000.

(b) **Indivisible projects** are those which must be undertaken completely or not at all. It is not possible to invest in a fraction of the project.

You may also encounter **mutually exclusive** projects when one, and only one, of two or more choices of project can be undertaken.

1.3 Single period rationing with divisible projects

With **single period capital rationing**, investment funds are a limiting factor in the current period. The total return will be maximised if management follows the decision rule of maximising the return per unit of the limiting factor. They should therefore **select those projects whose cash inflows have the highest present value per $1 of capital invested.** In other words, rank the projects according to their **profitability index**.

LEARN

$$\text{Profitability index} = \frac{\text{NPV of project}}{\text{Initial cash outflow}}$$

Exam skills

The cash outflow should be in the year in which capital is rationed. This may not be Year 0 so make sure you read the question carefully.

Example: Single period rationing with divisible projects

Short O'Funds has capital of $130,000 available for investment in the forthcoming period, at a cost of capital of 20%. Capital will be freely available in the future. Details of six projects under consideration are as follows. All projects are independent and divisible. Which projects should be undertaken and what NPV will result?

Project	Investment required $'000	Present value of inflows at 20% $'000
P	40	56.5
Q	50	67.0
R	30	48.8
S	45	59.0
T	15	22.4
U	20	30.8

Solution

The first step is to rank the projects according to the return achieved from the limiting factor of investment funds.

Project	PV inflows $'000	Investment $'000	PV per $1 invested $	Ranking
P	56.5	40	1.41	4
Q	67.0	50	1.34	5
R	48.8	30	1.63	1
S	59.0	45	1.31	6
T	22.4	15	1.49	3
U	30.8	20	1.54	2

The available funds of $130,000 can now be allocated.

Project	Investment $'000		PV $'000
R	30		48.8
U	20		30.8
T	15		22.4
P	40		56.5
Q (balance)	25	(½)	33.5
	130	Maximum PV =	192.0

Project S should not be undertaken and only half of project Q should be undertaken.

The resulting total NPV generated will be 192.0 – 130 = $62,000.

Note that the PI can be used as a project appraisal method in its own right. The decision rule to apply will be to accept all projects with a PI greater than one (in which case, PV inflows > initial investment, ie NPV > 0).

1.3.1 Advantages of the PI method

(a) Similar to the NPV method, usually **giving the same result** on **individual projects**.
(b) Can be used to rank divisible projects in conditions of **capital rationing**.

1.3.2 Disadvantages of the PI method

(a) PI indicates **relative returns** and is not an absolute measure.
(b) The PI method may **rank projects incorrectly** (If cash is not rationed, it is preferable to look at the NPV, which is an absolute measure).
(c) **Establishing** what is the **initial investment** may **not be straightforward** (The PI method works well only if the project has an outflow of cash at time 0, followed by cash inflows which may be at various times).

1.4 Single period rationing with non-divisible projects 11/10

If the projects are **not divisible** then the method shown in the last paragraph may not result in the optimal solution. Another complication which arises is that there is likely to be a small amount of **unused capital** with each combination of projects. The best way to deal with this situation is to use **trial and error** and test the NPV available from different combinations of projects. This can be a laborious process if there are a large number of projects available. We will continue with the previous example to demonstrate the technique.

Example: Single period rationing with non-divisible projects

Short O'Funds now discovers that funds in the forthcoming period are actually restricted to $95,000. The directors decide to consider projects P, Q and R only. They wish to invest only in whole projects, but surplus funds can be invested. Which combination of projects will produce the highest NPV at a cost of capital of 20%?

Solution

The investment combinations we need to consider are the various possible pairs of projects P, Q and R.

Projects	Required investment $'000	PV of inflows $'000	NPV from projects $'000
P and Q	90	123.5	33.5
P and R	70	105.3	35.3
Q and R	80	115.8	35.8

Highest NPV - undertake projects P and R and invest the unused funds of $20,000 externally.

Question 13.1 — Capital rationing

Learning outcome: C(1)(d)

Bijoux is choosing which investment to undertake during the coming year. The following table has been prepared, summarising the main features of available projects.

	Cash outlays		Cash receipts	
Project	Time 0 €'000	Time 1 €'000	Time 1 €'000	Time 2 €'000
Diamond	24	60	24	96
Sapphire	48	42	48	66
Platinum	60	42	12	138
Emerald	48	18	12	90
Quartz	36	48	24	96

There will be no cash flows on any of the projects after time 2. All projects are regarded as being of equal risk. Bijoux uses only equity sources of finance at an estimated cost of 20% per annum.

The cash flows given above represent estimated results for maximum possible investment in each project; lower levels of investment may be undertaken, in which case all cash flows will be reduced in proportion.

Required

Prepare calculations to identify the optimal set of investment assuming that capital available is limited to €120,000 at time 0, and €240,000 at time 1; assume that the Platinum project and the Emerald project are mutually exclusive (*Hint:* firstly check in which years capital rationing occurs).

1.5 Practical methods of dealing with capital rationing

A company may be able to limit the effects of capital rationing and exploit new opportunities.

(a) It might **seek joint venture partners** with which to share projects.

(b) As an alternative to direct investment in a project, the company may be able to consider a **licensing** or **franchising agreement** with another enterprise, under which the licensor/franchisor company would receive royalties.

(c) It may be possible to **contract** out parts of a project to reduce the initial capital outlay required.

(d) The company may seek **new** alternative **sources of capital** (subject to any restrictions which apply to it) for example:

　(i)　Venture capital
　(ii)　Debt finance secured on projects assets
　(iii)　Sale and leaseback of property or equipment
　(iv)　Grant aid
　(v)　More effective capital management
　(vi)　Delay a project to a later period

Section summary

- **Capital rationing** may occur due to internal factors (**soft** capital rationing) or external factors (**hard** capital rationing).
- When capital rationing occurs in a **single period, divisible** projects are ranked in terms of a **profitability index**.
- **Trial and error NPV calculations** should be used to rank **indivisible projects**.

2 Equivalent annual cost

Introduction

When an asset is being replaced with an identical asset, the equivalent annual cost method is a technique which can be used to determine the **best time** to replace the asset.

When an investment is being evaluated in terms of annual running costs, it may be appropriate to convert the capital cost into an **annualised cost** at the company's cost of capital. For example, when the capital expenditure is only a relatively small feature of a project and annual running costs are a much more significant item, annual profitability is the key factor in the decision.

$$\text{Equivalent annual cost} = \frac{\text{PV of costs over n years}}{\text{n year annuity factor}}$$

(a) **'PV of costs'** is the **purchase cost**, minus the present value of any subsequent disposal proceeds at the end of the item's life.

(b) The **n-year annuity factor is** at the company's cost of capital, for the number of years of the item's life.

Example: Annualised cost

A project is being considered which would involve a capital expenditure of $500,000 on equipment. The annual running costs and benefits would be as follows.

	$	$
Revenues		450,000
Costs		
Depreciation	100,000	
Other	300,000	
		400,000
Profit		50,000

The equipment would have a five year life, and no residual value, and would be financed by a loan at 12% interest per annum. Using annualised figures, assess whether the project is a worthwhile undertaking. Ignore risk and taxation.

Solution

The annualised capital cost of the equipment is as follows.

$$\frac{\$500{,}000}{\text{PV of \$1 per annum for yrs 1 to 5 at 12\%}} = \frac{\$500{,}000}{3.605} = \$138{,}696$$

Annual profit = $450,000 − $138,696 − $300,000 = $11,304

Depreciation is ignored because it is a notional cost and has already been taken into account in the annualised cost.

The project is a worthwhile undertaking, but only by about $11,000 a year for five years.

2.1 Equivalent annual cost and asset replacement

The annualised cost method can be used to assess when and how frequently an asset should be replaced with another asset.

The equivalent annual cost method is the quickest method to use in a period of no inflation.

STEP 1 Calculate the **present value of costs** for each **replacement cycle** over **one cycle only**.

These costs are not comparable because they refer to different time periods, whereas replacement is continuous.

STEP 2 **Turn the present value** of costs for each replacement cycle into an **equivalent annual cost** (an annuity).

The equivalent annual costs is calculated as follows.

$$\frac{\text{The PV of cost over one replacement cycle}}{\text{The cumulative present value factor for the number of years in the cycle}}$$

For example if there are three years in the cycle, the denominator will be the present value of an annuity for three years (eg at 10% would be 2.487).

Example: Replacement of an identical asset

James operates a machine which has the following costs and resale values over its four year life.

Purchase cost: $25,000

	Year 1 $	Year 2 $	Year 3 $	Year 4 $
Running costs (cash expenses)	7,500	11,000	12,500	15,000
Resale value (end of year)	15,000	10,000	7,500	2,500

The organisation's cost of capital is 10%. You are required to assess how frequently the asset should be replaced.

Solution

STEP 1 Calculate the present value of costs for each replacement cycle over one cycle.

	Replace every year		Replace every 2 years		Replace every 3 years		Replace every 4 years	
Year	Cash flow $	PV at 10% $	Cash flow $	PV at 10% $	Cash flow $	PV at 10% $	Cash flow $	PV at 10% $
0	(25,000)	(25,000)	(25,000)	(25,000)	(25,000)	(25,000)	(25,000)	(25,000)
1	7,500	6,818	(7,500)	(6,818)	(7,500)	(6,818)	(7,500)	(6,818)
2			(1,000)	(826)	(11,000)	(9,086))	(11,000)	(9,086)
3					(5,000)	(3,755)	(12,500)	(9,388)
4							(12,500)	(8,538)
PV of cost over one replacement cycle		(18,182)		(32,644)		(44,659)		(58,830)

STEP 2 Calculate the equivalent annual cost.

We use a discount rate of 10%.

(a) Replacement every year:

Equivalent annual cost = $\frac{\$(18,182)}{0.909}$ = $(20,002)

(b) Replacement every two years:

Equivalent annual cost = $\frac{\$(32,644)}{1.736}$ = $(18,804)

(c) Replacement every three years:

Equivalent annual cost = $\frac{\$(44,659)}{2.487}$ = $(17,957)

(d) Replacement every four years:

Equivalent annual cost = $\frac{\$(58,830)}{3.170}$ = $(18,558)

The optimum replacement policy is the one with the lowest equivalent annual cost, every three years.

2.2 Equivalent annual annuity

The equivalent annual annuity = $\frac{\text{NPV of project}}{\text{Annuity factor}}$

For example, a project A with an NPV of $3.75m and a duration of 6 years, given a discount rate of 12%, will have an equivalent annual annuity of $\frac{3.75}{4.111}$ = 0.91. An alternative project B with an NPV of $4.45m and a duration of 7 years will have an equivalent annual annuity of $\frac{4.45}{4.564}$ = 0.98.

This method is a useful way to compare projects with **unequal lives**.

Section summary

- DCF techniques can assist in **asset replacement decisions.** When an asset is being replaced with an identical asset, the **equivalent annual cost method** can be used to calculate an **optimum replacement cycle.**
- **Equivalent annual annuities** are a useful way to compare projects with **unequal lives.**

3 Real options   3/11, 5/11, 3/12

Introduction

Real options theory is an attempt to incorporate real-life uncertainty and flexibility into the capital investment decision. A major capital investment may not always be set in stone.

Real options attempt to incorporate **flexibility** to adapt decisions in response to unexpected market developments. It is argued that traditional methods such as NPV fail to accurately capture the economic value of investments in an environment of widespread uncertainty and rapid change. The real options method applies **financial options theory** to quantify the value of this flexibility.

Call and put options are covered in Paper P3 *Performance Strategy*. An understanding of their meaning will help here, but remember we are talking about capital investment projects not currency and interest rate options.

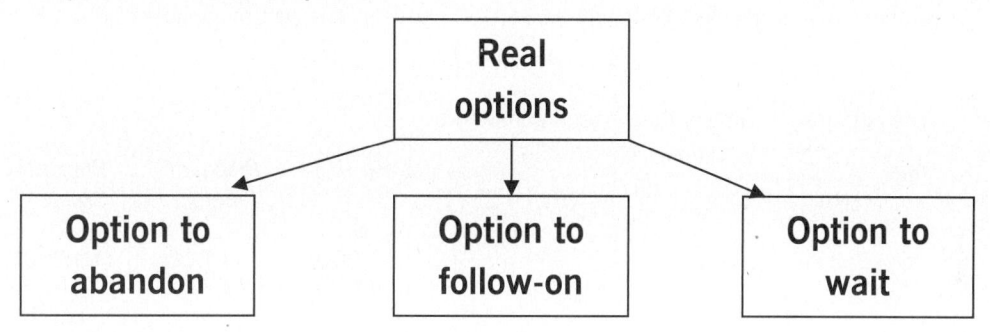

```
                    Real
                   options
          ┌───────────┼───────────┐
     Option to    Option to    Option to
     abandon     follow-on      wait
```

3.1 Option to follow-on

A follow-on option is a strategic option when the investment opportunity leads to follow-on wealth generating opportunities. For example buying new equipment could enable an organisation to develop experience and skills with the latest technology which may allow opportunities that would otherwise have been unavailable.

This is equivalent to a **call option**.

3.2 Option to abandon

An abandonment option refers to the ability to abandon the project at a certain stage in its life. If large sums are being spent, and prospects do not appear healthy, an abandonment option may be available. If the benefit streams from a project are highly **uncertain**, an option to abandon the project if things go wrong could be highly valuable. The **riskiness** of the project is reduced and the expected NPV increased.

This type of option is affected, for example, by the type of equipment needed for the project and the terms on which the equipment is acquired. If equipment is readily resalable this gives a more valuable abandonment option than if the equipment is highly specialised with no prospective second-hand purchasers.

This is equivalent to a **put option**.

3.3 Option to wait

An option to wait is a **timing option** which allows resolution of uncertainty. Investments are rarely 'now or never' opportunities but we do need to consider the cash flows foregone in the period of postponement. The cost of this is balanced against the value of waiting.

For example the possibility of 'doing nothing for a year' may be more valuable than a stated alternative because it will allow the **resolution of the uncertainty** surrounding legislation or to see if development status is granted on land.

This is equivalent to a **call option.**

3.4 Valuing real options

Real options can add value to projects, and should be taken into account in investment appraisal. Although the **valuation is difficult**, even a rough estimate is better than no estimate at all. Option theory provides a means for businesses to take into account:

(a) **Initial costs and benefits**
(b) The **present value of future benefits** and costs
(c) The **variability of future benefits** and costs
(d) The **timescale** directors are allowed to make the decision
(e) The **cost of capital**

3.5 Numerical example of real options

Libby Co is considering a three year project that has an initial cost of $10,000. Depending on the economic cycle the cash flows will either be $6,000 per year or $3,000 per year. There is a 60% probability that the cash flows will be $6,000 per year. The cost of capital is 10%.

This means that there is an expected cash flow per year of (6,000 × 0.6) + (3,000 × 0.4) = $4,800

The net present value of this project is therefore

Year	Cash flow	Discount factor	Present value
	$		$
0	(10,000)	1.000	(10,000)
1 – 3	4,800	2.487	11,938
			1,938

Wait option

However suppose that economic conditions after the first year are expected to remain the same for the **foreseeable future**. This means that Libby Co could wait one year to see which scenario occurs and then launch the project. This would gives the following NPVs

Best case

Year	Cash flow	Discount factor	Present value
	$		$
1	(10,000)	0.909	(9,090)
2 – 4	6,000	2.261*	13,566
			4,476

Worst case

Year	Cash flow	Discount factor	Present value
	$		$
1	(10,000)	0.909	(9,090)
2 – 4	3,000	2.261*	6,783
			(2,307)

* 4 year annuity factor – 1 year = 3.170 – 0.909 = 3.170 – 0.909 = 2.261

There is considerable value in the option to wait, in this case, because the NPV is increased by $4,476 – $1,938 = $2,538 as the downside risk is **eliminated** by waiting as in worst case scenario the project would not commence.

Abandonment option

Alternatively, if the project is started now, there may be the option to abandon the project after one year when the machinery used can be sold for $6,000.

This option would create the following possibilities at the end of year 1

Year (T_0 is now end of first year, when the decision is taken)	Cash flow $	Discount factor	Present value $
0	6,000	1.000	6,000
1	(6,000)	0.909	(5,454)
2	(6,000)	0.826	(4,956)
			(4,410)

Year	Cash flow $	Discount factor	Present value $
0	6,000	1.000	6,000
1	(3,000)	0.909	(2,727)
2	(3,000)	0.826	(2,478)
			795

This shows that if the cash flows are only $3,000 per year then the abandonment option should be taken as this has a positive NPV.

The abandonment option can then be incorporated into the NPV of the project as follows.

The expected value of the cash flows can be calculated as follows (including the scrap value for abandoning the project)

	Year 1			Year 2			Year 3	
Probability	$	EV	Probability	$	EV	Probability	$	EV
0.6	6,000	3,600	0.6	6,000	3,600	0.6	6,000	3,600
0.4	9,000	3,600	0.4	-	-	0.4	-	-
		7,200			3,600			3,600

The NPV would then be

Year	Cash flow $	Discount factor	Present value $
0	(10,000)	1.000	(10,000)
1	7,200	0.909	6,545
2	3,600	0.826	2,974
3	3,600	0.751	2,704
			2,223

The option to abandon has increased the overall NPV by $2,223 – $1,938 = $285

> **Section summary**
>
> **Options theory** can be applied to capital investments and can be used when managers are deciding whether to **wait**, **abandon** a project or make **follow-on** investments.

4 Adjusted present value

Introduction

We have seen that a company's gearing level has implications for its WACC. The viability of an investment project will depend partly on how the investment is financed, and how the method of finance affects gearing.

The adjusted present value method provides a better means of taking into account the effects of using loan finance than simple NPV analysis does.

The net present value method of investment appraisal is to **discount** the **cash flows** of a project at a **cost of capital**. This cost of capital might be the WACC, but it could also be another cost of capital, perhaps one which allows for the risk characteristics of the individual project.

An alternative method of carrying out project appraisal is to use the **adjusted present value (APV) method**.

4.1 Carrying out an APV calculation

The APV method involves two stages.

STEP 1 **Evaluate** the **project** first of all as if it was **all equity financed**, and so as if the company were an all equity company to find the 'base case NPV'

STEP 2 **Make adjustments** to allow for the effects of the method of financing that has been used

Example: APV method

A company is considering a project that would cost £100,000 to be financed 50% by equity (cost 21.6%) and 50% by debt (pre-tax cost 12%). The financing method would maintain the company's WACC unchanged. The cash flows from the project would be £36,000 a year in perpetuity, before interest charges. Tax is at 30%.

Appraise the project using firstly the NPV method and secondly the APV method.

Solution

	Cost %	Weighting	Product %
Equity	21.6	0.5	10.8
Debt (70% of 12%)	8.4	0.5	4.2
		WACC	15.0

Annual cash flows in perpetuity from the project are as follows.

	£
Before tax	36,000
Less tax (30%)	10,800
After tax	25,200

NPV of project = – £100,000 + (25,200 ÷ 0.15)
= – £100,000 + £168,000
= + £68,000

Note that the tax relief that will be obtained on debt interest is taken account of **in the WACC *not* in the project cash flows**.

Since £100,000 of new investment is being created, the value of the company will increase by £100,000 + £68,000 = £168,000, of which 50% must be debt capital.

The company must raise 50% × £168,000 = £84,000 of 12% debt capital, and (the balance) £16,000 of equity. The NPV of the project will raise the value of this equity from £16,000 to £84,000 thus leaving the gearing ratio at 50:50.

The **APV approach** to this example is as follows.

STEP 1 First, we need to know the **cost of equity in an equivalent ungeared company**. The MM formula we can use to establish this is as follows.

> Cost of ordinary (equity) share capital in a geared firm (with tax):
>
> $$k_{eg} = k_{eu} + [k_{eu} - k_d] \frac{V_D[1-t]}{V_E}$$

Remember k_d is the **pre-tax** cost of debt. Using the information from the question:

$$21.6\% = k_{eu} + \left[(k_{eu} - 12\%) \times \frac{50 \times 0.7}{50}\right]$$

$$21.6\% = k_{eu} + 0.70 k_{eu} - 8.4\%$$

$$1.70 k_{eu} = 30\%$$

$$k_{eu} = 17.647\%$$

Next, we calculate the **NPV of the project as if it were all equity financed**. The cost of equity would be 17.647%

$$NPV = \frac{£25,200}{0.17647} - £100,000 = £42,800$$

STEP 2 Next, we can use an MM formula for the relationship between the value of geared and ungeared companies, to establish **the effect of gearing on the value of the project**. £84,000 will be financed by debt.

$$V_g \text{ (APV)} = V_u + TB_c$$
$$= +£42,800 + (£84,000 \times 0.30)$$
$$= +£42,800 + £25,200.$$
$$= £68,000$$

The value TB_c (value of debt × corporate tax rate) represents the **present value of the tax shield on debt interest,** that is the present value of the savings arising from tax relief on debt interest.

This can be proved as follows.

Annual interest charge = 12% of £84,000 = £10,080

Tax saving (30% × £10,080) = £3,024.00

Cost of debt (pre-tax) = 12%

PV of tax savings in perpetuity $= \frac{£3,024}{0.12}$ (by coincidence only this equals the project net of tax cash flows)

$$= £25,200$$

TB$_c$ = £84,000 × 0.30 = £25,200 is a quicker way of deriving the same value. Note, however, this only works where the interest is payable in **perpetuity**. If not the PV of the tax shield will need to be computed by the 'long hand' method, above using an appropriate annuity factor.

Exam alert

Make sure you use the cost of debt to discount the tax relief on interest costs and not the cost of equity

Example: APV method and limited cash flows

Suppose in the above example the cash flows only lasted for five years, and tax was payable one year in arrears. Calculate the present value of the tax shield.

Solution

The tax saving will now only last for years 2 to 6. (Remember interest will be paid in years 1 to 5, but the tax benefits will be felt a year in arrears).

PV of tax savings = 3,024 × Annuity factor years 2 to 6
= 3,024 × (Annuity factors years 1 to 6 – Annuity factor year 1)
= 3,024 × (4.111 – 0.893)
= £9,731

The APV and NPV approaches produce the same conclusion.

4.2 APV and changes in gearing

However, the APV method can also be adapted to allow for financing which **changes the gearing structure** and the WACC.

In this respect, it is superior to the NPV method. Suppose, for example, that in the previous example, the **entire project were to be financed by debt**. The APV of the project would be calculated as follows.

(a) The NPV of project if all equity financed is:

$$\frac{£25,200}{0.17647} - £100,000 = +£42,800 \text{ (as before)}$$

(b) The adjustment to allow for the method of financing is the present value of the tax relief on debt interest in perpetuity.

DT$_c$ = £100,000 × 0.30 = £30,000

(c) APV = £42,800 + £30,000 = +£72,800

The project would increase the value of equity by £72,800.

Question 13.2 — APV

Learning outcome: C(1)(b)

A project costing $100,000 is to be financed by £60,000 of irredeemable 12% bonds and $40,000 of new equity. The project will yield an after-tax annual cash flow of £21,000 in perpetuity. If it were all equity financed, an appropriate cost of capital would be 15%. The tax rate is 30%. What is the project's APV?

4.3 Discounting tax relief at the risk-free rate

Often in exams you will be given the risk-free rate of return. As tax relief is allowed by the government and is almost certain, there is an argument for saying that **all tax relief** should be discounted at the **risk-free rate**. However there is the opposing argument that the **risk of the tax relief** is the same as the **risk of the debt** to which it relates, and therefore the tax relief should be discounted at the cost of debt. The risk-free rate would also not be used if the company was unlikely to be in a taxpaying position for some years.

In the exam we suggest that you make clear the reasons for choosing the discount rate that you have chosen to discount the tax relief, and add a comment that an alternative rate might be used.

4.4 Other elements in APV calculation

The tax shield may not be the only complication introduced into APV calculations.

4.4.1 Issue costs

The costs of issuing the finance needed for the project may also be brought into APV calculations.

Example: Issue costs

Edted is about to start a project with an initial investment of $20 million, which will generate cash flow over four years. The project will be financed with a $10 million 10 year bank loan and a rights issue. Issue costs are 5% of the amount raised.

Calculate the issue costs that will be used in the APV calculation.

Solution

Issue costs will not equal 5% of $10 million ($20 million − $10 million). The $10 million will be the figure left after the issue costs have been paid. Therefore $10 million must be 95%, not 100% of the amount raised, and the issue costs = $\frac{5}{95}$ × $10 million = $526,316

In the above example, the issue costs do not need to be discounted as they are assumed to be paid at time 0. The complication comes if issue costs are allowable for tax purposes.

Example: The tax implications of issue costs

Assume in the example above that issue costs are allowable for tax purposes, the tax is assumed to be 30% payable one year in arrears and the risk-free rate of return is assumed to be 8%.

Calculate the tax effect of the issuing costs to be included in the APV calculation.

Solution

Tax effect = Tax rate × Issue costs × Discount rate
= 0.3 × 526,316 × 0.926 = $146,211

4.4.2 Spare debt capacity

Projects may yield other incremental benefits, for example increased borrowing or debt capacity. These benefits should be included in the APV calculations, even if the debt capacity is utilised elsewhere.

Example: Spare debt capacity

Continuing with the Edted example, suppose the project increased the borrowing capacity of the company by $6 million, at the risk-free rate of return of 8%. Calculate the effect on the APV calculation.

Solution

Remember that we are concerned with the incremental benefit which is the **tax shield effect** of the increased debt finance.

Present value of tax shield effect	=	Increased debt capacity	×	Interest rate	×	Tax rate	×	Discount factor Years 2 to 5
	=	$6 million	×	8%	×	30%	×	3.067
	=	$441,648						

4.4.3 Subsidy

You may face a situation where a company can obtain finance at a lower interest rate than its normal cost of borrowing. In this situation you have to include in the APV calculation the tax shield effect of the cheaper finance and the effect of the saving in interest.

Example: Subsidy

Gordonbear is about to start a project requiring $6 million of initial investment. The company normally borrows at 12% but a government loan will be available to finance all of the project at 10%. The risk-free rate of interest is 6%.

Tax is payable at 30% one year in arrears. The project is scheduled to last for four years.

Calculate the effect on the APV calculation if Gordonbear finances the project by means of the government loan.

Solution

(a) The tax shield is as follows.

We assume that the loan is for the duration of the project (four years) only.

Annual interest = $6 million × 10% = $600,000

Tax relief = $600,000 × 0.3 = $180,000

This needs to be discounted over years 2 to 5 (remember the one year time lag). We do not however use the 10% to discount the loan and the tax effect; instead we assume that the government loan is risk-free and the tax effect is also risk-free. Hence we use the 6% factor in discounting.

NPV tax relief = $180,000 × Discount factor Years 2 to 5
= $180,000 × 3.269
= $588,420

(b) We also need to take into account the benefits of **being able** to pay a **lower interest rate**.

Benefits = $6 million × (12% – 10%) × 6% Discount factor Years 1 to 4
= $6 million × 2% × 3.465
= $415,800

(c) Total effect = $588,420 + $415,800 = $1,004,220.

4.5 The advantages and disadvantages of the APV method

The main advantages of the APV are as follows.

(a) APV can be used to **evaluate** all the **effects of financing** a product including:

(i) Tax shield
(ii) Changing capital structure
(iii) Any other relevant cost

(b) When using APV you do not have to adjust the WACC using assumptions of perpetual risk-free debt.

The main difficulties with the APV technique are:

(a) **Establishing** a **suitable cost of equity**, for the initial DCF computation as if the project were all-equity financed, and also establishing the all-equity β.

(b) **Identifying all the costs** associated with the method of financing.

(c) Choosing the correct discount rates used to discount the costs.

Exam alert

An article on adjusted present value can be found in the April 2011 issue of *Financial Management*.

Section summary

The **APV** method suggests that it is possible to calculate an **adjusted cost of capital** for use in project appraisal, as well as indicating how the net present value of a project can be increased or decreased by project **financing effects**.

- Evaluate the project as if it was all equity financed
- Make adjustments to allow for the effects of the financing method

Chapter Roundup

- **Capital rationing** may occur due to internal factors (**soft** capital rationing) or external factors (**hard** capital rationing).
- When capital rationing occurs in a **single period, divisible** projects are ranked in terms of a **profitability index**.
- **Trial and error NPV calculations** should be used to rank **indivisible projects**.
- DCF techniques can assist in **asset replacement decisions**. When an asset is being replaced with an identical asset, the **equivalent annual cost method** can be used to calculate an **optimum replacement cycle**.
- **Equivalent annual annuities** are a useful way to compare projects with unequal lives.
- **Options theory** can be applied to capital investments and can be used when managers are deciding whether to **wait**, **abandon** a project or make **follow-on** investments.
- The **APV** method suggests that it is possible to calculate an **adjusted cost of capital** for use in project appraisal, as well as indicating how the net present value of a project can be increased or decreased by project **financing effects**.
    - Evaluate the project as if it was all equity financed
    - Make adjustments to allow for the effects of the financing method

Quick Quiz

1. *Hard capital rationing* occurs when a restriction on an organisation's ability to invest capital funds is caused by an internal budget ceiling imposed by management.

    True ☐
    False ☐

2. Profitability Index (PI) = $\dfrac{(1)}{(2)}$

    What are (1) and (2)?

3. Equivalent annual cost = $\dfrac{\text{PV of costs over n years}}{\text{n year annuity factor}}$

    Explain briefly what is meant by:

    (a) PV of costs
    (b) n year annuity factor

4. Identify three common types of 'real option' found in relation to capital projects.

5. What is an indivisible project?

6. Give three reasons why hard capital rationing may occur.

7. What is the best way to find the optimal solution in a situation of single period rationing with indivisible projects?

8. What is the best way to find the optimal solution in a situation of single period rationing with divisible projects?

9   What are the two steps involved in calculating an APV?

10 What are the difficulties involved in using the APV technique?

Answers to Quick Quiz

1   1   False. This describes *soft* capital rationing.

2   (1) Present value of cash inflows
    (2) Initial investment

3   (a) The purchase cost, minus the present value of any subsequent disposal proceeds at the end of the item's life

    (b) The annuity factor at the company's cost of capital, for the number of years of the item's life

4   (a) The option to make follow-on investments
    (b) The option to abandon a project
    (c) The option to wait before making an investment

5   A project that must be undertaken completely or not at all.

6   Any *three* of:

    (a) Raising money through the stock market may not be possible if share prices are depressed.
    (b) There are restrictions on lending due to government control.
    (c) Lending institutions may consider the organisation to be too risky.
    (d) The costs associated with making small issues of capital may be too great.

7   Use trial and error and test the NPV available from different project combinations.

8   Rank the projects according to their profitability index.

9   Step 1: Calculate the NPV as if ungeared using k_{eu}

    Step 2: Adjust for the financing effects

10 (a) Establishing a suitable cost of equity, for the initial DCF computation as if the project were all-equity financed, and also establishing the all-equity β

    (b) Identifying all the costs associated with the method of financing

    (c) Choosing the correct discount rates used to discount the costs

Answers to Questions

13.1 Capital rationing

Optimal investments for Bijoux

First we need to determine in which year(s) capital is rationed, taking account of the fact that only one of the Platinum and Emerald projects will be undertaken.

	Cash flows with Platinum		Cash flows with Emerald	
Project	Time 0	Time 1	Time 0	Time 1
	€'000	€'000	€'000	€'000
Diamond	(24)	(36)	(24)	(36)
Sapphire	(48)	6	(48)	6
Platinum	(60)	(30)		
Emerald			(48)	(6)
Quartz	(36)	(24)	(36)	(24)
Total	(168)	(84)	(156)	(60)
Capital available	120	240	120	240

To rank the projects the basic PI as previously defined cannot be used as this would ignore outlays at time 1. One option would be to use a PI defined as $\frac{\text{PV of inflows}}{\text{PV of outlays}}$ but this is not entirely appropriate as capital is not rationed at Time 1.

An alternative, used here, is to use a PI defined as $\frac{\text{NPV project}}{\text{Initial capital invested}}$

It is therefore concluded that effective capital rationing exists only at Time 0 ie a single period of capital rationing situation.

	Cash flows			PV of cash flows @ 20%					
Project	0	1	2	0	1	2	NPV	PI	Rank
	€'000	€'000	€'000	€'000	€'000	€'000	€'000		
Diamond	(24)	(36)	96	(24)	(30.0)	66.6	12.6	0.525	1
Sapphire	(48)	6	66	(48)	5.0	45.8	2.8	0.058	5
Platinum	(60)	(30)	138	(60)	(25.0)	95.8	10.8	0.180	4
Emerald	(48)	(6)	90	(48)	(5.0)	62.5	9.5	0.198	3
Quartz	(36)	(24)	96	(36)	(20.0)	66.6	10.6	0.294	2

In time 0 with only €100,000 available projects would be introduced in order of profitability as shown.

Platinum without Emerald

Project	Proportion accepted	Funds used at Time 0	Total NPV
	%	€'000	€'000
Diamond	100	24	12.6
Quartz	100	36	10.6
Platinum	100	60	10.8
Sapphire	Nil	NIL	NIL
Funds utilised and available		120	34.0

Emerald without Platinum

Project	Proportion accepted %	Funds used at Time 0 €'000	Total NPV €'000
Diamond	100	24	12.6
Quartz	100	36	10.6
Emerald	100	48	9.5
Sapphire	25	12	0.7
Funds utilised and available		120	33.4

Platinum without Emerald is to be preferred as it yields a higher NPV.

Note. Platinum is selected in preference to Emerald even though it has a lower profitability index.

This is because the choice is effectively between investing €60,000 in Platinum with an NPV of €10,800 (PI = 0.18) or a package containing a €48,000 investment in Emerald and a €12,000 investment in Sapphire with a combined NPV of €10,200. This package has a profitability index of only 0.17 and is therefore rejected.

13.2 APV

	$
NPV if all equity financed: $21,000/0.15 − $100,000	40,000
PV of the tax shield: $60,000 × 12% × 30%/0.12	18,000
APV	58,000

Now try these questions from the Exam Question Bank

Number	Level	Marks	Time
Q21	Introductory	12 marks	22 mins
Q22	Examination	25 marks	45 mins
Q23	Examination	25 marks	45 mins

CONTROL OF INVESTMENT PROJECTS

In this chapter we discuss how investments, particularly investment projects are controlled. The first section concentrates on the various **phases of projects**. Certain key stages will be the same whatever the nature of the investment.

In the rest of the chapter we examine certain processes in more detail. Whatever the investment, it is vital that it is carefully assessed for **feasibility** and we look at feasibility studies in Section 2. Section 3 deals with the steps businesses can take if problems arise or changes have to be made to the initial specification for the investment. Section 4 deals with assessment of whether the investment was a success and the wider issues that a **post-completion audit** covers.

All of this chapter overlaps with the other two strategic level papers.

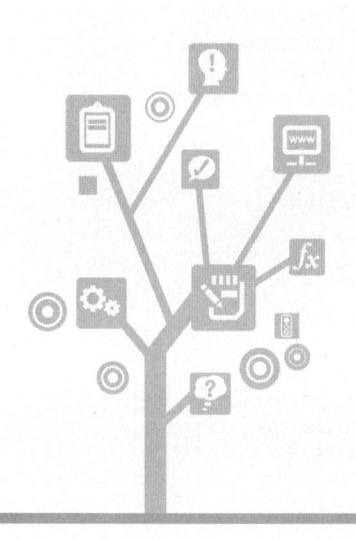

topic list	learning outcomes	syllabus references	ability required
1 Investments and projects	C(3)(a)	C(3)(i)	evaluation
2 Feasibility study	C(3)(a)	C(3)(i)	evaluation
3 Project control	C(3)(a)	C(3)(i)	evaluation
4 Investment performance and post-completion audits	C(3)(a)	C(3)(ii)	Evaluation

1 Investments and projects

Introduction

Investments, particularly projects, need to be carefully planned and controlled. Managers must consider the need for investments, choose the best option, control development and implementation and review whether the investment has fulfilled its aims.

1.1 Investment cycle

The investment process can be summarised as a cycle as follows

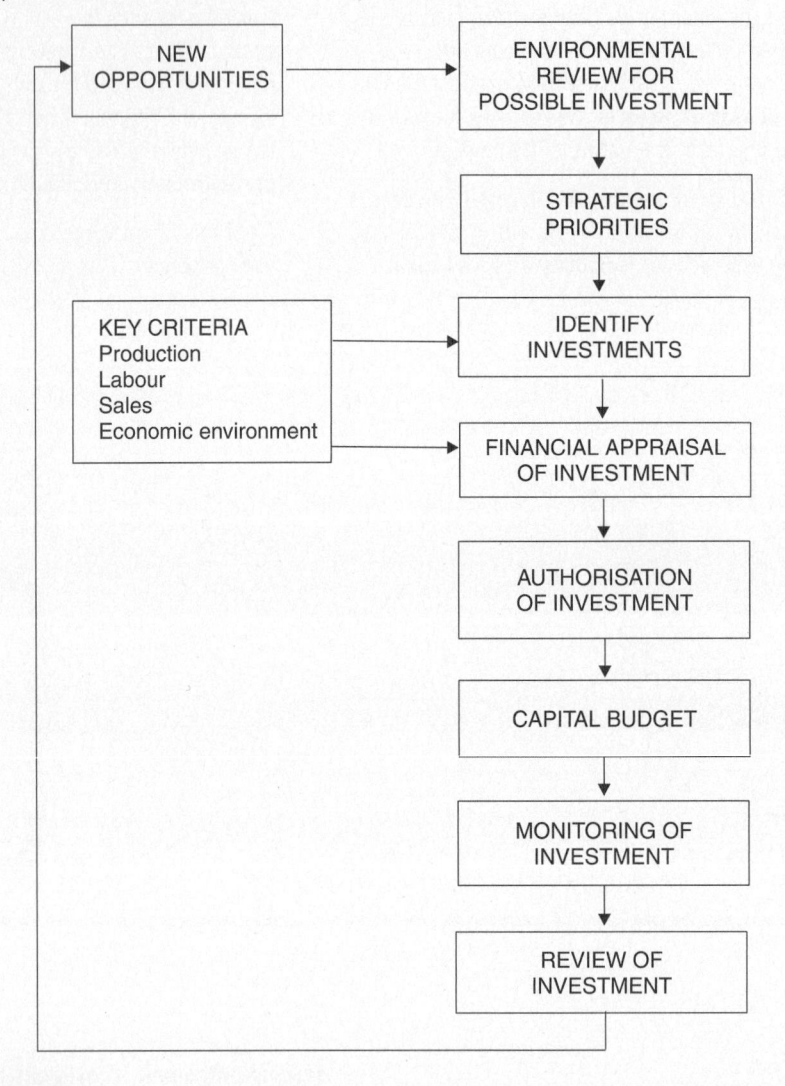

```
NEW OPPORTUNITIES
   ↓
ENVIRONMENTAL REVIEW FOR POSSIBLE INVESTMENT
   ↓
STRATEGIC PRIORITIES
   ↓
IDENTIFY INVESTMENTS   ← KEY CRITERIA
   ↓                     Production
FINANCIAL APPRAISAL      Labour
OF INVESTMENT            Sales
   ↓                     Economic environment
AUTHORISATION OF INVESTMENT
   ↓
CAPITAL BUDGET
   ↓
MONITORING OF INVESTMENT
   ↓
REVIEW OF INVESTMENT
   ↑ (loops back to NEW OPPORTUNITIES)
```

Question 14.1 — New product investment

Learning outcome: C(3)(a)

Why would a company extend its product mix with the introduction of new products?

1.2 Nature of projects

A business may undertake major investments in different contexts. Some investments will be undertaken to enhance ongoing operations, and benefits and costs may be indefinite. Other investments may be specific projects.

Investment projects generally have the following characteristics:

(a) They have a defined beginning and end.
(b) They have resources allocated to them, although often on a shared basis.
(c) They are intended to be done only once.
(d) They follow a plan towards a clear intended end-result.
(e) They often cut across organisational and functional lines.

Question 14.2 — IT system

Learning outcome: C(1)(a)

Identify the potential costs and benefits of a new IT system.

1.3 Project success factors

Projects, small or large, are prone to fail unless they are appropriately managed and some effort is applied to ensure that factors that might contribute to success are present. Here are some of the key factors.

(a) **Clearly defined mission and goals** effectively communicated to and understood by all participants.
(b) **Top management support** that is visible is important in sending out the right messages regarding the importance of the project.
(c) **Competent project manager** with the necessary skills.
(d) **Competent team members** with the appropriate knowledge, skills and attitudes.
(e) **Sufficient resources** in terms of finance, materials, people and processes.
(e) **Excellent communication channels** to ensure information is shared and there are no misunderstandings.
(f) **Clear client focus** so that all work is done bearing in mind the needs of internal and external customers.

1.4 Project phases and stages

The phases of a project can be broken down into a number of stages. The number of stages identified varies depending on type of project and the conventions of the organisation undertaking the project.

Project phases

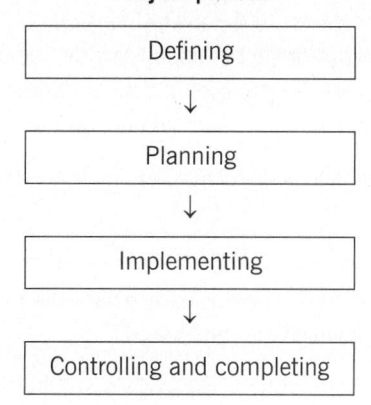

Defining
↓
Planning
↓
Implementing
↓
Controlling and completing

We now will look at each of these phases and stages.

1.5 Defining phase

The **defining phase** of a project is concerned with deciding whether a project should begin and committing to do so.

1.5.1 Initiation

Project initiation describes the beginning of a project. At this point certain management activities are required to ensure that the project is established with clear reference terms, an appropriate management structure and a carefully selected **project team**.

Projects originate from the **identification of a problem** or the **opportunity** to do something new. It is often not clear precisely what the problem is. The project team will have to study, discuss and **analyse** the problem, from a number of different aspects (eg technical, financial).

At the start of a project, documentation should be drawn up, setting out the **terms of reference** for the project.

1.5.2 Formation

The formation stage involves selecting the personnel who will be involved with the project, including a project manager and perhaps a project team.

1.5.3 Objective setting

Before specific objectives can be set it is necessary to establish more general **project goals**. Clear goals and objectives give team members **quantifiable targets** to aim for. This should improve motivation and performance, as attempting to achieve a challenging goal is more inspiring than simply being told 'do your best.'

1.6 Planning phase

The **planning phase** of a project aims to devise a workable scheme to accomplish the overall project goal.

1.6.1 Task planning

After the project team is in place and project goals and objectives have been set, the project should be broken down into **manageable tasks**.

Tasks should be:

(a) **Clear**. Eg 'Design the layout of the general sports halls.'

(b) **Self-contained**. No gaps in time should be apparent on work-units grouped together to form a task. All work-units within a task should be related.

1.6.2 Feasibility and fact finding

A more realistic judgement as to the **overall feasibility** of the project can now be made. Some large projects may involve a **pre-project feasibility study**, which establishes whether it is feasible to undertake the project at all. For complex projects, a detailed **feasibility study** may be required to establish if the project can be achieved within acceptable **cost and time constraints**.

We shall consider feasibility studies in more detail in Section 2.

1.6.3 Position analysis, options generation and options evaluation

Once the current situation has been clearly established, options can be generated for a range of projects or services, only one of which can be chosen.

Each course is analysed in terms of how well it would meet the project aims. A weighted scoring or ranking system may be useful here. Eventually the optimum course is chosen.

1.7 Implementing phase

The **implementing phase** is concerned with co-ordinating people and other resources to carry out the project plan.

1.7.1 Design and development

The design and development stage is where the actual product, service or process that will be the end result of the project is worked on. The activities carried out in this stage will vary greatly depending on the type of project. For example, in a software implementation, this is when the programming of the software would take place; in a construction project, the building design would be finalised.

The main aim is to produce a design that will meet user requirements; for this to happen, the **design** has to be **tested** against what users want. Subsequent phases may have to be altered if the product design changes as a result of the testing process.

1.7.2 Implementation

After the process, service or product has been developed it will be **made available** or **installed** so it is available to be used.

Products can be launched globally, or on a country-by-country basis, depending on the markets involved. **Launch plans** may have to be **modified** if competitors change their response.

If the project involves a new system or process, a period of **parallel running** alongside the existing system or process may be carried out. This enables results to be checked, and any last-minute problems to be ironed out before the organisation is fully reliant on the new system or process. However implementation is not the time for adding new features or enhancements in response to user comments. Pressure for new features should have been dealt with earlier; if demand arises at this stage, there may need to be a follow-on project.

At this stage **communication** with **internal users** and **customers** is essential to ensure that they are happy and will start using what has been developed. Communication needs to be two-way, with those affected by the project being able to discuss their initial needs and requirements for ongoing support.

1.8 Controlling phase

The **controlling phase** is concerned with ensuring project objectives are met by monitoring and measuring progress and taking corrective action when necessary.

Actual performance should be **reviewed** against the objectives identified in the project plan. If performance is not as expected, **control action** will be necessary.

1.9 Completing phase

Completion involves formalising acceptance of the project and bringing it to an orderly end.

Following installation and review there should be a **review meeting** to:

(a) Check that all products are complete and delivered.
(b) Check the status of any outstanding requests for change.
(c) Check all project issues have been cleared.
(d) Approve the project completion report.
(e) Arrange for a post completion audit (discussed later in this chapter).

Investment appraisal may include investments in IS/IT which is covered in Paper E3 *Enterprise Strategy*.

> **Section summary**
> - Investment projects need to be carefully **planned** and **controlled**.
> - The **phases of a project** can be broken down into defining, planning, implementing, controlling and completing.

2 Feasibility study

> **Introduction**
> A **feasibility study**, covering all aspects of a project's feasibility, and undertaken by a carefully selected team is a vital stage in assessing whether an investment is worthwhile. Feasibility studies are essential for investments and projects that are likely to be long and complicated.

2.1 Carrying out a feasibility study

If a major investment is to be successful, its feasibility needs to be carefully assessed before the organisation commits to it. A feasibility study should be carried out because a new investment:

(a) Might be complicated and costly.
(b) Disrupt operations during development and implementation (eg staff and management time).
(c) Have far reaching consequences in a way an organisation conducts future business.
(d) Impact on organisation strategy and structure.

2.2 The feasibility study team

A feasibility study team might be appointed to carry out the study (although individuals might be given the task in the case of smaller projects).

(a) Members of the team should be drawn from the **departments affected by the investment**.
(b) At least one person must have relevant **detailed technical knowledge**, and one other person be able to assess the **organisational implications** of the new system.
(c) It is possible to hire **consultants** to carry out the feasibility study, but their **lack of knowledge about the organisation** may adversely affect the usefulness of their proposals.
(d) Before selecting the members of the study group, the steering committee must ensure that they possess **suitable personal qualities**, eg the ability to be **objectively critical**.

2.3 Conducting the feasibility study

2.3.1 Terms of reference

The terms of reference for a feasibility study group may be set out by a steering committee, the information director or the board of directors. They should include defining whether **additional investment** is required, **specifying targets**, **selecting possible options**, **assessing the options** for **feasibility** and **recommending the best option**.

2.3.2 Option evaluation

This stage involves suggesting a number of **options** for the new investment, evaluating them and recommending one for adoption. It concludes with a final **feasibility study report**.

STEP 1 Create the **base constraints** in terms of expenditure, implementation and design time, and system requirements, which any system should satisfy.

STEP 2 Create outlines of **options**, describing, in brief, each option.

STEP 3 Assess the **impact** each proposal has on the operations of the relevant department and/or the organisation as a whole.

STEP 4 **Review** these proposals with the people affected, who should indicate those options they favour for further analysis.

Question 14.3 — Base constraints

Learning outcome: C(3)(a)

What are the base constraints likely to be for a computerised system?

2.4 Key areas of feasibility

There are five key areas in which a project must be feasible if it is to be selected.

- Operational feasibility
- Technical feasibility
- Social feasibility
- Ecological feasibility
- Economic feasibility

2.4.1 Operational feasibility

Operational feasibility is a key concern. If an investment makes technical sense but **conflicts with the way the organisation does business**, the solution is not feasible. Thus an organisation might reject a solution because it forces a change in management responsibilities, status and chains of command, or does not suit regional reporting structures, or because the costs of redundancies, retraining and reorganisation are considered too high.

2.4.2 Technical feasibility

The requirements, as defined in the feasibility study, must be technically achievable. For a computer system for example, any proposed solution must be capable of being implemented using available hardware, software and other technology. Technical feasibility considerations could include the following.

- **Volume** of transactions that can be processed within a given time
- **Capacity** to hold files or records of a certain size
- **Response times** (how quickly the computer does what you ask it to)
- **Number of users** that can be supported without deterioration in the other criteria

2.4.3 Social feasibility

An assessment of social feasibility will address a number of areas, including the following.

- **Personnel** policies
- Redrawing of **job specifications**
- Threats to **industrial relations**
- Expected **skills requirements**
- **Motivation**

2.4.4 Ecological feasibility

Ecological feasibility relates to environmental considerations. A particular course of action may be rejected on the basis that it would cause too much damage to the environment. In some markets customers may prefer to purchase ecologically sound products. Ecological feasibility issues could include the following.

- What **waste** products are produced?
- How is waste **disposed** of?
- Is use of the product likely to damage the **environment**?
- Could the production process be '**cleaner**'?
- How much **energy** does the process consume?

2.4.5 Economic feasibility

Any project will have economic costs and economic benefits. Economic feasibility has three strands.

- The benefits must justify the costs.

- The project must be the 'best' option from those under consideration for its particular purpose.

- The project must compete with projects in other areas of the business for funds. Even if it is projected to produce a positive return and satisfies all relevant criteria, it may not be chosen because other business needs are perceived as more important.

> **Section summary**
>
> A **feasibility study** is a vital stage in assessing whether an investment is worthwhile, particularly for projects that are likely to be long and complicated.

3 Project control

> **Introduction**
>
> For projects to be successful, they must be carefully controlled and problems swiftly dealt with.

3.1 Project organisation

Projects should have an **organisation chart** and **terms of reference** defining **objectives**, **timescales** and the roles of the **key individuals**, including taking steps to minimise the chances of loss of key individuals. The **resources** required need to be specified, and their availability confirmed.

Also in the initial stages, managers need to establish a **reporting structure**, so that project progress is regularly communicated to the right managers and staff.

3.2 Project monitoring

At the start of each project, an **overall project plan** needs to be produced to enable the business to monitor project delays. This should be supplemented by **detailed project plans and budgets** describing the tasks, resources and links. Techniques that you will have come across in your previous studies such as **Gantt charts** will be helpful here.

At the initial stage, the plan needs to highlight **resource and time constraints**, and also **project date constraints**.

Quality standards also need to be established before the project commences and ongoing quality control procedures defined.

Managers and **project monitoring committees** should be kept informed of progress, with achievements measured against the project's critical success factors being regularly reported. **Cost control systems** also need to be established that will monitor actual against planned expenditure.

3.3 Project risk management

At the initial stage, risks that could affect project implementation need to be carefully identified. Once this has happened, risks need to be **ranked** according to their **seriousness** and **likelihood**, and measures taken to transfer, minimise, accept or eliminate project risks. What happens to the risk will depend on the **severity** of the risk and the **cost** of management action.

The risk situation also needs to be reviewed every time key project decisions are taken.

3.4 Dealing with problems

An organisation could face serious problems if major investments are late, over budget or do not fulfil the objectives that they were meant to meet.

3.4.1 Types of difficulty

- The investment may be **poorly managed**; there may be conflict between managers and users, and there may be a lack of **monitoring and control**
- **Deadlines** may be **unrealistic**
- The **requirements** that the investment is designed to fulfil may change
- The investment process may be poorly **timetabled** and **resourced**
- There may be a **conflict** between time, cost and quality

3.4.2 Dealing with slippage

When an investment has slipped behind schedule there are a range of options open to the project manager. Some of these options are summarised in the following table.

Action	Comment
Do nothing	After considering all options it may be decided that things should be allowed to continue as they are.
Add resources	It may be possible to recover some lost ground.
Work smarter	Consider whether the methods currently being used are the most suitable, and seek changes.
Replan	If the assumptions the original plan was based on have been proved invalid a more realistic plan should be devised.

Action	Comment
Reschedule	A complete replan may not be necessary – it may be possible to recover some time by changing the phasing of certain deliverables.
Introduce incentives	Incentives such as bonus payments could be linked to work deadlines and quality.

3.4.3 Change procedure

Some of the reactions to slippage discussed above would involve changes that would significantly affect the investment. Other possible causes of changes to the original investment plan include:

- The availability of new technology
- Changes in personnel
- A realisation that requirements were misunderstood
- Changes in the business environment
- New legislation eg Data protection

The **earlier** a change is made the **less expensive** it should prove. However, changes will cost time and money and should not be undertaken lightly.

When considering a change **an investigation** should be conducted to discover:

- The consequences of **not** implementing the proposed change
- The impact of the change on **time**, **cost** and **quality**
- The expected **costs and benefits** of the change
- The **risks** associated with the change, and with the status-quo

The process of ensuring that proper consideration is given to the impact of proposed changes is known as **change control**.

Changes will need to be implemented into the project plan and communicated to all stakeholders.

You will have covered project management in your earlier studies and this material also links to Paper E3 *Enterprise Strategy*.

Section summary

Projects must be **carefully controlled** and swift action taken to deal with problems.

---

4 Investment performance and post-completion audits 11/11

Introduction

How do we assess if an investment has been successful? Post-completion audits are one way in which an assessment can be made.

4.1 Reviewing investment performance

Performance reviews will vary in content from organisation to organisation, and from investment to investment. Organisations will need to consider carefully the following factors.

- **What is evaluated**
- Who decides **what constitutes performance** and whether it is **good or bad**
- Does the **investment** have a **single clear purpose**, or a number of different purposes which will complicate the targets that are set for it
- How important will **quantitative measures** be and how important will **qualitative measures** be

4.2 Assessment of investment

Financial measures are an important measure of many investments' success. Organisations will assess whether the investment is generating the **expected positive cash flows** and whether it is fulfilling other targets, for example a **payback period** of less than a certain number of years, or a target return on investment.

However other targets may also be important. This is particularly true in **customer-focused** organisations, where the financial success of an investment in generating extra revenues is likely to be viewed in the context of other significant indicators.

Customer rejects: total sales	Ratio monitors customer satisfaction, providing a check on the efficiency of quality control procedures
Deliveries late: Deliveries on schedule	Whether production efficiency and production scheduling have reached acceptable levels
Flexibility measures	Whether the investment has improved responsiveness to market needs
Number of people served and speed of service	Future sales may be lost if these are inadequate
Customer satisfaction	Expressed through questionnaires, surveys etc

With other investments, the key success indicators factors are likely to be direct **improvements in production**. Likely important measures here include:

- Number of customer complaints and warranty claims
- Rework
- Delivery time
- Non-productive hours
- Machine down time
- Stock-outs

Some investments will be undertaken to **improve internal procedures**, and will be assessed on the basis of whether they have fulfilled the needs that prompted the investment. The performance of a computer system for example will be evaluated on the basis of whether it meets the basic needs to **provide information** of the **required quality** (timely, accurate, relevant to business needs, clear etc), or improves **turnaround time** for information.

Question 14.4 — Assessment of investment

Learning outcome: C(3)(a)

What performance measures are likely to be important in assessing the success of a new computerised sales processing system?

4.3 Post-completion audits

Pilot paper

A **post audit** or a **post-completion audit** is a review of the cash inflows to and outflows from a project after it has reached the end of its life, or at least some years after it began. As far as possible, the actual cash flows should be measured and compared with the estimates contained in the original capital expenditure appraisal. The manager **responsible** for the project should be asked to explain any **significant variances**.

KEY TERM

A POST-COMPLETION AUDIT is an objective, independent assessment of the success of a capital project in relation to plan. Covers the whole life of the project and provides feedback to managers to aid the implementation and control of future projects.

4.3.1 Benefits of post-completion audits

Post completion audit checking cannot reverse the decision to make the capital expenditure, because the expenditure will already have taken place. However, it does have a certain control value.

(a) If a manager asks for and gets approval for a capital project, and knows that in due course the project will be subject to a post-completion audit, then the manager will be more likely to pay attention to the **benefits** and the **costs** than if no post audit were threatened.

(b) If the post audit takes place before the project life ends, and if it finds that the benefits have been less than expected because of management inefficiency, steps can be taken to **improve efficiency** and earn greater benefits over the remaining life of the project. Alternatively, the post-completion audit may highlight those projects which should be discontinued.

(c) A post-completion audit can help to identify managers who have been **good performers** and those who have been poor performers.

(d) A post-completion audit might **identify weaknesses** in the forecasting and estimating techniques used to evaluate projects, and so should help to improve the quality of forecasting for future investment decisions.

(e) A post-completion audit might reveal areas where **improvements** can be made in methods so as to achieve better results from capital investments in general.

(f) The **original estimates** may be **more realistic** if managers are aware that they will be monitored, but post-completion audits should not be unfairly critical.

It may be too **expensive** to post-completion audit all capital expenditure projects; therefore managers may need to select a **sample** for a post-completion audit. A reasonable guideline might be to audit all projects above a certain size, and a random sample of smaller projects.

4.3.2 Problems with post-completion audits

(a) There are **many uncontrollable factors** in long-term investments such as environmental changes. Since such factors are outside management control there may be little to gain by identifying the resulting variances.

(b) This means that it **may not be possible to identify separately the costs and benefits** of any particular project or, due to uncertainty, to identify the costs and benefits at all.

(c) Post-completion audit can be a **costly and time-consuming exercise**. Labour, which may be a scarce resource, is required to undertake the task.

(d) Applied punitively, post-completion audit exercises may lead to **managers becoming over cautious** and unnecessarily risk averse.

(e) The **strategic effects** of a **capital investment project** may take years to materialise and it may never be possible to identify or quantify them effectively.

Exam alert

The benefits and limitations of post-audits often come up in exams, generally for as many as 6-8 comparatively easy marks.

Section summary

- The nature of an investment or project will determine how its success is measured.
- A **post-completion audit** is designed to identify improvements not only over the remaining life of a project, but also in the entity's budgeting and management procedures.

Chapter Roundup

- ✓ Investment projects need to be carefully **planned** and **controlled**.
- ✓ The **phases of a project** can be broken down into defining, planning, implementing, controlling and completing.
- ✓ A **feasibility study** is a vital stage in assessing whether an investment is worthwhile, particularly for projects that are likely to be long and complicated.
- ✓ Projects must be **carefully controlled** and swift action taken to deal with problems.
- ✓ The nature of an investment or project will determine how its success is measured.
- ✓ A **post-completion audit** is designed to identify improvements not only over the remaining life of a project, but also in the entity's budgeting and management procedures.

Quick Quiz

1. What are the four key project phases?

2. Which of the following are key areas that a feasibility study should assess?

    A   Operational feasibility
    B   Technical feasibility
    C   Social feasibility
    D   Strategic feasibility
    E   Economic feasibility
    F   Ecological feasibility

3. What are the main elements in the option evaluation stage?

4. On what factors should a ranking of risks be based?

5. If an investment slips behind schedule, an organisation's best course of action may be to do nothing.

    True ☐
    False ☐

6. Give three indicators, other than increased sales revenues, that indicate that an investment has led to better products or a better service being offered to customers.

7. A .... is an objective and independent appraisal of the measure of success of a capital expenditure project in progressing the business as planned.

Answers to Quick Quiz

1.
   - Defining
   - Planning
   - Implementing
   - Controlling and completing

2. A Operational, B Technical, C Social, E Economic, F Ecological. D Strategic concerns relate to whether a project is suitable.

3.
   - Create the base constraints
   - Create outlines of options
   - Assess the impact of each proposal
   - Review proposals with people affected

4. The likelihood of their happening and the severity of their consequences

5. True

6.
   - Customer rejects: Total sales
   - Deliveries late: Deliveries on schedule
   - Flexibility measures
   - Number of people served and speed of service
   - Customer satisfaction

7. A **post-completion audit/post audit** is an objective and independent appraisal of the measure of success of a capital expenditure project in progressing the business as planned.

Answers to Questions

14.1 New product investment

(a) To meet the **changing needs/wants of customers**: a new product may meet a new need (eg for environmentally friendly alternatives) or meet an existing need more effectively (eg digital cameras). Needs may change due to technological breakthroughs resulting in higher customer expectations or because of wider changes in society

(b) To **pace (or outpace) competitors**: responding to innovations and market trends before or shortly after competitors, so as not to miss marketing opportunities.

(c) To respond to **environmental threats and opportunities**: capitalising on opportunities presented by new technology, say (digital cameras), or other products (accessories and supplies for digital cameras); minimising the effects of threats such as environmental impacts (developing 'green' alternatives) or safety concerns (developing new safety features).

(d) To **extend the product portfolio** as part of a product development or diversification growth strategy. New products can bring new customers to the brand, enable cross-selling of products in the mix and so on.

(e) To **extend the life of a product**, by modifying it to maintain interest, simulate re-purchase (because it is 'new and improved') and/or target as yet unreached market segments.

(f) To **refresh the product portfolio**. Some products may become obsolete and need updating. Others will simply be deleted, and the company will need to replace them in the product mix in order to maintain brand presence and profitability.

14.2 IT system

Cost	Example
Hardware costs	• Computers and peripherals
Installation costs	• New buildings (if necessary) • The computer room (wiring, air-conditioning if necessary) • Desks, security systems etc
Development costs	• Costs of measuring and analysing the existing system • Costs of looking at the new system. • Software/consultancy work • Systems analysis • Programming. • Changeover costs, particularly file conversion, may be very considerable.
Personnel costs	• Staff training • Staff recruitment/relocation • Staff salaries and pensions • Redundancy payments • Overheads
Operating costs	• Consumable materials (tapes, disks, stationery etc) • Maintenance • Accommodation costs • Heating/power/insurance/telephone • Standby arrangements, in case the system breaks down
Intangible costs	Some costs are **harder to quantify**. • 'Learning curve' – staff will work slower until they become familiar with the new system • Staff morale may suffer from the enforced changes • Investment opportunities forsaken – the opportunity cost • Incompatibility with other systems may mean an unforeseen change is required elsewhere in the organisation

Direct benefits

(a) **Savings** because the old system is no longer operating.

(b) **Efficiency savings**

(c) **Extra cost savings or revenue benefits** because of the improvements or enhancements that the new system should bring. These include more sales revenue. There may also be operational efficiencies such as better inventory control and so fewer inventory losses from obsolescence and deterioration, reduced bad debts from a new receivables system or increased capacity utilisation. Cost savings may also derive from **better IT security and hence fewer losses.**

(d) Possibly, **some one-off revenue benefits** from the sale of equipment which the new system does not require. However, computer equipment depreciates very quickly. It is also possible that the new system will use **less office space**, possibly providing an opportunity to sell or rent the spare space.

Intangible benefits

Many of the benefits are **intangible**, or impossible to give a money value to.

- Improved **staff morale** from working with a more efficient system
- **Better management information**
- Automating routine decisions and tasks should provide **more time for planning**
- More informed **decision making**
- Further savings in staff time
- Benefits accruing from gaining **competitive advantage** through better quality and enhanced products
- Greater **customer satisfaction** and **loyalty**, arising from better customer service and equity
- **Better relationships** with **other supply chain participants**

14.3 Base constraints

The constraints will include:

- **Operations** (for example faster processing, larger volumes, greater security, greater accuracy, better quality)
- Information **output**
- **Volume of processing**
- **General system requirements** (eg accuracy, security and controls, audit trail, flexibility, adaptability)
- Compatibility/integration with existing systems

14.4 Assessment of investment

Important measures are likely to include the following.

(a) The **growth rates in file sizes** and the **number of transactions processed** by the system. Trends should be analysed and projected to assess whether there are likely to be problems with lengthy processing time or an inefficient file structure due to the volume of processing.

(b) The **clerical manpower** needs for the system, and deciding whether they are more or less than estimated.

(c) The identification of any **delays in processing** and an assessment of the consequences of any such delays.

(d) An assessment of the **efficiency of security procedures**, in terms of number of breaches, number of viruses encountered.

(e) A check of the **error rates** for input data. High error rates may indicate inefficient preparation of input documents, an inappropriate method of data capture or poor design of input media.

(f) An examination of whether output from the computer is being used to **good purpose**. (Is it used? Is it timely? Does it go to the right people?)

(g) **Operational running costs**, examined to discover any inefficient programs or processes. This examination may reveal excessive costs for certain items although in total, costs may be acceptable.

Now try this question from the Exam Question Bank	Number	Level	Marks	Time
	Q24	Introductory	n/a	35 mins

BUSINESS VALUATIONS

In the final chapters of the Study Text we shall be concentrating on **methods of calculating the valuations** of organisations of different types. We shall cover the **main methods of valuation** in this chapter, and demonstrate how **market efficiency** and **changing capital structure** impact upon valuation. The most important use of valuation techniques is in a merger or acquisition situation, and therefore Chapter 16 concentrates on these.

Because valuation is examined frequently, this chapter is one of the most important in the Text. You need to be able to use a range of measures in practical situations, also to discuss why they show different values and which measure is the most useful.

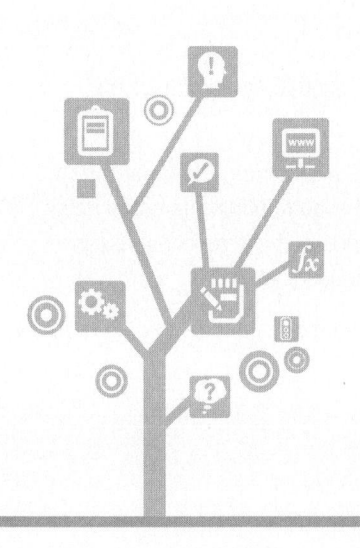

topic list	learning outcomes	syllabus references	ability required
1 Reasons for valuations	C(1)(c)	C(1)(x)	evaluation
2 Asset valuation bases	C(1)(c)	C(1)(ix),(x)	evaluation
3 Earnings valuation bases	C(1)(c)	C(1)(ix),(x)	evaluation
4 Dividend valuation bases	C(1)(c)	C(1)(ix),(x)	evaluation
5 Cash flow valuation methods	C(1)(c)	C(1)(ix),(x)	evaluation
6 Valuation issues	C(1)(c)	C(1)(xii),P(xiii)	evaluation
7 Intangible assets and intellectual capital	C(1)(c)	C(1)(xi)	evaluation

1 Reasons for valuations

Introduction
There are a number of different ways of putting a value on a business. Valuation is a key part of the investment decision as it is very important not to pay too much for an acquisition.

1.1 When valuations are required

Given quoted share prices on the Stock Exchange, why devise techniques for estimating the value of a share? A share valuation will be necessary:

(a) For **quoted companies**, when there is a takeover bid and the offer price is an estimated 'fair value' in excess of the current market price of the shares

> **KEY TERM**
> A TAKEOVER is the acquisition by a company of a controlling interest in the voting share capital of another company, usually achieved by the purchase of a majority of the voting shares.
> *(CIMA Official Terminology)*

(b) For unquoted companies, when:

  (i) The company wishes to 'go public' and must fix an issue price for its shares
  (ii) There is a scheme of merger
  (iii) Shares are sold
  (iv) Shares need to be valued for the purposes of taxation
  (v) Shares are pledged as collateral for a loan

(c) For **subsidiary companies**, when the group's holding company is negotiating the sale of the subsidiary to a management buyout team or to an external buyer

(d) For **any company**, where a shareholder wishes to dispose of his or her holding. Some of the valuation methods we describe will be most appropriate if a large or controlling interest is being sold. However even a small shareholding may be a significant disposal, if the purchasers can increase their holding to a controlling interest as a result of the acquisition

(e) For **any company**, when the company is being broken up in a liquidation situation or the company needs to obtain additional finance, or re-finance current debt

1.2 Stakeholder concerns

Exam skills
Remember that valuation should never be a purely mechanical exercise. When discussing how realistic your valuation methods are, you should bear in mind the impact of stakeholders on the valuation process.

1.2.1 Legal issues

In a number of situations, stakeholders will be given important **legal rights.** As we shall see in the next Chapter, in **merger and acquisition situations** shareholders have rights to be treated fairly by the directors of the companies that are joining together. Governments may also be interested if the merger leads to an organisation that is considered to be too large or dominant in its markets.

Insolvency legislation will give creditor stakeholders prior rights to receive the proceeds of dissolution, and may give them rights to object to arrangements designed to avoid insolvency.

1.2.2 Other situations

In certain circumstances the **attitude of stakeholders** other than shareholders will significantly influence valuation. A good example is a **takeover situation** where the acquiring company is paying for the skills and expertise of its target's employees. If **key employees** are unhappy with the takeover, and decide to leave, then the valuation of the target will be impaired.

1.3 General factors affecting valuation

As well as the calculations, buyers and sellers will also take into account the **industry situation**, the **fixed and human assets** of the company, and a number of factors relating to **shareholdings**:

- The **size** of shareholding to be acquired
- The **distribution** of other shareholdings
- The **rights** related to the shares
- Any **restrictions** on transfers

Exam skills

In an exam question as well as in practice, it is unlikely that one method would be used in isolation. Several valuations might be made, each using a different technique or different assumptions. The valuations could then be compared, and a final price reached as a compromise between the different values. Remember that some methods may be more appropriate for valuing a small parcel of shares, others for valuing a whole company.

1.4 Valuation of listed or unlisted company?

1.4.1 Listed companies

A **listed company** will have a **current stock market value** also known as its market capitalisation. Where small holdings of shares are being traded, this is the relevant price for the transaction.

However, if one company is looking to purchase another by buying shares, this value will **not give a suitable price** because the current shareholders will not have any extra incentive to sell their holdings at the current market price.

As a result a premium to the existing market price is normally offered. Therefore, in an exam question the current stock market price should be used as a **base figure** for calculations to give a suitable price.

1.4.2 Unlisted companies

Since an unlisted company has no stock market price determining a valuation may be more difficult. There is likely to be **less available information** to help a potential purchaser assess the value of the company. Typically this process will involve using a similar listed company (proxy company).

The techniques we are now going to cover produce a **range of values** which can be summarised as follows:

Maximum value ↑   Value the cash flows or earnings under new ownership

                Value the dividends under the existing management

Minimum value ↓   Value the assets

Section summary

There is no one correct business valuation. It makes sense to use several methods of valuation, and to compare the values they produce.

2 Asset valuation bases 9/11, 11/11

Introduction

We start by looking at the lowest valuation of a business. The asset basis can be used to provide a minimum value which can be useful if a business is difficult to sell.

2.1 The net assets method of share valuation

Using this method of valuation, the value of a share in a particular class is equal to the **net tangible assets,** divided by the **number of shares. Intangible assets** (including goodwill) should be **excluded**, unless they have a market value (for example patents and copyrights, which could be sold). The valuation of intangible assets in general, and intellectual capital in particular, is discussed at the end of this chapter.

Example: Net assets method of share valuation

The summary statement of financial position of Cactus is as follows.

	$	$	$
Non-current assets			
Land and buildings		160,000	
Plant and machinery		80,000	
Motor vehicles		20,000	
			260,000
Goodwill			20,000
Current assets			
Inventory		80,000	
Receivables		60,000	
Short-term investments		15,000	
Cash		5,000	
		160,000	
Current liabilities			
Payables	60,000		
Taxation	20,000		
Proposed ordinary dividend	20,000		
		(100,000)	
			60,000
			340,000
12% bonds			(60,000)
Deferred taxation			(10,000)
Total net assets			270,000
Ordinary shares of $1		80,000	
Reserves		140,000	
			220,000
4.9% preference shares of $1			50,000
Total equity and reserves			270,000

What is the value of an ordinary share using the net assets basis of valuation?

Solution

If the figures given for asset values are not questioned, the valuation would be as follows.

	$	$
Total value of assets less current liabilities	340,000	
Less intangible asset (goodwill)	(20,000)	
Total value of assets less current liabilities		320,000
Less: preference shares	50,000	
bonds	60,000	
deferred taxation	10,000	
		120,000
Net asset value of equity		200,000
Number of ordinary shares		80,000
Value per share		$2.50

2.2 Choice of valuation bases

The difficulty in an asset valuation method is establishing the **asset values** to use. Values ought to be realistic. The figure attached to an individual asset may vary considerably depending on whether it is valued on a **going concern** or a **break-up** basis.

Possibilities include:

- **Historic basis** – unlikely to give a realistic value as it is dependent upon the business's depreciation and amortisation policy

- **Replacement basis** – if the assets are to be used on an on-going basis

- **Realisable basis** – if the assets are to be sold, or the business as a whole broken up. This won't be relevant if a minority shareholder is selling his stake, as the assets will continue in the business's use

The following list should give you some idea of the factors that must be considered.

(a) Do the assets need **professional valuation?** If so, how much will this cost?

(b) Have the **liabilities** been accurately quantified, for example deferred taxation? Are there any contingent liabilities? Will any balancing tax charges arise on disposal?

(c) How have the **current assets** been valued? Are all receivables collectable? Is all inventory realisable? Can all the assets be physically located and brought into a saleable condition? This may be difficult in certain circumstances where the assets are situated abroad.

(d) Can any **hidden liabilities** be accurately assessed? Would there be redundancy payments and closure costs?

(e) Is there an **available market** in which the assets can be realised (on a break-up basis)? If so, do the balance sheet values truly reflect these break-up values?

(f) Are there any **prior charges** on the assets?

(g) Does the business have a regular **revaluation and replacement** policy? What are the bases of the valuation? As a broad rule, valuations will be more useful the better they estimate the **future cash flows** that are derived from the asset.

(h) Are there factors that might indicate that the **going concern valuation** of the business **as a whole** is **significantly higher** than the valuation of the individual assets?

(i) What shareholdings are being sold? If a minority interest is being disposed of, realisable value is of limited relevance as the assets will not be sold.

2.3 Use of net asset basis

The net assets basis of valuation might be used in the following circumstances.

(a) As a **'floor value'** for a business that is up for sale – shareholders will be reluctant to sell for less than the NAV. However, if the sale is essential for cash flow purposes or to realign with corporate strategy, even the asset value may not be realised.

(b) **As a measure of the 'security' in a share value**. The **asset backing** for shares provides a measure of the **possible loss** if the company fails to make the expected earnings or dividend payments. Valuable tangible assets may be a good reason for acquiring a company, especially freehold property which might be expected to increase in value over time.

(c) **As a measure of comparison in a scheme of merger**

A **merger** is essentially a business combination of two or more companies, of which none obtains control over any other.

For example, if company A, which has a low asset backing, is planning a merger with company B, which has a high asset backing, the shareholders of B might consider that their shares' value ought to reflect this. It might therefore be agreed that a something should be added to the value of the company B shares to allow for this difference in asset backing.

For these reasons, it is always advisable to calculate the **net assets per share**.

Section summary

The **net assets valuation** method can be used as one of many valuation methods, or to provide a lower limit for the value of a company. By itself it is unlikely to produce the most realistic value.

3 Earnings valuation bases

Introduction

The highest business valuation is usually calculated by valuing the earnings under new ownership. This method uses the P/E ratio which shows the stock market's view of the growth prospects of a company.

3.1 The P/E ratio (earnings) method of valuation   9/11, 11/11

This is a common method of valuing a **controlling interest** in a company, where the owner can decide on **dividend** and **retentions policy**. The P/E ratio relates earnings per share to a share's value.

Since P/E ratio = $\frac{\text{Market value}}{\text{EPS}}$, then market value per share = EPS × P/E ratio

Remember that earnings per share (EPS) = $\frac{\text{Profit / loss attributable to ordinary shareholders}}{\text{Weighted average number of ordinary shares}}$

The P/E ratio produces an **earnings-based** valuation of shares by deciding a suitable P/E ratio and multiplying this by the EPS for the shares which are being valued.

Market valuation or capitalisation = P/E ratio × Earnings per share

The EPS could be a historical EPS or a prospective future EPS. For a given EPS figure, a higher P/E ratio will result in a higher price.

3.2 Significance of high P/E ratio

A high P/E ratio may indicate:

(a) **Expectations that the EPS will grow rapidly**

A **high price is being paid for future profit prospects**. Many small but successful and fast-growing companies are valued on the stock market on a high P/E ratio. Some stocks (for example those of some internet companies in the late 1990s) have reached high valuations before making any profits at all, on the strength of expected future earnings.

(b) **Security of earnings**

A well-established low-risk company would be valued on a higher P/E ratio than a similar company whose earnings are subject to greater uncertainty.

(c) **Status**

If a quoted company (the predator) made a share-for-share takeover bid for an unquoted company (the target), it would normally expect its own shares to be valued on a **higher P/E ratio** than the target company's shares. This is because a quoted company ought to be a **lower-risk** company; but in addition, there is an advantage in having shares which are quoted on a stock market: the shares can be **readily sold**. The P/E ratio of an unquoted company's shares might be around 50% to 60% of the P/E ratio of a similar public company with a full Stock Exchange listing.

3.2.1 Problems with using P/E ratios

However using the price-earnings ratios of quoted companies to value unquoted companies may be problematic.

(a) Finding a quoted company with a **similar range of activities** may be difficult. Quoted companies are often **diversified**.

(b) A **single year's P/E ratio** may not be a good basis, if earnings are volatile, or the quoted company's share price is at an abnormal level, due for example to the expectation of a takeover bid

(c) If a P/E ratio trend is used, then **historical data** will be being used to value how the unquoted company will do in the future.

(d) The quoted company may have a **different capital structure** to the unquoted company.

CASE STUDY

Some sample P/E ratios taken from the Financial Times on 20 April 2011:

Market indices

FTSE 100	13.91
FTSE all-share	14.43

Industry sector averages (main market)

Chemicals	19.62
Construction and materials	14.22
Food producers	8.73
General retailers	10.59
Health care equipment and services	16.29
Mobile telecommunications	7.83
Software and computer services	19.44

Example: Earnings method of valuation

Spider is considering the takeover of an unquoted company, Fly. Spider's shares are quoted on the Stock Exchange at a price of £3.20 and since the most recent published EPS of the company is 20p, the company's P/E ratio is 16. Fly is a company with 100,000 shares and current earnings of £50,000, 50p per share. How might Spider decide on an offer price?

Solution

The decision about the offer price is likely to be preceded by the estimation of a 'reasonable' P/E ratio in the light of the particular circumstances.

(a) If Fly is in the **same industry** as Spider, its P/E ratio ought to be lower, because of its lower status as an unquoted company.

(b) If Fly is in a **different industry**, a suitable P/E ratio might be based on the P/E ratio that is typical for quoted companies in that industry.

(c) If Fly is thought to be **growing fast**, so that its EPS will rise rapidly in the years to come, the P/E ratio that should be used for the share valuation will be higher than if only small EPS growth is expected.

(d) If the acquisition of Fly would **contribute substantially to Spider's own profitability and growth**, or to any other strategic objective that Spider has, then Spider should be willing to offer a higher P/E ratio valuation, in order to secure acceptance of the offer by Fly's shareholders.

Of course, the P/E ratio on which Spider bases its offer will probably be lower than the P/E ratio that Fly's shareholders think their shares ought to be valued on. Some haggling over the price might be necessary.

Spider might decide that Fly's shares ought to be valued on a P/E ratio of 60% × 16 = 9.6, that is, at 9.6 × 50p = £4.80 each.

Fly's shareholders might reject this offer, and suggest a valuation based on a P/E ratio of, say, 12.5, that is, 12.5 × 50p = £6.25.

Spider's management might then come back with a revised offer, say valuation on a P/E ratio of 10.5, that is, 10.5 × 50p = £5.25.

The haggling will go on until the negotiations either break down or succeed in arriving at an agreed price.

3.3 Guidelines for a P/E ratio-based valuation

When a company is thinking of acquiring an **unquoted** company in a takeover, the final offer price will be agreed by **negotiation**, but a list of some of the factors affecting the valuer's choice of P/E ratio is given below.

(a) General **economic** and **financial** conditions

(b) The type of **industry** and the prospects of that industry. Use of current P/E ratios may give an unrealistically low valuation if these ratios are being affected by a lack of confidence throughout the industry.

(c) The **size** of the undertaking and its **status** within its industry. If an unquoted company's earnings are growing annually and are currently around £300,000 or so, then it could probably get a quote in its own right on the Alternative Investment Market, and a higher P/E ratio should therefore be used when valuing its shares.

(d) **Marketability**. The market in shares that do not have a Stock Exchange quotation is always a restricted one and a higher yield is therefore required.

(e) The **diversity** of shareholdings and the **financial status** of any principal shareholders

(f) The **reliability** of profit estimates and the past profit record. Use of profits and P/E ratios over time may give a more reliable valuation, especially if they are being compared with industry levels over that time.

(g) **Asset backing** and **liquidity**

(h) The **nature of the assets**, for example whether some of the non-current assets are of a highly specialised nature, and so have only a small break-up value

(i) **Gearing**. A relatively high gearing ratio will generally mean greater financial risk for ordinary shareholders and call for a higher rate of return on equity.

(j) The extent to which the business is dependent on the **technical skills** of one or more individuals

(k) The predator may need to be particularly careful when valuing an unlisted company of using a P/E ratio of a **'similar' listed company**. The predator should obtain reasonable evidence that the listed company does have the same risk and growth characteristics, and has similar policies on significant areas such as directors' remuneration.

Exam skills

For examination purposes, you should normally **take a figure around one half to two thirds** of the industry average when valuing an unquoted company.

3.3.1 Use of predator's P/E ratios

A predator company may sometimes use their higher P/E ratio to value a target company. This use of a higher P/E ratio is known as **bootstrapping.** This assumes that the predator **can improve the target's business**, which may be a dangerous assumption to make. The predator's intentions will also be important; the choice of P/E ratio may depend on whether the predator envisages demerging some of the target's operations, or retaining them all. It may be better to use an adjusted industry P/E ratio, or some other method.

3.3.2 Use of forecast earnings

When one company is thinking about taking over another, it should look at the target company's **forecast earnings**, not just its historical results.

Forecasts of **earnings growth** should only be used if:

(a) There are good reasons to believe that earnings growth will be achieved

(b) A reasonable estimate of growth can be made

(c) Forecasts supplied by the target company's directors are made in good faith and using reasonable assumptions and fair accounting policies

Question 15.1 — Earnings valuation

Learning outcome: C(1)(c)

Flycatcher wishes to make a takeover bid for the shares of an unquoted company, Mayfly. The earnings of Mayfly over the past five years have been as follows.

20X0	$50,000	20X3	$71,000
20X1	$72,000	20X4	$75,000
20X2	$68,000		

The average P/E ratio of quoted companies in the industry in which Mayfly operates is 10. Quoted companies which are similar in many respects to Mayfly are:

(a) Bumblebee, which has a P/E ratio of 15, but is a company with very good growth prospects
(b) Wasp, which has had a poor profit record for several years, and has a P/E ratio of 7

What would be a suitable range of valuations for the shares of Mayfly?

3.4 The earnings yield valuation method

$$\text{Earnings yield (EY)} = \frac{\text{EPS}}{\text{Market price per share}} \times 100\%$$

This method is effectively a variation on the P/E method (the EY being the reciprocal of the P/E ratio), using an appropriate earnings yield effectively as a discount rate to value the earnings:

$$\text{Market value} = \frac{\text{Earnings}}{\text{EY}}$$

Exactly the same guidelines apply to this method as for the P/E method. Note that where **high growth** is envisaged, **the EY will be low,** as current earnings will be low relative to a market price that has built in future earnings growth. A stable earnings yield may suggest a company with low risk characteristics.

3.5 The accounting rate of return (ARR) method of share valuation

This method considers the **accounting rate of return** which will be required from the company whose shares are to be valued. It is therefore distinct from the P/E ratio method, which is concerned with the **market** rate of return required.

The following formula should be used.

$$\text{Value} = \frac{\text{Estimated future profits}}{\text{Required return on capital employed}}$$

For a takeover bid valuation, it will often be necessary to adjust the profits figure to allow for **expected changes** after the takeover. Those arising in an examination question might include:

(a) New levels of directors' remuneration

(b) New levels of interest charges (perhaps because the predator company will be able to replace existing loans with new loans at a lower rate of interest, or because the previous owners had lent the company money at non-commercial rates)

(c) A charge for notional rent where it is intended to sell existing properties or where the rate of return used is based on the results of similar companies that do not own their own properties

(d) The effects of product rationalisation and improved management

Note that such adjustments can also apply to earnings used in a P/E valuation approach.

Example: ARR method of share valuation

Chambers is considering acquiring Hall. At present Hall is earning, on average, $480,000 after tax. The directors of Chambers feel that after reorganisation, this figure could be increased to $600,000. All the companies in the Chambers group are expected to yield a post-tax accounting return of 15% on capital employed. What should Hall be valued at?

Solution

$$\text{Valuation} = \frac{\$600,000}{15\%} = \$4,000,000$$

This figure is the maximum that Chambers should be prepared to pay. The first offer would probably be much lower.

An ARR valuation might be used in a takeover when the acquiring company is trying to assess the **maximum amount it can afford to pay**.

Section summary

- **P/E ratios** are used when a large block of shares, or a whole business, is being valued. This method can be problematic when quoted companies' P/E ratios are used to value unquoted companies.
- Other earnings methods include the **earnings yield** valuation method and the **accounting rate of return** method.

4 Dividend valuation bases

Introduction

The dividend valuation method involves the present value of the future dividends. It will produce a mid-range valuation that is generally more relevant to small shareholdings rather than the whole company.

4.1 Using the dividend valuation model

The dividend valuation model is based on the theory that an equilibrium price for any share (or bond) on a stock market is:

- The **future expected stream of income** from the security
- **Discounted** at a suitable **cost of capital**

Equilibrium market price is thus a **present value** of a **future expected income stream**. The annual income stream for a share is the expected dividend every year in perpetuity.

Using the **dividend growth model** we have:

$$P_0 = \frac{d_0(1+g)}{(k_e - g)} \text{ or } P_0 = \frac{d_1}{(k_e - g)}$$

Where
- d_0 = Current year's dividend
- g = Growth rate in earnings and dividends
- k_e = Shareholders' required rate of return
- $d_0(1 + g)$ = Expected dividend in one year's time (d_1)
- P_0 = Market value excluding any dividend currently payable

We looked at how to determine 'g' and k_e in Chapter 8.

Question 15.2 DVM

Learning outcome: C(1)(c)

Target paid a dividend of $250,000 this year. The current return to shareholders of quoted companies in the same industry as Target is 12%, although it is expected that an additional risk premium of 2% will be applicable to Target, being a smaller and unquoted company. Compute the expected valuation of Target, if:

(a) The current level of dividend is expected to continue into the foreseeable future.
(b) The dividend is expected to grow at a rate of 4% pa into the foreseeable future.
(c) The dividend is expected to grow at a 3% rate for three years and 2% afterwards.

4.2 Assumptions of dividend models

The dividend models are underpinned by a number of assumptions that you should bear in mind.

(a) Investors act **rationally** and **homogenously** and have **perfect information** available. The model fails to take into account the **different expectations** or **different marginal costs of capital of** shareholders, nor how much they are motivated by dividends vs future capital appreciation on their shares.

(b) The d_0 figure used does **not vary significantly** from the **trend or risk of dividends**. If d_0 does appear to be a rogue figure, it may be better to use an adjusted trend figure, calculated on the basis of the past few years' dividends.

(c) The **estimates** of future dividends and prices used, and also the cost of capital are **reasonable**. As with other methods, it may be difficult to make a confident estimate of the cost of capital. Dividend estimates may be made from historical trends that may not be a good guide for a future if for example there is a takeover, or derived from uncertain forecasts about future earnings, which assumes that there are **enough profitable projects** in the future to **maintain dividend levels**.

(d) Investors' attitudes to receiving different cash flows at different times can be modelled using **discounted cashflow arithmetic.**

(e) Directors use dividends to **signal** the strength of the company's position (however companies that pay zero dividends do not have zero share values).

(f) Dividends either show **no growth** or **constant growth**. If the growth rate is calculated using g=bR, then the model assumes that b and R are constant

(g) **Other influences** on share prices are **ignored**.

(h) The company's **earnings** will **increase** sufficiently to maintain dividend growth levels.

(i) The **discount rate** used exceeds the **dividend growth rate**.

(j) **Tax and issue expenses** are ignored.

PART C INVESTMENT DECISIONS AND PROJECT CONTROL   15: Business valuations

> **Section summary**
>
> The dividend valuation model is based on the present value of the future dividends being generated by the **existing** management. It is generally more relevant for **small shareholdings**.

5 Cash flow valuation methods   11/11, 3/12

> **Introduction**
>
> The discounted cash flow method calculates the present value of the future cash flows that will be generated by the new management.

5.1 The discounted future cash flows method of share valuation

This method of share valuation may be appropriate when one company intends to buy the assets of another company and to make further investments in order to **improve cash flows** in the future.

Example: Discounted future cash flows method of share valuation

Diversification wishes to make a bid for Tadpole. Tadpole makes after-tax profits of $40,000 a year. Diversification believes that if further money is spent on additional investments, the after-tax cash flows (ignoring the purchase consideration) could be as follows.

Year	Cash flow (net of tax) $
0	(100,000)
1	(80,000)
2	60,000
3	100,000
4	150,000
5	150,000

The after-tax cost of capital of Diversification is 15% and the company expects all its investments to pay back, in discounted terms, within five years. What is the maximum price that the company should be willing to pay for the shares of Tadpole?

Solution

The maximum price is one which would make the return from the total investment exactly 15% over five years, so that the NPV at 15% would be 0.

Year	Cash flows ignoring purchase consideration $	Discount factor (from tables) @ 15%	Present value $
0	(100,000)	1.000	(100,000)
1	(80,000)	0.870	(69,600)
2	60,000	0.756	45,360
3	100,000	0.658	65,800
4	150,000	0.572	85,800
5	150,000	0.497	74,550
Maximum purchase price			101,910

Exam skills

You may also need to calculate the value of cash flows in perpetuity using the formula given to you in the exam.

5.2 Selection of an appropriate cost of capital

In the above example, Diversification used its own cost of capital to discount the cash flows of Tadpole. There are a number of reasons why this may not be appropriate.

(a) The **business risk** of the new investment may not match that of the investing company. If Tadpole is in a completely different line of business from Diversification, its cash flows are likely to be subject to differing degrees of risk, and this should be taken into account when valuing them.

(b) The **method of finance** of the new investment may not match the current debt/equity mix of the investing company, which may have an effect on the cost of capital to be used.

5.3 Free cash flow

Under NPV, valuation of a new company = cash subscribed/paid for investment + NPV of proposed activities.

The **present value** of future **free cash flows model** (also known as the **surplus project cash flow model**) focuses on the strategic need of companies to reinvest in new plant to maintain or increase current operating cash flows. This investment expenditure does not generally equal the depreciation charge in the accounts. Free cash flow takes into account this difference.

In the free flow cash flow model:

Operating free cash flow	=	Revenues
	−	Operating costs
	+	Depreciation
	−	Debt repayments and lease obligations
	−	Working capital increases
	−	Taxes
	−	Replacement capital expenditure

Using this model, the value of a company is the **sum** of **future discounted free cash flows**.

You may see other definitions of free cash flow used by different companies.

The advantage of including strategic value as well as existing project value in the definition of free cash flow is that **strategic value** can often be a significant element of **company value**.

Free cash flows can also be used as an element in ratio calculations. For example, the dividend cover ratio can be adjusted to take account of free cash flow.

$$\text{Dividend cover} = \frac{\text{Free cash flow}}{\text{Dividends paid}}$$

This emphasises the importance of having cash available to pay dividends.

Possible disadvantages are that free cash flows may **fluctuate significantly** and will depend considerably on the company's **capital replacement policy**.

Free cash flow is also an important element in shareholder value analysis.

5.4 Shareholder value analysis

Shareholder value analysis (SVA) focuses on value creation using the net present value (NPV) approach.

KEY TERM

SHAREHOLDER VALUE is the total return to shareholders in terms of both dividends and share price growth, calculated as the present value of future free cash flows of the entity discounted at the weighted average cost of capital of the entity less the market value of debt.

Many leading companies (including, for example, Pepsi, Quaker and Disney) have used SVA as a way of linking management strategy and decisions to the creation of value for shareholders.

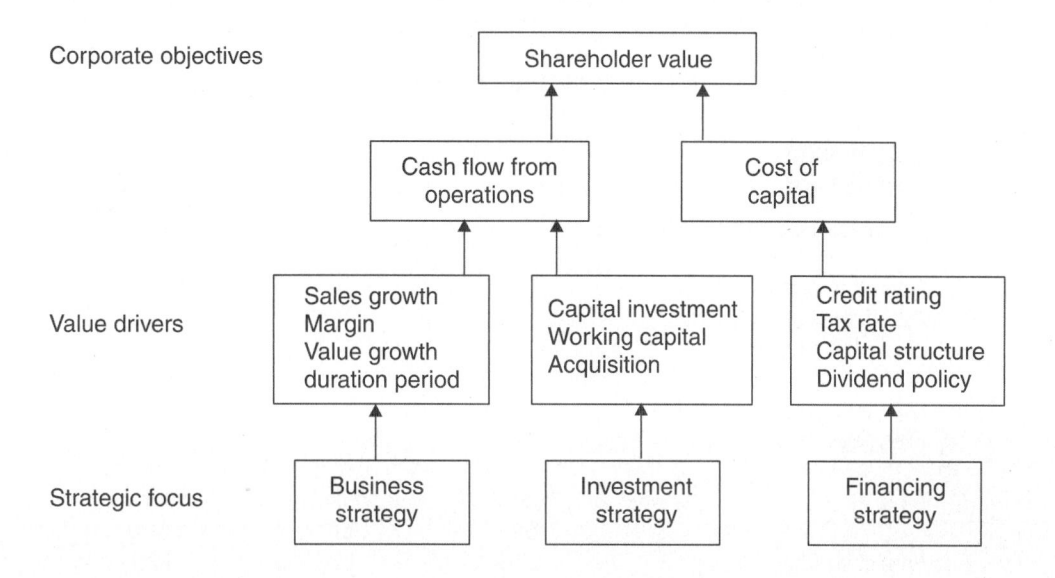

```
Corporate objectives              Shareholder value
                                    ↑
                       ┌────────────┴────────────┐
                  Cash flow from              Cost of
                   operations                 capital
                       ↑                        ↑
          ┌────────────┴────┐         ┌─────────┴─────────┐
          │                 │         │                   │
     Sales growth      Capital investment        Credit rating
Value drivers  Margin          Working capital          Tax rate
     Value growth       Acquisition              Capital structure
     duration period                             Dividend policy
          ↑                 ↑                         ↑
     Business          Investment              Financing
Strategic focus  strategy          strategy               strategy
```

5.4.1 SVA approach

(a) Key decisions with implications for cash flow and risk are specified. These may be **strategic**, **operational**, **related to investment** or **financial**.

(b) **Value drivers** are identified as the factors having the greatest impact on shareholder value, and management attention is focused on the decisions which influence the value drivers.

Value drivers are identified as being fundamental to the determination of value:

(i)   Sales growth rate
(ii) Operating profit margin
(iii) Tax rate
(iv) Fixed capital investment
(v)   Working capital investment
(vi) The planning horizon
(vii) The required rate of return

5.4.2 SVA assumptions

(a) The model assumes a **constant percentage** rate of sales growth and a **constant** operating profit margin.

(b) Tax is assumed to be a **constant percentage** of operating profit.

(c) Fixed and working capital investments are assumed to be a **constant percentage** of changes in sales.

5.4.3 Calculating shareholder value

Using the free cash flows, corporate value is then computed at a rate reflecting the **company's risk**.

A question covering this area may well indicate the rate that you should use to discount free cash flows. If you are not told the rate to use, the rate you should use should reflect the company's risk. This may be the weighted average cost of capital, but the WACC should not be used if **interest** has been included in the calculation of free cash flows. After tax cost of equity (ungeared) should be used if interest has been included in the free cash flow calculation, or if debt is assumed to be risk-free.

Example: SVA

Rackets is a quoted company. Its forecast operating profit for the year is $156 million after deduction of a $4 million depreciation charge. Tax on profits is estimated to be $48 million. Shareholders require a return of 8% per annum.

Non-current assets will be sold during the year and receipts are estimated to be $12 million. There will be investment in non-current assets and working capital during the year of $16 million. Free cash flows for the following three years are estimated to be $120 million.

Required

Calculate the value of Rackets using the SVA approach.

Solution

Free cash flow forecast for Year 1

	$m
Operating profit	156
Add depreciation	4
Less tax on profits	(48)
Add sale of assets	12
Less Investment in assets	(16)
Free cash flow	108

	Year 1 $m	Year 2 $m	Year 3 $m	Year 4 $m
Free cash flow	108	120	120	120
Discount factor @ 8%	0.926	0.857	0.794	0.735
Present value	100	103	95	88
Total present value	**386**			

The present value of the free cash flow in perpetuity = 120/0.08 × 0.735 = $1,103m

Value of Rackets = $(386 + 1,103)m = $1,489m

5.4.4 Advantages of SVA

(a) It is inclusive of the cost of capital and risk.
(b) It is not sensitive to the choice of accounting policies.
(c) It is relatively simple to apply.
(d) It is consistent with the concept of share valuation by DCF.
(e) It acts as a spur to management awareness of the key long-term value variables (drivers).

5.4.5 Disadvantages of SVA

(a) The **constant percentage assumptions** may be **unrealistic**.

(b) The **input data** may **not** be **easily available** from current systems, particularly to outsiders. It may not be easy to test whether the assumptions on which the forecasts are based are realistic.

(c) It may be **misused in target setting** – giving managers a 12-month target cash flow may discourage longer term profitable investment. On the other hand a longer-term target may be very difficult to set because of uncertainties over future cash flows.

(d) Other models have been suggested with **different value drivers**.

5.5 Economic Value Added (EVA®)

EVA® is closely associated with SVA and gives the economic value or profit added per year. It can be used as a means of **measuring managerial performance,** by assessing the net present value of revenues (profits) less resources used (capital employed). It is **not** a measure of share valuation.

EVA® = NOPAT − (cost of capital × capital employed)

where NOPAT = Net operating profit after tax adjusted for non-cash expenses (see below)

(cost of capital × capital employed) = imputed charge for the capital consumed, the cost of capital being the weighted average cost of capital for the firm's **target capital structure**

Adjustments may be needed to the profit figures in the accounts to arrive at NOPAT.

(a) **Interest** and **tax relief on interest** should be excluded from NOPAT, as they are taken into account in the imputed capital charge.

(b) **Investing cash flows** should be excluded from NOPAT **but** allowed for in **capital employed.** These include **goodwill, research and development** and **advertising**, and other expenditure designed to build the business up over the next few years. The amount added to capital employed should be a figure that reflects the expenditure that has affected profit this year, say the research and development charge for the last four years or goodwill that has previously been written off. (In some calculations a small charge for research and development is included in the income statement to reflect the economic depreciation of the capitalised value.)

(c) **Lease charges** should be excluded from NOPAT but added in as part of capital employed.

(d) The **depreciation** figure in the accounts can be used as an approximation for economic depreciation.

Economic depreciation = the fall in asset value due to wear and tear and obsolescence

If a separate figure is calculated for economic depreciation, accounting depreciation should be excluded from NOPAT.

5.5.1 Advantages of EVA®

(a) The economic value added approach focuses on **long-term** net present value.

(b) By including a **financing element**, it brings home to managers the costs of capital used, emphasising the importance of careful investment and control of working capital.

5.5.2 Disadvantages of EVA®

(a) EVA® may cause managers to **avoid projects** with poor initial returns or large initial expenditure (for example on research and development) if they are primarily being judged on short-term performance.

(b) The economic value added approach also suffers from the usual problems of being based on **historical accounting figures** that can be distorted.

(c) There may be **other value drivers** that are important, such as non-capitalised goodwill.

5.6 Market value added

Market value added (MVA) is the difference between:

(a) The **contribution** put into the business by investors (the purchase price of their shares **and** the re-investment of profits that would otherwise have been distributed)

(b) The increase in **current market value of their shares** resulting from the contribution

The MVA figure tends to correspond closely to the difference between the market value of equity and the book value of equity. To assess whether MVA is reasonable, you need to assess what economic value added will be for several years into the future; this may not be easy. Market value added also does not adjust for size differences for comparisons.

5.7 Drawbacks of cash flow methods

Cash flow methods of valuation can be used to place a **maximum value** on an entity and incorporate the **time value of** money.

However, whichever method is used, cash flow methods suffer from the following general drawbacks.

(a) As we have seen above, selection of an **appropriate cost of capital** may prove difficult.

(b) **Estimating future cash flows**, particularly of companies that are being acquired, may be **very difficult**.

(c) Cash flows are most appropriate for valuing **controlling interests**, which might have a significant influence on whether expected cash flows are attained.

5.8 Summary of valuation techniques

MAXIMUM VALUE (under new management)

- NPV/SVA
    - includes expected synergies
    - discount free cash flows at target's WACC
- P/E method
    - adjust P/E
    - P/E × EPS

FAIR VALUE (under existing method)

- Dividend valuation – use target's growth rate, most suitable for valuing a minority holding

MINIMUM VALUE

- Assets basis – most appropriate for a capital intensive business

---

Section summary

Discounted future cash flows valuation may be used to value a company. **Free cash flows** are a development of the DCF method. **Shareholder value analysis** focuses on the key decisions affecting value and risk.

Question 15.3
Business valuation

Learning outcome: C(1)(c)

Profed provides a tuition service to professional students. This includes courses of lectures provided on their own premises and provision of study material for home study. Most of the lecturers are qualified professionals with many years' experience in both their profession and tuition. Study materials are written and word processed in-house, but sent out to an external printer.

PART C INVESTMENT DECISIONS AND PROJECT CONTROL   15: Business valuations

The business was started fifteen years ago, and now employs around 40 full-time lecturers, 10 authors and 20 support staff. Freelance lecturers and authors are employed from time to time in times of peak demand.

The shareholders of Profed mainly comprise the original founders of the business who would now like to realise their investment. In order to arrive at an estimate of what they believe the business is worth, they have identified a long-established quoted company, City Tutors, who have a similar business, although they also publish texts for external sale to universities, colleges etc.

Summary financial statistics for the two companies for the most recent financial year are as follows.

	Profed	City Tutors
Issued shares (million)	4	10
Net asset values (£m)	7.2	15
Earnings per share (pence)	35	20
Dividend per share (pence)	20	18
Debt: equity ratio	1:7	1:65
Share price (pence)		362
Expected rate of growth in earnings/dividends	9% pa	7.5% pa

Notes

1. The net assets of Profed are the net book values of tangible non-current assets plus net working capital. However:
   - A recent valuation of the buildings was £1.5 million above book value.
   - Inventory includes past editions of text books which have a realisable value of £100,000 below their cost.
   - Due to a dispute with one of their clients, an additional allowance for bad debts of £750,000 could prudently be made.

2. Growth rates should be assumed to be constant per annum; Profed's earnings growth rate estimate was provided by the marketing manager, based on expected growth in sales adjusted by normal profit margins. City Tutors' growth rates were gleaned from press reports.

3. Profed uses a discount rate of 15% to appraise its investments, and has done for many years.

Required

(a) Compute a range of valuations for the business of Profed, using the information available and stating any assumptions made.

(b) Comment upon the strengths and weaknesses of the methods you used in (a) and their suitability for valuing Profed.

Exam skills

In a business valuation question, there is no one 'correct' answer. You need to be able to present a well reasoned report that takes into account a number of different view points whilst making reasonable assumptions

As well as assessing valuation issues in the TOPCIMA exam, you may also have to consider whether a premium should be paid to secure a particularly desirable acquisition.

6 Valuation issues

Introduction

In this section we look at the impact of market efficiency and change in capital structure on business valuations. We also look at how to value unlisted companies using geared and ungeared betas. We have looked at all of these issues earlier in the Study Text but now relate them to business valuations.

6.1 Impact of market efficiency

In Chapter 5 we discussed the significance of market efficiency and in this section we examine how market efficiency impacts upon the company valuation process.

6.1.1 Availability of information

The different methods we have discussed above are built upon different levels of efficiency. Broadly speaking, methods based on **historical or current position** require the market to have a **lower** degree of efficiency than methods that are based on **future cash flows** or **dividend flows**.

As most studies suggest that stock markets are **semi-strong efficient**, share prices are based on analysis of all **known information**. Directors therefore need to take the correct investment, financing and risk management decisions and make this information public.

6.1.2 Mergers and takeovers

Market efficiency is particularly important when companies are considering making an offer for another company. If the market is semi-strong efficient, the target's shares will be valued at a **fair price**; hence any premium offered on those shares has to be justified in terms of post-acquisition gains or savings.

However if the market is **very efficient**, arguably it will anticipate that a merger will take place and these gains will be realised. There is some evidence from the major stock exchanges that mergers are anticipated some months in advance. The more this happens, and the more likely benefits from anticipated mergers are factored into the share price, the less a premium is likely to be value for money for an acquiror.

6.2 Share valuation and change in capital structure

In Chapter 9 we considered the different viewpoints concerning the effect of capital structure on the cost of capital. In this section we look in greater detail on how capital structure impacts upon the valuation of companies.

6.2.1 Traditional approach

Remember that the traditional view was that the optimum level of gearing is where the company's weighted average cost of capital is minimised and therefore the company's total market value is maximised.

Example: Traditional approach

Gearing has the following capital structure (no tax):

		Constant annual payments to investors $m	Market value $m
Equity	dividends	27	150
Debt	interest	3	30
		30	180

The current cost of equity: $k_e = \dfrac{d_0}{P_0} = \dfrac{27}{150} = 18\%$

The current cost of debt: $k_d = \dfrac{i}{P_0} = \dfrac{3}{30} = 10\%$

WACC: $\dfrac{150}{180} \times 18\% + \dfrac{30}{180} \times 10\% = 16.67\%$

Note that in the case of constant dividends and interest, the WACC can be computed as:

$$\text{WACC} = \dfrac{\text{Total payments to investors}}{\text{Total MV}} = \dfrac{\$30m}{\$180m} = 16.67\%$$

Conversely, discounting the total payments to investors by the WACC in perpetuity can derive the total MV:

$$\text{Total MV} = \dfrac{\text{Total payments to investors}}{\text{WACC}} = \dfrac{\$30m}{0.1667} = £180m$$

Current gearing level, equity:debt, is 150:30 or 5:1

Now suppose the **gearing is to be increased** to Method (1) 3:1 or Method (2) 3:2 by the repurchase of shares, funded by new debt. It is estimated that the cost of equity will rise to compensate for the increase in gearing risk, by (1) 0.75% and (2) 3%, and that the cost of debt will rise, in the case of (2) only, by 0.5%.

What are the effects on WACC and total MV of each change?

New WACC under (1): $3/4 \times 18.75\% + 1/4 \times 10\% = 16.56\%$

and, since total payments to investors will be unchanged,

Total MV under (1) $= \dfrac{\$30m}{0.1656} = \$181.16m$

New WACC under (2) $= 3/5 \times 21\% + 2/5 \times 10.5\% = 16.8\%$

Total MV under (2) $= \dfrac{\$30m}{0.168} = \$178.57m$

Method (1), with the lower increase in gearing, had a small associated increase in the cost of equity, and the WACC went down – the impact of more cheaper debt outweighed the effect of the increased cost of equity. This led to a rise in the total MV.

Under Method (2), with the percentage of total capital represented by debt more than doubling, there was a much higher increase in the cost of equity, accompanied by an increase in the cost of debt. Despite the much higher proportion of cheap debt, the WACC went up, and the total MV fell.

Question 15.4 — Change in capital structure

Learning outcome: C(1)(c)

AB has a WACC of 16%. It is financed partly by equity (cost 18%) and partly by debt capital (cost 10%). The company is considering a new project which would cost $5,000,000 and would yield annual profits of $850,000 before interest charges. It would be financed by a loan at 10%. As a consequence of the higher gearing, the cost of equity would rise to 20%. The company pays out all profits as dividends, which are currently $2,250,000 a year.

(a) What would be the effect on the value of equity of undertaking the project?

(b) To what extent can you analyse the increase or decrease in equity value into two causes, the NPV of the project at the current WACC and the effect of the method of financing?

Ignore taxation. The traditional view of WACC and gearing is assumed in this exercise.

6.2.2 Net operating income approach

We saw earlier in this text that Modigliani and Miller stated in their basic theory that the level of gearing would not affect the value of shares in a tax-less world. However if taxation was introduced, the weighted average cost of capital will continue to fall as gearing increased.

You will remember that Modigliani and Miller argued that since WACC falls as gearing rises, and the value of a company should rise as its WACC falls, **the value of a geared company (V_g) will always be greater than its ungeared counterpart (V_u)**, but only by the amount of the debt-associated tax saving of the geared company, assuming a permanent change in gearing.

$$V_g = V_u + TB_c.$$

The additional amount of value in the geared company, TB_c is known as the value of the '**tax shield**' on debt.

However, the positive tax effects of debt finance will be exhausted where there is insufficient tax liability to use the tax relief which is available. This is known as **tax shield exhaustion**.

Example: MM with taxes

Notnil and Newbegin are companies in the same industry. They have the same business risk and operating characteristics, but Notnil is a geared company whereas Newbegin is all equity financed. Notnil earns three times as much profit before interest as Newbegin. Both companies pursue a policy of paying out all their earnings each year as dividends.

The market value of each company is currently as follows.

		Notnil $m		Newbegin $m
Equity	(10m shares)	36	(20m shares)	15
Debt	($12m of 12% bonds)	14		
		50		15

The annual profit before interest of Notnil is $3,000,000 and that of Newbegin is $1,000,000. The rate of tax is 30%. It is thought that the current market value per ordinary share in Newbegin is at the equilibrium level, and that the market value of Notnil's debt capital is also at its equilibrium level. There is some doubt, however, about whether the value of Notnil's shares is at its equilibrium level.

Apply the MM formula to establish the equilibrium price of Notnil's shares.

Solution

$V_g = V_u + TB_c$

V_u = the market value of an equivalent ungeared company. Equivalence is in both size and risk of earnings. Since Notnil earnings (before interest) are three times the size of Newbegin's, V_u is three times the value of Newbegin's equity:

$3 \times \$15,000,000 = \$45,000,000$.

$TB_c = \$14,000,000 \times 30\% = \$4,200,000$

$V_g = \$45,000,000 + \$4,200,000 = \$49,200,000$.

Since the market value of debt in Notnil is $14,000,000, it follows that the market value of Notnil's equity should be $49,200,000 − $14,000,000 = $35,200,000.

Value per share = $\dfrac{\$35,200,000}{10,000,000}$ = $3.52 per share

Since the current share price is $3.60 per share, MM would argue that the shares in Notnil are currently over-valued by the market, by $800,000 in total or 8c per share. MM argue that this discrepancy would be rapidly removed by the process of arbitrage until the equity value of Notnil was as predicted by their model.

Question 15.5 — WACC and MM theory

Learning outcome: C(1)(c)

CD and YZ are identical in every respect except for their gearing. The market value of each company is as follows.

	CD $m		YZ $m
Equity (5m shares)	?	(8m shares)	24
Debt ($20m of 5% bonds)	10		
	?		24

According to MM theory, what is the value of CD shares, given a corporation tax rate of 30%?

6.3 Valuation prior to flotation

There is a problem with valuing unlisted companies using earnings or dividends bases as a cost of equity (k_e) is needed. There are two methods of calculating a cost of equity, the CAPM and the dividend model, but both are difficult to apply to an unlisted company.

To deal with this problem, we can use the beta of a listed company to help to calculate k_e. We looked at **gearing and ungearing betas** in Chapter 8 in the context of a project specific cost of capital. We can use a very similar approach to calculate a geared cost of equity and then the value of a company as follows.

STEP 1 Find the equity beta of a similar listed company and strip out the effect of gearing to create an ungeared beta.

$$\beta_u = \beta_g \frac{V_E}{V_E + V_D(1-t)}$$

STEP 2 Regear the beta using the company's gearing using the formula

$$\beta_g = \beta_u + (\beta_u - \beta_d) \frac{V_D(1-t)}{V_E}$$ and calculate the k_e geared.

STEP 3 Use this k_e geared to calculate the value of the company using the formula

$$P_0 = \frac{d_0(1+g)}{k_e - g}$$

Example: Valuation prior to flotation

Blogs Co is going to obtain a stock market listing and a valuation therefore needs to be calculated for the company.

Blogs debt:equity ratio is 2:5, its annual earnings this year were $600,000 and it regularly pays 50% of earnings as dividends, with 5% growth expected each year.

A listed company in the same industry as Blogs has a debt:equity ratio of 1:2 and a beta of 1.62.

The risk-free return is 4%, the market return is 9% and tax is at 30%.

Solution

STEP 1

$$\beta_u = 1.62\left[\frac{2}{2+1(1-0.3)}\right] = 1.2$$

STEP 2

$$\beta_g = 1.2 + 1.2\left[\frac{(2(1-0.3))}{5}\right] = 1.54$$

$$k_e = 4\% + (9\% - 4\%)1.54 = 11.7\%$$

STEP 3

$d_0 = 50\% \times 600{,}000 = 300{,}000$

$g = 5\%$

$$P_0 = \frac{300{,}000(1+0.05)}{0.117 - 0.05} = \$4{,}701{,}493$$

Section summary

- The reliability of the various methods used to value shares may be affected by the **level of market efficiency**.

- The **traditional view of gearing** states that **market value** should be **maximised** at the optimum capital structure, where cost of capital is minimised. **Modigliani and Miller** state that in a world with taxes, market value should continue to rise as gearing rises, because tax benefits arise from interest paid.

- It can be difficult to **value unlisted companies** as obtaining a **cost of equity** is difficult. The **beta of a listed company** can be used to calculate the cost of equity.

7 Intangible assets and intellectual capital

Introduction

The valuation of intangible assets and intellectual capital is particularly difficult. This section looks at the various types of intangible assets that a business may benefit from and how they might be valued.

7.1 Valuation of intangibles

The asset based valuation method discussed earlier specifically excluded most intangible assets from the computation. This rendered this method unsuitable for the valuation of most established businesses, particularly those in the **service industry**.

7.1.1 Intangible assets and goodwill

KEY TERMS

INTANGIBLE ASSETS are identifiable non-monetary assets without physical substance which must be controlled by the entity as the result of past events and from which the entity expects a flow of future economic benefits. *(IAS 38)*

GOODWILL (acquired) is future economic benefits arising from assets that are not capable of being individually identified and separately recognised. *(IFRS 3)*

The above definition of intangible assets distinguishes:

(a) Intangible assets from tangible assets, by the phrase 'do not have physical substance'.

(b) Intangible assets from goodwill, by the word 'identifiable', an identifiable asset is legally defined as one that can be disposed of separately without disposing of a business of the entity.

The strict accounting distinctions do not need to concern us here. We are interested in any element of business that may have some value.

Certain intangible assets can be recorded at their **historical cost**. Examples include patents and trademarks being recorded at **registration value** and franchises being recorded at **contract cost**. However over time these historical values may become poor reflections of the assets' value in use or of their market value.

7.1.2 Intellectual capital

INTELLECTUAL CAPITAL is knowledge which can be used to create value. Intellectual capital includes:

(a) Human resources: the collective skills, experience and knowledge of employees

(b) Intellectual assets: knowledge which is defined and codified such as a drawing, computer program or collection of data

(c) Intellectual property: intellectual assets which can be legally protected, such as patents and copyrights

(CIMA Official Terminology)

As the demand for **knowledge-based products** grows with the changing structure of the global economy, knowledge plays an expanding role in achieving competitive advantage. **Employees** may therefore be extremely valuable to a business, and they should be included in a full assets based valuation.

The principles of valuation discussed below should be taken as applying to all assets, resources or property that are defined as intangible assets or intellectual capital, which will include:

- Patents, trademarks and copyrights
- Franchises and licensing agreements
- Research and development
- Brands
- Technology, management and consulting processes
- Know-how, education, vocational qualification
- Customer loyalty
- Distribution channels
- Management philosophy

7.2 Measurement of intangible assets of an enterprise

The **expanding intellectual capital** of firms accentuates the need for methods of valuation for comparative purposes, for example when an acquisition or buy-out is being considered.

Ramona Dzinkowski (The measurement and management of intellectual capital, Management Accounting, February 2000) identifies the following three indicators, which are derived from audited financial statements and are independent of the definitions of intellectual capital adopted by the firm.

- Market-to-book values
- Tobin's 'q'
- Calculated intangible value

7.2.1 Market-to-book values

This method represents the value of a firm's intellectual capital as **the difference between the book value of tangible assets and the market value of the firm**. For example, if a company's market value is $8 million and its book value is $5 million, the $3 million difference is taken to represent the value of the firm's intangible (or intellectual) assets.

Although obviously **simple**, this method's simplicity merely serves to indicate that it fails to take account of **real world complexities.** There may be imperfections in the market valuation, and book values are subject to accounting standards which reflect historic cost and amortisation policies rather than true market values of tangible non-current assets.

In addition, the accounting valuation does not attempt to value a company as a whole, but rather as a **sum of separate asset values** computed under particular accounting conventions. The market, on the other hand, values the entire company as a **going concern**, following its defined strategy.

7.2.2 Tobin's 'q'

The Nobel prize-winning economist James Tobin developed the 'q' method initially as a way of predicting investment behaviour.

'q' is the ratio of the **market capitalisation of the firm** (share price × number of shares) to the **replacement cost** of its assets.

If the replacement cost of assets is **lower** than the market capitalisation, **q is greater than unity** and the company is enjoying higher than average returns on its investment ('monopoly rents'). Technology and so called 'human-capital' assets are likely to lead to high q values.

Tobin's 'q' is affected by the same variables influencing market capitalisation as the market-to-book method. In common with that method, it is used most appropriately to make comparisons of the value of intangible assets of companies within an industry which serve the same markets and have similar tangible non-current assets. As such, these methods could serve as **performance benchmarks** by which to appraise management or corporate strategy.

7.2.3 Calculated intangible values

NCI Research has developed the method of **calculated intangible value (CIV)** for calculating the fair market value of a firm's intangible assets. CIV calculates an 'excess return' on tangible assets. This figure is then used in determining the **proportion of return** attributable to intangible assets.

A step-by-step approach would be as follows.

STEP 1 Calculate average pre-tax earnings and average year end tangible asset values over a time period.

STEP 2 Divide earnings by average assets to get the return on assets.

STEP 3 Multiply the industry average return on assets percentage by the entity's average tangible asset values. Subtract this from the entity's pre-tax earnings to calculate the excess return.

STEP 4 Subtract tax from the excess return to give the after-tax premium attributable to intangible assets.

STEP 5 Calculate the NPV of the premium by dividing it by the entity's cost of capital.

Whilst this seemingly straightforward approach, using readily available information, seems attractive, it does have two problems.

(a) It uses **average industry ROA** as a basis for computing excess returns, which may be **distorted by** extreme values.

(b) The choice of **discount rate** to apply to the excess returns to value the intangible asset needs to be made with care. To ensure comparability between companies and industries, some sort of **average cost of capital** should perhaps be applied. This again has the potential problems of **distortion.**

7.3 Valuation of individual intangible assets

7.3.1 Relief from royalties method

This method involves trying to determine:

(a) The value obtainable from licensing out the right to exploit the intangible asset to a third party, or

(b) The royalties that the owner of the intangible asset is relieved from paying through being the owner rather than the licensee

A **notional royalty rate** is estimated as a percentage of revenue expected to be generated by the intangible asset. The estimated royalty stream can then be **capitalised**, for example by discounting at a risk-free market rate, to find an estimated market value.

This relatively simple valuation method is easiest to apply if the intangible asset is already subject to licensing agreements. If they are not, the valuer might reach an appropriate figure from other comparable licensing arrangements.

7.3.2 Premium profits method

The premium profits method is often used for **brands**. It bases the valuation on capitalisation of the **extra profits generated** by the brand or other intangible asset in excess of profits made by businesses lacking the intangible asset or brand.

The premium profits specifically attributable to the brand or other intangible asset may be estimated (for example) by comparing the price of branded products and unbranded products. The estimated premium profits can then be capitalised by discounting at a risk-adjusted market rate.

7.3.3 Capitalisation of earnings method

With the capitalised earnings method, the **maintainable earnings accruing to the intangible asset** are estimated. An **earnings multiple** is then applied to the earnings, taking account of expected risks and rewards, including the prospects for future earnings growth and the risks involved. This method of valuation is often used to value **publishing titles**.

7.3.4 Comparison with market transactions method

This method looks at **actual market transactions** in similar intangible assets. A multiple of revenue or earnings from the intangible asset might then be derived from a similar market transaction.

A problem with this method is that many **intangible assets are unique** and it may therefore be difficult to identify 'similar' market transactions, although this might be done by examining acquisitions and disposals of businesses that include similar intangible assets.

The method might be used alongside other valuation methods, to provide a comparison.

> **Section summary**
>
> The valuation of **intangible assets** and **intellectual capital** presents special problems. Various methods can be used to value them including the relief from royalties, premium profits and capitalisation of earnings methods.

Chapter Roundup

- There is no one correct business valuation. It makes sense to use several methods of valuation, and to compare the values they produce.

- The **net assets valuation** method can be used as one of many valuation methods, or to provide a lower limit for the value of a company. By itself it is unlikely to produce the most realistic value.

- **P/E ratios** are used when a large block of shares, or a whole business, is being valued. This method can be problematic when quoted companies' P/E ratios are used to value unquoted companies.

- Other earnings methods include the **earnings yield** valuation method and the **accounting rate of return** method.

- The dividend valuation model is based on the present value of the future dividends being generated by the **existing** management. It is generally more relevant for **small shareholdings**.

- **Discounted future cash flows valuation** may be used to value a company. **Free cash flows** are a development of the DCF method. **Shareholder value analysis** focuses on the key decisions affecting value and risk.

- The reliability of the various methods used to value shares may be affected by the **level of market efficiency**.

- The **traditional view of gearing** states that **market value** should be **maximised** at the optimum capital structure, where cost of capital is minimised. **Modigliani and Miller** state that in a world with taxes, market value should continue to rise as gearing rises, because tax benefits arise from interest paid.

- It can be difficult to **value unlisted companies** as obtaining a **cost of equity** is difficult. The **beta of a listed company** can be used to calculate the cost of equity.

- The valuation of **intangible assets** and **intellectual capital** presents special problems. Various methods can be used to value them including the relief from royalties, premium profits and capitalisation of earnings methods.

Quick Quiz

1. Give four circumstances in which the shares of an unquoted company might need to be valued.
2. How is the P/E ratio related to EPS?
3. What is meant by 'multiples' in the context of share valuation?
4. Value = Estimated future profits/Required return on capital employed. What is the name of this valuation model?
5. Suggest two circumstances in which net assets might be used as a basis for valuation of a company.
6. There is one correct value for a business
    True ☐
    False ☐

7   Give six examples of types of intangible assets.

8   Identify three methods of valuing the intellectual capital of a business.

9   Identify four methods of valuing individual intangible assets.

Answers to Quick Quiz

1   (a) Setting an issue price if the company is floating its shares
    (b) When shares are sold
    (c) For tax purposes
    (d) When shares are pledged as collateral for a loan

2   P/E ratio = Share price/EPS

3   The P/E ratio: the multiple of earnings at which a company's shares are traded

4   Accounting rate of return method

5   (a) As a measure of asset backing
    (b) For comparison, in a scheme of merger

6   False. In a business valuation, there is no one correct answer. A range of valuations should be calculated.

7   Patents; trade marks; brands; copyrights; franchises; research and development

8   Market-to-book values; Tobin's q; calculated intangible value

9   Relief from royalties; premium profits; capitalisation of earnings; comparison with market transactions

Answers to Questions

15.1 Earnings valuation

(a) **Earnings**. Average earnings over the last five years have been $67,200, and over the last four years $71,500. There might appear to be some growth prospects, but estimates of future earnings are uncertain.

A low estimate of earnings in 20X5 would be, perhaps, $71,500.

A high estimate of earnings might be $75,000 or more. This solution will use the most recent earnings figure of $75,000 as the high estimate.

(b) **P/E ratio**. A P/E ratio of 15 (Bumblebee's) would be much too high for Mayfly, because the growth of Mayfly earnings is not as certain, and Mayfly is an unquoted company.

On the other hand, Mayfly's expectations of earnings are probably better than those of Wasp. A suitable P/E ratio might be based on the industry's average, 10; but since Mayfly is an unquoted company and therefore more risky, a lower P/E ratio might be more appropriate: perhaps 60% to 70% of 10 = 6 or 7, or conceivably even as low as 50% of 10 = 5.

The valuation of Mayfly's shares might therefore range between:

high P/E ratio and high earnings: 7 × $75,000 = $525,000 and

low P/E ratio and low earnings: 5 × $71,500 = $357,500.

15.2 DVM

$k_e = 12\% + 2\% = 14\% (0.14)$ $\qquad d_0 = \$250,000 \qquad$ g (in (b)) = 4% or 0.04

(a) $\quad P_0 = \dfrac{d_0}{k_e} = \dfrac{\$250,000}{0.14} = \$1,785,714$

(b) $\quad P_0 = \dfrac{d_0(1+g)}{k_e - g} = \dfrac{\$250,000\,(1.04)}{0.14 - 0.04} = \$2,600,000$

(c)

	Time 1	Time 2	Time 4	Time 4 onwards
Dividend ($'000)	258	266	274	279
Annuity to infinity $(1/k_e - g)$				8.333
Present value at year 3				2,325
Discount factor @ 14%	0.877	0.769	0.675	0.675
Present value	226	205	185	1,569
Total	**$2,185,000**			

15.3 Business valuation

(a) The information provided allows us to value Profed on three bases: net assets, P/E ratio and dividend valuation.

All three will be computed, even though their validity may be questioned in part (b) of the answer.

Assets based

	£'000
Net assets at book value	7,200
Add: increased valuation of buildings	1,500
Less: decreased value of inventory and receivables	(850)
Net asset value of equity	7,850
Value per share	£1.96

P/E ratio

	Profed	City Tutors
Issued shares (million)	4	10
Share price (pence)		362
Market value (£m)		36.2
Earnings per shares (pence)	35	20
P/E ratio (share price ÷ EPS)		18.1

The P/E for a similar quoted company is 18.1. This will take account of factors such as marketability of shares, status of company, growth potential that will differ from those for Profed. Profed's growth rate has been estimated as higher than that of City Tutors, possibly because it is a younger, developing company, although the basis for the estimate may be questionable.

All other things being equal, the P/E ratio for an unquoted company should be taken as between one half to two thirds of that of an equivalent quoted company. Being generous, in view of the possible higher growth prospects of Profed, we might estimate an appropriate P/E ratio of around 12, assuming Profed is to remain a private company.

This will value Profed at 12 × £0.35 = £4.20 per share, a total valuation of £16.8m.

Dividend valuation model

The dividend valuation method gives the share price as

$$\dfrac{\text{Next year's dividend}}{\text{Cost of equity - growth rate}}$$

which assumes dividends being paid into perpetuity, and growth at a constant rate.

For Profed, next year's dividend = £0.20 × 1.09 = £0.218 per share

Whilst we are given a discount rate of 15% as being traditionally used by the directors of Profed for investment appraisal, there appears to be no rational basis for this. We can instead use the information for City Courses to estimate a cost of equity for Profed. This is assuming the business risks to be similar, and ignoring the small difference in their gearing ratio.

Again, from the DVM, cost of equity = $\dfrac{\text{next year's dividend}}{\text{market price}}$ + growth rate

For City Tutors, cost of equity = $\dfrac{£0.18 \times 1.075}{£3.62}$ + 0.075 = 12.84%

Using, say, 13% as a cost of equity for Profed:

Share price = $\dfrac{£0.218}{0.13 - 0.09}$ = £5.45

valuing the whole of the share capital at £21.8 million

Range for valuation

The three methods used have thus come up with a range of value of Profed as follows.

	Value per share £	Total valuation £m
Net assets	1.96	7.9
P/E ratio	4.20	16.8
Dividend valuation	5.45	21.8

(b) **Comment on relative merits of the methods used, and their suitability**

Asset based valuation

Valuing a company on the **basis of its asset values** alone is rarely appropriate if it is to be sold on a going concern basis. Exceptions would include property investment companies and investment trusts, the market values of the assets of which will bear a close relationship to their earning capacities.

Profed is typical of a lot of service companies, a large part of whose value lies in the **skill, knowledge and reputation of its personnel**. This is not reflected in the net asset values, and renders this method quite inappropriate. A potential purchaser of Profed will generally value its intangible assets such as knowledge, expertise, customer/supplier relationships, brands etc more highly than those that can be measured in accounting terms.

Knowledge of the net asset value (NAV) of a company will, however, be important as a **floor value** for a company in financial difficulties or subject to a takeover bid. Shareholders will be reluctant to sell for less than the net asset value even if future prospects are poor.

P/E ratio valuation

The P/E ratio measures the **multiple of the current year's earnings** that is reflected in the **market price** of a share. It is thus a method that reflects the earnings potential of a company from a market point of view. Provided the marketing is efficient, it is likely to give the most meaningful basis for valuation.

One of the first things to say is that the market price of a share at any point in time is determined by supply and demand forces prevalent during small transactions, and will be dependent upon a lot of factors in addition to a realistic appraisal of future prospects. A downturn in the market, economies and political changes can all affect the day-to-day price of a share, and thus its prevailing P/E ratio. it is not known whether the share price given for City Tutors was taken on one particular day, or was some sort of average over a period. The latter would perhaps give a sounder basis from which to compute an applicable P/E ratio.

Even if the P/E ratio of City Tutors can be taken to be **indicative of its true worth**, using it as a basis to value a smaller, unquoted company in the same industry can be problematic.

The status and marketability of shares in a quoted company have tangible effects on value but these are difficult to measure.

The P/E ratio will also be affected by **growth prospects** – the higher the growth expected, the higher the ratio. The growth rate incorporated by the shareholders of City Tutors is probably based on a more rational approach than that used by Profed.

If the growth prospects of Profed, as would be perceived by the market, did not coincide with those of **Profed management** it is difficult to see how the P/E ratio should be adjusted for relative levels of growth.

In the valuation in (a) a crude adjustment has been made to City Tutors' P/E ratio to arrive at a ratio to use to value Profed's earnings. This can result in a very inaccurate result if account has not been taken of all the differences involved.

Dividend based valuation

The dividend valuation model (DVM) is a **cash flow based approach**, which valued the dividends that the shareholders expect to receive from the company by discounting them at their required rate of return. It is perhaps more appropriate for valuing a minority shareholding where the holder has no influence over the level of dividends to be paid than for valuing a whole company, where the total cash flows will be of greater relevance.

The practical problems with the dividend valuation model lie mainly in its **assumptions**. Even accepting that the required 'perfect capital market' assumptions may be satisfied to some extent, in reality, the formula used in (a) assumes constant growth rates and constant required rates of return in perpetuity.

Determination of an **appropriate cost of equity** is particularly difficult for a unquoted company, and the use of an 'equivalent' quoted company's data carries the same drawbacks as discussed above. Similar problems arise in estimating future growth rates, and the results from the model are highly sensitive to changes in both these inputs.

It is also highly dependent upon the **current year's dividend** being a representative base from which to start.

The dividend valuation model valuation provided in (a) results in a higher valuation than that under the P/E ratio approach. Reasons for this may be:

- The **share price** for City Courses may be currently **depressed below its normal level**, resulting in an inappropriately low P/E ratio.

- The **adjustment** to get to an **appropriate P/E ratio** for Profed may have been too harsh, particularly in light of its apparently better growth prospects.

- The **cost of equity** used in the dividend valuation model was that of City Courses. The validity of this will largely depend upon the relative levels of risk of the two companies. Although they both operate the same type of business, the fact that City Courses sells its material externally means it is perhaps less reliant on a fixed customer base.

- Even if business risks and gearing risk may be thought to be comparable a prospective buyer of Profed may consider investment in a **younger, unquoted company** to carry **greater personal risk**. His required return may thus be higher than that envisaged in the dividend valuation model, reducing the valuation.

15.4 Change in capital structure

(a)

	$
Current profits and dividends	2,250,000
Increase in profits and dividends	
($850,000 less extra interest 10% × $5,000,000)	350,000
New dividends, if project is undertaken	2,600,000
New cost of equity	20%

	$
New MV of equity	13,000,000
Current MV of equity	
($2,250,000 ÷ 0.18)	12,500,000
Increase in shareholder wealth from project	500,000

(b) (i) NPV of project if financed at current WACC = $\dfrac{\$850,000}{0.16} - \$5,000,000 = +\$312,500$

(ii) The effect of financing on share values must be to increase the MV of equity by the remaining $187,500, which indicates that the effect of financing the project in the manner proposed will be to increase the company's gearing, but to reduce its WACC.

15.5 WACC and MM theory

Value of CD in total $V_g = V_u + TB_c$ where V_u is the value of YZ.

V_g = $24,000,000 + $10,000,000 × 30% = $27,000,000.

CD's equity is valued at $27,000,000 – debt of $10,000,000 = $17,000,000, or $3.40 per share.

Now try these questions from the Exam Question Bank

Number	Level	Marks	Time
Q25	Examination	25	45 mins
Q26	Introductory	n/a	45 mins

AMALGAMATIONS AND RESTRUCTURING

In this final very important chapter, we are concerned with the issues of **business combinations** and **restructuring** from the point of view of financial management and financial strategy.

Questions in this area are likely to involve some calculations so you will need to bring in your knowledge of company valuation. However, questions will not be purely numerical. Topics you might be asked to discuss include why companies might choose to make an offer in a particular form, takeover tactics, the effect on shareholders, the different types of consideration and what happens after the takeover. Questions on the subjects discussed in this chapter will be **regularly** set in the compulsory section of this paper.

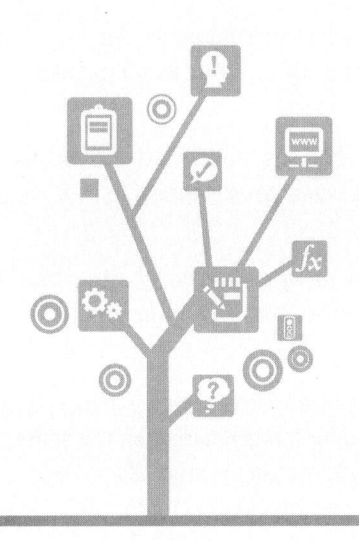

topic list	learning outcomes	syllabus references	ability required
1 Mergers and takeovers (acquisitions)	C(2)(a)	C(2)(ii)	evaluation
2 The conduct of a takeover	C(2)(a)	C(2)(i)	evaluation
3 Payment methods	C(2)(a)	C(2)(iii)	evaluation
4 Valuation of mergers and takeovers	C(2)(a)	C(2)(iii)	evaluation
5 Regulation of takeovers	A(1)(c)	A(1)(vii)	analysis
6 Post-acquisition integration	C(2)(a)	C(2)(iv)	evaluation
7 Impact of mergers and takeovers on stakeholders	C(2)(a)	C(2)(i)	evaluation
8 Exit strategies	C(2)(b)	C(2)(v),(vi),(vii)	evaluation

1 Mergers and takeovers (acquisitions)

> **Introduction**
>
> In this section we explain what is meant by the terms mergers, takeovers and acquisitions and the reasons why they happen.

1.1 Definition of mergers and takeovers

KEY TERMS

TAKEOVER: the **acquisition** by a company of a controlling interest in the voting share capital of another company, usually achieved by the purchase of a majority of the voting shares.*(CIMA Official Terminology)*

REVERSE TAKEOVER: when the smaller company takes over the larger one, so that the predator company has to increase its equity by over 100% to complete the takeover.

MERGER: a business combination that results in the creation of a new reporting entity formed from the combining parties, in which the shareholders of the combining entities come together in a partnership for the mutual sharing of the risks and benefits of the combined entity, and in which no party to the combination in substance obtains control over any other, or is otherwise seen to be dominant, whether by virtue of the proportion of its shareholders' rights in the combined entity, the influence of its directors or otherwise.
(FRS 6) (CIMA Official Terminology)

HORIZONTAL INTEGRATION is characterised by a firm adding new products to its existing market, or new markets to its existing products.

VERTICAL INTEGRATION, or vertical diversification, occurs when a company becomes either its own supplier of raw materials or components (ie **backward** vertical integration) or its own distributor or sales agent (ie **forward** vertical integration).

CONCENTRIC DIVERSIFICATION occurs when a company seeks to add new products that have technological and/or marketing synergies with the existing product line. These products will normally appeal to new classes of customer.

CONGLOMERATE DIVERSIFICATION consists of making entirely new products for new classes of customers. These new products have no relationship to the company's current technology, products or markets.

The distinction between mergers and takeovers (acquisitions) is not always clear, for example when a large company 'merges' with another smaller company. The methods used for mergers are often the same as the methods used to make takeovers. In practice, the number of genuine mergers is small relative to the number of takeovers.

> **Exam skills**
>
> Business amalgamations (mergers and takeovers) are likely to be a key topic for exam questions in *Financial Strategy* and the TOPCIMA exams. There is a significant amount of overlap with Paper E3 *Enterprise Strategy*.

Mergers or acquisitions should be undertaken to make profits **in the long term** as well as in the short term.

(a) **Acquisitions** may provide a means of entering a market at a **lower cost** than would be incurred if the company tried to develop its own resources, or a means of acquiring the business of a competitor. Acquisitions or mergers which might reduce or eliminate competition in a market may be prohibited by competition authorities.

(b) **Mergers** have tended to be more common in industries with a history of little growth and low returns. Highly profitable companies tend to seek acquisitions rather than mergers.

1.2 Reasons for mergers and takeovers

KEY TERM

SYNERGY is where the present value of the combined enterprise is greater than the sum of the net present value of the individual firms.

When two or more companies join together, there should be a **'synergistic'** effect. Synergy can be described as the **2 + 2 = 5** effect, whereby a group after a takeover achieves combined results that reflect a better rate of return than was being achieved by the same resources used in two separate operations before the takeover.

The main reasons why one company may wish to acquire the shares or the business of another may be categorised as follows.

Operating economies	Elimination of duplicate facilities and many other ways
Management acquisition	Acquisition of competent and go-ahead team to compensate for lack of internal management abilities
Diversification	Securing long-term future by spreading risk through diversification
Asset backing	Company with high earnings: assets ratios reducing risk through acquiring company with substantial assets
Quality of earnings	Reducing risk by acquiring company with less risky earnings
Finance and liquidity	Improve liquidity/ability to raise finance through acquisition of more stable company
Growth	Cheaper way of growing than internal expansion
Tax factors	Tax-efficient way of transferring cash out of corporate sector. In some jurisdictions, means of utilising tax losses by setting them against profits of acquired companies
Defensive merger	Stop competitors obtaining advantage
Strategic opportunities	Acquiring a company that provides a strategic fit (see below)
Asset stripping	Acquiring an undervalued company in order to sell off the assets to make a profit.

1.3 A strategic approach to takeovers

A strategic approach to takeovers would imply that acquisitions are only made after a full analysis of the underlying strengths of the acquirer company, and identification of candidates' **'strategic fit' with its existing activities**. Possible strategic reasons for a takeover are matched with suggested ways of achieving the aim in the following list from a publication of 3i (Investors in Industry), which specialises in offering advice on takeovers.

Strategic opportunities	
Where you are	How to get to where you want to be
Growing steadily but in a mature market with limited growth prospects	Acquire a company in a younger market with a higher growth rate
Marketing an incomplete product range, or having the potential to sell other products or services to your existing customers	Acquire a company with a complementary product range
Operating at maximum productive capacity	Acquire a company making similar products operating substantially below capacity

Strategic opportunities	
Where you are	**How to get to where you want to be**
Under-utilising management resources	Acquire a company into which your talents can extend
Needing more control of suppliers or customers	Acquire a company which is, or gives access to, a significant customer or supplier
Lacking key clients in a targeted sector	Acquire a company with the right customer profile
Preparing for flotation but needing to improve your balance sheet	Acquire a suitable company which will enhance earnings per share
Needing to increase market share	Acquire an important competitor
Needing to widen your capability	Acquire a company with the key talents and/or technology

1.4 Synergies

The following types of synergy may arise:

- **Operating** – for example economies of scale and eliminating inefficiency
- **Financial** – for example reduced risk through diversification, perhaps giving a lower cost of capital
- **Other effects** – for example management talent or increased market power

The types of synergy that arise through a particular merger or takeover will depend on the specific scenario. It is important to bear in mind that **projected** synergies may not be realised in practice.

1.5 Factors in a takeover decision   11/10

Several factors will need to be considered before deciding to try to take over a target business. These include the following.

Price factors

(a) What would the **cost** of acquisition be?

(b) Would the acquisition be **worth** the price?

(c) Alternatively, factors (a) and (b) above could be expressed in terms of:

What is the **highest price** that it would be worth paying to acquire the business?

The value of a business could be assessed in terms of:

(i) Its earnings
(ii) Its assets
(iii) Its prospects for sales and earnings growth
(iv) How it would contribute to the strategy of the 'predator' company

The valuation of companies was covered in the previous chapter of this Study Text.

Other factors

(d) Would the takeover be regarded as **desirable** by the predator company's shareholders and (in the case of quoted companies) the stock market in general?

(e) Are the owners of the target company **amenable** to a takeover bid? Or would they be likely to adopt defensive tactics to resist a bid?

(f) What form would the **purchase consideration take?** An acquisition is accomplished by buying the shares of a target company. The purchase consideration might be cash, but the purchasing company might issue new shares (or loan stock) and exchange them for shares in the company taken over. If purchase is by means of a share exchange, the former shareholders in the company taken over will acquire an interest in the new, enlarged company.

(g) How would the takeover be **reflected in the published accounts** of the predator company?

(h) Would there be any **other potential problems** arising from the proposed takeover, such as future dividend policy and service contracts for key personnel?

Exam skills

In the exam you may be asked to value a company and then discuss the strategic implications of the proposed acquisition.

Section summary

- **Takeovers** often target companies that are good **strategic fits** with the acquiring companies, often to acquire a new product range or to develop a presence in a new market.
- **Mergers** have been more common in industries with low growth and returns.

2 The conduct of a takeover

Introduction

In this section we look at what can happen when a takeover is announced. The target company may resist the takeover and we discuss possible defensive tactics.

2.1 Will the bidding company's shareholders approve of a takeover?

When a company is planning a takeover bid for another company, its board of directors should give some thought to **how its own shareholders might react** to the bid. A company does not have to ask its shareholders for their approval of every takeover.

(a) When a large takeover is planned by a listed company involving **the issue of a substantial number of new shares by the predator company** (to pay for the takeover), Stock Exchange rules may require the company to obtain the formal approval of its shareholders to the takeover bid at a general meeting (probably an extraordinary general meeting, called specifically to approve the takeover bid).

(b) If shareholders, and the stock market in general, think the takeover is not a good one the **market value of the company's shares is likely to fall**. The company's directors have a responsibility to protect their shareholders' interests, and are accountable to them at the annual general meeting of the company.

A takeover bid might seem **unattractive** to shareholders of the bidding company because:

(a) It might **reduce the EPS** of their company.
(b) The **target company** is in a risky industry, or is in danger of going into liquidation.
(c) It might **reduce the net asset backing** per share of the company, because the target company will probably be bought at a price which is well in excess of its net asset value.

2.2 Will a takeover bid be resisted by the target company?

Quite often, a takeover bid will be resisted. Resistance comes from the target company's board of directors, who adopt defensive tactics, and ultimately the target company's shareholders, who can refuse to sell their shares to the bidding company.

Resistance can be overcome by offering a higher price.

(a) In cases where an **unquoted** company is the target company, if resistance to a takeover cannot be overcome, the takeover will not take place, and negotiations would simply break down.

(b) Where the target company is a **quoted company**, the situation is different. The target company will have many shareholders, some of whom will want to accept the offer for their shares, and some of whom will not. In addition, the target company's board of directors might resist a takeover, even though their shareholders might want to accept the offer.

Because there are likely to be major **differences of opinion** about whether to accept a takeover bid or not, companies in most jurisdictions are subject to formal rules for the conduct of takeover bids. These and other regulatory issues are covered later in the chapter.

2.3 Contesting an offer

The directors of a target company must **act in the interests of their shareholders, employees and creditors**. They may decide to contest an offer on several grounds.

(a) The offer may be **unacceptable** because the **terms are poor**. Rejection of the offer may lead to an improved bid.

(b) The merger or takeover may have **no obvious advantage**.

(c) **Employees** may be **strongly opposed** to the bid.

(d) The **founder members of the business** may oppose the bid, and appeal to the loyalty of other shareholders.

When a company receives a takeover bid which the board of directors considers unwelcome, the directors must act quickly to fight off the bid.

2.4 Defensive tactics

The steps that might be taken to **thwart a bid** or **make it seem less attractive** include:

(a) **Revaluing assets** or **issuing a forecast of attractive future profits and dividends** to persuade shareholders that to sell their shares would be unwise, that the offer price is too low, and that it would be better for them to retain their shares.

(b) **Lobbying** to have the offer referred to the competition authorities

(c) Launching an **advertising campaign** against the takeover bid (one technique is to attack the accounts of the predator company)

(d) Finding a '**white knight**', a company which will make a welcome takeover bid (see below)

(e) Making a **counter-bid** for the predator company (this can only be done if the companies are of reasonably similar size)

(f) Arranging a **management buyout**

(g) Introducing a '**poison-pill**' anti-takeover device (see below)

(h) Introducing a '**shark repellent**' – changing the company's constitution to require a large majority to approve the takeover

CASE STUDY

Swiss pharmaceutical company Roche launched a hostile takeover bid for US diagnostics company Illumina in early 2012. Illumina adopted defensive tactics and announced that it would adopt a "poison pill" to protect its shareholders This meant that Illumina shareholders can buy new shares if any bidder acquires 15 per cent of the company's shares. This move protects the company by making Illumina more expensive to acquire. As a result of defensive tactics Roche let its offer expire in April 2012.

2.5 Costs of contested takeover bids

Takeover bids, when contested, can be very expensive, involving:

- Costs of professional services, eg merchant bank and public relations agency
- Advertising costs
- Underwriting costs
- Interest costs
- Possible capital loss on buying/selling the target company's shares

2.6 Gaining the consent of the target company shareholders

A takeover bid will only succeed if the predator company can persuade enough shareholders in the target company to sell their shares. Shareholders will only do this if they **are dissatisfied with the performance** of their company and its shares, or they are **attracted by a high offer** and the chance to make a good capital gain.

> **Section summary**
>
> A takeover may be **resisted** by the target company, if its directors believe that the terms are poor or there are no obvious advantages. Possible **defensive tactics** include issuing a forecast of attractive future profits, lobbying or finding a white knight (a company that would make a welcome takeover bid).

3 Payment methods

> **Introduction**
>
> In this section we look at how an acquisition can be financed and discuss the factors that will influence the choice of method of payment.

3.1 Methods of payment

The terms of a takeover will involve a purchase of the shares of the target company for **cash** or for **'paper'** (shares, or possibly bonds). A purchase of a target company's shares with shares of the predator company is referred to as a **share exchange**.

3.2 Cash purchases

If the purchase consideration is in **cash**, the shareholders of the target company will simply be bought out. For example, suppose that there are two companies.

	Big	Small
Net assets (book value)	$1,500,000	$200,000
Number of shares	100,000	10,000
Earnings	$2,000,000	$40,000

Big negotiates a takeover of Small for $400,000 in cash.

As a result, Big will end up with:

(a) Net assets (book value) of:

$1,500,000 + $200,000 − $400,000 cash = $1,300,000

(b) 100,000 shares (no change)

(c) Expected earnings of $2,040,000, minus the loss of interest (net of tax) which would have been obtained from the investment of the $400,000 in cash which was given up to acquire Small

How to obtain the cash is a **gearing decision** which has been covered in Part B of this Study Text.

Exam skills

You may be asked in the exam about the consequences of using different finance sources to support a cash offer. Exam questions typically ask you to evaluate whether a cash bid or a paper bid is more appropriate.

3.3 Purchases by share exchange

One company can acquire another company by **issuing shares** to pay for the acquisition. The new shares might be issued:

(a) **In exchange** for shares in the target company. Thus, if A acquires B, A might issue shares which it gives to B's shareholders in exchange for their shares. The B shareholders therefore become new shareholders of A. This is a takeover for a 'paper' consideration. Paper offers will often be accompanied by a **cash alternative.**

(b) **To raise cash** on the stock market, which will then be used to buy the target company's shares. To the target company shareholders, this is a cash bid.

Sometimes, a company might acquire another in a share exchange, but the shares are then **sold immediately** on a stock market to raise cash for the seller.

Whatever the detailed arrangements of a takeover with paper, the end result will be an **increase in the issued share capital of the predator company**.

Example: Share consideration (1)

Arcturus has agreed to acquire all the ordinary shares in Mira and has also agreed a share-for-share exchange as the form of consideration. The following information is available.

	Arcturus £m	Mira £m
Operating profit	100	20
Net profit before taxation	80	14
Net profit after taxation	60	10
Share capital – £0.50 ordinary shares	£20m	£5m
Price/earnings ratio	10	12

The agreed share price for Mira will result in its shareholders receiving a premium of 25% on the current share price.

How many new shares must Arcturus issue to purchase the shares in Mira?

PART C INVESTMENT DECISIONS AND PROJECT CONTROL   16: Amalgamations and restructuring   **329**

Solution

Market value Arcturus (10 × £60m) = £600m

Value per share (£600m/40m) = £15 per share

Market value Mira (12 × £10m) = £120m

Value of bid (£120m × 1.25) = £150m

Number of shares issued (£150m/£15) = 10 million shares

Example: Share consideration (2)

Demeter wishes to take over Semele. The following information relates to the two companies:

	Number of ordinary shares in issue	Market price per ordinary share
Demeter	20 million	£10.00
Semele	6 million	£3.00

The market price of each company's shares is regarded as an accurate reflection of their intrinsic value.

The takeover is expected to lead to research and development savings after taxation that have a present value of £12 million. The bid offer consists of one share in Demeter for every three shares held in Semele, plus £1.00 in cash for every three shares held in Semele.

By how much would the wealth of a shareholder who owns 3,000 shares in Semele increase if the takeover was successful?

Solution

Number of shares to be issued	=	6m × 1/3 = 2 million
Total number of shares in issue after takeover	=	20m + 2m = 22 million
Cash payment	=	£2 million
Value of combined company after takeover	=	£200m + 18m + 12m − 2m
	=	£228 million
Value of 1,000 shares after takeover	=	£228m × 1,000/22,000,000 = £10,364

	£
Share value	10,364
Cash	1,000
	11,364
Value of 3,000 shares before take over (3,000 × £3)	9,000
	2,364

Example: Share consideration (3)

X and Y are both listed companies.

	X plc	Y plc
Profit before tax for the year just ended	£4m	£3.5m
Profit after tax for the year just ended	£2.75m	£2.4m
Number of shares	10m	5m
P/E ratio (current)	12	10

X has made an offer to acquire all the share capital of Y. The offer price is 5 new shares in X for every 3 shares in Y.

What is the premium in % in the price offered to the shareholders of Y?

Solution

EPS, X = (£2.75 million/10 million shares) = £0.275

Share price, X = £0.275 × 12 = £3.30

EPS, Y = (£2.4 million/5 million shares) = £0.48

Share price, Y = £0.48 × 10 = £4.80

Offer = 5 shares in X, value 5 × £3.30, £16.50, for 3 shares in Y

Current market value of 3 shares in Y = 3 × £4.80 = £14.40

The premium in the offer price is therefore (£16.50 – £14.40)/ £14.40 = 14.6%

3.4 Use of bonds

Alternative forms of paper consideration, including debentures, loan notes and preference shares, are not so commonly used, due to:

- Difficulties in **establishing a rate of return** that is attractive to target shareholders
- The **effects on the gearing levels** of the acquiring company
- The **change in the structure of the target shareholders'** portfolios
- The **securities being potentially less marketable**, and lacking voting rights

Issuing **convertible bonds** will overcome some of these drawbacks, by offering the target shareholders the option of partaking in the future profits of the company if they wish.

Example: Loan consideration

Trim offers to buy 100% of the equity shares of Slim from its three owners. The purchase price will be £7 million, made up of 1.5 million new shares of Trim and £2 million in 10% bonds. The annual profits before tax of Slim have been £1 million for each of the past three years, after making suitable adjustments for directors' salaries and differences in accounting policies, and this level of profits is expected to continue after the takeover by Trim.

Trim has announced its intention of paying a dividend of £0.12 per share next year.

Assuming no synergy as the result of the acquisition, by how much will the earnings of Trim be expected to increase next year, when the profits of Slim are taken into account? Company tax is 30%.

Solution

	£'000	£'000
Slim profit before tax		1,000
Less: tax (30%)		300
		700
Interest on bonds	200	
Less: tax reduction	60	
Net increase in interest		140
Increase in profit after tax for Trim		560

3.5 The choice between a cash offer and a paper offer

The choice between cash and paper offers (or a combination of both) will depend on how the different methods are viewed by the company and its existing shareholders, and on the attitudes of the shareholders of the target company. The **factors** that the directors of the bidding company must consider include the following.

Company and its existing shareholders	
Dilution of EPS	Fall in EPS attributable to existing shareholders may occur if purchase consideration is in equity shares
Cost to the company	Use of bonds to back cash offer will attract tax relief on interest and have lower cost than equity. Convertible bonds can have lower interest
Gearing	Highly geared company may not be able to issue further bonds to obtain cash for cash offer
Control	Control could change considerably if large number of new shares issued
Authorised share capital increase	May be required if consideration is in form of shares. This will involve calling a general meeting to pass the necessary resolution
Borrowing limits increase	General meeting resolution also required if borrowing limits have to change
Taxation	If consideration is cash, many investors may suffer immediate liability to tax on capital gain
Income	If consideration is not cash, arrangement must mean existing income is maintained, or be compensated by suitable capital gain or reasonable growth expectations
Future investments	Shareholders who want to retain stake in target business may prefer shares
Share price	If consideration is shares, recipients will want to be sure that the shares retain their values

CASE STUDY

In January 2010, UK confectionery company Cadbury finally capitulated to a hostile takeover bid by Kraft, the US company that manufactures such well-known products as Kraft cheese slices and Toblerone. The £11.6 billion takeover – which valued Cadbury's shares at £8.50 per share (including a special dividend of 10p) – was financed partly by cash and partly by shares. Kraft sold its North American frozen pizza business to Nestle for $3.7 billion and used the proceeds to help fund the cash element of the bid. Of the £8.50 per share, £5 was paid in cash and the remainder in shares, with Cadbury shareholders receiving 0.1874 Kraft shares for every one Cadbury share.

3.6 Mezzanine finance and takeover bids

When the purchase consideration in a takeover bid is cash, the cash must be obtained somehow by the bidding company, in order to pay for the shares that it buys. Occasionally, the company will have sufficient cash in hand to pay for the target company's shares. More frequently, the cash will have to be raised, possibly from existing shareholders, by means of **a rights issue** or, more probably, by **borrowing from** banks or other financial institutions.

When cash for a takeover is raised by borrowing, the loans would normally be **medium-term** and **secured**.

However, there have been many takeover bids, with a **cash purchase option** for the target company's shareholders, where the bidding company has arranged loans that:

(a) Are short-to-medium term

(b) Are unsecured (that is, 'junior' debt, low in the priority list for repayment in the event of liquidation of the borrower)

(c) Because they are unsecured, attract a much higher rate of interest than secured debt (typically 4% or 5% above LIBOR)

(d) Often, give the lender the option to exchange the loan for shares after the takeover

This type of borrowing is called **mezzanine finance** (because it lies between equity and debt financing) – a form of finance which is also often used in **management buyouts** (which are discussed later in this chapter).

3.7 Earn-out arrangements

The purchase consideration may not all be paid at the time of acquisition. Part of it may be deferred, payable upon the target company reaching certain performance targets.

An EARN-OUT ARRANGEMENT is a procedure whereby owners/managers selling an entity receive a portion of their consideration linked to the financial performance of the business during a specific period after the sale. The arrangement gives a measure of security to the new owners, who pass some of the financial risk associated with the purchase of a new enterprise to the sellers. *(CIMA Official Terminology)*

For example, the consideration may be structured as follows.

(a) An initial amount payable at the time of acquisition

(b) A guaranteed minimum amount of deferred consideration, payable in, say, three years time

(c) An additional amount of deferred consideration, payable if a specified target performance is achieved over the next three years.

The total of the **initial and guaranteed deferred consideration** amounts may be based upon an **assets based approach to valuation**, or on an **earnings basis**, using, for example, the average level of expected profits over a given future period.

The **additional amount of deferred consideration** might be payable if the acquired company's **average profits or revenues** over the next three years exceeds a certain amount.

This method would only be appropriate if the acquired company was to be **run independently** of the **buyer's company**, at least for the period upon which the contingent consideration is based. If the acquired business were to be immediately integrated within the buyer's, it would be difficult to identify separately the relevant sales or profits.

Under these types of arrangement, then, the **overall valuation** of the business will have a **variable element**. The buyer will need to estimate the minimum, maximum and expected total amounts they may have to pay, with corresponding probabilities relating to the likelihood of the business reaching the specified targets. In particular, they will have to ensure that they could, if necessary, afford to pay the maximum amount, regardless of how unlikely that is to arise.

Exam alert

In the exam, you could well get a question where the cash v shares decision is finely balanced, and financing the cash offer may be the critical issue.

Section summary

Payment can be in the form of **cash**, a **share exchange** or **convertible bonds**. The choice will depend on available cash, desired levels of gearing, shareholders' taxation position and changes in control.

4 Valuation of mergers and takeovers 11/10

Introduction

Shareholders of both of the companies involved in a merger or acquisition will be very aware of the effect on share prices and earning per share. In this section we look at various examples illustrating what can happen.

4.1 The market values of the companies' shares during a takeover bid

Share prices can be very important during a takeover bid. Suppose that Velvet decides to make a takeover bid for the shares of Noggin. Noggin shares are currently quoted on the market at £2 each. Velvet shares are quoted at £4.50 and Velvet offers one of its shares for every two shares in Noggin, thus making an offer at current market values worth £2.25 per share in Noggin. This is only the value of the bid so long as Velvet's shares remain valued at £4.50. If their value falls, the bid will become less attractive.

Companies that make takeover bids with a **share exchange offer** are thus always concerned that the market value of their shares **should not fall** during the takeover negotiations, before the target company's shareholders have decided whether to accept the bid.

If the market price of the target company's shares rises above the offer price during the course of a takeover bid, the bid price will seem too low, and the takeover is then likely to fail, with shareholders in the target company refusing to sell their shares to the bidder.

4.2 EPS before and after a takeover

If one company acquires another by issuing shares, its EPS will go up or down according to the P/E ratio at which the target company has been bought.

(a) If the **target company's shares** are bought at a **higher P/E ratio** than the predator company's shares, the **predator company's shareholders** will suffer a **fall in EPS**.

(b) If the **target company's shares** are **valued at a lower P/E ratio**, the **predator company's shareholders** will benefit from a **rise in EPS**.

Example: mergers and takeovers (1)

Giant takes over Tiddler by offering two shares in Giant for one share in Tiddler. Details about each company are as follows.

	Giant	Tiddler
Number of shares	2,800,000	100,000
Market value per share	£4	–
Annual earnings	£560,000	£50,000
EPS	20p	50p
P/E ratio	20	

By offering two shares in Giant worth £4 each for one share in Tiddler, the valuation placed on each Tiddler share is £8, and with Tiddler's EPS of 50p, this implies that Tiddler would be acquired on a P/E ratio of 16. This is lower than the P/E ratio of Giant, which is 20.

If the acquisition produces no synergy, and there is no growth in the earnings of either Giant or its new subsidiary Tiddler, then the EPS of Giant would still be higher than before, because Tiddler was bought on a lower P/E ratio. The combined group's results would be as follows.

	Giant group
Number of shares (2,800,000 + 200,000)	3,000,000
Annual earnings (560,000 + 50,000)	610,000
EPS	20.33p

If the P/E ratio is still 20, the market value per share would be £4.07, which is 7p more than the pre-takeover price.

The process of buying a company with a higher P/E in order to boost your own P/E is known as **bootstrapping**. Whether the stock market is fooled by this process is debatable. The P/E ratio is likely to fall after the takeover in the absence of synergistic or other gains.

Example: mergers and takeovers (2)

Redwood agrees to acquire the shares of Hawthorn in a share exchange arrangement. The agreed P/E ratio for Hawthorn's shares is 15.

	Redwood	Hawthorn
Number of shares	3,000,000	100,000
Market price per share	£2	–
Earnings	£600,000	£120,000
P/E ratio	10	

The EPS of Hawthorn is £1.20, and so the agreed price per share will be £1.20 × 15 = £18. In a share exchange agreement, Redwood would have to issue nine new shares (valued at £2 each) to acquire each share in Hawthorn, and so a total of 900,000 new shares must be issued to complete the takeover.

After the takeover, the enlarged company would have 3,900,000 shares in issue and, assuming no earnings growth, total earnings of £720,000. This would give an EPS of:

$$\frac{£720,000}{3,900,000} = 18.5p$$

The pre-takeover EPS of Redwood was 20p, and so the EPS would fall. This is because Hawthorne has been bought on a higher P/E ratio (15 compared with Redwood's 10).

4.3 Buying companies on a higher P/E ratio, but with profit growth

Buying companies on a higher P/E ratio will result in a fall in EPS unless there is **profit growth** to offset this fall. For example, suppose that Starving acquires Bigmeal, by offering two shares in Starving for three shares in Bigmeal. Details of each company are as follows.

	Starving	Bigmeal
Number of shares	5,000,000	3,000,000
Value per share	£6	£4
Annual earnings		
Current	£2,000,000	£600,000
Next year	£2,200,000	£950,000
EPS	40p	20p
P/E ratio	15	20

Starving is acquiring Bigmeal on a higher P/E ratio, and it is only the profit growth in the acquired subsidiary that gives the enlarged Starving group its growth in EPS.

		Starving group
Number of shares (5,000,000 + 2,000,000)		7,000,000
Earnings		
If no profit growth (2,000,000 + 600,000) £2,600,000		EPS would have been 37.24p
With profit growth (2,200,000 + 950,000) £3,150,000		EPS will be 45p

If an acquisition strategy involves buying companies on a higher P/E ratio, it is therefore essential for continuing EPS growth that the acquired companies offer prospects of strong profit growth.

4.4 Further points to consider: net assets per share and the quality of earnings

You might think that dilution of earnings must be avoided at all cost. However, there are three cases where a dilution of earnings might be accepted on an acquisition if there were other advantages to be gained.

(a) **Earnings growth** may hide the dilution in EPS as above.

(b) A company might be willing to accept earnings dilution if the **quality of the acquired company's earnings** is superior to that of the acquiring company.

(c) A trading company with high earnings, but with few assets, may want to increase its assets base by acquiring a company which is strong in assets but weak in earnings so that assets and earnings get more into line with each other. In this case, **dilution in earnings is compensated for by an increase in net asset backing.**

Example: mergers and takeovers (3)

Intangible has an issued capital of 2,000,000 £1 ordinary shares. Net assets (excluding goodwill) are £2,500,000 and annual earnings average £1,500,000. The company is valued by the stock market on a P/E ratio of 8. Tangible has an issued capital of 1,000,000 ordinary shares. Net assets (excluding goodwill) are £3,500,000 and annual earnings average £400,000. The shareholders of Tangible accept an all-equity offer from Intangible valuing each share in Tangible at £4. Calculate Intangible's earnings and assets per share before and after the acquisition of Tangible.

Solution

(a) Before the acquisition of Tangible, the position is as follows.

Earnings per share (EPS) = $\dfrac{£1,500,000}{2,000,000}$ = 75p

Assets per share (APS) = $\dfrac{£2,500,000}{2,000,000}$ = £1.25

(b) Tangible's EPS figure is 40p (£400,000 ÷ 1,000,000), and the company is being bought on a multiple of 10 at £4 per share. As the takeover consideration is being satisfied by shares, Intangible's earnings will be diluted because Intangible is valuing Tangible on a higher multiple of earnings than itself. Intangible will have to issue 666,667 shares valued at £6 each (earnings of 75p per share at a multiple of 8) to satisfy the £4,000,000 consideration. The results for Intangible will be as follows.

EPS = $\dfrac{£1,900,000}{2,666,667}$ = 71.25p (3.75p lower than the previous 75p)

APS = $\dfrac{£6,000,000}{2,666,667}$ = £2.25 (£1 higher than the previous £1.25)

If Intangible is still valued on the stock market on a P/E ratio of 8, the share price should fall by approximately 30p (8 × 3.75p, the fall in EPS) but because the asset backing has been increased substantially the company will probably now be valued on a higher P/E ratio than 8.

The shareholders in Tangible would receive 666,667 shares in Intangible in exchange for their current 1,000,000 shares, that is, two shares in Intangible for every three shares currently held.

(a) *Earnings*

	£
Three shares in Tangible earn (3 × 40p)	1.200
Two shares in Intangible will earn (2 × 71.25p)	1.425
Increase in earnings, per three shares held in Tangible	0.225

(b) *Assets*

	£
Three shares in Tangible have an asset backing of (3 × £3.5)	10.50
Two shares in Intangible will have an asset backing of (2 × £2.25)	4.50
Loss in asset backing, per three shares held in Tangible	6.00

The shareholders in Tangible would be trading asset backing for an increase in earnings.

4.5 Valuation using post-merger dividends or cash flows

An alternative method to using the P/E ratios, is to consider the dividends or cash flows of the merged company. Reliable **cash flow estimates** should take into account the effects of the merger such as economies of scale and greater combined power.

4.5.1 Dividend method

The steps are as follows:

- Estimate the **initial dividends** of the **combined company** and the **dividend growth rate**

- Estimate the **new cost of capital**; if the cost of the two old companies differs significantly, some sort of weighted average method will be required

- Calculate the **value of the combined company** using the dividend valuation model

- Compare the **value of the combined company** with the **pre-merger value** of the acquiror. The excess is the value of the target

In practice, the level of dividends and dividend cover expected by shareholders in both companies may create difficulties before the merger or takeover is agreed.

4.5.2 Cash flow method

The steps here are as follows.

- Estimate the **cash flows of the combined company**, including the acquired's, the acquiror's and the additional cash flows arising from the beneficial effects of the merger

- Estimate the **new cost of capital** as above

- Calculate the **net present value** of the combined cash flows

- Compare the **value of the combined cash flows** with the acquiror's cash flows if no merger took place. The excess is the value of the target.

Question 16.1

Bid terms

Learning outcome: C(2)(a)

Themis is a fast-growing business which operates a chain of motels situated in motorway service stations throughout the UK. The company is committed to an aggressive strategy of expansion through acquisition and has recently made a bid for the shares of Arethusa that operates a chain of restaurants also situated in motorway service stations throughout the UK. Themis has offered 1 share for every 3 shares held in Arethusa. The following financial data concerning each company is available.

STATEMENTS OF COMPREHENSIVE INCOME FOR THE YEAR ENDED 31 MAY 20X9

	Themis £m	Arethusa £m
Revenue	564	242
Profit from operations	181	41
Finance costs	9	2
Net profit before taxation	172	39
Taxation	45	11
Net profit after taxation	127	28
Dividends	16	24
Accumulated profits	111	4

STATEMENT OF FINANCIAL POSITION AS AT 31 MAY 20X9

	Themis £m	Arethusa £m
Non-current assets	261	117
Net current assets	82	45
	343	162
Less: payables due beyond one year	62	6
	281	156
Capital and reserves		
Ordinary share capital	150	50
Accumulated profits	131	106
	281	156

The ordinary share capital of Themis consists of £0.50 shares and the ordinary share capital of Arethusa consists of £1 shares. The board of directors of Themis believes there is a strong synergy between the two businesses which will lead to an increase in after-tax profits of £15m per year following acquisition.

Share prices for each company in recent years have been as follows:

Year ended 31 May	20X6 £	20X7 £	20X8 £	20X9 (ie present) £
Themis	3.50	4.80	6.90	9.30
Arethusa	2.40	3.20	3.40	2.90

A shareholder in Arethusa has expressed concern over the bid. He points out that, following acquisition, the annual dividends are likely to be lower as Themis normally pays small dividends. As the shareholder relies on dividend income to cover his living expenses, he is concerned that he will be worse off following acquisition of Arethusa. He also believes that the price offered for the shares of Arethusa is too low.

Required

(a) Calculate:

    (i) The total value of the proposed bid

    (ii) The earnings per share of Themis following the successful takeover of Arethusa

    (iii) The share price of Themis following the takeover, assuming the price-earnings ratio of the company is maintained and the synergy achieved.

(b) Discuss the bid from the viewpoint of the shareholders of Arethusa and include in your discussion the shareholder's concerns mentioned above.

Question 16.2

Post-merger valuation

Learning outcome: C(2)(a)

Nyasa is committed to increasing its earnings per share through a policy of acquisition. The company has acquired several businesses in the past five years and is now considering the acquisition of Turkana. Financial information relating to Nyasa and Turkana is as follows:

ABBREVIATED STATEMENTS OF CONSOLIDATED INCOME FOR THE YEAR ENDED 30 APRIL 20X1

	Nyasa £m	Turkana £m
Revenue	120.4	80.9
Profit from operations	15.8	8.4
Finance costs	9.5	3.8
Profit before taxation	6.3	4.6
Taxation	2.1	1.6
Profit after taxation	4.2	3.0

STATEMENTS OF FINANCIAL POSITION AS AT 30 APRIL 20X1

	Nyasa £m	Turkana £m
Non-current assets	50.5	28.6
Net current assets	12.4	8.2
	62.9	36.8
Less Payables due beyond one year	4.6	3.1
	58.3	33.7
Capital and reserves		
£1 Ordinary shares	40.0	12.0
Reserves	18.3	21.7
	58.3	33.7
Price earnings ratio prior to bid	18	14

Nyasa has offered the shareholders of Turkana four shares in Nyasa for every three shares held. After-tax savings in overheads of £1.5m per annum are expected from the acquisition of Turkana.

Required

(a) Calculate:

    (i) The total value of the proposed bid

    (ii) The earnings per share for Nyasa following the successful takeover of Turkana

    (iii) The share price of Nyasa following the takeover, assuming that the price earnings ratio is maintained and the savings achieved

(b) Calculate the effect of the proposed acquisition from the perspective of a shareholder who holds 3,000 ordinary shares in:

    (i) Nyasa, and
    (ii) Turkana.

Comment on your results.

Section summary

Shareholders of both the companies involved in a merger will be sensitive to the effect of the merger on **share prices** and **earnings per share**.

5 Regulation of takeovers

> **Introduction**
>
> During an acquisition a company must be careful to comply with regulations and legislation. This section looks at the types of regulation to be aware of.

5.1 Takeover regulation

The UK **takeover panel** was formed in 1968 to regulate the conduct of parties in a takeover situation. It issued and administers the **City Code** which is designed to ensure that shareholders are treated fairly during the bid process.

The code is **voluntary**, although this is changing as a result of the **EU Takeover Directive**, and any listed company that does not comply may have its membership of the London Stock Exchange suspended.

5.1.1 The City Code: general principles

The City Code is divided into general principles and detailed rules which must be observed by persons involved in a merger or takeover transaction. The general principles include the following.

(a) 'All shareholders of the same class of an offeree company must be **treated similarly** by an offeror.' In other words, a company making a takeover bid cannot offer one set of purchase terms to some shareholders in the target company, and a different set of terms to other shareholders holding shares of the same class in that company.

(b) 'During the course of a takeover, or when such is in contemplation, neither the offeror nor the offeree company ...may **furnish information** to **some shareholders** which is **not made available** to all shareholders.'

(c) 'Shareholders must be given **sufficient information** and **advice to enable them to reach a properly informed decision** and must have sufficient time to do so. No relevant information should be withheld from them.'

(d) Directors of a target company are **not permitted** to **frustrate a takeover bid**, nor to prevent the shareholders from having a chance to decide for themselves.

(e) 'Rights of control must be **exercised in good faith** and the oppression of a minority is wholly unacceptable.' For example, a holding company cannot take decisions about a takeover bid for one of its subsidiaries in such a way that minority shareholders would be unfairly treated.

(f) 'Where **control of a company is acquired** ... a **general offer** to all other shareholders is **normally required**.' Control is defined as a 'holding, or aggregate holdings, of shares carrying 30% of the voting rights of a company, irrespective of whether that holding or holdings gives *de facto* control'.

5.1.2 The City Code: rules

In addition to its general principles, the City Code also contains a number of detailed rules, which are intended to govern the conduct of the parties in a takeover bid. These rules relate to matters such as:

(a) How the approach to the target company should be made by the predator company
(b) The announcement of a takeover bid
(c) The obligation of the target company board to seek independent advice (eg from a merchant bank)
(d) Conduct during the offer
(e) A time barrier to re-bidding if an offer fails

Exam skills

The details of this code do not need to be memorised but you do need to be aware of its existence and purpose.

5.2 Competition legislation   11/11

As we saw in Chapter 2, takeovers and mergers may be investigated by **competition authorities** to ensure that one company cannot **dominate** a market.

CASE STUDY

In March 2012, an acquisition of BMI (a loss-making subsidiary of German airline Lufthansa) by IAG (owner of British Airways and Iberia) was given the go-ahead by the EU Competition Commission despite the dominant position that this would give IAG in the airline industry, particularly out of London Heathrow airport.

The decision was approved because IAG agreed to relinquish up to 14 take-off and landing slots that BMI held.

In contrast, in March 2009 the UK's Competition Commission reported on the dominant position of BAA and ownership of airports in the UK.

The Commission observed that BAA had dominance of the market in the south-east of England and in the Scottish lowlands.

BAA was ordered to sell Gatwick, Stansted and Edinburgh or Glasgow airports by the commission.

BAA sold Gatwick for £1.5 billion in 2009 before the commission issued its ruling and in late 2011 decided to sell Edinburgh rather than Glasgow.

The sale of Stansted has not yet been completed due to the issue being subject to continued legal dispute between BAA and the Competition Commission.

Section summary

Directors of companies of any size must treat all shareholders **fairly** and give them **sufficient information** about the takeover. Larger mergers will be of interest to the **competition authorities**.

6 Post-acquisition integration   9/10, 9/11

Introduction

Many takeovers fail to achieve their full potential because of lack of attention paid to what happens after the takeover. In this section we look at what problems occur and how they can be addressed.

6.1 Problems of integration

Failures of takeovers often result from **inadequate integration** of the companies after the takeover has taken place. There is a tendency for senior management to devote their energies to the next acquisition rather than to the newly-acquired firm. The particular approach adopted will depend upon the **culture** of the organisation as well as the **nature** of the company acquired and **how it fits** into the amalgamated organisation (eg horizontally, vertically, or as part of a diversified conglomerate).

6.2 Drucker's Golden Rules

P F Drucker has suggested Five Golden Rules for the process of post-acquisition integration.

Rule 1	Within a year, the acquiring company should put top **M**anagement with relevant skills in place.
Rule 2	The acquiring company must ensure it can **A**dd value to the target (that is, ensure targets are set, communicated to customers and synergies are realised).
Rule 3	The acquiring company must show **R**espect to the products, management and track record of the target.
Rule 4	Ensure there is a **C**ommon core of unity (for example take actions to ensure systems are compatible).
Rule 5	Strategies should be developed for **H**olding onto existing staff (for example, loyalty bonuses).

Remember the mnemonic '**MARCH**'.

6.3 Jones's Integration Sequence

C S Jones has proposed a five-step 'integration sequence'.

STEP 1 — **Decide on and communicate initial reporting relationships**

This will reduce uncertainty. The issue of whether to impose relationships at the beginning, although these may be subject to change, or to wait for the organisation structure to become more established (see Step 5 below) needs to be addressed.

STEP 2 — **Achieve rapid control of key factors**

This will require access to the right accurate information. Control of information channels needs to be gained without dampening motivation. Note that it may have been poor financial controls which led to the demise of the acquiree company.

STEP 3 — **Resource audit**

Both physical and human assets are examined in order to get a clear picture. This includes examining the roles of each of the main stakeholders (staff, customers and suppliers) and evaluating the products sold.

STEP 4 — **Re-define corporate objectives and to develop strategic plans**

These should harmonise with those of the acquiror company as appropriate, depending on the degree of autonomy managers are to have to develop their own systems of management control.

STEP 5 — **Revise the organisational structure**

Successful post-acquisition integration requires careful management of the 'human factor' to avoid loss of motivation. Employees in the acquired company will want to know how they and their company are to fit into the structure and strategy of the amalgamated enterprise. Morale can, hopefully, be preserved by **reducing uncertainty** and by providing appropriate performance incentives, staff benefits and career prospects. If redundancies are felt to be necessary, voluntary redundancies should be offered first.

6.4 Service contracts for key personnel

When the target company employs certain key personnel, on whom the success of the company has been based, the predator company might want to ensure that these key people do not leave as soon as the takeover occurs.

To do this, it might be necessary to insist as a condition of the offer that the key people should agree to sign **service contracts**, tying them to the company for a certain time (perhaps three years). Service contracts would have to be attractive to the employees concerned, perhaps through offering a high salary or other benefits such as share options in the predator company. Where key personnel are shareholders, they might be bound not to sell shares for a period.

6.5 Merging systems

The degree to which the information, control and reporting systems of the two companies involved in a takeover are merged will depend to some extent upon the **degree of integration** envisaged. There are two extremes of integration:

(a) **Complete absorption of the target firm**, where the cultures, operational procedures and organisational structures of the two firms are to be fused together. This approach is most suitable where significant cost reductions are expected to be achieved through economies of scale, and/or combining marketing and distribution effort can enhance revenues.

(b) **The preservation approach**, where the target company is to become an independent subsidiary of the holding company. This would be most beneficial for the merger of companies with very different products, markets and cultures.

In the circumstances of a complete absorption, the two companies will become one, and thus a **common operational system** must be developed. The acquiring company's management should not impose immediately their own systems upon the target company's operations, assuming them to be superior. This is likely to **alienate** acquired employees.

It is probably best to **use the system already in place**, in the acquired company, initially supplemented by requests for additional reports felt to be immediately necessary for adequate information and control flows between the two management bodies. As the integration process proceeds, the best aspects of each of the companies' systems will be identified and a **common system developed.**

Where the two companies are to operate independently, it is likely that some changes will be needed to financial control procedures to get the two group companies in line. Essentially, however, the target company's management may **continue with their own cultures, operations and systems.**

Exam alert

Any discussion of post-merger value enhancing strategies must involve more than just a list of bullet points and must be relevant to the entities involved.

6.6 Failure of mergers and takeovers

The aim of any takeover will be to **generate value for the acquiring shareholders.** Where this does not happen, there may be a number of reasons, including **a strategic plan that fails to produce the benefits expected,** or **over-optimism** about future market conditions, operating synergies and the amount of time and money required to make the merger work.

A third recurring reasons for failure is **poor integration management**, in particular:

(a) **Inflexibility** in the application of integration plans drawn up prior to the event. Once the takeover has happened, management must be prepared to adapt plans in the light of changed circumstances or inaccurate prior information.

(b) **Poor man management**, with lack of communication of goals and future prospects of employees, and failure to recognise and deal with the uncertainty and anxiety invariably felt by them.

Section summary

Many takeovers fail to achieve their full potential because of lack of attention paid to **post-acquisition integration**. A clear programme should be in place, designed to re-define objectives and strategy, and take appropriate care of the human element.

7 Impact of mergers and takeovers on stakeholders   11/10, 9/11, 3/12

Introduction

We need to consider the effect of mergers and takeovers on stakeholders other than shareholders.

7.1 To what extent do the stakeholders in a merger or takeover benefit from it?

The following comments are based upon extensive empirical research.

(a) **Acquiring company shareholders**

At least half of mergers studied have shown a decline in profitability compared with industry averages. Returns to equity can often be poor relative to the market in the early years, particularly for equity-financed bids and first time players. Costs of mergers frequently outweigh the gains.

(b) **Target company shareholders**

In the majority of cases, it is the target shareholders who benefit most from a takeover. Bidding companies invariable have to offer a significant premium over the market price prevailing prior to the bid in order to achieve the purchase.

(c) **Acquiring company management**

The management of the newly enlarged organisation will often enjoy increased status and influence, as well as increased salary and benefits.

(d) **Target company management**

Whilst some key personnel may be kept on for some time after the takeover, a significant number of managers will find themselves out of a job. However, a 'golden handshake' and the prospect of equally remunerative employment elsewhere may lessen the blow of this somewhat.

(e) **Other employees**

Commonly the economy of scale cost savings anticipated in a merger will be largely achieved by the loss of jobs, as duplicated service operations are eliminated and loss-making divisions closed down. However, in some instances, the increased competitive strength of the newly enlarged enterprise can led to expansion of operations and the need for an increased workforce.

(f) **Financial institutions**

These are perhaps the outright winners. The more complex the deal, the longer the battle, and the more legal and financial problems encountered, the greater their fee income, regardless of the end result.

Section summary

Don't forget that **managers, employees** and **financial institutions** are key stakeholders in mergers as well as shareholders.

8 Exit strategies

> **Introduction**
>
> An **exit strategy** is a way to terminate ownership of a company or the operation of part of the company. You need to be able to discuss the types of exit strategy that are available and their implications.

8.1 Divestment

KEY TERM

A DIVESTMENT is disposal of part of its activities by an entity. *(CIMA Official Terminology)*

Mergers and takeovers are not inevitably good strategy for a business. In some circumstances, strategies of internal growth, no growth or even some form of divestment might be preferable.

Businesses must though have regard for the impact on:

- The **performance** of the company
- **Workforce morale** and performance
- **Stock market reaction** – the market dislikes uncertainty so must be given as much information as soon as possible

8.2 Demergers

A **demerger** is the opposite of a merger. It is the **splitting up of a corporate body into two or more separate and independent bodies.** For example, the ABC Group might demerge by splitting into two independently operating companies AB and C. Existing shareholders are given a stake in each of the new separate companies.

Demerging, in its strictest sense, stops short of selling out, but is an attempt to ensure that share prices reflect the true value of the underlying operations. In large diversified conglomerates, so many different businesses are combined into one organisation that it becomes difficult for analysts to understand them fully.

In addition, a management running ten businesses instead of two could be seen to lose some focus.

The potential disadvantages with demergers are as follows.

(a) **Economies of scale may be lost**, where the demerged parts of the business had operations in common to which economies of scale applied.

(b) The smaller companies which result from the demerger will have **lower revenue, profits and status** than the group before the demerger.

(c) There may be **higher overhead costs** as a percentage of **revenue**, resulting from (b).

(d) The ability to **raise extra finance**, especially debt finance, to support new investments and expansion may be **reduced**.

(e) **Vulnerability** to takeover may be **increased**.

CASE STUDY

In March 2010, Liberty International, the UK real estate company, confirmed the demerger of its central London properties from its regional shopping centres. Two new companies – Capital Shopping Centres and Capital & Counties – are expected to be listed on the London Stock Exchange as early as summer 2010.

David Fischel, Liberty's chief executive, commented

'The Capital & Counties business... [is] a very different business to the shopping centre business... The demerger will enable Capital Shopping Centres and Capital & Counties to achieve greater value for shareholders over time than the current Liberty International would as one combined business.'

Source: *Financial Times*, 9 March 2010

8.3 Sell-offs

A **sell-off** is a form of **divestment** involving the sale of part of a company to a third party, usually another company. Generally, cash will be received in exchange.

A company may carry out a sell-off for one of the following reasons.

(a) As **part of its strategic planning**, it has decided to restructure, concentrating management effort on particular parts of the business. Control problems may be reduced if peripheral activities are sold off.

(b) It **wishes to sell off a part of its business** which makes losses, and so to improve the company's future reported consolidated profit performance. This may be in the form of a management buy-out (MBO) – see below.

(c) In order to **protect the rest of the business from takeover**, it may choose to sell a part of the business which is particularly attractive to a buyer.

(d) The company may be **short of cash**.

(e) A subsidiary with **high risk** in its operating cash flows could be **sold**, so as to reduce the business risk of the group as a whole.

(f) A **subsidiary** could be **sold at a profit**. Some companies have specialised in taking over large groups of companies, and then selling off parts of the newly-acquired groups, so that the proceeds of sales more than pay for the original takeovers.

A sell-off may however **disrupt** the rest of the organisation, especially if key players within the organisation disappear as a result.

8.4 Liquidations

The extreme form of a sell-off is where the entire business is sold off in a **liquidation**. In a voluntary dissolution, the shareholders might decide to close the whole business, sell off all the assets and distribute net funds raised to shareholders.

CASE STUDY

Woolworths, the UK High Street chain, went into administration in November 2008 with debts of £385m. The administrator, Deloitte, sold off the assets (including inventory and fixtures and fittings) at discount prices.

8.5 Spin-offs

In a **spin-off**, a new company is created whose shares are owned by the shareholders of the original company which is making the distribution of assets. There is no change in the ownership of assets, as the shareholders own the same proportion of shares in the new company as they did in the old company. Assets of the part of the business to be separated off are transferred into the new company, which will usually have different management from the old company. In more complex cases, a spin-off may involve the original company being split into a number of separate companies.

For a number of possible reasons such as those set out below, a spin-off appears generally to meet with favour from stock market investors.

(a) The change may make a **merger or takeover** of some part of the business **easier** in the future, or may protect parts of the business from predators.

(b) There may be **improved efficiency** and **more streamlined management** within the new structure.

(c) It may be **easier** to **see the value of the separated parts** of the business now that they are no longer hidden within a conglomerate.

(d) The **requirements** of **regulatory agencies** might be **met more easily** within the new structure, for example if the agency is able to exercise price control over a particular part of the business which was previously hidden within the conglomerate structure.

(e) After the spin-off, shareholders have the **opportunity to adjust the proportions** of their **holdings** between the different companies created.

CASE STUDY

In April 2012 Chesapeake Energy, the second largest US natural gas producer, filed details of its plan to spin off its oilfield services division via an IPO with an estimated value of $862.5m. This is part of a plan to bolster Chesapeake's finances and to reduce its debt levels.

8.6 Going private

A public company **'goes private'** when a **small group of individuals**, possibly including existing shareholders and/or managers and with or without support from a financial institution, **buys all of the company's shares.** This form of restructuring is relatively common in the USA and may involve the shares in the company ceasing to be listed on a stock exchange.

Advantages in going private could include the following.

(a) The costs of meeting listing requirements can be saved.

(b) The company is protected from volatility in share prices which financial problems may create.

(c) The company will be less vulnerable to hostile takeover bids.

(d) Management can concentrate on the long-term needs of the business rather than the short-term expectations of shareholders.

(e) Shareholders are likely to be closer to management in a private company, reducing costs arising from the separation of ownership and control (the 'agency problem').

CASE STUDY

The San Francisco Business Times reported that several companies were considering going private, particularly young companies with shares under pressure in public markets. Tighter scrutiny of public company finances, together with new federal disclosure laws, had added to the cost of financing through public equity markets. Going private would allow greater flexibility to restructure operations, and a potential increase in value for those companies whose cash at bank or non-current assets were worth far more than the depressed stock market value.

8.7 Management buyouts (MBOs) 5/10, 9/11

KEY TERM

A MANAGEMENT BUYOUT is the purchase of a business from its existing owners by members of the management team, generally in association with a financing institution. *(CIMA Official Terminology)*

A **management buyout** is the purchase of all or part of a business from its owners by its managers. For example, the directors of a subsidiary company in a group might buy the company from the holding company, with the intention of running it as proprietors of a separate business entity.

(a) **To the managers,** the buyout would be a method of setting up in business for themselves.

(b) **To the group**, the buyout would be a method of **divestment**, selling off the subsidiary as a going concern.

A **large organisation's board of directors** may agree to a management buyout of a subsidiary for any of a number of different reasons.

(a) The **subsidiary** may be **peripheral** to the group's mainstream activities, and no longer fit in with the group's overall strategy.

(b) The group may wish to **sell off a loss-making subsidiary**, and a management team may think that it can restore the subsidiary's fortunes.

(c) The parent company may need to **raise cash quickly**.

(d) The subsidiary may be part of a **group that has just been taken over** and the new parent company may wish to sell off parts of the group it has just acquired.

(e) The **best offer price** might come from a **small management group** wanting to arrange a buyout.

(f) When a group has taken the decision to sell a subsidiary, it will probably **get better co-operation** from the management and employees of the subsidiary if the sale is a management buyout.

A **private company's shareholders** might agree to sell out to a management team because they need cash, they want to retire, or the business is not profitable enough for them.

CASE STUDY

According to a survey in 2011 by private bank Coutts the number of business owners considering a management buy-out (MBO) has risen by a third in the past three years but only accounts for 18 per cent of would-be sellers. In addition only 30 per cent of those who had completed an MBO said that it represented the best form of exit, and 55 per cent said it was the only way they could exit the business or it offered best value.

8.7.1 The parties to a buyout

There are usually three parties to a management buyout.

(a) A **management team** wanting to make a buyout. This team ought to have the skills and ability to convince financial backers that it is worth supporting.

(b) **Directors** of a group of companies

(c) **Financial backers** of the buyout team, who will usually want an equity stake in the bought-out business, because of the **venture capital risk** they are taking. Often, several financial backers provide the venture capital for a single buyout.

8.7.2 The role of the venture capitalist

Venture capitalists are far more inclined to fund MBOs, management buy-ins (MBI) and corporate expansion projects than the more risky and relatively costly early stage investments such as start-ups. The minimum investment considered will normally be around £100,000, with average investment of £1–£2 million.

Whilst the return required on venture capital for the high-risk, early stage investments may be as high as 80%, where the funding is for a well established business with sound management, it is more commonly around the 25–30% mark. Whilst this may be achieved by the successful investments, of course there will be many more that fail, and the overall returns on venture capital funds averages out at around 10–15%.

For MBOs and MBIs the venture capitalist will not necessarily provide the majority of the finance. A £50 million buy-out may be funded by, say, £15 million venture capital, £20 million debt finance and £15 million mezzanine debt.

Venture capital funds may require:

- A 20-30% shareholding
- Special rights to appoint a number of directors
- The company to seek their prior approval for new issues or acquisitions

Venture capitalists generally like to have a predetermined **target exit date,** the point at which they can recoup some or all of their investment in an MBO. At the outset, they will wish to establish various **exit routes**, the possibilities including:

- The sale of shares following a **flotation** on a recognised stock exchange
- The **sale** of the company to another firm
- The **repurchase** of the venture capitalist's shares by the company or its owners
- The sales of the venture capitalist's shares to an **institution** such as an investment trust

8.7.3 The appraisal of proposed buyouts

Management-owned companies seem to achieve better performance probably because of:

- A **favourable buyout price** having been **achieved**
- **Personal motivation and determination**
- **Quicker decision-making** and so **more flexibility**
- **Keener decisions** and action on pricing and debt collection
- **Savings in overheads**, eg in contributions to a large head office

However, many management buyouts, once they occur, begin with some redundancies to cut running costs.

An institutional investor (such as a venture capitalist) should evaluate a buyout before deciding whether or not to finance. Aspects of any buyout that ought to be checked are as follows.

(a) Does the management team have the **full range of management skills** that are needed (for example a technical expert and a finance director)? Does it have the right blend of experience? Does it have the commitment?

(b) Why is the **company for sale**? The possible reasons for buyouts have already been listed. If the reason is that the parent company wants to get rid of a loss-making subsidiary, what evidence is there to suggest that the company can be made profitable after a buyout?

(c) What are the **projected profits and cash flows of the business**? The prospective returns must justify the risks involved.

(d) What is **being bought**? The buyout team might be buying the shares of the company, or only selected assets of the company. Are the assets that are being acquired sufficient for the task? Will more assets have to be bought? When will the existing assets need replacing? How much extra finance would be needed for these asset purchases? Can the company be operated profitably?

(e) What is **the price**? Is the price right or is it too high?

(f) What **financial contribution** can be made by members of the management team themselves?

(g) What are the **exit routes** and when might they be taken?

8.7.4 Problems with buyouts

A common problem with management buyouts is that the managers have little or no experience in **financial management** or **financial accounting**. Managers will also be required to take tough decisions. A good way of approaching the problem is **scenario analysis** addressing the effect of taking a major decision in isolation. However, the results may be painful, including the ditching of long established products.

Other problems are:

(a) Tax and legal complications

(b) Difficulties in deciding on a fair price to be paid

(c) Convincing employees of the need to change working practices or to accept redundancy

(d) Inadequate resources to finance the maintenance and replacement of tangible non-current assets

(e) The maintenance of employees' employment or pension rights

(f) Accepting the board representation requirement that many sources of funds will insist upon

(g) The loss of key employees if the company moves geographically, or wage rates are decreased too far, or employment conditions are unacceptable in other ways

(h) Maintaining continuity of relationships with suppliers and customers

(i) Lack of time to make decisions

The issues discussed in this chapter may be very important when you come to take the TOPCIMA exam. You may be asked to consider various options including mergers, strategic alliances (and doing nothing)

Section summary

- A **demerger** is the splitting up of corporate bodies into two or more separate bodies, to ensure share prices reflect the true value of underlying operations.

- A **sell-off** is the sale of part of a company to a third party, generally for cash.

- A **spin-off** is the creation of a new company, where the shareholders of the original company own the shares

- A company **goes private** when a small group of individuals buys all the company's shares. Going private may **decrease costs** and make the company **less vulnerable** to hostile takeover bids.

- A **management buyout** is the purchase of all or part of the business by its managers. Management buy-outs can be the best way of maintaining links with a subsidiary, and can ensure the co-operation of management. The main complication with **management buyouts** is obtaining the consent of all parties involved. Venture capital may be an important source of financial backing.

Chapter Roundup

- **Takeovers** often target companies that are good **strategic fits** with the acquiring companies, often to acquire a new product range or to develop a presence in a new market.

- **Mergers** have been more common in industries with low growth and returns.

- A takeover may be **resisted** by the target company, if its directors believe that the terms are poor or there are no obvious advantages. Possible **defensive tactics** include issuing a forecast of attractive future profits, lobbying or finding a white knight (a company that would make a welcome takeover bid).

- Payment can be in the form of **cash**, a **share exchange** or **convertible bonds**. The choice will depend on available cash, desired levels of gearing, shareholders' taxation position and changes in control.

- Shareholders of both the companies involved in a merger will be sensitive to the effect of the merger on **share prices** and **earnings per share**.

- Directors of companies of any size must treat all shareholders **fairly** and give them **sufficient information** about the takeover. Larger mergers will be of interest to the **competition authorities**.

- Many takeovers fail to achieve their full potential because of lack of attention paid to **post-acquisition integration**. A clear programme should be in place, designed to re-define objectives and strategy, and take appropriate care of the human element.

- Don't forget that **managers**, **employees** and **financial institutions** are key stakeholders in mergers as well as shareholders.

- A **demerger** is the splitting up of corporate bodies into two or more separate bodies, to ensure share prices reflect the true value of underlying operations.

- A **sell-off** is the sale of part of a company to a third party, generally for cash.

- A **spin-off** is the creation of a new company, where the shareholders of the original company own the shares

- A company **goes private** when a small group of individuals buys all the company's shares. Going private may **decrease costs** and make the company **less vulnerable** to hostile takeover bids.

- A **management buyout** is the purchase of all or part of the business by its managers. Management buyouts can be the best way of maintaining links with a subsidiary, and can ensure the co-operation of management. The main complication with **management buyouts** is obtaining the consent of all parties involved. Venture capital may be an important source of financial backing.

Quick Quiz

1   **Fill in the blank.**

    .... is 'the acquisition by a company of a controlling interest in the voting share capital of another company, usually achieved by the purchase of a majority of the voting shares.' (CIMA Official Terminology)

2   What is meant by a 'white knight'?

3   What is a 'poison pill' in the context of takeovers and mergers?

4   A smaller company takes over a larger one, so that the smaller company must increase its voting equity by over 100% to complete the takeover. What is this process called?

5   What is the name of the arrangement where part of the purchase consideration is only paid when the target company reaches certain performance targets?

6   What are Drucker's five golden rules for post-acquisition integration?

7   If the target company's shares are valued at a lower P/E ratio, the predator company's shareholders will suffer a fall in EPS.

True ☐

False ☐

8   Why might management owned companies achieve improved performance?

9   What are the main exit routes for a venture capitalist?

Answers to Quick Quiz

1   A takeover

2   A company which will make a welcome takeover bid

3   An anti-takeover device

4   A reverse takeover

5   An earn-out arrangement

6   (1)   Common sense of unity shared by acquiror and acquiree

    (2)   Acquiror should ask 'what can we offer them'?

    (3)   Acquiror should treat products, markets and customers of acquired company with respect

    (4)   Acquiring company should provide top management with relevant skills for managing acquired company within one year

    (5)   Cross-company promotions of staff within one year

7   False. The predator company's shareholders will benefit from a rise in earnings per share.

8   (a)   Personal motivation and determination
    (b)   Quicker and more flexible decision making
    (c)   Keener decisions, eg on pricing
    (d)   Overhead savings

9
- The sale of shares following a **flotation** on a recognised stock exchange
- The **sale** of the company to another firm
- The **repurchase** of the venture capitalist's shares by the company or its owners
- The sales of the venture capitalist's shares to an **institution** such as an investment trust

Answers to Questions

16.1 Bid terms

(a) (i) *Number of shares in Arethusa: 50 million*

Themis shares issued to acquire Arethusa (1 for 3): 50 million/3 = 16,666,667

Value of the bid, at £9.30 per Themis share = 16,666,667 × £9.30 = £155 million.

(ii)

	£m
After-tax profits:	
Themis	127
Arethusa	28
Increase due to synergy	15
Earnings of combined group	170

Number of Themis shares in issue

Prior to takeover (150 m × £1/50p)	300,000,000
Issued to finance takeover	16,666,667
	316,666,667

EPS after the takeover = £170 million/316,666,667 shares = 53.7p per share, say 54p per share.

(iii) EPS of Themis before the takeover = £127 million/300 million share = 42.3p

P/E ratio of Themis before the takeover = £9.30/£0.423 = 21.99, say 22.

Share price of Themis after the takeover = 54p × 22 = £11.88.

(b) Arethusa shareholders are being offered shares in Themis, currently valued at £9.30 each, in exchange for every three shares they hold in Arethusa, currently valued at (3 × £2.90) £8.70. The offer price represents a **premium** to the current market price of Arethusa shares of just £0.60 per £8.70 of shares, which is about 5%. This **bid premium** seems very low.

The **current share price of Themis** is £9.30, having risen from £6.90 last year. The possibility that the share price will remain at this level (a P/E ratio of 22), or might even rise after the takeover, should be questioned. A fall in the Themis share price of about 5% or more (to less than £8.70) would mean that Arethusa shareholders would suffer a loss by agreeing to the takeover offer.

In contrast, the **current EPS of Arethusa** is (£28 million/50 million shares) 56p and the P/E ratio is therefore just 5.2 (£2.90/56p). There is a very **large difference** between the **P/E ratios** at which the two companies are currently valued, adding weight to the concern that either Themis shares are currently over-valued or Arethusa shares are under-valued by the market.

On the other hand, Arethusa shareholders might take the view that shares in Themis are likely to **rise still further** in value after the takeover. Accepting the offer from Themis would therefore enable them to make a further capital gain after the takeover has occurred.

Arethusa shareholders might want to invest in a company with a **high dividend payout policy**, and so would not want to hold on to their Themis shares after a takeover. If so, they should sell their Themis shares and invest in a different company. Concerns about dividend policy should not affect the response of Arethusa shareholders to the takeover offer.

16.2 Post-merger valuation

(a) *Workings*

Nyasa current EPS = $\dfrac{\text{Total earnings}}{\text{Number of shares}} = \dfrac{£4.2 \text{ million}}{40 \text{ million}} = 10.5\text{p}$

P/E ratio = 18

Current market price of Nyasa shares = 18 × 10.5p = 189p.

Turkana current EPS = $\dfrac{£3.0 \text{ million}}{12 \text{ million shares}} = 25\text{p}$

P/E ratio = 14

Current price of Turkana shares = 14 × 25p = 350p.

(i) The bid price is 4 Nyasa shares for every 3 Turkana shares.

This values 3 Turkana shares at (4 × 189p) = 756p.

Bid value per Turkana share = 756p/3 = 252p per share.

The total value of the proposed bid, given 12 million Turkana shares:

12 million × 252p = £30.24 million.

The bid, if successful, would result in the issue of (12 million × 4/3) 16 million new Nyasa shares.

(ii) Total earnings after takeover

	£m
Nyasa earnings	4.2
Turkana earnings	3.0
Savings from the acquisition	1.5
	8.7
Number of shares (40 million + 16 million)	56m

EPS following the takeover: £8.7 million/56 million = £0.155, ie 15.5p.

(iii) Share price of Nyasa after the takeover, assuming a P/E ratio of 18:

15.5p × 18 = £2.79

(b) **Holder of 3,000 shares in Nyasa**

	£
Value of shares before the takeover (× £1.89)	5,670
Value of shares after the takeover (× £2.79)	8,370
Increase in value of investment	2,700

Holder of 3,000 shares in Turkana

	£
Value of 3,000 shares before the takeover (3,000 × £3.50)	10,500
Value of shares after the takeover (4,000 × £2.79)	11,160
Increase in value of investment	660

The takeover would **increase the total value** of the **equity shares** of the companies, on the assumption that a P/E ratio of 18 can be maintained. There are two reasons for this increase in value.

(i) The earnings of Turkana will be re-rated from a P/E of 14 to a P/E of 18.
(ii) There will be savings of £1.5 million, adding (× 18) £27 million to equity values.

Under the terms of the current bid, Nyasa shareholders would enjoy an **increase in the value of their investment** by (£2,700/£5,670) almost 50%. Turkana shareholders would also expect some increase in the value of their investment but only by (£660/£10,500) about 6%. Most of the increase in the equity valuation arising from the acquisition would therefore be enjoyed by the Nyasa shareholders.

The estimated increase in the equity valuation is dependent on the assumption of savings of £1.5 million and the assumption that a **P/E ratio of 18** will be **maintained**. If these assumptions turn out to be over-optimistic, the value of Nyasa shares after the takeover will be lower than £2.79, and there would be a serious risk that the value of the investment of Turkana shareholders would fall as a result of the takeover.

The offer from Nyasa is therefore too low, and the directors of Turkana would recommend rejection of the bid on these grounds.

Now try these questions from the Exam Question Bank

Number	Level	Marks	Time
Q27	Examination	25	45 mins
Q28	Examination	20	36 mins
Q29	Examination	25	45 mins
Q30	Examination	50	90 mins

Exam skills

The 50 mark Section A question in your exam will comprise a pre-seen scenario (released about six weeks before the exam) supplemented by additional unseen material you will receive when you sit the exam.

We have included a sample Section A question, including the pre-seen and unseen material after the Exam Question Bank in this Study Text.

You should attempt this question now as well.

However, please note the pre-seen scenario included here is NOT the scenario you will be given for your exam.

BPP produce a Strategic Case Study Kit based on the pre-seen scenarios for each exam, and these Kits are available to purchase separately during the six weeks before the exam.

APPENDIX 1: DISCOUNTED CASH FLOW

This appendix is designed to refresh your memory of discounted cash flow techniques. It is essential that you are comfortable with these techniques as they are used in numerous parts of the syllabus. Work through the content and questions carefully to ensure you can do the necessary calculations and are familiar with the terminology used.

1 Discounted cash flow

Discounted cash flow, or **DCF** for short, is an investment appraisal technique which takes into account both the timings of cash flows and also total profitability over a project's life.

Two important points about DCF are as follows.

(a) DCF looks at the **cash flows** of a project, not the accounting profits. Cash flows are considered because they show the costs and benefits of a project when they actually occur and ignore notional costs such as depreciation.

(b) The **timing** of cash flows is taken into account by **discounting them**. The effect of discounting is to give a bigger value per $1 for cash flows that occur earlier: $1 earned after one year will be worth more than $1 earned after two years, which in turn will be worth more than $1 earned after five years, and so on.

1.1 Compounding

Suppose that a company has $10,000 to invest, and wants to earn a return of 10% (compound interest) on its investments. This means that if the $10,000 could be invested at 10%, the value of the investment with interest would build up as follows.

(a) After 1 year $10,000 × (1.10) = $11,000
(b) After 2 years $10,000 × (1.10)^2 = $12,100
(c) After 3 years $10,000 × (1.10)^3 = $13,310 and so on.

This is **compounding**. The formula for the future value of an investment plus accumulated interest after n time periods is:

$$FV = PV(1+r)^n$$

Where   FV   is the future value of the investment with interest

PV   is the initial or 'present' value of the investment

r   is the compound rate of return per time period, expressed as a proportion (so 10% = 0.10, 5% = 0.05 and so on)

n   is the number of time periods.

1.2 Discounting

Discounting starts with the future value, and converts a future value to a present value. For example, if a company expects to earn a (compound) rate of return of 10% on its investments, how much would it need to invest now to have the following investments?

(a) $11,000 after 1 year
(b) $12,100 after 2 years
(c) $13,310 after 3 years

The answer is $10,000 in each case, and we can calculate it by discounting. The discounting formula to calculate the present value of a future sum of money at the end of n time periods is:

$$PV = FV \frac{1}{(1+r)^n}$$

(a) After 1 year, $11,000 \times \dfrac{1}{1.10} = \$10,000$

(b) After 2 years, $12,100 \times \dfrac{1}{1.10^2} = \$10,000$

(c) After 3 years, $13,310 \times \dfrac{1}{1.10^3} = \$10,000$

Discounting can be applied to both money receivable and also to money payable at a future date. By discounting all payments and receipts from a capital investment to a present value, they can be compared on a common basis at a value which takes account of when the various cash flows will take place.

1.3 Present value tables

Present value tables are provided in your exam (and in Appendix 2 of this study text), and give the present value factor or **discount factor** for given values of n and r. They can only be used for whole numbers up to 20% and are rounded so lose some accuracy, but they simplify and speed up your calculations.

Look up the discount factor in the table and multiply the value of the cash flow by the discount factor.

(a) Calculate the present value of $60,000 at year 6, if a return of 15% per annum is obtainable.
(b) Calculate the present value of $100,000 at year 5, if a return of 6% per annum is obtainable.

Solution

(a) Present value = 60,000 × 0.432 = $25,920
(b) Present value = 100,000 × 0.747 = $74,700

1.4 Annuity tables

To calculate the present value of a constant annual cash flow, or annuity, we can multiply the annual cash flows by the sum of the discount factors for the relevant years. These total factors are known as **cumulative present value factors** or **annuity factors**. As with 'present value factors of $1 in year n', there are tables for annuity factors, which are shown in Appendix 2 of this text. For example, the cumulative present value factor of $1 per annum for five years at 11% per annum is in the column for 11% and the year 5 row, and is 3.696.

(a) What is the present value of $1,000 in contribution earned each year from years 1–10, when the required return on investment is 11%?

(b) What is the present value of $2,000 costs incurred each year from years 3 - 6 when the cost of capital is 5%?

Solution

(a) $1,000 × 5.889 = $5,889

(b)

PV of $1 per annum for years 1–6 at 5%	5.076
Less PV of $1 per annum for years 1–2 at 5%	1.859
PV of $1 per annum for years 3–6	3.217

PV = $2,000 × 3.217 = $6,434

1.5 Annual cash flows in perpetuity

You need to know how to calculate the cumulative present value of $1 per annum for every year in perpetuity (that is, forever).

When the cost of capital is r, the cumulative PV of $1 per annum in perpetuity is **$1/r**.

For example, the PV of $1 per annum in perpetuity at a discount rate of 10% would be $1/0.10 = $10.

Similarly, the PV of $1 per annum in perpetuity at a discount rate of 15% would be $1/0.15 = $6.67 and at a discount rate of 20% it would be $1/0.20 = $5.

2 The net present value method

The NPV method compares the **present value** of all the **cash inflows** from an investment with the **present value** of all the **cash outflows** from an investment. The NPV is thus calculated as the PV of **cash inflows** minus the PV of **cash outflows**.

NPV	
NPV positive	Return from investment's cash inflows in excess of cost of capital ⇒ undertake project
NPV negative	Return from investment's cash inflows below cost of capital ⇒ don't undertake project
NPV 0	Return from investment's cash inflows same as cost of capital

2.1 Example: NPV

A company is considering a capital investment, where the estimated cash flows are as follows.

Year	Cash flow $
0 (ie now)	(100,000)
1	60,000
2	80,000
3	40,000
4	30,000

The company's cost of capital is 15%. You are required to calculate the NPV of the project and to assess whether it should be undertaken.

Solution

Year	Cash flow $	Discount factor @ 15%	Present value $
0	(100,000)	1.000	(100,000)
1	60,000	0.870	52,200
2	80,000	0.756	60,200
3	40,000	0.658	26,320
4	30,000	0.572	17,160
		NPV =	56,160

Note. The discount factor for any cash flow 'now' (year 0) is always = 1, regardless of what the cost of capital is. The PV of cash inflows exceeds the PV of cash outflows by $56,160, which means that the project will earn a DCF yield in excess of 15%. It should therefore be undertaken.

2.2 Timing of cash flows: conventions used in DCF

Discounted cash flow applies discounting arithmetic to the relevant costs and benefits of an investment project. Discounting, which reduces the value of future cash flows to a present value equivalent, is clearly concerned with the timing of the cash flows. As a general rule, the following guidelines may be applied.

(a) A cash outlay to be incurred at the beginning of an investment project (**'now'**) occurs in **year 0**. The present value of $1 now, in year 0, is $1 regardless of the value of r.

(b) A cash outlay, saving or inflow which occurs **during the course of a time period** (say, one year) is assumed to occur all at once **at the end of the time period** (at the end of the year). Receipts of $10,000 during year 1 are therefore taken to occur at the end of year 1.

(c) A cash outlay or receipt which occurs **at the beginning of a time period** (say at the beginning of one year) is taken to occur **at the end of the previous year**. Therefore a cash outlay of $5,000 at the beginning of year 2 is taken to occur at the end of year 1.

3 The internal rate of return method

The **internal rate of return (IRR)** method is to calculate the **exact DCF rate of return** which the project is expected to achieve, in other words the rate at which the **NPV is zero**. If the expected rate of return (the IRR or DCF yield) **exceeds** a **target rate** of return, the project would be worth undertaking (ignoring risk and uncertainty factors).

To calculate the IRR.

STEP 1 Calculate the net present value using a 10% discount rate

STEP 2 Calculate the NPV using a second discount rate
(a) If the NPV is **positive**, use a second rate that is **greater** than the first rate
(b) If the NPV is **negative**, use a second rate that is **less** than the first rate

STEP 3 Use the two NPV values to **estimate the IRR**. The formula to apply is as follows.

$$IRR \approx a + \left(\left(\frac{NPV_a}{NPV_a - NPV_b}\right)(b-a)\right)\%$$

Where a   =   the lower of the two rates of return used
       b   =   the higher of the two rates of return used
       NPV_a =   the NPV obtained using rate a
       NPV_b =   the NPV obtained using rate b

3.1 Example: the IRR method

A company is trying to decide whether to buy a machine for $80,000 which will save costs of $20,000 per annum for 5 years and which will have a resale value of $10,000 at the end of year 5. If it is the company's policy to undertake projects only if they are expected to yield a DCF return of 10% or more, ascertain whether this project should be undertaken.

Solution

STEP 1 Calculate the first NPV, using the company's cost of capital of 10%

Year	Cash flow $	PV factor 10%	PV of cash flow $
0	(80,000)	1.000	(80,000)
1–5	20,000	3.791	75,820
5	10,000	0.621	6,210
		NPV =	2,030

This is positive, which means that the IRR is more than 10%.

STEP 2 Calculate the second NPV, using a rate that is **greater** than the first rate, as the first rate gave a positive answer.

Suppose we try 12%.

Year	Cash flow $	PV factor 12%	PV of cash flow $
0	(80,000)	1.000	(80,000)
1–5	20,000	3.605	72,100
5	10,000	0.567	5,670
		NPV =	(2,230)

This is fairly close to zero and **negative**. The IRR is therefore greater than 10% (positive NPV of $2,030) but less than 12% (negative NPV of $2,230).

STEP 3 Use the two NPV values to estimate the IRR.

The interpolation method assumes that the NPV rises in linear fashion between the two NPVs close to 0. The IRR is therefore assumed to be on a straight line between NPV = $2,030 at 10% and NPV = –$2,230 at 12%.

Using the formula

$$IRR \approx a + \left(\left(\frac{NPV_a}{NPV_a - NPV_b}\right)(b-a)\right)\%$$

$$IRR \approx 10 + \left[\frac{2,030}{2,030 + 2,230} \times (12-10)\right]\% = 10.95\%, \text{ say } 11\%$$

If it is company policy to undertake investments which are expected to yield 10% or more, this project would be undertaken.

APPENDIX 2: MATHEMATICAL TABLES AND EXAM FORMULAE

PRESENT VALUE TABLE

Present value of 1.00 unit of currency ie $(1+r)^{-n}$ where r = interest rate, n = number of periods until payment or receipt.

Periods (n)	1%	2%	3%	4%	5%	6%	7%	8%	9%	10%
1	0.990	0.980	0.971	0.962	0.952	0.943	0.935	0.926	0.917	0.909
2	0.980	0.961	0.943	0.925	0.907	0.890	0.873	0.857	0.842	0.826
3	0.971	0.942	0.915	0.889	0.864	0.840	0.816	0.794	0.772	0.751
4	0.961	0.924	0.888	0.855	0.823	0.792	0.763	0.735	0.708	0.683
5	0.951	0.906	0.863	0.822	0.784	0.747	0.713	0.681	0.650	0.621
6	0.942	0.888	0.837	0.790	0.746	0.705	0.666	0.630	0.596	0.564
7	0.933	0.871	0.813	0.760	0.711	0.665	0.623	0.583	0.547	0.513
8	0.923	0.853	0.789	0.731	0.677	0.627	0.582	0.540	0.502	0.467
9	0.914	0.837	0.766	0.703	0.645	0.592	0.544	0.500	0.460	0.424
10	0.905	0.820	0.744	0.676	0.614	0.558	0.508	0.463	0.422	0.386
11	0.896	0.804	0.722	0.650	0.585	0.527	0.475	0.429	0.388	0.350
12	0.887	0.788	0.701	0.625	0.557	0.497	0.444	0.397	0.356	0.319
13	0.879	0.773	0.681	0.601	0.530	0.469	0.415	0.368	0.326	0.290
14	0.870	0.758	0.661	0.577	0.505	0.442	0.388	0.340	0.299	0.263
15	0.861	0.743	0.642	0.555	0.481	0.417	0.362	0.315	0.275	0.239
16	0.853	0.728	0.623	0.534	0.458	0.394	0.339	0.292	0.252	0.218
17	0.844	0.714	0.605	0.513	0.436	0.371	0.317	0.270	0.231	0.198
18	0.836	0.700	0.587	0.494	0.416	0.350	0.296	0.250	0.212	0.180
19	0.828	0.686	0.570	0.475	0.396	0.331	0.277	0.232	0.194	0.164
20	0.820	0.673	0.554	0.456	0.377	0.312	0.258	0.215	0.178	0.149

Periods (n)	11%	12%	13%	14%	15%	16%	17%	18%	19%	20%
1	0.901	0.893	0.885	0.877	0.870	0.862	0.855	0.847	0.840	0.833
2	0.812	0.797	0.783	0.769	0.756	0.743	0.731	0.718	0.706	0.694
3	0.731	0.712	0.693	0.675	0.658	0.641	0.624	0.609	0.593	0.579
4	0.659	0.636	0.613	0.592	0.572	0.552	0.534	0.516	0.499	0.482
5	0.593	0.567	0.543	0.519	0.497	0.476	0.456	0.437	0.419	0.402
6	0.535	0.507	0.480	0.456	0.432	0.410	0.390	0.370	0.352	0.335
7	0.482	0.452	0.425	0.400	0.376	0.354	0.333	0.314	0.296	0.279
8	0.434	0.404	0.376	0.351	0.327	0.305	0.285	0.266	0.249	0.233
9	0.391	0.361	0.333	0.308	0.284	0.263	0.243	0.225	0.209	0.194
10	0.352	0.322	0.295	0.270	0.247	0.227	0.208	0.191	0.176	0.162
11	0.317	0.287	0.261	0.237	0.215	0.195	0.178	0.162	0.148	0.135
12	0.286	0.257	0.231	0.208	0.187	0.168	0.152	0.137	0.124	0.112
13	0.258	0.229	0.204	0.182	0.163	0.145	0.130	0.116	0.104	0.093
14	0.232	0.205	0.181	0.160	0.141	0.125	0.111	0.099	0.088	0.078
15	0.209	0.183	0.160	0.140	0.123	0.108	0.095	0.084	0.074	0.065
16	0.188	0.163	0.141	0.123	0.107	0.093	0.081	0.071	0.062	0.054
17	0.170	0.146	0.125	0.108	0.093	0.080	0.069	0.060	0.052	0.045
18	0.153	0.130	0.111	0.095	0.081	0.069	0.059	0.051	0.044	0.038
19	0.138	0.116	0.098	0.083	0.070	0.060	0.051	0.043	0.037	0.031
20	0.124	0.104	0.087	0.073	0.061	0.051	0.043	0.037	0.031	0.026

CUMULATIVE PRESENT VALUE TABLE

This table shows the present value of 1.00 unit of currency per annum, receivable or payable at the end of each year for n years $\frac{1-(1+r)^{-n}}{r}$.

Periods (n)	1%	2%	3%	4%	5%	6%	7%	8%	9%	10%
1	0.990	0.980	0.971	0.962	0.952	0.943	0.935	0.926	0.917	0.909
2	1.970	1.942	1.913	1.886	1.859	1.833	1.808	1.783	1.759	1.736
3	2.941	2.884	2.829	2.775	2.723	2.673	2.624	2.577	2.531	2.487
4	3.902	3.808	3.717	3.630	3.546	3.465	3.387	3.312	3.240	3.170
5	4.853	4.713	4.580	4.452	4.329	4.212	4.100	3.993	3.890	3.791
6	5.795	5.601	5.417	5.242	5.076	4.917	4.767	4.623	4.486	4.355
7	6.728	6.472	6.230	6.002	5.786	5.582	5.389	5.206	5.033	4.868
8	7.652	7.325	7.020	6.733	6.463	6.210	5.971	5.747	5.535	5.335
9	8.566	8.162	7.786	7.435	7.108	6.802	6.515	6.247	5.995	5.759
10	9.471	8.983	8.530	8.111	7.722	7.360	7.024	6.710	6.418	6.145
11	10.368	9.787	9.253	8.760	8.306	7.887	7.499	7.139	6.805	6.495
12	11.255	10.575	9.954	9.385	8.863	8.384	7.943	7.536	7.161	6.814
13	12.134	11.348	10.635	9.986	9.394	8.853	8.358	7.904	7.487	7.103
14	13.004	12.106	11.296	10.563	9.899	9.295	8.745	8.244	7.786	7.367
15	13.865	12.849	11.938	11.118	10.380	9.712	9.108	8.559	8.061	7.606
16	14.718	13.578	12.561	11.652	10.838	10.106	9.447	8.851	8.313	7.824
17	15.562	14.292	13.166	12.166	11.274	10.477	9.763	9.122	8.544	8.022
18	16.398	14.992	13.754	12.659	11.690	10.828	10.059	9.372	8.756	8.201
19	17.226	15.679	14.324	13.134	12.085	11.158	10.336	9.604	8.950	8.365
20	18.046	16.351	14.878	13.590	12.462	11.470	10.594	9.818	9.129	8.514

Periods (n)	11%	12%	13%	14%	15%	16%	17%	18%	19%	20%
1	0.901	0.893	0.885	0.877	0.870	0.862	0.855	0.847	0.840	0.833
2	1.713	1.690	1.668	1.647	1.626	1.605	1.585	1.566	1.547	1.528
3	2.444	2.402	2.361	2.322	2.283	2.246	2.210	2.174	2.140	2.106
4	3.102	3.037	2.974	2.914	2.855	2.798	2.743	2.690	2.639	2.589
5	3.696	3.605	3.517	3.433	3.352	3.274	3.199	3.127	3.058	2.991
6	4.231	4.111	3.998	3.889	3.784	3.685	3.589	3.498	3.410	3.326
7	4.712	4.564	4.423	4.288	4.160	4.039	3.922	3.812	3.706	3.605
8	5.146	4.968	4.799	4.639	4.487	4.344	4.207	4.078	3.954	3.837
9	5.537	5.328	5.132	4.946	4.772	4.607	4.451	4.303	4.163	4.031
10	5.889	5.650	5.426	5.216	5.019	4.833	4.659	4.494	4.339	4.192
11	6.207	5.938	5.687	5.453	5.234	5.029	4.836	4.656	4.486	4.327
12	6.492	6.194	5.918	5.660	5.421	5.197	4.988	4.793	4.611	4.439
13	6.750	6.424	6.122	5.842	5.583	5.342	5.118	4.910	4.715	4.533
14	6.982	6.628	6.302	6.002	5.724	5.468	5.229	5.008	4.802	4.611
15	7.191	6.811	6.462	6.142	5.847	5.575	5.324	5.092	4.876	4.675
16	7.379	6.974	6.604	6.265	5.954	5.668	5.405	5.162	4.938	4.730
17	7.549	7.120	6.729	6.373	6.047	5.749	5.475	5.222	4.990	4.775
18	7.702	7.250	6.840	6.467	6.128	5.818	5.534	5.273	5.033	4.812
19	7.839	7.366	6.938	6.550	6.198	5.877	5.584	5.316	5.070	4.843
20	7.963	7.469	7.025	6.623	6.259	5.929	5.628	5.353	5.101	4.870

EXAM FORMULAE

Valuation models

(i) Irredeemable preference share, paying a constant annual dividend, d, in perpetuity, where P_0 is the ex-div value:

$$P_0 = \frac{d}{k_{pref}}$$

(ii) Ordinary (equity) share, paying a constant annual dividend, d, in perpetuity, where P_0 is the ex-div value:

$$P_0 = \frac{d}{k_e}$$

(iii) Ordinary (equity) share, paying an annual dividend, d, growing in perpetuity at a constant rate, g, where P_0 is the ex-div value:

$$P_0 = \frac{d_1}{k_e - g} \text{ or } P_0 = \frac{d_0[1+g]}{k_e - g}$$

(iv) Irredeemable (undated) bonds, paying annual after tax interest, $i(1-t)$, in perpetuity, where P_0 is the ex-interest value:

$$P_0 = \frac{i[1-t]}{k_{dnet}}$$

or, without tax:

$$P_0 = \frac{i}{k_d}$$

(v) Total value of the geared firm, V_g (based on MM):

$$V_g = V_u + TB_c$$

(vi) Future value S, of a sum X, invested for n periods, compounded at r% interest:

$$S = X[1 + r]^n$$

(vii) Present value of 1.00 payable or receivable in n years, discounted at r% per annum:

$$PV = \frac{1}{[1+r]^n}$$

(viii) Present value of an annuity of 1.00 per annum, receivable or payable for n years, commencing in one year, discounted at r% per annum:

$$PV = \frac{1}{r}\left[1 - \frac{1}{[1+r]^n}\right]$$

(ix) Present value of 1.00 per annum, payable or receivable in perpetuity, commencing in one year, discounted at r% per annum:

$$PV = \frac{1}{r}$$

(x) Present value of 1.00 per annum, receivable or payable, commencing in one year, growing in perpetuity at a constant rate of g% per annum, discounted at r% per annum:

$$PV = \frac{1}{r - g}$$

Cost of capital

(i) Cost of irredeemable preference shares, paying an annual dividend d in perpetuity, and having a current ex-div price P_0:

$$k_{pref} = \frac{d}{P_0}$$

(ii) Cost of irredeemable bonds, paying annual net interest $i(1 - t)$, and having a current ex-interest price P_0:

$$k_{d\,net} = \frac{i[1 - t]}{P_0}$$

(iii) Cost of ordinary (equity) shares, paying an annual dividend d in perpetuity, and having a current ex div price P_0:

$$k_e = \frac{d}{P_0}$$

(iv) Cost of ordinary (equity) shares, having a current ex div price, P_0, having just paid a dividend, d_0, with the dividend growing in perpetuity by a constant g% per annum:

$$k_e = \frac{d_1}{P_0} + g \quad \text{or} \quad k_e = \frac{d_0[1 + g]}{P_0} + g$$

(v) Cost of ordinary (equity) shares, using the CAPM:

$$k_e = R_f + [R_m - R_f]\beta$$

(vi) Cost of ordinary (equity) shares in a geared firm, (with tax):

$$k_{eg} = k_{eu} + [k_{eu} - k_d]\frac{V_D[1 - t]}{V_E}$$

(vii) Weighted average cost of capital, k_0 or WACC:

$$WACC = k_e\left[\frac{V_E}{V_E + V_D}\right] + k_d(1 - t)\left[\frac{V_D}{V_E + V_D}\right]$$

(viii) Adjusted cost of capital (MM formula)

$$k_{adj} = k_{eu}[1 - tL] \quad \text{or} \quad r^* = r[1 - T^*L]$$

(ix) Ungear β:

$$\beta_u = \beta_g\left[\frac{V_E}{V_E + V_D(1 - t)}\right] + \beta_D\left[\frac{V_D(1 - t)}{V_E + V_D(1 - t)}\right]$$

(x) Regear β:

$$\beta_g = \beta_u + (\beta_u - \beta_d)\frac{V_D(1 - t)}{V_E}$$

(xi) Adjusted discount rate to use in international capital budgeting (International Fisher effect)

$$\frac{1 + \text{annual discount rate B\$}}{1 + \text{annual discount rate A\$}} = \frac{\text{Future spot rate A\$/B\$ in 12 months' time}}{\text{Spot rate A\$/B\$}}$$

Where A$/B$ is the number of B$ to each A$.

Other formulae

(i) Expectations theory:

$$\text{Future spot rate A\$/B\$} = \text{Spot rate A\$/B\$} \times \frac{1 + \text{nominal country B interest rate}}{1 + \text{nominal country A interest rate}}$$

Where:

A$/B$ is the number of B$ to each A$
A$ is the currency of country A and B$ is the currency of country B.

(ii) Purchasing power parity (Law of one price)

$$\text{Future spot rate A\$/B\$} = \text{Spot rate A\$/B\$} \times \frac{1 + \text{country B inflation rate}}{1 + \text{country A inflation rate}}$$

(iii) Link between nominal (money) and real interest rates

[1 + nominal (money) rate] = [1 + real interest rate][1 + inflation rate]

(iv) Equivalent annual cost

$$\text{Equivalent annual cost} = \frac{\text{PV of costs over n years}}{\text{n year annuity factor}}$$

(v) Theoretical ex-rights price

$$\text{TERP} = \frac{1}{N+1} [(N \times \text{Cum rights price}) + \text{Issue price}]$$

(vi) Value of a right

$$\text{Value of right} = \frac{\text{Theoretical ex rights price - Issue price}}{N}$$

where N = number of rights required to buy one share.

EXAM QUESTION AND ANSWER BANK

What the examiner means

The very important table below has been prepared by CIMA to help you interpret exam questions.

Learning objectives	Verbs used	Definition
1 Knowledge What are you expected to know	• List • State • Define	• Make a list of • Express, fully or clearly, the details of/facts of • Give the exact meaning of
2 Comprehension What you are expected to understand	• Describe • Distinguish • Explain • Identify • Illustrate	• Communicate the key features of • Highlight the differences between • Make clear or intelligible/state the meaning of • Recognise, establish or select after consideration • Use an example to describe or explain something
3 Application How you are expected to apply your knowledge	• Apply • Calculate/ compute • Demonstrate • Prepare • Reconcile • Solve • Tabulate	• Put to practical use • Ascertain or reckon mathematically • Prove with certainty or to exhibit by practical means • Make or get ready for use • Make or prove consistent/compatible • Find an answer to • Arrange in a table
4 Analysis How you are expected to analyse the detail of what you have learned	• Analyse • Categorise • Compare and contrast • Construct • Discuss • Interpret • Prioritise • Produce	• Examine in detail the structure of • Place into a defined class or division • Show the similarities and/or differences between • Build up or compile • Examine in detail by argument • Translate into intelligible or familiar terms • Place in order of priority or sequence for action • Create or bring into existence
5 Evaluation How you are expected to use your learning to evaluate, make decisions or recommendations	• Advise • Evaluate • Recommend	• Counsel, inform or notify • Appraise or assess the value of • Propose a course of action

Guidance in our Practice and Revision Kit focuses on how the verbs are used in questions.

BPP LEARNING MEDIA

1 Earnings per share   45 mins

Learning outcome: A(1)(a)

(a) 'Financial managers need only concentrate on meeting the needs of shareholders by maximising earnings per share – no other group matters.'

Discuss. **(10 marks)**

(b) Many decisions in financial management are taken in a framework of conflicting stakeholder viewpoints. Identify the stakeholders and some of the financial management issues involved in the following situations.

(i) A private company converting into a public company.

(ii) A highly geared company, such as Eurotunnel, attempting to restructure its capital finance.

(iii) A large conglomerate 'spinning off' its numerous divisions by selling them, or setting them up as separate companies (eg Hanson).

(iv) Japanese car-makers, such as Nissan and Honda, building new car plants in other countries. **(15 marks)**

(Total = 25 marks)

2 News For You   45 mins

Learning outcome: A(1)(c)

News For You operates a chain of newsagents and confectioners shops in the south of England, and is considering the possibility of expanding its business across a wide geographical area. The business was started in 20X2 and annual turnover grew to $10 million by the end of 20X6. Between 20X6 and 20X9 turnover grew at an average rate of 2% per year.

The business still remains under family control, but the high cost of expansion via the purchase or building of new outlets would mean that the family would need to raise $2 million in equity or debt finance. One of the possible risks of expansion lies in the fact that both tobacco and newspaper sales are falling. New income is being generated by expanding the product range inventoried by the stores, to include basic foodstuffs such as bread and milk. News For You purchases all of its products from a large wholesale distributor which is convenient, but the wholesale prices leave News For You with a relatively small gross margin. The key to profit growth for News For You lies in the ability to generate sales growth, but the company recognises that it faces stiff competition from large food retailers in respect of the prices that it charges for several of its products.

In planning its future, News For You was advised to look carefully at a number of external factors which may affect the business including government economic policy, and in recent months the following information has been published in respect of key economic data.

(i) Bank base rate has been reduced from 5% to 4.5%, and the forecast is for a further 0.5% reduction within six months.

(ii) The annual rate of inflation is now 1.2%, down from 1.3% in the previous quarter, and 1.7% 12 months ago. The rate is now at its lowest for twenty-five years, and no further falls in the rate are expected over the medium/long term.

(iii) Personal and corporation tax rates are expected to remain unchanged for at least twelve months.

(iv) Taxes on tobacco have been increased by 10% over the last twelve months, although no further increases are anticipated.

(v) The government has initiated an investigation into the food retail sector, focusing on the problems of 'excessive' profits on certain foodstuffs created by the high prices being charged for these goods by the large retail food stores.

Required

(a) Explain the relevance of each of the items of economic data listed above to News For You.

(13 marks)

(b) Explain whether News For You should continue with its expansion plans. Clearly justify your arguments for or against the expansion.

(12 marks)

(Total = 25 marks)

3 Lavinia Products　　　　　　　　　　　　　　　　　　　　45 mins

Learning outcome: A(2)(b)

Assume you are a consultant working for Lavinia Products. It is now May 20X3. You have been assigned to the company to advise on its objectives and financial situation. As well as being provided with financial statements for the year to 31 December 20X2, the company's accountant gives you the following information.

(1) Sales and cost of sales are expected to increase by 10% in each of the financial years ending 31 December 20X3, 20X4 and 20X5. Operating expenses are expected to increase by 5% each year. The cost of sales percentage increase includes any adjustments necessary due to changes in inventory.

(2) The company expects to continue to be liable for tax at the marginal rate of 33%. Assume tax is paid or refunded 12 months after the year end.

(3) The ratios of *receivables to revenue* and *payables to cost of sales* will remain the same for the next three years.

(4) The non-current assets are land and buildings which are not depreciated in the company's books. Capital allowances on the buildings may be ignored. All other assets used by the company (machinery, cars etc) are rented.

(5) Dividends will grow at 25% in each of the financial years 20X3, 20X4 and 20X5, as per the company's objectives.

(6) The company intends to purchase new machinery to the value of $500,000 during 20X3 although an investment appraisal exercise has *not* been carried out. It will be depreciated straight line over ten years. The company charges a full year's depreciation in the first year of purchase of its assets. Capital allowances are available at 25% reducing balance on this expenditure.

(7) Additional inventory was purchased for $35,000 at the beginning of 20X3. The value of inventory after this purchase is likely to remain at $361,000 for the foreseeable future.

(8) No decision has been made on the type of finance to be used for the expansion programme. However, the company's directors think they can raise new medium-term secured debt if necessary.

(9) The average P/E ratio of listed companies in the same industry as Lavinia Products plc is 15.

The company's objectives include the following.

- To earn a pre-tax return on the closing book value of shareholders' funds of 35% per year.
- To increase dividends per share by 25% per year.
- To obtain a quotation on a recognised stock exchange within the next three years.

A summary of the financial statements for the year to 31 December 20X2 is set out below.

LAVINIA PRODUCTS
SUMMARISED STATEMENT OF CONSOLIDATED INCOME FOR THE YEAR TO 31 DECEMBER 20X2

	$'000
Revenue	1,560
Cost of sales	950
Gross profit	610
Operating expenses	325
Interest	30
Tax liability	84
Net profit	171
Dividends declared	68

SUMMARISED STATEMENT OF FINANCIAL POSITION AT 31 DECEMBER 20X2

	$'000
Non-current assets (net book value)	750
Current assets	
Inventory	326
Receivables	192
Cash and bank	50
	1,318
Current liabilities	
Trade payables	135
Other payables (including tax and dividends)	152
Financing	
Ordinary share capital (ordinary shares of $1)	500
Retained profits to 31 December 20X1	128
Retentions for the year to 31 December 20X2	103
10% debenture redeemable 20Y8	300
Total financing	1,318

Required

(a) Using the information in the scenario:

   (i) Prepare forecast statements of consolidated income for the years 20X3, 20X4 and 20X5, and calculate whether the company is likely to meet its stated financial objective (return on shareholders' funds) for these three years. **(7 marks)**

   (ii) Prepare cash flow forecasts for the years 20X3, 20X4 and 20X5, and estimate the amount of funds which will need to be raised by the company to finance its expansion. **(9 marks)**

   Notes

   (1) You should ignore interest or returns on surplus funds invested during the three-year period of review.

   (2) This is *not* an investment appraisal exercise; you may ignore the timing of cash flows within each year and you should not discount the cash flows.

   (3) Ignore inflation.

(b) Plan a report to the directors of Lavinia Products which:

   (i) Discusses the key aspects and implications of the financial information you have obtained in your answer to part (a) of the question, in particular noting whether the company is likely to meet its stated objectives. **(5 marks)**

   (ii) Discusses whether the objectives as stated are suitable for the company at the present stage of its development, and discusses alternative objectives which the directors could consider. **(4 marks)**

(iii) Recommends additional methods of financial forecasting which could be used with advantage by the company's management. You should assume that the only forecasts prepared by the company at present are similar to those you have prepared for your answer to part (a) of this question.

(Total = 25 marks)

4 Subsidiaries   35 mins

Learning outcome: A(2)(b)

Your company has two subsidiaries, X and Y, both providing computer services, notably software development and implementation. The UK market for such services is said to be growing at about 20% a year. The business is seasonal, peaking between September and March.

You have available the comparative data shown in the Appendix to this question below. The holding company's policy is to leave the financing and management of subsidiaries entirely to the subsidiaries' directors.

Required

In the light of this information, compare and contrast the performance of the two subsidiaries.

It may be assumed that the difference in size of the two companies does not invalidate a comparison of the ratios provided.

Appendix

Data in this Appendix should be accepted as correct. Any apparent internal inconsistencies are due to rounding of the figures.

	X	Y
Revenue in most recent year (€'000)		
Home	2,856	6,080
Export	2,080	1,084
Total	4,936	7,164
Index of revenue 20X9 (20X6 = 100)		
Home	190%	235%
Export	220%	150%
Total	200%	220%
Operating profit 20X9 (€'000)	840	720
Operating capital employed 20X9 (€'000)	625	1,895

Ratio analysis

		X 20X9	X 20X8	X 20X7	Y 20X9	Y 20X8	Y 20X7
Return on operating capital employed	%	134	142	47	38	40	52
Operating profit: Sales	%	17	16	6	10	8	5
Sales: Operating capital employed	×	8	9	8	4	5	10
Percentages to sales value:							
Cost of sales	%	65	67	71	49	49	51
Selling and distribution costs	%	12	11	15	15	16	19
Administration expenses	%	6	6	8	26	27	25
Number of employees		123	127	88	123	114	91
Sales per employee	€'000	40	37	31	58	52	47
Average remuneration per employee	€'000	13	13	12	16	4	13
Tangible non-current assets turnover rate	×	20	21	14	9	11	14
Additions, at cost	%	57	47	58	303	9	124
Percentage depreciated	%	45	36	20	41	60	72
Product development costs carried forward as a percentage of revenue	%	0	0	0	10	8	6
Receivables: Sales	%	18	18	22	61	41	39
Inventory: Sales	%	0	1	0	2	2	1

		X			Y		
		20X9	20X8	20X7	20X9	20X8	20X7
Cash: Sales	%	7	9	2	1	1	0
Trade payables: Sales	%	2	2	3	32	21	24
Trade payables: receivables	%	11	14	15	53	50	62
Current ratio (:1)		1.5	1.3	1.2	1.1	1.1	0.9
Liquid ratio (:1)		1.5	1.3	1.2	1.0	1.0	0.9
Liquid ratio excluding bank overdraft		0	0	0	1.4	1.5	1.2
Total debt : Total assets	%	61	71	109	75	72	84

5 ZX   45 mins

Learning outcome: A(2)(d)

ZX is a relatively small US-based company in the agricultural industry. It is highly mechanised and uses modern techniques and equipment. In the past, it has operated a very conservative policy in respect of the management of its working capital. Assume that you are a newly recruited management accountant. The finance director, who is responsible for both financial control and treasury functions, has asked you to review this policy.

You assemble the following information about the company's forecast end-of-year financial outcomes. The company's year end is in six months' time.

	US$'000
Receivables	2,500
Inventory	2,000
Cash at bank	500
Current assets	5,000
Non-current assets	1,250
Current liabilities	1,850
Forecast sales for the full year	8,000
Forecast operating profit (18% of sales)	1,440

You wish to evaluate the likely effect on the company if it introduced one or two alternative approaches to working capital management. The finance director suggests you adjust the figures in accordance with the following parameters.

	'Moderate' policy	'Aggressive' policy
Receivables and inventory	– 20%	– 30%
Cash	Reduce to $250,000	Reduce to $100,000
Non-current assets	No change	No change
Current liabilities	+10%	+20%
Forecast sales	+ 2%	+4%
Forecast profit	No change in percentage profit/sales	

Required

Write a report to the finance director that includes the following.

(a) A discussion of the main aspects to consider when determining policy in respect of the investment in, and financing of, working capital, in general and in the circumstances of ZX.   **(10 marks)**

(b) Calculations of the return on net assets and the current ratio under each of three scenarios shown below.

   (i)   The company continues with its present policy.
   (ii) The company adopts the 'moderate' policy.
   (iii) The company adopts the 'aggressive' policy.   **(8 marks)**

(c) A recommendation for the company of a proposed course of action. Your recommendation should be based on your evaluation as discussed above and on your opinion of what further action is necessary before a final decision can be taken.   **(7 marks)**

(Total = 25 marks)

6 Cuando   36 mins

Learning outcome: A(2)(d)

Cuando is an on-line retailer of books, CDs and DVDs. The company was set up five years ago by a wealthy entrepreneur, David Nile, and has now grown to the point where the Board of Directors has decided that a listing should be sought on the local stock exchange. David Nile owns 80 per cent of the ordinary shares and has agreed to sell all of these as part of the public offering.

Recently, the Board of Directors began to debate the future dividend policy of the company, assuming that the stock exchange listing would be successful. However, there was a clear divergence of views. The Chairman felt that the current dividend policy was unacceptable and needed to be changed. He argued that the company had been investing heavily in its distribution methods and in advertising in the early years and that dividend policy had not been a pressing issue. However, the proposed listing must now lead to a reconsideration of the importance of dividends. The Chief Operating Officer, on the other hand, felt that the Chairman's concerns were unfounded as the pattern of dividends had no effect on shareholder wealth.

Information concerning the company since it was first set up is as follows:

Year ended 30 November	Net profits after taxation £000s	Ordinary dividends £000s	Ordinary shares in issue 000s
20X0	650	320	800
20X1	520	150	1,000
20X2	760	480	1,000
20X3	1,240	600	1,500
20X4	1,450	540	1,500

Required

(a) Evaluate the views expressed by the Chief Operating Officer and by the Chairman. **(10 marks)**

(b) Analyse the dividend policy that has been pursued to date and discuss whether a change would be in the interests of shareholders. **(6 marks)**

(c) Discuss the key points that should be taken into account when establishing an appropriate dividend policy for the company. **(4 marks)**

(Total = 20 marks)

7 Carpets Direct   36 mins

Learning outcome: B(1)(b)

Carpets Direct wishes to increase its number of retail outlets. The board of directors has decided to finance this expansion programme by raising the funds from existing shareholders through a one for four rights issue. The most recent statement of consolidated income of the company is as follows.

Statement of consolidated income for the year ended 30 April 20X5

	$m
Sales revenue	164.5
Profit from operations	12.6
Interest	6.2
Profit for year	6.4
Corporation tax	1.9
Profit after taxation	4.5
Ordinary dividends	2.0

The share capital of the company consists of 120 million ordinary shares with a par value of $0.50 per share. The shares of the company are currently being traded on the Stock Exchange at a price/earnings ratio of 22 times and the board of directors has decided to issue the new shares at a discount of 20% on the current market value.

Required

(a) In the context of share issues, explain what is meant by the term 'pre-emptive rights'. What are the advantages and disadvantages of pre-emptive rights from both the shareholders and the company's viewpoint? **(6 marks)**

(b) Calculate the theoretical ex-rights price of an ordinary share in Carpets Direct. **(6 marks)**

(c) Calculate the price at which the rights in Carpets Direct are likely to be traded. **(2 marks)**

(d) Identify and evaluate, at the time of the rights issue, each of the options arising from the rights issue to an investor who holds 4,000 ordinary shares before the rights announcement. **(6 marks)**

(Total = 20 marks)

8 Sundown Carehomes   34 mins

Learning outcome: B(1)(b)

Sundown Carehomes (Sundown) is planning to purchase for £1.6 million, a small private company, Thirdage. Originally Sundown suggested an all-share offer, but the owners of Thirdage insisted on payment in cash. Sundown are considering four ways to raise the money required;

(a) By making a '1 for 4' rights issue at £4. Sundown shares currently stand at £4.75.

(b) By issuing £1.6 million in 8% 20-year loan notes (maturing 20X0) at par.

(c) By issuing 20-year zero-coupon bonds with a redemption yield of 8% and repayable at par.

(d) By issuing £1.6 million in 6% 20-year convertible bonds, at par, with the option to convert into 5 shares at £20 per share on maturity of the bond in 20X0.

Current redemption yield of a 7% Government bond maturing in 20X0 is 5%.

Required

(a) Explain what is meant by the phrase 'redemption yield of a 7% Government bond'. **(3 marks)**

(b) Explain why Sundown Carehomes would issue bonds with a 8% redemption yield when yield on Government bonds is only 5%. **(3 marks)**

(c) Describe the features of a zero-coupon bond and explain why a company might issue such a bond and why investors might find it attractive. **(3 marks)**

(d) Calculate the theoretical share price immediately after making the proposed rights issue, if there is 100% take-up of the issue. **(3 marks)**

(e) Calculate the issue price of the zero coupon bond. **(3 marks)**

(f) Calculate the net present value of the convertibility option, assuming a discount rate of 8%, and explain what this tells you about expectations for Sundown's profitability or business performance. **(4 marks)**

(Total = 19 marks)

9 PG　　　　　　　　　　　　　　　　　　　　　　　　　　　　　　35 mins

Learning outcome: B(1)(b)

(a) PG has a paid-up ordinary share capital of £4,500,000 represented by 6 million shares of 75p each. It has no loan capital. Earnings after tax in the most recent year were £3,600,000. The P/E ratio of the company is 15.

The company is planning to make a large new investment which will cost £10,500,000, and is considering raising the necessary finance through a rights issue at 800p.

Required

(i) Calculate the current market price of PG's ordinary shares.

(ii) Calculate the theoretical ex-rights price, and state what factors in practice might invalidate your calculation.

(iii) Briefly explain what is meant by a deep-discounted rights issue, identifying the main reasons why a company might raise finance by this method.

(b) As an alternative to a rights issue, PG might raise the £10,500,000 required by means of an issue of convertible bonds at par, with a coupon rate of 6%. The bonds would be redeemable in seven years' time. Prior to redemption, the bonds may be converted at a rate of 11 ordinary shares per £100 nominal.

Required

(i) Explain the term conversion premium and calculate the conversion premium at the date of issue implicit in the data given.

(ii) Identify the advantages to PG of issuing convertible bonds instead of the rights issue to raise the necessary finance.

10 Ducey　　　　　　　　　　　　　　　　　　　　　　　　　　30 mins

Learning outcome: B(1)(d)

Ducey has decided to acquire some new plant and machinery and is now considering whether to buy or to lease it. The machinery in question has a useful life of four years and is expected to have no residual value at the end of that time. It would cost £176,000 to buy which would be financed by borrowing. Alternatively it could be leased for four years at an annual rental of £55,000 payable annually in advance.

The tax rate is 30%. If purchased the machine would attract tax-allowable depreciation of 25% (reducing balance basis) per annum. A balancing allowance or charge would be made on disposal. If leased, the rental would be allowed fully against tax. Tax is paid (and allowances received) one year in arrears.

The before tax cost of borrowing to Ducey is estimated to be 19%.

Required

(a) Advise Ducey whether to buy or to lease the machine on the assumption that the company has sufficient taxable profits to fully absorb all tax allowances rising from the buy or lease decision.

(b) Advise Ducey whether to buy or to lease the machine on the basis that the company is in a permanent non-tax paying position.

(c) Describe briefly any other factors which the company should take into account when making the lease or buy decision.

11 Nile plc 27 mins

Learning outcome: B(1)(c)

Nile plc is considering an investment of capital to be raised from the issue of new ordinary shares and debentures in a mix which will hold its gearing ratio approximately constant. It wishes to estimate its weighted average cost of capital.

The company has an issued share capital of 1 million ordinary shares of £1 each; it has also issued £800,000 of 8% debentures. The market price of ordinary shares is £4.76 per share (ex div) and debentures are priced at £69 per cent (ex interest). Debentures are redeemable at par in twenty years' time.

A summary of the most recent statement of financial position runs as follows.

	£'000		£'000	£'000
Ordinary share capital	1,000	Non-current assets		1,276
Reserves	1,553	Current assets	4,166	
Deferred taxation	164	Less: current		
Debentures	800	Liabilities	1,925	
				2,241
	3,517			3,517

Dividends have been as follows.

	Dividends £'000
20X4	200
20X5	230
20X6	230
20X7	260
20X8	300

Assume that there have been no changes in the system or rates of taxation during the last five years, that the rate of corporation tax is 35%. Assume that 'now' is 20X8.

Required

(a) Calculate Nile plc's weighted average cost of capital. **(10 marks)**
(b) Discuss briefly any difficulties and uncertainties in your estimation. **(5 marks)**

(Total = 15 marks)

12 Incorrect manual 27 mins

Leaning outcome: B(1)(c)

Your company has produced a draft guidance manual to assist in estimating the cost of capital to be used in capital investment appraisal. Extracts from the manual are reproduced below.

Relevant data:

	Book value $m	Market values $m
Equity (50 million ordinary shares)	140	214
Debt: 6% bank loans	85	85

	Per share Pence	Annual growth rates %
Dividends	24	6
Earnings	67	9

The beta value of the company is 1:1.

Other information

	%
Market return	14
Risk free rate	6
Corporate tax rate	30

Illustration 1 – When the company is diversifying its activities:

The asset (ie geared) beta of a similar company in the industry in which your company proposes to diversify is 0.90. Gearing of the similar company:

	Book values $m	Market values $m
Equity	165	230
Debt	65	60

Cost of equity

The beta of the comparator company is used as a measure of the systematic risk of the new investment. As the gearing of the two companies differs, the beta must be adjusted for the difference in gearing.

Ungearing

$$\text{Beta equity} = \text{beta asset} \times \frac{V_E}{V_E + V_D(1-t)}$$

$$\text{Beta equity} = 0.90 \times \frac{230}{230 + 60(1-.3)} = 0.76$$

Using the capital asset pricing model

$K_e = Rf + (Rm - Rf) \text{ beta} = 6\% + (14\% - 6\%) \, 0.76 = 12.08\%$

Cost of debt

This remains at 6.0%

Weighted average cost of capital:

$$12.08\% \times \frac{214}{299} + 6\% \times \frac{85}{299} = 10.36\%$$

The cost of capital to be used in the investment appraisal when diversifying is 10.36%

Required

Produce a revised version of this draft manual, correcting the errors in Ilustration 1. **(15 marks)**

13 ABC   45 mins

Learning outcome: B(1)(b)

ABC is a large professional service company listed on a major international stock exchange. ABC has recently appointed a new Finance Director who is concerned about the financing of the company.

Forecast statement of financial position at 31 May 20X4:

	$m
Non-current assets	555
Current assets	195
	750

Issued share capital (per value 25 cents)	200
Reserves	250
	450
Debentures 7% annual coupon (nominal value)	
(redeemable 31 May 20X8 at par)	150
Bank loans	100
Current liabilities	50
	750

On 31 May 20X4, market values are $107 per cent ex interest for debentures and $0.75 ex dividend for each share. Interest on the bank loan is 5% per annum and the loans are not scheduled to be repaid before 31 May 20X7.

The following earnings and closing shareholder funds have been forecast for the next three years:

Year ending	31 May 20X5	31 May 20X6	31 May 20X7
	$m	$m	$m
Earnings before interest and tax (EBIT)	58.0	50.0	54.0
Closing shareholder funds at year end	446.8	437.9	431.9

Debenture covenants

There are two covenants relating to the debentures, as follows:

'At no time will the debt ratio of prior charge capital/shareholders' funds exceed 60%, based upon book values.'

'The ratio of EBIT/total interest payable shall not fall below 3.5 times.'

Restructuring funding

The Finance director is concerned that the company is close to breaching debenture covenants and is considering ways of restructuring the company's funding to eliminate this risk.

Two alternatives are being considered.

One scheme is to redeem the debentures on 31 May 20X4 at market value, funded by a new bank loan. The company's bank has quoted an annual coupon of 5% for a loan maturing on 31 May 20X8.

An alternative scheme, being recommended by ABC's merchant bank, is a rights issue of 1 for 5 shares to raise $100 million of funds to repay the current bank loan.

Assume that tax is recoverable at 30% on interest payments at the time that the interest is paid and that all interest payments are made annually in arrears. Ignore any taxation implications of the redemption premium on the debenture.

Required

(a) Calculate gearing and interest cover ratios for the years ending 31 May 20X5 to 31 May 20X7, and indicate whether ABC is likely to breach either of the two debenture covenants over the next three years. (Ignore any restructuring funding proposals.) **(4 marks)**

(b) Calculate the cost of debt for the existing debenture based on the current market value on 31 May 20X4 and advise the Finance director whether or not it is likely to be cheaper to redeem the debenture with a bank loan. Identify what other factors would need to be taken into account when deciding whether to redeem the debenture with a bank loan. (No further calculations are required). **(10 marks)**

(c) Calculate the issue price and ex-rights price of the proposed rights issue. Discuss the advantages of the merchant bank's recommendation to repay the bank loan by raising new equity finance compared with the merits of redeeming the debentures by entering into a new bank loan.

(Note: No further gearing or interest cover calculations are required.) **(11 marks)**

(Total = 25 marks)

14 Treasury management — 20 mins

Learning outcome: B(2)(a)

Many large international organisations have a central treasury department, which might be a separate profit centre within the group. The responsibilities of this department will include the management of business risk and market risk for the group as a whole.

Required

(a) Describe the functions of a central treasury department.

(b) Describe the information that the treasury department needs, from inside and outside the organisation, to perform its function.

15 Risk reduction — 25 mins

(a) Explain the development of portfolio theory when more than two securities are available, including the availability of risk-free investments.

(b) Explain the practical implications of portfolio theory to a fund manager and to the projects manager of a company.

16 Mezen — 35 mins

Learning outcome: C(1)(a),(b)

Mezen is currently considering the launch of a new product. A market survey was recently commissioned to assess the likely demand for the product and this showed that the product has an expected life of four years. The survey cost $30,000 and this is due for payment in four months' time. On the basis of the survey information as well as internal management accounting information relating to costs, the assistant accountant prepared the following profit forecasts for the product.

Year	1 $'000	2 $'000	3 $'000	4 $'000
Sales	180	200	160	120
Cost of sales	(115)	(140)	(110)	(85)
Gross profit	65	60	50	35
Variable overheads	(27)	(30)	(24)	(18)
Fixed overheads	(25)	(25)	(25)	(25)
Market survey written off	(30)	–	–	–
Net profit/(loss)	(17)	5	1	(8)

These profit forecasts were viewed with disappointment by the directors and there was a general feeling that the new product should not be launched. The Chief Executive pointed out that the product achieved profits in only two years of its four-year life and that over the four-year period as a whole, a net loss was expected. However, before a meeting that had been arranged to decide formally the future of the product, the following additional information became available:

(i) The new product will require the use of an existing machine. This has a written down value of $80,000 but could be sold for $70,000 immediately if the new product is not launched. If the product is launched, it will be sold at the end of the four-year period for $10,000.

(ii) Additional working capital of $20,000 will be required immediately and will be needed over the four-year period. It will be released at the end of the period.

(iii) The fixed overheads include a figure of $15,000 per year for depreciation of the machine and $5,000 per year for the re-allocation of existing overheads of the business.

The company has a cost of capital of 10%.

Ignore taxation.

Required

(a) Calculate the incremental cash flows arising from a decision to launch the product. **(9 marks)**

(b) Calculate the approximate internal rate of return of the product. **(4 marks)**

(c) Explain, with reasons, whether or not the product should be launched. **(2 marks)**

(d) Outline the strengths and weaknesses of the internal rate of return method as a basis for investment appraisal. **(5 marks)**

(Total = 20 marks)

17 DIN — 35 mins

Learning outcome: D(ii)

(a) Explain the difference between real rates of return and money rates of return and outline the circumstances in which the use of each would be appropriate when appraising capital projects under inflationary conditions.

(b) DIN has just developed a new product to be called Rance and is now considering whether to put it into production. The following information is available.

  (i) Costs incurred in the development of Rance amount to €480,000.

  (ii) Production of Rance will require the purchase of new machinery at a cost of €2,400,000 payable immediately. This machinery is specific to the production of Rance and will be obsolete and valueless when that production ceases. The machinery has a production life of four years and a production capacity of 30,000 units per annum.

  (iii) Production costs of Rance (at year 1 prices) are estimated as follows.

	€
Variable materials	8.00
Variable labour	12.00
Variable overheads	12.00

  In addition, fixed production costs (at year 1 prices), including straight line depreciation on plant and machinery, will amount to €800,000 per annum.

  (iv) The selling price of Rance will be €80.00 per unit (at year 1 prices). Demand is expected to be 25,000 units per annum for the next four years.

  (v) The retail price index is expected to increase at 5% per annum for the next four years and the selling price of Rance is expected to increase at the same rate. Annual inflation rates for production costs are expected to be as follows.

	%
Variable materials	4
Variable labour	10
Variable overheads	4
Fixed costs	5

  (vi) The company's weighted average cost of capital in money terms is expected to be 15%.

Required

Advise the directors of DIN whether it should produce Rance on the basis of the information above.

Notes

Unless otherwise specified all costs and revenues should be assumed to rise at the end of each year. Ignore taxation.

18 Harry   45 mins

Harry is financial manager of RP. He is nearing retirement. You have been appointed as his deputy with a view to taking over from him in 12 months' time.

The company is considering an investment in a new product which will cost €1,200,000 in new machinery and will result in profit before depreciation and tax of €375,000 per annum in real terms for five years. At the end of the five years, the machinery can be sold for its written-down tax value. The investment will require working capital of €100,000 in real terms from the start of year 1.

The following notes are relevant.

1. At the end of year 5, the total working capital can be released in cash back to the company.

2. Inflation is expected to be 4% per annum on all operating cash flows and working capital for the period under review. Working capital will not increase for any other reason.

3. The company pays tax at the rate of 30%. Tax is payable in the year profits are earned.

4. Tax relief is available on capital expenditure at 25% on a reducing balance. The company also depreciates its plant and equipment on this basis. The first claim is made in year 1. The machine is sold at its tax written down value at the end of year 5.

5. Assume all cash flows occur at the end of the year *except* the purchase of the new machinery. This occurs at the beginning of the year.

6. The company's long-term capital structure is shown below.

	€'000
Ordinary shares €1 each	1,000
Reserves	8,794
	9,794
10% debenture (€100 par value)	1,000
	10,794

7. The current ex dividend market value of shares is 250c and the current ex interest market value of debentures is €95.

8. The debenture is redeemable in 3 years' time at par.

9. A dividend of 20c per share has just been paid on the shares. Dividends have grown consistently at 10% over the past few years, and this pattern is expected to continue.

Required

(a) Calculate the company's weighted average cost of capital.   **(7 marks)**

(b) Evaluate the investment using the company's WACC, as suggested by Harry. *Note.* If you are unable to complete part (a) of the question, you may assume a nominal cost of capital of 16%.
                                                                                (11 marks)

(c) Whatever your own answer to part (b), assume the results of your financial evaluation suggest the investment is worthwhile (ie the NPV is positive). You think that some of Harry's assumptions are unrealistic. In particular, you are concerned about the uncertainty surrounding each year's cash flows and the use of the WACC as the discount rate.

Write a memo to Harry which explains how the evaluation might be refined, or developed, to overcome your concerns.   **(7 marks)**

Note. You are not required to revise your calculations for part (b) of the question to answer part (c) of the question.

(Total = 25 marks)

19 PG plc   36 mins

Learning outcome: C(1)(b)

PG plc is considering investing in a new project in Canada which will have a life of four years. The initial investment is C$ 150,000, including working capital. The net after-tax nominal cash flows which the project will generate are C$ 60,000 per annum for years 1, 2 and 3 and C$ 45,000 in year 4. The terminal value of the project is estimated at C$50,000, net of tax.

The current spot rate is £/C$1.700. Economic forecasters expect the pound to strengthen against the Canadian dollar by 5% per annum over the next four years.

The company evaluates UK projects of similar risk at 14%.

Required

(a) Calculate the NPV of the Canadian project using the following two methods:

  (i) Convert the currency cash flows into sterling and discount the sterling cash flows at a sterling discount rate

  (ii) Discount the cash flows in C$ using an adjusted discount rate

  and explain briefly the theories and/or assumptions which underlie the use of the adjusted discount rate approach in (ii). **(12 marks)**

(b) The company had originally planned to finance the project with internal funds generated in the UK. However, the finance director has suggested that there would be advantages in raising debt finance in Canada.

Required

Discuss the advantages and disadvantages of matching investment and borrowing overseas as compared with UK-sourced debt or equity.

Wherever possible, relate your answer to the details given in this question for PG plc. **(8 marks)**

(Total = 20 marks)

20 Pressley plc   30 mins

Learning outcome: C(1)(b)

Pressley plc, a UK-based company, has the opportunity to buy a factory in Europe. The factory will make the same product that Pressley currently exports to the continent. Pressley expects projects to yield a discounted payback period of four years using a cost of capital of 12%.

Purchase and fitting of the factory would cost an immediate €2,500,000. There are no relevant tax consequences of this investment amount.

The contribution (in nominal terms) earned by the European factory in the next four years will be:

Year	1	2	3	4
€'000	1,400	2,200	2,500	2,800

Corporation tax rate in the host country is 20%. This is expected to stay constant for the purpose of this appraisal.

In the same four year period, contribution from Pressley's exports from UK to Europe would have been expected to be as shown in the table below.

Year	1	2	3	4
£'000	350	400	440	470

Corporation tax in the UK is charged at 30%. This is expected to remain constant for the foreseeable future. Full tax treaties exist between the UK and European countries.

The exchange rate is currently €/£ 0.6279. Inflation in the UK is 2.3% whilst inflation in mainland Europe averages 4.7%.

All tax is payable at the end of the year in which the profits arise.

Required

Calculate whether the proposed factory would be acceptable to Pressley.

21 Fund restrictions   22 mins

Learning outcome: C(1)(d)

A company can invest in the following four projects. The timing and amounts of the cash flows are shown below.

	T_0 $'000	t_1 $'000	t_2 $'000	NPV (15%) $'000	IRR %
Project A	(150)	100	105	14.22	9
Project B	(200)	150	135	28.27	14
Project C		(175)	230	21.74	12
Project D	(300)	200	220	35.01	12

Required

(a) If the company has a present restriction of $450,000 for investment, calculate which projects it would invest in. Assume that all projects are divisible. **(5 marks)**

(b) If there are no fund restrictions and these four projects are mutually exclusive, explain with reasons which project the company should choose. **(2 marks)**

(c) Explain why capital rationing occurs. **(5 marks)**

(Total = 12 marks)

22 ANT   45 mins

Learning outcomes: C(1)(d)

ANT, a multi-product company, is considering four investment projects, details of which are given below.

Development costs already incurred on the projects are as follows.

A $	B $	C $	D $
100,000	75,000	80,000	60,000

Each project will require an immediate outlay on plant and machinery, the cost of which is estimated as follows.

A $	B $	C $	D $
2,100,000	1,400,000	2,400,000	600,000

In all four cases the plant and machinery has a useful life of five years at the end of which it will be valueless.

Unit sales per annum, for each project, are expected to be as follows.

A	B	C	D
150,000	75,000	80,000	120,000

Selling price and variable costs per unit for each project are estimated below.

	A $	B $	C $	D $
Selling price	30.00	40.00	25.00	50.00
Materials	7.60	12.00	4.50	25.00
Labour	9.80	12.00	5.00	10.00
Variable overheads	6.00	7.00	2.50	10.50

The company charges depreciation on plant and machinery on a straight line basis over the useful life of the plant and machinery. Development costs of projects are written off in the year that they are incurred. The company apportions general administration costs to projects at a rate of 5% of selling price. None of the above projects will lead to any actual increase in the company's administration costs.

Working capital requirements for each project will amount to 20% of the expected annual sales value. In each case this investment will be made immediately and will be recovered in full when the projects end in five years time.

Funds available for investment are limited to $5,200,000. The company's cost of capital is estimated to be 18%.

Required

(a) Calculate the NPV of each project. **(12 marks)**

(b) Calculate the profitability index for each project and advise the company which of the new projects, if any, to undertake. You may assume that each of the projects can be undertaken on a reduced scale for a proportionate reduction in cash flows. Your advice should state clearly your order of preference for the four projects, what proportion you would take of any project that is scaled down, and the total NPV generated by your choice. **(5 marks)**

(c) Discuss the limitations of the profitability index as a means of dealing with capital rationing problems. **(8 marks)**

Ignore taxation. **(Total = 25 marks)**

23 Trosoft 45 mins

Learning outcomes: C(1)(d)

Trosoft is a Singapore-based company specialising in the development of business software. The company's managers believe that its future growth potential in the software sector is limited, and are considering diversifying into other activities. One suggestion is Internet auctions, and a member of the management team has produced the following draft financial proposal.

Internet auctions project

	Year 0 S$000	Year 1 S$000	Year 2 S$000	Year 3 S$000	Year 4 S$000
Auction fees	–	4,300	6,620	8,100	8,200
Outflows					
IT maintenance costs	–	1,210	1,850	1,920	2,125
Telephone	–	1,215	1,910	2,230	2,420
Wages	–	1,460	1,520	1,680	1,730
Salaries	–	400	550	600	650
Allocated head office overhead	–	85	90	95	100
Marketing	500	420	200	200	–
Royalty payments for use of technology	680	500	300	200	200
Market research	110	–	–	–	–
Rental of premises	–	280	290	300	310
Total outflows	1,290	5,570	6,710	7,225	7,535
Profit before tax	(1,290)	(1,270)	(90)	875	665
Tax	316	311	22	(214)	(163)
Other outflows					
IT infrastructure	(2,700)	–	–	–	–
Working capital	(400)	(24)	(24)	(25)	(26)
Net flows	(4,074)	(983)	(92)	636	476

Additional information:

(i) All data include the estimated effects of inflation on costs and prices wherever relevant. Inflation in Singapore is forecast to be 2% per year for the foreseeable future.

(ii) The investment in IT infrastructure and the initial working capital will be financed by a six year 4.5% fixed rate term loan. Other Year 0 outlays will be financed from existing cash flows.

(iii) Highly skilled IT staff would need to be taken from other activities resulting in a loss of S$80,000 per year pre-tax contribution for three years.

(iv) Head office cash flows for overheads will increase by S$50,000 as a result of the project in year 1, rising by S$5,000 per year after Year 1.

(v) Corporate tax is at a rate of 24.5% per year, payable in the year that the tax liability arises. The company has other profitable projects.

(vi) Tax allowable depreciation on IT infrastructure is 20% for the first year, and straight-line thereafter. The IT infrastructure has an expected working life of six years after which major new investment would be required.

(vii) The company's current weighted average cost of capital is 7.8%.

(viii) The company's equity beta is 1.05.

(ix) The average equity beta of companies in the Internet auctions sector is 1.42.

(x) The market return is 9.5% per year and the risk free rate 4% per year.

(xi) Trosoft's capital gearing is:

Book value 55% equity, 45% debt
Market value 70% equity, 30% debt

(xii) The average gearing of companies in the Internet auction sector is 67% equity, 33% debt by market values.

(xiii) The market research survey was undertaken three weeks ago.

(xiv) After tax operating net cash flows after year 4 are expected to stay approximately constant in real terms. The royalty payment will remain at S$200,000 in money terms.

(xv) Issue costs on debt are 1.5%. These costs are not tax allowable.

Required

Acting as an external consultant you have been asked to prepare a report on the proposed diversification of the company into Internet auctions. The report must include a revised financial analysis. You should use the adjusted present value method for this purpose. Include in your report discussion of other financial and non-financial factors, including real options, that Trosoft might consider prior to making the investment decision. **(25 marks)**

24 Feasibility study 35 mins

Learning outcome: C(3)(a)

An important step in the implementation of any computer system is the feasibility study. Senior staff in an organisation may be unconvinced of the value of the study.

Required

(a) Briefly explain what is meant by a computer feasibility study, and what such a study should achieve.

(b) Explain the importance of each of the main sections that should be contained in the feasibility study report.

(c) Identify three members of a 'typical' feasibility study team, and provide a one sentence description of their role.

(d) Discuss briefly on the suggestion that if a special purpose package is to be purchased, then there is no need for such a study.

(e) List four major factors which might justify the introduction of a computer system for production planning and scheduling in a manufacturing company.

25 Bases of valuation 45 mins

Learning outcome: C(1)(c)

The directors of Carmen plc, a large conglomerate, are considering the acquisition of the entire share capital of Manon Ltd, which manufactures a range of engineering machinery. Neither company has any long-term debt capital. The directors of Carmen plc believe that if Manon is taken over, the business risk of Carmen will not be affected.

The accounting reference date of Manon is 31 July. Its statement of financial position as on 31 July 20X4 is expected to be as follows.

		£	£
Non-current assets (net of depreciation)			651,600
Current assets:	Inventory and work in progress	515,900	
	Receivables	745,000	
	Bank balances	158,100	
			1,419,000
			2,070,600
Current liabilities:	Payables	753,600	
	Bank overdraft	862,900	
			1,616,500
Capital and reserves:	Issued ordinary shares of £1 each		50,000
	Distributable reserves		404,100
			2,070,600

Manon's summarised financial record for the five years to 31 July 20X4 is as follows.

Year ended 31 July	20X0	20X1	20X2	20X3	20X4 (estimated)
	£	£	£	£	£
Profit before non-recurring items	30,400	69,000	49,400	48,200	53,200
Non-recurring items	2,900	(2,200)	(6,100)	(9,800)	(1,000)
Profit after non-recurring items	33,300	66,800	43,300	38,400	52,200
Less: dividends	20,500	22,600	25,000	25,000	25,000
Added to reserves	12,800	44,200	18,300	13,400	27,200

The following additional information is available.

(a) There have been no changes in the issued share capital of Manon during the past five years.

(b) The estimated values of Manon's non-current assets and inventory and work in progress as on 31 July 20X4 are as follows.

	Replacement cost	Realisable value
	£	£
Non-current assets	725,000	450,000
Inventory and work in progress	550,000	570,000

(c) It is expected that 2% of Manon's receivables at 31 July 20X4 will be uncollectable.

(d) The cost of capital of Carmen plc is 9%. The directors of Manon Ltd estimate that the shareholders of Manon require a minimum return of 12% per annum from their investment in the company.

(e) The current P/E ratio of Carmen plc is 12. Quoted companies with business activities and profitability similar to those of Manon have P/E ratios of approximately 10, although these companies tend to be much larger than Manon.

Required

(a) Estimate the value of the total equity of Manon Ltd as on 31 July 20X4 using each of the following bases.

    (i) Statement of financial position value
    (ii) Replacement cost of the assets
    (iii) Realisable value of the assets
    (iv) The dividend valuation model
    (v) The P/E ratio model   **(13 marks)**

(b) Explain the role and limitations of each of the above five valuation bases in the process by which a price might be agreed for the purchase by Carmen plc of the total equity capital of Manon Ltd.

(7 marks)

(c) State and justify briefly the approximate range within which the purchase price is likely to be agreed. **(5 marks)**

Ignore taxation. **(Total = 25 marks)**

26 Perseus 45 mins

Learning outcome: C(1)(c)

Perseus is a wholly-owned subsidiary of Minos. Although the subsidiary has provided satisfactory levels of performance, Minos is considering the sale of the subsidiary to another conglomerate. Minos is experiencing trading problems in other parts of its operations and needs to sell Perseus in order to raise much-needed finance. The most recent statement of financial position of Perseus is as follows:

Statement of financial position as at 30 November 20X2

	$m	$m	$m
Non-current assets			
Freehold land and buildings at cost		58.5	
Less: Accumulated depreciation		10.2	
			48.3
Fixtures and fittings at cost		8.6	
Less: Accumulated depreciation		2.9	
			5.7
Motor vehicles at cost		3.2	
Less: Accumulated depreciation		1.4	
			1.8
			55.8
Current assets			
Inventory at cost	49.5		
Trade receivables	23.4		
Cash at bank	21.5		
		94.4	
Less: Payables: amounts falling due within one year			
Trade payables	25.9		
Tax	5.4		
		31.3	63.1
			118.9
Bonds			
Less: payables: amounts falling due after one year			49.0
			69.9
Capital and reserves			
Ordinary $0.50 shares			25.0
Accumulated profits			44.9
			69.9

Extracts from the statement of consolidated income for the year ended 30 November 20X2 are as follows:

	$m
Net profit after taxation	10.7
Dividend proposed and paid	3.3

The following details were taken from a financial newspaper concerning the shares of Tityus, a similar business operating in the same industry that is listed on the Stock Exchange.

20X1 – 20X2

High	Low	Stock	Price	± or	Dividend (net)	Cover (times)	Yield (gross %)	P/E (times)
640c	580c	Tityus	615c	+ 5c	12.0c	2.5	2.2	20.5

An independent valuer has recently estimated the current realisable value of the company's assets as follows:

	$m
Freehold land and buildings	104.2
Fixtures and fittings	3.5
Motor vehicles	0.4
Inventory	58.0

The statement of financial position values of the remaining assets were considered to reflect their net realisable values.

Tax on dividends is at the lower rate of income tax of 10%.

Required

(a) Calculate the value per share of Perseus using the following valuation methods:

   (i) Net assets (liquidation) basis
   (ii) Dividend yield basis; and
   (iii) Price/earnings ratio basis

(b) Briefly evaluate the strengths and weaknesses of each of the share valuation methods set out in (a) above.

27 Gasco   45 mins

Learning outcome: C(2)(a)

Gasco, a public limited company with a market value of around £7 billion, is a major supplier of gas to both business and domestic customers. The company also provides maintenance contracts for both gas and central heating customers using the well-known brand name Gas For All. Customers can call emergency lines for assistance for any gas-related incident, such as a suspected leak. Gasco employs its own highly-trained workforce to deal with all such situations quickly and effectively. The company also operates a major new credit card, which has been extensively marketed and which gives users concessions, such as reductions in their gas bills.

Gasco has recently bid £1.1bn for CarCare, a long established mutual organisation (ie it is owned by its members) that is the country's leading motoring organisation. CarCare is financed primarily by an annual subscription to its 4.4 million members. In addition the organisation also obtains income from a range of other activities such as a high profile car insurance brokerage, a travel agency and assistance with all types of travel arrangements. Its main service to members is the provision of a roadside break-down service, which is now an extremely competitive market with many other companies involved. Although many of its competitors use local garages to deal with breakdowns, CarCare uses its own road patrols.

CarCare members have to approve the takeover, which once completed provided them each with a windfall of around £300 each.

Gasco intend to preserve the CarCare name which is extremely well-known by consumers.

Required

(a) Discuss the possible reasons why Gasco is seeking to buy CarCare. **(9 marks)**

(b) Discuss how the various stakeholders of CarCare might react to the takeover. **(8 marks)**

(c) Discuss the potential problems that may face Gasco in running CarCare now that the takeover has been achieved. **(8 marks)**

(Total = 25 marks)

28 Olivine 36 mins

Learning outcome: C(2)(a)

Olivine is a holiday tour operator that is committed to a policy of expansion. The company has enjoyed record growth in recent years and is now seeking to acquire other companies in order to maintain its growth momentum. It has recently taken an interest in Halite, a charter airline business, as the Board of Directors of Olivine believes that there is a good strategic fit between the two companies. Both companies have the same level of risk. Abbreviated financial statements relating to each company are set out below.

Abbreviated statement of consolidated income for the year ended 30 November 20X3

	Olivine £m	Halite £m
Sales	182.6	75.2
Operating profit	43.6	21.4
Interest charges	12.3	10.2
Net profit before taxation	31.3	11.2
Company tax	6.3	1.6
Net profit after taxation	25.0	9.6
Dividends	6.0	4.0
Accumulated profits for the year	19.0	5.6

Summarised statements of financial position as at 30 November 20X3

	Olivine £m	Halite £m
Non-current assets	135.4	127.2
Net current assets	65.2	3.2
	200.6	130.4
Payables due after more than one year	120.5	104.8
	80.1	25.6
Capital and reserves		
£0·50 ordinary shares	20.0	8.0
Retained profit	60.1	17.6
	80.1	25.6
Price/earnings ratio before the bid	20	15

The Board of Directors of Olivine is considering making an offer to the shareholders of Halite of five shares in Olivine for every four shares held. It is believed that a rationalisation of administrative functions arising from the merger would reap after tax benefits of £2·4m.

Required

(a) Calculate:

   (i) The total value of the proposed offer

   (ii) The earnings per share of Olivine following the successful acquisition of Halite

   (iii) The share price of Olivine following acquisition, assuming that the benefits of the acquisition are achieved and that the price/earnings ratio declines by 5%. **(10 marks)**

(b) Calculate the effect of the proposed takeover on the wealth of the shareholders of each company. **(5 marks)**

(c) Discuss your results in (a) and (b) above and state what recommendations, if any, you would make to the directors of Olivine. **(5 marks)**

(Total = 20 marks)

29 K and H 45 mins

Learning outcomes: C(2)(a)

K wishes to acquire H. The directors of K are trying to justify the acquisition to the shareholders of both companies on the grounds that it will increase the wealth of all shareholders. The supporting financial evidence produced by K's directors is summarised below.

	K £'000	H £'000
Operating profit	12,400	5,800
Less interest payable	4,431	2,200
Profit before tax	7,969	3,600
Less taxation	2,789	1,260
Earnings available to ordinary shareholders	5,180	2,340
Earnings per share (pre-acquisition)	14.80 pence	29.25 pence
Market price per share (pre-acquisition)	222 pence	322 pence
Estimated market price (post-acquisition)	240 pence	
Estimated equivalent value of one old H share (post-acquisition)		360 pence

Payment is to be made with K ordinary shares, at an exchange ratio of 3 K shares for every 2 H shares.

Required

(a) Demonstrate how the directors of K produced their estimates of post-acquisition value and, if you do not agree with these estimates, produce revised estimates of post-acquisition values. All calculations must be shown. State clearly any assumptions that you make. **(10 marks)**

(b) If the acquisition is contested by H, using K's estimate of its post-acquisition market price calculate the maximum price that K could offer without reducing the wealth of its existing shareholders.
(3 marks)

(c) The board of directors of H later informally indicate that they are prepared to recommend to their shareholders a 2 for 1 share offer.

Further information regarding the effect of the acquisition on K is given below.

(i) The acquisition will result in an increase in the total pre-acquisition after tax operating cash flows of £2,750,000 a year indefinitely.

(ii) Rationalisation will allow machinery with a realisable value of £7,200,000 to be disposed of at the end of the next year.

(iii) Redundancy payments will total £3,500,000 immediately and £8,400,000 at the end of the next year.

(iv) K's cost of capital is estimated to be 14% a year.

All values are after any appropriate taxation. Assume that the pre-acquisition market values of K and H shares have not changed.

Recommend, using your own estimates of post-acquisition values, whether K should be prepared to make a 2 for 1 offer for the shares of H. **(6 marks)**

(d) Disregarding the information in (c) above and assuming no increase in the total post-acquisition earnings, evaluate whether this acquisition is likely to have any effect on the value of debt of K.
(6 marks)

(Total = 25 marks)

30 Premoco   90 mins

Background information

It is currently November 20X7. Premoco operates in oil and related industries. Its shares are quoted on the London Stock Exchange. In its retailing operations the company has concentrated on providing high-quality service and facilities at its service stations rather than competing solely on the price of petrol. Approximately 75% of its revenue and 60% of its profits are from sales of petrol, the remainder coming from other services (car wash and retail sales from its convenience stores which are available at each service station).

The company has been highly profitable in the past as a result of astute buying of petroleum products on the open market. The company does not enter into supplier agreements with the major oil companies except on very short-term deals. However, profit margins are now under increasing pressure as a result of intensifying competition and the cost of complying with environmental legislation.

Future strategy

The managing director of the company, David Wong, is assessing three possible acquisitions which would help the company increase the percentage of its non-petroleum revenue and profits.

Option 1. Nafco owns fifteen service stations in the south of England. These sites are of poor image, the company having, in the past, aimed at selling petrol at the lowest possible prices and providing little in the way of other services. However, the sites are in good locations and therefore suitable for renovation and development. The institutional investors in Nafco are known to be dissatisfied with the company's recent performance and can be expected to support a bid if the terms are right. Nafco's service stations are too small for the major oil companies to want to operate, so Premoco foresees little competition from alternative buyers. One of Premoco's suppliers of petroleum products has indicated it might be willing to provide development finance for up to 50% of the acquisition cost at only 5% interest per annum, repayable over ten years. However, this would involve Premoco entering into a long-term supply agreement for all fifteen sites.

Option 2. Oiltrans specialises in oil distribution from the depots owned by the major oil companies to their retail outlets. Its shares have been quoted on the stock market for the past two years. It operates a fleet of oil tankers, some owned and some leased. Premoco has used Oiltrans' services in the past and knows it has an up-to-date and well-managed fleet. However, a bid for Oiltrans would almost certainly be regarded as hostile and, as 40% of the shares are owned by the directors and their families, a successful bid is far from assured.

Option 3. Carsals owns six car showrooms in prestige locations, all of which operate the franchise of a major motor manufacturer. It is a long-established family-owned business which is not listed on a stock market. The managing director and major shareholder is planning to retire shortly and his children have shown no interest in taking over the business. He has therefore approached David Wong, whom he has known for some years, asking if Premoco would be interested in buying Carsals.

Premoco's financial advisors have produced estimates of the expected NPV and the first full-year post-merger earnings of Premoco with each of the three acquisition options. These are as follows.

	Estimated post-merger earnings in first full year following merger £m	*Estimated NPV of combined organisation* £m
Premoco plus Nafco	32	512
Premoco plus Oiltrans	35	595
Premoco plus Carsals	23	368

Financial statistics and other information on Premoco and the three possible acquisitions are shown below.

Extracts from Premoco's statement of financial position at 30 June 20X7

	£m	£m
Non-current assets (NBV)		140.00
Current assets:		
Inventory and receivables	120.00	
Bank and cash	80.00	
		200.00
		340.00
Ordinary £1 share capital: (authorised £30 million)		
Issued		20.00
Reserves		180.00
Secured loan stock 8% redeemable in 8 years time		50.00
Current liabilities		90.00
		340.00

Summary financial statistics

	Premoco	Nafco	Oiltrans	Carsals
Last year end	30.6.X7	30.6.X7	30.6.X7	31.3.X7
Shares in issue (millions)	20	10	12	0.5
Earnings per share (pence)	103	75	85	160
Dividend per share (pence)	31	55	42	112
Share price (pence)	1,648	675	1,530	N/a
Net asset value (£ million)	250	60	65	6
Debt ratio (outstanding debt as % of total market value)	13.0	30.0	15.0	0
Forecast annual growth rate %	11	5	14	9
Beta co-efficient	1.2	0.9	1.3	1.25

(1) The forecast growth rates have been provided by Premoco's financial advisors. They are based on **publicly available information** and assume all companies continue to operate independently and that dividend policies, capital structure and risk characteristics remain unchanged.

(2) The beta shown for Carsals is the **equity beta** of a **larger, quoted company** in a similar line of business. This company has a gearing ratio (debt : debt + equity) of 20%. Assume a debt beta of zero.

You should ignore any taxation issues throughout this question.

Required

(a) Calculate, for Premoco and, where relevant, for the three acquisition options before the merger:

    (i) The current market value and P/E ratio
    (ii) The cost of equity using the CAPM
    (iii) The prospective market value using the constant growth dividend valuation model

assuming the return on the market is 12% and the return on the risk-free asset is 6%.

(10 marks)

(b) You now have up to three values for each company as an independent entity. These are the current market value and the value using the dividend valuation model (as you have calculated for part (a)), and asset value (given in the scenario).

Discuss the usefulness and limitations of each of these methods of company valuation to Premoco in its acquisition decision. **(12 marks)**

(c) Assume you are working as one of Premoco's financial advisors. Write a report to David Wong, the managing director, which discusses the following issues for *each* acquisition option:

(i) The price to be offered to the target company's shareholders. You should recommend a range of terms within which Premoco should be prepared to negotiate

(ii) Whether cash or a share exchange would be the most appropriate method of financing the bid

(iii) The business implications (effect on existing operation, growth prospects, risk etc)

You should recognise that there is no single correct solution to the issues raised in this part of the case. The exercise is to assess and analyse the information available (state any assumptions you make), and then use your judgement to offer credible advice. **(28 marks)**

(Total = 50 marks)

1 Earnings per share

> **Top tips.** You would not get a complete question on stakeholders, but might well need to bring them into discussions about the consequences of a merger or the results of an investment. You could take a less even-handed approach than we have in (a) provided you justified your arguments and gave some attention to opposing arguments. However if you take a fairly extreme position, you have to discuss the problems of doing so. On the one hand will government wish to intervene to prevent anti-social behaviour; on the other hand how do you measure success in fulfilling the requirements of stakeholders? What happens if those requirements conflict?
>
> In (b) note how the interests of stakeholders who are **not directly involved** in decisions may be affected. Note also the potential **conflicts** – a sell-off may benefit shareholders but not employees. Instead of trying to avoid damaging stakeholder interests, a more practical solution may be to **compensate** them for damage incurred. Alternatively the damage may spur them to action – for example competitors damaged by a new car plant.

(a) **Profit maximisation**

One of the principles of the market economy is that if the owners of businesses attempt to achieve **maximum profitability** and **earnings** this will help to increase the wealth of society. As a result, it is usually assumed that a proper objective for private sector organisations is profit maximisation. This view is substantially correct. In general, the market economy has out-performed planned economies in most places in the world. Two key objectives of financial managers must therefore be the **effective management** of shareholders' funds and the provision of financial information which will help to increase shareholder wealth.

Problems with profit maximisation

However, profit-seeking organisations can also cause problems for society. For example, **monopolists** are able to earn large returns which are disproportionate to the benefits they bring to society. The **costs of pollution** fall on society rather than on the company which is causing it. A company may increase profitability by making some of its work-force redundant but the costs of unemployed people fall on society through the social security system.

The question that then follows is 'Should individual companies be concerned with these market imperfections?'

Government's role

There are two opposing viewpoints. On the one hand it can be argued that companies should only be concerned with **maximisation of shareholders' wealth**. It is the role of government to pick up the problems of market imperfections (eg by breaking up monopolies, by fining polluters and by paying social security benefits).

Stakeholder interests

An alternative viewpoint is that a company is a coalition of **different stakeholder** groups: shareholders, lenders, managers, employees, customers, suppliers, government and society as a whole. The objectives of all these groups, which are often in conflict, need to be considered by company managers when making decisions. From this viewpoint, financial managers cannot be content with meeting the needs of shareholders only.

Consideration of stakeholders

The truth is somewhere in between. The over-riding objective of companies is to create **long-term wealth for shareholders**. However this can only be done if we consider the likely behaviour of other stakeholders. For example, if we create extra short-term profits by cutting employee benefits or delaying payments to creditors there are likely to be **repercussions** which reduce longer term shareholder wealth. Or if we fail to motivate managers and employees adequately, the costs of the resulting inefficiencies will ultimately be borne by shareholders.

Conclusion

In summary, the financial manager is concerned with **managing the company's funds** on behalf of shareholders, and **producing information** which shows the likely effect of management decisions on shareholder wealth. However management decisions will be made after also considering other stakeholder groups and a good financial manager will be aware that financial information is only one input to the final decision.

> **Top tips.** Only three of the situations need be addressed in your answer.

(b) (i) **A private company converting into a public company**

When a private company converts into a public company, some of the existing shareholder/managers will sell their shares to outside investors. In addition, new shares may be issued. The **dilution of ownership** might cause loss of control by the existing management.

The stakeholders involved in potential conflicts are as follows.

(1) **Existing shareholder/managers**

They will want to sell some of their shareholding at as high a price as possible. This may motivate them to overstate their company's prospects. Those shareholder/managers who wish to retire from the business may be in conflict with those who wish to stay in control – the latter may oppose the conversion into a public company.

(2) **New outside shareholders**

Most of these will hold **minority stakes** in the company and will receive their rewards as **dividends only**. This may put them in conflict with the existing shareholder/managers who receive rewards as salaries as well as dividends. On conversion to a public company there should be clear policies on dividends and directors' remuneration.

(3) **Employees, including managers who are not shareholders**

Part of the reason for the success of the company will be the efforts made by employees. They may feel that they should benefit when the company goes public. One way of organising this is to create **employee share options** or other bonus schemes.

(ii) **A highly geared company attempting to restructure its capital finance**

The major conflict here is between **shareholders** and **lenders**. If a company is very highly geared, the shareholders may be tempted to take very high risks. If the gamble fails, they have limited liability and can only lose the value of their shares. If they are lucky, they may make returns many times the value of their shares. The problem is that the shareholders are effectively gambling with money provided by lenders, but those lenders will get no extra return to compensate for the risk.

Removal of risk

In restructuring the company, something must be done either to shift risk away from the lenders or to reward the lenders for taking a risk.

Risk can be **shifted away** from lenders by taking **security** on previously unsecured loans or by **writing restrictive covenants** into loan agreements (eg the company agrees to set a ceiling to dividend pay-outs until gearing is reduced, and to confine its business to agreed activities).

Lenders can be **compensated** for taking risks by either negotiating increased interest rates or by the issue of 'sweeteners' with the loans, such as share warrants or the issue of convertible loan stock.

Other stakeholders

Other stakeholders who will be interested in the arrangements include **trade creditors** (who will be interested that loan creditors do not improve their position at the expense of themselves) and **managers**, who are likely to be more risk averse than shareholders if their livelihood depends on the company's continuing existence.

(iii) **A large conglomerate spinning off its divisions**

Large conglomerates may sometimes have a market capitalisation which is less than the total realisable value of the subsidiaries. This is referred to as **'conglomerate discount'**. It arises because more synergy could be found by the combination of the group's businesses with competitors than by running a diversified group where there is no obvious benefit from remaining together.

For many years, Hanson Trust was the exception to this situation, but subsequently it decided to break up the group.

The stakeholders involved in potential conflicts are as follows.

(1) **Shareholders**

They will see the chance of immediate gains in share price if subsidiaries are sold.

(2) **Subsidiary company directors and employees**

They may either gain opportunities (eg if their company becomes independent) or suffer the threat of job loss (eg if their company is sold to a competitor).

(iv) **Japanese car makers building new car plants in other countries**

The stakeholders involved in potential conflicts are as follows.

(1) **The shareholders and management of the Japanese company**

They will be able to gain from the combination of advanced technology with a cheaper workforce.

(2) **Local employees and managers engaged by the Japanese company**

They will gain enhanced skills and better work prospects.

(3) **The government of the local country, representing the tax payers**

The **reduction** in **unemployment** will ease the taxpayers' burden and increase the government's popularity (provided that subsidies offered by the government do not outweigh the benefits!)

(4) **Shareholders, managers and employees of local car-making firms**

These will be in conflict with the other stakeholders above as existing manufacturers lose market share.

(5) **Employees of car plants based in Japan**

These are likely to **lose work** if car-making is relocated to lower wage areas. They will need to compete on the basis of **higher efficiency**.

2 News For You

> **Top tips.** In (a) you may find it helpful to look at each of the circumstances separately, and then to consider the positive and negative effects of each, before concluding what is the most likely overall effect of that circumstance. Bear in mind the particular nature of News For You's business eg type of products sold, profit margins, major competitors.
>
> In (b) you should not only consider the pros and cons of expansion, but also try to draw some conclusions and make recommendations. You could also think about some alternative developments that News For You could consider.

(a) (i) **Reduction in bank base rate**

   (1) **Change in costs of borrowing**

   Directly through the change in the cost of borrowing and therefore the cost of capital. A **fall in interest rates** will make borrowing cheaper, and therefore reduce the cost of **raising the finance** for the proposed expansion. This is likely to apply to whatever means of finance News for You chooses, since corporate borrowing rates are generally set at a certain **premium above base rate.** If News For You applies DCF techniques in evaluating the expansion, the reduction in the cost of capital will lead to an increase in the level of the NPV for the proposals.

   (2) **Level of demand**

   Indirectly through the effect of interest rates on the level of demand within the economy. Economic theory contends that a fall in the level of interest rates will increase the **demand for money**, and hence the overall level of demand within the economy. Other theories, on the other hand, believe that the level of consumer demand is unaffected by changes in interest rates. New For You is trading in **low value basic products** for which the level of demand is relatively inelastic. Even if a fall in interest rates does increase overall demand, this is unlikely to have any significant effect on the level of demand for News For You's products.

   (3) **Economic confidence**

   Economic theory would also suggest that the reduction in the interest rate will **increase general economic confidence and encourage expansion.** Again though it is likely that the level of confidence will not have much impact on the type of products News For You sells.

   (4) **Summary**

   To summarise, the reduction in the bank's base rate is likely to reduce the cost of the expansion plans, but will probably have little effect on the level of sales.

(ii) **Effects of present and forecast rates of inflation**

   (1) **Interest rates**

   Interest rates are **unlikely to rise** if inflation remains so low.

   (2) **Costs of purchases**

   The **cost of the products** that News For You purchases should **remain stable**. **Wage rates** may be less affected; there may be pressures other than inflation rates that cause wage increases.

(3) **Price increases**

In conditions of low inflation, it is **hard to make** any **price increases** without losing business. News For You is vulnerable to supermarket chains using basic products such as bread and milk as loss leaders, thereby reducing its ability to compete.

Low inflation is therefore likely to present more of a threat than an opportunity to News For You.

(iii) **Effects of stable tax rates**

(1) **Consumer demand**

Changes in personal tax rates can affect **consumer demand**, but as was discussed above, demand for News For You's products is inelastic, and therefore the stability or otherwise of tax rates is unlikely to have much effect on sales.

(2) **Tax relief**

When planning the expansion, it is easier to plan with confidence since the levels of **tax relief available** to both the company and individual equity investors are **known**.

Stable personal and corporate tax rates will therefore help in developing the expansion plans.

(iv) **Price sensitivity of consumers**

It is not clear whether the recent drop in demand for tobacco products is due to the recent tax increases or to other factors. These products are one of the higher value items sold in the shops, and therefore customers are likely to be **more price sensitive**. There is a risk that other retailers such as supermarkets and garages could use their superior buying power to offset the increase in tax with price reductions, with which News For You may find it hard to compete. **Health issues,** including strengthening of government health warnings on cigarettes, may also be significant.

(v) **Competition in supermarket sector**

Food retailing is a relatively new area for News For You, and has been entered with a view to increase sales. However, basic foodstuffs carry a **very low margin** and there is a risk that the supermarkets may respond to the government investigation by cutting prices in an attempt to prove their competitiveness. This could have severe repercussions for News For You, since it does not have large and profitable higher value product ranges over which to spread the loss. Recent growth figures suggest that prospects for expansion are limited.

(b) **Arguments in favour of expansion**

(i) **Need to increase sales**

Due to the low level of gross margins, News For You needs to **increase the level of sales** in order to trade profitably. In view of the low level of recent sales growth, in spite of the addition of new products, it seems that the only way to increase sales significantly is by the opening of new outlets.

(ii) **Bulk order discounts**

Expansion of the business will **increase the level of purchases and** could lead to an improvement in the level of buying power with suppliers, and the ability to take advantage of **bulk order discounts**. This would in turn have a positive impact on gross margins and profitability.

(iii) **Wider geographical spread**

A wider geographical spread will make the business **less vulnerable to local events**, such as an increase in the level of unemployment or the opening of a new superstore.

(iv) **Economies of scale**

Expansion could lead to some **economies of scale**, for instance in the wider deployment of regional management.

Arguments against expansion

(i) **Nature of products**

Expansion will not change the fundamental weakness of the business, which is that most of the business is in **low value products** with **strong price competition**. There is limited potential to grow, and other factors, the greater convenience of being able to **buy practically all products** required at a **single large store**, are working against the business.

(ii) **Long-term demand for newspapers**

The expansion of electronic and other mass media make it likely that demand for newspapers will continue to decline. Businesses such as News For You depend on customers for newspapers **making other purchases** on their regular visits. If these visits are reduced, then the pressure on sales is likely to continue, regardless of any expansion.

(iii) **Competitive pressures**

Strong price competition due to **low inflation** and the **position of the supermarket sector** is likely to continue for the foreseeable future.

Conclusion

In conclusion, News for You should think very carefully before committing to the expansion, since this is unlikely to do much to increase margins and profitability, given the current competitive climate for newspapers, tobacco and basic foodstuffs. The company could perhaps consider an alternative strategy of selling **different higher added value products**, and changing the whole style of the operation. For example it could think about expanding into areas such as hand made chocolates, or supplying local organic produce.

3 Lavinia Products

Top tips. Use a logical, clear structure and presentation for your forecast statements. Always make it easy for the marker to award you marks by showing your workings. This type of question is likely to be very time pressured in the exam so you need to practise doing forecasts at speed. The temptation is to concentrate on the calculations and ignore the discussion parts but that is a very bad idea. There will be plenty of marks for discussions and explanations so you must get into the habit of providing full answers to all parts of a question.

(a) (i) Lavinia Products statements of consolidated income

	Actual 20X2 $'000	20X3 $'000	Forecast 20X4 $'000	20X5 $'000
Revenue (increase 10% pa)	1,560	1,716	1,888	2,076
Cost of sales (increase 10% pa)	(950)	(1,045)	(1,150)	(1,264)
Gross profit	610	671	738	812
Operating expenses (increase 5% pa)	(325)	(341)	(358)	(376)
Depreciation (10% pa × $500,000)		(50)	(50)	(50)
Profit from operations	285	280	330	386
Interest (assumed constant)	(30)	(30)	(30)	(30)
Profit before tax	255	250	300	356
Taxation (see working)	(84)	(58)	(85)	(111)
Net profit	171	192	215	245
Dividend (25% growth pa)	(68)	(85)	(106)	(133)
Retained profit	103	107	109	112
Reserves b/f	128	231	338	447
Reserves c/f	231	338	447	559
Share capital	500	500	500	500
Year end reserves	231	338	447	559
Year end shareholders' funds	731	838	947	1,059
Pre-tax return on shareholders funds	34.9%	29.8%	31.7%	33.6%

On the basis of these figures, the financial objective of a pre-tax return of 35% of year-end shareholders' funds is not achieved in any of the years.

Working: Tax payable

It is assumed that the company does not account for deferred taxation.

	Actual 20X2 $'000	20X3 $'000	Forecast 20X4 $'000	20X5 $'000
Profit before tax	255	250	300	356
Add back depreciation		50	50	50
Less: capital allowance (25% red./bal)		(125)	(94)	(70)
Taxable profit	255	175	256	336
Tax at 33%	84	58	85	111

(ii) **Cash flow forecasts**

The 20X2 statement of financial position figure for 'other payables (including tax and dividends)' is in fact simply the sum of tax and dividends in the statement of consolidated income. It is assumed that this will continue to be the case in the following three years. The annual change in net current assets can be computed as follows.

Changes in net current assets

	Actual 20X2 $'000	20X3 $'000	Forecast 20X4 $'000	20X5 $'000
Inventory (scenario note (7))	326	361	361	361
Receivables (12.31% of sales) *	192	211	232	256
Trade payables (14.21% of cost of sales) *	(135)	(148)	(163)	(180)
Tax and dividends payable	(152)	(143)	(191)	(244)
Net current assets	231	281	239	193
Increase/(decrease) net current assets		50	(42)	(46)

* Alternatively receivables and payables can be computed as a 10% increase each year.

The cash flow forecasts can then be constructed.

Cash flow forecasts

	20X3 $'000	20X4 $'000	20X5 $'000
Retained profit for the year	107	109	112
Add back depreciation	50	50	50
(Investment in working capital)/release of working capital (see working)	(50)	42	46
Expenditure on non-current assets	(500)		
Surplus/(deficit) for the year	(393)	201	208
Cash/(deficit) b/f	50	(343)	(142)
Cash/(deficit) c/f	(343)	(142)	66

The company will need to find finance of $343,000 in 20X3 but this can be completely repaid in the following two years. However, interest costs have been ignored in this computation.

Appendices

1 *Cash receipts and payments*

	20X3 $'000	20X4 $'000	20X5 $'000
Receipts			
Cash from sales (sales + opening receivables – closing receivables)	1,697	1,867	2,053
Payments			
For purchases (cost of sales + opening payables – closing payables)	1,032	1,135	1,248
Operating expenses	341	358	376
Additional inventory purchase	35		
Machinery	500		
Interest (current year)	30	30	30
Tax (previous year)	84	58	85
Dividends (previous year)	68	85	106
	2,090	1,666	1,845
Net cash flow	(393)	201	208
Cash/(deficit) b/f	50	(343)	(142)
Cash/(deficit) c/f	(343)	(142)	66

(b) To: The directors of Lavinia Products
From: RT Consultants
Date: 22 May 20X3

Report on the objectives and financial forecasts of Lavinia Products

As requested by the terms of reference, I have prepared forecast statement of consolidated incomes and cash flow forecasts for the years 20X3 to 20X5. These are shown as Appendix 1 to this report [part (a) of this solution]. In Appendix 2, I have added some additional calculations to assist with the interpretation of the forecasts.

(i) **Key aspects of the financial information and the likelihood of achieving the objectives**

The three key objectives given to me were concerned with **return on shareholders' funds, growth in dividends per share and the ability to gain a stock market quotation**.

Although the company is making good profits, the calculations show that the objective of continuing to earn a pre-tax return of 35% on the book value of shareholders' funds is unlikely to be achieved over the next three years. The results for 20X3 show that the return will fall to 30%. In fact this figure will be further reduced by interest costs on the funding requirement of $343,000 if medium-term capital is used. The figures for 20X4 to 20X5 show a slow improvement in the return.

Although the company will earn sufficient profits to enable it to increase dividend per share by 25% each year, this will result in a steadily increasing **pay-out ratio** (rising from 40% to 54% of equity earnings) because earnings per share will increase at a rate of only 12% to 14% per year. The large increase in dividend pay-out is one of the contributory factors to the high funding requirement in 20X3. A better alternative is probably to lower the targeted dividend growth.

The effect of the additional borrowing requirement in 20X3 will be to increase **gearing**. Measured as Total long-term/medium-term debt *to* Book value of shareholders' funds, this will reach a maximum of (300 + 343)/838 = 77% in 20X3, which may be too high for comfort. Although interest cover (operating profit/interest) is safe in 20X2 at 9.5 times, this figure will fall to less than half if borrowing more than doubles. These effects are not revealed by Appendix 1 [part (a) of the question] because of the assumptions made.

When evaluating the suitability of the company for a flotation, analysts will be more concerned with **sustainable growth in equity earnings** than with an artificially high growth rate in dividends. The projected growth in earnings per share is good but not exciting and the company will probably need a longer track record before it can achieve a quotation. Alternatively, it should look for investments with faster growth opportunities. If, however, a flotation were obtained after three years, the likely valuation of the company's shares, at a P/E of 15, is $3.68 million.

In summary, the projections show that the company is profitable, with a reasonable growth rate, but that dividend growth should be held back in line with earnings growth in order to reduce the borrowing requirement in 20X3. A stock exchange quotation before the year 20X6 is unlikely.

(ii) **Suitability of the objectives as stated**

The **target return on shareholders' funds** of 35% pre-tax seems to be based on results for 20X2. This figure is, however, too high to be used as a target. If used as the basis for investment decisions it is likely that the company will reject projects which are adequately profitable even though they earn less than 35%. This will slow down its growth, allowing competitors to gain from its rejected opportunities. In addition, replacement of non-current assets may be postponed because it would depress the rate of return. The directors may attempt to squeeze short-term profits at the expense of long-term sustainability.

What is needed is a fundamental objective based on the company's ability to generate wealth for its shareholders. Research shows that return on shareholders' funds is a very bad indicator of this ability. More effective measurements are based on the principles of **shareholder value analysis** (SVA) or related techniques such as **economic value added** (EVA) or **cash flow return on investment** (CFROI). We would be happy to explain the principles of these techniques to you in a further report.

The objective of a 25% growth in dividends is also over-ambitious since this is clearly not matched by the expected growth in earnings or available cash flow. If the company were to be floated on a stock market, the dividend policy needs to be reviewed in detail. It is generally considered that a steady growth in dividends is a good thing but that the rate of growth should signal the company's long-term growth prospects. Dividend policy is, however, a complex subject and we would be happy to explore this further with you.

Finally, the objective of seeking a stock exchange quotation should be carefully reviewed against other possibilities for the company's development. The advantages of a quotation are that it becomes much easier to raise share capital from outside investors and your own shareholdings will significantly increase in value. However you must seriously consider the proportion of shares which you wish to retain and the consequent effect on control of the company. **Alternatives to a flotation** include:

- Continuing to grow using a combination of retained earnings and borrowings
- Identifying suitable individuals or organisations who wish to take a stake in your company
- Selling out to another company which wants to acquire your business

The choice of a way forward will depend on your own personal goals, which may be different for each director and will need careful and honest discussion.

(iii) **Additional methods of financial forecasting**

The forecasts prepared for this report are prepared on the basis of the assumptions given to me, which are very generalised and over-simple. For example, the relationship between sales, costs, receivables and payables remain the same over the period, no additional stockholdings have been budgeted after 20X3 and interest on additional borrowings (which is a significant figure) has been omitted.

A more detailed set of forecasts needs to be prepared, on a month-by-month basis, within the context of the company's strategic plans. A computerised planning model would be appropriate for assembling this information. Input to the forecasts will include the following.

- Marketing, production and purchasing plans; estimates from line managers of sales, costs, inventory and so on
- Statistical analysis of the relationship between the variables in the model and a cross-check against the managers' detailed estimates
- Estimates of general economic factors and their likely effect on the company and the industry as a whole
- Estimates of any likely changes in the behaviour and attitudes of competitors, customers and suppliers
- The results of capital investment appraisal and other decisions

There are many ways of handling **risk** and **uncertainty** in the estimates. Suitable techniques need to be chosen from the following options.

- The preparation of best and worst case estimates
- Use of data tables to show ranges of possible results
- Sensitivity analysis and the identification of 'key' variables
- Assignment of probabilities to estimates
- Use of simulation for complex repetitive uncertain events
- Scenario planning and the development of contingency plans.

Appendix 2 – further calculations to assist with interpretation of the results

		20X2	20X3	20X4	20X5
Equity earnings (profit after tax)	($'000)	171	192	215	245
Total dividend	($'000)	68	85	106	133
Number of $1 shares	('000)	500	500	500	500
Earnings per share	(pence)	34.2	38.4	43.0	49.0
Dividend per share	(pence)	13.6	17.0	21.2	26.6
Annual growth in EPS	%		12.3%	12.0%	14.0%
Dividend payout ratio (dps/eps)	%	40%	44%	49%	54%
Market capitalisation of shares at a P/E of 15	($ million)	2.57	2.88	3.23	3.68

4 Subsidiaries

> **Top tips.** The very important point that current appearances might be deceptive is made first. The answer brings out other points you may need to consider when undertaking a financial analysis:
>
> - Distortions built into various ratios, for example the effects of recent investments in assets
> - Problems making comparisons, for example different classifications of costs
> - Dubious accounting policies such as carrying forward product development costs
> - The implications of involvements in different markets, particularly the overseas market
> - Increased costs bringing, for example, more sales
>
> The discussion on working capital suggests that Y may be suffering some of the signs of over-trading - remember the remedy is more long-term capital.
>
> A conclusion is helpful here.

Profitability

X is the **more profitable** company, both in **absolute terms** and in **proportion to sales** and to **operating capital employed**. This may indicate that X is much better managed than Y, but this is not the only possibility, and a study of the other data shows that Y's profitability, while at present lower, may be more sustainable.

Asset usage

While Y appears to be making worse use of its assets than X, with **asset turnover ratios** lower than X's and falling, this seems to be largely because Y has recently acquired substantial new assets. It may be that within the next few years X will have to undertake a major renewals programme, with consequent adverse effects on its asset turnover ratios.

Sales

A higher percentage of Y's sales are to the home market, while it has still achieved fairly substantial export sales. This suggests that Y could have done better in **exploiting** the **export market**, but also that Y is less exposed than X to **exchange rate fluctuations** and the possible imposition of **trade barriers**. The prospects for the home market appear good, and should give scope for adequate growth. Y has achieved higher growth in total revenue than X over the past three years.

Y is making **sales per employee** about 50% higher than X, and has consistently done so over the past three years. X shows no sign of catching up, despite the fact that its total number of employees has recently fallen slightly. The modest rises in sales per employee over the past three years in both X and Y may be due largely to inflation.

Costs

Y seems to be significantly better than X at **controlling** the cost of sales (49% of sales in Y, and 65% in X), though X has made improvements over the past three years while there has been little change in Y. On the other hand, X's **administration expenses** have been only 6% of sales, while Y's have been 26% of sales. This contrast between the two types of cost suggests that different categorisations of costs may have been used. If we combine the cost of sales and administration expenses, then for X they total 71% of sales and for Y they total 75% of sales. There is thus little difference between the companies, though X has shown improved cost control while Y has not. X has also had **lower selling and distribution costs**.

One must however bear in mind that X will have had a lower depreciation element in its costs than Y, because Y has **recently invested substantially** in non-current assets. Y's costs will also be increased by its **higher salaries**, which may pay off in **better employee motivation** and hence higher sales per employee. On the other hand, Y's costs have been kept down by the carrying forward of an increasing amount of **product development costs**, an accounting policy which may well be imprudent.

Working capital management

In working capital management, X has the edge. Y has **very high receivables**, and these have recently risen sharply as a proportion of revenue. Y also carries rather more **inventory** than X, and has very little cash. While both companies have **tolerable current and liquid ratios**, X's are certainly safer. Y achieves a liquid ratio of 1:1 almost entirely by relying on its receivables. If it suffers substantial bad debts, or if the bank should become concerned and call in the overdraft, Y could suffer serious **liquidity problems**. It also depends heavily on **trade credit** to finance its receivables. While it is sensible to take advantage of trade credit offered, Y may depend too much on the continued goodwill of its **suppliers**. This may indicate the **need** for a fresh **injection of equity**.

Conclusion

On balance, X seems to be a sounder company than Y, with better financial management.

5 ZX

> **Top tips.** The key point to emphasise is that holding too much working capital is expensive whereas holding too little can result in system breakdown. However, modern manufacturing techniques and re-engineering of business processes can help achieve the best of both worlds: low working capital *and* efficient production and sales systems.
>
> Avoid the temptation to discuss the procedures for managing working capital rather than concentrating on the higher level policy decisions that are more important at final level.

To: Finance Director
From: Financial Manager
Date: 4 December 20X1
Subject: Working capital policy

(a) **Policy for investment and financing of working capital**

Choice of policies

The level of investment in working capital should be chosen after considering **manufacturing**, **marketing** and **financing factors** and other relevant stakeholder relationships. There is a range of possible investment policies, lying along a spectrum from conservative to aggressive.

Conservative policy

A conservative policy, such as we adopt at present, aims to **reduce the risk of system breakdown** by holding high levels of working capital. Thus customers are allowed **generous payment terms** to stimulate demand, **inventory** of finished goods is **high** to ensure availability for customers, and raw materials and work in progress are high to minimise the risk of running out of inventory and consequent downtime in the manufacturing process. Suppliers are paid promptly to ensure their goodwill, again to minimise the chance of stock-outs.

Effects of conservative policy

However, the cumulative effect on these policies can be that the firm carries a high burden of **unproductive assets**, resulting in a **financing cost** that can destroy profitability. A period of rapid expansion may also cause **severe cash flow problems** as working capital requirements outstrip available finance. Further problems may arise from inventory obsolescence and lack of flexibility to customer demands.

Aggressive working capital policy

An aggressive working capital investment policy aims to reduce this financing cost and increase profitability by **cutting inventory, speeding up collections from customers**, and **delaying payments to suppliers**. The potential disadvantage of this policy is an increase in the chances of **system breakdown** through **running out of inventory** or **loss of goodwill** with customers and suppliers.

However, modern manufacturing techniques encourage inventory and work in progress reductions through just–in–time policies, flexible production facilities and improved quality management. Improved customer satisfaction through quality and effective response to customer demand can also enable the shortening of credit periods. Our **modern production facility** gives the company the potential to implement radical new management techniques, including those mentioned above, and to move along the working capital policy spectrum towards a more aggressive stance.

Short-term or long-term finance

Whatever the level of working capital in the business, there is a choice as to whether the investment is financed by short term or longer term funds. In this sense, a **conservative policy** would finance using **longer term loans or share capital** whereas an **aggressive policy** would finance using **shorter term measures** such as **bank overdraft**, **factoring of debts**, or **invoice discounting**. The advantage of short term finance is that it can be cheaper but its disadvantage is that it is more easily withdrawn in the event of a cash crisis.

(b) **Ratio analysis**

Policy:	Conservative (present) $'000	Change %	Moderate $'000	Change %	Aggressive $'000
Receivables	2,500	–20	2,000	–30	1,750
Inventory	2,000	–20	1,600	–30	1,400
Cash at bank	500		250		100
Current assets	5,000		3,850		3,250
Current liabilities	(1,850)	10	(2,035)	20	(2,220)
Net current assets	3,150		1,815		1,030
Non-current assets	1,250		1,250		1,250
Net assets	4,400		3,065		2,280
Forecast sales	8,000	2	8,160	4	8,320
Operating profit margin	18%		18%		18%
Forecast operating profit	1,440		1,469		1,498
Return on net assets	33%		48%		66%
Current ratio	2.70		1.89		1.46

Notes

- Return on net assets = operating profit / net assets.

- There is no logical reason why sales should increase as a result of a more aggressive working capital policy. The reasoning behind this assumption is unclear.

(c) **Recommended course of action**

The conclusion to be drawn from the figures in (b) above is that **substantial funds** can be released by moving from a conservative to an aggressive working capital position ($4.40m – $2.28m = $2.12m). These funds could be **repaid to shareholders**, **invested** or used to **reduce borrowings** depending on the company's situation.

Moderate working capital position

My first recommendation is that the company should attempt to move towards a moderate working capital position by **tightening up** its **debt collection procedures**, **buying inventory** in **smaller batches** and **negotiating longer credit periods** from suppliers. Our small size does not help us in this respect but, if achievable, this would result in a significant increase in return on net assets and an acceptable current ratio.

Use of modern techniques

However, further moves towards more aggressive working capital arrangements should be the outcome rather than the driver of policy changes. The key changes that need to be made in our firm are concerned with the adoption of **modern supply chain** and **manufacturing techniques**. These will enable us not only to reduce working capital while avoiding system breakdown but also to improve quality and flexibility and to increase customer demand. At the moment, we have modern equipment but are not taking full advantage of its potential. I therefore recommend that a **comprehensive study** of our **key business processes** is undertaken. I will be happy to evaluate the financial effects of the possible scenarios.

6 Cuando

> **Top tips.** Exam questions may involve a discussion of different views being expressed by different directors. Answers on dividend policy should mix the theory (M&M) with the practical arguments against M&M. This question requires some planning so that you don't repeat in part (c) what you said in part (a). Note that part (a) takes into account the position of the main shareholder; spread of shareholdings will be a significant issue in many dividend questions.

(a) **Chairman's views**

At present the company has only one major shareholder, David Nile, who owns 80% of the shares. The extent to which Mr Nile has been involved in the management of the company is not clear, but it seems likely that he has been **involved in and has approved** previous decisions regarding dividends, probably in response to the investment needs of the company, and perhaps with an eye to his own individual tax position at different times. The **Chairman** is therefore surely correct to point out that the company has not needed to worry about the signals sent by its dividend policy in the past because it has been retaining profits as needed to develop the business.

Chief Operating Officer's views

The **Chief Operating Officer** says that the pattern of dividends has no effect on shareholder wealth, presumably following the theory put forward by Modigliani and Miller (MM) that dividend policy is irrelevant to shareholders because they can make their own adjustments (buying or selling shares) to achieve the level of income they require from their investments.

This may have been true in the case of David Nile, who probably began with a 100% stake and may since have sold 20% of his shares. But on the other hand to retain this stake he must have invested more money in the company in the meantime (in 20X3), given the increase in share capital from 800,000 shares to 1.5 million, so the argument does not really make sense.

Arguments against MM

In any case, there are strong arguments against MM's view that dividend policy is irrelevant as a means of affecting shareholder's wealth.

(i) **Differing rates of taxation on dividends** and **capital gains** can create a preference for a high dividend or one for high earnings retention.

(ii) Due to imperfect markets and the possible difficulties of selling shares easily at a fair price, shareholders might need **high dividends** in order to have funds to invest in opportunities outside the company.

(iii) **Markets are not perfect**. Because of **transaction costs** on the sale of shares, investors who want some cash from their investments should prefer to receive dividends rather than to sell some of their shares to get the cash they want.

(iv) **Information available** to shareholders is **imperfect**, and they are not aware of the future investment plans and expected profits of their company. Even if management were to provide them with profit forecasts, these forecasts would not necessarily be accurate or believable.

(v) As a consequence of imperfect information, companies are normally **expected at least to maintain the same level of dividends** from one year to the next. They are expected to pay a constant dividend or an increased dividend, but not a lower dividend than the year before. Failure to maintain the dividend level would undermine investors' confidence in the future.

(vi) Perhaps the strongest argument against the MM view is that shareholders will tend to prefer a **current dividend** to future capital gains (or deferred dividends) because the future is more uncertain.

Dividend policy in practice

In practice, dividend policy is significant to shareholders and the **Chairman's** view that a listing, putting all of the shares into public hands, will make dividend policy a **more pressing issue** is exactly in line with conventional thinking about dividend policy.

Unexpected changes in dividend payments will have an **effect on the share price**, and to avoid upsetting the market, a company might try to apply a policy of a consistent payout ratio (ratio of dividends to distributable profits for the year).

Companies will often also **'smooth' dividend payments**, ignoring 'temporary' fluctuations in annual profitability. Shareholders might therefore expect to receive dividends from a company that grow each year.

Market expectations can therefore be **a major factor in the formulation of dividend policy**, and listed companies are likely to be extremely reluctant to permit the kind of fluctuations in dividend level that have occurred in the case of Cuando in the past.

(b) The figures that are available can be analysed as follows.

	Net profits £'000	Annual growth %	Dividends £'000	Shares In issue '000	Earnings per share £	Dividends per share £	Dividend payout ratio %
20X0	650	–	320	800	0.81	0.40	49.23
20X1	520	(20.00)	150	1,000	0.52	0.15	28.85
20X2	760	46.15	480	1,000	0.76	0.48	63.16
20X3	1,240	63.16	600	1,500	0.83	0.40	48.39
20X4	1,450	16.94	540	1,500	0.97	0.36	37.24

Cuando's earnings have increased steadily apart from a dip in its second year. However, without more detailed information no clear pattern to the growth can be discerned. Most growth was achieved in 20X3.

Earnings per share are typically around 80p with a dividend payout ratio of around 50% of this, but there is no consistent pattern at all. A higher than usual dividend was paid in 20X2, presumably to compensate shareholders for the much smaller dividend in 20X1, but in the following year, 20X3 (when the most spectacular growth occurred), the dividend fell back again to its 20X0 level. Despite the rise in earnings per share in 20X4 the dividend per share fell once more.

As mentioned in part (a) this policy has presumably been acceptable to the one major shareholder, but when his shares are sold to the public a change seems very desirable on the grounds that shareholders typically expect consistency, at the very least, and prefer steady growth to wild fluctuations for no apparent reason.

(c) Besides matters already mentioned in this answer there are a number of other factors that affect dividend policy, including the following.

(i) The purpose of retaining profits should usually be to **invest in new projects**, in order to develop and grow the business. Unless there are profitable investments available to invest in, there should be no reason to retain the profits instead of paying them out as dividends.

(ii) Companies are **prevented by law from distributing dividends in excess of the distributable reserves** of the company. Broadly speaking, distributable profits are accumulated profits. A loss-making company might therefore find its ability to pay dividends is restricted.

(iii) Dividends have to be **paid in cash** (given that scrip dividends are uncommon). In order to make a dividend payment, a company must therefore **have sufficient free cash flow** to afford to make the payment. It is quite possible for a company to make profits but have insufficient cash to pay a suitable dividend.

(iv) The board of directors might want to use dividend policy to provide signals to the market about **expectations for future profits and growth**. An increase in dividends could be used to signal optimism about the future. If the signal is well-received, the share price could be boosted.

7 Carpets Direct

> **Top tips.** Remember in (c) that the value of rights is **not** the cost of the rights share. In part (d), make sure you make the point that the wealth of the shareholder would be unaffected, whether the rights were taken up or sold, but would be reduced if the rights were allowed to lapse.

(a) **Pre-emptive rights**

Pre-emptive rights give existing shareholders in a company the right to be offered any new shares to be issued by the company **before** an offer is made to outside investors. In the UK, companies wishing to make an issue of new equity shares for cash are **legally obliged** to offer the shares, in the first instance, to existing shareholders.

Advantages

The advantage of pre-emptive rights is that it can **prevent dilution of control** for **existing shareholders**. Providing the rights are taken up and new shares are offered in proportion to existing shareholdings, existing shareholders will maintain the same level of control following the new share issue as before the issue.

If new shares were offered to **external investors**, there is a real prospect of some dilution of control for existing shareholders. Moreover, shares may have to be offered to outside investors at a **discount**, thereby depressing share prices.

From the company viewpoint, a rights issue is a **less expensive** and **quicker** method of issuing shares than a public issue.

Disadvantages

The disadvantage of pre-emptive rights is that it places **restrictions on new share issues**. It **prevents greater competition** for new shares which, in turn, can **increase the cost of capital** for a company.

Although a rights issue may be a cheaper way of issuing shares than a public issue, a **placement** of shares is usually an even cheaper and quicker method of issuing shares.

If a **rights issue fails** through lack of support, the company may then have to undertake some other form of issue in order to raise the finance required. This will increase the time and expense involved in raising the necessary finance.

(b) Earnings per share $\frac{\$4.5m}{120m}$ = $0.0375

Market value per share ($0.0375 × 22) = $0.825

Theoretical ex-rights price

	$
Original shares 4 at $0.825	3.30
Rights share 1 at $0.66	0.66
	3.96

Value of share following the rights issue $\frac{\$3.96}{5}$ = 79.2c

(c) *Value of rights*

	$
Value of share following rights issue	79.2c
Cost of acquiring a rights share	66.0c
Value of rights	13.2c

(d) *Evaluation of options*

(i) *Take up rights issue*

	$
Value of holding after rights issue [(4,000 + 1,000) × 79.2p]	3,960
Less cost of acquiring rights shares (1,000 × 66p)	660
	3,300

(ii) *Sell rights*

	$
Value of holding after rights issue (4,000 × 79.2p)	3,168
Add sale of rights (1,000 × 13.2p)	132
	3,300

(iii) *Do nothing*

	$
Value of holding after rights issue (4,000 × 79.2p)	3,168

The above calculation reveals that the investor will be in the **same financial position** whether the rights offer is taken up or sold.

If the investor **does nothing** and, therefore, allows the rights issue to lapse, he/she will be **worse off** than under the other two options. However, in practice, a company may sell, **on behalf of the investor**, any rights not taken up and pay over the proceeds in order to ensure the investor is no worse off. This is usually done subject to there being a certain minimum value for the rights.

8 Sundown Carehomes

> **Top tips.** The question is made easier to answer because it is broken down into short sections which can be answered independently.

(a) The **redemption yield** is the true annual return received by an investor in the bond, taking into account both the interest received (in this case 7% before tax -referred to as the 'interest yield') and the gain or loss in capital value of the bond over the period to redemption.

The **gain or loss in capital value** arises because the current market value of the bond will be **dependent on its interest yield** compared with the market interest rate, and can be above or below par. For example, a 7% bond will sell at *above par* if the market interest rate is only 5%. If the bond is held to redemption, it will *redeemed at par value*, creating a capital loss, which will bring the redemption yield down to approximately 5%.

(b) Any public company suffers a **risk of bankruptcy** and/or default on its interest payments. In normal circumstances this **default risk is higher** than that of the national government. Because investors require compensation for risk, the company must offer to pay a higher interest rate than that paid by the government. Furthermore, the company will not be able to obtain the economies of scale on loan issue costs which are available to the government.

(c) A **zero coupon bond** pays **no interest**. If it is to be redeemed at par, it must be issued at a **large discount on par value**, giving the investor a return which consists entirely of the capital gain between redemption value and issue price.

A company would find such a **zero interest bond attractive** if it needs to finance a project through a start-up period of several years in which all cash generated is needed for reinvestment. The bond would be suitable provided that by the redemption date sufficient cash or refinancing is available to pay the lenders a much larger sum than was originally borrowed.

Investors who **prefer to make capital gains** rather than receive interest would find this **type of bond attractive**, because it has growth characteristics without the risk of equity shares. Although investors may prefer capital gains for tax reasons, any advantage depends on the tax rules of the country concerned.

(d) For every 4 shares at £4.75, one new share is issued at £4.00. The theoretical ex-rights price will therefore be (4 × £4.75) + £4.00 / 5 = £4.60.

(e) The zero coupon bond must show an 8% return over 20 years. If redemption is at £100, the issue price should be £100/1.08^{20} = £100 × 0.215 = £21.50.

This means the company must issue £7.44m nominal of bonds in order to raise £1.6m.

(f) Assuming the **convertible bond's par value** is £100, and it is issued at par, there is no gain on conversion in 20 years' time, which means there is no advantage to investing in it; 5 shares at £20 each are worth only £100. The NPV will be heavily negative, as follows:

Year	Cash flow £	Discount factor @ 8%	Present Value £
0	(100)	1.000	(100.0)
1–20	6	9.818	58.9
20	100	0.215	21.5
			(19.6)

The company's shares are projected to rise from £4.75 to £20 in 20 years, from which the expected average annual return is calculated as £4.75 × $(1 + r)^{20}$ = £20.

Thus $1/(1 + r)^{20}$ = 4.75/20 = 0.2375, from which r is approximately 7%, representing poor business performance from Sundown.

9 PG

Top tips. Be warned if you got (a) (i) wrong that manipulation of the earnings and price formulae may come up in this paper. (a)(ii) brings out the limitations of the theoretical ex rights price calculation. Actual price movements depend on the state of the market, the degree of market efficiency and, very importantly, the risk profile.

In (b) (ii) you are only asked about the advantages of issuing convertible bonds; the principal feature is short-term benefits from being able to raise funds at limited cost, with possible adverse consequences (dilution of earnings, change in control) only happening long-term.

(a) (i) The **current market price** can be found by multiplying the earnings per share (EPS) by the price/earnings (P/E) ratio.

EPS is £3.6/6m = 60p per share

P/E ratio is 15

Market price of shares is 15 × 60p = **£9.00 per share**

(ii) In order to raise £10,500,000 at a price of 800 pence, the company will need to issue an additional 1,312,500 (£10,500,000/£8.00) shares.

Following the investment, the total number of shares in issue will be 7,312,500 (6,000,000 + 1,312,500).

At this point, the total value of the company will be:

(6m × £9) + £10,500,000 = £64,500,000

The **theoretical ex-rights price** will therefore be £64.5m/7.3125m = **£8.82**.

Problems with calculations

(1) The **costs of arranging the issue** have not been included in the calculations.

(2) The **market view** of the **quality of the new investment** will affect the actual price of the company's shares.

(3) If the **issue** is **not fully subscribed** and a significant number of shares remain with the underwriters, this will **depress the share price**.

(4) The effect of the new investment on the **risk profile** of the company and the expected **future dividend stream** could also cause the share price to differ from that predicted.

(5) The price of the shares depends not only on the financial performance of the company, but also on the **overall level of demand** in the stock market. If the market moves significantly following the announcement of the issue, this will affect the actual price at which the shares are traded.

(iii) **Features of deep discounted rights issue**

In a **deep-discounted** rights issue, the new shares are priced at a **large discount** to the current market price of the shares. The purpose of this is to ensure that the issue is well subscribed and that shares are not left with the underwriters, and thus this form of issue pricing is attractive when the stock market is particularly volatile. However, the shares cannot be issued at a price which is below their nominal value.

Disadvantage of deep discounted rights issue

The main drawback to this approach is that a **larger number of shares** will need to be **issued** in order to raise the required amount of finance, and this will lead to a larger dilution of earnings per share and dividends per share.

(b) (i) **Conversion premium**

The **conversion premium** is the **difference** between the **issue value** of the **bonds** and the **conversion value** as at the date of issue. In other words it is the measure of the additional expense involved in buying shares via the convertible bonds as compared with buying the shares on the open market immediately.

In this case, £100 bonds can be converted into 11 ordinary shares. The **effective price** of these shares is therefore £9.09 per share.

The **current market price** of the shares is £9.00. The **conversion premium** is therefore £9.09 − £9.00 = **9 pence**. This can also be expressed in percentage terms as **1%** (0.09/9).

(ii) **Advantages of issuing convertible bonds**

(1) **Convertibles** should be **cheaper than equity** because they offer greater security to the investor. This may make them particularly attractive in fast growing but high-risk companies.

(2) **Issue costs** are **lower** for bonds than for equity.

(3) **Interest** on the **bonds** is **tax deductible**, unlike dividends on ordinary shares.

(4) There is **no immediate change** in the **existing structure** of control, although this will change over time as conversion rights are exercised.

(5) There is no **immediate dilution** in **earnings** and **dividends per share**.

10 Ducey

> **Top tips.** In part (a) it is helpful to show clearly how the tax allowable depreciation has been calculated and how they have been allocated over time. In part (b) state clearly the clear assumptions surrounding your choice of interest rate for evaluating the financing alternatives.

(a) First calculate the NPV cost of the plant if it is acquired using a bank loan. The discount rate to be used will be 13%, this being the approximate after-tax cost of the bank loan (19% × 70%).

Tax-allowable depreciation will be claimed as follows.

All figures £'000

Year	Basis of claim	Value (× 30%)	Claimed in year
1	176 × 25% = 44.00	13.2	2
2	(176 – 44) × 25% = 33.00	9.9	3
3	(176 – 44 – 33) × 25% = 24.75	7.425	4
4	Balance = 74.25	22.275	5

The NPV cost of the project can now be calculated.

Year	Plant £	Tax £	Cash flow £	Disc factor	NPV £
0	(176.00)		(176.00)	1.000	(176.00)
1			0	0.885	0.00
2		13.2	13.2	0.783	10.34
3		9.9	9.9	0.693	6.86
4		7.425	7.425	0.613	4.55
5		22.275	22.275	0.543	12.10
NPV cost of purchase					(142.15)

The NPV cost of leasing the plant can be calculated using the discount rate of 13%.

Year	Lease £	Tax relief £	Cash flow £	Disc factor	NPV £
0	(55.00)		(55.00)	1.000	(55.00)
1	(55.00)	16.5	(38.5)	0.885	(34.07)
2	(55.00)	16.5	(38.5)	0.783	(30.15)
3	(55.00)	16.5	(38.5)	0.693	(26.68)
4		16.5	16.5	0.613	10.11
NPV cost of leasing					(135.79)

The NPV cost of leasing is lower than buying outright using a bank loan and is therefore financially more advantageous to Ducey.

(b) If the company is in a permanent non-tax paying situation, then the alternative sources of finance can be evaluated on the basis of their **direct NPV costs** excluding tax allowances.

The NPV cost of purchase in year 0 is £176,000.

The NPV cost of leasing can be found by multiplying the annual rental payments in years 1 to 3 by the value of a three year annuity at 19%, and adding this to the year 0 PV of £55,000. Since the company is not paying tax, it will be unable to receive the tax benefits of any interest payments and therefore the before tax cost of borrowing (ie 19%) will be used to evaluate the lease:

NPV = £55,000 + (2.140 × £55,000) = £172,700.

Leasing is still therefore more financially advantageous than outright purchase.

(c) Other factors to be considered when the company is making the lease or buy decision include the following.

(i) **Running expenses**

It is assumed in the calculations that these are the same under the two financing alternatives. However in practice, items such as insurance, maintenance etc may vary.

(ii) **Current liquidity**

The effect of taking out and servicing an immediate loan of £176,000 on the overall liquidity and borrowing capacity must be considered.

(iii) **Accuracy of estimates**

The company must be certain that the life of the machine has been estimated correctly at four years. If there is a possibility that the life could be shorter than this then the alternatives should be re-evaluated.

(iv) **Effect on reported profits**

The effect of the alternatives on the reported profits should be taken into account, since this in turn could affect the dividend policy and therefore the valuation of the company's shares.

(v) **Change in interest rate**

The calculations assume that the interest rate will be fixed for the life of the machine. If the rate changes then this will have financial implications which should be evaluated.

11 Nile plc

Top tips. Part (a) is a fairly straightforward calculation of WACC, remember to consider the post-tax cash flows when working out the cost of debt. The discount rates chosen will determine the cost of debt, and therefore the WACC, but answers should be around the figures given. In an exam full credit will be given for correct workings for any sensible discount rates.

(a) The net dividend has increased 1.5 times from the end of 20X4 to the end of 20X8, a period of 4 years. This represents an approximate annualised growth rate of 10.67% (being $\sqrt[4]{1.5}$).

Cost of ordinary share capital in after tax terms $\simeq \dfrac{30(1.1067)}{476} + 0.1067 = 0.176$ or 17.6%

Cost of debentures: = £69 is the current market price per cent. The cost of debentures (%) is the internal rate of return of the following cash flows:

Year	MV £	Interest £	Tax Saving £	Cash Flow £
0	(69)			(69.0)
1-20		8	(2.8)	5.2
20		100		100.0

At a discount rate of 7% the NPV is + £11.9, and at a discount rate of 9% the NPV is − £3.7. The IRR is (by interpolation)

$$7\% + \left(\frac{11.9}{11.9 + 3.7} \times 2\%\right) = 8.5\%$$

It is assumed that the new issue of shares and debentures will be weighted in accordance with the existing gearing ratio as measured by market values.

The **weighted average cost of capital** is:

	Cost %	Market Value £'000
Ordinary share capital	17.6	4,760
Debentures	8.5	552
		5,312

Weighted average cost of capital (K_o) = (17.6 × 4760/5312) + (8.5 × 552/5312) = **16.7%**

(b) The following **difficulties** and **uncertainties** should be mentioned.

(i) Will the **growth rate** in dividend remain the same as in previous years?

(ii) Should a **premium for risk** be added to the weighted average cost of capital; e.g. should the test discount rate for projects be, say, 20% or more rather than 16.7% (or 17%)?

12 Incorrect manual

> **Top tips.** For this question you need to realise the error in illustration 1 is that the cost of equity calculated is an ungeared beta which needs to be adjusted before calculating the WACC.

Illustration 1 – when the company is diversifying without changing its gearing

The equity beta of a similar sized company in the industry that you want to move into is 0.90.

Gearing of the similar company is debt $60m and equity $230m (market values).

Cost of equity

The beta needs to be adjusted for differences in gearing.

Asset beta = Equity beta × $\dfrac{V_E}{V_E + V_D(1-t)}$

Asset beta = $0.90 \times \dfrac{230}{230 + 60(1 - 0.3)} = 0.76$

CAPM

$K_e = R_f + (R_m - R_f)$ beta

6 + (14 − 6) 0.76 = 12.08%

This is an ungeared K_e.

Now to reflect our own company's gearing use this formula.

$K_{adj} = K_{eu}(1 - tL)$

$L = \dfrac{85}{85 + 214}$

K_{adj} = 12.08 (1 − 0.3 × 0.284) = **11.05%**

Alternatively

Regear the asset beta using our own company's gearing

$$0.76 = \text{Equity beta} \times \frac{214}{214 + 85(1-0.3)}$$

$$\frac{0.76}{0.7825} = \text{Equity beta} = 0.9712$$

Using this in the capital asset pricing formula:

$$K_e = R_f + (R_m - R_f) \text{beta}$$

$$6 + (14 - 6)\,0.9712 = 13.77\%$$

Now using the normal K_o formula for the weighted average cost of capital

$$K_o = (13.77 \times 214/299) + (6 \times 0.7 \times 85/299) = \mathbf{11.05\%}$$

13 ABC

> **Top tips.** This is a question from an old syllabus Paper 4 Finance exam so is not at strategic level. It does however provide excellent practice at some very important calculations. You will need to be completely comfortable with, and quick at, these types of calculations in your exam.

(a) **Gearing ratios**

$$\text{Gearing} = \frac{\text{Prior charge capital}}{\text{Shareholders' funds}}$$

20X5 $\dfrac{250}{446.8} = 56\%$

20X6 $\dfrac{250}{437.9} = 57.1\%$

20X7 $\dfrac{250}{431.9} = 57.9\%$

These are slightly below the covenant level of 60% and therefore appear acceptable. However, it would only take a fall of $5 million per annum in shareholder funds for gearing to rise to an unacceptable level.

Interest cover		$m
Interest on debentures =	7% × $150m =	10.5
Interest on bank loans =	5% × $100m =	5.0
Total interest		15.5

20X5 $\dfrac{58}{15.5} = 3.74$ times

20X6 $\dfrac{50}{15.5} = 3.23$ times

20X7 $\dfrac{54}{15.5} = 3.48$ times

The covenant for EBIT/total interest is 3.5 times so interest cover falls below acceptable limits in 20X6 and 20X7.

There is a significant risk that ABC will breach the debenture covenants so urgent action is required to obtain alternative finance or restructure the business to improve gearing and interest cover.

(b) **Cost of debt for existing debenture**

Year		Cash flow $m	Discount factor @ 3%	PV $m	Discount factor @ 4%	PV $m
0	Market value	(107.00)	1.000	(107.00)	1.000	(107.00)
1–4	Interest (after tax)	4.90	3.717	18.21	3.630	17.79
4	Capital repayment	100.00	0.888	88.80	0.855	85.50
				0.01		(3.71)

After tax cost of debt = 3.00%

Pre-tax cost of debt = $\dfrac{3.00}{1-0.3}$ = 4.29%

Cost of debt for a 5% pre-tax bank loan

Year		Cash flow $m	Discount factor @ 3%	PV $m	Discount factor @ 4%	PV $m
0	Loan	(107.00)	1.000	(107.00)	1.000	(107.00)
1–4	Interest (after tax)	3.745*	3.717	13.92	3.630	13.59
4	Loan repayment	107.00	0.888	95.02	0.855	91.49
				1.94		(1.92)

*107 × 0.05 = 5.35 × (1 – 0.3) = 3.745

After tax cost of debt = $3 + \dfrac{1.94}{1.94+1.92} = 3.5\%$

Pre-tax cost of debt = $\dfrac{3.5}{1-0.3} = 5\%$

The debenture is therefore cheaper than the proposed replacement bank loan.

Other factors to consider

(i) The identity of the debenture holders and whether the debenture covenant could be renegotiated.

(ii) The security or loan covenants that may be required by the bank and whether these are any more flexible than the current debenture covenant.

(iii) The possibility of reducing the interest charge by offering non-current assets as security. The statement of financial position contains a high level of non-current assets.

(iv) Alternative and cheaper sources of finance may be available.

(v) Planned dividend payouts are in excess of earnings which could be a serious concern for providers of finance.

(c) **Issue price of proposed rights issue**

Current number of shares $= \dfrac{200}{0.25} = 800$ million

Number of new shares to be issued $= \dfrac{800}{5} = 160$ million

$100 million is needed so the issue price $= \dfrac{100}{160} = \$0.625$ per share

	$
5 shares @ $0.75	3.750
1 share @ 0.625	0.625
	4.375

$\dfrac{4.375}{6} = \$0.73$

Alternative solution

$$\text{Ex-rights price} = \dfrac{(N \times \text{cum-rights price}) + \text{issue price}}{N+1}$$

$$= \dfrac{(5 \times 0.75) + 0.625}{6}$$

$= \$0.73$ per share

Advantages of new equity finance

- Avoidance of the redemption premium costs
- Improved gearing and interest cover
- Dividends are more flexible than loan interest as they do not have to be paid when profits are low
- It is a permanent form of finance and will not need to be restructured after four years
- It provides a good foundation for raising future debt finance

Advantages of the bank loan:

- Loan interest tends to be cheaper as it is tax deductible and constant unlike dividends where growth is expected
- The high value of non-current assets on the statement of financial position could be used as security for a bank loan
- Debt can be repaid and is therefore more flexible than equity finance
- It is easier to arrange and administer and there is less risk involved.

14 Treasury management

Top tips. A few easy marks may be available for discussing the role of the treasury function. (b) looks at the role from another angle.

(a) **Management of cash**

A central treasury department will normally have the responsibility for the **management of the group's cash flows** and borrowings. Subsidiaries with surplus cash will be required to submit the cash to the treasury department, and subsidiaries needing cash will borrow it from the treasury department, not from an external bank.

Borrowing

A central treasury will also be given the **responsibility for borrowing** on behalf of the group. If a subsidiary needs capital to invest, the treasury department will borrow the money required, and lend it on to the subsidiary. The subsidiary will be responsible for **paying interest** and **repaying the capital** to the treasury department, which will in turn be responsible for the interest and capital payments to the original lenders.

Risk management

Another function of the treasury department will be to **manage the financial risk** of the group, such as currency risk and interest rate risk. Within broad guidelines, the treasurer might have authority to decide on the balance between fixed rate and floating rate borrowing, and to use swaps to adjust the balance. The department would also be responsible for arranging forward exchange contracts and other hedging transactions.

Taxation

The central treasury department could also be responsible for the **tax affairs** of the group, and an objective would be to minimise the overall tax bill. To accomplish this effectively, the treasury must have **authority to manage transfer prices** between subsidiaries in the group, as a means of transferring profits from high-tax countries to lower-tax countries.

(b) The treasury function needs information from within and from outside the organisation to carry out its tasks.

- (i) From each subsidiary within the group, it will need **figures for future cash receipts and payments**, making a distinction between definite amounts and estimates of future amounts. This information about cash flows will be used to **forecast the cash flows of the group**, and identify any future borrowing needs, particularly short-term and medium-term requirements. Figures should be provided regularly, possibly on a daily basis.

- (ii) Information will also be required about **capital expenditure requirements**, so that long-term capital can be made available to fund it.

- (iii) Subsidiary finance managers should be encouraged to **submit information** to the **treasury department** about local market and business conditions, such as prospects for a change in the value of the local currency, or a change in interest rates.

- (iv) From outside the group, the treasury will need a **range of information** about current market prices, such as exchange rates and interest rates, and about which banks are offering those prices. Large treasury departments will have a link to one or more information systems such as Reuters and Bloomberg.

- (v) The treasury department should be alert to any **favourable market opportunities** for raising new debt capital. The treasurer should maintain regular contact with several banks, and expect to be kept informed of opportunities as they arise.

- (vi) Where the treasury is responsible for the group's tax affairs, information will also be needed about **tax regulations** in each country where the group operates, and changes in those regulations.

15 Risk reduction

> **Top tips.** You may be asked for a few marks to explain the importance of portfolio theory and the subject matter of this question is fairly typical. The last point about individuals being better able than companies to diversify is important, and you should bear it in mind when considering acquisitions of companies in different sectors.

(a) **Assumptions of portfolio theory**

In portfolio theory, investors are assumed to be **profit maximising** and **risk averse**. This means that they will trade off portfolio return against risk such that an 'efficient portfolio' will have the highest possible return for any given risk level and the lowest risk for any given return.

Two security portfolio

Investigation of the two-security portfolio reveals that, for two risky investments, only **some proportional combinations** will be efficient. The remaining possible combinations can be 'eliminated', that is they will be considered unattractive by investors.

As more risky investments are added to the portfolio, it is found that only a relatively **small proportion** of possible combinations are **efficient**. Portfolio theory shows how these efficient portfolios lie on part of the boundary of the set of all possible portfolios.

Investigation of a two-security portfolio consisting of a risk free investment and a risky investment shows that in this case there are **no inefficient portfolios** resulting from different proportional combinations. The set of possible portfolios simply gives a straight line trade-off between return and risk.

Optimal combination

Combining the effects described in the two preceding paragraphs, it is found that the optimal investment combination is a mix of **risk free investments** with an **efficient portfolio** of **risky securities.** When this is done, it becomes apparent that the best portfolio of risky securities would be one that consisted in theory of all possible investments. This is known as the market portfolio and is approximated by a diversified share portfolio of twenty or more shares.

Portfolio theory therefore arrives at the conclusion that all investors should split their funds between risk free investments (eg bank deposits, Treasury bills) and a diversified portfolio of risky investments (eg shares). The proportion invested in each category is, however, a personal choice for each investor and depends on their individual attitude to risk.

(b) The practical implications of portfolio theory to a fund manager are highly significant, and are increasingly put into practice as competition for investment funds becomes keener.

Diversification by companies

Portfolio theory suggests that fund managers should **diversify the risk-bearing part** of their holdings into at least twenty different shares or securities. When taken in conjunction with the efficient market hypothesis, portfolio theory suggests that investors cannot consistently achieve a better risk return trade-off than that offered by the stock market index (eg the FTSE index for London shares). To satisfy the demand for diversified portfolios, index tracking funds are now available. These are popular in UK and US but are of less relevance in less efficient stock markets.

Diversification by individuals

At first sight it may appear that the projects manager of a company should seek to diversify the company's business into as many different fields as possible, in order to reduce the company's risk. However, the manager should realise that investment decisions are made on behalf of shareholders, who are able to **diversify their overall portfolios** by buying shares in many different companies. For such shareholders the overall risk of any individual company is irrelevant. What matters is the incremental risk that an individual project adds to the market portfolio.

16 Mezen

> **Top tips.** In (a), if you failed to identify which costs were relevant correctly, make sure you understand why. (c) makes the important point about sensitivity of cash flows. Even if a project has a positive NPV, or an acceptable IRR, a company may not go ahead if the profits are felt to be too marginal, and the risk of loss too great. Although you will have encountered questions on the weaknesses of IRR in lower level papers, they still might sneak into *Financial Strategy*.

(a) **Incremental cash flows**

The survey has been undertaken already, even though it has not yet been paid for, and therefore the $30,000 is a sunk cost.

The depreciation charge of $15,000 is not a cash-flow. The re-allocated fixed overheads will be incurred whether or Mezen goes ahead with the product. Both of these amounts may be subtracted from the $25,000 of fixed overheads in the original calculations.

The company forgoes $70,000 of immediate income from the sale of the machine.

	Time 0 $'000	Time 1 $'000	Time 2 $'000	Time 3 $'000	Time 4 $'000	NPV $'000
Sales		180	200	160	120	
Cost of sales		(115)	(140)	(110)	(85)	
Variable overheads		(27)	(30)	(24)	(18)	
Fixed overheads		(5)	(5)	(5)	(5)	
Machine	(70)				10	
Working capital	(20)				20	
Incremental cash flows	(90)	33	25	21	42	
× 10% discount factor	1.00	0.91	0.83	0.75	0.68	
Present value	(90.00)	30.03	20.75	15.75	28.56	5.09

(b) **Approximate internal rate of return**

	Time 0 $'000	Time 1 $'000	Time 2 $'000	Time 3 $'000	Time 4 $'000	NPV $'000
Incremental cash flows	(90)	33	25	21	42	
× 14% discount factor	1.00	0.88	0.77	0.68	0.59	
Present value	(90.00)	29.04	19.25	14.28	24.78	(2.65)

$$IRR = a + \frac{NPV_a}{NPV_a - NPV_b}(b-a)$$

Where a is the lower rate of return, b is the higher rate of return, NPV_a is the NPV discounted at a, and NPV_b is the NPV discounted at b.

$$IRR = 10 + \left[\frac{5.09}{5.09 - (-2.65)} \times (14-10)\right]\% = 12.63\%$$

(c) The product has a positive net present value and an IRR that exceeds the company's cost of capital, and this suggests that it should be launched.

The decision is very marginal, however. It would certainly not be worthwhile if the market survey had not yet been commissioned, in which case the cost of $30,000 would need to be included. A relatively small drop in sales or a small increase in costs would result in a negative NPV. The company may well be able to find better uses for the $20,000 that will be spent now, and for the immediate income of $70,000 on the sale of the machine.

(d) The **internal rate of return (IRR)** is the rate of return that results in a NPV of zero. The rule with the **internal rate of return (IRR)** method of project evaluation is that a project should be undertaken if it is expected to achieve a return in excess of the company's cost of capital. A project that has an IRR in excess of the cost of capital must have a positive NPV.

Strengths

The main **advantage** of the IRR method is that the information it provides may be more easily understood by managers, especially non-financial managers.

It is sometimes said that IRR is difficult to calculate, but **both** NPV and IRR are actually **very easy to calculate** with a **spreadsheet**.

Weaknesses

However, it might be tempting for some managers to **confuse IRR** and **accounting return** on capital employed (ROCE). The accounting ROCE and the IRR are two completely different measures. If managers were given information about both ROCE (or ROI) and IRR, it might be easy to get their relative meaning and significance mixed up.

The IRR method also ignores the **relative size of investments**: for example a project with an annual return of $50 on an initial investment of $100 would have the same IRR as a project with an annual return of $5,000 on an initial investment of $10,000, although the latter is clearly preferable.

IRR **favours projects that are less sensitive to increases in the discount rate** and therefore the IRR method may sometimes indicate that a project that yields a smaller increase in shareholder wealth should be preferred to one that yields a larger increase, whereas the opposite is the case. NPV should therefore be used to **decide** between **mutually exclusive projects**.

17 DIN

> **Top tips.** In (a) you have to explain why the real rate of return is a significant figure and state the clues that questions will give you about whether cash flows are real or nominal.
>
> In (b) if you are working out the cost element of unit price, a table is always helpful. Brief narrative can also be helpful to show the examiner what you've done and highlight the points for which you will gain marks, such as excluding sunk costs.

(a) The **real rate of return** is the rate of return which an investment would show in the absence of inflation. For example, if a company invests €100, inflation is 0%, and the investment at the end of the year is worth €110, then the real rate of return is 10%.

In reality however, there is likely to be an element of inflation in the returns due to the change in the purchasing power of money over the period. In the example above, if inflation was running at 5%, then to show a real rate of return of 10%, the investment would need to be worth €115.50 at the end of the year. In this case the money rate of return is 15.5% which is made up of the real return of 10% and inflation at 5%.

The relationship between the nominal ('money') rate of return and the real rate of return can be expressed as follows.

(1 + nominal rate) = (1 + real rate) × (1 + inflation rate)

The rate to be used in discounting cash flows for capital project appraisal will depend on the way in which the **expected cash flows** are **calculated**. If the cash flows are expressed in terms of the actual number of pounds that will be received or paid on the various future dates, then the nominal rate must be used. If however they are expressed in terms of the value of the pound at year 0, then the real rate must be used.

(b) *Workings*

	Year 1	Year 2	Year 3	Year 4
Sales volume	25,000	25,000	25,000	25,000
Unit price (€)	80	84	88	93
Variable material cost (€)	8.00	8.32	8.65	9.00
Variable labour cost (€)	12.00	13.20	14.52	15.97
Variable overhead (€)	12.00	12.48	12.98	13.50

Notes

(i) Development costs of €480,000 are sunk costs and will be excluded from the calculations.

(ii) Depreciation does not involve any movement of cash and will be excluded from the fixed overheads (€600,000 in year 1).

(iii) All figures have been adjusted for the appropriate rate of inflation. The investment will therefore be evaluated using the WACC expressed as a nominal rate of 15%.

Evaluation of investment

	Year 0 €'000	Year 1 €'000	Year 2 €'000	Year 3 €'000	Year 4 €'000
Capital outlay	(2,400)				
Sales		2,000	2,100	2,205	2,315
Direct costs					
Materials		(200)	(208)	(216)	(225)
Labour		(300)	(330)	(363)	(399)
Overhead		(300)	(312)	(324)	(337)
Fixed overheads		(200)	(210)	(221)	(232)
Gross cash flow	(2,400)	1,000	1,040	1,081	1,122
Discount at 15%	1.000	0.870	0.756	0.658	0.572
Present value	(2,400)	870	786	711	642
NPV	609				

The investment yields a net present value at the end of four years of €609,000. In the absence of other factors such as capital rationing, production of the Rance should be undertaken.

18 Harry

Top tips. This question shows how different areas of the syllabus can be combined into one question. If you get stuck, make an assumption and move on, and don't forget to use a proforma layout for the NPV calculation.

(a) **Cost of equity**

$$k_{eg} = \frac{d_0(1+g)}{P_0} + g$$

$$= \frac{20(1+0.1)}{250} + 0.1$$

$$= 18.8\%$$

Cost of debt can be estimated by comparing the current market value of the debt with the discounted payments due to be made by the company up to the redemption date.

Year	Cash flow €	8% discount factor	PV €	10% discount factor	PV €
0	(95)	1.000	(95.00)	1.000	(95.00)
1–3	10 (1 – 0.3)	2.577	18.04	2.487	17.41
3	100	0.794	79.40	0.751	75.10
			2.44		(2.49)

Interpolating:

Post tax cost of debt, k_{dnet} = $8\% + \dfrac{2.44}{2.44 + 2.49} \times (10 - 8)$

= 9.0%

$$\text{WACC} = k_{eg}\left[\dfrac{V_E}{V_E + V_D}\right] + k_{dnet}\left[\dfrac{V_D}{V_E + V_D}\right]$$

= $18.8\left(\dfrac{250}{250+95}\right) + 9\left(\dfrac{95}{250+95}\right)$

= 16.1%, say 16%

(b)

	Time 0 €'000	Time 1 €'000	Time 2 €'000	Time 3 €'000	Time 4 €'000	Time 5 €'000
Profit (nominal values)		390.0	405.6	421.8	438.7	456.2
Tax (30%)		(117.0)	(121.7)	(126.5)	(131.6)	(136.9)
Capital outlay	(1,200.0)					
Machinery sale (W1)						284.8
Tax allowances (W1)		90.0	67.5	50.6	38.0	28.5
Working capital	(100.0)	(4.0)	(4.2)	(4.3)	(4.5)	117.0
Net cash flow	(1,300.0)	359.0	347.2	341.6	340.6	749.6
Discount factor @ 16%	1.000	0.862	0.743	0.641	0.552	0.476
Present value	(1,300.0)	309.5	258.0	219.0	188.0	356.8
PV cumulative	(1,300.0)	(990.5)	(732.5)	(513.5)	(325.5)	31.3

NPV is therefore positive €31,300.

Workings

(1) *Tax allowances and resale value*

		€'000	Time
1st allowance	1,200 × 25% × 30%	90.0	1
2nd allowance	75% of previous	67.5	2
3rd allowance	75% of previous	50.6	3
4th allowance	75% of previous	38.0	4
5th allowance	75% of previous	28.5	5

There is no balancing allowance since the machinery is sold at its written down value.

Written down value = €1,200,000 × 0.75^5 = €284,766

(2) *Working capital requirements*

	Time 0 €'000	Time 1 €'000	Time 2 €'000	Time 3 €'000	Time 4 €'000	Time 5 €'000
Amounts	100.0	104.0	108.2	112.5	117.0	
Increment	(100.0)	(4.0)	(4.2)	(4.3)	(4.5)	117.0

(c) **To:** Financial Manager
From: Deputy Financial Manager
Date: 12 May 20X8
Subject: Evaluation of proposed new product investment

Evaluation of project

The financial evaluation of the proposed investment on the original basis suggests that the project will just about be viable since the NPV at the end of five years is positive. However, the size of the **profit** is relatively small in relation to the size of the project, and it is worth considering the **assumptions** underlying the evaluation to ensure that these are appropriate. Otherwise, we run the risk of **making a loss**. Areas that merit further work include the following.

Use of the WACC as the discount rate

The **WACC approximates** to the **overall cost of capital** to the business. However, this investment amounts to €1.3 million (including working capital), and is therefore a relatively large investment. We should therefore consider whether undertaking the project would in itself affect the cost of capital to the business. If it does, then the WACC should be adjusted to take account of this. Further, it is assumed that the project carries the same level of risk as the existing operations. If the risk profile is different, then the cost of capital should be adjusted to reflect this.

The timescale of the project

The project is evaluated over a five-year time frame, taking into account the tax effects, which is a long time in forecasting terms. In practice it is unlikely that the **same discount rate** will be **appropriate** to the **whole of this period**, and it would be helpful to adjust the current WACC for the expected movements in the general economic situation, and in particular the level of interest rates during that period.

The nature of the cash flows

Single values have been used for each element of the cash flow projections. In practice, each of the different elements is likely to be subject to **different levels of risk**. For example, the projected level of sales could be affected by the speed of technological change within the industry as well as by more general economic influences. We should therefore attempt to estimate the **levels of uncertainty** in the forecast cash flows. The most likely cash flows can then be reduced in line with our perceived risk aversion before being discounted at a rate appropriate to each year.

The sensitivities inherent in the project

It is likely that certain elements within the cash flow projections are more important than others in determining the eventual outcome of the project. It would therefore be useful to undertake some form of sensitivity analysis to identify both the key variables and the likely impact of their deviating from forecasts on the financial outcome of the project.

I would be happy to discuss any of these areas further with you, and look forward to receiving your comments.

19 PG plc

> **Top tips.** This question illustrates the two methods of performing international investment appraisal and why they should be the same. It also considers whether borrowing in Canadian dollars would be beneficial.

(a)

		Year 0	Year 1	Year 2	Year 3	Year 4
(i)	Method 1 C$					
	Initial investment	(150,000)				50,000
	Other cash flows		60,000	60,000	60,000	45,000
	Net cash flows	(150,000)	60,000	60,000	60,000	95,000
	C$ per £	1.700	1.785	1.874	1.968	2.066
		(88,235)	33,613	32,017	30,488	45,983
	4% pa discount factors	1.000	0.877	0.769	0.675	0.592
	Discounted £	(88,235)	29,479	24,621	20,579	27,222
	Cumulative discount £	(88,235)	(58,756)	(34,135)	(13,556)	13,666
(ii)	Method 2					
	C$ net cash flows as above	(150,000)	60,000	60,000	60,000	95,000
	19.7% pa discount factors	1.000	0.835	0.698	0.583	0.487
	Discounted C$	(150,000)	50,100	41,888	34,980	46,265
	Discounted £ (@ £/C$ 1.700)	(88,235)	29,479	24,621	20,579	27,222
	Cumulative discounted £	(88,235)	(58,756)	(34,135)	(13,556)	(13,666)

For the two approaches to yield the **same** net present value, the discount rate applied to the Canadian $ cash flows needs to be the combination of the sterling discount rate (14% pa) and the projected strengthening of the pound.

$$(1 + C\$ \text{ discount rate}) = (1 + £ \text{ discount rate}) \times \frac{\text{Exchange rate in 12 months £/C\$}}{\text{Spot rate £/C\$}}$$

$$= (1 + 0.14) \times \frac{1.785}{1.700} = 1.197$$

Therefore, C$ WACC = 19.7%

A forecast of a 5% per annum strengthening of the pound against the dollar will, generally, be associated with UK inflation rates/interest rates being 5% points per annum below the corresponding Canadian figures. It is surprising, therefore, to see that the Canadian cash flows are expected to be constant. It would be worth checking that they are nominal, and not inadvertently real.

(b) As the barriers to international trade come down, and globalisation becomes a reality, exchange rate risk management becomes a **higher priority** in financial management.

This particular project looks viable given the assumptions as regards future exchange rates. However, they are **only forecasts** and the actuals could turn out to be significantly different. If the pound were to **strengthen by more than forecast**, the value of the project to PG plc's shareholders would fall and could even become negative. If PG plc's managers are sufficiently **risk averse**, they may wish to protect the company's cash flows against that possibility.

Borrowing Canadian dollars (as opposed to allowing UK borrowings to rise) would offer such protection. If the pound were to strengthen, the number of pounds required to service/repay the loan would be fewer. Lower trading receipts, in other words, would be **offset** by lower financing payments.

The **interest rate** is likely to be different in the two countries. In the particular situation described, it could afford to be up to five percentage points per annum higher in Canada than in the UK before it adds to PG plc's costs. Interest payable is usually deductible in arriving at **taxable profits**, which could add further value.

The other side of the coin, however, is that financing a project in the local currency could reduce its value if the currencies move in the **opposite direction** to that feared. In this case, for example, choosing not to borrow in Canada would be seen to have been the right move if sterling **weakens** against the dollar.

It is most unlikely that additional UK equity would be raised for such a small (in the context of a plc) investment. It may, indirectly, affect the decision as to **how much dividend** to declare, but it is likely to be overwhelmed by other considerations.

20 Pressley plc

> **Top tips.** Make sure you know how to use purchasing power parity to forecast future exchange rates as this is required for this question. This question also tests the effect of double taxation on investment appraisal.

	Year 1	Year 2	Year 3	Year 4
€'000	1,400	2,200	2,500	2,800
€ tax @20%	(280)	(440)	(500)	(560)
Net remitted	1,120	1,760	2,000	2,240
@ Exchange rate (W1)	0.6135	0.5994	0.5857	0.5723
£ receipt	£687	£1,055	£1,171	£1,282
Further UK cash flows				
Lost contribution	(350)	(400)	(440)	(470)
Tax saving (30%)	105	120	132	141
UK tax on Euro contribution	(86)	(132)	(146)	(160)
Net relevant £	356	643	717	793
Discount factors @ 12%	0.893	0.797	0.712	0.636
Present Value	*318*	*512*	*511*	*504*
Cumulative PV				1,845
Investment (0.6279 × 2,500)				1,570
Net Present Value				275

Workings

(1) PPP

$$\text{Year 1} = 0.6279 \times \frac{1.023}{1.047} = 0.6135$$

$$\text{Year 2} = 0.6135 \times \frac{1.023}{1.047} = 0.5994$$

$$\text{Year 3} = 0.5994 \times \frac{1.023}{1.047} = 0.5857$$

$$\text{Year 4} = 0.5857 \times \frac{1.023}{1.047} = 0.5723$$

(2) *UK tax on overseas earnings*

Example year 1

	€
Overseas contribution	1,400
UK Tax liability	420
Double Tax Relief	280
Net UK charge	140

At exchange rate for year 1 (€/£ 0.6135) = £85.9. Note: use the exchange rate for the year of the profit *not* the tax payment.

Note. Taxing the euro cash flows at the **UK rate** of 30% gives the same answer.

If you use this method in the exam, you will need to state that because tax will ultimately be paid at the UK rate and the company does not care who it is paying tax to, then you are using the 30% tax rate.

Here are your cash flows using this method, they are the same in net terms as those presented at the top of the page:

€'000	Year 1	Year 2	Year 3	Year 4
	1,400	2,200	2,500	2,800
€ tax @30%	(420)	(660)	(750)	(840)
Net remitted	980	1,540	1,750	1,960
@ exch. Rate (W1)	0.6135	0.5994	0.5857	0.5723
£receipt	601	923	1,025	1,122
Lost contribution	(350)	(400)	(440)	(470)
Tax saving (30%)	105	120	132	141
Net relevant £	356	643	717	793

21 Fund restrictions

Top tips. In part (a) you should state any further assumptions that you make about the constraints on investment. The Profitability Index approach should be used. In part (c) it is helpful to consider the reasons why cash shortages may arise and to relate these to the capital budget constraints.

(a) It is assumed that the **restriction on investment** applies to the total period under consideration, and that this **amount cannot be incremented** after period 0 by using funds generated from the projects selected earlier. The projects will be ranked using the Profitability Index (PI), which is calculated as the NPV per $1 invested.

Project	NPV	Investment	PI	Ranking
	$'000	$'000	$'000	
A	14.22	150	0.0948	4
B	28.27	200	0.1414	1
C	21.74	175	0.1242	2
D	35.01	300	0.1167	3

On this basis, the company should invest $200,000 in project B, $175,000 in project C, and the remaining $75,000 in project D. This will generate an expected NPV of $67,515.

(b) If there are no fund restrictions and the projects are mutually exclusive, the company should select the project that has the **highest NPV** since this will make the greatest contribution to increasing the net worth of the business, and on this basis project D would be chosen.

(c) A period of capital rationing is often associated with more general problems of cash shortage. Possible reasons for this include the following.

   (i) The business has become **loss making** and is unable to cover the depreciation charge. Since one purpose of the depreciation charge is to allow for the cost of the assets used in the profit and loss account, the implication is that there will be insufficient cash with which to replace these assets when necessary.

   (ii) High inflation may mean that even though the business is profitable in historical cost terms, it is still **failing to generate sufficient funds** to replace assets.

   (iii) If the business is growing it may face a **shortage of working capital** with which to finance expansion, and this may result in a period of capital rationing.

   (iv) If the business is seasonal or cyclical it may face **times of cash shortage** despite being fundamentally sound. In this situation, there may be a periodic need for capital rationing.

   (v) A large one-off item of expenditure such as a property purchase may mean that the company faces a **temporary shortage of cash** for further investment.

A further reason for capital rationing arises in the situation where the company has more investment opportunities available than the funds allocated to the capital budget permit. This means that projects must be ranked for investment, taking into account both financial and strategic factors.

22 ANT

> **Top tips.** A table setting out each element of unit cost is helpful. When doing the NPV calculations it is important to show them, but show them in a way that minimises the writing you have to do. If you were not able to fit your answer to (a) across the page, you could have stated the discount factors at the start of the answer and then done the calculations. Note also that we have taken the short cut of using annuity factors. Don't forget the 'reclaiming of working capital' in year 5.
>
> In (b) you are using **total inflows** to calculate the profitability index, not net present value. When setting out your workings a column on cumulative outlay should help you ensure you take the correct proportion of the partial project.
>
> (c) starts off by stating the **assumptions**, and then goes on to discuss **complications** in which the NPV approach could not be used.

(a) The first step is to calculate the **annual contribution** from each project, together with the working capital cash flows. These cash flows, together with the initial outlay, can then be **discounted** at the **cost of capital** to arrive at the NPV of each project. Development costs already incurred are irrelevant. There are no additional administration costs associated with the projects, and depreciation is also irrelevant since it has no cash effect.

First, calculate annual contribution.

	A	B	C	D
Unit sales	150,000	75,000	80,000	120,000
	$	$	$	$
Selling price per unit	30.00	40.00	25.00	50.00
Material cost per unit	7.60	12.00	4.50	25.00
Labour cost per unit	9.80	12.00	5.00	10.00
Variable overheads per unit	6.00	7.00	2.50	10.50
	$'000	$'000	$'000	$'000
Sales per annum	4,500	3,000	2,000	6,000
Materials	1,140	900	360	3,000
Labour	1,470	900	400	1,200
Variable overheads	900	525	200	1,260
Annual contribution	990	675	1,040	540
	$'000	$'000	$'000	$'000
Working capital requirement (20% annual sales value)	900	600	400	1,200

It is assumed that working capital will be recovered at the end of year 5. The initial outlay will be made in year 0.

The NPV of each project can now be calculated.

Cash flows

Year	A		B		C		D		Discount
	Gross pa	Net	Gross pa	Net	Gross pa	Net	Gross pa	Net	Factor
	$'000	$'000	$'000	$'000	$'000	$'000	$'000	$'000	18%
0	(3,000)	(3,000)	(2,000)	(2,000)	(2,800)	(2,800)	(1,800)	(1,800)	1
1–4	990	2,663	675	1,816	1,040	2,798	540	1,453	2.690
5	1,890	826	1,275	557	1,440	629	1,740	760	0.437
		489		373		627		413	

(b) The **profitability** index provides a **means of optimising the NPV** when there are more projects available which yield a positive NPV than funds to invest in them. The profitability index measures the ratio of the present value of **cash inflows** to the **initial outlay** and represents the net present value per $1 invested.

Project	PV of inflows $'000	Initial outlay $'000	Ratio	Ranking
A	3,489	3,000	1.163	4
B	2,373	2,000	1.187	3
C	3,427	2,800	1.224	2
D	2,213	1,800	1.229	1

Project D has the highest PI ranking and is therefore the first choice for investment. On this basis the funds available should be invested as follows.

Project	Initial outlay $'000	Total NPV $'000	% taken	Cumulative outlay $'000	Actual NPV $'000
D	1,800	413	100	1,800	413
C	2,800	627	100	4,600	627
B	2,000	373	30	5,200	112
A	3,000	491	0	5,200	0
Total NPV generated					1,152

(c) The profitability index (PI) approach can be applied only if the projects under consideration fulfil certain criteria, as follows.

(i) There is **only one constraint on investment**, in this case capital. The PI ensures that maximum return per unit of scarce resource (capital) is obtained.

(ii) **Each investment** can be **accepted** or **rejected** in its entirety or alternatively accepted on a partial basis.

(iii) The NPV generated by a given project is **directly proportional** to the percentage of the investment undertaken.

(iv) Each investment can only be **made once** and not repeated.

(v) The company's aim is to **maximise overall NPV**.

If **additional funds** are **available** but at a higher cost, then the simple PI approach cannot be used since it is not possible to calculate unambiguous individual NPVs.

If certain of the projects that may be undertaken are **mutually exclusive** then **sub-problems** must be **defined** and **calculations made** for different combinations of projects. This can become a very lengthy process. These assumptions place limitations on the use of the ratio approach. It is not appropriate to multi-constraint situations when linear programming techniques must be used. Each project must be infinitely divisible and the company must accept that it may need to undertake a small proportion of a given project. This is frequently not possible in practice. It is also very unlikely that there is a simple linear relationship between the NPV and the proportion of the project undertaken; it is much more likely that there will be discontinuities in returns.

Possibly a more serious constraint is the assumption that the company's only concern is to **maximise NPV**. It is possible that there may be long-term strategic reasons which mean that an investment with a lower NPV should be undertaken instead of one with a higher NPV, and the ratio approach takes no account of the relative degrees of risk associated with making the different investments.

23 Trosoft

> **Top tips.** This question might look daunting in terms of where to start but remember an APV calculation always starts with the base case NPV and, if you use a clear layout and work through all the information methodically, you will gain marks throughout.

To: Directors of Trosoft
From: Financial Management Consultant

Report on the proposed diversification into Internet auctions

Introduction

Our assessment of the proposed investment takes into account **financial and non-financial factors** and considers the **effect of the diversification** on the **overall business strategy** of the company.

Time period of analysis

Four years of financial estimates were provided in your original brief. However, because the **IT infrastructure** underlying the project is expected to last six years before renewal is required, **the estimates have been extended to six years**, assuming that costs (apart from royalty payments and depreciation) and working capital rise at the current rate of inflation, 2% per year after year 4.

Method of analysis

The **adjusted present value** method has been used for the financial evaluation, first computing the base case NPV and then the PV of financial side effects.

Base case NPV

	Year 0 S$'000	Year 1 S$'000	Year 2 S$'000	Year 3 S$'000	Year 4 S$'000	Year 5 S$'000	Year 6 S$'000
Auction fees		4,300	6,620	8,100	8,200	8,364	8,531
Costs							
IT maintenance costs		1,210	1,850	1,920	2,125	2,168	2,211
Telephone costs		1,215	1,910	2,230	2,420	2,468	2,518
Wages		1,460	1,520	1,680	1,730	1,765	1,800
Salaries		400	550	600	650	663	676
Incremental head office overhead (W2)		50	55	60	65	66	68
Marketing	500	420	200	200	–	–	–
Royalty payments for use of technology	680	500	300	200	200	200	200
Lost contribution from other activities		80	80	80	–	–	–
Rental of premises		280	290	300	310	316	323
Tax allowable depreciation (W3)		540	432	432	432	432	432
	1,180	6,155	7,187	7,702	7,932	8,078	8,228
Profit before tax	(1,180)	(1,855)	(567)	398	268	286	303
Tax (24.5%)	289	454	139	(98)	(66)	(70)	(74)
	(891)	(1,401)	(428)	300	202	216	229
Add back depreciation:		540	432	432	432	432	432
Other outflows:							
IT infrastructure	(2,700)						
Working capital (W4)	(400)	(24)	(24)	(25)	(26)	(10)	509
Net flows	(3,991)	(885)	(20)	707	608	638	1,170
Discount factors at 10% (W5)	1	0.909	0.826	0.751	0.683	0.621	0.564
Present values	(3,991)	(804)	(17)	531	415	396	660

The expected base case NPV is **(S$2,810,000)**.

Workings

(1) The market research cost has been left out of the computation, as it is a sunk cost.

(2) Only incremental head office overheads have been included. Other allocated overheads are irrelevant.

(3) Depreciation = $\frac{2,700}{5}$ = 540 Year 1 and $\frac{(2,700-540)}{5}$ = 432 in Years 2–6.

(4) Working capital in Year 5 is assumed to increase by the 2% inflation rate. Accumulated working capital at Year 4 = 400 + 24 + 24 + 25 + 26 = 499. 2% × 499 = 10. Total working capital at Year 5 (509) is assumed to be released at the end of Year 6.

(5) **Cost of equity**

For the base case NPV the ungeared cost of equity has been used for the new project as the discount rate. To find this we ungeared the average equity beta of companies in the internet auction sector to find the asset beta:

Assuming corporate debt to be virtually risk free:

$\beta_a = \beta_e E/[E + D](1 - t)]$

$\beta_a = 1.42 \times 67/[67 + 33 (1 - 0.245)] = 1.035$

Using CAPM

$K_{eu} = R_f + (R_m - R_f) \beta_a$

$K_{eu} = 4\% + (9.5\% - 4\%) 1.035 = 9.69\%$

We have approximated this result to 10% as the discount rate for the base case NPV computation.

Financing side effects

Tax shield (tax relief on interest payments)

The six year term loan covers IT infrastructure S$2.7 million plus working capital S$0.4 million = S$3.1 million.

The interest rate is 4.5%.

Annual interest = S$3.1m × 4.5% = S$139,500

Annual tax relief = 24.5% × S$139,500 = S$34,177

Discount this at the risk free rate 4%

The present value of tax relief for six years is: S$34,177 × 5.242 = S$179,156

Alternatively the tax shield could be based upon the percentage debt capacity of the company.

Issue costs

Issue costs are S$3,100,000 × 1.5% = **S$46,500**

Adjusted present value

The estimated APV of the investment is –S$2,810,000 + S$179,156 – S$46,500 = (S$2,677,344)

Results of evaluation

On the basis of the financial estimates made, the **investment is not worthwhile**, having a large negative adjusted present value. Alternative investment opportunities are likely to produce much better results, and should be investigated. However, the negative APV of this project is subject to a **large margin of error**, as there are major potential benefits and uncertainties that have not been valued in the computation, such as **realisable value**, or **benefits after six years**.

The discount rate used is based on the **capital asset pricing model**, which has a number of theoretical weaknesses. However, any errors in the discount rate are probably immaterial compared with **uncertainties in the cash flows** themselves. Some of the **cash flow estimates** may be **wrong** because of **lack of underlying information**. More information should be obtained to substantiate the forecast sales figures, and **sensitivity** and/or **simulation analysis** should be used to investigate the impact of different assumptions on net cash flows.

Other factors

Real options

There are several possible alternatives that have not been brought into the evaluation. These will add value as real options. They include the **option to sell the project as a going concern** at various points in its life (a **put option**), the **option to increase investment and market share**, and the **option to cross-sell other company products** to the project's clientele (**call options**). Although valuing these options is difficult, it is better to attempt an estimate rather than ignore their value altogether.

Lack of experience

The company has **no experience in this field of business** and may make **management mistakes** as it goes through the learning curve. For example, there may be **technological problems or legal regulations** that have not been fully explored. Also, marketing and pricing may prove difficult if existing suppliers decide to react to the **increased competition**.

Strategic considerations

Before engaging in a different market sector it is always wise to **revisit the company's overall business strategy**. A major risk is that this investment may divert management resources from the core business and cause long-term problems.

24 Feasibility study

> **Top tips.** This question may seem rather peripheral to the *Financial Strategy* syllabus but feasibility studies are a key stage in project implementation and control that you do need to consider. Feasibility studies should identify the wider relevant costs and benefits that you may also have to discuss.

(a) A computer feasibility study is intended to evaluate the appropriateness of computerising an application which had been accomplished manually or by using another system. It is intended to accomplish three things.

  (i) **Assess the information processing requirements** found in an application.

  (ii) **Identify and investigate various alternatives** which could satisfy the requirements identified.

  (iii) **Inform management** about the options and the costs, benefits, technology, risks, labour implications etc of each.

(b) **The assessment of needs provides the foundation for all other analysis.** Here one identifies what tasks are to be computerised and quantifies the requirements in terms of volume, speed, accuracy, security etc. Without this understanding of what the system will need to do it is most unlikely that an effective or economical system will be obtained. This phase looks primarily at the **functions to be performed** and the required performance standards.

  Given the required tasks and performance standards a **variety of alternatives** may be reviewed and compared. The objective here is to keep an open mind and consider a full range of options. Several options might satisfy all performance criteria and then be referred to management for a final decision, perhaps with a recommendation for one.

  The information provided to management on costs, benefits, etc allows them to consider any systems acquisition, development or upgrade. This information allows systems to be **compared more effectively**.

(c) The study would normally be carried out by a **feasibility study team**. This team would include:

  (i) Someone from the **software house** having a detailed knowledge of computers and systems design

  (ii) One or two **senior managers** having a detailed knowledge of the workings and staff of the departments affected

  (iii) An **accountant** to carry out cost-benefit analyses of the proposed system, and prepare a detailed budget for installing it

(d) The best solution for the organisation is best identified through a thorough **investigation**, as would be provided by the feasibility study. The understanding gained by studying an existing system and formalising its operation **will aid in designing** a new system, or in **developing a specification** for one. Any purchase of a package without first developing **a sound specification** is likely to leave the company with a system unsuited to their needs.

(e) Four factors which would justify **introducing a new computer system** for production planning and scheduling would be these.

  (i) **Better control over the handling of customer orders** so that these are dealt with more expeditiously.

  (ii) **Improved production planning** to allow the company to fill orders more effectively and deliver production in a more timely fashion.

  (iii) **Inventories will be more closely monitored** and improved production planning will reduce the amount of work in progress. These reductions will reduce the company's need for working capital to yield a direct improvement in cash flow.

  (iv) By improving its production scheduling it will find that **better use of both equipment and labour will result**. This will improve profits, perhaps significantly.

25 Bases of valuation

> **Top tips.** For this question it is important not only to be able to use the various valuation methods required, but also to know the limitations of each method. In an exam question it is likely that you will need to recommend a realistic purchase price for a company.

(a) (i) **Statement of financial position value** = £454,100

(ii) **Replacement cost value** = £454,100 + £(725,000 − 651,600) + £(550,000 − 515,900) = £561,600

(iii) **Realisable value** = £454,100 + £(450,000 − 651,600) + (570,000 − 515,900) − £14,900 = £291,700

Bad debts are 2% × £745,000 = £14,900. Bad debts are assumed not to be relevant to statement of financial position and replacement cost values.

(iv) The **dividend growth model value** depends on an estimate of growth, which is far from clear given the wide variations in earnings over the five years.

1 The lowest possible value, assuming zero growth, is as follows.

$$\text{Value} = \frac{£25,000}{0.12} = £208,333$$

It is not likely that this will be the basis taken.

2 Looking at dividend growth over the past five years we have:

20X4 dividend = £25,000

20X0 dividend = £20,500

If the annual growth rate in dividends is g

$$(1 + g)^4 = \frac{(25,000)}{20,500} = 1.2195$$

$$1 + g = 1.0508$$

$$g = 0.0508, \text{ say } 5\%$$

Then, MV ex div = $\dfrac{\text{Dividend in 1 year}}{0.12 - g}$

$$= \frac{25,000(1.05)}{0.07}$$

$$= £375,000$$

3 Using the rb model, we have:

Average proportion retained = $\dfrac{12,800 + 44,200 + 18,300 + 13,400 + 27,000}{33,300 + 66,800 + 43,300 + 38,400 + 52,200}$

= 0.495 (say b = 0.5)

$$\text{Return on investment this year} = \frac{53{,}200}{\text{average investment}}$$

$$= \frac{53{,}200}{(454{,}100 + 454{,}100 - 27{,}200)/2}$$

$$= 0.1208 \text{ (say r = 12\%).}$$

Then g = 0.5 × 12% = 6%

So MV ex div = $\frac{25{,}000(1.06)}{0.06}$ = £441,667

(v) *P/E ratio model*

Comparable quoted companies to Manon Ltd have P/E ratios of about 10. Manon is much smaller and being unquoted, its P/E ratio would be less than 10, but how much less?

If we take a P/E ratio of 5, we have MV = £53,200 × 5 = £266,000

If we take a P/E ratio of 10 × ²/₃, we have MV = £53,200 × 10 × ²/₃ = £354,667

If we take a P/E ratio of 10, we have MV = £532,000

(b) (i) *The statement of financial position value*

The statement of financial position value should not play a part in the negotiation process. **Historical costs** are **not relevant** to a decision on the future value of the company.

(ii) *The replacement cost*

This gives the cost of setting up a **similar business**. Since this gives a higher figure than any other valuation in this case, it could show the **maximum price** for Carmen to offer. There is clearly no goodwill to value.

(iii) *The realisable value*

This shows the cash which the shareholders in Manon could get by **liquidating the business**. It is therefore the **minimum price** which they would accept.

All the methods (i) to (iii) suffer from the limitation that they do not look at the **going concern value** of the business as a whole. Methods (iv) and (v) do consider this value. However, the realisable value is of use in assessing the risk attached to the business as a going concern, as it gives the base value if things go wrong and the business has to be abandoned.

(iv) *The dividend model*

The figures have been calculated using Manon's k_e (12%). The relevance of a dividend valuation to Carmen will depend on whether the **current retention** and **reinvestment policies** would be continued. Certainly the value to Carmen should be based on 9% rather than 12%. Both companies are **ungeared** and in the same **risk class** so the different required returns must be due to their **relative sizes** and the fact that Carmen's shares are more **marketable**.

One of the main limitations on the dividend growth model is the problem of estimating the **future value of g**.

(v) *The P/E ratio model*

The P/E ratio model is an attempt to get at the value which the **market** would put on a company like Manon. It does provide an external yardstick, but is a very crude measure. As already stated, the P/E ratio which applies to larger quoted companies must be **lowered** to allow for the size of Manon and the non-marketability of its shares. Another limitation of P/E ratios is that the ratio is very dependent on the expected future growth of the firm. It is therefore not easy to find a P/E ratio of a 'similar firm'.

(c) The minimum price which the shareholders of Manon will accept will be the realisable value of the assets, **£291,700**. The **maximum price** Carmen will pay is the earnings basis using a P/E of 10 at **£532,000**.

The dividend basis gives a value of about 5% gives a value of £375,000. This looks optimistic given the lack of dividend growth over the last couple of years.

So the eventual purchase price will probably be in the range £291,700 and £375,000.

26 Perseus

> **Top tips.** If you struggled on either part of this question, you should go back over the material again, as valuation will occur in practically every sitting, often in the compulsory question. Remember that the examiner will never just want you to carry out valuation calculations. You should **always** comment on the methods you use, even if you are not explicitly asked to in the question as you are here.

(a) (i) *Net assets basis*

	$m
Freehold land and buildings	104.2
Fixtures and fittings	3.5
Motor vehicles	0.4
Inventory	58.0
Trade receivables	23.4
Cash	21.5
Trade payables	(25.9)
Tax	(5.4)
Bonds	(49.0)
Net assets	130.7

$$\text{Value per share} = \frac{\$130.7m}{50m} = \$2.61 \text{ per share}$$

(ii) *Dividend yield basis*

$$\text{Dividend per share in Perseus (gross)} = \frac{\$3.3m \times 10/9}{50m} = 7.33 \text{ c}$$

It is assumed that this dividend will remain constant in future years.

Gross dividend yield of Tityus = 2.2%

Adjust upwards for lesser marketability/greater risk of an unlisted company - say 2.6%*

$$\text{Value per share in Perseus} = \frac{\text{Dividend per share}}{\text{Dividend yield}} = \frac{0.073}{0.026} = \$2.81 \text{ per share}$$

*(Alternatively, since this is a very arbitrary adjustment, it would be acceptable to use the unadjusted yield to get a value of $3.22, then add a note to acknowledge that this is likely to be an over-valuation.)

(iii) *Price/earnings ratio basis*

$$\text{Earnings per share of Perseus} = \frac{\$10.7m}{50m} = 21.4c$$

P/E ratio of Tityus = 20.5

Adjust downwards for lesser marketability/ greater risk of an unlisted company – say 15**

Value per share in Perseus = $0.214 × 15 = $3.21

**(A similar note to that at the end of (ii) applies here, with an unadjusted value of $4.39)

(b) **Net assets basis**

The **net assets (liquidation)** basis is a method of valuation that can be used if the company is to be liquidated and the individual assets sold off to pay the shareholders. If the company is a going concern then the actual business **should be worth** a lot more than the break up value of the assets, due to the future earnings and cash flows of the business and unrecorded assets such as goodwill. Therefore if the business is to be sold as a going concern then the net asset value is far too low a value. However it can be used as a bottom line figure to give an indication of the absolute lowest figure that could be accepted from a bidder.

Dividend yield basis

The **dividend yield method** of valuation is a conceptually sounder method of valuation for a business that is being valued as a going concern. The dividend valuation model is used to find the **present value of future dividends** based on the shareholders' required dividend yield.

However there are a number of problems with this method. Firstly **a suitable dividend yield** has to be determined. It is possible, as above, to use the published dividend yield of a similar listed company; however when valuing the shares of a private company the dividend yield must be adjusted upwards to reflect the lack of marketability of private company shares and the increased perceived risk compared to a listed company. This adjustment is arbitrary. In addition, the published dividend yield will incorporate an **expected level of growth** (the higher the growth the lower the yield) which may not match growth expectations in the company to be valued.

Secondly a **suitable dividend figure** must be used. This could be the latest year's dividend, an average of a number of past years or an estimate of the actual future dividends.

There is a further problem with the use of the dividend yield for the valuation of an entire company. The dividend yield method is suitable for the **valuation of a small holding** in a company but if the entire company is to be purchased then the new owners may have an entirely different dividend policy and therefore it is the earnings of the company rather than the dividends which are of importance.

Price/earnings method

The price/earnings method of valuation is therefore a good method to use for the purchase of an entire company as it is based upon the last reported earnings of the company.

Again however there are problems with **determining an appropriate price/earnings ratio** and sustainable earnings. The price/earnings ratio of a similar listed company can be used but as with the dividend yield this must be adjusted to reflect the **lack of marketability**, increased risk and difference in growth expectations. This time however the adjustment should be downwards and is again an arbitrary one. The earnings figure that is used could be the current earnings figure, an average of a number of years past earnings or the future earnings that the purchaser expects from the company.

27 Gasco

> **Top tips.** This case study is a welcome change to most 'general questions' on mergers and takeovers as it provides a lot of detail for use as illustrations of synergy, stakeholder expectations and post-merger problems. You should state the general principles involved and illustrate them with examples drawn from the question.

(a) There is frequently a mix of good and bad reasons behind a takeover bid. Amongst the good reasons, the most significant is the possibility of creating **synergy,** which means that the value of cash flows from the combined business is higher than the value of cash flows from the two individual businesses. Although CarCare and Gasco are in different market sectors, there are a number of areas which may generate synergy.

(i) **Elimination of duplicated resources**. The most obvious areas are the marketing systems, the call centre systems and local offices and training facilities for mobile repair/emergency staff. Head office overheads may also be reduced.

(ii) **Cross-selling**. Opportunities exist to cross-sell products to customers on the other company's database.

(iii) **Building a critical mass** for non-core business. This might apply to the financial services areas of both businesses. The credit card and insurance businesses may gain from a combined brand name.

(iv) **Reduction in the risk of the company's cash flow profile**. CarCare receives membership subscriptions in advance, whereas Gasco's customers will pay mainly in arrears. The combined cash flows will be perceived as less risky by shareholders and lenders.

(v) The takeover of CarCare will **abolish its mutual status** and will allow equity funds for expansion to be raised more easily, by share issues made by the parent company, reducing the cost of capital.

Amongst the many possible bad reasons for takeover are:

(i) The directors of Gasco **seeking the prestige** of a larger company
(ii) Diversification with **no real strategic objective**
(iii) Gasco using up surplus cash, **again with no strategic objective**

(b) **Stakeholders**

The major stakeholders of CarCare are its members, who are both owners and customers, its directors and employees, and its creditors. Competitors will also be highly interested in the takeover.

Members

The members will have **mixed reactions.** The replacement of mutual status with marketable equity shares or cash will give them an immediate **'windfall' gain,** which many will welcome. However, the cost of this is **lost influence** on the future direction of CarCare. As customers, many may fear a reduction in the quality of service, particularly in the light of increased competition in the market and the fact that GasCo has to demonstrate that it is making a **return on its investment**. Others may disagree, on the basis that Gasco will be able to raise money for expansion, modernisation and improvements more easily than CarCare could as a mutual organisation.

CarCare's directors have a duty to ensure that they act in the **best interest** of **members.** However they will also be concerned about their own positions after the takeover and will wish to seek suitable positions in the new company's management structure. Some may fear loss of their jobs.

Employees

Employees will have **mixed reactions** depending on whether they are likely to be presented with additional opportunities or loss of status or redundancy. There is likely to be some **rationalisation** of the workforce except for those with highly specific skills, and for those who remain there may also be the threat of relocation. Employees will be seeking answers to these questions before the takeover happens, but are unlikely to receive comprehensive answers.

Creditors

Creditors, including bankers, will probably be **happy** with the **merger** provided that Gasco has no financial problems.

Competitors

Some competitors will fear that they will **lose market share** if the takeover enables new finance for expansion, improvement and marketing of CarCare. Others will be more optimistic, believing that CarCare will become less sensitive to the needs of customers.

(c) Gasco may face a number of problems after the takeover has been achieved.

    (i) Former members of Gasco who did not agree with the takeover, and who may have been actively resisting it, may decide to **change their service provider** to another organisation. The parent company will have to be pro-active in giving confidence to all its CarCare customers.

    (ii) The two organisations probably had **different management styles**, Gasco being a stock exchange quoted company with a clear need for financial results and CarCare being more orientated to serving its customers and acting as a pressure group to represent their needs. Conflicts may arise between directors, managers and employees of CarCare after the takeover as a result of an enforced change in management style from Gasco.

    (iii) Actual and feared redundancies, relocations, changes in work practice, training methods and other problems may **demotivate CarCare employees,** causing resistance and a drop in productivity. In this respect, delays in information provision and decision making can make the situation worse.

    (iv) **Competitors may take advantage** of reorganisation problems at CarCare in order to gain market share.

28 Olivine

Top tips. Our answer to part (a)(ii) assumes that the administrative savings have been achieved. Otherwise the answer to (a)(ii) is £(25 + 9.6)m/60m = 57.7 pence per share, and subsequent answers also change.

(a) (i) **The total value of the share offer**

Earnings per share = £25m/40m = £0.625

P/E ratio = 20

Share price = 20 × £0.625 = £12.50 per share

Share offer = 5 shares × (16m shares/4) = 20m shares issued

Value of share offer = £12.50 × 20 million = £250 million

(ii) **Olivine earnings per share**

Earnings = £25m + £9.6m + £2.4m = £37.0m

Number of shares = 40m + 20m = 60 million

Earnings per share = £37.0m/60m = 61.7 pence per share

(iii) **Share price of Olivine**

Earnings per share (part ii) = 61.7 pence per share

Price earnings ratio = 20 × (100 − 5)% = 19

Share price = 19 × £0.617 = £11.72 per share

(b) **Effect on wealth of shareholders**

Olivine shareholders

Original holding = 40m shares @ £12.50 per share = £500m

New share price = £11.72

New share value = 40m shares @ £11.72 = £468.8m

Loss in shareholder wealth = £500m − £468.8m = £31.2m or 6.24%

Halite shareholders

Original earnings per share = £9.6m/16m shares = £0.60

Price/earnings ratio = 15

Share price = 15 × £0.60 = £9.00 per share

Original holding = 16m shares @ £9.00 = £144m

New holding = 20m shares @ £11.72 = £234.4m

Gain in shareholder wealth = £234.4m – £144m = £90.4m or 62.78%

(c) The **market capitalisation** of the separate businesses is (40m × £12.50) + (16m × £9.00) = £644m. When combined the market capitalisation will be 60m × £11.72 = £703.2m so there are benefits to be gained in overall terms.

Effect on share price

The **total share value** of Halite prior to the acquisition is £144 million. However the intended share issue by Olivine of 20 million shares has a value at Olivine's current share price of £250 million. The issue of so many shares to achieve this premium means that there is a small reduction in the size of the earnings per share of Olivine even when the earnings of Halite and the benefits of the acquisition are taken into account. This reduction in earnings per share together with a 5% reduction in the price/earnings ratio of Olivine after the acquisition would lead to a reduction in Olivine's share price from £12.50 per share before the acquisition to £11.72 per share after the acquisition. The estimate of the revised P/E ratio is possibly too high and needs further scrutiny.

This reduction in share value for Olivine shareholders would **result in a loss in shareholder value** from the acquisition of £31.2 million (6.24%). In contrast the generous premium being considered for the shares of Halite would lead to an increase in the value of the shares held by former Halite plc shareholders of £90.4 million (62.78%).

Beneficiaries of offer

If the proposed offer is made all of the benefit of the acquisition will accrue to the Halite plc shareholders and the Olivine shareholders will suffer a loss in share value. However, the dividend per share for Halite shareholders is likely to be lower in the future than it is at present.

The directors of Olivine might wish to consider a less generous offer than the current premium of £106 million (£250m – £144m) on the purchase of Halite. For example a share for share exchange would value the offer at £200 million (16 million shares @ £12.50 per share) thereby still providing a substantial premium to the Halite shareholders but with no loss to the Olivine shareholders.

29 K and H

> **Top tips.** The stages used in (a) are:
>
> - Calculate combined earnings
> - Calculate earnings per share
> - Calculate p/e ratio using share price given in the question
>
> and then comment on the lack of realism, suggesting a better method.
>
> Note in (b) that the 240p estimate is an assumption which should be questioned.
>
> In (c) you have to find out what the excess (premium) on acquisition is, and compare it with the change in earnings that will result from the acquisition. The key to (d) is explaining the significance of the enhancement in size.

(a)

	K	H
Earnings	£5,180,000	£2,340,000
EPS	14.8p	29.25p
Number of shares	35,000,000	8,000,000

An offer of three shares in K for two shares in H would result in the equity of K increasing to 47,000,000 shares.

In order to establish how the estimated post-acquisition market price of K was reached, we must look at **P/E ratios**.

	K	H
Pre-acquisition price	222	322
EPS	14.8	29.25
P/E ratio, pre-acquisition	15	11

The post-acquisition earnings, assuming no synergy or growth, would be (5,180 + 2,340) £7,520,000 or (÷ 47 million shares) 16p a share.

The estimated post-acquisition share price of K is 240p. On the assumption that the post-acquisition EPS is 16p, the P/E ratio would be 15.

It would therefore seem that the estimated post-acquisition market price of K shares has been derived by applying the **pre-acquisition P/E ratio** of K to an estimated post-acquisition EPS (assuming no profits growth through synergy).

The estimated post-acquisition equivalent market value of an old H share is 1.5 times 240 pence, because three K shares will be exchanged for two H shares, giving a relative value of 3:2 or 1.5.

These estimates cannot be realistic, because it is incorrect to assume that on a takeover where neither company is minuscule relative to the other, the post-acquisition P/E ratio will be the same as the pre-acquisition P/E ratio of the more highly rated company in the takeover.

K is hoping to take over a public company with a **lower P/E ratio** than its own, and its directors must expect K's post-acquisition P/E ratio to fall accordingly.

A better estimate of the post acquisition P/E ratio would be the *weighted average* of their pre-acquisition P/Es as follows.

	Earnings £'000		Market value £'000
K	5,180	(35m × 222p)	77,700
H	2,340	(8m × 322p)	25,760
Combined	7,520		103,460

Weighted average P/E ratio $\dfrac{103{,}460}{7{,}520} = 13.758$

Applying this to a post-acquisition EPS of 16p, an estimated post-acquisition market price of K shares would be (13.758 × 16p) 220p each. This would make the post-acquisition equivalent MV of an old H share (220 × 1.5) = 330p.

There would be a very slight gain for H shareholders at the expense of K shareholders, but not much. This is because the share exchange ratio of three for two reflects almost exactly the pre-acquisition market prices per share of 322:222 = 1.45 or nearly 1.50, which is 3:2.

(b)
	£'000
Value of 35 million K shares:	
Estimated post-acquisition value (× 240p)	84,000
Pre-acquisition value (× 222p)	77,700
Gain to K shareholders from acquisition (× 18p)	6,300

K could raise its offer by £6,300,000 without reducing the wealth of its shareholders, but only assuming that the 240p estimate of the post-acquisition share price is correct. This extra value might be offered in **cash** (£0.7875 per share in H) or in **more shares** in K.

(c) The pre-acquisition market value of K is unchanged at 222p, and so a two-for-one share exchange offer would value each share in H at 444p as well, compared with its current 322p.

	£'000
Offer value for 8,000,000 shares in H (× 444p)	35,520
Current value of 8,000,000 shares in H (× 322p)	25,760
Excess	9,760

The revised offer would only maintain the wealth of current shareholders if the combined share values of the post-acquisition company were to increase by at least £9,760,000.

It is assumed that the value of the post-acquisition company will be increased by the NPV of the asset disposals, savings in running costs and extra redundancy costs, discounted at K's cost of capital of 14% per year.

Year	Item	Amount £'000	Discount factor @ 14%	Present value £'000
0	Redundancy costs	(3,500)	1.000	(3,500.0)
1	Redundancy costs	(8,400)	0.877	(7,366.8)
1	Fixed asset disposals	7,200	0.877	6,314.4
1 – ∞	Savings in running costs	2,750	(1 ÷ 0.14) = 7.14	19,642.9
			Net present value	15,090.5

We might therefore conclude that because of redundancies and rationalisation, the combined value of the post-acquisition companies will increase by about £15,000,000 which is more than the £9,760,000 needed to fund the extra price being offered for their shares to H shareholders. Of the increase in share values, H shareholders would benefit by the first £9,760,000, leaving the remaining £5,240,000 to be shared between all shareholders in the post-acquisition company.

A **two for one offer** should therefore be made.

(d) Assuming no increase in total post-acquisition earnings, the group will have a fairly low interest cover ratio. The interest cover in the 'old' K is (12,400 ÷ 4,431) 2.8 times and in the 'old' H is (5,800 ÷ 2,200) = 2.6 times. In the combined company it will be (12,400 + 5,800) ÷ (4,431 + 2,200) = 2.75 times.

Although we do not have statement of financial position details, this low interest cover indicates **high gearing**, and the cost of the existing debt capital might therefore be high.

The takeover will create an **enlarged company**, and because of this, it is fairly reasonable to assume that the **risk of default** will be less than with either of the 'old' companies taken individually. This **reduction in default risk**, if perceived to be significant, might reduce the return that investors in debt capital seek from the company. A reduction in the required return on marketable fixed interest capital would raise its **market value**. In this respect, the acquisition would have some effect on the **market value** of K's debt.

Of course, K's debt might be **non-marketable bank loans** and **overdrafts**, in which case the acquisition would not have any effect on the market value of the debt, since such debt has no market value.

30 Premoco

> **Top tips.** This is a wide-ranging question that requires a good all-round grasp of the factors involved in the acquisition decision. In part (a) set out your ratio calculations clearly and make sure you recognise when there is a need to ungear and gear betas. In part (b) you must comment on each method. In part (c) there is no one right or wrong answer. Follow the question requirements directly in the report.

(a) (i) *Current market values and P/E ratios*

The market value of the company's shares (market capitalisation) is the share price multiplied by the number of shares in issue.

The P/E ratio (price/earnings ratio) is the share price divided by the latest earnings per share.

No figures are available for Carsals, which is a private company.

	Premoco	Nafco	Oiltrans
Share price (pence)	1,648	675	1,530
Number of issued shares (million)	20	10	12
Total market value of shares (£ million)	329.6	67.5	183.6
Earnings per share (pence)	103	75	85
P/E ratio	16	9	18

(ii) *Cost of equity (k_e) using the CAPM (capital asset pricing model)*

This is given by: $k_e = R_f + (R_m - R_f)\beta_g$

The market return, R_m, is 12% and the risk free rate, R_f, is 6%. The equity beta factor (β_g) for the first three companies is given directly, but for Carsals it is estimated by de-gearing the equity beta of a similar quoted company to get the asset beta or ungeared beta, β_u. This is because Carsals has no debt in its capital structure.

The no tax formula is $\beta_u = \beta_g \dfrac{V_E}{V_E + V_D}$

Thus for Carsals $\beta_u = 1.25 \times \dfrac{80}{80+20} = 1.0$

	Premoco	Nafco	Oiltrans	Carsals
Beta factor	1.2	0.9	1.3	1.0
Cost of equity = 6% + (12% – 6%)β	13.2%	11.4%	13.8%	12.0%

(iii) *Prospective market value using the constant growth dividend valuation model*

The formula is $P_0 = \dfrac{d_1}{k_e - g}$ where d_1 (next year's dividend) $= d_0 (1 + g)$.

	Premoco	Nafco	Oiltrans	Carsals
Latest dividend per share (d_0) (pence)	31	55	42	112
Expected growth, g	11%	5%	14%	9%
Next year's dividend, d_1 (pence)	34.41	57.75	47.88	122.08
Estimated value per share $d_1/(k_e - g)$ (£)	15.64	9.02	N/A	40.69
Number of issued shares (million)	20	10		0.5
Total prospective market capitalisation (£m)	312.8	90.2		20.3

(b) **Usefulness of the three types of valuation in the acquisition decision**

Summarised values for the four companies

	Premoco	Nafco	Oiltrans	Carsals
	£m	£m	£m	£m
Current market value	329.6	67.5	183.6	N/A
Prospective market value	312.8	90.2	N/A	20.3
Net asset value	250	60	65	6

(i) *Current market value method*

(1) The **current market value** shows the value of each of the listed companies to its existing shareholders. The efficient market hypothesis (semi-strong form) implies that the market value of each company is the best estimate of its fundamental value, based on public information. Despite criticisms of the EMH, there is a large body of evidence which shows that the **semi-strong form** is substantially correct. However, when making an acquisition decision, Premoco is concerned with the value of each target company to itself, not to that company's existing shareholders. Adjustments may therefore be needed

(2) During the negotiations, information which is not known to the public may emerge. This will cause Premoco to adjust its valuations. Premoco may also have plans for **generating synergy** when it combines a new business with its own (eg by elimination of duplicated assets and costs). This will affect the value of the new business to Premoco. However, extreme caution must be exercised when using estimates of synergy to adjust market values, because the market may already have anticipated the merger taking place and may have increased the price of the target company to allow for possible synergy. This effect can make the market values of companies unreliable if takeover rumours start.

(3) Premoco will probably find it necessary to offer a price higher than the **existing market** value in order to induce target company shareholders to sell.

(4) There is, of course, no market value for the private company, which cannot be valued by this method.

(ii) *Dividend valuation method*

The **prospective value based on the constant growth dividend valuation model** is one method of attempting to compute the fundamental going concern value of the business from basic data concerning the company. The model itself is, however, very crude, assuming that dividend growth will be at a constant rate to perpetuity. More complex versions of this model exist where **varying growth rates** can **be postulated**. In particular, the model becomes meaningless if g exceeds the cost of equity and very unreliable when the two figures are close together, as for Premoco itself.

(iii) *Net asset values*

The **net asset values** of the companies are probably based on **historical** cost, although some oil companies do use a current cost basis for reporting.

(1) **Historical cost**

In terms of relevance for an acquisition, historical cost is irrelevant except as an approximation to either net realisable value or current cost.

(2) **Current cost**

Current cost, or replacement cost, is useful in showing the cost of setting up a similar business from scratch but it is *not* a valuation of the business concerned. It ignores goodwill and intangible assets and, if Premoco did decide to set up a competing business from scratch, the original target company would still exist as a competitor.

(3) **Net realisable value**

Net realisable values of the business assets are probably the most useful asset figures which can be provided. This is obviously true if the business is acquired to be broken up but NRV asset values are also useful when viewing the business as a going concern: the break-up value of the business shows the worst-case scenario if the business is acquired as a going concern but fails. In other words, it is NRV which should be used as the basis of the 'asset backing' calculation, not historical cost.

(iv) *Conclusion*

In practice the businesses cannot be valued separately if they are going to be joined together, and a valuation method may well involve a combination of computing the present value of future improved operating cash flows together with the net realisable value of assets which are to be sold. The company will find the 'estimated NPV of the combined organisation' more useful than any of the stand-alone valuations of the businesses.

(c) **To:** David Wong
From: Financial Adviser
Date: 12 November 20X7
Subject: Report on three possible acquisitions available to Premoco

Introduction

I have examined the information which you have supplied to me on the three potential acquisitions and set out my views on the strategic implications of each, bearing in mind your **wish to diversify away from petroleum**. Relevant calculations are shown in the Appendix. I have assumed that the existing market value of Premoco, £329.6 million, is a fair estimate of its true value.

Nafco

(i) *Price to be offered*

(1) On the basis of the financial advisers' figures (see Appendix), the combination will increase equity earnings by £3.9 million and creates added value (synergy) of £114.9 million (29%). The **absolute maximum price** which can be paid for Nafco is £182.4 million, which is £18.24 per share. The minimum that can be offered is the existing market price of £6.75 per share. You should not of course offer the maximum price. If the shareholders of Premoco are to get their fair share of value added from the merger, they should not pay more than 29% more than the current market price per share of Nafco. This gives a price of **£8.71 per share** (£87.1 million in total).

(2) A **suggested range for negotiation** is therefore £7 to £9 per share. If your intelligence is correct, Nafco's institutional shareholders would be pleased to accept a reasonable offer from a more up-market firm like yours and there should be no reason to go above the figure of £8.71 unless a competing bid emerges.

(ii) *Suggested terms of the offer*

(1) A price of £87.1 million could be financed substantially by cash in the bank but this would leave no investment funds for improving Nafco's operations. If you wish to pursue the cash route, you will need to borrow over the medium or long term. The gearing of Premoco is not high and borrowing will not be a problem, but you must recognise that **group gearing** will **increase** if this acquisition is made, because Nafco's **debt ratio** is much **higher** than your own.

(2) If you intend to borrow, one option is to take up the supplier's offer of cheap loan finance in return for a long-term supply agreement. Acceptance of the offer would reduce Premoco's cost of capital. However, the decision on this source of finance should not be regarded as **part of the acquisition decision**. It is something which needs to be investigated in its own right as it would involve a major **change in strategy** from the existing policy of buying petrol in the open market.

(3) The alternative to increasing borrowing is to **issue shares** in Premoco to the shareholders of Nafco (a share-for-share swap). The share price of Premoco (£16.48) is roughly twice the offer price for Nafco, so the terms of the offer would be approximately 1 for 2. This would have the advantage of **keeping gearing low** and would probably be very acceptable to the disaffected institutional shareholders of Nafco, who would be able to retain their investment in the petroleum industry and maintain the balance of their portfolios. However, the transactions costs of share issues are much higher than for borrowing. Share issues become more obviously advantageous for larger acquisitions.

(iii) *Business implications*

(1) The acquisition of Nafco would result in **horizontal integration expanding** the company's operations in **retailing of petroleum** and expanding the company's market share. Large economies of scale could be generated, which accounts for the very high synergy expected from the merger. A choice needs to be made as to whether Nafco's garages should be adapted to run in the same **up-market** way as Premoco's or whether they should concentrate on their existing **low-price** strategy. Whatever the strategy, substantial investment will be needed to improve the image with consumers and hence to improve on the company's existing growth prospects, which are low.

(2) The acquisition of Nafco does not in itself represent a **diversification** away from petroleum products and is therefore not what you appear to be looking for at the moment. However, it appears to be a **good buy** if the price can be kept relatively low and there is much **scope for developing convenience stores** on the Nafco sites.

Oiltrans

(i) *Price to be offered*

Using the same arguments as were put forward for Nafco plc, the **absolute maximum value** of Oiltrans (on the basis of NPV of the combined organisation) is £265.4 million or £22 per share, compared with the current price of £15.30. The added value generated by the merger is 16% which, when added to the current market price, gives £17.75. The suggested **range of prices** for negotiation is **£16** to **£18 per share** but, because the bid is hostile, you might have to be prepared to go higher.

(ii) *Terms of the offer*

(1) At £17.75 per share, the total cost of the acquisition is £213 million. This is too large to be financed entirely by cash, and **borrowing** would **increase gearing significantly**. A share issue or a mixture of shares and debt is the most likely route for financing this acquisition. The share-for-share swap would be in the region of 1 for 1 (see tutorial note above) which would mean the issue of 12 million new shares.

(2) Since only 10 million shares are available for issue, this would mean that the **authorised share capital** would need to be **increased**, and this in turn would signal to the market that something major was about to happen. To avoid an increase in authorised share capital, the company could offer a **choice of shares or a cash alternative**. In cases like this, the cash alternative is usually less than the equivalent share value because it is less risky.

(3) A **further problem** of a large share issue is that existing share ownership of Premoco will become diluted and large shareholders in Oiltrans may become dominant in the combined company.

(iii) *Business implications*

(1) The acquisition of Oiltrans would be a **vertical integration** of an **existing supplier** into the company's business. This represents more of a diversification than the acquisition of Nafco and is therefore more in line with your stated strategy but, judging from the figures, less synergy can be created because of the different nature of the two businesses. Oiltrans has significantly higher growth prospects than the existing business of Premoco.

(2) Your problem with diversifying into a business of this type is that you **cannot easily demonstrate expertise** and **experience** at managing such companies. In the event of a contested takeover, shareholders will probably back the existing management unless you can demonstrate that they are inefficient in some way. Note that for most large shareholders there is **no benefit** if your company diversifies purely to **reduce risk** because these shareholders will already hold diversified portfolios. Indeed it is quite likely that they already own shares in Oiltrans plc as well as Premoco.

(3) If the takeover succeeds, the existing management would probably resign, and we lose their skills which appear to have been a **significant influence** on Oiltrans' success.

(4) When two companies of similar size consider merging there is a real problem as to who will end up running the company. The directors of Oiltrans may turn the tables on you by arranging a **counter-bid** for the shares of Premoco. Alternatively, to agree bid terms, you will need to decide which directors from both sides should head the combined group.

Carsals

(i) *Price to be offered*

(1) The **absolute maximum amount** that could be paid for Carsals (on the basis of NPV of the combined organisation) is £38.4 million, which is £76.80 per share. Our dividend valuation model approach gave a figure of £40.69 per share. Synergy generated by the merger is 5%, so to give your own shareholders their fair share of this gain, the price paid should not be more than £42.72 per share, giving a total price of £21.36 million.

(2) The **price paid** would depend on how quickly the **existing major shareholder needs to make the sale** and on **what other offers** he is likely to receive. One major problem is that other car dealers can generate synergy from the acquisition and can therefore afford to pay more than Premoco. Before agreeing the price, you must be sure of the terms of the franchise, in particular the period for which it lasts and the renewal terms.

(ii) *Terms of the offer*

This company could be purchased using existing cash. However a **share-for-share exchange** could be used as a means of tying in the existing managing director, and solving the problem of appointing a suitable managing director (see below). A generous earn-out arrangement may also persuade the existing managing director to stay on, and reduces the risk of loss of customers.

(iii) *Business implications*

(1) Carsals represents a **complete product diversification** from the existing business but maintains the **same up-market image** in prestige locations. There will be no problems of control arising from the acquisition. The business is predicted to show reasonable growth but there will be **no immediate synergy** available from the business combination. The sort of longer term synergy available is in marketing the superior image for both cars, petroleum & other retail services. In addition there may be scope to sell some **properties**.

(2) You will need to appoint a **suitable managing director** from the car sales business if the owner has not groomed a suitable successor. The terms of the franchise must be investigated carefully and, finally, you must be aware that the success of this business depends to a large extent on the continued success of the motor manufacturer.

Conclusions

Despite your wish to diversify, I feel on balance that the opportunity of **expanding the existing business** by the acquisition of Nafco presents much higher wealth-producing opportunities than a contested bid for Oiltrans, which may well drain company resources and come to nothing. The acquisition of Carsals should also be followed up promptly, as a quick purchase may result in a bargain.

Signed: Financial Adviser

APPENDIX

	Premoco £m	Nafco £m	Oiltrans £m	Carsals £m
Total equity earnings	20.6	7.5	10.2	0.8
Existing value of shares*	329.6	67.5	183.6	20.3
Company combination		P+N	P+O	P+C
Sum of existing earnings		28.1	30.8	21.4
Estimated post-merger earnings		32.0	35.0	23.0
Additional earnings predicted		3.9	4.2	1.6
Sum of existing valuations		397.1	513.2	349.9
Estimated NPV of combined organisation		512.0	595.0	368.0
Increase in value from the combination		114.9	81.8	18.1
Maximum price that can be paid for the acquisition**		182.4	265.4	38.4

*Dividend valuation model used for Carsals.

**NPV of combination minus value of Premoco £329.6 million.

SAMPLE PRE-SEEN QUESTION

Question 1

Pre-seen case study

Introduction

M plc is a long established publisher of newspapers and provider of web media. It is based in London and has had a full listing on the London Stock Exchange since 1983. The company has three operating divisions which are managed from the United Kingdom (UK). These are the Newspapers Division, the Web Division and the Advertising Division.

Newspapers Division

The Newspapers Division publishes three daily newspapers and one Sunday newspaper in the UK. The Division has three offices and two printing sites. Between them the three offices edit the three daily newspapers and the Sunday newspaper. The Newspaper Division has two subsidiary publishing companies, FR and N. FR is based in France within the Eurozone and N in an Eastern European country which is outside the Eurozone. Printing for all the Division's publications, except those produced by FR and N, is undertaken at the two printing sites. FR and N have their own printing sites.

Web Division

The Web Division maintains and develops 200 websites which it owns. Some of these websites are much more popular in terms of the number of "hits" they receive than others. Web material is an increasing part of M plc's business. In the last ten years, the Web Division has developed an online version of all the newspapers produced by the Newspapers Division.

Advertising Division

The sale of advertising space is undertaken for the whole of M plc by the Advertising Division. Therefore, advertisements which appear in the print media and on the web pages produced by the Newspapers Division (including that produced by FR and N) and the Web Division respectively are all handled by the Advertising Division.

Group Headquarters

In addition to the three operating divisions, M plc also has a head office, based in the UK, which is the group's corporate headquarters where the Board of Directors is located. The main role of M plc's headquarters is to develop and administer its policies and procedures as well as to deal with its group corporate affairs.

Mission statement

M plc established a simple mission statement in 2005. This drove the initiative to acquire FR in 2008 and remains a driving force for the company. M plc's mission is "to be the best news media organisation in Europe, providing quality reporting and information on European and world-wide events".

Strategic objectives

Four main strategic objectives were established in 2005 by M plc's Board of Directors. These are to:

1. Meet the needs of readers for reliable and well informed news.
2. Expand the geographical spread of M plc's output to reach as many potential newspaper and website readers as possible.
3. Publish some newspapers which help meet the needs of native English speakers who live in countries which do not have English as their first language.
4. Increase advertising income so that the group moves towards offering as many news titles as possible free of charge to the public.

Financial objectives

In meeting these strategic objectives, M plc has developed the following financial objectives:

i. To ensure that revenue and operating profit grow by an average of 4% per year.

ii. To achieve steady growth in dividend per share.

iii. To maintain gearing below 40%, where gearing is calculated as debt/(debt plus equity) based on the market value of equity and the book value of debt.

Forecast revenue and operating profit

M plc's forecast revenue and net operating profit for the year ending 31 March 2012 are £280 million and £73 million respectively.

Extracts from M plc's forecast income statement for the year ending 31 March 2012 and forecast statement of financial position as at 31 March 2012 are shown in the appendix.

Comparative divisional performance and headquarters financial information

The following information is provided showing the revenue generated, the operating profit achieved and the capital employed for each division and the operating costs incurred and capital employed in M plc's headquarters. This information covers the last two years and also gives a forecast for the year ending 31 March 2012. All M plc's revenue is earned by the three divisions.

Newspapers Division

	Year ended 31.3.2010 £million	Year ended 31.3.2011 £million	Forecast for year ending 31.3.2012 £million
Revenue external	91	94	94
Revenue internal transfers	90	91	96
Net operating profit	45	46	48
Non-current assets	420	490	548
Net current assets	4	8	(10)

Web Division

	Year ended 31.3.2010 £million	Year ended 31.3.2011 £million	Forecast for year ending 31.3.2012 £million
Revenue internal transfers	55	60	66
Net operating profit	10	13	16
Non-current assets	37	40	43
Net current assets	1	1	(2)

Advertising Division

	Year ended 31.3.2010 £million	Year ended 31.3.2011 £million	Forecast for year ending 31.3.2012 £million
Revenue external	162	180	186
Internal transfers	(145)	(151)	(162)
Net operating profit	10	18	19
Non-current assets	3	6	7
Net current assets	1	1	(2)

Headquarters

	Year ended 31.3.2010 £million	Year ended 31.3.2011 £million	Forecast for year ending 31.3.2012 £million
Operating costs	8	9	10
Non-current assets	37	39	43
Net current assets	1	1	(1)

Notes:

1. The Advertising Division remits advertising revenue to both the Newspapers and Web Divisions after deducting its own commission.

2. The Web Division's entire revenue is generated from advertising.

3. The revenues and operating profits shown for the Newspapers Division include those earned by FR and N. The converted revenue and operating profit from N are forecast to be £20 million and £4 million respectively for the year ending 31 March 2012. FR is forecast to make a small operating profit in the year ending 31 March 2012. The Board of M plc is disappointed with the profit FR has achieved.

Additional information on each of M plc's divisions

Newspapers Division

FR is wholly owned and was acquired in 2008. Its financial statements are translated into British pounds and consolidated into M plc's group accounts and included within the Newspaper Division's results for internal reporting purposes.

Shortly after it was acquired by M plc, FR launched a pan-European weekly newspaper. This newspaper, which is written in English, is produced in France and then distributed throughout Europe. M plc's board thought that this newspaper would become very popular because it provides a snapshot of the week's news, focused particularly on European issues but viewed from a British perspective. Sales have, however, been disappointing.

N, which publishes local newspapers in its home Eastern European country, is also treated as part of the Newspapers Division. M plc acquired 80% of its equity in 2010. At that time, M plc's board thought that Eastern Europe was a growing market for newspapers. The subsidiary has proved to be profitable mainly because local production costs are lower than those in the UK relative to the selling prices.

The Newspapers Division's journalists incur a high level of expenses in order to carry out their duties. The overall level of expenses claimed by the journalists has been ignored by M plc in previous years because it has been viewed as a necessary cost of running the business. However, these expenses have risen significantly in recent years and have attracted the attention of M plc's internal audit department.

There has been significant capital investment in the Newspapers Division since 2009/10. The printing press facilities at each of the two printing sites have been modernised. These modernisations have improved the quality of output and have enabled improved levels of efficiency to be achieved in order to meet the increasing workloads demanded in the last two years. Surveys carried out before and after the modernisation have indicated higher levels of customer satisfaction with the improved quality of printing.

The increased mechanisation and efficiency has reduced costs and led to a reduction in the number of employees required to operate the printing presses. This has led to some dis-satisfaction among the divisional staff. Staff in the other divisions have been unaffected by the discontent in the Newspapers Division. Staff turnover has been relatively static across the three divisions, with the exception of the department which operates the printing presses in the Newspapers Division where some redundancies have occurred due to fewer staff being required since the modernisation.

Web Division

The web versions of the newspapers are shorter versions of the printed ones. There is currently no charge for access to the web versions of the newspapers. Revenues are generated from sales by the Advertising Division of advertising space on the web pages. Some of the websites permit unsolicited comments from the public to be posted on them and they have proved to be very popular. The Web Division is undertaking a review of all its costs, particularly those relating to energy, employees and website development.

The Web Division's management accounting is not sophisticated: for example, although it reports monthly on the Division's revenue and profitability, it cannot disaggregate costs so as to produce monthly results for each of the 200 websites. The Division is at a similar disadvantage as regards strategic management accounting as it lacks information about the websites' market share and growth rates. This has not mattered in the past as M plc was content that the Web Division has always been profitable. However, one of M plc's directors, the Business Development Director (see below under The Board of Directors and group shareholding) thinks that the Web Division could increase its profitability considerably and wants to undertake a review of its 200 websites.

Advertising Division

The Advertising Division remits advertising revenue to both the Newspapers and Web Divisions after deducting its own commission. In addition, the Advertising Division offers an advertising service to corporate clients. Such services include television and radio advertising and poster campaigns on bill boards. Advertisements are also placed in newspapers and magazines which are not produced by M plc, if the client so wishes. An increasing element of the work undertaken by the Advertising Division is in providing pop-up advertisements on websites.

Planning process

Each division carries out its own planning process. The Newspapers Division operates a rational model and prepares annual plans which it presents to M plc's board for approval. The Web Division takes advantage of opportunities as they arise and is operating in a growth market, unlike the other two divisions. Its planning approach might best be described as one of logical incrementalism. Increased capital expenditure in 2010/11 helped the Advertising Division to achieve an 11% increase in revenue in that year. The Divisional Managers of both the Web Division and the Advertising Division are keen to develop their businesses and are considering growth options including converting their businesses into outsource service providers to M plc.

The Board of Directors and group shareholding

M plc's Board of Directors comprises six executive directors and six non-executive directors, one of whom is the Non-executive Chairman. The executive directors are the Chief Executive, and the Directors of Strategy, Corporate Affairs, Finance, Human Resources and Business Development. The Business Development Director did not work for M plc in 2005 and so had no part in drafting the strategic objectives. She thinks that objective number four has become out-dated as it does not reflect current day practice. The Business Development Director has a great deal of experience working with subscription-based websites and this was one of the main reasons M plc recruited her in March 2011. Her previous experience also incorporated the management of product portfolios including product development and portfolio rationalisation.

There are divisional managing directors for each of the three divisions who are not board members but report directly to the Chief Executive.

One of M plc's non-executive directors was appointed at the insistence of the bank which holds 10% of M plc's shares. Another was appointed by a private charity which owns a further 10% of the shares in M plc. The charity represents the interests of print workers and provides long-term care to retired print workers and their dependents. Two other non-executive directors were appointed by a financial institution which owns 20% of the shares in M plc. The remaining 60% of shares are held by private investors. The board members between them hold 5% of the shares in issue. None of the other private investors holds more than 70,000 of the total 140 million shares in issue.

It has become clear that there is some tension between the board members. Four of the non-executive directors, those appointed by the bank, the charity and the financial institution, have had disagreements with the other board members. They are dissatisfied with the rate of growth and profitability of the company and wish to see more positive action to secure M plc's financial objectives.

Some board members feel that the newspapers market is declining because fewer people can make time to read printed publications. Some of the non-executive directors think that many people are more likely to watch a television news channel than read a newspaper.

Editorial policy

M plc's board applies a policy of editorial freedom provided that the published material is within the law and is accurate. The editors of each of the publications printed in the UK and France and of the websites have complete autonomy over what is published. They are also responsible for adhering to regulatory constraints and voluntary industry codes of practice relating to articles and photographs which might be considered offensive by some readers.

There is less scrutiny of the accuracy of the reporting in N's home country than in other countries. The Eastern European country in which N is situated has become politically unstable in the last two years. Much of this unrest is fuelled by the public distaste for the perceived blatant corruption and bribery which is endemic within the country's Government and business community. It is well known that journalists have accepted bribes to present only the Government's version of events, rather than a balanced view. There is also widespread plagiarism of published material by the country's newspapers and copyright laws are simply ignored.

Corporate Social Responsibility

A policy is in place throughout M plc in order to eliminate bribery and corruption among staff especially those who have front line responsibility for obtaining business. This policy was established 15 years ago. All new employees are made aware of the policy and other staff policies and procedures during their induction. The Director of Human Resources has confidence in the procedures applied by his staff at induction and is proud that no action has ever been brought against an employee of M plc for breach of the bribery and corruption policy.

M plc is trying to reduce its carbon footprint and is in the process of developing policies to limit its energy consumption, reduce the mileage travelled by its staff and source environmentally friendly supplies of paper for its printing presses. The Newspapers Division purchases the paper it uses for printing newspapers from a supplier in a Scandinavian country. This paper is purchased because it provides a satisfactory level of quality at a relatively cheap price. The Scandinavian country from which the paper is sourced is not the same country in which N is situated.

Strategic Development

The Board of Directors is now reviewing M plc's competitive position. The Board of Directors is under pressure from the non-executive directors appointed by the bank, the charity and the financial institution (which between them own 40% of the shares in M plc), to devise a strategic plan before June 2012 which is aimed at achieving M plc's stated financial objectives.

Extracts from M plc's forecast group income statement and forecast statement of financial position

Forecast income statement for the group for the year ending 31 March 2012

	Notes	£ million (GBP million)
Revenue		280
Operating costs		(207)
Net operating profit		73
Interest income		1
Finance costs		(11)
Corporate income tax	1	(19)
FORECAST PROFIT FOR THE YEAR		44

Forecast statement of the group financial position as at 31 March 2012

	Notes	£ million (GBP million)
ASSETS		
Non-current assets		641
Current assets		
Inventories		2
Trade and other receivables		27
Cash and cash equivalents		2
Total current assets		31
Total assets		672
EQUITY AND LIABILITIES		
Equity		
Share capital	2	140
Share premium		35
Retained earnings		185
Non-controlling interest		16
Total equity		376
Non-current liabilities		
Long term borrowings	3	250
Current liabilities		
Trade and other payables		46
Total liabilities		296
Total equity and liabilities		672

Notes:

1. The corporate income tax rate can be assumed to be 30%.

2. There are 140 million £1 shares currently in issue.

3. The long-term borrowings include £83 million of loan capital which is due for repayment on 1 April 2013 and the remainder is due for repayment on 1 April 2019.

End of pre-seen material

Unseen material for Case Study

Background

Assume today is 1 December 2011.

M plc currently has 140 million £1 ordinary shares in issue and, on 30 November, its shares were trading at 283 pence ex-dividend. Dividends for M plc for the year ended 31 March 2012 are expected to be 22 pence per share, maintaining the 4% annual increase in dividends that has been achieved in recent years. For simplicity, dividends should be assumed to be declared and paid on 31 March each year.

Investment project

A new investment opportunity has been identified by the Newspaper division for a Europe-wide sports-only newspaper, to be called Sports Fan, which it proposes to commence at the start of April 2012. The paper would be published in English and would feature in-depth reporting of a range of popular European sports.

This proposal has been under consideration since March 2011 and M plc has been reported by Media Monthly, a specialist magazine covering the media sector, to have showed dummy copies of the twice-weekly paid-for title to a number of media agencies during the summer.

The project is expected to be launched in the UK initially and then extended into Europe gradually over time. New printing facilities would be added to FR's site to support this investment.

The project has been evaluated over a 6-year period beginning 1 April 2012 and the project net operating cash flows have been estimated to be as follows:

Year	£ million	€ million
1	3	-1
2	8	11
3	13	19
4–6	15	23

All cash flows should be assumed to arise on 31 March of each year. It should also be assumed that annual cash flows, less tax, are paid across to the UK on the final day of each year.

The cost of the initial investment in plant and other equipment at the beginning of April 2012 is €90 million and this is subject to depreciation charged on a straight line basis at 5% per annum. An additional €5 million will be required to finance working capital at the beginning of April 2012.

In addition to these cash flows it is hoped that the development of mobile phone apps would generate further revenue, which could add up to 5% to the net operating cash flows from year 4 of the investment. This estimate is based on the 'gut feel' of the Sales Director and has not been verified.

Tax

M plc would pay overseas corporation tax at a rate of 20%. In FR's home country tax depreciation allowances are calculated on the same basis as accounting depreciation allowances. As the project involves investment in France the tax authorities there will treat all of the operating cash flows as taxable, irrespective of where they are generated. The rate of corporation tax in the UK is 30%, but a double tax treaty allows taxes charged in France to be deducted from UK taxes charged in the same period. Assume that overseas taxes are payable in the year in which they are incurred and that UK taxes are payable one year in arrears.

Exchange rates

At 31 March 2012 the spot exchange rate is expected to be £/€1.1 (that is, £1 = €1.1). The euro is expected to weaken against the British pound (sterling) in line with the differential in long term interest rates between the two regions over the life of the project. Long term interest rates are expected to remain stable at 0.5% per annum in the UK and 1.5% per annum in Europe for the foreseeable future.

Financing the project

The total initial investment of €95 million will be funded by M plc at the beginning of April 2012, by a rights issue. The printing press will not be operational immediately, but the impact of the lead time required for this to be fully operational is reflected in the lower cash inflows in year 1.

It is estimated that the realisable residual value for the plant and equipment will be €63 million; this amount will be repaid in full to the UK without any taxes being payable.

Press statements

In March 2011, M plc responded to questions from journalists by announcing that it was evaluating the potential for the Sports Fan magazine. On the same day, it announced its plans to use a 1 for 4 rights issue to fund the €95 million capital investment in the event of the proposal being accepted.

The Sports Fan proposal was accepted two weeks ago and a press release issued to announce M plc's intention to proceed with the project without delay. The press statement also announced M plc's intention to temporarily reduce dividend growth rates during the development stage of the project.

Investment criteria

Criterion 1

M plc assesses overseas investment projects based on the net present value of the forecast £ sterling cash flows using a risk adjusted £ sterling discount rate of 12%.

Criterion 2

M plc requires overseas projects to generate an accounting rate of return of at least 25% per annum. Accounting rate of return is defined as:

$$\frac{\text{average annual accounting profit before interest and taxes}}{\text{average annual (written down) investment}}$$

Required

(a) Show, by calculation, that the proposed investment project met:

(i) the NPV investment criteria **(14 marks)**

(ii) the ARR investment criteria set by M plc **(5 marks)**

(b) Discuss the major risk issues that should have been considered by M plc when evaluating the project **(7 marks)**

(c) The board of M plc has been concerned about the unusually volatile movements in the share price in the current financial year and has asked you, an external management consultant, to draft a report to the board of M plc that critically addresses the issues detailed below. Assume a semi-strong efficient market applies.

(i) Explain the possible reasons for the unusually volatile movements in M plc's share price in the current financial year. No calculations are required. **(5 marks)**

(ii) Advise what would have been a fair market price for M plc's shares following the announcement of the acceptance of the proposal and after adjusting for the proposed rights issue. As part of your answer, calculate M plc's share price on each of the bases listed below and discuss the relevance of each result in determining a fair market price for the entity's shares:

- The theoretical ex-rights price *before* adjusting for the project cash flows
- The theoretical ex-rights price *after* adjusting for the project cash flows **(11 marks)**

(iii) Advise on the impact of the proposal on M plc's financial objectives and on shareholder wealth. **(5 marks)**

In addition up to 3 marks are available for structure and presentation. **(3 marks)**

(Total = 50 marks)

Question 1

Marking scheme

	Marks
Requirement (a) (i)	
Tax	2
Operating cash flows	1
Working capital	1
UK tax including double taxation relief (1 for recognition of double taxation, 1 for timing)	4
Initial investment and residual value	2
Exchange rate forecasting	3
NPV and comment	1
Requirement (a) (ii)	
Annual accounting profit	1
Average profit	1
Average investment	1
ARR and comment	2
MAXIMUM FOR REQUIREMENT	19
Requirement (b)	
Up to 3 marks per risk discussed and applied to the scenario eg	
• business risks	
• political risks	
• financial risks	
MAXIMUM FOR REQUIREMENT	7
Requirement (c)(i)	
Efficient market hypothesis – explanation of semi-strong form	Max 3
Impact of changes in economic or business conditions on the share price	1
Market perception of likely outcome of bid and profitability of project	1
Extent to which the information has been anticipated by the market	1
MAXIMUM FOR REQUIREMENT	5
Requirement (c)(ii)	
Calculation of TERP before project cash flows	Max 3
Calculation of TERP after project cash flows	Max 2
Discussion of results/alterative calculations	Max 6
Conclusion	Max 2
MAXIMUM FOR REQUIREMENT	11
Requirement (c)(iii)	
Up to 2 marks per issue discussed eg	
• shareholder wealth	
• gearing (2 marks for calculations)	Max 5
Structure and presentation (1 for heading, 1 for format, 1 for neatness)	Max 3
TOTAL FOR QUESTION	50

(a) (i)

Project cash flows

Working	Time	0	1	2	3	4	5	6	7
1	from euro cash flows		-0.9	9.8	16.8	20.1	19.9	19.7	0.0
	from uk sales		3.0	8.0	13.0	15.0	15.0	15.0	
	total		2.1	17.8	29.8	35.1	34.9	34.7	0.0
2	tax overseas		0.4	-2.8	-5.2	-6.2	-6.2	-6.2	0.0
	UK			0.2	-1.4	-2.6	-3.1	-3.1	-3.1
1	investment	-81.8						54.0	
1	w.cap	-4.5						4.3	
	net	-86.3	2.5	15.2	23.2	26.3	25.6	83.7	-3.1
	df 12%	1.000	0.893	0.797	0.712	0.636	0.567	0.507	0.452
	pv	-86.3	2.2	12.1	16.5	16.7	14.5	42.4	-1.4
	npv	**16.7**							

Working	Time	0	1	2	3	4	5	6
1	exchange rate	1.100	1.111	1.122	1.133	1.144	1.156	1.167
	euro cash flows		-1	11	19	23	23	23
	£ cash flows		-0.9	9.8	16.8	20.1	19.9	19.7
	plant	81.8						
	working cap	4.5						
2	pre tax cash flows		2.1	17.8	29.8	35.1	34.9	34.7
	depreciation		-4.1	-4.0	-4.0	-3.9	-3.9	-3.9
	pre tax profit		-2.0	13.8	25.8	31.2	31.0	30.8
	tax payable 20%		0.4	-2.8	-5.2	-6.2	-6.2	-6.2
	tax payable in the uk 10%			0.2	-1.4	-2.6	-3.1	-3.1	-3.1

Exchange rates have been forecast using **interest parity theory** i.e. multiplying the spot rate by 1.015 (1 + the overseas interest rate) / 1.005 (1 + UK interest rate).

Tax allowances on the plant and equipment are the **same** as the accounting depreciation. Because M plc has other projects in Europe, it is assumed that its loss in year 1 will be used to reduce these profits.

The net present value of the project is approximately £17m; this may be considered a 'prudent' evaluation because it ignores the Sales Director's 'gut feel' about the potential for higher revenue on top of these cash flows. This is a high positive net present value, indicating that investment criterion 1 is satisfied.

(a) (ii)

ARR

	Total time 1-6	Workings	
average PBIT	21.77	total inflows	154.4 in £ms from NPV
		total depreciation	-23.8
		total profit	130.6
average investment	72.3	opening	86.3 in £ms from NPV
		closing	58.3
		average	72.3

ARR **30.1%**

Accounting rate of return = 30%. This is well above the minimum investment criterion of 25% per annum.

(b) *Major risk issues*

When evaluating the project there is a wide range of risks that need to be considered. Although overlapping, these can be grouped into business risk, political risk and financial risks.

Business risk

These are the risks associated with the project. A key risk will be that the magazine is not popular; M plc already has experience of pan-European publications that have failed – however these took a UK perspective of European issues and this venture will have learned form this experience and may well adopt a more European perspective. Nevertheless, there will be a risk that readers will be more interested in their national sports, but will be less interested in a European perspective. There will also be a risk that the advertising revenue anticipated within the magazine does not materialise, this will be especially likely if sales of the magazine are disappointing.

The **realisable value estimated for plant and equipment** is a major assumption and there is a significant risk that this could prove to be over-optimistic. The present value of this disposal value is £54m × 0.507 = £27.4m. This means that the disposal value would have to fall by 62% (17m / 27.4m) for the project NPV to fall to zero.

Political risks

The government (or a future government headed by another political party) may take action that is **detrimental to the profitability** of M plc's operations. For example, it may **increase taxation** or **introduce exchange controls** on repatriated profits. These risks should be minimised so far as possible by conducting research and signing agreements with the government (eg on tax rates and profit repatriation).

Financial risks

The financial risks that M plc will face will be an extension of what it already faces in Europe: gearing, interest rate risk and currency risk. Since the project is all equity financed, the directors have chosen **not to increase gearing** or **interest rate risk.** This policy increases the **currency risk** of their operations, because a significant proportion of their operating profit and the £ value of the asset base will vary with fluctuations in the value of the Euro. Declines in the value of the euro will need to be countered by **price increases,** which may damage sales. An alternative method of financing which could hedge some of this currency risk is to take out a **substantial loan** in **euros.**

(c) To: The Board of Directors of M plc

From: Management Consultants

Report on share price volatility and estimation of a fair valuation of the shares of M plc

You have asked us to provide some possible explanations for the increased volatility of M plc's share price in the current financial year, to advise on a fair market price for the shares, and to explain how and to what extent the directors can influence the price of the company's shares.

(i) *Volatility of share price movements*

No perfect models of share valuation or share price movements exist. The following notes are therefore intended as partial explanations for the share price volatility; they are based on the **efficient market hypothesis.**

Efficient markets hypothesis

The **efficient market hypothesis** (semi-strong form) postulates that share prices **swiftly and rationally reflect all information** that is **publicly available**. During this whole period, the market has reacted to any favourable or unfavourable information about the Sports Fan project by marking M plc shares up or down accordingly.

March announcement

The announcement in March ended speculation on the company's intentions but added to market uncertainties for many reasons including:

- The **proposed project** was **so large**
- It would require a **major rights issue**, which is unpopular with some shareholders
- There was **no proposed mechanism** for hedging currency risk on the project
- The proposal could have been **rejected or delayed**.

In November, the Board's press release **clarified the company's intention to proceed with the project** but the accompanying comments on future dividends may have been treated with some scepticism, resulting in further uncertainties and fluctuations in the share price.

(ii) *Fair market price for M plc's shares*

The **fairest** valuation for a company's shares would be based on **all relevant information** at the time. However, the implication of the efficient market hypothesis (semi-strong form) is that the actual share price will be based on **public information only**; this will include some financial information on the likely returns on this new project

Effect of the rights issue on the share price

The share price at 30 November was 283 pence ex div, and the market capitalisation was 140m x 2.83 = £396m. The effect of the 1 for 4 rights issue on this price (in isolation of any project effects) can be easily computed.

The number of shares issued to fund the plant and equipment (1 for 4 rights issue) is $\frac{1}{4} \times$ 140 million = 35 million. This implies an issue price of approximately £86.4m / 35m = £2.47 (ignoring issue costs).

The theoretical ex rights price of the shares (ignoring the project NPV which is not public information) is **276 pence,** as shown below

	£m
amount raised from rights issue	86.4
value before rights issue	396
value post rights issue	482.4
no shares post rights issue	175
TERP	2.76

Effect of the project NPV

If the market was told that the **proposed project** has a **positive expected NPV** of approximately £17 million, and if this figure were believed by the market, then the shares should increase in value by £17 million to a total value of £499 million, that is a **yield adjusted** value per share of (499/175) **285 pence**. This is the closest we can get to a fair value of the shares.

(iii) *Impact on M plc's objectives*

The project will make it difficult for M plc to achieve their dividend growth objective. However, despite the short term impact on the dividend, this project should offer strong benefits to shareholders; shareholder wealth maximisation is a key objective for any listed company.

The yield adjusted share price of £2.85 indicates a market capitalisation of:

175m share x 2.85 = £499m

Compared to a pre rights issue value of £396m, this is an increase of £17m (the project NPV) in shareholders wealth (after recognising that they have put in another £86m with the rights issue).

This represents a rise in shareholder wealth of 17/ 396 = 4.3% and may be understated if the possible benefit of mobile phone apps materialises.

It also has a beneficial impact on the gearing ratio:

Before this initiative the gearing was 39% (250 / (250 + 396)), this is very close to the 40% target for maximum gearing. However after the project gearing has fallen to 33% (250 / (250 + 499)).

In summary, despite its short-term impact, this project should allow M plc to increase wealth and to reduce risk.

INDEX

Note: **Key terms** and their references are given in **bold**

3 E's, 12

Abandonment option, 257
Accounting rate of return, 200
Accounting rate of return (ARR) method of share valuation, 296
Acquisition, 322
Adjusted payback, 220
Adjusted present value, 260
Agency problem, 10, 20
Agency theory, **10**
Allocative efficiency, 93
Alpha value, 146
Alternative Investment Market (AIM), 78
Amalgamations, 322
American option, **237**
Annualised cost, 254
Arbitrage, **169**
Arbitrage pricing theory, 190, 191
Asset replacement, 255
Asset turnover, 36
Asset valuation bases, 290

Balanced scorecard, 7
Bank of England, 25
Barter, **233**
Base constraints, 277
Beta, 172
Beta factor, **142**
Bilateral netting, 235
Bonds, 103
Bonus issue, **90**
Bootstrapping, 295
Business risk, 137, 153, 165, 300
Business strategy, 20

Calculated intangible values, 312
Capital asset pricing model (CAPM), 141, 190
Capital investment appraisal, 200
Capital markets, 78
Capital rationing, **250**
Capital structure, **162**, 306
Capital structure decision, 162
Capitalisation issue, **90**
Capitalisation of earnings method, 313
Cash budgets, **41**
Cash flow valuation methods, 299
Cash forecasts, 41
Cash operating cycle, 38
Cash purchases, 327
Cash surpluses, 52
Centralised cash management, 185
Certainty equivalent method, **215**
Changes in economic variables, 51
Chartists, 92
City Code on Takeovers and Mergers, 326, 339

Comparison with market transactions method, 313
Competition authorities, 23
Competition legislation, 340
Competition regulation, 22
Concentric diversification, **322**
Conduct of a takeover, 325
Conglomerate diversification, **322**
Constraints on financial strategy, 20
Contesting an offer, 326
Contingency funding, 52
Contractual joint venture, 231
Conversion premium, 108
Conversion value, 108
Convertible bonds, 330
Convertible debt, **108**
Corporate governance, **11**, **22**
Correlation between investments, 189
Cost of capital, **136**, 201, 300
Cost of debt, 147
Cost of equity, 137
Cost of preference shares, 141
Counterpurchase, **233**
Countertrade, **233**
Country risks, 234
Coupon, 103
Credit rating, 20
Creditworthiness, 102
Cum div, **138**
Cum rights, 86
Currency option, **237**
Current ratio, 37
Current re-investment level, 140

Debentures, 103
Debt and gearing, 37
Debt ratio, 37
Debt/equity, 37
Decision trees, 219
Deep discount bond, **104**
Defensive tactics, 326
Demerger, 344
Dilution, **85**, 335
Discounted future cash flows, 304
Discounted future cash flows method of share valuation, 299
Discounted payback period, 201
Discounting, 201
Diversification, 230
Diversifying, 189
Divestment, **344**, 347
Dividend, **63**
Dividend cover, 39
Dividend decisions, 15
Dividend growth model, 138
Dividend payout ratio, 39
Dividend policy, 63, 73
Dividend validation on model, 91
Dividend valuation bases, 297

Dividend valuation model, 137, 138, 297
Dividend yield, 38

Divisible projects, 250
Double taxation agreement, 240
Double taxation relief (DTR), 240
Drucker's Golden Rules, 341

Earnings per share (EPS), 39
Earnings valuation bases, 292
Earnings yield, 39, 296
Earnings yield valuation method, 296
Earnings: method of valuation, 292
Earn-out arrangements, 332
Economic constraints, 23
Economic value added, 303
Efficient market hypothesis, 93
Environmental accounting, 70
EPS before and after a takeover, 333
Equity, 91
Equity share capital, 91
Equivalent annual annuity, 256
Equivalent annual cost, 254
Eurobond, 113
Eurocredits, 113
Eurocurrency, 112
Eurodollars, 112
European option, 237
Ex div, 138
Ex rights, 86
Excess return, 312
Exchange rate risk, 28
Exchange rates, 28
Exit strategies, 344
Expectations, 26
Expected return of a porfolio, 188
Exporting, 232
External hedging techniques, 236

Failure of mergers and takeovers, 342
Feasibility study, 276
Finance lease, 120
Financial distress costs, 162
Financial objectives, 4
Financial risk, 5, 137, 153, 162, 164, 172
Financial targets, 5
Financing decisions, 14, 27
Financing overseas investments, 233
Financing requirements, 52
Fixed charge, 104
Floating charge, 104
Floating rate debt, 150, 153
Floor value, 109, 292
Flotation, 80, 348
Follow-on option, 257
Forecast, 41
Forecast financial statements, 45
Forecasting exchange rates, 241
Foreign Direct Investment (FDI), 230
Foreign exchange constraints, 29

Foreign exchange risk, 114
Foreign exchange risks, 234
Foreign subsidiaries, 231
Forward contracts, 236
Free cash flow, 300
Free rate, 216
Fundamental analysis, 91
Fundamental theory of share values, 91, 138
Funding constraints, 20
Funding deficit, 43
Futures contracts, 237

Geared betas, 173
Gearing, 64, 67, 162, 164, 295
Gearing and ungearing betas, 309
Goal congruence, 10
Going private, 67, 346
Goodwill, 310
Gordon's growth approximation, 140
Government departments, 12
Government securities, 78
Growth rate, 139

Hard capital rationing, 250
Hedging, 235
Hire purchase, 124
Historic growth, 139
Horizontal integration, 322

Impact of mergers and takeovers on stakeholders, 343
Indivisible projects, 250
Industry regulators, 22
Inflation, 23, 207, 241
Information processing efficiency, 93
Initial public offer (IPO), 80
Institutional investors, 78
Intangible assets, 310
Integration sequence, 341
Intellectual capital, 311
Interest cover, 37, 166
Interest rate parity, 243
Interest rates, 24
Internal hedging techniques, 235
Internal rate of return (IRR), 148, 208
International constraints, 29
International debt finance, 112
International investment, 230
International investment appraisal, 241
Introduction, 82
Inventory days, 38
Investment decisions, 14
Investments and projects, 272
Investor relations, 20
Investors in Industry, 323
Invoicing in the home currency, 235
Irredeemable, 105
Irredeemable debt, 107, 147
Irrelevancy theory, 65

Issue costs, 263
Issues in financial reporting, 68
Issuing house, 80

Joint venture, 231, 253
Jones's Integration Sequence, 341

Leading and lagging, 52, 235
Lease or buy decisions, 125
Leasing, 120
Legislation, 21
Licensing, 232
Life cycle, 64
Limiting factor, 250
Liquidations, 345
Liquidity, 37, 64
Litigation risk, 234
Loan note, 103
Loss of goods in transit, 234

Management buyouts (MBOs), 102, **347**
Management charges, 232
Marginal cost of capital, 153
Market capitalisation, 312
Market efficiency, 306
Market risk, 142
Market risk premium, 144
Market segmentation theory, 26
Market valuation or capitalisation, 292
Market value, 91
Market value added, 303
Market values, 5, 165
Marketability, 90
Market-to-book values, 312
Matching, 112, 235
Maturity matching, 61
Merger, 292, 322
Mergers and takeovers, 306, 322
Merging systems, 342
Mezzanine finance, 102, 331
Modified internal rate of return (MIRR), 210
Modigliani and Miller, 65, 169, 308
Monetary Policy Committee, 25
Money market hedge, 236
Money rate of return, 207
Money terms, 207
Multilateral netting, 235
Multinational, 63, 185, 186
Multinational company, 29, 231
Mutually exclusive projects, 209, 251

Net assets method of share valuation, 290
Net assets per share, 39
Net operating income, 169, 308
Net present value, 201
Netting, 235
Nominal rates of interest, 24
Nominal value, 91
Non-annual cash flows, 202

Non-financial objectives, 7
Non-quoted company, 5
Non-systematic risk, 142
Not-for-profit organisations, 12
NPV layout, 203

Objectives, 4
OECD Model Agreement, 240
Offer for sale, 80
Offers for sale by tender, 80
Offsets, 233
Operating gearing, 37, 165
Operating leases, 120
Operational efficiency, 93
Opportunity cost, 136
Overdrafts, 102
Overseas taxes, 239
Overtrading, 37, 62

P/E ratio, 39
P/E ratio (earnings) method of valuation, 292
Paper bid, 328
Payables payment period, 38
Payback method, 201, 327
Performance analysis, 34
Performance related pay, 10
Placing, 82
Poison-pill, 326
Political risk, 29, 234
Portfolio, 141, 188
Post-acquisition integration, 340, 341
Post-completion audit, 281
Preference shares, 84
Premium profits method, 313
Present value of future free cash flows model, 300
Pricing shares, 83
Primary markets, 78
Prior charge capital, 84
Private equity, 83
Probability analysis, 216
Process specialisation, 230
Profit margin, 36
Profit maximisation, 4
Profitability and return, 36
Profitability index, 251
Project control, 278
Project phases and stages, 273
Project specific cost of capital, 172
Project success factors, 273
Prospectus issue, 81
Published forecasts, 69
Purchasing power parity, 241

Quick ratio, 37

Random walk theory, 92
Ratio analysis, 34
Rational, 93

Real options, 257
Real rate of return, 207
Real rates of interest, 24
Real terms, 207
Receivables collection period, 38
Redeemable debt, 148
Redemption, 105
Redemption yield, 106
Regulation of takeovers, 339
Regulatory bodies, 21
Reinvestment assumption, 210
Relevant costs, 201
Relief from royalties method, 313
Residual theory, 65
Resist a takeover, 326
Return on capital employed, 36, 200
Return on equity, 36
Return on investment, 200
Reverse takeover, 322
Rghts issue, 85
Risk, 25, 136, 141, 165, 184, 189, 213
Risk and returns, 143
Risk and reward, 188
Risk and uncertainty, 212
Risk management, 279
Risk-adjusted discount rates, 220
Risk-free rate of return, 137
Risks of overseas investments, 234
Role of capital markets, 78
Royalty, 232

Sale and leaseback, 124
Scrip dividends, 67
Scrip issue, 90
Secondary markets, 78
Security, 292
Sell-offs, 345
Semi-strong form efficiency, 94, 306
Sensitivity analysis, 51, 213
Service contracts for key personnel, 341
Share exchange, 328
Share options, 10
Share price, 5
Share price behaviour, 91
Share repurchase, 67
Share splits, 90
Shareholder value, 301
Shareholder value analysis, 11, 301
Shareholders, 63
Shareholders' preferences between risk and return, 190
Short-term targets, 6
Short-termism, 83
Signalling effect, 64
Simulation models, 219
Small and medium-sized entities, 114
Social accounting, 70
Social feasibility, 278
Soft capital rationing, 250
Spare debt capacity, 264

Spin-offs, 346
Stakeholders, 9, 343
Start-up investments, 230
Statement of financial position based forecasts, 41
Stock market, 5, 78
Strategic approach to takeovers, 323
Strategic financial management, 4
Strategic fit, 323
Strategy, 4
Strike price, 238
Strong form efficiency, 94
Subsidy, 264
Synergy, 323
Systematic risk, 142, 173

Takeover, **288**, 322
Takeover panel, 339
Takeovers by share exchange, 78
Tax allowable depreciation, 204
Tax exhaustion, 172
Tax relief on interest, 149
Tax shield, 20, 261, 308
Tax shield exhaustion, 308
Taxation, 204, 239
Technical analysis, 92
Technical feasibility, 277
Term loans, 102
Theoretical ex-rights price, 86
Theories of capital structure, 168
Tie-breaker clauses, 240
Timing option, 258
Tobin's 'q', 312
Traditional view of dividend policy, 65
Traditional view of WACC, 168
Transfer pricing, 232
Treasury function, 182

Uncertainty, 213
Underwriting, 82, 113
Ungeared betas, 173
Unlisted companies, 309
Unquoted company, 294, 326
Unsystematic risk, 142

Valuation of mergers and takeovers, 333
Valuation prior to flotation, 309
Valuation using post-merger dividends or cash flows, 336
Value drivers, 11, 301
Value for money, 12
Value of rights, 88
Venture capital, 83, 348
Vertical integration, 322
View of WACC, 169

Warrants, 102, 111
Weak form efficiency, 94
Weighted average cost of capital, 151

White knight, 326
Working capital, 203
Working capital financing, 61
Working capital management, 60

Yield adjusted ex-rights price, 87
Yield curve, 26
Yield to maturity, 106

Zero coupon bond, 104

Notes

Notes

Review Form – Paper F3 Financial Strategy (6/12)

Please help us to ensure that the CIMA learning materials we produce remain as accurate and user-friendly as possible. We cannot promise to answer every submission we receive, but we do promise that it will be read and taken into account when we update this Study Text.

Name: _____   **Address:** _____

How have you used this Study Text?
(Tick one box only)
- [ ] Home study (book only)
- [ ] On a course: college _____
- [ ] With 'correspondence' package
- [ ] Other _____

Why did you decide to purchase this Study Text? *(Tick one box only)*
- [ ] Have used BPP Texts in the past
- [ ] Recommendation by friend/colleague
- [ ] Recommendation by a lecturer at college
- [ ] Saw information on BPP website
- [ ] Saw advertising
- [ ] Other _____

During the past six months do you recall seeing/receiving any of the following?
(Tick as many boxes as are relevant)
- [ ] Our advertisement in *Financial Management*
- [ ] Our advertisement in *Pass*
- [ ] Our advertisement in *PQ*
- [ ] Our brochure with a letter through the post
- [ ] Our website www.bpp.com

Which (if any) aspects of our advertising do you find useful?
(Tick as many boxes as are relevant)
- [ ] Prices and publication dates of new editions
- [ ] Information on Text content
- [ ] Facility to order books off-the-page
- [ ] None of the above

Which BPP products have you used?

Text	[✓]	Success CD	[ ]
Kit	[ ]	i-Pass	[ ]
Passcard	[ ]	Interactive Passcard	[ ]

Your ratings, comments and suggestions would be appreciated on the following areas.

	Very useful	Useful	Not useful
Introductory section	[ ]	[ ]	[ ]
Chapter introductions	[ ]	[ ]	[ ]
Key terms	[ ]	[ ]	[ ]
Quality of explanations	[ ]	[ ]	[ ]
Case studies and other examples	[ ]	[ ]	[ ]
Exam skills and alerts	[ ]	[ ]	[ ]
Questions and answers in each chapter	[ ]	[ ]	[ ]
Fast forwards and chapter roundups	[ ]	[ ]	[ ]
Quick quizzes	[ ]	[ ]	[ ]
Question Bank	[ ]	[ ]	[ ]
Answer Bank	[ ]	[ ]	[ ]
OT Bank	[ ]	[ ]	[ ]
Index	[ ]	[ ]	[ ]

Overall opinion of this Study Text	Excellent [ ]	Good [ ]	Adeqate [ ]	Poor [ ]

Do you intend to continue using BPP products?   Yes [ ]   No [ ]

On the reverse of this page is space for you to write your comments about our Study Text We welcome your feedback.

The BPP Learning Media author of this edition can be e-mailed at: andrewfinch@bpp.com

Please return this form to: Stephen Osborne, CIMA Publishing Manager, BPP Learning Media Ltd, FREEPOST, London, W12 8BR

TELL US WHAT YOU THINK

Please note any further comments and suggestions/errors below. For example, was the text accurate, readable, concise, user-friendly and comprehensive?